LOBBYING FOR EQUALITY

JACQUES GODARD AND THE STRUGGLE FOR JEWISH CIVIL RIGHTS DURING THE FRENCH REVOLUTION

Pastel portrait of Jacques Godard by an unidentified artist, painted in 1807. The portrait bears a label in handwritten script pasted on the reverse side which reads in French: "Jacques Godard avocat with the Parlement of Paris, member of the first legislature, born on August 7, 1762 [sic], first son of Mr. Jacques Godard, auditor at the Chambre des Comptes of Dijon, died in Paris on November 4, 1791 on St. Gervais and St. Protais's Day as a result of a putrid and malign fever, at the age of 29. This portrait was made 16 years after the death of Jacques Godard and copied from a small portrait made in pencil." (From the author's personal collection.)

LOBBYING FOR EQUALITY

JACQUES GODARD AND THE STRUGGLE FOR JEWISH CIVIL RIGHTS DURING THE FRENCH REVOLUTION

GERARD LEVAL

HEBREW UNION COLLEGE PRESS

HEBREW UNION COLLEGE PRESS

©2021 Hebrew Union College Press
Cover design by Elena Barschazki
Set in Arno Pro by Elena Barschazki

Printed in the United States of America

Library of Congress Cataloging-in-Publication Data
Names: Leval, Gerard, author.
Title: Lobbying for equality: Jacques Godard and the struggle for
Jewish civil rights during the French Revolution / Gerard Leval.

Description: Cincinnati, OH: Hebrew Union College Press, 2021. |
Includes bibliographical references and index. | Summary: "A history of
the life and work of Jacques Godard, a young French avocat, who was
influential in the granting of civil rights to the Jews of France during the
French Revolution"-- Provided by publisher.
Identifiers: LCCN 2020042702 | ISBN 9780878202256 (hardback) |
ISBN 9780878202263 (ebook)
Subjects: LCSH: Jews--Legal status, laws, etc.--France--History--
Revolution, 1789-1799--Sources. | Jews--France--Social conditions x
History--18th century--Sources. | Equality before the law--France--
History--18th century--Sources. | Citizenship--France--History--18th
century--Sources. | France--Ethnic relations--History--18th century--
Sources. | France--History--Revolution, 1789-1799. | Godard, Jacques,
1762-1791. | Lawyers--France--Biography.
Classification: LCC KJV4207.J49 L48 2021 | DDC 342.4408/73--dc23
LC record available at https://lccn.loc.gov/2020042702

And he shall be thy spokesman unto the people; and it shall come to pass, that he shall be to thee a mouth, and thou shalt be to him in God's stead.

Exodus 4:15–16

In memory of
Robert and Jeanne Geissmann, A"H,
my maternal grandparents, who instilled in me
a deep respect for Jewish tradition & an abiding
affection for France, its culture and its history

Table of Contents

PROLOGUE

In the elaborately decorated great hall of the Hôtel de Ville of Paris, in 1790—just over six months after the great upheavals that had shaken France and had launched the events that have come to be known as the French Revolution—a delegation of eight men hesitatingly approached the long table at the front of the chamber in which the General Assembly of the Representatives of the Commune of Paris was convening. The Assembly comprised a very somber group of three hundred men, consisting of five representatives from each of the sixty districts located within the French capital. These men were charged, on an interim basis pending the installation of a more permanent municipal government, with the governance of the city of Paris—a city in the midst of an effervescent transformation characterized by extraordinary social and political turmoil.

The members of the delegation who walked cautiously toward the table at which the Assembly's officers sat were middle-aged to elderly. They were all rather stocky and somewhat overdressed. One member was dressed in the colorful military uniform of the newly formed Paris National Guard, and, upon close examination, did not appear to be French at all.

A ninth individual, who joined the delegation as the group moved slowly toward the officers' table, was a handsome, much younger man appearing to be not yet thirty. The young man, who accompanied the eight other men to the front of the hall, had risen from a seat within

the Assembly itself. He was dressed soberly and fashionably in the manner of most of the other members of the Assembly, his head covered
by a powdered wig from which emerged a small ponytail held in place
by an attractive ribbon. He now stood at the front of the group as they
approached the Assembly's officers. He walked confidently. The older
men, as they followed him, were hesitant in their gait, looking around
uncomfortably and visibly ill at ease. Upon their arrival near the front of
the chamber, the young man left the group and strode confidently to the
table, where, with suitable deference, he acknowledged the president of
the Assembly, a Catholic priest in full clerical garb. The priest extended
his hand in welcome and with a small gesture invited the young man to
speak. The older men moved respectfully to the side, hats in hand.

Reading from a prepared text, the young man began to address the
Assembly, making it obvious at the outset that he was both a member of
the Assembly and a sometime advocate for those on the margins of society. "I have left for just a moment the place that I occupy in your midst,"
he declared, "to assume the one that suits me when I speak on behalf of
supplicants and I serve as the the interpreter for the unfortunate."[1]

As he plunged into his remarks, it became apparent that he was an
experienced public speaker. He spoke with fluency and with the distinct
rhetorical flourishes that characterized members of the French legal profession. From the very beginning of his speech, the young man made it
unmistakeably clear that he was acting, not in his capacity as a member
of the Assembly he was addressing, but rather as an adviser and spokesman for a long-oppressed minority now asserting itself in the midst of
the greatest political upheaval in modern European history. His remarks
summarized an analysis of the legal and moral arguments for making
France's Ashkenazi Jews, who were then considered as foreigners and
as members of a separate "nation," full "active" citizens of France, with
identical rights to those granted to all other Frenchmen.[2]

---

1. Jacques Godard, *Discours prononcé le 28 Janvier 1790 par M. GODARD, Avocat
au Parlement, l'un des Représentans de la Commune, en présentant à l'Assemblée générale de la Commune, une Députation des JUIFS de Paris* (Paris: L'Imprimerie de
Lottin l'aîné & Lottin de St. Germain, 1790). All translations from the French are
the author's, unless otherwise noted.
2. Ashkenazi Jews, also known as German Jews, lived mostly in the eastern
provinces of France. Numbering approximately fifty thousand (out of a total
French population of slightly more than 28 million), they were mostly poor and

Subsequently published and thereby saved for posterity, the young man's plea was an important volley in the battle for equality for the long-suffering Ashkenazi Jewish community of France and, indirectly, for all the Jews of Europe at large. On the prior evening, the young man had arranged to have delivered to each member of the French National Constituent Assembly—the newly established and autoproclaimed national legislative body of France—the text of a lengthy and comprehensive petition addressing the very same issue in an effort to convince the members of the nascent national legislature to take immediate action in favor of Jewish equality. The petition filed with the National Assembly and the pleas made to the Paris Assembly constituted the initial steps of a determined political effort of lobbying on behalf of the Ashkenazi Jews of France, as they sought full integration into the nation they called home. The struggle would extend over nearly two years, but these dual steps marked a symbolic turning point. They would have a decisive effect on the struggle to destroy one of the oldest prejudices infecting the Western world, a struggle to fulfill for the Ashkenazi Jewish community of France its deep-seated desire to become fully integrated into French society while remaining faithful to its religious practices.

The young man, Jacques Godard, a Catholic from a modest noble family of the Burgundy region, without any personal links to Jews or Judaism but with a profound sense of fairness and justice and a deep respect for legal processes, would play a pivotal role in the fight for Jewish equality. With his guiding hand, his pen, and his voice, he spearheaded a campaign which would ultimately lift the Jews of France to formal legal equality with their fellow-citizens—a status that constituted a first in the history of modern Europe. Many individuals contributed to this achievement. But no non-Jew labored as intensively, as intelligently, and as devotedly as Godard.

Godard's life was brief, cut short by illness possibly caused by the pressures imposed on his health as a result of his considerable labors and ambitions. Today he is scarcely remembered. Perhaps, in part, this is because he died of natural causes, a death which denied him the dramatic

---

unassimilated. A few thousand Sephardic Jews (the descendants of refugees from the Iberian Peninsula and usually referred to as Spanish or Portuguese Jews) lived in southwestern France. They tended to be far more affluent and were generally much more assimilated than their Ashkenazi brethren. In addition, some five hundred Jews of mixed Ashkenazi and Sephardic ancestry, lived in Paris.

martyrdom under the blade of the guillotine that secured immortality for so many of his revolutionary contemporaries. He is barely a footnote in the story of the turbulent French Revolution and little more in the history of the Jewish people. But he assuredly deserves more. He was a tireless advocate for concepts of justice that we now take for granted. His abbreviated career was marked by powerful advocacy on behalf of a number of marginalized individuals and groups, including individuals falsely accused of crimes, a Black slave, a Protestant, and Jews. The story of Godard's life, with an emphasis on the energetic and skillful assistance he provided to the Ashkenazi Jews of France as they sought to achieve the elusive right to be free and equal citizens of the nation in which they resided, is a story that merits being told and remembered.

In order to tell this story appropriately, it is important to describe the historical, political, and social context in which it took place. Jacques Godard rendered his services in a particularly agitated epoch, where changing attitudes and their accompanying conflicts—political, social, and physical—were rapidly reshaping French society. To appreciate the role Godard played in the drama that led to the first achievement of full-fledged legal equality for a diaspora Ashkenazi Jewish community, it is necessary to examine the history and complex backdrop which constituted the setting for that role. Thus, in tracing and rendering the life of Jacques Godard, I have sought to describe the history of the Jewish people in France and the nature of the society in which Godard and they lived, as well as the forces which made that society what it was. I have also endeavored to describe the prominent personalities with whom Godard interacted and the turbulent political events in which the struggle for Jewish equality took place as viewed from Godard's point of reference.

In our time of growing religious extremism, increasing intolerance, and resurgent antisemitism, when fundamental democratic values and basic human rights, as well as the rule of law itself are in many places throughout the world under siege, the story of this struggle, not just for tolerance, but for true legal equality for a much-maligned religious minority in a nation that had been hostile to that minority for centuries, is a drama of special and consequential relevance—as is the life of an individual who was instrumental in achieving that equality.

CHAPTER 1

SEMUR-EN-AUXOIS

The Burgundian town of Semur-en-Auxois is located fewer than fifty miles to the northwest of Dijon, the mid-sized capital of the region best known for its wine and mustard production. Semur sits in the verdant Côte d'Or sector of eastern France, high above a sharp bend in the winding Armançon River. It is, as it has been for generations, a picturesque town, dominated by four ancient towers, the remnants of an important medieval fortress, and a prominent Gothic church whose origins date back to the eleventh century.[1] The streets are narrow and winding, lined with an assortment of centuries-old two- and three-story houses. Many of the houses are modest, but the town also has well over a dozen large and impressive mansions, a number of which date back to the eighteenth century and some even earlier, alluding to the wealth of a few of the town's residents. It has been asserted that Semur is one of the oldest towns in France, and its various ruins and monuments suggest that the claim has some merit.[2] It may have been founded as early as the fifth century.

---

1. This picturesque town has served as the backdrop for scenes in a number of movies, including the 1957 American film, "The Happy Road," directed by Gene Kelly and in which Kelly starred.
2. Alfred de Vaulabelle, *Histoire générale de Semur-en-Auxois* (Semur-en-Auxois: L. Horry Imprimeur-Editeur, 1905), 264. See also Benjamin Guérard, "Semur-en-Auxois," in *Histoire des Villes de France,* edited by Aristide Guilbert. Paris: Furne et Cie. – Perrotin – H. Fournier, 1848.

Favored by the waters of its river, by ample forests, and by the protective nature of the sharp bends in the Armançon River which enclosed its fortress on three sides, Semur grew steadily over the centuries. Then its population stabilized, and has not varied very much since the mid-eighteenth century, continuing to number approximately 4,500 individuals until this day. A certain lethargy, if not stagnancy, seems to have characterized the town during the eighteenth century.[3] In that era, Semur shared many of the physical, legal, and social attributes of other French towns of its size. Like many other such towns, until the French Revolution, residency was severely restricted and outsiders were generally unwelcome. Jews—the perennial pariahs of Western Christendom—were not allowed to live or carry out any commercial activity in the town.[4]

In this modest town, on July 1, 1762,[5] Jeanne-Baptiste Jassot,[6] the wife of Louis-Charles-Jacques Godard, gave birth to a son.[7] She and her husband gave the child the traditional Godard family Christian name of Jacques. According to an entry in the official records of Semur-en-Auxois, he was baptized on August 8 of the year of his birth. His godfather, Jacques Jassot,

---

3. In the words of one scholar, in 1789 the town was "without much activity" ("*cette petite ville bourguingnonne, sans grande activité*") and even "asleep" ("*la ville est endormie*"). Régine Robin-Aizertin, "Les structures sociales à Semur-en-Auxois en 1789," *Actes du Quatre-vingt onzième Congrès National des Sociétés Savantes* (Rennes, 1966), Section d'Histoire Moderne et Contemporaine, vol. 2, *Ancien Régime et Révolution* (Paris: Bibliothèque Nationale, 1969), 241, 249.

4. Ibid., 264.

5. Jean Baptiste Louis Joseph Billecocq, Letter of November 5, 1791, eulogizing Jacques Godard. *Mercure Universel*, vol. 9, no. 230, pp. 86–88.

6. *Archives départementales de la Côte d'Or, Semur-en-Auxois, État-civil de la Côte d'Or-Registres paroissiaux et/ou d'état civil: 1759–1773*, p. 122.

7. Louis-Charles-Jacques Godard was born in Semur-en-Auxois on January 17, 1730, the son of Jacques Godard and Marie-Colombe Pasquier. He died on March 3, 1807, in Semur "in his house on rue Montbelliard." Since the elder Jacques Godard's death was attested to by his forty-three-year-old son, Jean-François Dominique Godard, we know that Jacques Godard had at least one younger brother. Archives départementales de la Côte d'Or, Semur-en-Auxois, an XIII-1810 – FRAD021EC 603/026 – Vue 292/532. Dominique Godard, who was an ordained priest, would become mayor of Semur during Year V (1796–1797), serving for three years. He would die in Paris in 1811, at the age of 48. Vaulabelle, *Histoire générale de Semur-en-Auxois*, 290. Godard also had a younger sister, Marie-Colombe, born in 1766.

was his grandfather, an avocat (a lawyer[8]) registered with the Parlement of Dijon. His godmother, Marie-Colombe Godard, was likely his aunt or great-aunt and was the widow of Philibert Rousseau, also an avocat registered with the Parlement of Dijon.[9]

It is noted in the entry concerning the younger Godard's baptism that his father was similarly an avocat registered with the very same Parlement in Dijon. However, just a few years later, in 1767, the senior Godard was to become an auditor of the *Chambre des Comptes* of Dijon, the governmental Commission of Auditors (and precursor of today's *Cour des Comptes*) charged with overseeing government finances.[10] The various *Chambres des Comptes*, scattered across the regions of France, were austere bodies which slowly and meticulously reviewed the inflow of revenues and the outflow of expenses from the national and regional treasuries.

Godard's father, as a member of a body tasked with the oversight of government finances and the descendant of a long line of distinguished public servants, likely valued intellectual rigor and had a strong sense of public duty. Charged with verifying the proper application of government funds, he was undoubtedly imbued with a belief in proper ethical conduct and would have infused his own family with that same sense of moral responsibility. He would also have been a conscientious and jealous guardian of both the prerogatives of the administrative bodies on which he and other members of his family served and of his place in the social hierarchy of his community. Jacques Godard, the father, also appears to have been a man of intellectual curiosity. He spent considerable sums building the family library, notably with volumes of the *Encyclopédie*, the

---

8. See Chapter 2, p. 11n1.

9. The Parlements in eigtheenth-century France were not legislative bodies, rather, they were administrative and judicial entities which registered royal decrees in their local areas, a prerequisite to the enforceability of such decrees in those regions. As such, for generations, the Parlements had served as one of the very few checks on the power of France's absolute monarchs, both through their judicial decisions and by their occasional refusals to register royal decrees. In addition, the Parlements served as courts of appeal, reviewing decisions of lower courts and sometimes, as we will observe, their own prior decisions. Their role in the events leading to the French Revolution was to be of the utmost significance. See Chapter 9 below.

10. Henri Beaune and Jules d'Arbaumont, *La Noblesse aux États de Bourgogne de 1350 à 1789* (Dijon: La Marche Libraire-Editeur, 1864), 106; Robin-Aizertin, op. cit., 234.

great compilation of contemporary knowledge that the Enlightenment *philosophes* Denis Diderot and Jean-Baptiste le Rond d'Alembert edited and assembled in the second half of the eighteenth century, and whose presence in a home library was a sign of the owner's interest in the pursuit of knowledge and of an enlightened view of the world.[11]

The Godard family had relationships with regional intellectuals, in particular with the renowned Burgundian naturalist George-Louis Leclerc de Buffon, one of the most prominent scientists of the time, as well as with Buffon's circle of friends.[12] Buffon reportedly had a "special affection" for the young Godard, an affection which seems to have been reciprocated in abundance.[13] In 1788, when Buffon died, Jacques Godard would write an obituary for the *Journal de Paris,* in which he highlighted that relationship, noting that he had "lived for some time in the intimate company of Buffon."[14] Emphasizing in the obituary that his familiarity with Buffon dated to his youngest days, Godard wrote that "since childhood [he] had had a relationship with the great man, and still had a relationship with

11. There exist two unpublished documents that attest to the senior Godard's interest in books. One is a copy of a purchase order dated December 10, 1776, from Jacques Godard, "*auditeur de la Chambre des Comptes,*" to Dijon's most prominent bookseller, Jean-Baptiste Capel, acknowledging an obligation to purchase the most recent edition of the *Encyclopédie.* The other is a receipt dated March 29, 1780, from Capel acknowledging payment-in-full from Jacques Godard, "auditeur de la Chambre des Comptes," for the purchase of certain volumes of the *Encyclopédie.* (From the author's personal collection.)
12. Following a medical education and studies in mathematics, Georges-Louis Leclerc, Comte de Buffon (1707–1788) was appointed supervisor of the royal botanical garden, which was to become the *Jardin des Plantes* in Paris, a preeminent center for the study of botany. As a consequence of this appointment, he prepared a survey of natural history. The product was a fifty-volume work, entitled *Histoire naturelle, générale et particulière.* The work was left unfinished at Buffon's death, but dominated the study of the natural sciences in France for generations. In recognition of his scientific accomplishments, Buffon was elected to the Académie Française in 1753, and in 1782 became an honorary foreign member of the American Academy of Arts and Sciences. He spent much of his life on his estate at Montbard, just a few miles from Semur, and was both a local and a national celebrity.
13. J.B.L.J. Billecocq, letter in *Mercure Universel,* vol. 9, no. 230, pp. 86–89.
14. *Journal de Paris,* May 3, 1788, no. 124, pp. 545–47, and May 4, 1788, no. 125, pp. 549–51.

most of his friends."[15] Encounters with so prominent a scholar undoubtedly had an impact on the young man, minimally making him aware of the intellectual ferment that was going on all around him.

Louis-Charles-Jacques Godard's ancestry and his position in the Chambre des Comptes of Dijon brought an important social standing that would have provided the Godard family with advantages in an era in which belonging to the proper social class was absolutely essential to achieving material success. The significance of status in the small towns of France of the late eighteenth century can scarcely be overemphasized. Almost every aspect of life revolved around that status. Where a family lived, the schools attended by its children, its circle of friends and acquaintances, as well as its relationships with neighbors, authorities, and with suppliers of goods and services were all governed by its status in the community. Familial status was also critical in assuring that the next generation could pursue a meaningful career.

The Godard family had benefited from regional prominence for many generations. It is possible to ascertain that, as early as 1499, a certain Guillaume Godard from Semur held the position of public prosecutor (*procureur du Roi*) in Dijon. He served in that important position until 1507.[16]

The familial tradition of public service is echoed a number of generations later when a descendant of Guillaume, a certain Jean Godard,[17] served in the 1690s as an "*officier au grenier à sel et au bailliage*" (an officer of the salt attic and of the bailiwick) of Semur, receiving the specific title of "*garde-scel en la chancellerie*" (guardian of the salt in the chancery) and then of "*conseiller au bailliage*" (counselor at the bailiwick).[18] Effectively, the holder of a post relating to "salt" was a tax collector, with the right to collect and store the tangible evidence of one of the most significant of the indirect taxes assessed by the Bourbon monarchy, a tax on salt (the so-called "*gabelle*").[19] The tax was levied through required payments to

15. Ibid., May 3, 1788, no. 124, p. 545.
16. Jules d'Arbaumont, *Armorial de la Chambre des Comptes de Dijon, d'après le manuscrit inédit du Père Gautier* (Dijon: Lamarche, Librairie-Editeur, 1881), 387.
17. Ibid., 351.
18. The term "bailiwick" refers to a judicial district. However, the judicial districts were sometimes indistinct. Overlapping bailiwicks existed and conflicts could arise as assertions of authority caused clashes among officials.
19. See *Tarifs et sentence de Messieurs les Officiers du Grenier à Sel de Paris portant*

the monarchy upon delivery of a quantity of salt (which was a product of great value, especially in the interior of the nation). The officer would store the collected salt in a special place called euphemistically a "*grenier*" (attic) and collect taxes in connection with its purchase. However, the officer also acted as an administrator, an accountant, and a judge. His judicial role was primarily related to deciding issues concerning fraud with respect to the salt tax. The various components of this office carried with them both remunerative benefits and social status. The position also served to provide the officer with an intimidating and resented role as a feared government official.[20]

In 1718, Jean Godard was replaced in his role as *conseiller* by his son, Jacques, the grandfather of the Jacques Godard of interest to us. Jean and his son Jacques had been privileged to have, since the 1690s, a coat of arms, a critical symbol of their family's prominence. The Godard coat of arms was a crest "of gold color with an azure band on which are embedded three sets of antlers [or horns] in a silver color."[21] This emblem evidenced that certain members of the Godard family, those registered with a Parlement, were part of the nobility of the robe (*noblesse de robe*), the second tier of French nobility. While this status was far from that enjoyed by the nobility of the sword (*noblesse d'épée*)—the true elites of that era—it reflected a family's significant social standing within its provincial community. In keeping with its status, the family appears to have lived comfortably. During the latter half of the eighteenth century, they lived on rue du Rampart in the heart of Semur. Although the precise location of their residence is not known, it is likely that the family lived in one of the street's still extant half-dozen large and attractive eighteenth-century mansions.[22]

---

règlement pour le prix du sel, tant de la ville de Paris, que de la Campagne (Paris: L'Imprimerie de Charles Huguier, 1710).

20. Philibert Rousseau, the late husband of Jacques Godard's godmother, had held the same position prior to Godard's birth. (État civil, 122.)

21. Charles D'Hozier, *Armorial Général de France, Recueil Officiel dressé en vertu de l'Edit de 1696*, Généralité de Bourgogne, vol. 1 (Dijon: Imprimerie Darantière, 1875); cf. d'Arbaumont, *Armorial de la Chambre des Comptes de Dijon*. A simplified black and white version of this coat of arms appears on a Godard family document in the author's private collection.

22. In his history of Semur-en-Auxois, Vaulabelle indicates that, at certain times, the street currently known as rue du Rampart bore the name rue de Montbeillard—the name of the street identified in the elder Jacques Godard's death certificate as the location of the house in which he died. Vaulabelle, *Histoire générale*

The younger Jacques Godard was born into this relatively prominent provincial family just as the long and bloody Seven Years' War was coming to an inglorious end for France. Another in the series of internecine European conflicts that had been tearing the continent apart for centuries, the Seven Years' War had a global component. In North America, it became known as the French and Indian War, the conflict which cemented English control of most of the continent and which helped to establish the military reputation of a young soldier in the British army named George Washington. Regardless of the name ascribed to it, for France the war was a watershed—and not a particularly felicitous one. As the war drew to a close, France was on the verge of losing most of its overseas empire to its perennial enemy, Great Britain. Canada had effectively been lost just a couple of years before when, in 1761, British troops, commanded by General James Wolfe, surreptitiously climbed up the side of the great fortress at Quebec and defeated the French defenders under the leadership of the Marquis de Montcalm. The French defeat at the Battle of Quebec proved fatal for France's ambition to remain a major presence in North America, leaving only the tiny islands of St. Pierre and Miquelon off the coast of Canada as a sad consolation prize. A treaty of peace that would formalize the loss was less than a year away. Partially as a consequence of the war, the mood in France at this time was suitably gloomy. Due to the confluence of a number of dramatic and adverse occurrences, it would get much worse over the course of the next several decades.

By 1762, Louis XV, the fourth member of the Bourbon dynasty to rule France, had been king for forty-seven years. He had been the nominal head of the French kingdom since his ascent to the throne at the age of five on the death of his great-grandfather, Louis XIV, the glorious Sun King. Louis XV lived most of his life in the shadow of his illustrious predecessor, isolated from the realities of the people he ostensibly governed. His reign began with a regency headed by his distant cousin, the Duc d'Orléans,[23] during which the morals of the ruling class had reached a

---

de Semur-en-Auxois, 98.

23. The Dukes of Orléans were descended from Philippe d'Orléans, the younger brother of Louis XIV. At many points in the ensuing centuries, the descendants of this royal brother posed serious challenges to the elder related branch of the Bourbon royal family. The fraternal competition of half a dozen generations before remained a powerful force in the political conflicts of the late eighteenth century. It became particularly venomous around the time of the French Revo-

nadir and financial failures had severely tarnished the standing of the French nation. Financial and moral scandals as well as ruinous wars would continue to punctuate Louis XV's reign.

In 1762, Louis XV was only fifty-two years old. But, having lived a dissolute and listless life, he was prematurely old and tired, and was uninterested in the details of governing. Living in the isolation of rigid court etiquette in the splendor of the vast palace at Versailles, just over ten miles to the southwest of Paris, he spent most of his time hunting, partying, and womanizing, leaving the work of governing to an array of ministers. Most prominent among the ministers serving the king in 1762 was Étienne-Francois de Choiseul.[24] At this stage of Louis XV's reign, Choiseul held most of the power of the state. In this role, he was required to develop close relationships with suppliers to the royal armies. Particularly noteworthy among these suppliers was a certain Berr Cerf Berr, a wealthy, resourceful, and prominent Jew from Alsace, with whom Choiseul developed an uncommon bond. This bond would provide Cerf Berr with an opportunity to play a critical role in leading the Ashkenazi

---

lution, when the head of the Orléans family fomented opposition to his cousin the king and then voted to send him to his death on the guillotine, only to follow him there a few months later. The competition between the two familial branches would continue through the nineteenth century when Bourbon and Orléans kings of France alternated as monarchs. The competition ended definitively when the last Bourbon descendant, Henri, Comte de Chambord, Charles X's grandson and Louis XVI's grandnephew, died childless in 1883, thereby conceding claims to the throne of France to the Orléans branch. The Orléanist claims continue to this day.

24. Étienne François, Marquis de Stainville, Duc de Choiseul (1719–1785), was descended from an aristocratic family from the Lorraine region. Initially, he served in the military and then as a diplomat, first as French ambassador to Rome and then, more importantly, to Vienna, where he cemented an alliance between the French and Austrian monarchies. His diplomatic success led him to rise rapidly through the ranks from Foreign Minister to, in 1761, principal minister of Louis XV's government. In that capacity, he was responsible for negotiating the Treaty of Paris which ended the Seven Years' War, for the annexation of Corsica to France, for the incorporation of Lorraine into France, and for the formal establishment of the several French colonies in the Antilles. He was removed from power and exiled to his country estate in 1770, in part as a result of a conflict with Madame DuBarry, the king's mistress. Although his exile ended when Louis XVI ascended the throne, he never regained any actual power within the government.

Jewish community in the struggle for Jewish equality.[25] In this context, Cerf Berr would come into close contact with Jacques Godard and become Godard's client.

The absence of a strong leader at the apex of French society was sowing the seeds of disintegration inside the complex and dysfunctional hierarchy of the French governmental structure. Battle lines were being drawn between royal authority and regional spheres of power—between the entrenched and dissolute nobility and a rising and ambitious bourgeoisie led in considerable measure by members of the legal profession. Supplemented, or perhaps stimulated, by the intellectual liberation spurred by the Enlightenment and the concomitant weakening of the Catholic Church, these battles were on the verge of becoming explosive and would soon culminate in a conflagration that we have come to call the French Revolution, which would unravel the fragile fabric of French society and destroy the old order.

Far from Versailles, in his hometown of Semur, Jacques Godard developed as a precocious child, given to writing and speech-making from an early age. His family's social standing, with its local prominence and status within the administration of France, as well as his father's role as an auditor in the *Chambre des Comptes* of Dijon and his family's friendship with regional intellectuals, suggest that the young Godard must have overheard and then participated in wide-ranging conversations about philosophy, politics, and the growing social turmoil. On the basis of a portrait of the young Godard, painted some sixteen years after his death, but based upon a pencil sketch apparently made from life, we can surmise that he was a handsome young man. In the extant pastel image of Godard, he is depicted with dreamy eyes, full lips, a slight cleft in his chin, a somewhat plump but pleasant face and a distinctly aristocratic dignity. The artist depicted him wearing a somber outfit appropriate for a youthful professional of the era with a prominent white-powdered wig adorning his head. The overall impression created by this image of Jacques Godard is of an attractive, purposeful, intelligent and thoughtful individual.[26]

---

25. See Chapter 14.
26. The portrait of Jacques Godard by a unidentified artist, owned by the author, bears a label in handwritten script pasted on the reverse side which reads: "Jacques Godard avocat with the Parlement of Paris, member of the first legislature, born on August 7, 1762 [*sic*], first son of Mr. Jacques Godard, auditor at the *Chambre des Comptes* of Dijon, died in Paris on November 4, 1791 on St. Gervais

The blend of his prominent provincial familial environment and tradition, his own intellectual qualities, and his good looks, charm, and interpersonal skills likely were the factors that led him to decide to become a member of the legal profession. The civil service and enlightenment values of his father may also have served to prompt him to devote a portion of his brief legal career to assisting those who stood on the margins of his society and generally to work toward the public good.

---

and St. Protais's Day as a result of a putrid and malign fever, at the age of 29. This portrait was made 16 years after the death of Jacques Godard and copied from a small portrait made in pencil." ⸱⸱

CHAPTER 2

MOVING TO PARIS –
BECOMING AN AVOCAT

As a very young man, Jacques Godard chose to leave his native province
and move to Paris in pursuit of his goal of becoming an avocat and of ac-
quiring a measure of fame.[1] By the time he was nineteen, he had settled in

1. The term "avocat," as that term was used in the eighteenth-century context,
is not readily translated. David Bell, in his important work on the French legal profession of the eighteenth century, translates the term as "barrister"—an
individual who would represent his clients in front of courts. I believe that the
term avocat is somewhat more expansive. However, the educational requirements were minimal; a simple and not very difficult to obtain university degree
seemed to suffice. A short clerkship followed by sponsorship by an avocat who
had been in practice for at least twenty years was perceived as being adequate
to finalize the qualifications. To actually practice as a "barrister," however, an
avocat had to be registered with the Order of Avocats affiliated with a Parlement. Only a small proportion of qualified avocats were in fact registered; many
qualified avocats chose to pursue other, potentially more lucrative, careers. The
actual tasks of an avocat were ill-defined and ranged from pleading as a barrister
in the courts to assisting with simple legal formalities. As we will see, as the
Revolution approached, avocats also became advocates of their clients before
legislative bodies. To avoid any confusion about the definition of an "avocat," I
have chosen to use the French term rather than to translate it. Had I chosen to
translate the term, I probably would have used the generic English word "lawyer" rather than "barrister" (which to American lawyers has a very British tone
and suggests an activity exclusively related to litigation), in order to encompass
the wide range of activities carried out under that designation. See David Bell,

Paris in a modest lodging owned by a Monsieur Thérigny, located at 42, rue des Fossés-Montmartre.[2] His lodging was just off the elegant place des Victoires and a few blocks behind the Palais-Royal, the residence of the Orléans family, cousins and competitors of the ruling Bourbon dynasty.

With approximately six hundred thousand inhabitants, Paris was by far France's largest city and second in population size only to London among all European cities. It was not the beautiful city of broad boulevards and uniform architecture we know today. Rather, it was still a maze of medieval streets and rundown buildings, afflicted by great poverty, but accented by a smattering of large plazas adorned by spectacular monumental public buildings and with a few neighborhoods in which stately aristocratic mansions dominated.[3] It was the economic, intellectual, and cultural center of France, where fortune and misfortune could be found in abundance. In the early 1780s Paris was a city in ferment, especially intellectually, where Enlightenment philosophy and notions of political reform regarding the institutions of France's government were fiercely debated.

In the spring of 1774, Louis XV succumbed to smallpox and was replaced by his grandson, Louis-Auguste, who ascended the throne at the age of nineteen as Louis XVI. The new king's consort was the youngest daughter of the Austrian Empress Maria-Theresa—the archduchess, Marie-Antoinette. The marriage was the product of a political arrangement that was intended to cement the recent alliance between France and Austria that had been engineered by the Duc de Choiseul. In stark contrast to his grandfather, the young monarch seemed very interested in being an involved and benevolent ruler. However, raised in the rarified

Lawyers and Citizens: The Making of a Political Elite in Old Regime France (New York: Oxford University Press, 1991), 26, et seq.

2. Rue des Fossés-Montmartre was the street which is today the segment of rue d'Aboukir that runs from the particularly attractive and chic seventeenth-century place des Victoires to the very ordinary rue Montmartre. By the standards of the times, it was rather distant from the center of the city of Paris and especially from the Palace of Justice and Châtelet where avocats plied their trade. It was a kind of suburban area, and thus would have been significantly less expensive than the neighborhoods closer to the Seine. In 1788, Godard moved, as will be discussed later, to a residence in the heart of the concentrated and bustling Marais district on rue des Blancs-Manteaux.

3. See Graham Robb, *Parisian: An Adventure History of Paris* (London & Paris: W. W. Norton & Company, 2010) and Joan DeJean, *How Paris Became Paris: The Invention of the Modern City* (New York: Bloomsbury, 2014).

atmosphere of the Court at Versailles, he was ill-prepared for his tasks and was far too young and inexperienced to assume the role of absolute monarch. His undistinguished physical appearance and natural shyness, combined with an apparent indolence and lack of intellectual acuity, created a perception of weakness within the executive power structure. This perceived vacuum at the apex of the French government created both complexity and opportunity. Most importantly, the French involvement in the American War of Independence, upon which the young Louis XVI decided to embark in 1777 in hopes of avenging France's terrible losses in the Seven Years' War and thereby enhancing the image of the Bourbon monarchy, was on the verge of bankrupting the state. The American war also served to popularize many of the republican political concepts that were developing in these rebellious British colonies. In France, a volcanic explosion was in the offing, and avocats were destined to be at the forefront of the conflagration.

It is in the midst of this slowly brewing storm that, at the young age of nineteen, on July 10, 1781, Jacques Godard was accepted as an avocat in Paris. However, it was only on February 22, 1783, that he officially became a member of the *Ordre des avocats* (Order of Lawyers) of Paris and was registered as an avocat authorized to pursue a legal practice—including an appellate practice before the *Parlement de Paris*, the highest court of appeals of the city.[4] By that time, he had obtained a university degree and rapidly completed a clerkship, entitling him to accede formally to the ranks of the legal profession. As was the custom, upon becoming a member of the Order, he was assigned a specific seat on one of the benches in the great hall of the Palace of Justice. The seat to which he was assigned was located on the fifth bench near the *Bonne-Foi* ("Good Faith") column (which was the sixth column from the front of the hall).[5] The great hall still exists today, and, although it is now devoid of benches, it is readily possible to stand on the spot where Godard's designated seat was located.

In the late eighteenth century, becoming an avocat was not particularly difficult.[6] Legal education was a relatively perfunctory matter mostly involving the payment of fees, without the expenditure of much intellectual effort. A "*stage*" or clerkship with an established avocat was the most

---

4. See *Almanach Royal*, 1790, 363.
5. Claude-Nicolas Sanson, *Tableau des Avocats au Parlement* (Paris, 1787), 41.
6. Bell, *Lawyers and Citizens*, 27.

onerous requirement.[7] Being accepted into the *Ordre des avocats* required the sponsorship of an avocat with twenty years of seniority. Although compared to the large number of attorneys in the contemporary United States the number may seem modest, eighteenth-century France had a large number of avocats and they were becoming increasingly organized and influential.[8] In a recent detailed study of the legal profession of the era, it was noted that, although France had thousands of qualified avocats, only an average of just over five hundred were actually practicing in each year between 1700 and 1789.[9] The majority of individuals who became avocats did not continue to pursue the profession, choosing other activities once they had obtained the title. Importantly, there was a marked tendency among young men to follow in their fathers' footsteps into the profession, with well over fifty percent of avocats of that era being themselves the sons of avocats, notaries, or members of the high administration.[10] Consequently, since so many members of Godard's family had been avocats in prior generations, young Jacques Godard's choice to become an avocat would have been a natural one. Only his determination to leave his native province for Paris was somewhat unusual (albeit not entirely uncommon) and suggests a strong streak of ambition.

Godard was well aware of the relatively simple path to becoming an avocat.[11] However, as he would several years later inform his cousin Jean Cortot—an avocat originally from Semur who had himself become a member of the Bar of the city of Dijon at the age of twenty-two (in 1748) and was to spend his entire career there as an avocat and as the librarian of the royal library of the city—any young man wishing to enter the profession in Paris had to pass through a multitude of barriers.[12] Godard

---

7. Ibid., 28.

8. Cf. Hervé Leuwers, *L'Invention du Barreau français 1660–1830. La Construction Nationale d'un Groupe Professionnel* (Paris: Editions de l'École des hautes études en sciences sociales, 2006).

9. Bell, *Lawyers and Citizens*, 28.

10. Ibid.

11. Letter from Jacques Godard to Jean Cortot, June 19, 1785 (Archives de la Côte d'Or, Serie E, Nos. 642 & 643).

12. Jean Cortot (1726–?) was an avocat and also served as a royal censor and inspector general of the library of the duchies of Bourgogne and nearby provinces in Dijon (1784). See p. 29, *Inventaire-sommaire des Archives Communales Antérieures à 1790*, written by MM. Le Gouvenain and Ph. Vallée, archivists, Ville de Dijon, vol. 3 (Dijon: Imprimerie Typographique et Lithographique de F. Carré, 1892). Cor-

explained that, in order to become an avocat, it was necessary to clerk for "four years" and that during those years, every prospective avocat was "observed," and that "attention is paid to your morality, to your conduct."[13] Furthermore, he wrote, "the two representatives of each column" [the physical columns located in the great hall of the Paris Palace of Justice near which each avocat registered with the Parlement was assigned a specific seat] "visit you in order to ascertain that you are decently lodged, that you have a sufficient number of books." He went on to indicate that a full report was then delivered to a commission made up of avocats (two from each of the ten "columns") and current and former leaders of the Bar. Ultimately, certain senior members of the Bar would vote to determine whether the young postulate would be admitted or not.[14] Once an avocat had been admitted, Godard noted, the Order of Avocats "kept watch over [the young avocat] with the greatest severity." He specified the nature of the controls exercised on a young avocat: "An inappropriate pleading is eliminated, irregular conduct, failure to be courteous, everything is punished, either by a reprimand or by a suspension."[15] Thus, although the barriers to entry into the profession were modest, not everyone could be admitted, and the members of the Bar exercised a certain amount of self-policing to maintain standards.

If admission to the Bar posed modest challenges, achieving success as an avocat was an altogether different and much more daunting matter.

---

tot was born in Dijon on March 25, 1726, the son of Étienne Cortot and Huguette Mouchot, whose family came from Godard's hometown of Semur-en-Auxois. The precise familial link between Godard and Cortot is not entirely clear. Godard always referred to Cortot as his "cousin" while Cortot would refer to Godard as his "relative." In any event, the relationship between the two men appears to have been rather strong for a while, but ended abruptly when their politics began to diverge dramatically as the Revolution approached and Godard became increasingly supportive of the movement to restructure France's governing institutions. Cortot was and remained a traditional royalist. It is because of Cortot's royalist leanings, which resulted in his hasty departure and exile from Dijon in 1792, with the subsequent confiscation of his personal papers, that the correspondence between the "cousins" was preserved.

13. In spite of Godard's specific mention of a four-year clerkship, the time which elapsed between his acceptance as an avocat and his registration with the Bar suggests that his clerkship was considerably shorter, likely less than two years.

14. Letter from Godard to Cortot, October 28, 1788. Archives départementales de la Côte d'Or, Archives civiles – Série E, nos. 642 & 643.

15. Ibid.

As it has been noted, the French pre-Revolutionary legal system was immensely complex and convoluted, even byzantine. "The operative concepts of [the French] government [of that era] were duplication, ambiguity and competition."[16] Learning the essentials of the legal profession and how to maneuver through the various layers of overlapping and frequently conflicting jurisdictions and the multitude of tribunals and regulatory agencies was a complex and time-consuming effort. Developing contacts, both within the profession and outside of it, was also an essential ingredient to a successful career, and equally difficult. It took diligence and ambition to navigate this system successfully. Godard was well-suited to the task. He was a young man who appeared resolved to achieve success, at all levels, and quickly.

A friend and mentor of the young Godard, a priest from Godard's hometown of Semur named Théodoric, writing to Godard on May 1, 1784, alluded to Godard's driving ambition, and expressed a prophetic concern that Godard's "love of glory, that the desire for a precocious reputation" could lead him to cause harm to his health. The friend went on to note that Godard was gifted with "wit, good judgment and a happy disposition," and that he should rely on those attributes and "develop good working habits." Théodoric also urged Godard to form professional relationships with the most prominent avocats of the time, who, he speculated, would be best positioned to appreciate Godard's "talents and morals."[17] Godard seems to have taken this latter advice to heart.

By 1785, as he was in the initial stages of his legal career, the young Godard demonstrated an eagerness not merely to become an avocat, but to penetrate Parisian society and to climb as rapidly as possible into the very limited ranks of the most celebrated jurists of his time. He was, as his friend Théodoric had noted in his 1784 letter, ambitious and sought without hesitation to develop and use connections.[18] On June 19, 1785, barely two years after being registered as an avocat, Godard wrote about his new profession to his cousin Cortot. He wrote with the enthusiasm

---

16. Bell, *Lawyers and Citizens,* 22.
17. Letter dated May 1, 1784, to Jacques Godard from Théodoric, Lyon, près place des Terreaux. (From the author's personal collection.)
18. In his 1788 obituary of Buffon, Godard would write approvingly that Buffon worked extremely long hours and subordinated all else to the search for glory, suggesting that Godard regarded self-promotion as a positive quality to be pursued and lauded. *Journal de Paris,* May 3, 1788, no. 124, p. 546.

suitable to a newly initiated professional, remarking that he was "young and everything looks beautiful in the career I have chosen." He held a lofty view of his chosen profession, writing, "I believe there is no better station in life than ours." However, he also demonstrated a realism less typical for his age, indicating to his cousin that being an avocat "is really only a social station (*état*) when one gives it some consideration. The title of avocat by itself is the smallest of all titles, because it is the easiest to obtain."[19]

Godard was to carry on a lengthy and prolific correspondence with Cortot. The correspondence gave Godard an opportunity to solicit advice from Cortot, but also provided Godard with an outlet through which he could express both professional and political views. It would provide a window to his efforts to develop his skills and connections, as well as to his increasingly strong opinions about the turbulent times in which he lived. There may have been an additional purpose to Godard's frequent (sometimes, even daily) letters to Cortot: Cortot seems to have been an important source of financial assistance to the young Godard. In a letter to Cortot, written on December 9, 1787, Godard alluded to the happy prospect of being able to repay his debt to his cousin upon his return to Paris following a visit to his hometown of Semur.[20] With access to financial resources a challenge throughout his career, Godard would not have been above maintaining a close relationship with someone who could help to alleviate his financial pressures.

Godard made no secret of his ambition. In the June 19, 1785 letter to his cousin Cortot, the young Godard expressed his willingness to work very hard, indicating that "Work, patience and adequate time, these are the three great instruments of my desires."[21] Then he confessed to his strenuous efforts to become well introduced into the legal world, essentially through networking: "When I need rest, I go to become electrified by the great avocats of the capital. Gerbier wishes me well, but I am particularly linked to Élie de Beaumont and Target."[22]

Godard selected well in the creation of his network. Of all the members of the Paris *Ordre des Avocats* in the decade preceding the French Revolution, Pierre-Jean-Baptiste Gerbier was perhaps the most prominent

---

19. Letter from Godard to Cortot, June 19, 1785.
20. Letter from Godard to Cortot, December 9, 1787.
21. Ibid.
22. Ibid.

and admired for his persuasive abilities.[23] Gerbier, born in Rennes, was
one of the ambitious provincials who chose at a young age to seek fame
and fortune in the capital as members of the legal profession, becoming
renowned as a result of their legal and oratorical skills. Gerbier achieved
superstar-like status among the members of the Bar of his era, successfully pleading on behalf of a wide variety of plaintiffs and defendants. As
a measure of their respect for him, his colleagues gave him the moniker,
"Eagle of the Bar."[24] His skills were primarily as an orator, but very few
of his pleadings have survived.[25] As a final testimonial to the respect in
which he was held by his brethren in the profession, Gerbier was elected
president of the Paris Bar in 1787, shortly before he succumbed to illness
and died. Learning the elements of oratory from Gerbier could only enhance Godard's career.

Jean-Baptiste-Jacques Élie de Beaumont, the second individual mentioned by Godard in his letter to Cortot, was a Protestant member of
the *Ordre des avocats*, registered with the Parlement of the capital of
Normandy, Rouen.[26] Protestants represented a small minority within
the population of France and, although they could now live in relative

---

23. Pierre-Jean-Baptiste Gerbier de la Massillays (1725–1788), born in the provincial town of Rennes, was registered as an avocat with the Parlement de Paris
in 1745. He became a prominent avocat and noted orator. During the 1770s, he
alienated many of his fellow members of the Bar by siding with Maupeou, Louis
XV's chancellor (Minister of Justice), when the latter sought to suppress the Parlements. However, he reconciled with his colleagues, who elected him president
of the Paris Bar in 1787, shortly before his death.
24. Thiéblin, Henri, *Éloge de Gerbier* (Paris: Typographie de E. Plon, 1875), 7.
25. The terrible fires that swept through many public buildings—including the
Paris Palais de Justice and Hôtel de Ville—during the uprising of the Paris Commune in 1871, resulted in the destruction of many documents related to the legal
profession. As a consequence, the pleadings of the avocats of the Bar of the Ancien Régime are now very incomplete. Copies of Gerbier's written pleadings are,
in large part, lost to posterity. Henri Thiéblin, ibid.
26. Jean-Baptiste-Jacques Élie de Beaumont (1732–1786), originally from Normandy, registered with the Paris Parlement in 1752. Despite his Protestant faith,
he achieved considerable success as an avocat. But it is for his representation, in
1762, of the martyred Protestant Jean Calas's family that he attained great fame.
His membership in the most important of Paris's Masonic Lodges, the *Loge des
Neufs-Soeurs* (Lodge of the Nine Sisters) provided him with status and high-level
social connections. Among the members of the Lodge was Benjamin Franklin,
with whom Élie de Beaumont seems to have had significant contact.

security, they had not yet attained full legal equality. Consequently, Élie de Beaumont's religious affiliation put him in a somewhat precarious position in overwhelmingly Catholic France, although it also provided him with a special perspective from which to carry out his legal work. Born in 1732 in the Cotentin section of Normandy, which borders the English Channel, Élie de Beaumont was yet another provincial who acquired fame in Paris.

Just like Godard a generation later, Élie de Beaumont moved to Paris to participate in the great legal movements of his time. He became known throughout France as a result of of the brief he filed in 1762 in the celebrated case of Jean Calas. Jean Calas was, like Élie de Beaumont, a Protestant. He was falsely accused of killing his son, allegedly because the son was about to convert to Catholicism. Calas was tortured and found guilty of the murder. Ultimately, he was brutally executed, despite having ceaselessly proclaimed his innocence. The liberal forces in France, locked in a protracted struggle with the Catholic hierarchy and its reactionary tendencies, fought against this injustice during the legal proceedings and then later sought to overturn Calas's conviction despite the implementation of the sentence. Élie de Beaumont's efforts in representing the Calas family, joined by eloquent appeals from many *philosophes* and, most notably, Voltaire, were ultimately, but belatedly, successful.[27] Some years after his execution, Calas was fully exonerated and Louis XV was compelled to pay compensation to the Calas family. Élie de Beaumont was acclaimed for his success in the Calas case and achieved great fame as a consequence. He formed part of a vanguard of avocats who fought intolerance and obscurantism in mid- and late eighteenth-century France during the years leading to the French Revolution and who contributed to the moderate and tolerant ideology that prevailed in its earliest phase.

The Target to whom Godard referred in his letter to Cortot was Guy-Jean-Baptiste Target, another of the true giants of the Paris Bar of the pre-revolutionary period. A Parisian by birth, he was universally recognized as one of the era's most prominent avocats, "one of the premier orators of the Bar," in the words of a colleague, and as a significant personality. He was a man who frequented the best salons and knew the

---

27. Élie de Beaumont. *Mémoire à Consulter pour la Dame Anne-Rose Caribel, veuve Calas, & pour les Enfans.* Imprimerie de Le Breton, 1762.

leading thinkers of his time.[28] As was the custom of the era, he was a prolific letter writer. Among the many letters he penned are two dated July 13
and 31, 1782, to Benjamin Franklin, then living in Paris as a representative
of the nascent United States of America, thereby indicating that Target
had, at least, a passing acquaintance with the great American.[29] Indeed,
Target's fame spread beyond the boundaries of France, even to the United States. On May 9, 1782, Target, along with ten other Frenchmen, was
declared an honorary citizen of the city of New Haven, Connecticut. The
certificate which evidenced this honor was signed by Roger Sherman,
a signer of the American Declaration of Independence.[30] It proclaimed
that, by reason of Target's "sincere zeal for the rights of mankind, the
liberty and glory of the United States and the Commerce of this city," the
Freemen of New Haven were giving him "all of the rights, privileges and
immunities of the City."[31] In the words of the avocat Charles Lacretelle
(the younger brother of another celebrated avocat of the pre-revolutionary period, Pierre-Louis Lacretelle), who also courted Target's favor, he
was a man of "wit, knowledge, and good sense" (although, as a cautionary note, Lacretelle indicated that Target "was not a skillful writer").[32]

---

28. Statement made by Boucher d'Argis, the founder of the Paris legal aid society.
See *Recueil de pièces concernant l'Association de Bienfaisance Judiciaire, Fondée en
1787* (Paris: Clousier, 1789), 42.
29. The letters, although merely transmittal letters, indicate that Target had an acquaintance with Franklin. In the first, he wrote: "I have the honor of presenting
my respectful homage to Mr. Franklin, and to send him a work in English [Letters
from an American Farmer] which Mr. Michel-Guillaume Jean de Crèvecœur has
asked me to send him. I owe thanks to Mr. de Crèvecœur for having given me the
opportunity to have Mr. Franklin remember me and to offer Him the assurance of
my devotion and of my respect. /s/ Target" (Founders Online, National Archives.
http://founders.archives.gov/documents/Franklin/01-37-02-0405. Source: *The
Papers of Benjamin Franklin, March 16 through August 15, 1782*, vol. 37, ed. Ellen R.
Cohn. (New Haven, CT and London: Yale University Press, 2003), 628–29.
30. A copy of the certificate can be found among the illustrations in a book
published by Target's grandson. Paul-Louis Target, *Un Avocat du XVIIIe siècle*
(Paris: Alcan-Lévy, Imprimeur de l'Ordre des Avocats, 1893).
31. Louis de Bachaumont, *Mémoires secrets pour servir l'histoire de la république des
lettres* (London, 1777–89), vol. 29, p. 135. Target had had translated and disseminated
the pamphlet *Observations on the importance of the American Revolution and the means
of rendering it a benefit to the World* by the British theologian and philosopher Richard
Price. (See M. Muraire, *Eloge de G.J.B. Target* (Paris: Imprimerie de Xhrouet, 1807), 24,
32. Charles LaCretelle, *Dix Années d'Epreuves pendant la Révolution* (Paris: Chez

In 1785, the Académie Française, the most prestigious intellectual establishment in France then as now, elected Target as its first avocat member in nearly one hundred years, acknowledging his intellectual and literary prominence. A few years later, Target would be given credit for playing a critical role in drafting the Constitution of 1791. This was, however, a credit of questionable value since that Constitution holds the dubious record of having been the shortest-lived implemented constitution in French history and is generally considered to have been unwieldy and impractical.

Godard engaged in a concerted and relentless effort to cultivate a special relationship with Target and was immensely successful in achieving his objective. Over the course of the next few years, he became Target's disciple and principal assistant.[33] Establishing this connection was assuredly a wise move for a young avocat, since Target stood at the highest level of the French legal profession of his time and at the center of a large social and political network.

Becoming a friend of Target or, even better, his disciple and secretary, was clearly a worthwhile effort for Godard. Target was renowned for his loyalty to those close to him and many vied for the privilege of being associated with him and basking in his reflected glory. In 1783, the *Gazette des Tribunaux*, a publication intended primarily for the Paris legal community, published a poem, whose author remained anonymous, lauding Target's faithfulness to his friends and disciples. The poem, laced with a considerable dose of sarcasm, also suggests that Target's loyalty was part of a character that consisted of generous quantities of vanity and pomposity:

TARGET, daigne agréer l'hommage	TARGET, deigns to accept homage
D'un Disciple a peine connu,	From a disciple barely known
Qu'a toujours flatté l'avantage	Always flattered by the advantage
De venir faire sous ses yeux	Of coming to perform under his eyes
L'utile & noble apprentissage	The useful and noble apprenticeship
D'un art que tu reçus des cieux	Of an art which you received from the skies
Pour mieux protéger sur la terre	To better protect on earth
La Justice & la Vérité.	Justice and Truth
Ah! l'innocent persécuté	Oh! The persecuted innocent

A. Allouard, Libraire, 1842), 8.
33. Bell, *Lawyers and Citizens*, 172.

Que défend ta voix tutélaire,	Defended by your tutelary voice
Dans son espoir n'est point trahi ;	In his hope is not betrayed;
Mais heureux cent fois le	But a hundred times happy the
Confrère	Colleague
Dont ton cœur a fait son AMI.[34]	Whom your heart has made its FRIEND.

Godard and Charles Lacretelle were not alone in seeking out Target as a mentor. He was renowned for gathering young avocats around himself in his home where, according to a eulogy given in 1807 by the then president of France's highest court, Target "exercised an honorable patronage of beneficence and encouragement" and "thereby prepared men for the future tied to the cult of justice and honor, who would never allow the sacred fire to be extinguished."[35] The young avocats who associated with Target not only benefited from Target's legal instruction, but were inspired to "render service to society."[36] Occasional rumors suggested that the relationships between master and disciples were not solely professional, but there is nothing to substantiate those rumors.[37]

Lacretelle, in his memoirs, noted the presence of Raymond Romain DeSèze—another young avocat already in the midst of a lengthy and

34. *Gazette des Tribunaux*, 1783, vol. 15, no. 9, pp. 141–42.
35. Muraire, M., *Éloge de G.J.B. Target*, 14–15.
36. Lacretelle, P.-L.,*Oeuvres de P. L. Lacretelle, aîné*, vol. 2 (Paris: Bossange Frères, Libraires, 1823), 438.
37. Target, who was a bachelor for most of his life, married Lisa Jeanne-Louise Leroy on September 19, 1791, when he was fifty-seven years old and she was thirty-one. They had four children, the last of whom was born when Target was seventy-one. His marriage late in life seems to have added fuel to the rumors respecting possible relationships with the cadre of young men who hovered around Target in the many years prior to his marriage. There is at least one allusion to Target's potentially unconventional sexuality in a series of satirical writings about him by André-Boniface-Louis Riqueti, Vicomte de Mirabeau (and known as *Mirabeau-Tonneau* [Mirabeau-Barrel], due to his considerable girth) (1754–1792), the younger brother of the revolutionary orator Honoré de Mirabeau. In the fifth of five pamphlets entitled sarcastically *Bulletin de couches de M. Target, Père et mère de la Constitution...* [Bulletin of the bedsheets of Mr. Target, Father and Mother of the Constitution...], Mirabeau refers to Target as "this great hermaphrodite." Mirabeau, *Facéties du Vicomte de Mirabeau, Cinquième Bulletin de couches de Me. Target, Père et mère de la Constitution...*, March 20, 1790, 3.

illustrious career—at Target's table.[38] He also indicated the participation of Camille Desmoulins, a brilliant, impulsive young avocat whose talents were somewhat marred by his distracting stammer, but who was to become a journalist and one of the most prominent and tragic of the revolutionaries.[39] The competition for Target's attention and affection must have been fierce. In that vein, many years later, the elder of the Lacretelle brothers, Pierre-Louis, would brag that he had been Target's closest associate and that he believed Target "had loved no one more than me, nor I anyone more than he."[40] It is very likely that Godard, had he had the opportunity, would have objected to Lacretelle's characterization and might himself have asserted the status of most-favored friend.

Target, the son of an avocat, had for a generation been a prominent avocat in Paris. His had been a varied practice. His orations, filled with the circumlocutions and the pompous rhetoric popular in his time, had made him one of the best-known and most highly regarded members of

38. Raymond Romain de Sèze or DeSèze (1750–1828) was an avocat from Bordeaux whose most significant claim to fame is that he was one of the three members of the defense team (the others being Francois Tronchet and Chrétien-Guillaume de Lamoignon de Malesherbes) that unsuccessfully represented Louis XVI during his trial before the Convention in December 1792 and January 1793. Unlike some other defenders of the king, although he was briefly imprisoned during the Terror—the period when normal legal protections were suspended and summary executions became a means of enforcing radical policies—DeSèze avoided execution by the radical revolutionaries and went on to have a successful legal career during the Empire and Restoration. He became president of the Court of Cassation in 1815. He was also elected to membership in the Académie Française in 1816 and named a Count by Louis XVIII. A descendant of one of DeSèze's siblings has indicated to the author that, in the DeSèze family, Raymond DeSèze has always been referred to as "le Défenseur" (the Defender) for his courageous and risky defense of the king.

39. Camille Desmoulins (1760–1794), an avocat by training who was admitted to the Paris Bar in 1785, spent most of his professional career as a journalist and pamphleteer. His meteoric political career began when he delivered a fiery speech on July 12, 1789, in the gardens of the Palais Royal. That speech is generally considered to have been the spark that set off the rioting which led to the assault on the Bastille. As a member of the National Convention, he became an ally and close confidant of Georges-Jacques Danton and was sentenced to death and executed along with Danton when Robespierre turned on Danton and his colleagues in the spring of 1794. Barely one week later, Desmoulins' young wife, accused of having been a co-conspirator with her husband, followed Desmoulins to the scaffold.

40. Lacretelle, *Oeuvres de P. L. Lacretelle, aîné*, vol. 2, p. 437.

the Paris Bar. The philosopher Voltaire was among his admirers, having written to him in February 1767 that "for a long time, I have joined the masses of citizens who view you as their defender."[41] But he was not without his detractors. At least one of his fellow avocats considered that "he had none of the advantages that give such power to the orator. His pronunciation was heavy, his face lacking in grace, his eyes shifty."[42]

Over the course of his pre-revolutionary career, Target had acted across a wide spectrum of civil and criminal matters. His clients had included members of the aristocracy and the clergy as well as Protestants and Jews. In the 1770s, he had garnered a certain amount of fame through his representation of the noted playwright Beaumarchais in a domestic dispute. Among his other important cases was one which included an unusual religious dispute where his client had been the wife of one of the wealthiest Portuguese Jews of Bordeaux.[43]

In 1762, the Portuguese-Jewish businessman Samuel Peixotto decided to divorce his wife, Sara Mendes d'Acosta. Peixotto moved to Paris and sought the approval of the secular courts to confirm the divorce that he had unilaterally given Sara in accordance with Jewish law. Sara contested the civil proceedings. She enlisted Target's assistance and he provided her with a vigorous representation. The secular court ultimately determined, as had been requested by Sara with the advice and assistance of Target, that the issue of divorce was a religious issue to be decided in accordance with the customs and usages of the Portuguese (i.e., Sephardic) Jews.[44]

---

41. Letter from Voltaire to Target of February 1767, in Voltaire, *Correspondence and Related Documents*, ed. Theodore Besterman (Oxford: Voltaire Foundation, 1974), vol. 31, p. 357 D 13964, cited in Xavier Martin, "A Propos d'un livre, Target, Bentham et le Code Civil," *Revue d'Histoire des Facultés de Droit* (SHFD/Librairie générale de droit et de jurisprudence, 2001): 121–48, 122.

42. E.-A. Hua, *Mémoires d'un avocat au Parlement de Paris député à l'Assemblée législative* (Poitiers: Henri Oudin Librairie-Editeur, 1871), 16.

43. *Répertoire Universel et Raisonné de Jurisprudence*, vol. 3 (Paris: Chez Garnery, 1807), 726. See also *Causes célèbres, curieuses et intéressantes de toutes les cours souveraines du royaume avec les jugements qui les ont décidés*, vol. 65, Paris, 1780.

44. The religious authorities hesitated to rule due to the importance and power of the parties. Ultimately, the matter was mooted when Samuel Peixotto went to Spain and converted to Catholicism. Arthur Hertzberg, *The French Enlightenment and the Jews: The Origins of Modern Anti-Semitism* (New York: Schocken, 1968), 207–8; See also *Mémoire à Consulter et Consultation pour Dame Sara Mendez d'Acosta, épouse du Sieur Samuel Peixotto*, 1777.

The secular court ruled that the religious authorities in Bordeaux alone had the authority to decide upon the validity of the divorce. Target had triumphed on behalf of his client (although the elder Lacretelle claimed credit for drafting the memorandum that decided the case).[45] However, by means of his victory, Target had also established that, when it came to family law matters, even the highly assimilated Portuguese Jews of south-western France, for all the legal rights that had been given them centuries before by French monarchs and which had been reaffirmed by Louis XV, had their own laws and dispute resolution mechanisms and were not subject to secular courts. The conclusion to be drawn was inevitable. The Jews, even the most assimilated of Jews with rights of citizenship, were not full-fledged Frenchmen.

Target's reputation was such that he was called upon to defend the Archbishop of Strasbourg, Cardinal de Rohan, in connection with his role as one of the principal actors in perhaps the most gripping scandal of the era, an event that has come to be known as the Affair of the Necklace.[46] The scandal involved an attempt to sell a spectacular and spectacularly expensive diamond necklace to the young queen, Marie-Antoinette, under false pretenses.[47] All of France was gripped by the scandal which engulfed the queen in 1786 and served to severely discredit the royal family at a time when royal authority was under siege. The scandal arose when

45. Lacretelle, *Oeuvres de P. L. Lacretelle, aîné*, vol. 2, p. 437.

46. It has been suggested that it was due to Target being a Freemason (specifically as a member of the *Loge des Neufs Sœurs*, the most prominent of the Parisian Masonic Lodges of the era) that he was selected to defend the Cardinal, since the Cardinal received considerable support from the Masonic lodges. In 1788, many of those who assisted the Cardinal in his travails during the Necklace scandal formed a club called the *Société des Trente* (the Society of Thirty). That group included some of the most prominent early revolutionaries and became one of the more cohesive clubs in the early months of the Revolution, helping to coordinate strategy and legislation at the National Assembly. Target was among its leaders and, even though Godard does not appear to have joined the club, he must have met many of its members through his relationship with Target. See Jean-André Faucher and Achille Ricker, *Histoire de la Franc-maçonnerie en France (avec Lettre liminaire de Me Richard Dupuy)*, 179, et seq. and Louis Amiable, *Une loge maçonnique d'avant 1789: la loge des Neuf Sœurs. Augmenté d'un commentaire et de notes critiques de Charles Porset* (Paris: Edimaf, 1989).

47. The queen was defended in the legal proceedings by Raymond DeSèze, who would go on to be one of the defense attorneys for Louis XVI in his trial before the revolutionary Convention.

the Cardinal, in an effort to ingratiate himself to the queen, participated (probably as a dupe) in a scam to sell her the necklace. Opponents of the monarchy sought to use the scandal to reinforce the growing anger fueled by the perception that members of the royal family were arrogantly and frivolously squandering public funds.

Target, in defending one of the most illustrious of the protagonists in the affair, was elevated to a summit of prominence. Godard was by his side as Target worked skillfully to exculpate the Cardinal.[48] Target's representation of the discredited Cardinal did not discredit the avocat. On the contrary, it served to enhance his already well-established reputation. Godard loyally credited the Cardinal's ultimate public relations success, as well as his exoneration from all criminal charges, "entirely" to Target's pleadings. He noted that, upon the issuance of the verdict in favor of the Cardinal, Target "shared in all of the honors of this triumph."[49]

However, following his successful defense of the Cardinal, Target retired from the active practice of law, at least as a barrister. He became, instead, a counselor to whom individuals and the royal government would turn for advice and assistance. He did, however, continue to file briefs in selected matters. When the Revolution began, he entered politics and for some time his legal career was sidelined. Active in electoral politics in the early years of the Revolution, he was elected to the Estates-General and continued his service as a member of the National Assembly, elevated for a time to serve as its president. He became a municipal judge in the later years of the Revolution. His career as an adviser to governments would continue long past the Revolution and into the years of the Napoleonic Empire.[50]

---

48. Godard did not fail to mention in several of his letters to his cousin Cortot that he was by Target's side as Target represented the besieged Cardinal. See Letters from Godard to Cortot, May 21, 1786, May 30, 1786 and June 2, 1786.

49. Letter from Godard to Cortot, June 2, 1786.

50. He died on September 9, 1806. His tomb, located in the cemetery of Mollières in the Essonne District just a dozen miles south of Paris, is adorned with a monument topped by a bust of Target and bearing an epitaph which contains a lengthy tribute to his legal career and which does not fail to note Target's extraordinary loyalty to his friends. The epitaph reads: "Eloquent orator, Distinguished scholar, Profound legal counselor, Because of his talent, he was an ornament of the Bar. The oppressed innocent, the widow and the orphan found in him an ardent and unbiased defender, the unfortunate a humble helper, the citizens an honest judge. Good father, sensitive husband, dependable and loyal friend. He was a model of all of the virtues."

In spite of his early retirement, in the spring of 1787 Target entered the fray in a case involving the civil equality of Protestants. On June 20 of that year he filed a *"Consultation"*—a memorandum of applicable legal principles, a kind of legal opinion[51]—in defense of the Marquise d'Anglure, a woman whose father had been a Protestant.[52] On the basis of the notion that Protestants could not enter into valid marriages, the Marquise's nephews challenged the very legitimacy of her birth and thus her right to inherit from her father in order that they, rather than the daughter, allegedly illegitimate, might acquire their uncle's entire estate.[53] Target defended the Marquise's right to inherit, arguing that, as a legal matter, based upon extensive precedent as well as upon practical considerations, her father's Protestantism did not support the claim that she was illegitimate. In his *Consultation*, Target espoused a laudable tolerance for divergent religious opinions, suggesting that individuals should not be required to abjure their faith (that they should not "lie to God" and that, once the law had recognized their legal existence, "they have the right to practice their faith").[54] He was forceful in his appeal for acceptance of Protestants as full-fledged members of French society, eloquently declaring, "They are men, your fellow citizens, your friends and your brothers, subjects of the same king, children of the same father, members of the same society."[55] He then reminded his readers that "even Jews" were not deprived of the right to marry, suggesting that this was yet another

51. The *"Consultation"* was not, strictly speaking, a pleading. Rather, it was the opinion of an avocat, intended to bolster the pleadings in a case. Félix Liouville, in a series of lectures that he delivered in the mid-nineteenth century, noted that "a *Consultation* is not like the Pleadings and Memorials, it is, more precisely, the decision of a private judge." *De la Profession d'Avocat, Discours prononcés par Felix Liouville*, fourth edition (Paris: Cosse, Marchal et Cie, 1868), 184. See also Gustave Duchaine and Edmond Picard, *Manuel Pratique de la Profession d'Avocat* (Paris: A Durand et Pedone Lauriel, 1869), 383.
52. Guy Target, *Consultation sur l'Affaire de la dame Marquise d'Anglure contre les Sieurs Petit, au Conseil des Dépêches, dans laquelle l'on traite du mariage et de l'état des Protestants* (Paris: Imp. Nyon, 1788).
53. Ironically, the principal challenger to the Marquise's legitimacy, her father's nephew, was himself a Protestant, who, as a contemporary observer wryly noted, was "a man who by his religious principles should detest the very laws that he is asserting." *Causes célèbres, curieuses et intéressantes*, vol. 93, p. 11.
54. *Consultation sur l'Affaire de la dame Marquise d'Anglure*, 155–56.
55. Ibid., 177.

clear indication that Protestants should also benefit from that right.[56] He prevailed in his defense of the Marquise; she was declared her father's legitimate heir, authorized to inherit from him and to benefit from the protection of the law.

Not surprisingly, at a time when Enlightenment philosophy was all the rage and many in France were endeavoring to shed their society's most onerous prejudices, the d'Anglure case attracted a great deal of attention. Among those who closely followed the case and paid particular attention to the Marquise's defense was Chrétien-Guillaume de Lamoignon de Malesherbes, one of Louis XVI's principal ministers and closest advisers. Malesherbes, in a letter to Pierre-Louis Lacretelle, urged Lacretelle to press Target to publish his brief in support of the Marquise because, Malesherbes wrote, "I foresee that this brief will provide the occasion for advancing the general cause."[57] This "general cause" was the goal of providing full civil rights to Protestants.

Indeed, as a result of his representation of the Marquise, and with his growing reputation as a wise counselor, Target was shortly thereafter asked by Louis XVI to assist Malesherbes in drafting an edict respecting the civil rights of Protestants in France. Styled as an "Edict of the King concerning those who do not espouse the practice of the Catholic Religion," and within mere months enacted into law, it became the ultimate edict of tolerance for France's long-suffering Protestant minority.[58] It is easy to surmise that, with Target actively involved in this major legislative project, Godard must have spent considerable time discussing the issue of Protestant equality with Target and may perhaps even have assisted in drafting parts of the Edict's text. That likelihood is buttressed by the role that Godard would play shortly thereafter in a very similar case.[59] The general topic of religious liberty, a subject of increasing concern in the era, would, therefore, have been much on the minds of the

---

56. Ibid. In his *Consultation*, Target made just four passing references to Jews, alluding only to the fact that their marriages were recognized because they had their own special laws.

57. Armand Lods, "L'Avocat Target défenseur des Protestants," in *Bulletin de la société d'histoire du protestantisme français*, vol. 43 (1885). Target did not long resist Malesherbes' suggestion; a complete version of his *Consultation* on behalf of the Marquise d'Anglure appeared in print in 1788.

58. "*Edit du Roi, concernant ceux qui ne font pas profession de la Religion Catholique.*"

59. See the discussion of the Brisset case below.

two avocats as they together navigated the turmoil of the times. It is also very likely that, as a result of Target's work on this project, Godard may have come into significant contact with Malesherbes himself.

Malesherbes stood out as one of the most remarkable personalities of his era. His eventual martyrdom would make him one of the truly tragic figures of the time. Descended from a noble family of distinguished public servants and an avocat by training, Malesherbes, born in 1721, rose to become one of Louis XVI's principal advisers. He was a man of great integrity, marked by a strong sense of duty to his nation and to his monarch. In spite of living in one of the oldest and most beautiful mansions in Paris (today the site of the Bibliothèque Historique de la Ville de Paris on rue Pavée in the Marais section of the city),[60] he was modest and unpretentious, with little interest in status or even appearance.[61] During much of Malesherbes' career, he was a strong defender of the prerogatives of the Parlements, so much so that in 1771 Louis XV issued a *"lettre de cachet"* exiling him to his chateau some fifty miles south of Paris.[62] When, following the accession of Louis XVI, Malesherbes was allowed to return to the Court, he became, with some encouragement from Louix XVI, a prominent, albeit rather unsuccessful, proponent of government reform. As part of his plan of reform, he labored, this time successfully, for the legal equality of Protestants. Shortly after completing that effort, he would be charged by Louis XVI with reviewing the status of the Jews of France.

---

60. Jacques Hillairet, *Dictionnaire Historique de Rues de Paris*, vol. L/Z (Paris: Editions de Minuit, 1961), 248.

61. A statement by François Antoine de Boissy d'Anglas, cited in a speech about Malesherbes by Louis-Eugene Peyrusse in December 1840, describes Malesherbes as follows: "When you saw him for the first time, with his brown suit with large pockets, his gold buttons, his sleeves of muslin, his ruffle stained with tobacco, and his round wig poorly combed and badly placed on his head, and you heard him speak with so little affectation and guile, although with such a great sense of erudition and thought, it was impossible to imagine that he was the son of a Chancellor of France." Louis-Eugène Peyrusse, *Éloge de Lamoignon de Malesherbes* (Toulouse: Imprimerie de Jean-Matthieu Douladoure, 1840), 6n1.

62. The *"lettres de cachet"* were warrants that could be issued by the French monarch without any just cause or due process against any person in the kingdom. They could result in exile or lengthy imprisonment without trial and without recourse. Although infrequently used during the reign of Louis XVI, the *"lettres de cachet"* were considered a repugnant symbol of the autocratic power of the monarchy and generated much resentment in the years prior to the Revolution.

In 1787, Malesherbes began his work regarding the rights of Jews in France. Although he was not able to conclude his work due to the start of the Revolution, while pursuing his research he came into contact with many leaders of the Jewish community—of the Ashkenazi Jews (from the area in and contiguous to German states) and of the so-called Portuguese Jews (the descendants of Spanish and Portuguese Jews residing in southwestern France), as well as with a mixture of both groups to be found in small numbers in Paris.[63] He apparently compiled significant notes

---

63. As previously noted, Ashkenazi Jews are Jews of central and eastern European descent. At the time of the French Revolution, those Jews, sometimes referred to as "German" Jews, lived predominantly along the eastern and northeastern borders of France, in Alsace, Lorraine and the areas constituted by the three dioceses of Metz, Verdun, and Toul, known as the Three Bishoprics. They are distinct from the Sephardic Jews (or *Sephardim*, in the Hebrew formulation), who are descended from non-European and Iberian Jews. Many Sephardim were descended from Jews who lived in Spain and Portugal during a period euphemistically referred to as the "Golden Age of Spain," when Muslims controlled the area. Some of them left Spain and Portugal as Christians regained control of the Iberian Peninsula in the fourteenth and fifteenth centuries and the persecution of Jews became widespread (although some Jews had already left when radical Muslims, known as the Almohades had conquered parts of the peninsula). At the time of the expulsion of Jews from Spain in 1492 and from Portugal in 1497, some Jews settled in the Arab world and other Muslim countries with a few coming to France. Others stayed in Spain and Portugal and nominally converted to Catholicism. But in the ensuing years, some of the converts left the Iberian Peninsula, headed to southern France, and slowly returned to their ancestral beliefs. The Iberian Jews, whose customs were quite different from those of the Ashkenazi Jews and who came to southwestern France either at the time of the expulsions or some time later, as we shall see, had a markedly different history and benefited from a different legal status. Although we will primarily focus on the Ashkenazi experience, because of the intertwining of the two groups in the pursuit of equality in France, we will also give some consideration to the Sephardim and their efforts. It is important to note that the Sephardic communities of southwestern France in the eighteenth century were quite different in their origins from France's current large Sephardic Jewish community. Today's Sephardic community came to France very largely from North Africa—Morocco, Algeria and Tunisia—after those nations obtained their independence from France in the early 1960s. As France's Chief Rabbi Haïm Korsia emphasized to me in our conversation about this book, they are not the descendants of the Sephardim living in Bordeaux, Bayonne, Saint-Esprit and other southwestern communities at the time of the Revolution. In order to draw this important distinction, I will, generally, refer to these latter Jews in the manner in which they were euphemistically identified in the eighteenth century, namely, as

regarding the legal status of the French Jewish communities and may have developed a basic framework for approaching the task of providing them with juridical existence. His files disappeared in the turmoil of the era, rendering it impossible to know just how advanced he was in his efforts when the Revolution commenced, or the content of what he ultimately intended to recommend to the king regarding the rights to be given to Jews. The start of the Revolution put an abrupt end to Malesherbes' work. It is not certain whether Target was involved in Malesherbes' work regarding the Jewish community, but it is very likely that he was. If so, then Godard also likely participated in discussions with his mentor regarding the status of the Jews in France well before the start of the Revolution.

Despite his great renown and his impressive network of connections, Guy Target's reputation was not without stain. He was disdained by both the right and the left for his relative moderation and political vacillations. His reliance on the convoluted oratory of French avocats when he became a member of the Estates-General (which would become the National Assembly) made him the butt of jokes and sarcastic remarks. Royalists would later hold him in particular disdain[64] in substantial part due to his failure to accept Louis XVI's request that he defend the king in his trial for treason before the revolutionary National Convention in 1792.[65] In

---

"Portuguese Jews." It is, however, appropriate to add the observation made by the *Journal de Paris* in its January 30, 1790 edition when it wrote: "What do we mean when we refer to 'Spanish and Portuguese' Jews who, for two or three centuries from father to son have been born and have lived in France? They were Spanish and Portuguese two or three hundred years ago, but it seems to us that they have had the time to become French..." *Journal de Paris*, no. 30, January 30, 1790, p. 118.

64. The royalist avocat and historian Jean-François Fournel, in his *History of the Bar of Paris*, published in 1816, demonstrating the strong antipathy that the royalists had understandably developed toward Target, was especially harsh in his evaluation of Target, writing: "In the Assembly, he did not justify the fame that he had accumulated. His obsession with reasoning on the great work of the regeneration of the kingdom, his political ejaculations, his eternal preaching of harmony and unity, followed by peace and tranquility, and other grotesque phrases, covered him with ridicule which was a source of amusement in Paris and was food for the newspapers. Leaving the National Assembly incognito, he fell back to the position of district judge, and the great legislator descended from the highest regions to sit in a monastic refectory." Jean-François Fournel, *Histoire du Barreau de Paris dans le cours de la Révolution* (Paris: Maradan, 1816), 83.

65. The National Convention was the assembly elected in September 1792 on the basis of universal male suffrage, following the attack on the Tuileries which effec-

light of Target's stellar legal reputation, the king, recognizing the extreme danger of his situation, had sought to obtain Target's assistance. However, Target invoked his advanced age (he was fifty-nine years old) and alleged ill health (he would live for another twelve years) as the grounds for declining the king's request. It is more generally assumed that he was, with some justification, concerned about his own safety and simply felt it was too risky to undertake this task. In an attempt to limit the damage to his reputation, Target published a short pamphlet arguing against the accusations brought against the king on jurisdictional grounds.[66]

When Target turned down the king's request, Louis XVI then requested that Malesherbes represent him. Malesherbes responded affirmatively and (at the age of seventy-one) came out of retirement to defend the king. With a team of avocats which included DeSèze, Malesherbes worked diligently to mount a persuasive defense on behalf of the king. This defense of the king, although thoughtful and well-prepared, did not prevent the condemnation and eventual execution of Louis XVI. The price paid by Malesherbes for his role in defending his king was extraordinarily high. In April 1794 Malesherbes, his daughter, and his granddaughter were sent together to the guillotine.[67] Unlike Malesherbes, Target had demonstrated life-saving caution, but, as a consequence, he has gone down in history as lacking courage, his reputation forever tarnished by his failure to defend the doomed Louis XVI.

Nonetheless, Godard had every reason to wish to associate himself closely with Target and, rather blatantly, made every effort to become part of Target's circle of friends and disciples. Godard bragged to his cousin

tively overthrew the monarchy in August of that year. This governing body replaced the Legislative Assembly of 1791 and instituted the First Republic on September 22, 1792. The notion of convening a "Convention" appears to have been derived from the role played by the American Constitutional Convention of 1787, which drafted the Constitution that has been the primary governing document of the United States since that time. Once the Republic had been created, the National Convention set about drafting a new constitution. However, that constitution, the "Constitution of 1793," was never actually implemented and the National Convention operated on a kind of ad hoc basis until it was replaced in 1795 by the Directory.
66. G. J-B. Target, *Observations de Target sur le procès de Louis XVI* (Paris, 1792).
67. Another granddaughter, Louise Madeleine Marguerite Le Peletier de Rosanbo, was spared from execution, albeit barely. She married Hervé de Tocqueville. One of their sons was the noted social commentator, Alexis de Toqueville, author of *Democracy in America*.

Cortot about these efforts: "I often dine at his residence and, every time that I see him, I leave more satisfied with myself than when I entered. You cannot imagine how much there is to gain with a man like him; superior in his profession, as you know, he is a stranger to no science, nor to any state. He has a prodigious variety of acquaintances and speaks of everything with an indescribable ease and charm."[68] Godard was not shy about imposing himself on Target, conceding that he would ask to arrange a visit whenever he ran into the great jurist on the street. The frequency of his success was highlighted when Godard informed his cousin Cortot that he dined with Target at least once a week.[69] The relationship with Target would provide Godard with a platform upon which the younger man could build his legal career and inject himself into the public arena.

Being associated with Target provided Godard with excellent connections and placed him in the middle of the accelerating struggle for civil rights for all French citizens. In spite of Target's retirement from the active practice of law in 1787, he remained involved in political and social activities. Godard, as Target's close associate, was in a particularly good position to take on those matters that came to Target's door, but which the great jurist was no longer prepared to handle.

Godard remained close to Target professionally, and, in September 1788, physically as well. At that time, he moved to more spacious quarters at 56 rue des Blancs-Manteaux,[70] just "behind the residence of Mr. Target," at 20, rue Sainte-Croix de la Bretonnerie[71] in the crowded Marais

---

68. Letter from Godard to Cortot, June 19, 1785.

69. Ibid.

70. In the almanacs of the era, Godard's address is listed as 56, rue des Blancs-Manteaux. (See, for example, *Almanach Royal*, 1790.) Today, rue des Blancs-Manteaux ends at number 42. None of the maps of the era indicate that there was ever a 56. With the generous assistance of Mme. Valentine Weiss of the *Centre de Topographie parisienne* of the *Archives Nationales*, I have determined that the building within which Godard rented his quarters on rue des Blancs-Manteaux was likely located where a large building bearing the number 22 currently stands. In his *Dictionnaire Historique des Rues de Paris*, Jacques Hillairet indicates that over the course of several centuries the building that stood on the site housed various legal professionals, lending considerable plausibility to the likelihood that this was, indeed, the location of Godard's last residence and office. See Hillairet, *Dictionnaire Historique de Rues de Paris*, vol. A/K, 202.

71. The 1696 mansion on rue Sainte-Croix de la Bretonnerie, near the intersection with rue Aubriot, in which Target lived, practiced law, and where he died

neighborhood. Rue des Blancs-Manteaux was then, as now, a long and narrow street running along a generally east-west trajectory (although in a somewhat undulating manner, following the curvature of the Seine), lined mostly with three and four-story buildings. Even though he seems to have preferred his former neighborhood near Place des Victoires, which he referred to as "the beautiful neighborhood,"[72] Godard moved to rue de Blancs-Manteaux, in his own words, for "professional reasons": so he could be nearer the center of his activities as an avocat, as well as in closer proximity to his long-time mentor.[73] Godard would reside at this location for the rest of his life. The neighborhood, then known as the 7th *arrondissement*, counted a significant number of avocats and other legal professionals among its residents. It also happened to be in close proximity to the largest concentration of the approximately five hundred Jews then living in Paris. That situation would become particularly important within but a few short years.

---

in 1806, was demolished in 1929. Today, a large, unattractive and non-contextual red brick building from the 1930s stands on the site. See Hillairet, *Dictionnaire Historique de Rues de Paris*, vol. L/Z, 493.

72. Letter from Godard to Cortot, September 17, 1788.

73. Ibid.

CHAPTER 3

SOCIAL CLIMBING

Godard made ample use of the brotherhood among the avocats who
frequented the Palace of Justice, where the Paris Parlement met, and
the Châtelet, where the criminal courts, certain civil courts, and one of
the local prisons were located.[1] His brethren in the profession quickly
provided him with the opportunities and access necessary for the development of a successful legal career. This contact with distinguished
avocats, who themselves both represented and were befriended by
wealthy and well-connected individuals, provided Godard with a pathway not only to professional development but also to social standing.
At this time of deep social and intellectual upheaval, being part of a
group of socially prominent intellectuals was essential to a successful

---

1. The Palace of Justice (Palais de Justice) was (and remains to this day) part of a
large complex of buildings on the *Ile de la Cité* which includes portions of a medieval royal palace. The Châtelet, located along the banks of the Seine at the foot
of rue St. Denis, across the river from the Palace of Justice, was a sinister group of
buildings. The buildings existing in the decade before the Revolution had been
rebuilt a hundred years before on the site of a fortress whose origins dated back
a thousand years. The complex incorporated courts, prisons, and a morgue. It
was insalubrious, malodorous, and unattractive. It was a far more active site of
legal proceedings than the Palace of Justice, where appellate proceedings pre-
dominated. Not long after the Revolution, during the Napoleonic Empire, the
buildings were demolished to make way for the large plaza adorned by a fountain
and flanked by two large theaters that now occupies the site.

professional life. Such connections were additionally a means of entering into the political and social discourse that dominated the turbulent
years preceding the fall of the Bastille.

During the 1780s Paris prided itself on its multitude of "salons" hosted
by prominent individuals, most often women, where intellectuals, government officials, the enlightened aristocracy, and the wealthy gathered
to debate the issues of the day and to while away their time.[2] Literary
criticism, political thought, and visions for society percolated in this
milieu. The proliferation of salons helped to promote both a great deal
of cross-pollination and a reinforcement of ideas among the upper and
bourgeois classes. Much of the intellectual energy that would fuel the first
phase of the Revolution would emerge from these salons.

Godard frequented a number of these salons. He became part of the
social circle of Jean-François Marmontel,[3] a playwright, librettist, and author who contributed to Diderot's and d'Alembert's *Encyclopédie* and who
was elected to the Académie Française in 1763, becoming its perpetual
secretary in 1783.[4] Although Marmontel's gatherings, held in the suburbs

---

2. In her history of the French Revolution, Germaine de Staël highlighted the
role women played in elite French society prior to the Revolution. She wrote
that "in France, women [were] accustomed to lead almost all the conversation
that [took] place at their houses, and their minds [were] early formed to the
facility which this talent requires. Discussions on public affairs were thus softened by their means and often intermingled with kind and lively pleasantry."
Germaine de Staël, *Considerations on the Principal Events of the French Revolution*
(new translation of the 1818 English edition, ed. Aurelian Craiutu), (Indianapolis: Liberty Fund, Inc., 2008), 252–53.
3. Jean-François Marmontel (1723–1799), born in the Limousin section of central
France, moved to Paris as a young man, allegedly at the urging of Voltaire. He wrote
a number of books and essays, serving as the librettist for some of the most significant operatic composers of the time. As a consequence of his writings, he was
elected to the Académie Française in 1763 and subsequently became its permanent
secretary. His memoires, published posthumously, were widely read.
4. In March of 1783, Marmontel exchanged letters with John Adams, then U.S.
Minister to the Netherlands, but present in France to assist in the negotiation
of the peace treaty with England that acknowledged the independence of the
United States. Apparently, Marmontel had it in mind to write a history of the
American Revolution and sought Adams' assistance. In his letter to Adams of
March 8, 1783, Marmontel wrote: "Mr. Marmontel is honored to present his
compliments to Mr. Adams, and to return the excellent [but unspecified] letter
he so kindly entrusted to him. More than ever, this letter makes him realize how

rather than at the city's heart, were not at the apex of salon society, they nonetheless brought together interesting and significant individuals. Marmontel was perhaps best known for his librettos for operas composed by Grétry and Piccini, which were immensely popular in their time, but are now mostly forgotten. Indeed, music and especially opera occupied a very important role in French high society of the era—other than the philosophical and political battles of the times, nothing seemed more important than determining who was the greatest opera composer. In Paris in the 1770s and 1780s, the candidates for that title were Christoph Willibald Gluck and Niccolò Piccini.[5] The battle was ferocious and taken with the utmost seriousness.[6] Godard, because of his friendship with Piccini's sometime librettist, must have undoubtedly sided with Piccini.

---

greatly he needs Mr. Adams' help and insight to compose a reasonable account of the great revolution that constitutes the glory of North America and guarantees its happiness." However, in spite of this exchange, Marmontel never actually wrote a history of the American Revolution. Marmontel also became a close friend of Thomas Jefferson. Their friendship was such that, for a time, Jefferson and Marmontel dined together every Thursday. In his correspondence, Jefferson described Marmontel as being "a very amusing man." Kevin J. Hayes, The Road to Monticello: The Life and Mind of Thomas Jefferson (New York: Oxford University Press, 2008), 301.

5. Niccolò Piccini or Piccinni (1728–1800), an Italian by birth, became one of the most popular opera composers in France on the eve of the Revolution. He was a prolific composer of all types of musical compositions, but achieved fame as the composer of dozens of Italian operas, many of which were produced in Paris, and none of which are part of today's standard repertoire. Christoph Willibald Gluck (1714–1787), although raised in Bohemia, became a prominent composer of operas in Vienna. In 1773, he moved to Paris where he achieved great success with several operas that appealed to the French spirit and, notably, "Iphigenie en Tauride" and "Orfeo ed Euridice" which continue to be performed to this day. The battle between Piccini and Gluck would be echoed in the mid-nineteenth century in the competition between Richard Wagner and Giacomo Meyerbeer. This latter competition would be tinged with antisemitism since Meyerbeer was Jewish (his original name being Jakob Meyer Beer), and Wagner (who some believe could have been the illegitimate son of a Jewish father) attacked him relentlessly for his Jewishness, going so far as to publish an antisemitic pamphlet entitled Jewishness in Music (Das Judentum in der Musik) in an effort to discredit Meyerbeer and the by-then deceased Felix Mendelssohn.

6. In 1777, Marmontel wrote a lengthy essay on the importance of music in France, which he entitled Essai sur les révolutions de la musique en France (Essay on the revolutions in music in France).

Godard's ability to enter into Marmontel's circle was likely tied to Godard's family's friendship with George Buffon—the noted botanist who had become a member of the Académie Française in 1753 and was, therefore, an intellectual colleague of Marmontel's—but also to Marmontel's interest in legal issues. Although his social circle was predominantly constituted of some of the era's literary superstars, it also included some prominent members of the Paris Bar.

In his memoirs, entitled *Mémoires d'un père* (A Father's Memoir), published many years later, Marmontel noted that, in 1783, he would regularly gather an assortment of friends and acquaintances at his country estate in the village of Grignon, today part of the town of Thiais (in the southern suburbs of Paris just a short distance from what is now Orly Airport). These memoirs provide us with an insight into the circle of acquaintances into which Godard immersed himself as he began his career and developed his large network of professional colleagues and personal friendships. Marmontel identified Godard as a regular visitor at his estate, part of an eclectic and stimulating group that also included the author Guillaume Thomas Raynal—a defrocked priest who wrote a variety of treatises in conjunction with some of the *philosophes*, and, most notably, a book entitled *A Philosophical and Political History of the Settlements and Trade of the Europeans in the East and West Indies*.[7] In his book, Raynal highlighted the extensive freedom accorded to Jews in Surinam, and apparently influenced a portion of the memorandum prepared by the Jews of Bordeaux for submission to Malesherbes in his study of the status of the Jews of France.[8] Marmontel also mentioned Jean-Jacques Barthélmy,[9] a dilettante who had important government personalities among his

---

7. Guillaume Thomas Raynal (1713–1796) was a French writer during the Enlightenment. He wrote on contemporary history and economics and was welcomed into a number of the important salons as a result. He is particularly remembered for his economic history of the French West Indies. In 1791, he wrote a scathing critique of the work of the National Assembly, causing him to be ostracized from politics.

8. David Feuerwerker, *L'Émancipation des Juifs en France* (Paris: Éditions Albin Michel, 1976), 167.

9. Jean Jacques Barthélémy (1716–1795), the product of a Jesuit education, was a cleric best known for his travels to Italy in the company of the Duke and Duchess de Choiseul, with whom he had a noted friendship. In 1789, he was elected to the Académie Française. See Louis-Jules-Barbon Mancini Nivernois, "Essai sur la Vie de J.J. Barthélémy," in *Voyage du Jeune Anacharsis en Grèce dans le milieu du quatrième siècle avant l'ére vulgaire*, vol. 1 (London: Charles Dilly, 1796).

close friends, including, most significantly, Louis XV's sometime principal minister, the Duc de Choiseul; the Marquis of Célesia,[10] a Genoan
diplomat; Louis de Bréquigny,[11] an academic historian; Marin Carbury
de Céphalonie,[12] an officer in the Russian army; the Abbé Nicolas Thyrel
de Boismont,[13] a prominent cleric; Raymond Romain DeSèze, the young
avocat from Bordeaux, and the Abbé Jean-Sifrein Maury.[14] Maury, who
would, in 1785, become one of Marmontel's colleagues at the Académie
Française, was an extreme conservative whose reactionary positions
would make him a standout in national politics during the Revolution
and would elevate him to a leadership position in the effort to prevent
minorities, including, notably, Jews, from achieving equality. Over the
course of the coming years, Maury would become one of the principal
antagonists in Godard's efforts on behalf of Jews.

When, many years later, he wrote his reminiscences, Marmontel described his guests in complimetary and generous terms. His description of
Godard, as "having the verve of a gaiety full of intelligence," was similarly

---

10. Pietro Paolo, Marquis of Célesia, (1732–1806) was a diplomat and a Genoan
statesman.

11. Louis-Georges-Oudard-Feudrix de Bréquigny (1714–1795), a historian, specialized in the history of French-English relations. He was a member of the Académie
Française and, as such, was a colleague of Marmontel in that august body.

12. Comte Marin Carbury de Céphalonie served as a lieutenant-colonel in the
armies of Russia and was a director of the cadet corps. He participated in the
effort to erect a monument to Peter the Great of Russia in St. Petersburg, which
resulted in the installation, under the patronage of Catherine the Great, of the
colossal statue of the Russian Emperor atop a pedestal made up of an enormous
rock which stands to this day.

13. Nicolas Thyrel de Boismont (1715–1786) was a priest and a highly regarded
pulpit orator. His eloquence led him to pronounce funeral orations for many
members of the royal family during the reign of Louis XV. He was elected to
the Académie Française (but, allegedly, only through the pressures placed
upon the Académie by his noble lover, the Duchess de Chaulnes).

14. Jean-Sifrein (or Siffrein) Maury (1746–1817) was both a cleric and an author of
some renown. He was very conservative in his views, opposing most of the liberal policies of the Revolution and, notably, the grant of equality to Jews, which
he fought with particular virulence. He was ultimately compelled to emigrate
from France during the Revolution. However, a certain pragmatism permeated
his politics and, eventually, he became a supporter of Napoleon, resulting in his
return. As a consequence, he was expelled from France during the Restoration
and while in Rome was imprisoned by the Pope.

generous.[15] The avocat DeSèze, who seems to have joined the circle of
friends somewhat later (Marmontel notes in his description of his social
circle that DeSèze "soon began to give to our gatherings even more uplift
and charm,") was, even then, a successful avocat who would be called
upon to represent high-profile clients.[16] His ultimate claim to fame would
be his eloquent, albeit unsuccessful, defense of Louis XVI in the king's
trial before the revolutionary National Convention, as co-counsel with
Malesherbes and François-Denis Tronchet.[17] Representing the king was
a feat that DeSèze was able to accomplish without putting his own head
in jeopardy. Not surprisingly and consistent with his tendency to engage
in vigorous networking, Godard soon became a close collaborator of
DeSèze. Some years later, in his role as editor of the literary *Mercure de
France*, Marmontel wrote of Godard, that he "is personally known to us
by his talents and most esteemed qualities."[18]

The social circle of which the young Godard became an integral part
also included Jean-Baptiste-Antoine Suard, a distinguished journalist,
editor, and literary critic, who had become a member of the Académie
Française in 1772 and was subsequently named as the royal government's
theatrical censor.[19] In spite of Suard's very conservative political outlook,

15. Marmontel, *Mémoires d'un Père*, Book 11, in *Mémoires de Marmontel, Secrétaire
Perpétuelle de l'Académie Française* (Paris: Librairie de Firmin Didot Frères, Imprimeurs de l'Institut, 1846), p. 418.
16. Ibid.
17. Francois-Denis Tronchet (1726–1806) was born to a family of avocats and
rose to prominence as a member of the Paris Bar. He became president of the Bar
and was elected to the Estates-General in 1789. He served on the Constitution
Committee of the National Assembly, which would play an important role in the
quest for Jewish equality. Following his service as part of Louis XVI's defense
team, he was forced to go into hiding. He resumed both his political and legal
careers during the Directory and subsequent regimes.
18. *Mercure de France*, January 22, 1791, vol. 140, no. 4, p. 301
19. Jean-Baptiste Antoine Suard (1732–1817) came from Besançon, where he
demonstrated his brilliance during the course of his secondary education. At 20,
he moved to Paris, where he began a career as an author and critic. Among the
individuals with whom he began his writing career was the noted avocat Gerbier.
In 1772, Suard was elected to the Académie Française, and served as its secretary.
Subsequently, he was selected by Louis XV to serve as the royal censor of theatrical
productions. He managed to avoid prosecution during the Terror by hiding out
in a small town. He and his wife then left France until the Directory was installed.

he and Godard became fast friends.[20] Suard's wife, Amélie Panckouke Suard, a brilliant woman from a prominent family, took a special interest in Godard. Born in 1743, she was the younger sister of Charles-Joseph Panckoucke, who in 1784 acquired the *Mercure de France*, and its affiliated publications, among the most significant literary newspapers of that era. Following his acquisition of the *Mercure*, Panckoucke entrusted the editorial control to his brother-in-law, Suard. In 1789, Panckoucke founded the *Gazette Nationale* (which also bore the name *Moniteur Universel*), a newspaper that would quickly become the most influential and widely read daily publication during the French Revolution.[21] Panckoucke's ownership of these two important publications made him a formidable force in French politics and society.[22]

Amélie Suard was substantially younger than her prominent husband and was by all accounts not only intelligent but attractive. She had many admirers. Among the most prominent of those was one of the most esteemed of the *philosophes* still living at the time of the Revolution, the mathematician and philosopher Nicolas de Condorcet.[23] He was held in

20. Suard's conservatism did not prevent him from decrying anti-Jewish prejudice. In an article about the English theater which he published as part of his memoires in 1804, commenting on the "barbaric and disgusting" topics which infused old British ballads, Suard wrote: "There are several [old British ballads] which are based upon this ridiculous opinion that the Jews crucified and ate little Christian children and this monstruous absurdity is always presented as a universally established fact." Jean-Baptiste Suard, "Coup-d'Oeil sur l'Histoire de l'Ancien Théatre français," in *Mélanges de Literature*, vol. 4 (Paris: Dentu, 1804), 363–64.
21. Over time, even though both names remained on the masthead of the newspaper, the name "*Moniteur*" would become the newspaper's principal appellation. It will, therefore, be referred to consistently as the "*Moniteur*."
22. Godard and Charles-Joseph Panckoucke became acquainted. As evidence that the two knew one another there is an indication that in May 1791 Panckoucke sent a letter to Godard requesting information regarding a commission report that Godard prepared regarding riots that had taken place in the Department of the Lot. *Archives Parlementaires, Première Série*, vol. 25, p. 286n1. (Virtually all references to the *Archives Parlementaires* are to the volumes in the *Première Série*, which covers the years 1789 to 1799. As a consequence, the reference to "*Première Série*" will intentionally not be included in citations to the *Archives Parlementaires*. References to *Archives Parlementaires* from any other series will cite the relevant series.)
23. Marie-Jean-Antoine-Nicolas de Caritat, Marquis de Condorcet (1743–1794), trained as a mathematician, achieved the pinnacle of fame as a late Enlightenment philosopher—arguably the last of that group. He advocated various re-

high regard throughout French intellectual society and was a frequenter of salons. He counted Thomas Jefferson among his friends.[24]

It was shortly after her marriage to Suard that Amélie and Condorcet pursued an intense relationship. Oddly, at one point, when Condorcet had been appointed Inspector-General of the Mint, the Suards and Condorcet shared housing quarters inside the Hôtel de la Monnaie (the Paris mint), a prominent edifice located along the Left Bank of the Seine.[25] The relationship between Amélie and Condorcet was—as was the case with so many amorous relationships of the era—complicated and convoluted, emotional and intellectual, deep and dramatic, as evidenced by their voluminous correspondence.[26] Amélie seems to have been in love with Condorcet, but

---

forms, including reform of the French educational system, and was an early and strong promoter of women's rights, believing in and advocating for fundamental principles of equality between the genders, including full citizenship rights for women. In 1788, as a result of his publication of a pamphlet which argued for a variety of human rights, including women's suffrage, entitled *Lettres d'un bourgeois de Newhaven à un citoyen de Virginie sur l'inutilité de partager le pouvoir législatif entre plusieurs corps* (Letters from a Bourgeois of New Heaven [*sic*] to a Citizen of Virginia on the Uselessness of Dividing the Legislative Power Among Various Bodies), Condorcet was named an honorary citizen of the city of New Haven, following Target in receiving this honor. In this tract, Condorcet presented an argument in favor of a separation of church and state, a very novel and forward-looking notion at the time of its writing that went well beyond anything that his contemporaries, including Godard, were then contemplating. Although he would be defeated by Jacques Godard in an early round of voting in the 1791 legislative elections, in a subsequent round he would ultimately be elected to a seat in the Legislative Assembly. There, he aligned himself with the moderate Girondins and, as a consequence, became a fugitive after their fall from grace in 1793. He was charged with treason, eventually arrested, and imprisoned. Shortly after his imprisonment, he was found dead in his cell, presumably by his own hand from swallowing poison that he carried inside a ring he wore. In the days preceding his arrest, his wife Sophie filed for divorce, most likely to protect her financial resources from confiscation due to the charges brought against Condorcet. A divorce was granted. However, it was granted only after Condorcet's death; Sophie was not informed of his death until several months after it had occurred and she continued to pursue the divorce proceedings after he had died— highlighting the dysfunctionality of the Revolutionary justice system.

24. Kevin J. Hayes, *The Road to Monticello*, 302.

25. In recognition of Condorcet's residency at the Hôtel de la Monnaie, today a large statue of Condorcet stands in tribute to him just a few steps to the west of the *Hôtel*.

26. René Doumic, "Lettres d'un Philosophe et d'une Femme sensible—Con-

she encouraged him to marry someone else (in light of her marriage to Suard, toward whom she demonstrated great loyalty and devotion, albeit only limited passion). Ultimately, Condorcet met, became infatuated with, and married the intelligent and pretty Sophie de Grouchy, the niece of the influential avocats Charles-Marguerite-Jean-Baptiste Mercier Dupaty[27] and Emmanuel-Marie-Michel-Philippe Fréteau de St. Just.[28] Sophie was also the sister of Emmanuel de Grouchy, who would become a Maréchal of France during the Napoleonic Empire and would achieve notoriety for his failure to bring his troops to Napoleon's aid during the battle of Waterloo, resulting in Napoleon's defeat and abdication. Despite Amélie having encouraged Condorcet to marry, she grew profoundly jealous of his involvement with Sophie.[29] Simultaneously, Amélie's husband appears to have been increasingly disturbed by Condorcet's attraction to his wife. The tortured nature of these relationships would have its repercussions. Many years later, when Condorcet was being sought for prosecution by the military forces of the revolutionary National Convention due to his relatively moderate positions

---

dorcet et Madame Suard d'après une Correspondence inédite," *Revue des Deux Mondes*, vols. 5, 6 & 7. See also *Lettres et manuscrits de J.A.N. Caritat, Marquis de Condorcet*, compiled February 1932, New Acquisition 23639, Bibliothèque Nationale de France, which contains copies of many autograph letters exchanged between Condorcet and Amélie Suard.

27. Charles-Marguerite-Jean-Baptiste Mercier Dupaty (1746–1788) was born in La Rochelle. He became an avocat and served as the president of the Parlement of Bordeaux. As we will note later, he and Godard had a close professional relationship in spite of their very different views of the world. Dupaty died just before the outbreak of the Revolution in 1788. It is interesting to note that, in 1797, Dupaty's daughter, Eléanor, married Armand Élie de Beaumont, the son of the noted Protestant attorney, Jean-Baptiste Élie de Beaumont, with whom Godard worked in the 1780s. (Antoine Guillois, *La Marquise de Condorcet, sa famille, son salon, ses amis 1764–1822* [Paris: Paul Olendorff, Ed., 1897], 86n1.)

28. Emmanuel-Marie-Michel-Philippe Fréteau de Saint-Just (1745–1794) served as a counselor to the Paris Parlement during the 1780s and sided with the Parlement against the monarchy, in spite of being a member of the nobility. His support of the Parlement resulted in his imprisonment. As a member of the National Assembly, he strongly supported a constitutional monarchy. It is a testament to the respect his fellow Assembly members had for him that he was twice elected as president of the Assembly. During the Terror, he was arrested on a charge of conspiring against the state and, deprived of the right to defend himself before the Revolutionary Tribunal, he was convicted, condemned to death, and executed, all on the same day, June 14, 1794.

29. Doumic, "Lettres d'un Philosophe et d'une Femme sensible," 68.

and sympathy for the opposition Girondins, he asked Suard to provide him with a safe haven on the Suard country estate in Fontenay-aux-Roses, just a few miles southwest of Paris. Suard allegedly agreed to do so. However, when Condorcet appeared at the estate while the Suards were away, he found that Suard had failed to leave any means of access to the residence leaving Condorcet without refuge. Condorcet's inability to find refuge, presumably as a result of Suard's change of heart, ultimately led to Condorcet's arrest and imprisonment and to his subsequent suicide while in prison. This failure to provide a suitable hiding place for Condorcet, perceived as a betrayal of the philosopher, has been ascribed to Suard's jealousy over Condorcet's well-known and reciprocated affection for Amélie.[30]

Amélie Suard grew to know Godard very well. In fact, she knew him so well that it is through a letter that she wrote and published years later that we have one of the very few references to Godard's physical appearance, confirming the image set out on the single extant portrait of Godard, but painted years after his death, and to his personal character traits (excluding Godard's own not very objective analyses, of course). Included among a compilation of her many essays, this lengthy letter, sent to her husband shortly following Godard's death, described, in almost hagiographic terms, his character and alluded to his good looks.

Just days after Godard's death, Amélie wrote to her husband, "You liked him, you told me, with the confidence that you gave to my own attachment to him; no, you liked him already for himself; you liked him for his polite physical appearance, faithful symbol of all of his kindness, of all of his candor and of all of his virtues."[31] She went on to describe Godard: "Few men

---

30. Antione Guillois, *Le salon de Madame Helvétius: Cabanis et les idéologues* (Paris: Calmann-Lévy, Editeur, 1894), 97–98; "Lettres d'un philosophe et d'une femme sensible, 57–81; Jules Michelet provides a slightly different analysis. Although he acknowledges the "well-known egotism of Suard," he suggests that it was Condorcet who chose not to stay in the Suard house (which was serving as a hideaway for the Suards) in order to avoid causing them difficulties with the revolutionary authorities. Jules Michelet, *Les Femmes de la Revolution* (Paris: Adolphe Delahays, Libraire-Editeur, 1855), 102.

31. The Letter is not signed "Amélie," but rather merely with an "A." There is little doubt, however, that this initial is a stand-in for Amélie Suard since the letter was ultimately published in a collection entitled *Lettres de Madame Suard à son Mari sur son Voyage de Ferney, Suivies de quelques autres inserées dans le Journal de Paris* (A. Dampierre, An X [1802]). Importantly, this same letter appeared in the November 8, 1791 edition of the *Journal de Paris*.

have been better treated by nature. His young and ardent soul brought him only good-hearted sentiments that could elevate and ennoble him. It was a stranger to all of those petty passions which degrade virtues and which often destroy them. I never surprised in him a movement which could not be attributed to goodness and justice."[32]

There is no indication that Godard had anything beyond a platonic relationship with Amélie, especially in light of her marriage to Suard and involvement with Condorcet, but it is clear that the young avocat had an effect on Mme. Suard that went beyond what would be usual for a mere acquaintance.[33] Indeed, a warm relationship between the two continued for many years, as evidenced by two letters from Godard to Amélie, one of which he wrote in 1789 and one likely in 1790.[34] Godard was effusive in his expressions of respect ("tender respect," as he wrote) for Amélie and appears to have spent much time with her, not hesitating to confide his burdens and his problems to her.[35] It is highly likely that Godard spent some time at Amélie's Paris salon, which she held every Tuesday and Saturday. Obviously, Condorcet attended, as did many of the literary and political giants of the pre-revolutionary years.

Amélie Suard wrote in her *Essais de Mémoire sur M. Suard*, that "L'abbé Arnaud, M. d'Alembert, M. Dupati [*sic*], who were among our most intimate friends, had the good fortune not to witness the revolution."[36] The reference to M. Dupati (actually, to Charles-Marguerite-Jean-Baptiste Mercier Dupaty) further reinforces the link between Godard's professional

---

32. J.B.A. Suard, *Mélanges de Litterature; publiés par J.B.A. Suard*, vol. 3 (Paris: Dentu, 1896), 528, et seq.
33. The extent of the relationship between Godard and Amélie is shrouded in mystery. When one of Amélie's admirers responded to the publication many years later of her tribute on the occasion of Godard's death, she in turn wrote to him that "six years have deprived me of three men, whose deaths have been a loss to the Nation...who deprived me of the pleasure of loving them." (A footnote identifies two of the three as "Cond** et Gar**." The "Cond**" is evidently Condorcet, and it is possible that the abbreviation "Gar**" refers to Godard.) Amélie Suard, *Essais de Mémoire sur M. Suard* (Paris: Imp. P. Didot, 1820),115.
34. Unpublished letters of Jacques Godard to Amélie Suard, dated November 19, 1789, and July 27, _____ (the year is not visible on the second of the surviving letters, but the contents of the letter strongly suggest that it is 1790), Archives of the Institut Voltaire, Geneva, Switzerland.
35. Ibid.
36. Amélie Suard, *Essais de Mémoire sur M. Suard*, 155n1.

life and his social life. Dupaty was a highly regarded and well-connected avocat (in addition to being the uncle of Condorcet's wife) with whom Godard would later work closely on a case concerning a robbery of items belonging to a Jewish family from the area near Metz—a case that appears to have had far-reaching repercussions for Godard's career.

As a consequence of his associations with Target, Marmontel, Suard (and his wife), Dupaty, and Condorcet, it remains possible, maybe even probable, that Godard also had access to and attended other prominent salons of the era. Those salons would have included the salons of Mme. Helvetius and Sophie de Condorcet herself, where Thomas Jefferson, then Ambassador of the United States to France, was a regular guest. There are indications that, during his lengthy stay in Paris, Jefferson also frequented Target's home on rue Sainte-Croix-de-la-Bretonnerie where intellectuals and other celebrities were guests of the lawyer in the years preceding the Revolution.[37] It is, therefore, very plausible that Jacques Godard may have had some, and possibly even frequent, contact with the author of the American Declaration of Independence and future president of the United States, and that Jefferson's opinions may have had an impact on Godard's intellectual development.

By moving to Paris and choosing to become an avocat registered with the Paris Parlement, Godard entered the very competitive heart of the French legal world. He had, of course, obvious connections to the Parlement of Dijon and to the avocats registered there. In addition, his family's prominence and connections in the Burgundy region would have provided a relatively comfortable and remunerative career path for the young Godard in his native province. However, the Dijon Parlement was merely a modest regional Parlement. The real action was in Paris.

The Paris Parlement, like all the seventeen Parlements in France, both registered royal edicts for its region (a condition to rendering any royal edict enforceable in that region) and acted as a regional court of appeals. It was by far the most important court in France, with a jurisdiction that covered a full third of the country.[38] The Paris *Ordre des avocats* was, in turn, the most prestigious of the French Bars. In 1789, there were 605 avocats registered with the *Ordre des avocats* in Paris. The next largest Bar in

---

37. "Discours prononcé par Paul Boulloche, à l'ouverture de la Conférence des Avocats le 26 Novembre 1892," in Target, *Un Avocat du XVIIIe siècle*, 32.
38. Bell, *Lawyers and Citizens*, 24.

France, the Order in Toulouse, had only 215 registered avocats. Being an avocat provided certain advantages and privileges, among them the right to defend clients directly before the Parlement.[39] The avocats authorized to practice before the Parlement of Paris were very likely to become the most prominent avocats in the kingdom and could expect, if they played their cards well, to assume a significant role in the juridical and even the political life of the nation. However, in the early stages of their careers, before they had developed reputations that would attract wealthy clients and generous fees, they could not expect to earn very much. Indeed, most young avocats in Paris, including Godard, lived on the edge of poverty.[40]

Godard's connections were a complement to his personal qualities. He rapidly developed a reputation as a gifted defense and appellate avocat, with particular skill as a serious writer and good legal tactician. He was an excellent draftsman of persuasive briefs.[41] He would, during his very short career, publish quite a few works of considerable length that would highlight those attributes. The combination of his organizational and writing skills with his intellectual abilities would eventually make him the most important chronicler of the accomplishments of the legislative body of the City of Paris during the first year of the Revolution.

In fact, shortly after joining the *Ordre des avocats de Paris*, Godard began to demonstrate his organizational and leadership skills. Early on, he founded and led a *"Conférence judiciaire"* (a Judicial Conference). Judicial Conferences were seminars where young avocats were encouraged to write essays and make presentations about the important civil and criminal jurisprudential issues of the time, where they were provided with opportunities "to hone their legal skills and to become known."[42] Godard

---

39. Michael Fitzsimmons, *The Parisian Order of Barristers and the French Revolution* (Cambridge, MA: Harvard, 1987), 2.

40. Godard alludes to the precarious nature of his finances in one of his unpublished letters to Amélie Suard. See unpublished letter from Jacques Godard to Amélie Suard, dated November 19, 1789 (Geneva, Switzerland, Archives of the Institut Voltaire, Cote IMV: MS AS 420).

41. Amélie Suard would write, regarding his legal skills, that "He had a natural method such that he would put everything in its place. The facts, the reflections, everything was so well organized..." Suard, *Essais de Mémoire sur M. Suard*, 107–8.

42. Letter from Godard to Cortot, December 5, 1785. In this letter Godard mentioned his judicial conference, which he referred to somewhat immodestly as being "one of the best at the Palace." Cf. *Moniteur*, Sunday, November 6, 1791, Letter from J.B.L.J. Billecocq, *Mercure Universel*, vol. 9, no. 230, pp. 86–89. See

created such a conference and, through this project, refined his own legal writing skills. But he also developed his own concepts of fundamental justice; not just justice in the purely legal sense, but also in the sphere of social and individual rights.[43]

Godard's devotion to the notion of providing justice to the less fortunate was further evidenced when, on December 1, 1787, he joined with many other members of the Paris legal community to form the *"Association de Bienfaisance judiciaire"* (the Association for Judicial Welfare). The group was, in the words of its founder, Antoine Gaspard Boucher d'Argis—a legal scholar who wrote extensively on criminal law matters—a legal aid society intended to: "Give to the poor free defense counsel and...[fulfill] the obligation to indemnify those who, having been accused, condemned, and imprisoned at the demand of the public prosecutor, have been subsequently absolved."[44] On December 21 Godard was the eighty-first member of the Paris legal community to become a member of the association,[45] following by but a few days the enrollment of his mentor Target, who had joined on December 10 as the forty-fifth member.[46] The association solicited contributions, and the names of the donors were made public (although some donors made their contributions anonymously). Godard made such a contribution of which, on December 23, the *Journal de Paris* made note.[47] Shortly after joining the association, Godard was elected to serve on the Third Subcommittee of the Judicial Committee, the group that determined which matters brought to the association were worthy of being accepted.[48] Participation in the *Association* was but another example of the ambitious young avocat's steadily growing involvement in matters relating to the public welfare, all while scaling the steps to the upper echelons of leadership in the legal profession and to the inner circles of the social world of pre-revolutionary Paris.

also David Bell, *Lawyers and Citizens*, 34.

43. "He did not take on any cause that his conscience had not already espoused. His talent was only at the service of truth: it alone prompted and excited him." Suard, *Essais de Mémoire sur M. Suard*, 109.

44. *Recueil de pièces concernant l'Association de Bienfaisance Judiciaire, Fondée en 1787* (Paris: Clousier, 1789), 17.

45. Ibid., 160.

46. Ibid., 145.

47. *Journal de Paris*, December 24, 1787, no. 358, p. 1547.

48. *Recueil de pièces concernant l'Association de Bienfaisance Judiciaire, Fondée en 1787*, p. A-5.

CHAPTER 4

DEVELOPING A LAW PRACTICE

Essential to any lawyer's development of a solid reputation is the opportunity to work on challenging and notable matters. Despite his young age, shortly after he had been admitted to the Paris *Ordre des avocats*—thanks to his intellect and rapidly developing skills, as well as to his growing connections with his legal colleagues—Jacques Godard managed to involve himself, in various capacities, in a large number of noteworthy legal proceedings. He participated directly or indirectly in a variety of cases that aroused public interest during the latter part of the critical decade before the outbreak of the Revolution. Godard's role in these cases gave him the opportunity not only to hone his legal skills, but also to become a player in the simmering political unrest that would soon boil over.

His practice was broad-based. As is true for most avocats, and as assuredly was the case in pre-revolutionary France with its tortured and overlapping maze of laws and jurisdictions, many of the cases he was hired to handle involved principally procedural matters. However, a number of the cases involved seemingly lost causes or matters involving individuals challenging accepted standards of society. Some of these cases were extremely important, even *causes célèbres*. This was of particular consequence since it has been noted that "sensational *causes célèbres* combined with the legal profession's special privileges...put barristers in the vanguard of reform and allowed them to behave, some

49

years before 1789, as if France were already a Republic."[1] In other words, Godard's professional activities, within the context of his legal practice, set him on a political course at a time of great political effervescence. Furthermore, in many of these high-visibility cases, he acted in concert with other avocats, many of whom were among the most prominent members of the Bar—individuals whose acquaintance he had cultivated from the moment he arrived in Paris. He would continue to have frequent contact with these individuals throughout his life as his career evolved from the pure practice of law to one largely focused on political activism.

One of the earliest cases in which Godard's name appears involved notarial malpractice. Notaries of the pre-revolutionary era played, as they still do today in France, a very important role in documenting and implementing commercial and real estate transactions. Importantly, they frequently served as intermediaries, "trustees," and escrow agents in such transactions.[2] Godard represented and filed a brief on behalf of one of several creditors of a notary who appears to have absconded with his client's funds. The matter, which was before the courts from mid-1785 until early 1786, was a criminal case in which procedural questions dominated. The notary was represented by Louis-Simon Martineau[3] who, in a subsequent matter, would soon have Godard join him in defending one of his clients.[4] Another of the creditors in the notarial case was represented by Raymond DeSèze, with whom Godard worked as early as 1784 in a case in which the adverse party was the financial director of the Comte d'Artois, Louis XVI's youngest brother and the future early nineteenth-century King Charles X.[5] Although the criminal case against the notary was focused

---

1. Bell, *Lawyers and Citizens*, 174.
2. See Chapter 36 below for a discussion of "trusts."
3. Louis-Simon Martineau (1733–1799), an avocat registered with the Parlement of Paris, was elected to the Estates-General in 1789. As a member of the National Assembly, he participated actively in the work of the Assembly, serving as a member of the Ecclesiastical Committee. In December 1789 he issued a report which was the precursor of the Civil Constitution of the Clergy, proposing to make all priests civil servants. The Civil Constitution was ultimately adopted in July 1790 and became one of the most divisive acts of the revolutionary government, creating a schism with the traditional Catholic hierarchy and causing immense discomfort to traditional Catholics (including Louis XVI), who still made up a very large proportion of the French population.
4. *Gazette des Tribunaux*, 1786, vol. 21, no. 11, 166, et seq.
5. *Mémoire pour le Sieur Jean-Baptiste Giroud, bourgeois de Paris, contre le sieur*

on purely procedural matters, it was considered to be of importance in the legal community, giving the avocats involved in the matter a certain amount of recognition. Emphasizing this, the *Gazette des Tribunaux* commented that the verdict was "impatiently awaited" because the case was "truly important to all of society" due to the "character of the public person who is accused." Godard was clearly very pleased when he "won" his case against the notary, as he proudly informed his cousin Cortot.[6]

In 1785, in yet another procedural matter, Godard represented a textile merchant named Jambe who was seeking to defend himself against a court order seizing certain goods that he had sold to a Spanish Grandee. Arguing that a tribunal could not seize goods of "first necessity" and that, furthermore, the court's order had not been registered in the proper jurisdiction, Godard sought to nullify the impact of the court's seizure order. Ultimately, Godard also prevailed in this case.[7]

Godard's various pleadings in both the minor and major cases he handled during his brief legal career display both his skill as an advocate and his talent as a writer, and highlight the wide scope of his interests. They also disclose the nature of his professional relationships, which were to become a pivotal component of his uncommon career. Furthermore, they reveal an emerging political philosophy.

THE SCIENTIST PRIEST

In early 1785 Godard made one of his first forays into high-profile legal proceedings, joining a team of avocats consisting of his mentor, Target, Jean-Jacques Piales,[8] Élie de Beaumont, Raymond DeSèze, Jacques

---

Gilbert de la Grye, employé au bureau de la Surintendance des finances de M. le Comte d'Artois (Signé: Giroud, Me. Godard avoc.), Consultation, Signé: De Sèze, Paris 5 mars 1784 (Paris: L'Imp. De Clousier, 1785 in 4°) [Ms. Joly de Fleury 1954 f° 107].

6. Letter from Godard to Cortot, October 13, 1785.

7. *Gazette des Tribunaux*, 1786, vol. 21, no. 11, 327. See also *Gazette des Tribunaux*, 1785, vol. 19, no. 23, 381.

8. Jean-Jacques Piales (1747–1789) was an avocat who specialized in legal matters affecting the Catholic Church. He wrote significant treatises respecting religious topics, including a couple relating to the intersection of canon and civil law. He remained an active avocat despite being afflicted by blindness as early as 1763. Since he died at the very onset of the Revolution, he did not have the opportunity to play a role in the dramatic changes that altered the relationship beween the government of France and the Catholic Church.

Blondel[9] and Levacher de Laterinière,[10] to defend the interests of a scholarly cleric named Jean-Louis Giraud-Soulavie.

Soulavie was a priest from the modest diocese of Viviers (in the Rhone-Alps region), a small, walled city established in the Middle Ages. Most importantly, he was the author of a remarkable eight-volume scientific treatise entitled: *The Natural History of Southern France.*[11] Another priest from Viviers (and allegedly a friend of Soulavie's), Augustin de Barruel,[12] virulently attacked Soulavie as being "a heretic, impious and an atheist" in a book entitled *Genesis, according to Mr. Soulavie,*[13] written and published with the clear support of the Catholic hierarchy. The charge against Soulavie was very simply that he held Enlightenment principles contrary to those of fundamental Christian theology, and most specifically contrary to the core Catholic notion that only God had revealed all truth.

In point of fact, Soulavie was not just a parish priest whose views deviated from Church theology; he was, significantly, a distinguished scientist. As a means of defending himself and protecting his reputation

---

9. Jacques Blondel, an avocat with the Parlement of Paris, joined the Bar in 1760. He lived on rue Saint Avoye just around the corner from rue des Blancs-Manteaux where Godard took up residence in the late 1780s. In 1789, Blondel became a member of the Assembly of representatives from the various city districts and would have been in close contact with Godard as they both pursued their municipal political careers.

10. Levacher de Laterinière (or Le Vacher de la Terrinière) became a member of the Parlement of Paris in 1778. He resided on rue Bourglabbé (or Bourg l'Abbé), a small street joining rue St. Martin to rue St. Denis in the Marais neighborhood, near Godard's residence, during the predominant portion of his career as an avocat. (*Almanach Royal*, 1790, p. 361.)

11. Jean-Louis Giraud Soulavie, *L'Histoire naturelle de la France méridionale* (Paris: Chez Quillau, Mérigot, Belin, 1782).

12. Augustin de Barruel (1741–1820) was ordained to the priesthood in the Jesuit order. He was profoundly opposed to the Enlightenment and staunchly supported the Ancien Régime. He was a prolific author who, in supporting Catholicism, espoused strongly anti-Masonic principles. He was initially exiled from France in the 1770s, when the Jesuits were expelled by Louis XV. He returned to France several years later, but left again in 1792, at which time he settled in England. During his second exile, he wrote his memoirs—a diatribe against the Jacobins which became one of the most popular books of its time. He never abandoned his energetic opposition to liberal thought, even during the years of the Empire.

13. Albin Mazon, *Histoire de Soulavie (Naturaliste, Diplomate, Historien)*, vol. 1 (Paris: Librairie Fischbacher, 1893), 38; citing an extract from the *Mémoires Secrètes of Bachaumont* (vol. 27, p. 78); cf. *Gazette des Tribunaux*, 1785, vol. 19, no. 22.

as an independent scholar, Soulavie brought charges of defamation against Barruel and sought the suppression of Barruel's book. Beyond the theological and defamatory components of the struggle between the two priests, there was also an undercurrent of personal animus. During private discussions between the two, Soulavie had confided in Barruel some of the theories that he was planning to include in future volumes of his treatise, with the understanding that the discussion was strictly between the two of them. When Barruel attacked Soulavie, he referred to the theories Soulavie had shared with him in confidence. This unauthorized disclosure especially antagonized Soulavie and added fuel to the litigation, as did the fact that Soulavie blamed Barruel's attacks for Soulavie's failure to receive promotions within the Catholic hierarchy. To do battle with Barruel, Soulavie assembled a distinguished legal team of veteran avocats, but it was the young Godard who took the lead in Soulavie's legal battle.

This case is of particular importance because, in his book, Soulavie was the first person to assert that it is possible to measure the age of the earth through an examination of layers of rock formations. Based upon his analysis, Soulavie posited that the earth was millions of years old, in direct contravention of the theology of the Catholic Church, which measured the age of the earth based upon biblical revelation. Arguably, Soulavie was one of the earliest modern examples of a member of the Catholic hierarchy who advocated the pure pursuit of science—the effort to seek out truth solely through tangible evidence. His opponent, on the other hand, espoused the conservative values of the Catholic religion.[14] It was, of course, a particular oddity in the case that both the antagonists were members of the Catholic clergy. Soulavie was accused by his fellow priest of "incredulity and materialism." However, Soulavie vigorously combatted this accusation, claiming that his scientific discoveries actually reinforced his faith. Although he was a scientist, he remained, at least at the time of the litigation, steadfastly devoted to his religion and asserted that, if he failed to resist the accusation of heresy, it would render him culpable in the very eyes of God.[15]

Godard wrote the brief in support of Soulavie, to which the other avocats on the team added their names. In his brief, which was filed on April 26, 1785, Godard argued two major procedural points on behalf of Soulavie, neither of which, because of the stage at which the proceedings

14. *Revue du Lyonnais*, 53.
15. *Gazette des Tribunaux*, 1785, vol. 19, no. 22, pp. 351–52.

stood, related to the substance of Soulavie's writings nor to the principle of free expression.[16] Godard noted that it was perfectly appropriate for Soulavie to attack Barruel since the latter had directly attacked both Soulavie's book and the author himself. Furthermore, he asserted that Barruel was fully aware that Soulavie's book had been officially authorized by the government (in other words had not been banned by the government's censors, one of whom was none other than Godard's friend Suard). Godard went on to note, as a further indication that Barruel's comportment was unacceptable, that the defamatory attack had been launched in a book that itself had not been authorized by the government.

Beyond drafting the initial brief, in his representation of the cleric the young avocat did not have much opportunity to demonstrate his legal skills, as the case was ultimately abandoned by Soulavie at the demand of his hierarchical superior, the Archbishop of Narbonne.[17] Initially, the Archbishop attempted to dissuade Soulavie from pursuing his legal battle through an offer that Soulavie instead join the scientific expedition headed by the Comte de la Pérouse on its around-the-world trip (a voyage that ultimately ended in disaster with the expedition disappearing without a trace in the South Pacific in 1788). When Soulavie refused the Archibishop's proposition, the Archbishop, quite desperate to bring the dispute to a rapid end, offered Soulavie a substantial pension and free housing as an incentive to renounce the legal proceedings.[18] Soulavie accepted this offer, bringing the litigation between the two priests to an inconclusive closure. The valiant efforts of the Catholic hierarchy to have Soulavie give up his legal efforts confirm that, even without a formal legal victory, Soulavie had the better argument in the lawsuit, as well demonstrated in Godard's pleadings.[19] Science has since unqualifiedly recognized that Soulavie understood the process by which the earth has been evolving.[20] The Catholic Church clearly did not want a secular judgment handed down in a dispute between two of its priests, especially a judgment in favor of Soulavie's position.

---

16. Mazon, *Histoire de Soulavie*, 44.

17. Henri Nadault Buffon, *Correspondance inédite de Buffon*, vol. 2 (Paris: Hachette, 1860), 378–79.

18. *Mémoires Secrets pour servir à l'histoire de la République des Lettres en France depuis MDCCLXII jusqu'à nos jours ou Journal d'un Observateur*, vol. 29, p. 7.

19. *Revue du Lyonnais*, 53.

20. Mazon, *Histoire de Soulavie*, 48.

In joining Soulavie's legal team, Godard had aligned himself with a liberal thinker of international renown. Soulavie was highly respected by the intellectuals of his time. In fact, during 1782 and 1783, Soulavie had met and corresponded extensively with Benjamin Franklin (then residing in France as an envoy of the newly independent thirteen American colonies). It was during his stay in Paris that Franklin, an immensely popular figure in France, negotiated the treaty which, when signed in 1783, confirmed that independence. The many exchanges between Soulavie and Franklin related, not to theology, but strictly to science, one of Franklin's abiding passions.

In many ways, the Soulavie case epitomized the growing conflict between France's conservative forces (heavily concentrated among the clergy and those who adhered strictly to Catholic theology and practice) and its enlightened elements, which encompassed most intellectuals as well as a growing segment of the liberal clergy and many among the developing middle, commercial, and professional classes, including many avocats. Godard's role in defending Soulavie placed him squarely in the midst of the enlightened avocats of Paris and helped to cement his relationships with liberals and freethinkers, providing him with essential credentials for the political struggles that were about to begin.

After the start of the Revolution, Soulavie became increasingly politically radical and, ultimately, anti-clerical. In 1792, he married a young woman from his home village of Largentière. In mid-1793, in the midst of the Revolution, he was named by the Revolutionary government as the French ambassador to Geneva, where to the dismay of the Genevans he militated for the annexation of Geneva to France. However, in the summer of 1794 he was repatriated, arrested, and imprisoned on the charge that he had been a supporter of the radical Jacobins. When he was liberated a year later, he retired from politics and spent the balance of his life in Paris writing historical texts and memoirs, some of which, oddly, were outright fabrications.

THE DEFENSE OF A SWISS SOLDIER

Among the many avocats with whom Godard associated in the early years of his legal career was Pierre-Louis Lacretelle, an avocat some ten years his senior.[21] Lacretelle was born in the northeastern city of Metz,

---

21. Pierre-Louis de Lacretelle (1751–1824) became active in politics during the

which at that time had the largest Jewish population of any French urban center. He had left his native city, just as Godard had left his, to become an avocat in Paris.

Lacretelle achieved early prominence through his writing skills. In 1784 he won an important writing prize awarded by the prestigious *Société royale des arts et des sciences* (Royal Society of Arts and Sciences) of the city of Metz. Each year, the Royal Society sponsored an essay contest on a question or topic the Society deemed to be of particular relevance to French society. The questions posed by the Society for its contest in 1784 were: "What is the origin of the opinion which extends to all of the members of a family a part of the shame attached to the ignominious penalties which are imposed on a guilty individual? This opinion, is it more harmful than useful? And, in the event that one should respond in the affirmative, what would be the means of remedying the disadvantages that result?" Of the twenty-two submissions, Lacretelle's lengthy essay, entitled *Discours sur le Préjugé des Peines infamantes* [On the Prejudice of Ignominious Punishments] was judged to be the best, even though the Society expressed qualms about all the essays, including his. He was, nonetheless, awarded first prize.[22]

However, in an unusual move, the Society decided also to award a second prize (but announced it to be "of the same value" as the first prize[23]). The second prize winner was Maximilien de Robespierre, a fellow avocat originally from Arras, a small city in the north of France, who was already practicing law in Paris.[24] His essay, uninspiringly entitled *Discours adressé*

Revolution. He was a moderate and, as such, as the Revolution veered toward radical politics, he was in imminent danger of being beheaded. Arrested by the forces of the National Convention, he survived the Terror only because Robespierre, the man over whom he had prevailed in the 1784 essay contest in Metz, was himself decapitated first. He wrote a variety of political and legal treatises and, in 1806, was elected to the Académie Française. His moderation and resourcefulness permitted him to survive the Revolution, the Napoleonic era, and the Restoration and to remain active during all these regimes.

22. Pierre Louis de Lacretelle, *Discours sur le Préjugé des Peines infamantes* (Paris: Chez Cuchet, 1784).

23. Ibid., vii.

24. Maximilien François Marie Isidore de Robespierre (1758–1794) was born in Arras in northern France, where he studied law. Although he was registered with the Parlement of Paris, he practiced law in his native city. He was elected to the Estates-General in 1789 and rapidly became known for his oratorical skills and

à Messieurs de la Société royale literaire de Metz [Remarks addressed to the Gentlemen of the Royal Literary Society of Metz], presented a powerful argument against the heavy-handed punishment of criminals. He appeared to favor leniency whenever possible. Robespierre's opinions, as expressed in his essay, would become a subject of much ironic commentary in the next few years, as he sent hundreds of his political opponents to their deaths. Not surprisingly, as a result of receiving his prize in tandem with Robespierre, Lacretelle's name has become inextricably bound with that of Robespierre (who would soon shed the embarrassing noble "de" in his family name), even though the two men shared few political opinions.

Lacretelle was among the many avocats who hovered around Target, albeit substantially before Godard did so. His younger brother, Charles, however, was among Target's disciples during the 1780s when Godard was spending much time with the eminent avocat. As such, we can presume that Godard was in frequent contact with Lacretelle and his older brother (generally referred to as Lacretelle, l'Ainé—Lacretelle, the Elder).

In 1786, the older Lacretelle invited Godard to join him in representing Baron François-Louis de Waldner de Freundenstein, from the city of Mulhouse in Alsace. At that time, Mulhouse was controlled by the Swiss, making the Baron a Swiss citizen. Waldner was the Chief of the Infantry Camp, Chevalier of the Grand Vassal of the Archbishopric of Bâle, the Swiss city just a few miles from Mulhouse.[25] Lacretelle and Godard represented Waldner against a claim asserted by the widow of Comte Christian-Frederic-Dagobert de Waldner de Freundenstein, a soldier in the armies of Louis XVI and the older brother of the plaintiff.[26]

---

his firmly held opinions. He supported the liberation of slaves, equality for Jews and the elimination of the death penalty. In 1792, he was elected to the National Convention, where, as a member of the radical Jacobins, he supported extreme revolutionary measures. When he became president of the National Convention he advocated for the implementation of a regime of terror, sending hundreds to their deaths on the guillotine. In the summer of 1794, Convention members, fearful for their own lives, turned on Robespierre and had him executed.

25. See Henriette-Louise de Waldner de Freudenstein, Mémoires de la Baronne d'Oberkirch, vol. 1, ed. Comte de Montbrison (Paris: Charpentier, Libraire-Editeur, 1853). (Paris: Charpentier, Libraire-Editeur, 1869).

26. Gazette des Tribunaux, 1786, vol. 22, no. 27; cf. Mémoire et Consultation sur les privilèges et les immunités du corps militaire suisse en France, 1786. In 1777, Dagobert de Waldner became Inspector of the Troops in Alsace and purchased a stately mansion in the heart of Strasbourg. Interestingly, the mansion was located di-

The litigation was a family struggle over rights to an estate. The widow of Comte de Waldner was his second wife, and twenty-one years his junior. Because of her common origins, she was intensely disliked by the Comte's family and considered unsuitable as a spouse for the Comte.[27] The pleadings indicate that the Comte's younger brother was endeavoring to prevent her from receiving a bequest under the Comte's will out of sheer disdain. This family dispute was clearly laced with all the bitterness that such intra-familial confrontations can involve when significant amounts of money are at stake.

The case pivoted on the rather banal procedural question of whether Swiss soldiers serving in France were subject to French jurisdiction. Although the Comte was nominally Swiss, virtually all his property was in France (including major properties in the Paris region) where he had lived most of his life. The French courts (at the Châtelet) had already sided with the widow, and the Comte's family was seeking to overturn that decision. In appealing the dismissal of the Comte's brother's suit, Lacretelle and Godard wrote eloquently in support of the theory that the Swiss mercenaries hired by the French monarchy were not subject to French jurisdiction. They argued that generations of treaties and other agreements between France and Switzerland served as evidence of the special relationship between the two countries. They contended that all the customs which were inculcated in the individuals brought up in Swiss territory were not to be relinquished merely because of service to an allied sovereign. Indeed, they posited that the Swiss soldiers remained fully within the control of their sovereign, notwithstanding that their sovereign had made their services available to a foreign nation. Lacretelle and Godard then went on to commend the Swiss for their devotion to liberty and independence. They proposed that a people so devoted to its

---

rectly across the street from the city's oldest known mikvah (Jewish ritual bath). When Dagobert de Waldner died, the mansion was purchased by the Princess Christine de Saxe, Louis XVI's mother's sister. Through a daughter from his first marriage, Dagobert de Waldner was the great-grandfather of the noted nineteenth-century French composer Hector Berlioz.

27. "À la fidelité et à la vertu des suisses, Christian-Frederic-Dagobert, premier comte de Waldner de Freundenstein, 1711–1783, bourgeois suisse au service du roi de France," *En passant par Soultz, Haut Rhin*, 2018. http://www.amisdesoultz.fr/index.php/site-er/christian-frederic-dagobert-premier-comte-de-waldner-de-freundstein.

own liberty could hardly be expected to become subject to the laws of another nation, especially when they had left their country to assist that other nation. In defense of their clients, they wrote:

> If Switzerland, even while it was subject to a foreign Prince [the Austrian monarch] had preserved its independence in such an important respect; if even then it benefitted from the right to be governed by Magistrates of its own selection and which it took to itself; it would never have accepted that when its Inhabitants came to France in the capacity of allies, they would be treated as subjects; it must have stipulated expressly for them the right to be governed by their own Judges, by Judges of their own Nation; and today, when several centuries of absolute liberty have served only to increase in it this strong love of independence, it will less than ever suffer the attacks that some would level at it.[28]

Godard and Lacretelle argued simply that, due to their history, the Swiss would never have agreed to such an arrangement. The argument was thoughtful and well-expressed, even if it was rather contrived in light of the actual facts of the case. Regrettably, the available record does not specify the outcome.

For Jacques Godard, far more important than the case itself and the role he played in it was the impact of his association with the older and far more experienced Lacretelle. Lacretelle was not just a prominent and successful avocat. In addition to also being a published author and an individual of significant renown, throughout his career Lacretelle was a staunch advocate for granting legal rights to minorities. He was a particularly determined defender of the Jews of his native city of Metz.[29] Lacretelle wrote extensively about the right of Jews to citizenship and spoke in glowing terms about the benefits that they brought to society, including in a pleading on behalf of two Jews that he filed in 1775 with the Parlement of Nancy.[30] There is an obvious likelihood that Lacretelle

---

28. *Mémoire et Consultation, sur les Privilèges et les Immunités du Corps Militaire Suisse en France*, 1786, p. 18.

29. Pierre-Louis LaCretelle, *Oeuvres de P-L LaCretelle*, vol. 1 (Paris: Bossange Frères, 1823), x.

30. See *Mémoires pour deux Juifs de Metz* in P.-L. LaCretelle, *Oeuvres de P-L LaCretelle*, vol. 1, pp. 213, et seq. See also Jules Sechehaye. *Allocution de M. le Bâtonnier et Éloge de P.-L. Lacretelle*, pp. 12–13.

and Godard had many occasions to discuss the plight of the Jews of Metz and, more generally, that of the Jews of France. Their conversations must have included discussion of the issue of Jewish legal rights. Furthermore, it may have been Lacretelle who later arranged to have Godard become involved in a major case involving Jews from the area of Metz (albeit as the antagonists), an involvement which would likely lead the younger avocat to an important role in the struggle for Jewish equality.

GODARD, THE MATRIMONIAL AVOCAT

Later in 1786 Godard represented a client in a more prosaic matter. His client was a woman, identified only as Mme. A.D.C., seeking a divorce from her philandering husband.[31] Godard filed a brief in which he contended that defamation, contempt, public repudiation (as a consequence of living apart), and notorious and scandalous adultery were equal grounds for the separation and ultimate divorce of a couple. Godard's brief involved a lengthy and persuasive analysis of the various grounds for divorce and focused specifically on the notorious and scandalous act of adultery (viewed as two separate grounds for the grant of a divorce). His pleading displays indignation at the husband's infidelity that reflects his rather rigid views of right and wrong, as well as his provincial conservatism and perhaps youthful enthusiasm for the marital ideal.[32]

Godard was associated in his representation of Mme. A.D.C. with the prominent avocat Louis-Simon Martineau, against whom he had pleaded a short time earlier in the matter involving the corrupt notary. Martineau, who lived on rue des Blancs-Manteaux just a few doors away from where Godard would come to live in 1788, was particularly reputed for specializing in family and matrimonial issues. His reputation had been significantly enhanced by his role in a high-profile matter involving the divorce of a woman named Lebrun in 1781.[33] The fact that the young Godard had been asked by the much older and more experienced Martineau to assist him and was given full credit for providing that assistance suggests that Godard was already held in considerable regard as an advocate and as a

31. In matters involving personal reputations, it was customary not to identify parties by their full names but to refer to them merely by their initials.

32. *Gazette des Tribunaux*, 1787, vol. 23, no. 23, sec. 11, p. 188.

33. *Annales du Barreau français ou choix des plaidoyers et mémoires les plus remarquables*, vol. 5 (Paris: B. Warée, 1824), 457, et seq.

skilled writer of briefs. Once again, unfortunately, the final outcome of this case is not available.

THE PRIEST PRACTICING MEDICINE

In the only recorded instance of Godard representing a client in multiple matters, he represented an elderly priest named de la Mote de Behringhen, from the small town of Montaulin, in the Champagne-Ardennes region near the city of Troyes. In 1786, the priest was charged with improperly preparing a baptismal certificate for an illegitimate child.[34] Purportedly, in an alleged effort to prevent the baby from being placed in legal limbo, the priest had inscribed the name of an individual, not related to the infant, as the father of the child without the individual's authorization. Godard, in his brief on behalf of the priest (to which a *Consultation* prepared by Target, Gerbier and DeSèze was attached), invoked his client's age and unblemished prior record as the vital elements in his defense. He observed that "the esteem of which his client was the beneficiary in his parish, the universal consideration which he has earned through his piety and his talents, eighty-five years of an irreproachable conduct, are the surest guaranties of his innocence and the most terrible argument against his accuser."[35] Yet again, we are left without the record of a verdict. However, we have ample evidence of Godard's skill and eloquence in the priest's defense.

In the same year, de la Mote, this time in a far more significant matter, was taken to court by the doctors of the nearby city of Troyes. The doctors asserted a charge against the priest of practicing medicine without a license. Priests giving medical advice and dispensing medications had generally been "tolerated" throughout France, so long as this was done without charge and within a restrained periphery, usually the priest's own parish. For some forty years, the priest of Montaulin had carried on his informal medical practice in his own community, but, as his reputation grew, his activities expanded into an ever-growing geographical area.

De la Mote's apparent medical success became a source of concern and irritation to the doctors of Troyes. Relying upon an Edict of March 1707, which prohibited the rendering of medical services by any individual

---

34. *Gazette des Tribunaux*, 1786, vol. 21, no. 25, pp. 397, et seq.
35. Ibid., 1786, vol. 21, no. 13, pp. 199–200.

who did not possess a degree from a recognized royal medical school, they chose to file suit. In response, de la Mote argued that it was customary for priests to provide some medical counseling and to occasionally provide medications to their parishioners, so long as it was free of charge. The priest, according to the plaintiffs, had been engaging in extensive medical activities throughout the greater region (and not just within his small community), thereby becoming a perceived threat to the physicians in the area. The physicians obtained a judgment against the priest which forbade him from "visiting any sick, carrying out and exercising Medicine, providing, selling, bringing or administering any remedies or medications of any type whatsoever, even gratuitously...except in the parish of Montaulin." Furthermore, the priest was condemned to pay all the expenses of the proceedings.

In the original case, Godard filed a brief, which was also supplemented by a *Consultation* written by Target, Gerbier, and DeSèze. Yet, in spite of the prestigious array of attorneys arguing on his behalf, the priest was handed an adverse verdict. In 1786, de la Mote appealed the judgment and Godard filed a brief in support. (Godard's brief was supplemented by a *Consultation* by François Menassier de l'Estre, another avocat registered with the Paris Parlement.[36]) He argued that it would be inappropriate to prevent de la Mote from providing all the beneficial services he was capable of providing, especially when he rendered these services without charge. Godard also asserted, somewhat contradictorily, that it was unjust that de la Mote had been ordered to refrain from receiving any compensation for his services even in his own parish. He further argued that this prohibition was inappropriate because it resulted from the physicians' false assertion that the priest was carrying on his medical work for the express purpose of making money. As a final argument, Godard suggested that since de

36. François Menassier de l'Estre was an early advocate for women's rights. In particular, he urged the elimination of the dowry, which served as a very serious obstacle for young women from poor families seeking to marry and especially for those seeking to marry above their own social station. In 1784, in a study about gender differences, he wrote: "When a woman will bring as a dowry nothing more than her virtue and her charms, both sexes, the law, and social mores will benefit. Then, not only will there be fewer unmarried persons, but spouses will be better suited to one another and divorces will be fewer." Menassier de l'Estre, *De l'honneur des deux sexes, et principes généraux sur les différentes espèces de rapts, de séduction, de subornation et de violence*, 28.

la Mote had been authorized to continue his medical practice in his own parish for which he was not compensated, it was inequitable for him to have been charged with all the expenses of the proceedings.

The doctors responded by asserting that the priest had regularly been paid and, furthermore, that certain of his patients had died from his "cures." They also noted the inconsistency in de la Mote's argument that he rendered his services without charge but objected to the constraint on his ability to be paid. They contended that this served as proof that the priest intended to continue to practice medicine for compensation, in violation of the law.

Godard's brief received a compliment from the editor of the *Gazette des Tribunaux*, who noted that the matter was interesting both because of the subject matter and "the manner in which it is discussed by M. Godard."[37] On May 10, 1786, the avocat-général of the Parlement (the individual charged with providing advice to the court on behalf of the public interest), Marie-Jean Hérault de Séchelles,[38] a future revolutionary

37. *Gazette des Tribunaux*, 1786, vol. 21, no. 13, p. 199.
38. Marie-Jean Hérault de Séchelles (1759–1794) was a prominent member of the legal profession of the pre-Revolutionary era, serving for a number of years as an avocat-général, or public advocate (a kind of magistrate charged with representing the public interest). In spite of his aristocratic origins (he was the grandson of Louis Georges Érasme de Contades, a Marshal of France, and a cousin of the Duchesse de Polignac, one of Marie-Antoinette's closest confidants), he participated in the assault on the Bastille. He was elected to the Legislative Assembly in the fall of 1791 and began a rapid transition toward radicalism. In 1793 he participated, together with Robespierre and Louis Antoine de St. Just, in drafting the Constitution of 1793, a strikingly radical document, which was never actually implemented. That Constitution included a far broader defense of religious freedom than did the Declaration of the Rights of Man and of the Citizen, specifying that religious observance regardless of the religion could not be prohibited (Constitution of June 24, 1793, Article 7). Hérault de Séchelles voted for the conviction of Louis XVI (although he was conveniently not in Paris for the vote on the king's execution) and was one of the promoters of the implementation of the Terror, serving for some six months on the revolutionary Committee of Public Safety. However, in contrast to the austere behavior of some of the revolutionaries, Hérault was an unabashed libertine and pursued an ostentatious personal life. Ultimately, having allied himself with Georges-Jacques Danton, he came to be viewed as a threat by Robespierre and was accused of corruption and counter-revolutionary activities. He was sent to the guillotine in the spring of 1794, along with Danton and Camille Desmoulins.

activist, issued a recommendation to affirm the original ruling, and, in spite of Godard's excellent brief, the Parlement handed Godard a loss by siding with the doctors.[39]

REPRESENTING PARISIAN BAKERS

Also in 1786, Godard was appointed as the avocat for the bread bakers (the *boulangers*) of Paris and filed a brief on their behalf in opposition to an appeal taken in an effort to overturn a ruling that had been issued in their favor. In this representation, Godard was positioned against two powerful individuals, the Archbishop of Paris and the Duc de Penthièvre. The Duc de Penthièvre[40] was not only an extraordinarily wealthy aristocrat, and as such an obviously formidable opponent; he was also the father-in-law of the Duc d'Orléans, the cousin of the king, and one of the chief challengers to Louis XVI's authority.[41] It was nothing short of audacious for so young a man to take on such prominent individuals. Indeed, it was actually quite contrary to the customary practices of the Paris Bar for a young avocat, early in his career, to risk attacking "the honor of powerful persons."[42] Few would have dared, but the ambitious Godard was not deterred.

The case arose in the context of the desire of the bakers to hold their twice weekly "wheat" market in the town of Brie-Comte-Robert—a small municipality some twelve miles to the southeast of Paris—on Mondays and Fridays, even when those days fell on religious holidays. In that town, the custom, if a major Catholic holiday such as Good Friday or Christmas fell on a Monday or Friday, was to hold the market on a proximate date. On April 6, 1786, the bakers of Paris were successful in obtaining an injunction that required the wheat market to be held systematically on

39. *Gazette des Tribunaux*, 1787, vol. 24, no. 43, pp. 257, et seq.

40. Louis Jean Marie de Bourbon, Duc de Penthièvre (1725–1793), was a direct descendant of Louis XIV, through his youngest son (who, though born of a liaison with a mistress, Madame de Montespan, was legitimized by the king). Both by reason of inheritance and connections with Louis XV he became one of the wealthiest men in France. His youngest daughter married Philippe d'Orléans and their son, Louis Philippe, became King of the French in 1830. Undoubtedly, it is only because of his death in the spring of 1793 that he was spared execution on the guillotine.

41. *Gazette des Tribunaux*, 1787, vol. 23, no. 17, pp. 258–61.

42. Boucher d'Argis, "Histoire abrégée de l'Ordre des Avocats," in M. Dupin, aîné, *Profession d'Avocat*, 3rd ed. (Brussels: Louis Haumann & Cie. Libraires, 1834), 57.

Mondays and Fridays, even when religious holidays occurred on those days. The bakers had ostensibly sought the order to ensure a steady flow of flour into Paris, so the city could be appropriately supplied with bread regardless of holidays (and, coincidently, they could continue to bake and sell bread and earn a livelihood). The legal argument that had prompted the issuance of the order was the assertion that other towns in the area, and, notably, the towns of Sceaux (half a dozen miles to the south of Paris) and Poissy (a dozen miles to the northwest of Paris), were permitted to hold their wheat markets on religious holidays.[43]

The Duc de Penthièvre, in his capacity as the lord of Brie-Comte-Robert, was the principal opponent of the order and was joined in his opposition by the Archbishop of Paris, in his capacity as the defender of Catholicism. On behalf of the bakers, Godard argued that the appeal had no basis in law. He cited numerous examples of markets in villages scattered throughout the Paris region that held their market days on religious holidays and did not make any concession to the holiday schedule. The appellants responded that the inappropriate actions of some towns could not justify a violation of proper behavior in Brie-Comte-Robert. Godard went on to argue that commerce in wheat was the sustaining economic activity of Brie-Comte-Robert and, therefore, everything should be done to promote that activity, including systematically and regularly holding the wheat market in the town on the designated days. He evoked a regulation of 1736 that had expressly recognized the importance of commerce in wheat in Brie-Comte-Robert.[44]

Notwithstanding Godard's arguments, on January 17, 1787, the Grand Chamber of the Paris Parlement, on the advice of the avocat-général, Hérault de Séchelles, sided with the Duke and the Archbishop and overturned the order. The Parlement ordered that the wheat market respect the schedule of holidays and that the rescheduling of the market as a consequence of holiday observances was to be announced at the immediately prior market, accompanied by the sound of "trumpets." Godard's loss was made even more crushing by an order that the bakers pay the costs of the proceedings.[45]

---

43. *Gazette des Tribunaux*, 1787, vol. 23, no. 17, pp. 259–61.
44. Ibid., 259
45. Ibid., 261.

CHAPTER 5

ADVOCATING FOR A SLAVE

The many cases which Godard handled in the earliest years of his legal career gave him the experience he would need as he began to play a role in various high-profile matters. By 1787, Godard had received a number of opportunities to use the skills that he had been developing and had participated in a series of cases that were of great legal and social significance. The quantity of cases Godard handled in a very short span during 1787 and the extraordinary skills he brought to bear in addressing both the details of the cases and the legal issues demonstrate his striking talents as an avocat and his impressive level of energy. Godard's work on these cases dramatically elevated his profile among the members of the Paris Bar and throughout the French legal profession. It also brought him to the attention of policymakers and provided him with intimations of the fame that, despite his protestations to the contrary, he seemed to crave. Much of this took place when he was just twenty-four years old, indicating the promise of a truly illustrious career to come.

In the late winter of 1787, with escalating political and social violence as a backdrop, and shortly following his representation of the Swiss soldier and the Paris bakers, Godard became involved in a particularly controversial and morally challenging case when he joined several other avocats in representing a slave named Julien Baudelle. The case was of considerable public interest and generated substantial publicity.[1] Even though Godard ultimately lost this important case, he very much prevailed in the court of public opinion and reinforced his reputation as an advocate for the disadvantaged.

The various phases of the case present an overview of the state of legal proceedings and the interrelationship of the judicial and executive components of the French government in the pre-revolutionary era. Godard's principal pleading on behalf of Julien provides a detailed description both of the facts of the case and the laws relating to slavery in France and its colonies.[2] The legal conclusions in the brief in support of Julien against his "owners" in Martinique—Henry Jacques Claude Ruste de Rezeville and his wife, Reine Baudelle (who was in France at the time of the proceedings), as well as against Pierre Ferdinand Ozenne,[3] who was Reine's lover and with whom Julien and Reine lived[4]—were supported by a succinct *Consultation* submitted by Louis-Simon Martineau, Raymond DeSèze, and a certain Bienaymé.[5] Godard's brief, entitled *"Réclamation de Liberté"* (Demand for Liberty), was filed on May 11, 1787.[6]

---

1. See *Causes célèbres, curieuses et intéressantes*, vol. 167 (Paris) 1788 (by M. des Essarts). Nicolas Toussaint Le Moyne des Essarts was the principal writer for this legal publication that disseminated information to the legal community respecting cases considered significant in their time. He devoted a very substantial portion of Volume 167 to this case, extensively quoting from Godard's pleading.

2. The literature regarding this matter generally refers to Julien by his first name. Therefore, although this may be considered patronizing, it is the manner in which he will be referred to in this section of the text.

3. Pierre Ferdinand Ozenne (1751–1823) was a shipping merchant involved in the slave trade, with connections to Benjamin Franklin and Silas Deane, the American representatives to France. He became the comptroller for the Duc d'Orléans and appears to have achieved considerable personal financial success. His home, where Julien resided, was located on rue du Mail, very near place des Victoires, and just a few steps from Godard's then residence on rue des Fossées-Montmartre.

4. Pierre Charet, "L'affaire Julien Baudelle, une affaire d'état Pierre Ferdinand Ozenne et le marquis de La Fayette," *Généalogie et Histoire de la Caraïbe*. http://www.ghcaraibe.org/articles/2017-art25.pdf

5. The reference to Bienaymé is probably a reference to the cleric Pierre-François Bienaymé or Bienaimé (1737–1806) who served as the Bishop of Metz. From a family of notaries, he studied both law and theology. Although it was rather unusual, he kept a foot in both camps—practicing as an avocat and serving as a priest in the Catholic hierarchy.

6. *Gazette des tribunaux*, 1787, vol. 23, no. 4, pp. 234, et seq. See also *Mémoires Secrets pour servir à l'histoire de la République des Lettres en France depuis MD-CCLXII jusqu'à nos jours ou Journal d'un Observateur*, vol. 35 (Londres: Chez

When ultimately published,[7] it was the avocat-général, Hérault de Séchelles, whose name appeared first and most prominently on the pleading.[8] It is, in fact, highly likely that the two men cooperated in the preparation of the brief, and that the far more prominent Hérault de Séchelles, with the prestige of his title as avocat-général giving him substantial credibility, was, therefore, ascribed a higher level of recognition in the published document. The two young avocats knew one another quite well. They not only collaborated professionally in several important matters, including the case of Julien Baudelle, but also had some social interactions. When, in the fall of 1785, Hérault de Séchelles traveled to Montbard in Burgundy to meet the renowned naturalist Buffon, he first stopped in Semur to meet Godard, where Godard, who was on one of his periodic visits to his hometown, provided him "an abundance of information" about Buffon in anticipation of the meeting.[9] In confirmation of this meeting, Godard alluded to the encounter in a letter of December 13, 1785, to his cousin Cortot, when he wrote that he might "have come this year to Dijon with M. Hérault," had there not been a smallpox epidemic in Dijon at the time.[10]

In spite of the greater prominence given to Hérault de Séchelles on the cover of the brief filed on behalf of Julien Baudelle, various commentators, including Nicolas des Essarts, gave Godard full credit for the authorship of the brief and suggest that Hérault de Séchelles, in his role

---

John Adamson, 1789), 89.

7. *Mémoire pour Julien Baudelle, Américain, Intimé; Contre le sieur Ruste de Rezeville, Négociant à la Martinique, & Demoiselle Reine Baudelle, son épouse, Appellans; En présence de M. le Procureur Général, Plaignant & Accusateur; contre la Dame Ruste & le sieur Ozenne* (Paris: Chez N. H. Nyon, Imprimeur du Parlement, rue Mignon Saint André-des-Arcs, 1787).

8. Ibid.

9. See Émile Dard, "Hérault de Séchelles avant la Révolution," in *La Revue de Paris*, vol. 4 (Paris: Bureaux de la Revue de Paris, 1906): 396; and, generally, Marie-Jean Hérault de Séchelles, *Voyage à Montbard*, edited by F.-A. Aulard, (Paris: Librairie de Bibliophiles, 1890); corroborated also by an unpublished letter from Hérault de Séchelles to Jacques Godard of September 20, 1785, in which Hérault de Séchelles indicates that he will be in Semur in a few days and, referring to Buffon, that "we will go together to the greatest writer of the century and the only genius remaining." (Letter sold at April 20, 2009, auction at Rossini, Maison de Vente, Item 242.)

10. Letter from Godard to Cortot, December 13, 1785.

as a public advocate, had lent his name to the pleading to give support to Godard.[11] There is ample reason to believe that Godard was likely the principal author of this important document upon which the two avocats collaborated closely in the defense of their joint client. This is reinforced by an undated letter from Hérault de Séchelles to Godard, which had to have been written around the time that Godard had completed the last brief on behalf of Julien. In that letter, Hérault, after noting that he was personally being reproached for each day that Julien was spending in prison, informed Godard that he was "delighted by the new brief that you have prepared for our client." He went on to praise the brief for being a "complete demonstration" (presumably of the rights of Julien) and that, as a consequence, "two and two do not equal four if this man [Julien] is not freed by the law."[12]

Even though the pleading on behalf of Julien is, as Hérault de Séchelles indicated, a remarkable piece of legal advocacy, opinions regarding its quality were not unanimous. The anonymous author of *Mémoires Secrets pour servir à l'histoire de la République des Lettres en France depuis MDCCLXII jusqu'à nos jours ou Journal d'un Observateur*, which reported on Godard's brief, was rather harsh, suggesting that "it was not more eloquent, not clearer, nor more methodical" than prior pleadings in the case, that it was merely repetitive. However, on June 18, when, prior to the Parlement's rendering of its final ruling, Godard submitted a shorter supplemental brief which he entitled "Decisive Reflections" ("*Réflexions décisives*"), the same anonymous author was more laudatory, indicating that "this second brief is much better written than the first, in that it is irresistible, at least with respect to its reasoning."[13]

Godard began his plea for Julien's liberty with an impassioned appeal against slavery generally, containing echoes of the philosophy of Jean-Jacques Rousseau:

> If the unhappy slaves of America, once they have touched the shores of France, obtain so readily from our courts the restitution of a liberty that they ought never to have lost; if, despite the burden of servitude that we wish to impose on them, and the different signs that we are

---

11. *Gazette des Tribunaux*, 1787, vol. 23, no. 4; *Mémoires Secrets*, op. cit.
12. Unpublished undated letter from M. Hérault de Séchelles to Jacques Godard. Bibliothèque Historique de la Ville de Paris, MS 814, Document 335.
13. *Gazette des tribunaux*, 1787, vol. 23, no. 4, p. 234.

accustomed to consider as those of slavery, they nonetheless permit to triumph this innate natural sentiment that demands that man should be free, Julien has only to expose his demand in order to cause all judges to become interested on his behalf and to arm them against his enemies.[14]

Before plunging into the details, Godard went on to summarize his view of the case based upon his perception of the fundamental equality of all men, writing "Julien has against him no title, nor any sign of enslavement, having left free from America, having arrived free in France." He continued by criticizing French authorities as being tools of Julien's "former" masters and as seeking to deprive Julien of his existing right to liberty. "[T]hey want," he asserted, "to send him back, as a slave, to the colonies in the midst of a herd of men, whom we have turned into animals; he does not ask for the restitution of his liberty, he asks for the preservation of his liberty."[15]

The facts of the case, as presented by Godard in his brief, are so fascinating that they merit a substantial retelling. According to Godard, Julien, the principal protagonist, had been born in the French colony of Martinique in 1765. He was the biological son of a prominent plantation owner, Julien-Rose Baudelle, and a Black woman named Julie Boudou (a slave who belonged to Baudelle). Julien was a servant of Reine Baudelle Ruste de Rezeville, his aunt, the sister of Julien's biological father. In 1777, when he was just twelve years old, Julien traveled with Mme. Ruste to France, entering the country with her at the port of Marseille. Sometime thereafter, the two went back to Martinique, returning to Paris again in 1783. (The visit to France followed by a return to Martinique and a subsequent return to France would be among the most significant facts in the legal proceedings which ensued.) According to Godard, Julien had faithfully remained with his mistress (his aunt) and continued to serve her with devotion and affection.

During the second stay in France, Julien became aware that Mme. Ruste, following the death of her brother (Julien's father) in Martinique, intended to send him back alone to the island, which would ensure his continued enslavement. Although, in spite of this information, he continued to serve her, according to Godard he had a profound desire

14. Ibid., 234–35.
15. *Causes Célèbres curieuses et intéressantes,* vol. 167 (Paris: 1788), 10.

to remain free. As a consequence, he sought an official confirmation of the freedom that he believed was his. On March 5, 1786, Julien (with the assistance of an unidentified avocat) secured a ruling from the French Admiralty[16]—a governmental agency with limited jurisdiction over commercial maritime matters, but which had jurisdiction over persons of color—declaring that he was and would remain free. The order also prohibited anyone, including Mme. Ruste, from infringing on his freedom in any manner. The basis for this determination was the critical fact, according to Godard, that Julien had become a free man when he had initially been brought to France in 1777.

Julien then arranged to have Mme. Ruste officially notified of the ruling confirming his freedom, believing, in Godard's analysis, that by doing this he would prove his great loyalty to her— demonstrating that he was choosing to stay with her voluntarily and not in his prior capacity as a slave. Mme. Ruste, however, had a dramatically different interpretation of Julien's actions and a very different intention. Despite the familial ties and Julien's obvious loyalty, Mme. Ruste clearly did not consider Julien to be an equal human being and was determined to keep him as her property.[17] Surreptitiously and unilaterally, on March 12, 1787, Mme. Ruste obtained her own judicial ruling: an injunction against the prior ruling issued to Julien, which authorized her to deliver him to her husband Henry Ruste de Rezeville in Martinique.[18] The judgment further authorized her to have Julien placed in Paris's notorious La Force Prison on rue du Roi de Sicile in the Marais neighborhood pending his return to Martinique.[19]

By means of rumors circulating through Mme Ruste's household, Julien became aware of Mme. Ruste's plans and of the new ruling. Without revealing that knowledge, he feigned illness, perhaps hoping that people would take pity on him. He then left his mistress to spend the night with his friend Vincent (who had himself been a servant of Julien's father years

---

16. *Mémoire pour Julien Baudelle*, 3. The Admiralty of France, although originally an important component of the Royal government and the military establishment, had since the reign of Louis XIV become primarily an agency concerned with private and commercial navigation. (*Amirauté de France et Conseil des Prises, Papiers Penthièvre*, Archives Nationales de France, Inventaire de la Sous-Série G, 1894, 1967).

17. Ibid., 3; cf. *Causes Célèbres Curieuses et Intéressantes*, vol. 167, 12–13.

18. *Mémoire pour Julien Baudelle*, 3.

19. *Causes Célèbres Curieuses et Intéressantes*, vol. 167, 13–14.

before). Without telling her where he had gone, Julien then wrote a letter to Mme. Ruste, which Godard characterized as "gentle" in tone, telling her that he was prepared to continue in her service, but that he simply did not want to be a slave. Through her attorney, a certain Delaval, Mme. Ruste responded harshly, ordering Julien to reconsider his actions and to return to her. She charitably suggested that, if he did so, despite his escape, he might "yet merit some kindness" from her.[20] Within a day, Julien had reiterated to Mme. Ruste his desire to return to her, but only if his freedom was assured.

Efforts were made to bring about a reconciliation among Mme. Ruste, her lover Ozenne, and Julien through a mediation conducted by Delaval. These efforts failed. However, Delaval was persuaded of the sound legal basis of Julien's right to remain free. Not subject to our current deontological concerns, he tried to have the March 12 judgment suspended, with Julien's freedom assured until a hearing on his motion. On March 19 the opposition to the judgment was filed with the court, which ordered that all actions should be deferred until the 23rd, expressly instructing the parties that "the current state [of the parties] was to remain unaltered" until that date. Suddenly, despite the court's order that he should remain at liberty until a decision had been reached by the court, Julien disappeared. It turns out that on March 20, while crossing the Seine on the Pont Neuf, he was arrested by a police inspector and sent back to La Force Prison.[21] Godard was particularly and appropriately disturbed by the intrusion of the royal administration in a pending judicial matter.

Julien was soon removed from the prison without leaving a trace. The authorities would not disclose his whereabouts and Delaval simply could not find him. However, Delaval engaged in some detective work and, by means of a search of the records of the carriage transportation companies in Paris, determined that Julien was somewhere on the road to Rouen in Normandy on his way to the port of Le Havre. Julien had apparently been taken from the prison in shackles and was being transported out of reach of the Paris courts. Continuing her efforts to regain her "property," Mme. Ruste unilaterally obtained an administrative order on March 21 confirming that the order of March 12 should be executed.[22] The new order was

---

20. *Mémoire pour Julien Baudelle*, 6.
21. Ibid., 9.
22. Ibid., 10.

obtained on the basis of an ex parte request to the Minister of the Navy, the Maréchal de Castries, who had issued his decision in the name of the king.[23] In his pleading, Godard, ever the believer in the fundamental justice that the law should produce, indicated that this approach "had an insulting quality to it, not only for Julien, but for justice itself."[24] Mme. Ruste had by herself determined she could deprive Julien of his liberty without even waiting for the court to reach a decision, and had been supported by the royal government, in defiance of the judicial process.[25] A Me. Rimbert now joined Julien's defense team and advocated for Julien with zeal. At the hearing held on March 23 everything that had transpired since March 19 was disclosed. A new hearing was then set for March 28, with further instructions given to the public prosecutor respecting potential violations of law.

Mme. Ruste, not to be deterred from her objective, filed another action on March 27 in which she simply asserted that Julien was her slave and that, since she did not have all the necessary elements of proof readily available, she should be given six months to prove that fact. The public advocate then spoke up, indicating that this case was no longer about whether Julien was a slave or free, but rather now revolved around the issue of whether in France a man could simply be abducted against the rules of law and of a court.[26] The court ordered that Mme. Ruste desist from her course of action. However, Delaval became concerned that it might be too late. On March 25 Delaval was informed that Julien, as a "possession" of Mme. Ruste, had been sent to a prison in the port city of Le Havre to be shipped to Martinique by order of the king. (In fact, only bad weather had prevented Julien from being sent to Martinique on March 30.) Delaval sent a memo to the prosecutor describing all that had transpired. He then

23. This order appears to have been tantamount to a "*lettre de cachet*," which could be issued without any opportunity for the party subject to the order to contest it. Obviously, as an avocat devoted to legal process, Godard could not but be incensed at such an order.

24. See *Causes célèbres, curieuses et intéressantes*, vol. 167 (Paris, 1788), 26.

25. Apparently, the Marquis de Lafayette, a staunch opponent of slavery, intervened with the Maréchal de Castries and sought to have him reverse the order he had issued in favor of Reine Ruste de Rezeville and worked with Julien's legal team to have Julien declared a free man. Charet, "L'affaire Julien Baudelle," 2.

26. Although not specifically named, the public advocate was Hérault de Séchelles. *Causes célèbres, curieuses et intéressantes*, vol. 167, p. 29.

received notice that Julien had expressed the fervent desire that Mme. Ruste not be prosecuted criminally for what she had done to him. Deeply moved by Julien's request, Delaval immediately sent money to Le Havre for Julien's needs. However, he quickly found out that Julien was already being brought back to Paris by the police inspector.

Julien was then once again incarcerated in La Force Prison, where no one, not even his avocat, could see him. Delaval, in an effort to communicate with his client, obtained an order authorizing him to meet Julien, but the warden of the prison simply refused to provide access. However, just as had occurred with Delaval, who had been retained to pursue Julien but ended up defending him, Julien won his jailers over to his cause. On April 11 Delaval, now joined by Godard, who had been brought on as a member of the defense team, went to the prison to see Julien, where the jailers acclaimed Godard and Delaval as though they had obtained Julien's liberty. But, in fact, they had not.

In writing about this episode in the appellate pleadings on behalf of Julien filed with the Paris Parlement, Godard optimistically articulated his faith in the French judicial system and in the king, as joint purveyors of justice. His analysis included an aspirational call for an abolition of slavery in its entirety. He wrote:

> Where are the laws, by virtue of which we would have the right to deprive Julien of his freedom? Is it not in the code of France that one should seek them? Despotism is despised in this empire; slavery is banned. There is one master [the king] and his subjects; but the master commands more by his goodness than by means of force; and the subjects obey him less by means of constraints than by love. Some vestiges of ancient servitude still dishonored the French Government, Louis XVI highlighted the beginning of his reign by abolishing them. Let us judge, by this act of generosity and grandeur, how much the very idea of slavery is repugnant to the paternal heart of our kings."[27]

Godard went on to note that slavery was still permissible on certain islands belonging to France and exhorted the king to add to his "title of glory" by promulgating the abolition of slavery altogether. However, reaffirming his belief in the rule of existing law, Godard went on to note

---

27. *Mémoire pour Julien Baudelle*, 16.

that so long as those laws existed, they had to be respected. Therefore, despite the revulsion he clearly felt toward the laws which permitted slavery, he expressed the view that it was important to review them to see whether they were favorable or unfavorable to Julien.

Godard proceeded to analyze four laws potentially applicable to Julien's situation. He began with the *"code-noir"* ("black code") of 1685, related to the control that masters could exercise over people of color, and quickly concluded that this code had nothing to do with the pending matter. He continued by describing the Edict of 1716, which, he argued, was intended to qualify the notion that slaves would automatically become free upon arriving in France, where slavery was not allowed. It prescribed the rules applicable to bringing slaves to France and the requirements that had to be complied with if slaves were not immediately to become free upon arriving on French soil. He then noted that slavemasters had manipulated the intricacies of the provisions of the Edict in order to avoid its impact, with the consequence that many slaves were then brought into France. However, when these individuals returned to the islands after growing accustomed to living far less restricted lives, antagonism with their masters and consequent difficulties ensued. In order to reduce this problem (but more likely in order to limit the number of Blacks in France), Louis XV adopted the Declaration of 1738. This Declaration provided that all slaves who came to France would automatically become legally free, but would in actuality become servants of the king, to be sent to the colonies to perform whatever work he chose. This, apparently, did not accomplish the unstated objective of restricting the presence of Blacks in France. As a result, in 1777 Louis XVI promulgated yet another new law simply forbidding the entry into France of any slave, regardless of his color.

In spite of this latter law, whites were allowed to bring one slave on visits to France, but he or she had to be immediately sent back when the owner returned home. Before leaving his colony of residence for a visit to France, the owner also had to deposit 4,000 *livres* as a bond.[28] If a master failed to post the bond, the slave immediately became free upon setting foot in France.

According to Godard, his review of the various relevant laws raised three fundamental questions about Julien: First, was Julien Mme. Ruste's

---

28. This was a very considerable sum since it is estimated that the *livre* in the 1780s was the equivalent of approximately 10€ or roughly US $11.00 in 2020.

slave? Second, if he was or had been, was he still her slave now that he was in France? Finally, could he be subject to confiscation while in France?[29]

To the question of whether Julien was Mme. Ruste's slave, Godard responded initially by stating that it was up to Mme. Ruste to prove his status as a slave.[30] Even though Mme. Ruste claimed that he was her slave, Godard insisted that the proper presumption, since Julien was a human being, was in favor of arguing that he was not a slave. In response to Mme. Ruste's request for a six-month period in which to prove that Julien was a slave, Godard wanted to know what would happen to Julien in the meantime. Slavery being such an odious condition, Godard suggested that if a claimant could not immediately prove the status of enslavement, then the individual in question simply had to be freed. He posited that perhaps Mme. Ruste could prove that Julien's mother was her slave, but then hastened to note that his mother's condition would have nothing to do with Julien's status.[31] Furthermore, Godard insisted that, even if Julien himself admitted that he was a slave, his mere concession of that point would by itself be insufficient to establish his actual status as a slave.

Next, Godard addressed the issue of whether, even if Julien had at one time been a slave, he was still Mme. Ruste's slave. He reminded the court that, in order for Julien to continue to be Mme. Ruste's slave in France, she would have had to have fully satisfied all of the formalities required by the applicable law—a failure to comply with any of the requirements and Julien would no longer be a slave. Godard then observed that Mme. Ruste had, in fact, failed to honor all these conditions. He pointed out that Mme. Ruste had even listed Julien on the manifest of the ship that brought him to France not as a slave, but as a free man. Consequently, he inquired, how could she even assert a claim that he was her slave? As a result, Godard concluded that, as of 1777, when Julien first came to France, Mme. Ruste had lost her ownership rights in him.[32]

All that was left to determine, according to Godard, was whether the king had a right to confiscate Julien for the king's service. Godard, delving into a topic with which he was particularly familiar through his service

29. *Mémoire pour Julien Baudelle*, 21.
30. Ibid., 22.
31. In fact, Julien's mother was no longer a slave, having managed to purchase her own freedom for 3,000 *livres* some years earlier. Charet, "L'affaire Julien Baudelle," 1.
32. *Mémoire pour Julien Baudelle*, 24.

as a member of the Bar of the Paris Parlement, then indicated that the law regarding confiscation of a former slave by the king had never been registered by that body. In light of this, therefore, the law was simply null and void. But Godard further insisted that, even if the law had been properly registered, only the king could have demanded confiscation—not Mme. Ruste. He continued by noting that the king could not have taken possession of Julien since the law applied only to Blacks who were slaves when on French soil, and it was obvious that Julien had never had the status of a slave while he was in France. Furthermore, in an analysis that speaks to the blatant racism of the era, Godard asserted that Julien was not actually a Black man; he was of mixed race since his father was a white Frenchman. In an effort to reinforce his argument, Godard even went so far as to analyze Julien's physical features and noted that they were not consistent with those of a Black man. In keeping with the racial perspectives of his time, Godard suggested that, because of his "white" looks, if Julien had children (presumably with a white woman) they would probably be deemed to be white and that, therefore, Julien could himself be considered to be white, and, assuredly, not Black.

Godard then went on to make an impassioned plea against Black slavery and in favor of remunerated labor, laced, however, with the racial stereotype of Black indolence: "Leave these unhappy Africans in the country that gave them life; employ in your colonies only free white people and you will see, whether with a smaller number of men, you do not obtain all of the produce which you currently obtain from America and to which you attach such a high value."[33] Godard continued: "Furthermore, do you persist in wanting to see the law implemented merely because it exists? Well, then! Yes, the law sends back to the colonies all of those who come from there, and with respect to whom immigration would be harmful to our culture. But this is only applicable to slaves and Julien is not a slave."[34]

As he proceeded with his argument, it became abundantly clear that Godard hoped that this case could turn out to be a test case respecting slavery itself. He noted that Julien did not have to fear a law which did not apply to him; that Julien was a subject of the king of France, and that, therefore, he was not a slave. He had, as Godard insisted, left Martinique free, had arrived in France free, and had every right to preserve his

---

33. Ibid., 61–62.
34. Ibid., 63.

freedom. No individual from America, he insisted, had ever presented a better case for highlighting the rights of former slaves in France.

Godard next appealed to the Parlement's emotions and to its prerogatives, highlighting how terribly Mme. Ruste had treated Julien after she had filed an appeal before the Parlement, and then asking: "Is this, then, how one behaves, with respect to men and the law and the judges? Invoking the Parlement's authority when it would have been possible to be heard before an ordinary court is, in the first instance, a grave crime against society; but to invoke the authority of both at once is even graver."[35]

Relying upon the rhetorical flourishes of his era, Godard then eloquently criticized those officers of the royal administration who wielded arbitrary power and who, in Julien's case, had been willing to allow Mme. Ruste to circumvent judicial proceedings: "Oh you, to whom the monarch has bestowed a portion of his power, distance yourselves from those who come before you with the title of accusers and realize that they are merely trying to seduce your goodness. Think that every person who solicits your authority, when he could invoke justice [through resort to the courts], already has proven that he is fearful of it and he condemns himself by his very demand; think that an accuser who addresses you outside of the presence of the accused is always suspect."[36] Here, Godard was reasserting his faith in proper process and in judicial justice. He was also lashing out against arbitrary royal prerogatives, one of the most obnoxious practices of the Ancien Régime.

Godard concluded by pleading with the members of the Parlement: "It is up to the magistrates, the protectors of the rights of citizens, to give to society the vengeance which it is owed for so many oppressive acts combined."[37] With assurance he asserted that Julien was not afraid of being sent back to America. He was, after all, according to Godard, free. Adding a supernatural gloss on his argument, he asserted that even the weather had favored Julien since he had been supposed to leave for Martinique on March 30, but inclement weather had prevented his departure and permitted him to have his day in a French court.

Going further, Godard then indicated that Julien should be entitled to damages for all that he had suffered, noting, with dramatic irony, that the

---

35. Ibid., 68–69.
36. Ibid., 69.
37. Ibid., 70–71.

damages should come from his aunt (since Mme. Ruste was, of course, the sister of Julien's biological father). The authors of the very brief *Consultation* which supplemented Godard's pleading emphasized Godard's argument against arbitrary royal power by urging that "a severe punishment" be inflicted upon Mme. Ruste for having "interrupted the course of Justice and having prevented the execution of the Judgments of the Court." They further supported the assessment of damages for the benefit of Julien "for all of the harm that she had inflicted upon him."[38]

In the presentation to the Parlement on Julien's behalf, the public advocate, Hérault de Séchelles, articulated the arguments presented by Godard, whose brief he had so ardently praised.[39] Unfortunately, none of this was sufficient to overcome the Parlement's perception of the provisions of Louis XV's Declaration of August 9, 1777, which the Parlement deemed to be protective of Mme. Ruste and her husband's property claim to Julien. Thus, on June 27, 1787, the Parlement discharged the accusation that Julien had lodged against Mme. Ruste. The order of March 5 was overturned and, as a consequence, it was declared that Julien belonged to Sieur and Mme. Ruste to do with as they saw fit. They were then authorized to send him back to Martinique, but enjoined to take care of his welfare and to treat him "humanely."[40]

Strangely, it appears as though Julien did not go back to Martinique. Rather, he continued to live with Reine Ruste and her lover, Ozenne, in Paris. Several years later, Ozenne even provided Julien with a *"rente,"* a cash flow that was sufficient to allow him to live comfortably. The payment may have been in exchange for Julien serving as a stalking horse or straw person in some potentially shady real estate transactions pursued

---

38. Ibid., 36.
39. In his summary of Godard's brief and the case in general, des Essarts notes that it is Godard who developed the principal arguments in Julien's appeal and that "they were subsequently discussed by the advocate general, Hérault de Séchelles." Thus, des Essarts effectively ascribes credit for the skillful argumentation in the appeal to Godard rather than to Hérault de Séchelles, who was, as des Essarts also notes, "an eloquent magistrate." (Ibid., 72.) It is appropriate to cite the observation made to me by Prof. Miranda Spieler, who noted that Hérault de Séchelles' support for Godard's position in the Julien Baudelle matter is an important triumph of principle over personal interest since Hérault de Séchelles was from a family that had been active in the slave trade for generations and that a substantial portion of the advocate general's wealth was the product of that trade.
40. *Mémoire pour Julien Baudelle,* 74.

by Ozenne. In 1815 Julien married, and continued to live in relative comfort until his death in Paris in 1837.[41]

For Godard, the adverse decision of the Paris Parlement in Julien's case was assuredly a painful loss. The tone of his pleadings suggests a deep belief in the arguments he made on Julien's behalf. However, despite his defeat, the young avocat had unambiguously demonstrated a willingness to lend his talents in the defense of the least fortunate of his society—in this case, the enslaved. He had lost a case, but enhanced his reputation markedly and potentially energized an important cause. As the journalist Billecocq would write some years later, Godard "lost this case...but he won it in the opinion of all of the friends of liberty and justice."[42] In a very real sense, Godard's pleadings in this case constituted an important volley in the battle for the emancipation of persons of color in continental France—an effort that would culminate in a complete, albeit temporary, victory in the wake of the French Revolution and a full and permanent triumph throughout territories controlled by France in the mid-nineteenth century. Indeed, just six months after Godard lost his battle on behalf of Julien Baudelle, a number of enlightened political leaders led by the future Revolutionary Jacques-Pierre Brissot de Warville created the Society of Friends of Blacks (Société des Amis des Noirs), a group devoted to the gradual abolition of Black slavery in the French colonies.[43] Among the founders of this group were some of the most prominent future leaders of the Revolution: Condorcet (who authored the Society's bylaws), Honoré de Mirabeau, the Marquis de Lafayette, Jérôme Pétion, Adrien Duport, Emmanuel-Joseph Sieyès, Alexandre Lameth, the Marquis de

---

41. Charet, "L'affaire Julien Baudelle," 4.

42. *Mercure Universel*, vol. 9, no. 230, p. 88.

43. Jacques-Pierre Brissot de Warville (or Ouarville) (1754–1793) sought in his youth to become a writer, but failed to achieve his ambition. As a result of an early attempt at writing a political tract against the queen, he spent a short time in the Bastillle. In 1789, he created the *"Patriote Français,"* a newspaper which achieved a certain amount of renown. He was elected to the Paris Assembly in 1789 and played a significant role, including on behalf of Jews, while he served as a member of that Assembly. Although he was a strong opponent of the monarchy and advocated for a war against Austria, he was generally moderate in his politics. In 1792 he joined the Girondins and, as a result, he ultimately became a political enemy of Robespierre, leading to his arrest for his political views and his execution in the fall of 1793 with his fellow Girondins.

Pastoret, and Henri Grégoire.[44] The Society would actively campaign for an end to slavery and would, within but a few years, on February 14, 1794, attain its objective, a remarkable achievement for the time (even though the achievement would be of short duration).[45] Although there is no direct evidence that Godard became a member of the group, it is difficult to imagine that his energetic defense of Julien Baudelle did not play an important role in stimulating the creation of the Society and the pursuit of its noble goal.

Of course, the United States, the nation whose founding principles served as the motivation for so many of the French experiments with freedom, would lag nearly three-quarters of a century behind in the struggle for the emancipation of slaves. It is, furthermore, interesting to speculate as to whether the American Ambassador to France and future president of the United States, Thomas Jefferson, took any interest in the case of Julien Baudelle. There is no mention of the case in Jefferson's extensive extant correspondence from Paris.[46] However, it would not have

---

44. Many of these individuals became important members of the *Société des Trente* (The Society of Thirty), which was a core group within the Estates-General that prompted many of the early developments within that body and its successor, the National Assembly.

45. On February 4, 1794, the National Convention decreed that "the enslavement of Negroes in all of the colonies is abolished; as a consequence, all men, without distinction for their color, residing in the colonies, are French citizens and will benefit from all of the rights granted by the Constitution." (*Moniteur*, 17 Pluviose An 2 [February 5, 1794], no. 137, p. 554.) However, this was hardly the end of the matter. In 1802, Napoleon reinstated slavery in the colonies and it would not be until 1848 that slavery was definitively abolished in all French territories by the government of the Second Republic.

46. Interestingly, just eight days after the decision on the Julien Baudelle matter was rendered by the Parlement, Jefferson sent a letter to Hérault de Séchelles. In his letter, he did not refer to the just-decided matter. Rather, he appeared to be responding to an inquiry from Hérault regarding Anglo-Saxon legal concepts. In his letter, Jefferson recommends that Hérault acquire forty-two law books (that he enumerates both by name and by price), indicating, at the top of his list, that "[a] person who would wish to have a good general idea of the laws of England, should read the following books..." Is this exchange between the two lawyers at that point in time a mere coincidence or is it the result of a dialogue between the two possibly related to the just-decided Julien Baudelle matter in light of Jefferson's potential interest in the case? There is nothing to indicate that the exchange is anything more than a coincidence, but if so, it is a most interesting coincidence. *The Papers of Thomas Jefferson*, vol. 11, 1 January–6 August 1787,

been surprising if he had paid some attention to the legal proceedings. The issues raised by the case would have undoubtedly been intellectually intriguing to him; they would also have been of great personal interest. After all, Jefferson had brought at least one of his slaves, the young Sally Hemings (the half-sister of his late wife, Martha), over to France, ostensibly as a companion to his own young daughter. Had the outcome of Julien's case been different and had Julien been granted his freedom, Sally Hemings could have relied on that outcome to assert her right to her freedom, since her situation was similar to that of Julien. But then again, Jefferson, in spite of his lofty beliefs in human rights, would likely not have been beyond actively seeking to protect his perceived property rights.[47] Faced with claims of freedom from his slave, he might very well have interposed a defense of diplomatic immunity to divert the impact of a decision adverse to those rights.

---

ed. Julian P. Boyd (Princeton, NJ: Princeton University Press, 1955), 547–49.
47. In her biography of Jefferson, Fawn Brodie highlights the ambivalence of Jefferson's views with respect to his ownership of slaves. She notes that it can be seen that "for a man theoretically intent upon emancipation of all slaves, Jefferson was extremely possessive about his own." Fawn M. Brodie, *Thomas Jefferson: An Intimate History* (New York: W. W. Norton & Co., 1974), 234–35.

CHAPTER 6

THE HERMIT OF BURGUNDY

The professional skills that Godard had been honing quickly provided him with further significant opportunities to demonstrate his legal talents in a very public manner. However, none of the cases that he took on did more to enhance his reputation than one in early 1787, which continued even as he was working on the Julien Baudelle matter. In the winter of 1787 Godard joined the effort to overturn the verdict rendered in the case that became known as the "Affair of the Burgundian Hermit" ("*l'Affaire de l'Hermite de Bourgogne*").[1] This case had already attracted attention as it had made its way through the complex French judicial system over the course of more than half a dozen years. Furthermore, and very importantly for Godard, it was a case with roots in his native region of Burgundy. In spite of his voluntary move to Paris, Godard remained attached to that province, perhaps with an eye to a political career, and this case, although not without some political risk to Godard, was particularly helpful in strengthening those ties.

The case originally arose in 1780 when Nicolas Maret (known to his neighbors as Frère Jean), who lived in the hermitage of St. Michel, fewer than thirty miles to the north and east of Jacques Godard's hometown of Semur-en-Auxois, was attacked by a group of brigands. Although his

---

1. *Gazette des Tribunaux*, 1787, vol. 23, no. 11, pp. 196–201; 1787, vol. 24, no. 31, pp. 71, et seq.

assailants attacked him from behind, and it is not likely that he actually
saw them, Frère Jean readily (but mistakenly) identified seven individuals.
At the conclusion of a brief trial, the accused were convicted by the local
court in the regional center of Chatillon-sur-Seine. In spite of the scant
evidence, in March 1782 two of the accused were sentenced to death and
promptly executed. Three other accused were given lesser, but nonetheless
extremely harsh, sentences. One was sent to the galleys, where he died. In
1783, however, the real culprits were identified, when, already imprisoned
for other crimes, they confessed. Following the confessions, the families
of the men who had originally been condemned petitioned Louis XVI for
a reversal of their convictions.

In 1786, the matter was sent to the Parlement of Dijon for reconsideration. Sometime thereafter, a group of Parisian avocats including Godard,
who assumed chief responsibility, undertook the representation of the
condemned men, both living and dead.[2] The confessions of the actual
aggressors suggest that this should not have been a difficult task. However, any effort to reverse a prior decision, especially one which resulted
in some of the defendants having been executed, and therefore requiring
admission of a terrible miscarriage of justice, presented monumental
challenges. Godard was charged with drafting the pleadings seeking to
reverse the judgment of guilt. He proved himself up to the task. Godard
produced significant pleadings, including a brief that was filed on April 22,
1787, which attracted the attention of the press.[3] The *Gazette des Tribunaux*
was laudatory of Godard's work, noting that the brief he submitted to
the Parlement "announces a great deal of talent and will assuredly attract
public attention."[4] Taking note of the simplicity and compelling nature of
Godard's pleading, the reviewer considered that Godard had "rendered
his recitation of the facts particularly interesting; his narration is simple
and it is by this simplicity that it becomes more touching."[5] The *Gazette
des Tribunaux* praised his mastery of the substance of the case:

---

2. *Journal politique, ou Gazette des Gazettes*, 1787, vol. 24, p. 49.

3. *Mémoires Secrets pour servir à l'histoire de la République des Lettres en France
depuis MDCCLXII*, vol. 35 (London: Chez John Adamson, 1789), 87. The
description of Godard's brief noted that a Consultation "signed by Me. Target
and supported by twelve of the most noted avocats" had been submitted in
support of the brief.

4. "*annonce beaucoup de talens, & fixera surement l'attention publique....*"

5. *Gazette des Tribunaux*, 1787, vol. 23, no. 11, p. 197.

Mr. Godard divides his methodology into two portions. In the first, he establishes that his clients are not guilty; he discusses with much orderliness the indications that may have decided their condemnation and he makes them disappear.

In the second, he amasses the proofs of the innocence of the accused and the circumstances which exclude any possibility that they committed the crime imputed to them. In so lengthy a discussion, without neglecting the specific methods of his cause, Mr. Godard brings himself to an examination of matters of public interest: he even knows how to broaden his subject matter by addressing questions which are so often debated, namely, the effects which the testimony of the complainants, of those who are accusers and of essential witnesses must, of necessity, cause, and of the danger of judging solely on the basis of presumptions."[6]

The *Gazette* went on to note Godard's fundamental concern with avoiding injustice. It stated that "Mr. Godard emphasizes with force the danger of presumptions, because he maintains that there was nothing against his clients other than such presumptions and he cries out, after having amassed a multitude of examples where such presumptions have sent innocents to their deaths: False and tragic science that are these tortures, must you again appear in our Books and in our Courts?"[7] The compliments were echoed by the anonymous author of the *Mémoires Secrets pour servir à l'histoire de la République des Lettres en France depuis MDCCLXII jusqu'à nos jours ou Journal d'un Observateur*, who wrote that Godard, described as "a young avocat," had submitted a brief that was "clear, methodical and nobly written."[8]

In his principal pleading, Godard highlighted the discovery of the actual culprits and the obvious occurrence of a tragic judicial error. But he also clearly sought to use the case as a means for promoting the much-needed legal reforms that were then being considered by the royal government. He noted with eloquence and flourish:

This great error, as a consequence of the new character that it will

6. Ibid., 197–98.
7. Ibid., 198.
8. *Mémoires Secrets pour servir à l'histoire de la République des Lettres en France depuis MDCCLXII*, vol. 35, p. 87.

acquire due to the additional evidence, will make the cause of the five unfortunates a national cause, in which citizens of all of the Orders will take part, because it will force them to turn their attention onto themselves and it will finally determine, let us not doubt this, this reform desired for such a long time and with such justification of our criminal laws; it will force all sensitive souls to groan over the impossibility of remedying the harm that those laws cause, and the death penalty, which alone renders this harm irreparable, instead of being handed down for all types of crimes, will be either eliminated or reserved solely for the most heinous crimes; it will provide for an examination of whether it would not be necessary to let a period of time elapse between sentencing and execution during which period truth will have the time to reach the judges, when they may have been in error; it will cause to reverberate to the ears of the legislators these touching words of one of the accused, of one of those who no longer lives: "An irreparable harm has been done to me and to mine because it was said: 'Here is a poor man who is alone with his children, who will not have any defense; we must strive to destroy him;'" but now the accused will have a defender…[9]

Godard went on to note that the royal government was already endeavoring to correct a system that had caused such a terrible miscarriage of justice. He reminded his audience that Lamoignon, the then Minister of Justice, following in the steps of his illustrious ancestor of one hundred years before who had served as a senior magistrate under Louis XIV, was even then drafting a new criminal code intended to remedy many of the existing injustices in the judicial structure.[10]

Godard was very proud of his pleading. He sent a copy to his cousin Cortot in Dijon. But in his transmittal letter he expressed some trepidation about the effect that his pleading might have on the members of the Parlement of Dijon. He emphasized that he hoped the members of the Parlement would not bear him ill-will by reason of "the truth that I was

---

9. *Gazette des Tribunaux*, 1787, vol. 23, no. 11, pp. 199–200.

10. Chrétien François de Lamoignon de Baville (1735–1789) served as Minister of Justice from April 1787 until September 1788. He was a nephew of Chrétien Guillaume de Lamoignon de Malesherbes, the royal adviser commonly referred to as "Malesherbes," who would play a pivotal role in bringing about the civil equality of Protestants and would go on to defend Louis XVI before the National Convention.

obliged to state." Godard assured his cousin (undoubtedly in the hope that the message would be transmitted to the members of the Parlement) that, in spite of the error committed by the Parlement, there had been no diminution in his respect for them.[11]

On August 15, 1787, the Parlement of Dijon—the very same body which had previously affirmed the conviction of the condemned men—made an extraordinary move and reversed itself. Godard had succeeded in achieving the complete exoneration of his clients, both living and dead. On August 28, with the real criminals having been convicted, and the innocence of Godard's clients having become unchallengeable, the judges then considered whether to make restitution to the victims' families. Godard made a powerful and impassioned appeal for such restitution—noting the terrible consequences that had ensued from the injustice that had been done. In his pleadings, he demonstrated a practical side as he sought to influence the court by asserting his local credentials and his attachment to his home province:

> Born in the province which you govern, brought up in the midst of numerous monuments to your wisdom, it is sweet for us to restate that which we have felt and to render publicly, the just homage which is due to you. Now, do not ask yourselves why a voice that you have not been accustomed to hearing arose suddenly in your midst. In becoming attached to the Bar of the capital, we did not break any of the links to our homeland. The unfortunates whom we represented had the right to our zeal. Could we possibly have failed to respond to their expectations![12]

He then concluded with an assertion of his perception of his role as the advocate of the less fortunate: "Judges, we will, therefore, celebrate having been brought before you by a solemn circumstance and to have given you proof that we have remained faithful to the oath that we have taken to defend the innocent and the truth."[13]

The Parlement determined that restitution had to be made to the wrongly condemned men and to their families. The king then provided the funds for the payment of this restitution and Godard was given the

---

11. Letter from Godard to Cortot, April 24, 1787.
12. *Journal Encyclopédique*, vol. 8, part 2, pp. 325, et seq.
13. Ibid.

task of distributing those funds "to the families of the unfortunates...
to repair the errors of the judges."[14] Furthermore, all criminal records
of each of the individuals wrongly condemned were ordered expunged
of any reference to the offenses and to their punishments and it was
further ordered that statements asserting their innocence were to be
published and disseminated throughout the region.[15]

---

14. *Mercure Universel,* vol. 9, no. 230, p. 87.
15. *Gazette des Tribunaux,* 1787, vol. 24, no. 31, p. 74.

CHAPTER 7

DEFENDING SEVEN GERMANS CONDEMNED
ON THE TESTIMONY OF TWO JEWS

Shortly after his victory in the Burgundian Hermit case, Godard had an opportunity to play a role in yet another high-profile case, one which bore an uncanny resemblance to the Burgundian Hermit matter. On July 26, 1787, Godard was called upon for assistance by the respected avocat Charles Marguerite Mercier Dupaty, who was part of Marmontel's social circle. (Dupaty was the uncle-in-law of the philosopher Condorcet, through Condorcet's marriage to Dupaty's niece, Sophie de Grouchy, and Godard undoubtedly knew Dupaty well through both his professional and social connections.) In addition to being a member of the Paris Bar, Dupaty was a renowned jurist, and assuredly among those whom Godard chose to frequent as he developed his skills and reputation and sought to advance his career. Dupaty asked Godard to participate in an effort to overturn the convictions of seven Germans who had been condemned by the Parlement of Metz in northeastern France for the aggravated theft of valuable objects in 1769.

Dupaty wrote a ninety-five-page memorandum in support of the condemned Germans. Godard delivered a seven-page *Consultation*. The short document was elegant and persuasive. It far outshone Dupaty's long and convoluted pleading.

Metz was home to the largest Jewish community in all of France at this time. Significantly, the condemnation of the seven Germans had been obtained exclusively upon statements from the two victims, Cerf Moyse and Salomon Cerf, both Jews. On September 24, 1768, the two Jews claimed that their house, within the jurisdiction of the tribunals of Metz (in the village of Mittlebron near the larger city of Phalsbourg), had been pillaged by a group of hooligans. The victims filed a complaint for theft with violence. Seven Germans from the vicinity were promptly arrested and charged with the crime.

The Germans were ultimately found guilty solely on the basis of the testimony provided by the two Jewish complainants. Four were condemned to death and promptly executed and three were sent to the galleys for life. Suddenly, in 1786, many years after the condemnations of the seven Germans, other individuals arrested for a different crime confessed to the robbery. Dupaty then sought the reversal of the condemnation of the seven Germans. Although he prepared all the basic pleadings, as was the custom, he sought the services of another avocat to provide a *Consultation*, which would supplement his written pleadings with legal arguments to buttress the factual and rhetorical arguments. Dupaty would call upon Godard to assist him in this way. In light of the great acclaim Godard was then receiving for his work on the similar Burgundian Hermit case (which he would shortly win), he would have been a natural choice.

As an addendum to Dupaty's extensive and meandering brief, Godard delivered his succinct arguments in defense of the condemned men.[1] Dupaty had devoted a substantial portion of his pleading to attacks against the presiding magistrate for having given any credence to the testimony of Jews against Catholics (which was the religion of the convicted Germans). His brief, dated July 20, 1787, was replete with accusations of bad faith leveled against the Jewish complainants. Dupaty deplored the very notion that Jews could provide testimony in a French legal proceeding. (In this context, it is important to remember that Ashkenazi Jews living in France were not citizens and had an ambiguous juridical status.) He emphasized that Jews could not even take usual oaths, and that if they took them they were null and void. He went so far as to cite as proof the words of the Kol Nidre prayer, the Aramaic-language prayer of renunciation of oaths recited three times in the synagogue on the evening of Yom Kippur (which, interestingly, Dupaty quoted in Latin). The Kol Nidre prayer is, in fact,

---

1. *Justification de sept hommes condamnés par le Parlement de Metz en 1769*, by Charles-Marguerite Mercier Dupaty, 95–103, in which the *Consultation* by Jacques Godard is cited in its entirety.

the product not of some implied right to disregard oaths made in judicial matters but, rather, the expression of an aspiration that God will permit the disavowal of undertakings made to God that are not, or cannot be, fully kept. The prayer has also sometimes been interpreted as a manifestation of the regrettable need that Jews have had across the ages to repudiate vows of abandonment of the Jewish faith made under torture and other constraints during times of persecution.

Dupaty's argument was replete with anti-Jewish prejudice. As an interesting parallel, Dupaty's great-great-grandson, Armand du Paty de Clam, who would become one of the principal antagonists in the Dreyfus Affair in 1894, placed a particular emphasis on Alfred Dreyfus's Jewishness and laced his attacks against Dreyfus with antisemitic venom. Perhaps as a means of emphasizing the strength of intractable prejudice, a yet-later descendant, Charles Mercier du Paty de Clam, would, in the nineteen forties, briefly head the Commissariat General for Jewish Affairs, the agency of the Vichy government charged with persecuting Jews.

In contrast to Dupaty's vitriolic attack against the Jewish witnesses, Godard, in his skillfully prepared *Consultation* on behalf of the condemned men, focused on the more abstract issue of justice itself.[2] He noted that the miscarriage of justice whose remediation was being sought was not the result of malice or vice by the complaining witnesses or the judge, but rather was the consequence of a simple error—an error that he was seeking to rectify. Unlike Dupaty, Godard did not place his emphasis on the disqualifying nature of the testimony of the Jewish complainants because they were Jews. Instead, he focused on important procedural matters and, in particular, on the human failings that can pervert and, in this case, had, in his view, perverted justice. It was not because the testimony that had led to the condemnation of the men was provided by Jews that a miscarriage of justice had occurred. It was, rather, because of the absence of any other tangible evidence that Godard expressed his indignation. Based upon the unverified testimony of witnesses, and that testimony alone, the accused were tortured to obtain confessions. To Godard, this was an underlying flaw in the French system of justice and a violation of fundamental principles of fairness.[3]

2. Filed in Paris on July 30, 1787. *Mémoires Secrets pour servir à l'histoire de la République des Lettres en France depuis MDCCLXII*, vol. 35, p. 364.

3. In a footnote to his *Consultation*, Godard saw fit to make reference to his mentor, Target, citing Target's well-known *Consultation* in the matter of the

Facing this second obvious and terrible miscarriage of French justice, Godard seized upon the opportunity to vociferously condemn the principle whereby every accused was presumed to be guilty. Eloquently, he declared: "Let us forever proscribe this strange system, which, converting every accused into a guilty party, would deliver them all, without exception, to the sword of the Law or, rather, of the Tribunals."[4] Then, in an effort to personalize his presentation and to emphasize the risk of miscarriages of justice that seemed to him to be inherent in the French system, as well as to point out the practical aspects of the crux of the matter, he went on to ask a direct question that highlighted the very real risk to every individual from such acts of injustice generally: "Is there anyone amongst us who can flatter himself to believe that never will chance, the meanness of man, some unpredictable circumstances, or perhaps some imprudence, assemble against him some degree of plausibility with respect to a crime that has been committed?"[5]

Godard also argued that the divergent penalties imposed on the seven defendants (as had occurred with the application of the various penalties imposed on the defendants in the case of the Hermit) undermined the very premise on which the verdict and sentence were based. "Nothing is more contrary to our holy notions of Justice than this difference of penalties between the accomplices of a similar crime," Godard asserted.[6] To him, unequal treatment equaled unfair treatment and could only destabilize elementary notions of justice.

He next proceeded to attack the use of torture, which had been applied to the condemned men (who had refused to confess even under the terrible effects of that torture). He went on to note that, in his view, the judge who had presided over the case, and also over the use of torture (a process that was fully acceptable under then-existing French law), was well-intentioned and that he had merely committed an error.[7] To

Marquise d'Anglure. (See Chapter 8 below.) He heaped praise upon Target, calling him "a great Orator" and lauded the Anglure *Consultation*, describing it as "eloquent and profound." *Justification de Sept Hommes Condamné par le Parlement de Metz, Consultation*, 99.

4. Ibid., 97.
5. Ibid.
6. Ibid., 98.
7. Torture was officially and definitively banned by Article 2 of the first section of the Penal Code adopted by the French National Assembly in 1791. Capital

drive home the importance of the error, however, Godard emphasized
that while injustice was actually rare, error was frequent and the criminal
justice system, therefore, needed to be modified in an effort to avoid
such errors. He concluded by noting somewhat immodestly that he,
personally, was in the business of carrying out justice, as he had in the
case before the Dijon Parlement, and that this was the reason he had
agreed to participate in the Metz case. "For we, who have carried out an
act of justice and of obligation, by defending the five men condemned
by the Parlement of Dijon, we believe that we are repeating such an act
today, by assisting in publicizing the defense of the seven unfortunates
condemned by the Parlement of Metz."[8]

Godard's pleading was both compelling and rational. He did not seek to
appeal to prejudice (against Jews or anyone else) or to the need to avenge
the death penalty and terrible punishments inflicted on the defendants.
Rather, he appealed to principle and to the fundamental need to reform
the justice system.

The Parlement of Paris overturned the verdict of the Parlement of Metz
and decried the irreversible punishments that had been inflicted, handing
Dupaty and Godard an important victory on behalf of their clients. Once
again, Godard had been successful in bringing about the exoneration
of previously condemned individuals. He thereby further burnished
his credentials as the defender of the less fortunate and of the victims
of injustice, and he enhanced his reputation as a persuasive and rational
advocate for justice.

In the summer of 1790, Godard would have another opportunity
to represent individuals wrongly sentenced to extreme punishments.
The matter involved two brothers by the name of Roux-Aymard, who
had been convicted and sentenced to death by hanging in 1766 (with
the spouse of one of the brothers sentenced to banishment for life) for
the crime of counterfeiting coins. They had managed to escape and
remained fugitives for twenty-four years.[9] In the proceedings following

---

punishment was abolished in 1981.

8. *Justification de sept hommes condamnés par le Parlement de Metz en 1769, Consultation*, 102–3.

9. *Jacques Godard, Mémoire justificatif pour Jean-François Roux Aymard et Joachim
Roux-Aymard, son frère, condamnés par jugement en dernier ressort du prévôt de la
maréchaussée de Burgey, du 2 septembre 1766 à être pendus, et encore pour Susanne
Michaud, femme de Jean-François Roux Aymard, condamnée par le même jugement*

their eventual capture, Godard pleaded for their exoneration on the grounds of the denial of their right to a presumption of innocence. He railed against the use of the threat of torture, which often caused defendants against whom there was no serious evidence of wrongdoing to plead guilty. He apparently made excellent use of his usual logic and rhetorical skills. The *Moniteur* described Godard's pleading in the matter as one "in which he has been able to spread out the kind of vivid and compelling interest which oppressed innocents always inspire when they are defended by brilliant pens."[10]

Although there is no specific evidence that confirms this, it is likely that Godard's role in the Metz case is another of the factors that brought him to the attention of Jewish leaders in Alsace, and facilitated his becoming acquainted with Berr Cerf Berr, the wealthy leader of the community who had, shortly before Godard became involved in the Metz case, acquired a large country estate in Lorraine, some fifteen miles from Metz.[11] Undoubtedly, the case of the seven Germans, because it involved a Jewish household and the testimony of Jewish witnesses, was closely followed by the region's Jewish community. Anyone who had participated in one of the most important and publicized legal proceedings of the region could not but have garnered attention. Godard's success in overturning the verdict against the German defendants, even though it involved discrediting the testimony of Jewish witnesses, must have impressed observers of the legal proceedings. This is especially so because the young avocat had eschewed the easy path of relying on anti-Jewish venom and instead sought to elevate equal justice for all defendants in his quest to vindicate his clients. Such an approach likely made its mark on the leaders of the local Jewish community, who might already have seen in him a potential champion for their own cause.

à un bannissement perpétuel hors du royaume.

10. *Moniteur*, July 15, 1790, no. 196, p. 122.

11. *État et société en France aux XVIIe et XVIIIe siècles: Mélanges offerts à Yves Durand*, ed. Jean-Pierre Bardet (Paris: Presses de l'Université de Paris-Sorbonne, 2000), 154n88, where it is noted that "Cerf Berr...had fully paid for the lands of Tromblaine and of Jarreville near the Meurthe...on 26 February 1786 for the amount of 410,000 [*livres*]."

CHAPTER 8

DEFENDING A PROTESTANT

In June 1787 Guy Target filed his lengthy *Consultation* in defense of the rights of the Marquise d'Anglure, a Protestant woman whose wealthy late father's family had begun legal proceedings against her in an effort to deprive her of property she received on her father's death. The grounds for their claim to the property were that, as a Protestant, the father had been unable to enter into a valid marriage, and, thus, his daughter was illegitimate and could not inherit from him. Target's efforts on behalf of the plaintiff, certainly one of his most important legal efforts, had engendered important repercussions leading, most importantly, to new legislation in favor of Protestants—the Edict of 1787. Interestingly, just a few months later and likely in coordination with Target, Godard filed his own extensive (eighty printed pages) brief in a lawsuit involving a strikingly similar set of circumstances.

In this case, it was a widower whose late wife had left him a life estate in all of her possessions who found himself obliged to defend himself against claims from her relatives. Pierre Brisset and Elisabeth Carré were civilly married in Niort in western France, on March 30, 1758. A religious wedding—a Protestant ceremony—had taken place a little over a year later. By Godard's account, the marriage was a happy one, with only their inability to have children placing a damper on the couple's happiness.[1]

---

1. Godard, *Mémoire pour Pierre Brisset... contre Pierre Simonnet et autres* (Paris:

In 1773, more than fifteen years after the couple had contracted their civil marriage, Elisabeth prepared a will. The will provided that her husband, for whom she indicated in the will her feelings of "friendship" and in recognition of "the care and attention" that he had bestowed on her, as well as "other good and just causes of which [she had] knowledge," would be the recipient of a life estate in all of her assets upon her death.[2] However, following her death in 1775, Elisabeth's brothers challenged the will, alleging that the marriage between their sister and Pierre Brisset had never been valid because it had not been celebrated in the church of her parish. Brisset found himself embroiled in a protracted legal battle with the brothers. Within a few months of Elisabeth's death, the brothers had secured a default judgement in their favor which deprived Brisset of his rights under the will. Brisset was apparently too poor to mount an effective defense and was unable to ward off the legal attack from his erstwhile brothers-in-law. Although Brisset appealed the judgment, his impoverishment did not permit him to do so with any zealousness and he eventually abandoned his efforts. However, some twelve years after the adverse judgment was handed down, Godard was induced to attempt to reinstate the appeal.

In undertaking this appeal, Godard clearly had public opinion in mind. His brief in support of Pierre Brisset focuses little on the relevant facts but extensively on certain fundamental principles of law and ethics, especially on the notion of religious tolerance. He began with a thorough discussion of the jurisdictional issue, namely the assertion that Elisabeth's brothers did not have any standing to question the validity of their sister's marriage. Godard based his argument on the fact that the marriage was a well-established matter, that the couple lived openly and notoriously for many years as a married couple, each recognizing the other as a legitimate spouse with their status acknowledged by everyone around them. To question the validity of such a status, Godard suggested, was contrary to settled law, going back to Roman law (which he amply cited). He argued that the manner in which the Brisset-Carré couple lived and the lengthy period of time during which they had done so created a powerful presumption that theirs was a valid marriage. "The affection, the decency, the honorable status in which two individuals live, is not a part

N.H. Nyon, 1788), 8.
2. Ibid., 9.

of concubinage; and if the public gives to these individuals the title of spouses, this is the title to which they are entitled," Godard asserted.[3] The alternative, he posited, was to allege that this couple had lived in a sinful and disreputable state. There was, he continued, a powerful presumption against this being the case.

Beyond the existence of a civil contract of marriage, Godard noted that, when a couple of years after Elisabeth's death Brisset remarried, he identified himself as (and the notary drawing up the second marriage contract had acknowledged that he was), "the widower of Elisabeth Carré."[4] This strengthened the fundamental notion that a valid marriage of lengthy duration had previously existed. Then, demonstrating his agility and resourcefulness, Godard delivered a coup-de-grâce by accusing the brothers of bad faith, noting that in challenging the will they had actually identified Brisset as "Elisabeth Carré's widower."[5] Thus, he concluded, even they had acknowledged the validity of the marriage that they were now challenging.

As Godard presented his arguments he focused on the discriminatory aspects of the laws against Protestants as the most important aspect of the case. In doing so, he took note of (and in many respects echoed) Target's by-then famous *Consultation* in the d'Anglure matter.[6] Of course, it was not enough to merely cite the text; he had to engage in an extensive panegyric, praising his mentor with an ardor that bordered on the sycophantic:

A profound *Consultation* appeared a few months ago [fn. *Consultation* of Mr. Target, for Madame the Marquise d'Anglure]. All of the principles on marriage and on the status of men, all of the Laws regarding Protestants, all of the Regulations, all of the Arrêts, all of the relevant facts to this class of men, separated from us by the diversity of belief are reported, examined, weighed with a rare wisdom, which has placed this Work among the ranks of the most distinguished.[7]

Deviating completely from his announced mission of demonstrating that Elisabeth Carré's brothers lacked standing to bring their claims against

3. Ibid., 22.
4. Ibid., 29.
5. Ibid., 32.
6. Guy Target, *Consultation sur l'Affaire de la dame Marquise d'Anglure.*
7. Godard, *Mémoire pour Pierre Brisset*, 38–39.

Brisset, Godard went on to launch a full-frontal attack on anti-Protestant prejudice and the need to remedy this injustice. He sought to establish that, in spite of laws asserting that no Protestants actually lived in France, it had for generations been recognized that Protestants did reside in France and, obviously, it was known that they adhered to their own religious practices, including their own marriage practices. More importantly, he suggested that the French had never sought to impose Catholic rites on Protestants, and thus, if Protestants were living in France and having children, they must of necessity have been validly married in accordance with their own rites and not Catholic rites. He concluded that, therefore, "a Protestant is legitimately married even though he is not married in the Church. His marriage is proven, either by the act of celebration by a Protestant minister, or by Possession."[8] Possession in this case was established by the actual act of living openly and notoriously over a lengthy period of time as husband and wife.

Godard continued with an exposition of the relationship between Catholics and Protestants and of the practical consequences of having the two groups living side-by-side within France. He then praised the new more tolerant attitudes that were taking hold, giving Protestants more rights. It is in this context that Godard, for the first time in any of his writings, turned his attention to the plight of French Jews.

In praising the recently announced Edict of 1787 in favor of Protestant rights, which had been drafted in large part by Target, Godard unexpectedly, and in a seemingly spontaneous desire to expand his analysis, set his sights on the status of the Jews.[9] He noted the contempt in which Jews had been held for centuries, indicating that the very name of the "nation" was deemed an "insult" and that "we are frightened by the name itself."[10] He then proceeded to echo a belief that would very shortly be widely disseminated by the noted cleric Henri Grégoire: if the horror and disdain that Jews inspired could be cast aside, they would merge into the French people through gradual assimilation and would ultimately accept the Catholic religion. Godard also espoused the notion that much of the

---

8. Ibid., 53.

9. The sudden focus on Jews could very well have been a consequence of the beginning of Target's work with Malesherbes on the issue of Jewish rights, a task which Louis XVI had just assigned to Malesherbes and with which Target likely was associated.

10. Godard, *Mémoire pour Pierre Brisset,* 72.

Jewish situation could be ascribed, not to the fault of the Jews, but rather to the actions of the society in which they lived:

> We reproach the Jews for isolating themselves, for being strangers to the sentiments of nature and society; but is it not our institutions which have forced them to be what they are?...We reproach them for consuming their lives in speculation and usury; but, since they are not allowed to enter other professions, how do we expect them not to be speculators and usurers?[11]

Godard, giving the impression that he believed that the Edict regarding Protestants—about which he had to have known quite a lot in light of his relationship with Target—was applicable to Jews, predicted that the regrettable predilections of the Jews would soon be eliminated because "[t]he Jews will no longer have a need to make of trickery an art, nor of bad faith a pursuit; they will have lost all of their vile passions, even before they have lost their name."[12] After this short but pointed detour into the subject of the Jews, Godard returned to his plea for tolerance for minorities generally, asserting that tolerance would be an asset to the nation and a protection for Catholicism itself; tolerance for Protestants in France would help to assure tolerance for French Catholics in nations where Catholics were in the minority.

The latter part of Godard's brief was distinctly different from the earlier sections where he had focused his pleading on arguments strictly on behalf of Pierre Brisset. This lengthy last portion was more in the nature of a political tract seeking to remedy long-standing wrongs. Since it is likely that Godard was retained not by the impoverished Brisset himself but by Protestants seeking to promote their cause (perhaps through the good offices of Target, who was appropriately perceived as a strong advocate for Protestant rights, or even of Malesherbes), this change of direction was undoubtedly fully responsive to the desires of his real clients. In this portion of his brief, he argued for tolerance and national unity, going on for many pages emphasizing the need to end the centuries-old prejudices against the Protestant minority.

In support of his plea for tolerance toward Protestants, Godard highlighted specific Protestants who were engaged in activities beneficial to

---

11. Ibid., 73–74.
12. Ibid., 34.

France. He focused on Jacques Necker and his spouse. Necker was the Genevan Protestant banker who had been appointed General Director of the Royal Treasury by Louis XVI at the beginning of his reign and, in that capacity, served as the administrator of France's deeply troubled finances. As part of his task, he had overseen the financing of France's efforts in the American War of Independence.[13] Necker's spouse, Suzanne, the daughter of a pastor, was well known in Paris for her engagement in charitable work. Godard's complimentary remarks about Necker and his wife, however, were apparently not merely intended to strengthen the persuasive power of the brief. There is evidence that, once it had been published, Godard personally sent a copy of his brief to the Neckers, leading to the conclusion that he had given careful thought to using his role on behalf of Brisset to enhance his social and, possibly, political standing. On November 25, 1788, Suzanne Necker sent a letter to Godard thanking him for "sending a *Mémoire*." (Although the note does not specify which *Mémoire* he had sent, in light of the date of the note, it is almost certain that the "*Mémoire*" in question was the Brisset brief.) Giving Godard the praise he must have been seeking, Mme. Necker replied: "One is willing to remain in a world where there is still misfortune to be relieved and eloquent men to espouse its cause."[14]

It is worth noting that Godard made no secret of his efforts to cultivate a relationship with the Neckers. He had apparently met them through his friendship with the Suards and must have encountered them in the salons that he frequented and possibly through his own attendance at Mme. Necker's prestigious salon. When in early 1788 Jacques Necker published a book on religion, entitled De l'Importance des opinions

---

13. In 1777, Necker was appointed by Louis XVI to be Director General of the Royal Treasury, but was not given the title of Minister of Finance due to his Protestant religion. Under strong pressure from the queen, he fell out of favor and resigned in 1781. He would return to direct France's finances in 1788 as the specter of bankruptcy hung over the nation, only to be dismissed in July 1789. This latter dismissal would be one of the events that would trigger the insurrection that launched the Revolution. Following the seizure of the Bastille, Necker was recalled to serve as Minister of Finance, but resigned the post in September 1790 and retired permanently to his estate in Coppet, Switzerland.

14. *The Collection of John Boyd Thacher of the Library of Congress, vol. 3, Catalogue of Autographs Relating to the French Revolution* (United States Government Printing Office, 1931), 10.

religieuses [Of the Importance of Religious Opinions],[15] Godard wrote to Necker extolling the book as "a veritable and magnificent treatise on happiness,"[16] adding that "the poor, the unfortunates, all of those who are crushed by our insensibility and by the injustice of our institutes, you console them in their misfortune."[17]

Godard seems to have been proud of his efforts to cultivate the Neckers and mentions them in other writings.[18] He also persisted in his correspondence with both Jacques and Suzanne Necker for several years, including at the beginning of 1789 when Mme. Necker responded to him that she was hastening to "express her gratitude to Monsieur Godard for the sentiments which he expresses and of which M. Necker feels the full value."[19] In a letter of September 11, 1789, Mme. Necker again lavished praise upon Godard, this time through an allusion Godard had made to her husband's book. Mme. Necker wrote that her husband's book had been written precisely for people like Godard, who, she affirmed, "has entered into a great career for beneficence and [to whom] success has already consecrated your virtues and given proof of your talents."[20] Exchanging letters and, especially, receiving compliments from one of the era's power couples, was assuredly an encouraging boost to Godard's ego and could only have incited him to become more active in the public arena.[21]

---

15. Jacques Necker, *De l'Importance des opinions religieuses* (London, 1788), 104.

16. André Encrevé, "La Réception des Ouvrages de J. Necker sur la Religion d'après sa correspondance privée," in *Cahiers Staëliens, organe de la Société des études staëliennes,* n.s., no. 55–2004.

17. Ibid., 102n89.

18. Letter from Godard to Cortot, September 7 (1788).

19. Unpublished letter from Suzanne Necker to Jacques Godard, dated February 9, 1789 (Alde, Maison de Vente, Auction of April 20, 2009, Item 320.)

20. Unpublished letter from Suzanne Necker to Jacques Godard, dated September 11, 1789. (Alde, Maison de Vente, Auction of April 20, 2009, Item 320.) Godard was so gratified by Mme. Necker's praise that he did not fail to return the favor. When writing his history of the Paris Assembly a couple of years later, he made a very flattering reference to her as "the virtuous and inseparable Companion of his [Jacques Necker's] destiny." Jacques Godard, *Exposé des Travaux de l'Assemblée des Représentants de la Commune de Paris* (Paris: Lottin, 1790), 8–9.

21. There is evidence (based upon the unpublished draft of a letter in Godard's handwriting that the author acquired in 2017) that Godard also knew and may have sought to develop a relationship with the Neckers' only child, Germaine de Staël. De Staël, born in 1766, was a frequent presence at some of the leading salons of pre-Revolutionary Paris and became a prominent author and intellectual

Godard concluded his brief on behalf of Brisset by invoking the patronizing but frequently heard notion that, even though non-Catholics were wrong in their beliefs, "they should be treated like men." For good measure, he added an expression of his respect for Louis XVI, who would, he asserted, be remembered as a "good" king.[22] This observation may have seemed necessary to the publication of his brief, and also useful as Godard contemplated carving out a career path, either in government service or with the support of government authorities.

Godard's pleading in the Brisset matter contained many powerful arguments. However, it is not possible to read the brief without concluding that Godard was thinking in far broader terms than the vindication of his client's position, or even in terms of justice for Protestants generally (or his own personal advancement, for that matter). Emulating Target in his pleading on behalf of the Marquise d'Anglure, Godard's text is clearly a political tract. It is, in fact, implausible that he was not seeking to promote an agenda and to have an impact on public opinion, and, in the process, elevate his personal profile for posterity. It does not appear, though, that Godard achieved his goal. In spite of a victory in the case—unlike Target's *Consultation* in the d'Anglure case, which was accompanied by public adulation—Godard's brief made barely a ripple. Regarding Protestant rights, it was simply too late. The question of fundamental rights for Protestants had already been addressed and generally redressed. Their rights were now yesterday's issue. And the issue of Jewish rights was not quite yet of mainstream interest. Godard's observation about the plight of the Jews was perhaps a premature volley into a controversial topic. However, even if not much noted, the brief marked Godard's first open articulation of the need for a reform of the rights of Jews in France and, as such, it was a precursor to the important work that he was to pursue just a little over a year later. He could not have known it, but it was this pursuit, which began in the Brisset brief, that was to provide him with the measure of fame and immortality that he appeared so eager to secure.

---

gadfly following the Revolution. She corresponded with countless personalities of her era, including Thomas Jefferson, with whom she exchanged several letters. (For an additional discussion of the draft letter involving Germaine de Staël, see Chapter 31, p. 394n44., below.)

22. Ibid., 80.

CHAPTER 9

THE AVOCATS OF FRANCE STRUGGLE WITH ROYAL AUTHORITY

The primary political battle in France in the late 1780s was a tug-of-war between royal authority in Versailles and the regional Parlements (and, most importantly, the Paris Parlement), all of which were heavily populated with avocats. This power struggle of the elites, whose ranks were filled with aggressive avocats, took place against a backdrop of financial stress, increasing social unrest, and natural disasters, all of which contributed to the ultimate dismantling of the existing system of government. Jean-François Fournel, a royalist avocat who would collaborate with Godard on a case in 1789, many years later took note of the important role that avocats played in the Revolution.[1] He wrote that "in general, the Bar and the Government [were] bound by relationships so close that the history of one [was] inextricably bound to that of the other." He went on critically to note that "it was the Bar which received the first [revolutionary] shocks and which either softened them or aggravated them."[2] This perspective was echoed by Jean-Sylvain Bailly, a distinguished astronomer of somber appearance, who would serve as the domineering and autocratic Mayor of Paris during the early years of the Revolution.[3]

1. *Gazette des Tribunaux*, vol. 28, no. 32, p. 85.
2. Jean-François Fournel, *Histoire du Barreau de Paris dans les cours de la Révolution* (Paris: Maradan, 1816), 7.
3. Jean-Sylvain Bailly (1736–1793), an astronomer best known for charting the course of Halley's comet, was elected Mayor of Paris by the Paris electors on

Describing avocats and their impact on the Revolution, Bailly was complimentary, explaining that "[a]vocats played a truly beautiful role, they constituted one of the most enlightened classes. They made their mark everywhere, by their numbers and by their opinions, in the districts of the capital, in their localities and in the electoral assemblies and in the legislative body."[4] Avocats were simply essential to the ferment leading to the Revolution and to its early development.

Godard was an interested bystander and modest participant in the brewing dispute between Versailles and the avocats of the Parlements. He was too young to play an influential role in this battle, which was largely waged by a somewhat older generation that was itself about to be displaced by younger colleagues, some of whom were only a very few years older than Godard himself. However, Godard's extensive correspondence with his distant cousin Cortot provides us both with a precious vantage point from which to view the struggle and with an understanding of Godard's personal views respecting this confrontation. This correspondence highlights Godard's strong desire to become involved in the evolving political struggles. His many letters to his cousin also served an important function in their own time as the means of purveying news from Paris to Burgundy. In an age where provincial newspapers were few and the dissemination of information from the capital to the provinces took a long time, private letters were often the principal means of providing relatively timely updates on current events. It is likely that Godard's letters were read not only by his cousin but also by others in Dijon who could thereby obtain news of what was taking place in Paris. The relatively sparse amount of personal details

---

July 15, 1789. Flesselles, the *"Prévôt des marchands de Paris"* (the provost of Paris merchants)—effectively the mayor of the city—had been massacred in front of the Hôtel de Ville immediately after the seizure of the Bastille, with his head placed on a pike and paraded around the city. The electors determined to replace Flesselles promptly and quickly settled on Bailly, giving him the newly created title of *"Maire"* (Mayor). Bailly was symbolically confirmed in this role by Louis XVI when the king came to Paris on July 17 (but was not given the benefit of a full and proper election until August of 1790). Following his selection, Bailly encouraged the districts to form a new municipal assembly, but then found himself repeatedly at odds with the Paris Assembly as it sought to curtail the prerogatives he repeatedly attempted to assert. In 1790, Godard would be in the forefront of efforts by the municipal assembly to confront the Mayor and to challenge his authority. See Godard, *Exposé des Travaux*, 5, et seq.
4. Jean-Sylvain Bailly, *Mémoires de Bailly* (Paris: Baudouin Frères, 1821), 55.

in the letters suggests that Godard was conscious that his letters might be read by persons other than his cousin and may have been written, at least in part, with a wider audience in mind.

The Godard-Cortot correspondence has survived only because Cortot was ultimately forced to leave France in the early 1790s due to his royalist leanings. His property, including his personal papers, was at that time confiscated by public authorities. Despite being incomplete, the extant letters (including some drafts of Cortot's responses) provide us with valuable insights into Godard's general thinking during this transformative era. Beginning in late 1787, Godard's letters to Cortot disclose a reform-minded activist interested in affirming the power of the Parlements against royal authority, but they also reveal a consummate moderate, with even a conservative bent—at least on social issues. Godard was eager to see change, but he remained a strong supporter of Louis XVI, a king in whom he had substantial faith, but whom he believed was poorly advised.[5]

On December 9, 1787, Godard began one of his intense exchanges of letters with Cortot. The backdrop for Godard's December 9 letter is the monarchy's attempt to rein in the increasingly restive and rebellious professional middle class. As part of that effort, certain leaders of the Paris Parlement had been arrested at the order of the king and exiled. In his letter Godard noted that the Parlement had repeatedly called for the return of the leaders—but to no avail. He proceeded to make a passing reference to "an edict concerning Protestants" then under consideration. This was, of course, the document prepared by Chrétien-Guillaume de Lamoignon de Malesherbes, Louis XVI's trusted senior advisor, with the assistance of Godard's mentor, Guy Target. The edict sought to give Protestants significant new legal rights for the first time since the issuance of the Edict of Nantes nearly two hundred years earlier. The adoption of this edict, which took place with alacrity once the subject matter had attracted the interest of the king, became one of the powerful incentives for the Ashkenazi Jews of France to consider seeking their own civil

5. Letter from Godard to Cortot, June 22, 1788. This view of a benign and misled monarch was commonly held among those members of the Third Estate who opposed the existing system. Georges Lefebvre writes that the bourgeoisie actually made "an idol of Louis XVI." This artificial distinction between the king and the royal government helped to fuel their opposition to the aristocracy. Lefebvre, *The Coming of the French Revolution*, trans. R.R. Palmer (New York: Vintage Books, 1947), 45.

equality. In his letter to Cortot, Godard gave the edict short shrift, noting that the members of the Paris Parlement were studying it, but he did not offer any opinion on the text.[6] At that time, Godard's focus was far more on the political power struggle with the king than on the more abstract issue of religious freedom, which he had previously addressed during his representation of the Protestant Pierre Brisset earlier in the year.

In spite of his specific interest in the political situation, Godard made a rhetorical detour in his letter to comment on what he perceived as an extraordinary act of kindness performed by Philippe, Duc d'Orléans, the king's distant cousin and his fierce competitor for popularity, as well as one of the principal agitators in the political turmoil of the time.[7] Godard cited an event that had taken place just a day or two prior to the date of his letter, when the duke and his servant, traveling by horseback, had to ford a stream. The duke quickly found that the stream was much deeper than anticipated and his horse drowned, forcing the duke to swim. The duke then called out to his servant to turn back, but the servant was already in the water. The duke grabbed him by the hair and dragged him to dry land, thereby saving his life. Godard, a product of his time, was impressed by the actions of the duke and found that this story brought him "much honor."[8] The notion that a noble of royal blood would risk his life for a servant was obviously uncommon and surprising even to a sophisticated young man like Godard.

---

6. Letter from Godard to Cortot, December 9, 1787.

7. As noted above (Chapter 1, p. 7n23) the Orléans family had sought for generations to undermine the Bourbon family's hold on the French monarchy. The growing political turmoil of the era was viewed as a moment of opportunity by the then head of the family, Philippe d'Orléans (later to become known as Philippe Egalité, as he sought to ingratiate himself with the revolutionaries). The residence of the Duc d'Orléans, the Palais Royal, and its connected galleries and gardens, became a center of anti-Bourbon activity. It also appears as though the Duc used his considerable fortune to foment discontent with the king and his entourage seemingly in the hope that he could supplant his cousin on the throne. He would fail dismally in his efforts, ending up guillotined in 1793. It would be left to the Duc's son, Louis-Philippe d'Orléans, to achieve the family's ultimate success, when he was elevated to the French throne during the July 1830 Revolution which overthrew Louis XVI's youngest brother, Charles X. The success was short-lived since Louis-Philippe was himself overthrown during the 1848 Revolution.

8. Letter from Godard to Cortot, December 9, 1787.

Three weeks later, on December 27, 1787, Godard once again wrote to Cortot, asking him to speak with Pierre-François Gauthier, a member of the Dijon Parlement, and to inform Gauthier of Godard's esteem for him. He also indicated that he intended to visit with the president of the Dijon Parlement, who was then in Paris. All of this seems to have been part of a concerted effort to cement Godard's relationship with the Parlement of his home province, certainly for the purpose of generating clients and, potentially, in the hope that he might become the Paris legal representative of the Parlement or some of its members.

In the same letter, Godard alluded to the decision of the Minister of Justice to establish a three-person commission for the reform of French criminal and civil laws. The letter mentioned that Godard's mentor Target was to become a member of the three-member commission (and, as Godard somewhat snidely mentioned, by far its highest paid member).[9] In light of Godard's obvious interest in altering and enhancing the French legal system, he must have been delighted that he would be so close to those charged with the reform and that his personal friend was to be a leader in the effort.

In 1788, after the Parlement of Paris had refused to register various edicts issued by Louis XVI, the king, at the urging of his most prominent ministers, implemented a structure that would bypass and potentially even eliminate the Parlements. Acting through his principal minister, the archbishop of Toulouse, Loménie de Brienne, the king proposed to create a single national plenary body charged with registering royal decrees.[10] Avocats throughout France were outraged at the prospect of one of their most important prerogatives being suppressed. Opposition to Loménie de Brienne became widespread within the legal community, as well as in the population at large. Avocats sought to convene assemblies throughout France to protest the attempt to deprive the Parlements and their members of their traditional role.

---

9. Ibid.

10. Étienne Charles de Lomenie de Brienne (1727–1794), a member of the clergy who became archbishop of Toulouse and subsequently was named a cardinal (although stripped of that title when he took the civil oath during the Revolution), did not inspire a great deal of respect from his contemporaries, nor has history been particularly kind to him. Georges Lefebvre, one of the preeminent French scholars of the Revolution, was unqualified in his contempt for the archbishop, referring to him as "an incompetent ignoramus." Lefebvre, *The Coming of the French Revolution*, 25.

Godard stood solidly with his brethren in the legal profession. He
was, not surprisingly, disdainful of the effort to destroy the Parlement
structure and replace it with the proposed single chamber. In his letters
to Cortot, he described the efforts by the king to suppress opposition to
his reform proposal. On May 7 he wrote in detail regarding the arrest of
two members of the Paris Parlement. Jean-Jacques Duval d'Eprémesnil,[11]
one of the Parlement's most eloquent younger members, and Goislart de
Montsabert,[12] a contemporary of Godard, were ordered arrested because
they had spoken out against the proposed elimination of the Parlements
and had submitted a resolution to that effect. Godard described how,
just before midnight on the evening of Sunday, May 4, the king had sent
hundreds of French and Swiss soldiers to surround the Paris Palace of
Justice in an effort to find and arrest d'Eprémesnil and Goislart. Although
Godard noted that he had left the premises at 10:30 that evening, he indicated that many of his fellow-avocats had chosen to stay and sleep in the
main hall of the Palace in solidarity with d'Eprémesnil and Goislart. In
fact, he wrote, when the soldiers came into the hall to arrest the two men,
the avocats demonstrated noteworthy courage in resisting the soldiers.
Initially, they told the soldiers that they could not have access to the main
hall, in which they allegedly benefited from a kind of right of sanctuary.
But when the soldiers returned a second time on the morning of May 5
(and this time Godard was present), the avocats simply refused to identify

---

11. Jean-Jacques Duval d'Eprémesnil (1745–1794). Born in the French colony
of Pondicherry in India, Duval d'Eprémesnil was an active participant in the
opposition to the monarchy in the years immediately preceding the Revolution.
During the deliberations leading to the calling of the Estates-General, he advocated for a vote by members of that body rather than by order, in support of
the position of the Third Estate and against the monarchy. He was then elected
to the Estates-General as a member of the nobility and served in the National
Assembly. His service in that body was, contrary to his comportment in the
Parlement, very supportive of the monarchy. As a consequence of his support
of a vote by each member of the Estates-General at a critical moment on the
road to the Revolution, d'Eprémesnil came to be known as the "Unintentional
Revolutionary." He narrowly escaped being killed during the September 1792
massacres, but was ultimately guillotined as a counter-revolutionary and English spy in April 1794.
12. Anne Louis François Goislart de Montsabert (1763–1814) served as a member of the Paris Parlement and joined d'Eprémesnil in vocal opposition to the
reformation of the parlements. He was killed in a duel just as Napoleon's empire
collapsed and the Bourbon monarchy was about to be restored.

the two objects of their quest as the soldiers searched the premises. Only when d'Eprémesnil and Goislart decided that resisting the royal arrest warrants would ultimately be futile and turned themselves in were the arrests made.[13] D'Eprémesnil was exiled to a sinister fortress on the island of Saint Marguerite—the fortress best known as the prison in which the so-called Man in the Iron Mask was incarcerated—and Goislart was imprisoned briefly in the Bastille in Paris.

As always, Godard was particularly affected by the mistreatment of others. He would later describe to Cortot his concern about how d'Eprémesnil was being treated: "M. d'Eprémesnil is locked in a cell of fifteen square feet with iron bars, where his health is deteriorating. He is treated very harshly by his jailer, who believes that by treating him in this manner he will ingratiate himself to his masters." Godard continued by noting that he had seen a letter from d'Eprémesnil in which d'Eprémesnil, although he allegedly expressed himself with the "softest and most courteous serenity," was in sufficient distress that he was "requesting his father-in-law to solicit for him the right to stroll in a small courtyard near his cell."[14] D'Eprémesnil's exile would not be lengthy; on September 23 he was liberated upon orders of the king.

Godard was clearly proud of his colleagues' resistance and rather pleased with himself. He wrote to his cousin that when he returned to the Palace of Justice on the morning of May 5, he had had great difficulty in entering and had been warned that once inside he could no longer leave, but, as he noted proudly, "I had determined to stay *eight days if that had been necessary*." [Godard provided the emphasis.[15]]

In his continuing description of the confrontation between the avocats and royal authority, Godard wrote to Cortot on May 9, 1788, that the new "bizarre" structure would not last more than "a month or two."[16] He also described in sarcastic terms the monarchy's attempt to intimidate the "grand chamber" of the Parlement of Paris, which had been summoned to Versailles.[17] He wondered how the edicts had been received

---

13. For a more complete description of the standoff at the Palace of Justice in May 1788, see J. Gaudry, *Histoire du Barreau de Paris*, vol. 2 (Paris: Auguste Durand Éditeur, 1864), 322–24.

14. Letter from Godard to Cortot, June 8, 1788.

15. Ibid., May 7, 1788.

16. Ibid., May 9, 1788.

17. The Grand Chamber of the Parlement was the room within the Paris Pal-

in the provinces and sought information about the Parlement of Dijon and its reaction. Further describing the situation in Paris, he took note that royal troops had imposed order at the Paris Palace of Justice and had prevented the Parlement from meeting. However, exhibiting his inherent conservatism and deference to authority, he indicated that he did not think that the Parlement would have met in any event since "I do not think that it would have permitted itself to contravene the orders of the king, who prohibited all of its functions until new orders."[18]

A week later, Godard once again wrote to Cortot to bring him up to date on events taking place in Paris. Now he indicated that avocats in Paris were refusing to render their services and that the criminal courts at the Châtelet—the large, decrepit, and forbidding complex just across the Seine from the Palace of Justice—were not functioning. He did not fail to note that he had dined with Target the previous evening, and had found out that Target had just shared a lunch with the Duc de Penthièvre, the wealthy father-in-law of the Duc d'Orléans, who was one of the defendants in the Paris bakers' case that Godard had handled in 1786. Apparently, also in attendance at that lunch were members of the "académie" (presumably the Académie Française), including a few members of the high nobility. Godard opined that Target had been successful in "making them taste his principles regarding all of this Revolution."[19] This allusion to a "Revolution" was, as had been Godard's prior reference, merely an allusion to the conflict between the monarchy and the Parlements, not to the overthrow of the monarchy that was about to occur. Suggesting that he needed a respite from the conflicts raging in Paris, he concluded his letter by noting that he was "leaving tomorrow for the country."[20]

The correspondence between the cousins continued as the battle between the monarchical power and the Parlements further escalated. Godard also kept tabs on the growing strife within the legal profession, and was so eager to convey to Cortot his view of the conflict that, with

---

ace of Justice where the Parlement would sit when it performed its important functions, including the review of significant judgments. This anthropomorphic language was an allusion to the core of the Parlement and the efforts of the monarchy to exercise control over it. The room which existed in 1788 was destroyed during the uprising of the Paris Commune in 1871.
18. Letter from Godard to Cortot, May 9, 1788.
19. Ibid., May 16, 1788.
20. Ibid.

uncharacteristic modesty, he never even mentioned that the *Journal de Paris* in its May 3 and 4 editions had carried the article in the form of a letter to the editors that he had written in memory of his friend Buffon, the recently deceased great Burgundian scientist.[21]

Godard remained focused on the struggles of the legal community and the context in which these struggles were taking place. The supposed confrontation among certain components of the monarchy—members of the royal family, the nobility of the blood and conservative ministers, and its institutions—and the king himself was also a source of much anguish to Godard. Noting in a letter sent on June 1, 1788, that a line from a current play, "Blind Prince or rather ministers who are also blind" had received wild applause during a recent performance, Godard reiterated his faith in the king, and his belief that foolish ministers, not the king, were to blame for the current crisis.[22]

As the days passed, Godard became increasingly concerned that, unlike many other provinces, his native Burgundy was not actively supporting the Parlements. He expressed shock that the nobility of that province had failed to react to the attempt to increase the concentration of power at Versailles. "Will the nobility of Burgundy be the only one which maintains its silence?" he railed in a letter to Cortot. "Doesn't it have a direct interest in this quarrel? And would it not be possible to deprive it of its privileges tomorrow?" He then lashed out at two Burgundian bailiwicks which had chosen to register the king's decree, castigating them as "dishonored forever and certainly without any benefit."[23]

Just a few days later, however, Cortot informed Godard that the Burgundians had demonstrated their opposition to the royal action. Godard expressed his pleasure with this turn of events, but also noted with some alarm the growing tensions throughout France.[24] His concern was well-placed. On June 12 Godard emphatically described the riots that had just occurred in Grenoble in support of the local Parlement. This was the famous Day of the Tiles when a local mob confronted royal troops and pelted them with roof tiles. Although he only referenced two deaths

---

21. Godard wrote a lengthy and thoughtful article on the occasion of Buffon's passing, but the official eulogy for Buffon, delivered at the Académie Française, was given by Condorcet.
22. Letter from Godard to Cortot, June 1, 1788.
23. Ibid., June 5, 1788.
24. Ibid., June 8, 1788.

occurring during the rioting, in fact, four individuals died. He could not have known it, but those individuals can properly be considered the very first of the hundreds of thousands of victims of the coming Revolution.

In his letters, Godard grew increasingly pessimistic about the ability of the monarchy to successfully work its way out of its financial crisis. He did not, however, seem optimistic about the prospects of a meeting of the infrequently convened Estates-General, the assembly in which representatives of the three principal segments of French society— the clergy (the First Estate), the nobility (the Second Estate) and the commoners (the Third Estate)—could come together for the purpose of considering and consenting to structural changes to the country's governing apparatus. In all past convenings of the Estates-General, each order had been given a single vote. The prospect of such an arrange-ment, with its obvious skewing of power in favor of the Church and the nobility, was evidently unpalatable to the professional class. And yet, if no national consensus could be found to solve the growing financial crisis, then changing the tax structure (taxing the untaxed assets of the clergy and subjecting a greater number of French citizens to a more equal tax burden) would simply require such a meeting. No French king had summoned an Estates-General since 1614, and it was unclear how the Estates-General would function if convened. It was, however, rather certain that political confusion, if not chaos, could ensue.

By June 22 Godard wrote to Cortot that "it appears to me to be impos-sible that we will escape holding an Estates-General; necessity is making it unavoidable."[25] At the end of his letter, he volunteered his view that recently the *Chambre des Comptes* of Dijon had made an unspecified "courageous" decision. Presumably, the nature of the decision was suffi-ciently well-known in Dijon that he did not have to describe it to Cortot, nor, of course, did he need to remind Cortot that his (Godard's) father was an officer of the Dijon *Chambre*.

Mere days later, Godard sent another letter to Cortot in which the preponderance of his text was a quote from a resolution issued by the Parlement of Rouen attacking the Minister of Justice for his en-forcement of the royal edict of May 8. The Minister of Justice was, of course, Lamoignon, the nephew of Chrétien-Guillaume de Lamoignon de Malesherbes, the royal counselor with whom Guy Target was then

---

25. Ibid., June 22, 1788.

working closely on legal reforms. Target's relationship with the Minister did not assuage Godard's disdain for Lamoignon.

Godard's frustration with royal authority grew rapidly. By July 4 he seemed ready to leave Paris. He declared to his cousin that, if matters were not straightened out or if Lamoignon's proposals prevailed, he would "leave his apartment, place all of his personal effects with friends and return to Burgundy until a more favorable turn of events warranted his return to Paris."[26] It is likely that the disturbances in Paris were having a nefarious impact on his already precarious income and that he might have to return to the care of his more affluent parents. He was undoubtedly also concerned that the elimination of the Parlements would bring to an end the most significant part of his professional work.

The developing political crisis led Godard to take a growing interest in working with the representatives of various provinces, including those of his native Burgundy. In early July Godard informed Cortot that he had visited with a delegation of Burgundians seeking to meet with the Minister of Justice in order to introduce them to Target, who could provide them with advice regarding a meeting with the Minister. Apparently, the meeting with Target went quite well. Target provided the Burgundians with considerable insights into the behavior they should adopt and methods they should use in order to achieve their objective if they could manage to meet Lamoignon.

Just a few days later, on July 16, Godard noted ominously that representatives of the nobility from Brittany had been unceremoniously thrown into the Bastille on the grounds that they had held a Parlement meeting in spite of the prohibition against such meetings. Godard informed his cousin that, in addition to the political turmoil raging in Paris, the weather also had deteriorated—a terrible storm had afflicted Paris and nearby regions. Hail the size of eggs had hit the city and its environs with such violence that crops had been destroyed, windows had been broken, and some people had actually been killed.[27] This meteorological catastrophe was yet another of the many calamities that were relentlessly afflicting France in this period. As a consequence of the difficulties being encountered by farmers resulting from the harsh weather, the price of bread was skyrocketing. Simultaneously, public finances were continuing to degrade

26. Ibid., July 4, 1788.
27. Ibid., July 16, 1788.

and the public markets were not doing well. Misfortune was piling up for an increasingly troubled and financially weakened France.

In mid-August Godard hosted a dinner for representatives from Burgundy and Grenoble, together with a prominent, but unidentified, citizen from Brittany. In his letter of August 11 he noted that his law colleagues Target, DeSèze, and Dupaty had also been in attendance at the dinner, as well as a certain Berquin (likely Arnaud Berquin, the author of many popular children's books and the private tutor of Charles-Joseph Panckoucke's two daughters).[28] The dinner had served as an occasion to toast various provincial emissaries, including those from Burgundy. This reinforced the fact that Godard was just beginning his role as a representative for special interests—in today's parlance, as a lobbyist—with its obligatory socializing. With France on the cusp of major political and institutional change, the prospect of playing such a role had to have appeared highly desirable to Godard, as he sought to find his place within the changing order.[29]

Godard added a personal note in his letter to Cortot. He expressed his regret that Cortot had not been able to join the Paris dinner. He hoped, he wrote, that if the situation in Paris stabilized, Cortot would come to Paris for a few days. Then, departing from his usual serious approach, he wrote that he would try to introduce Cortot "to some good citizens and to very pretty women," indicating that, in his view, "the one does not negate the other." This was a rare indication that the young bachelor was not solely focused on his work and networking, but that he may also have had a personal social life. Returning to his more serious mode, however, Godard added a postscript indicating he had just heard that the convening of the Estates-General had formally been set for May 1 of the following year.[30]

Days later, on August 20, Godard announced to his cousin that the king was incapable of meeting state financial obligations and would begin to issue notes to the holders of government bonds in lieu of actually making payments. The monarchy was now officially insolvent. Godard seems to

---

28. Ibid., August 11, 1788.
29. For additional observations relating to Godard's views of the developing Revolution, see Henri Carré, "La Tactique et les Idées de l'Opposition Parlementaire d'après la Correspondance Inédite de Cortot et de Godard (1788–1789)," in A. Aulard, *La Révolution française: Revue d'histoire moderne et contemporaine*, vol. 29 (Paris: La Société de l'Histoire de la Révolution, 1895), 99–121.
30. Letter from Godard to Cortot, August 11, 1788.

have wanted to see the effect for himself and visited the Paris stock market (then located in the Hôtel de Nevers on rue Colbert just a few blocks from his residence), "where he had never previously set foot.[31] Oddly, in spite of the spiraling difficulties and in a wildly inaccurate prediction, Godard wrote Cortot that "the people of Paris are so carefree that they will let themselves be crushed without saying a word." However, more accurately, he announced that "the worst winter is coming and already the streets are not safe at eleven o'clock in the evening."[32] In fact, Paris was seeing a large influx of vagabonds streaming to the capital from the countryside in search of food and employment. Increasing criminality—a by-product of the poverty of this growing indigent population—as well as the spiraling financial crisis, and the terribly cold weather beginning to sweep across much of France as autumn arrived were adding to the growing misery afflicting the nation.

In spite of the escalating financial crisis, Louis XVI's government moved forward with a matter of particular interest to Godard—the reform of the criminal legal system. In a letter to Cortot dated August 25 Godard described the new laws that were being crafted and adopted to implement these reforms. He happily informed his cousin that torture as a means of eliciting confessions had been abolished. This important development echoed Godard's plea in his *Consultation* on behalf of the seven Germans, in which he had urged the abolition of torture. However, Godard had hoped for more. With evident disappointment, he indicated that the right of the accused to counsel had not been included in the reform legislation.[33]

The continuing refusal of the king to permit the Parlements to reconvene also remained a topic of particular interest to Godard. He expressed to Cortot the hope that Jacques Necker, the Protestant Genevan banker so popular with the French middle class, would be elevated to the position of chief minister. Necker had extensive support among Paris's elites, both bourgeois and noble, but the royal family and the queen, in particular, opposed his appointment. Unspoken, but widely recognized, was the reluctance of the king and especially the queen to support a foreigner and, most particularly, a Protestant (considered by the king to be a heretic), for such a prominent post.

---

31. Ibid., August 20, 1788.
32. Ibid.
33. Ibid., August 25, 1788.

Godard's pessimism about the overall situation in Paris rose to the fore as yet again he informed his cousin of his precarious financial situation. He wrote, with a kind of despair, that "[i]f the hopes that we have [for the appointment of Necker] are not realized, I will not delay in returning to Burgundy. I am no longer in a condition to stay in Paris."[34]

But he did not have to wait long to convert his pessimism into a burst of joy. Just one day later, in a letter to Cortot, Godard waxed poetic about a new turn of events. "Blow all of the trumpets," he wrote exultantly, "announce it in the streets and in all the crossroads of your city that the archbishop [Loménie de Brienne, Minister of Finance and chief minister] has been dismissed and that Mr. NECKER [Godard wrote his name in capital letters] is the superintendent of finances."[35]

The optimism reflected in Godard's correspondence suddenly swept through Paris. For Godard, the most important factor was that Necker had made it clear he would permit the Parlement to return to Paris from its exile. Godard did not fail to articulate his hope that, despite his sponsorship of criminal reform, which Godard strongly favored, the Minister of Justice, Lamoignon, would quickly follow Loménie de Brienne out of his government position. That departure, he noted, would be the "second sacrifice" necessary in order to restore "peace with the Parlements and with the nation."[36]

Godard's letters of the next days were filled with descriptions of the celebrations that went on throughout Paris to commemorate the fall of Loménie de Brienne and the return of Necker. He recounted at length the activities that occurred on Place Dauphine, the small triangular public space just behind the Palace of Justice where avocats tended to congregate (as they still do today) and, most especially, on the grounds of the Palais Royal, the residence of the Duc d'Orléans and the preferred gathering place of the increasingly revolutionary middle class and of the liberal nobility. He reported on the displays of fireworks that lit the Paris evening sky in celebration of this government shakeup. Only one discordant note disturbed Godard. The departing archbishop had been promised a cardinal's hat, together with a prosperous archbishopric in the city of Sens, as well as some emoluments for members of his family, as compensation for his

---

34. Ibid.
35. Ibid., August 26, 1788.
36. Ibid.

unceremonious dismissal. Godard was distressed. "What a frightening abuse of grace!" he wrote indignantly.[37] With his firm sense of fairness and an awareness of his own impecuniousness, Godard could hardly cope with the notion that a disgraced public minister should be handsomely rewarded for his poor stewardship of state affairs.

The euphoria following Necker's appointment distracted Godard, who did not again write to his cousin until September 7. In that letter, he revealed the resurgence of his sycophantic streak, noting that he had exchanged correspondence with the new minister, whose favor he had been so actively courting, and whom he had met at some of the salons that he frequented: "Mr. Necker is somewhat ill, I received from him and Mme. Necker a very honest response to my compliments and good wishes."[38] (Just a short while later, of course, Godard would send a copy of his Brisset brief to the Neckers, eliciting additional compliments from them.) The increasingly self-serving nature of Godard's letters was beginning to irritate the provincial cousin, who would soon bring the correspondence to a brutal end.

Events began to move quickly, although not always in ways Godard and his fellow avocats might have hoped. As Godard wrote to Cortot on September 12, the return of the Parlement from its exile was conditioned upon various structural changes, which "the Parlement energetically protested," and would not accept.[39]

Just a couple of days later, Godard announced to his cousin that the Minister of Justice, Lamoignon de Baville, had been dismissed. His pleasure with this development, and the fact that the outgoing Minister did not receive the elevation to a dukedom to which he had apparently aspired, led Godard to incorporate a pun into his letter. He twisted the former Minister's hoped-for, but denied, title into an insult by separating the syllables of that aspired-to title and making a play on those syllables. He wrote to his cousin that Lamoignon was leaving, not as a newly elevated Duc de Baville, as Lamoignon had hoped, but rather as a low (*bas*) and vile (*vil*) individual. Godard also informed Cortot that his (Godard's) friends (and, perhaps, clients), the representatives of the Brittany region, had just been released from the Bastille.[40]

---

37. Ibid., August 28, 1788.
38. Ibid., September 7, 1788.
39. Ibid., September 12, 1788.
40. Ibid., September 12, 1788.

As September passed, Godard took note of the increasing violence in
the streets of Paris. Parisians sought to express their joy at the dismissal
of the Minister of Justice by burning him and other individuals in effigy.
Mingling with these crowds were also groups of individuals bent on causing chaos. The forces of order, including the King's Swiss Guard, sought
energetically to stop this activity. Godard reported that the troops had
attacked the populace with "sabers and bayonets" and, in a statement that
may have been an exaggeration, that approximately one hundred fifty had
been killed and wounded. Despite the violence the celebrations continued, some of which Godard personally witnessed. Before concluding his
letter of September 19 he informed Cortot that Dupaty, the attorney with
whom he had socialized and, most notably, whom he had assisted on
the Metz case involving the two Jewish complainants, had just died of a
"malignant fever."[41] Dupaty was just forty-eight years old.[42]

The letters of the next couple of days were devoted to announcing
the imminent return of the Parlement to Paris. Godard also noted, not
without some sense of satisfaction, that Lamoignon, the fallen Minister
of Justice, had substantial debts and that "several prosecutors who believe
that vengeance is sweet are getting ready to seize his assets as soon as the
Parlement has returned."[43] To justify his obvious satisfaction at Lamoignon's misfortune, he added that "[n]ever will it be possible to inflict on
him all of the evil which he committed."[44]

Finally, on September 24 Godard was able to tell his cousin that the
Parlement had returned to Paris to loud applause. He also took the opportunity to complain that Cortot was not responding to his many letters.[45]

His complaint had its effect, since on October 9 Godard expressed
his gratitude for Cortot's recent lengthy letter. In his letter, Godard took
note of Cortot's own position in the dispute between the king and the

---

41. Ibid., September 19, 1788.
42. As president of the Paris *Ordre des Avocats*, Dupaty was by then an important
and well-known personality. He was a man of such stature that Thomas Jefferson took note of his passing, albeit briefly, writing simply, "President Dupaty
is dead," in a letter sent to his (Jefferson's) personal secretary William Short on
September 20, 1788. *The Papers of Thomas Jefferson*, vol. 13, March 7– October
1788, ed. Julian P. Boyd (Princeton, NJ: Princeton University Press, 1956), 619–21.
43. Letter from Godard to Cortot, September 22, 1788.
44. Ibid.
45. Ibid., September 24, 1788.

Parlements, which appears to have been oriented toward creating a national legislature for France. Godard lauded his cousin for his views and sought to link them to those of Godard's mentor Guy Target. "I was delighted to learn from Mr. Gouget," Godard wrote, "that you were more national than parliamentary.[46] This is how one should be and this is how Mr. Target is, with whom all of your ideas appear to mesh perfectly."[47]

Target was also mentioned in Godard's next letter to Cortot. However, this time, his comment appears to have been based upon a misunderstanding. Cortot had made an allusion to a book concerning the rules of the Bar that Cortot ascribed to Target. Godard quickly disabused Cortot of the notion that Target had authored such a book. Nonetheless, he seized upon Cortot's comments to provide observations on the operations of the Paris Bar. He described in detail the rules applicable to young avocats who were seeking admittance to the Bar, providing an important perspective on the professional oversight functions of the Paris Bar of the era. He began by stating with apparent pride that a proposal setting a minimum amount of wealth as a prerequisite to becoming an avocat had been rejected. Then, he went on to write that the prerequisite "was rejected in order not to foreclose this career to poor men who may have talent. Wealth is therefore not a consideration, and for the same reason [one's station at] birth is also not a criterion."[48] When writing about poor men with talent, Godard was likely thinking of himself, as he continuously struggled to make ends meet. Godard went on to describe in detail the mentoring procedures that the Paris Bar had developed for its young

---

46. The "Mr. Gouget" to whom Godard referred was Maurice Gouget-Deslandres (1755–1827), a member of the Parlement of Dijon who would eventually become a judge in that city. He served in the National Guard and also became a member of the Dijon chapter of the *Société de la Constitution*. During the early years of the Revolution, he authored a number of pamphlets regarding the national debt and the availability of private credit. See Maurice Gouget-Deslandres, *Discours sur les finances, le crédit des assignats, la circulation de l'argent, & la baisse de l'intérêt de l'argent prononcé à la séance du 13 août 1790, de la Société des amis de la Constitution et à la séance du 22 août de la Société du club de mil sept cent quatre-vingt-neuf* (Paris: Chez Desennes, Cusac, 1790); *Procès-verbal de la confédération des gardes nationales des quatre départements formans ci-devant la province de Bourgogne et pays adjacens faite sous les murs de Dijon, le 18 mai 1790* (Dijon: l'Imprimerie de P. Causse, 1790), 5, 25.
47. Letter from Godard to Cortot, October 9, 1788.
48. Ibid., October 28, 1788.

avocats, procedures in which he had participated through the creation of a judicial conference at the very beginning of his career with the Paris Order of Avocats and from which he benefitted through his relationships with Target and others. At the end of his description, he emphasized that, if the supervisory committee in charge of reviewing the quality of new avocats determined to severely punish a young avocat, then the entire assembly of avocats would sit as a court of appeals, "because it sees with a jaundiced eye this newly created aristocracy."[49] Yet again, Godard seemed particularly interested in protecting those who might be vulnerable, in this case young avocats who might have made some error or offended someone in a position of authority.

Godard's letters continued at a rapid pace. In November, when he wrote to his cousin, he began by yet again singing the praises of Target, "whose opinions are given great value at the Assembly of Notables."[50] He was referring here to the second Assembly of Notables, which had been convened by the king many months after the suspension of the original Assembly of the same name for the purpose of hammering out the multitude of details relating to the convening of the Estates-General. Even as he sat as a member of the second Assembly of Notables, Target was also a member of the Paris Assembly of Electors, which was beginning to wrestle with the process of electing representatives from the city of Paris to the Estates-General. Godard would himself become involved in this latter process.

In his November letter, Godard noted with obvious satisfaction that, at the forthcoming gathering of the Estates-General, the Third Estate would have as many members as the First Estate and Second Estate combined, a first sign of royal acceptance of the growing power of the bourgeoisie. (He did not mention that, in spite of this concession to the Third Estate, the king had not acquiesced to permitting votes by individuals rather than by Order. The king's silence on this latter issue made the decision to increase the representation less than meaningful and would be a major source of conflict in the months to come.) Over the next months and years, Godard would demonstrate an increasing interest in electoral politics, both with respect to the technical aspects of determining who could vote and how they could do so, and in regard to his personal pursuit of elective office.

---

49. Ibid.
50. Ibid., November 16, 1788.

In concluding his November letter to his cousin, Godard bragged that he had been retained by the heirs of a certain individual from Dijon who had died leaving a substantial estate of 3,500,000 francs.[51] It is likely that this particular engagement provided some welcome remuneration to the young avocat and a modicum of relief from his chronic financial problems. It assuredly reaffirmed the importance to Godard of maintaining close ties with his home region as a significant client-development technique.

With the arrival of the end of 1788 and the beginning of 1789, Godard became an ever more enthusiastic supporter of the revolutionary fervor spreading through Paris. Although Godard's letters to his cousin from this period are not available (if he wrote any), a rather jarring response from Cortot to one of Godard's letters fills in the details. On February 3, 1789, Cortot sent his last letter to his cousin and kept a copy of the draft of this letter in his files. Cortot, clearly exasperated with Godard's enthusiasm for a movement with which he, Cortot—who remained a staunch royalist—did not agree, complained bitterly that Godard's revolutionary fervor was insensitive to his feelings. He criticized Godard's verbosity, a verbosity that was a natural by-product of his professional position in which flowery language was a staple, but which Godard had a tendency to overdo. Cortot wrote to Godard, "you do not fear aggravating my pain by directing toward me your irresistible itch to write, so as not to permit the public to fail to know that you are the zealous partisan of an opinion of which I disapprove."[52] He went on to reproach Godard, angrily suggesting that Godard's letters were merely self-serving—perhaps with a view to electoral success—and lacing his comments with angry sarcasm:

> Write then, since this seems to be necessary for the type of reputation that you are seeking to create, and to give me yet an additional excuse to add to the list which you are setting out before me, all of the peasants of our Burgundy whose votes you are going to capture. Send them, very specially, models of deliberations to be held, you will at least make them speak French.[53]

Cortot's letter continued in the same vein, with ever harsher rhetoric.

---

51. Ibid.
52. Letter from Cortot to Godard, February 3, 1789.
53. Ibid.

He declared that he "pitied" Godard. And, then he concluded by writing "frankly":

> I do not like either writers of fancy phrases nor exalted heads; when yours will be cooled down, you will let me know; in the meantime dispense with sending me this kind of writing which can only displease me since none of your rhetoric will make me feel better.[54]

Godard was certainly terribly hurt by the brutal tone of Cortot's letter, but he responded without anger. Rather, he expressed respectful regret. Asserting with his usual exaggeration that he would gladly sacrifice his very existence for his cousin, he noted, however, that "it did not depend on me to sacrifice my conscience." Following that declaration, he made a statement that was distinctly at odds with everything that he had been doing to enhance his reputation and to achieve worldly success. "It isn't reputation that I seek, but goodness that I desire; names are lost in the midst of all of these writings with which we are flooded, but I throw my brochures into the crowds without attaching my name." He defensively noted that he had had profound disagreements with others, but that he continued to engage in constructive dialogues with them. In particular, he reiterated an observation that he had made in his January letter to Cortot that he had "twice had strong altercations with Mr. d'Eprémesnil, and we, nonetheless, get along well."[55] As proof of his ability to maintain cordial relations with those with whom he disagreed, he informed Cortot that d'Eprémesnil had just arranged for him to have dinner with "Bergasse," the prominent avocat, who, according to Godard, being "desirous of getting to know me, has asked that we dine together."[56] He

---

54. Ibid.

55. Ibid.

56. Nicolas Bergasse (1750–1832) was registered as an avocat in 1775. He became a strong proponent of the work of Franz Anton Mesmer, who developed the concept of hypnosis, creating a group to support Mesmer's work in France. His reputation was significantly enhanced through his representation of the Baron Guillaume Kornmann in a case involving Kornmann's wife's adulterous relationship. That case led him into a very public conflict with Caron de Beaumarchais, the author and playwright, who had been represented by Target, providing Bergasse with great notoriety. Elected to the Estates-General from his native city of Lyon, he served for a few months as a member of the Constitution Committee of the National Assembly before his rather unique positions in government put him in conflict with many of his fellow members and he resigned. He became an

concluded his letter by telling Cortot that he did not wish to cause him any pain, but that, in any event, "I could never cause as much [pain] as your letter caused me."[57]

Not surprisingly, the correspondence between the cousins ceased. There are no further exchanges of letters to be found. Beyond the sad fact of a familial breakup and the end of a relationship between legal colleagues, the termination of this correspondence closes an important window into the mind and emotions of Jacques Godard. The cousins' nearly seventy-letter exchange represents not only a unique perspective on the character of two interesting avocats as the world in which they exercised their professions changed dramatically, but a rare personal analysis of the critical conflict among the monarchy, the aristocracy, and the legal professionals as France teetered on the brink of revolution.

The end of this exchange of letters would also mark, as Cortot had sensed, Godard's formal entry into the political fray gaining momentum around him. Of course, as Godard's professional activities were beginning to evolve, the world around him was about to dissolve with a speed that no one could have anticipated. The French Revolution was about to begin in earnest and Godard would make every effort to be in the center of the storm.

---

adviser to Louis XVI during the last days of the king's reign. Arrested in 1794, he survived the Terror, but did not reengage in political activities until the Restoration and then only as a writer of political tracts.

57. Letter from Godard to Cortot, February 6, 1789.

CHAPTER 10

LAW PRACTICE AS THE
REVOLUTION APPROACHES

Even as the turbulence of the approaching Revolution accelerated and as Godard became increasingly involved in the public arena, he continued to conduct an active legal practice. His civic activities, however, would steadily begin to draw him away from the practice of law. As the watershed year of 1789 approached, Godard's docket was filled with many important cases. In January 1789 he seemed overwhelmed by his caseload, writing to his cousin that, "I have many matters and I sleep very little."[1] As he closed his letter, he reiterated that, if he was writing somewhat less frequently, it was "because now I have more matters than it is possible for me to handle," adding that, "in the next month, I have three cases of the greatest importance to plead, in addition to the memorials and *consultations*."[2] Although Godard was prone to some exaggeration, based upon the public record of his legal activities, he was probably not exaggerating very much.

During this critical period in French history, the cases Godard took on addressed various interesting and challenging issues. In mid-1788, Godard was called upon to render a *Consultation* in a legal dispute that again involved a priest.[3] This time, however, Godard was aligned against

---

1. Letter from Godard to Cortot, undated (however, based on its sequencing, it can be determined to have been written in January 1789).

2. Ibid.

3. Jacques Godard, *Consultation à un Mémoire pour Antoine Lefevre, dit Barré, et al.* (Imprimerie de C. Simon, 1788). Three other avocats, Bitousé Deslignières,

the priest, a certain Sieur le Bée de Belicour, who served in the small town of Bourg near Laon, to the north of Paris. The priest had accused three members of the family of Antoine Lefevre of setting three fires that had devastated the town, and also of stealing his watch. During the investigation, it became apparent that the accuser was the actual perpetrator of the acts of arson and that he had pretended that his watch had been stolen by the twelve-year-old daughter of the accused couple in an effort to give additional plausibility to his accusations. A court in Laon exonerated the Lefevre family and assessed considerable damages against the priest due to the "calumnious" nature of his false accusations. The priest then appealed the assessment of damages. Godard wrote a brief in support of the enforcement of the judgment against the priest. His short four-page *Consultation* emphasized the terrible injustice that had been perpetrated against the Lefevre family and highlighted that the accuser was a priest who had made nefarious use of his position of trust—a strongly aggravating factor which fully justified the substantial damages. "By reason of his title of Priest," Godard asserted, the accuser "exposed [the defendants] to far greater dangers."[4] Effectively, Godard accused the priest of an abuse of his spiritual role and of having used his elevated status to cover his crimes. He also noted that the disrepute that the false accusations and the sixteen months of unjustified imprisonment that the family had experienced had irreparably harmed them and warranted the payment of consequential damages. He concluded his plea for enforcement of the judgment against the priest (even suggesting that it would be appropriate to augment it) by reminding the court that the humiliation visited upon the young daughter would likely doom her to "perpetual celibacy."[5]

A strong sense of disgust with the reprehensible conduct of the priest permeates Godard's pleading, again emphasizing Godard's provincial sense of morality. The powerful disdain expressed for the priest's misconduct may also have been a reflection of the fact that Godard's brother, Dominique, had just recently been ordained a priest and that le Bée's comportment was assuredly contrary to the Godard family's belief in the proper behavior of a priest. On a more practical level, it is probable that Godard's indignation with the priest in his official capacity as a representative of the Church

Duport Dutertre, and Brière de Lesmont, added their signatures in support of Godard's *Consultation*.

4. *Consultation à un Mémoire pour Antoine Lefevre, dit Barré, et al.*, 63.

5. Ibid., 64.

was a means of placing responsibility for the payment of damages on the Church itself rather than on the likely-indigent priest.

Undoubtedly the most important and highest-profile case which Godard handled at the end of 1788 and in the first months of 1789 involved the defense of the Leblanc family of the southeastern Paris suburb of Charenton.[6] The husband, wife, and son of the family had been convicted of the murder of Daniel-Louis-Fidel-Armand Bocquillon, a tax collector from Auxonne (in Burgundy), who allegedly had been killed inside the inn kept by the Leblancs. According to the allegations, the Leblanc family, with the assistance of a servant, stabbed Bocquillon and dropped his body into the nearby Seine River in their attempt to rob him. The family appealed the verdict and Godard represented Mr. Leblanc, who, by the time of the appeal, was the sole survivor of the family, since Mme. Leblanc and her son had died in prison. He filed a lengthy memorandum in support of Mr. Leblanc. His powerful pleading was yet another impassioned call for justice.

At the beginning of his brief, Godard took note that the members of the Leblanc family had always comported themselves in an exemplary manner. This formed the backdrop for his argument that, in the absence of the most convincing proof, it would simply be a miscarriage of justice to affirm the conviction of any individual. His was an argument that in our legal environment seems virtually self-evident, but which was far less so in late eighteenth-century France, namely, that in order to convict an accused it was necessary to provide proof beyond a reasonable doubt, or as Godard put it: "the proofs the most stringent, the least questionable, the most diverse; proofs which are persuasive and distance all of the court's doubts."[7]

In order to shed doubt on the earlier conviction of the Leblanc family, Godard evoked certain well-recognized terrible miscarriages of justice. He included in his list, most notably, the obviously unwarranted conviction, torture, and execution that had occurred just a few years previously in the Calas case.[8] He even evoked his own victory over injustice in the matter involving the Hermit of Burgundy. Interestingly, he did not refer to the Metz case involving the Jewish complainants. Aware of the power

---

6. *Gazette des Tribunaux*, 1789, vol. 27, no. 11, p. 169, et seq.; *Causes célèbres, curieuses et intéressantes*, vol. 173, part 1 (May 1789).

7. *Causes célèbres, curieuses et intéressantes*, vol. 173, part 1 (May 1789).

8. Ibid., 74.

of public opinion in celebrated cases, Godard argued that such public opinion should not have a place in a court of law and implored the court to reject such external pressures. He also noted the terrible suffering (and expense) that had been inflicted on the Leblanc family through the protracted legal proceedings and their imprisonment. Following a detailed analysis of the facts surrounding Bocquillon's murder, Godard posited that instead of a murder, what had actually transpired was a suicide. His arguments were logical, thorough, and ultimately persuasive. His defense was, however, controversial. Godard's cousin Cortot disapproved of Godard's representation of the Leblanc family, as did much of the public.[9] Nonetheless, Godard was able to boast to Cortot that he was pleased that his pleadings had ultimately been "approved by the opinion of the public, of [his] colleagues and of the judges" and that he had converted "the opinion of those who had been opposed" to his clients. He expressed his firm hope that he would prevail in the matter.[10]

The final decision reversing the conviction of the Leblanc family was handed down on March 17, 1789. With this victory, Godard achieved an important success at a particularly critical time. The legal publication which recorded Godard's pleadings in the Leblanc case offered him high praise. It noted that the young avocat's "talents are frequently remarked upon."[11] Another publication, the *Journal Politique de Bruxelles*, did not fail to remind its readers that Godard was the avocat who had achieved vindication for his clients in the Burgundian Hermit case.[12]

Also early in 1789, Godard was retained to represent a certain Mr. Cousin, the tutor of the minor son of a notary. His representation was in the context of an effort by the wife of a client of the notary (who also happened to be the notary's uncle) to recover from the tutor a large amount of money that had allegedly been entrusted to the notary by the plaintiff's late husband. According to the pleadings, the funds had been entrusted without the issuance of any documents evidencing a specific obligation to return them; allegedly, the notary and the plaintiff's late husband simply had an informal understanding regarding their return. In response to

---

9. Letter from Godard to Cortot, January 1789. In writing about the Leblanc case, Godard notes in his letter to his cousin that he is "very disappointed that you do not approve of the defense which I have undertaken."
10. Ibid.
11. *Gazette des Tribunaux*, 1789, vol. 27, no. 11, p. 170.
12. *Journal Politique de Bruxelles*, February 14, 1789, no. 7, pp. 91, et seq.

the claims for reimbursement, Godard argued that it was not plausible that anyone would have been able to take title to such a large amount of money without some tangible evidence of that transfer. The existence of a mere oral claim was, in Godard's view, completely insufficient to establish any rights of such importance. Godard noted that accepting an oral declaration of ownership in a matter such as this would leave important matters to pure chance and could make decisions involving critical issues subject to the whims of isolated testimony. (He might have added that permitting significant financial transactions without written documents would diminish the role of the legal profession in commerce.) The legal publication which reported the case noted that it would have been expected that a matter of this nature would be accompanied by a lengthy and "certainly thorny" discussion, but that Godard's elucidation of the issues had been, to the contrary, "clear and interesting."[13]

Godard's position in this civil matter echoed positions he had taken in prior criminal and civil proceedings. Rigorous adherence to legal processes and to direct rules were the hallmark of an orderly society. He believed in the integrity of the legal system and was committed to the application of legal processes.

Somewhat later in 1789, Godard joined with the avocats Ange-François Pantin,[14] Jean-François Fournel—the prominent royalist avocat and historian of the Paris Bar—and Nicolas-François Bellard,[15] all registered with the Paris Parlement, in defending the rights of a farmer. The farmer, François Saron, was a simple laborer who needed to cross over property owned by the local parish in order for his animals to access a small parcel of land he owned. The property that he had to traverse belonged to a parish other than his own, and the municipality and residents of the parish which asserted ownership objected strenuously to Saron crossing over property

13. Ibid., no. 26, pp. 411–12.

14. Ange-François Pantin was an avocat who was registered with the Parlement in Paris in 1788. He served as "*bâtonnier*" (president) of the Paris Bar in 1825–26. He died in 1840.

15. Nicolas-François Bellard (or Bellart) (1761–1826) served as a royal prosecutor prior to the Revolution. He became a defender of many of those accused of various crimes following the August 10, 1792, riots, but then fled Paris during the Terror. He later became a conservative supporter of the Bourbon Restoration following the fall of Napoleon and once again became a prosecutor for the royal government. His collected works were published posthumously in 1828. See *Oeuvres de N-F Bellart*, 6 volumes (Paris: J.-L.-J. Brière, 1827–1828).

they perceived as being theirs. They claimed that Saron could pass over their property as an incidental matter, but that he could not derive any commercial benefits from such access. Godard appears to have played a rather minor role in this case and, in the press review of the pleadings, it was Pantin who was singled out for praise in his presentation of Saron's defense. However, in this case, Godard was once again on the side of the weaker party, defending a peasant against both a municipal government and the Church hierarchy.[16]

Later in the year, Godard took up the defense of a party in a rather sordid domestic legal battle. He defended a widow against the claims of a mistress of her late husband.[17] The deceased husband, Claude Aps, a jeweler, had married Louise Lambert in 1771. Together, during the early years of their marriage, they had a child. However, a number of years into the marriage, Aps met a younger woman, Anne-Françoise le Court, who served as the domestic to a "kept" woman—making le Court a doubly undesirable woman for a man of a certain social standing. Aps and le Court had four illegitimate children together (although Aps had recognized and, thereby, legitimized one of them). In 1783, Aps signed a document acknowledging an indebtedness to le Court in the amount of 1,200 *livres*, with a promise to "repay" the indebtedness in 1785. Aps died in 1786, never having repaid the alleged debt.

A couple months after Aps's death, the mistress, le Court, asserted a claim to the 1,200 *livres* and demanded payment of that amount from the very modest estate that Aps had left behind. Aps's widow asked the court in Paris to declare the indebtedness null and void as being a fraudulent gift from Aps to his mistress. The court concurred with the widow. The mistress then appealed the judgment to the Parlement. In the appeal, Godard provided the *Consultation* to support the principal brief filed on behalf of the widow prepared by Bienaimé, the priest-avocat with whom Godard had worked in the defense of Julien Baudelle.

The mistress's attorneys made four arguments in favor of her claim of entitlement to payment of the alleged debt from the balance of the estate. First, they reminded the Parlement that the debt had been evidenced by a notarial instrument, giving it a presumption of validity. Then, they claimed that even if the debt was really a hidden gift, it was a valid gift.

16. *Gazette des Tribunaux*, 1789, vol. 28, no. 32, p. 85.
17. *Gazette des Tribunaux*, 1789, vol. 27, no. 23, p. 356.

Third, they argued that, minimally, le Court was entitled to payment as damages for having been seduced by Aps. Finally, they asserted that she was entitled to the payment of the debt as a form of child support for the four children that she and Aps had together.

In response, Godard argued on behalf of the widow that the debt instrument did not recite that any actual payment had been made by le Court to Aps (or that he had provided any acknowledgment of receipt of such payment). He asserted that it was implausible that a servant of a woman of questionable reputation could have had the resources which she claimed to have lent to Aps. Godard went on to assert, with the same disdain for adultery that he had previously articulated in the 1786 divorce case, that a woman who had given herself, outside of marriage, to a married man was not entitled to any kind of dowry or other support. Such a form of support would, he wrote, violate French social policy. He rejected the argument that le Court's seduction by Aps entitled her to support, suggesting that a thirty-year-old woman of dubious character could hardly claim to have been duped into a relationship. Then Godard disposed of the argument that the illegitimate children were entitled to child support by indicating that, although French law (which he contrasted to Roman law, a system that completely dismissed claims of out-of-wedlock children) contemplated support payments to illegitimates, the law would not permit such payments to be made to the detriment of legitimate children. The Aps estate being very small, Godard suggested that any payment to le Court would effectively deprive the legitimate child of support from the estate of his father.

On the basis of Godard's arguments, the advocate general, Hérault de Séchelles, urged that the earlier judgment be upheld. Hérault's recommendation was adopted by the Parlement and on April 25, 1789, the appeal was dismissed. The appellant was ordered to pay fines and expenses. Godard had achieved a victory. Following this victory, the public prosecutor, apparently not fully satisfied with the favorable outcome that had been obtained, pursued le Court on a charge that she had falsified the baptismal certificate of the "legitimized" child.[18]

It is interesting to note Godard's strong support of conservative social mores in this case—a case which could not have yielded him fees of any significance. In his pleading, he seemed highly offended by the assertions

18. *Gazette des Tribunaux*, 1789, vol. 27, no. 23, pp. 359–61.

of a woman who must have appeared to him as a kind of prostitute or, as we might say today, a gold-digger. Although in pre-Revolutionary Paris morals were quite loose, especially among the bourgeoisie and upper classes, the French provinces remained profoundly conservative and Godard, a child of provincial Burgundy, articulated and promoted those predilections in his handling of this case.

During the course of the year, Godard was involved in two additional cases related to testamentary matters. One of the cases has a very contemporary ring, namely, raising the issue of the capacity of an elderly individual to execute a testament.[19] Godard represented a former avocat, Me. Bodasse, the maker of a will which was challenged by family members on the grounds that Bodasse allegedly did not have the required mental capacity to do so.[20] The limited description of the matter in the contemporary *Gazette des Tribunaux* suggests that Bodasse's capacity to act on his own behalf had previously been challenged and determined to be legally inadequate. However, Godard specified that the judgment of lack of capacity occurred only after the execution of the will in question, and therefore should not have affected the capacity of the individual in the making of his will.[21] The summary description does not indicate the outcome of the matter and, since the *Gazette des Tribunaux* ceased publication in 1790, the ultimate decision in the matter is not known. However, it is apparent that Godard, consistent with his respect for legal processes and personal liberty, must have made a compelling case that, absent an existing judgment deciding on actual incapacity, there was a presumption of capacity and of each individual's right to exercise personal choice.

In a second case involving a testamentary bequest, Godard represented a medical student, with the charming family name of Dance, who had been named as the beneficiary of a will whose provisions were being challenged by several members of the family of the decedent.[22] Godard defended the medical student against claims both of his lack of qualification to receive the gift and of undue influence on the testator. The brief entry in the *Gazette des Tribunaux* does not provide very much detail, nor does it indicate the outcome of the matter. Yet, once again, Godard was

---

19. *Gazette des Tribunaux*, 1789, vol. 28, no. 21, p. 331.
20. When addressed in French, avocats are referred to as "Maître," or "Master." The title is abbreviated as "Me."
21. *Gazette des Tribunaux*, 1789, vol. 28, no. 21, p. 331.
22. *Gazette des Tribunaux*, 1789, vol. 28, no. 6, p. 93.

representing the less-powerful party. Students of medicine were rarely in a strong financial position and it is possible to conclude that Godard wished to assist a person who had presumably neither resources nor power.

Considering the growing pressures on Godard in the months before and following the convening of the Estates-General, it is remarkable that he was able to handle so many complex and challenging legal matters simultaneously. However, the character of a young man eager for fame and fortune and anxious to become an important player in an increasingly agitated world is reflected in Godard's every move, and makes it much easier to understand why he was prepared to take on so many cases, even as he sought to augment his role in the increasingly turbulent political environment of the time.

CHAPTER 11

THE STRUGGLES OF THE JEWISH COMMUNITY

Far from the world where the young Jacques Godard was born, grew up, and began to develop his skills as an avocat as well as to undertake his struggle to succeed in competitive Paris society, a struggle of a very different type was taking form. The leaders of small Jewish communities within and on the periphery of the Kingdom of France were beginning their efforts to have their communities share in the promise of the Enlightenment. This was especially true for the leaders of the Ashkenazi Jews of France's northeastern region—a population of approximately forty thousand individuals—as well as for the modest group of some five hundred Jews living in the Paris region. Their push for recognition and equality in the decades leading to the French Revolution was the product of a deep desire to shed centuries of precarious existence punctuated by repression, discrimination, and physical abuse. These efforts to achieve equality, however, would not be uniformly endorsed by the Jewish communities nor by the entirety of their leadership, especially the religious leadership. Interwoven into the nascent desire for equality was a fear of losing some of the autonomy from which they had benefited for centuries. Also underlying that fear was concern that full civil integration would expose the Jewish communities to the risk of assimilation and a loss of the precious religious identity they had retained since exile from the land of their origins.

Another set of French Jewish communities, the predominantly Sephardic communities of Avignon, Bordeaux, Bayonne, and other towns and

cities in southern and, especially southwestern, France, had not suffered
quite the same indignities as their Ashkenazi brethren. These commu-
nities were composed largely of refugees from Spain and Portugal, who
had found relative safety in France after the expulsions of 1492 and 1497.
These Jews, a large number of whom were "Marranos" or "Conversos"—
Jews who had converted to Catholicism to escape the persecutions of the
Spanish and Portuguese Inquisitions and then gradually left the Iberian
Peninsula—had slowly over the course of generations returned to their
Jewish origins. But they had also integrated into their surrounding societies, achieving a level of prosperity through a range of commercial
activities. In addition, since the sixteenth century, they had been the
recipients of Patent Letters from various French monarchs that afforded them significant civil rights. Therefore, for these Jews, rather than a
pursuit for additional civil rights, their priority would be to preserve the
rights they had accumulated over the centuries. The divergences between
the Ashkenazi communities of eastern France and the largely Sephardic
or "Portuguese" communities of the south and southwest would lead to
major differences as the communities sought to find their place in the
new world created by the French Revolution. They would often find it
necessary to compete rather than to cooperate.

The plight of the ancient Ashkenazi communities had always been much
more dire than that of the Portuguese Jews. For hundreds of years, since
the time of the Roman Empire, small communities of Ashkenazi Jews had
existed along the west bank of the Rhine River valley and in areas extending
to its west and northwest, primarily in what are today the French regions
of Alsace and Lorraine. Especially beginning with the Crusades in the late
eleventh century, when large groups of soldiers inspired by the leadership
of the Roman Church marched across the region on their way to liberate
the Holy Land from Muslim domination, these communities had been
subjected to countless episodes of violence and anti-Jewish prejudice. The
Jews of these small communities had lived through a very complicated and
frequently miserable history from their very arrival.

Jews appear to have first arrived in eastern regions of what is today
France at the time of the Roman conquest of large swaths of Gaul.[1]

---

1. H. Graetz, *Popular History of the Jews*, vol. 2, "The Epoch of the Diaspora, The
Transition Period," Chapter 9, p. 473. See also A. Marignan, *Études sur la Civilisation
française, vol. 1. La Société Mérovingienne* (Paris: Librairie Émile Bouillon, 1899), 62.

Although initially small Jewish communities lived in relative peace and security throughout western Europe, with the fall of the Roman Empire and the ever-increasing authority of the Roman Church, anti-Jewish regulations began to appear and were imposed with alarming regularity. A seemingly endless series of onerous, discriminatory, and restrictive laws and rulings emanated from every center of power in the lands that would become France, creating powerful legal precedents against the treatment of Jews as equal subjects of the region's rulers. Legal restrictions, echoing powerful religious prejudice, would set the tone for the struggle for Jewish equality at the end of the eighteenth century, and it is not surprising that the battle to overcome these long-entrenched juridical constraints would require tremendous effort.

Among the earliest laws targeting Jews was an edict of the Frankish King Childebert in 535 or 540 (mentioned in the writings of the Bishop Gregory of Tours) which prohibited Jews from appearing in public between holy Thursday and Easter Sunday, thereby keeping Jews out of sight of Christians during their holiest holidays (and perhaps also preventing violence against them due to the virulently anti-Jewish liturgy of those holidays). Childebert's decree further denied Jews the right to have any Christian servants.[2] By means of an edict issued in 614, Clotaire II, another early Frankish king, prohibited Jews from taking any public action (such as enforcing their legal rights in contractual disputes) against Christians.[3] At approximately the same time, the Council of Paris prohibited Jews from exercising any public function. Then, in 629, the legendary King Dagobert purportedly issued the first of a long line of orders of expulsion which mandated that Jews either convert to Catholicism or simply leave his kingdom.[4]

However, Dagobert's edict notwithstanding, most Jews apparently chose to remain despite the precarious nature of their economic and legal situation. They then found themselves on a legal and social rollercoaster of sorts. Brief periods of peace and prosperity, during which Jewish communities could thrive, were succeeded by periods of repression and varying degrees of violence. With the onset of the Crusades, the relatively peaceful times came to a sudden and devastating end. The rabble that

---

2. Ibid., 476.

3. Achille-Edmond Halphen, *Recueil des Lois Décrets, Ordonnances, Avis du Conseil d'État, Arrêtés et Règlements Concernant les Israélites depuis la Révolution de 1789* (Paris: Au bureau des archives Israélites de France, 1851), vii.

4. Ibid., 478.

constituted and accompanied each of the several Crusader armies was filled with religious and anti-Jewish fervor. Since the Crusaders were on their way to fight the infidels in the Holy Land, why not kill or harm infidels along the way? The systematic violence that was inflicted on the small and isolated Jewish communities of the Rhine valley and adjacent territories by the various Crusades left a traumatic legacy of fear and distrust of the surrounding gentile world. This kind of mass violence and psychological trauma, which was reflected liturgically by countless *"piyyutim"*—Hebrew poems bemoaning the violence inflicted and the consequent martyrdom created—would not again be experienced by the Jews of the region until the twentieth century.

In spite of the difficulties of this early period, Jewish scholarship thrived in France with the presence of scholars of unparalleled quality such as Rabbi Salomon ben Isaac (better known as Rashi) and his sons-in-law and grandchildren (known as the Tosaphists).[5] Rashi's commentaries remain, to this day, among the most widely read of all writings about the Torah. In fact, some of Rashi's analyses (which include words in old French dialect), incorporated as commentary in the Talmud and written in a distinctive Hebrew script, serve not only to further Jewish religious studies, but also provide insights into the origins of the French language itself.

The accession, in 1180, of the Capetian King Philippe II (known in history as "Philippe Auguste") began a new phase of legal oppression of Jews that was to continue for generations.[6] By an Edict issued in April 1182 Philippe Auguste ordered the Jews to leave his kingdom within three months, confiscated their real property and made them sell their personal property. Since many Jews had for generations been engaged in making small loans to their Christian neighbors, in a move to use France's Jews to enhance his financial and political situation, Philippe Auguste then issued a second decree effectively canceling all his subjects' obligations to Jews. He also required that the debtors contribute twenty percent of the forgiven debts to the royal coffers. It has been suggested that the concept of letters of credit developed as a consequence of this Edict and of the attempt by Jews to preserve the value of their assets in France even as many of them were forced to leave.[7]

---

5. Graetz, *Popular History of the Jews*, vol. 3, 161–64.

6. Halphen, *Recueil des Lois Décrets, Ordonnances*.

7. Baptiste Capefigue, *Histoire de Philippe-Auguste*, vol. 1, 1180–1191 (Paris: Dufey, Libraire, 1829), 249, et seq.

Oppressive legislation would thereafter frequently focus on Jewish financial activities. Ostensibly, such legislation would be targeted at relieving Christians of the obligations they had incurred to Jews, but usually the object was to permit the monarchy to reap financial benefits and the Church to obtain prestige and power from the restrictions imposed on the Jews, and to make Catholic theology appear triumphant.

Philippe Auguste, who personally participated in the Third Crusade along with Richard the Lion-Hearted of England, actively continued his campaign to harass the Jews and to benefit from their distress. In September 1198 he readmitted the Jews into his kingdom, but heavily taxed their lending activities in order to reap as much profit from those activities as possible. The imposition of restrictive regulations continued, although curtailed by the ever-expanding financial needs of the king. In 1204, despite countervailing pressures, Philippe Auguste reached an agreement with his barons and the clergy of France that those who bought or sold goods and services from or to Jews would not be excommunicated. However, as a compromise and as a highly symbolic act, he ruled that the Church could excommunicate wet-nurses who nursed the children of Jews. Business relations could continue, but close personal interactions would be forbidden. On September 1, 1206, Philippe Auguste issued regulations that affected many aspects of the debt obligations contracted with Jews and the rates of interest. These were augmented by yet more stringent regulations in February 1218. The regulations, however, also prohibited all debtors from committing any violence against Jews, subject to payment of a fine to the king in the event of a violation.[8]

In November 1223 Philippe Auguste's son and successor, Louis VIII, adopted similar regulations. He issued an ordinance which declared that all interest on sums due to Jews would cease to accrue as of the date of issuance of the ordinance and that, in order to receive any reimbursement of such debt obligations, Jews would have to formally register their loans within three months. This registration requirement was a means of generating revenue for the monarchy since registration involved the payment of taxes to the royal authorities. It also increased the cost of the loans, thereby heightening resentment against the Jewish moneylenders.[9]

---

8. Halphen, *Recueil des Lois Décrets, Ordonnances,* ix.

9. Jacqueline Rochette, *Histoire des Juifs d'Alsace des Origines à la Révolution* (Paris: Librairie Lipshutz, 1938), 10.

In 1230, Louis IX, known to history as the righteous and spiritual
Saint Louis but who was infused with a deep hatred of Jews, began his
anti-Jewish efforts by formally prohibiting Jews from entering into any
debt instruments.[10] In 1254, the king relieved Christians of one-third of
their registered obligations to Jews and imposed yet additional restrictions on existing debt obligations. Then, later that year, in Languedoc and
Languedoil (essentially all of what then constituted France), Jews were
expressly prohibited from the practices of usury (effectively all lending at
interest), blasphemy, and magic, and it was further decreed that the Talmud was to be burned, with all Jews not in compliance with the decree
to be expelled from France. Expulsions, as well as dramatic and massive
book burnings, followed this decree.[11]

In approximately 1257, Louis IX ordered the restitution to debtors of all
usury "extorted" by Jews and the confiscation of all real property owned
by Jews, except for synagogues and cemeteries. Then, in 1269, he commanded that Jews wear a distinctive mark on their clothes (in conformity
with the orders that had been issued by the Lateran Council in 1215). The
steady deterioration of the French Jewish community's legal situation
continued unabated. The following year, Jews were effectively refused access to courts, with testimony of Jews against Christians being rendered
null and void. Obviously, such legislation once again made enforcement
of loan instruments extremely difficult.[12] A decade later, in 1280, Louis
IX's son and successor, Philippe III, who ascended the throne when his
father died in Tunisia as he was returning from the Eighth Crusade, issued a decree prohibiting Christians from working for Jews.[13]

There were, however, occasional hiatuses from the onslaught of restrictive legislation against Jews. Sometimes these respites were the result of the
ongoing struggle between the secular authority and the Church. Philippe
IV was among the French monarchs who, in the earlier years of his reign,
sought to assert royal authority over clerical authority. In 1288, as part of

10. Graetz, *Popular History of the Jews*, vol. 3, p. 308.
11. Halphen, *Recueil des Lois Décrets, Ordonnances*, xii. Interestingly and oddly,
Léon Halévy suggests that this decision to burn the Talmud was an enlightened
action because it contemplated the destruction of books rather than people
(as was, he suggested, the practice in other countries). Léon Halévy, *Résumé de
l'Histoire des Juifs Modernes* (Paris: Chez Lecointe, Librairie, 1828), 59.
12. Halphen, *Recueil des Lois Décrets, Ordonnances*, xiii.
13. Halphen, *Recueil des Lois Décrets, Ordonnances*, xiv.

his struggle, he declared that Jews could not be incarcerated on the request of any cleric without obtaining an order from the secular authorities. However, just two years later, in 1290, all the Jews of Gascony were expelled.

As Philippe IV continued his efforts to limit the power of the Church, he issued an edict prohibiting Church inquisitors from exceeding their jurisdiction by trying to address issues of usury and other allegedly criminal activities of Jews. He further prohibited the secular authorities from arresting Jews at the request of these religious authorities.[14] But then, in August, 1306, the king ordered the secular authorities to sell at auction all of the real property and personalty that had been confiscated from the Jews and to pay over the amounts to the king.[15] Following an altogether too familiar pattern, once again, in 1309, the king released all Christian debtors from their obligations to Jews.[16]

On August 22, 1311, Philippe IV, then in dire need of financial resources, followed the established pattern and expelled the Jews from his kingdom, with the attendant benefit of seizing the property the Jews were compelled to abandon or to sell at very substantial discounts. However, the exodus of the community rapidly led to economic distress. As a consequence, Philippe's successor, Louis X, by an ordinance issued in 1315, recalled the Jews to France. Pursuant to that ordinance, it was specified that Jews could lend money, but only at modest rates of interest. The ordinance also limited the amount of property, real and personal, that Jews could own, but it did allow them to own property and to carry on their religious practices. However, it reinforced the obligation that Jews wear a distinctive mark on their clothing—the same mark that had been imposed by the Lateran Council one hundred years before.[17] Shortly thereafter, Louis X's successor, Philippe V, authorized Jews to own residences.[18] However, yet again, in 1321, Philippe V expelled the Jews from France, ostensibly in response to the accusation that they had poisoned the fountains and cisterns of the kingdom.[19]

The situation of Jews living in proximity to France, and especially in Alsace and Lorraine, where Jewish communities were concentrated,

---

14. Halphen, *Recueil des Lois Décrets, Ordonnances,* xv.
15. Graetz, *Popular History of the Jews,* vol. 4, p. 1.
16. Halphen, *Recueil des Lois Décrets, Ordonnances,* xv.
17. Rochette, *Histoire des Juifs d'Alsace,* 12–13.
18. Ibid., 10.
19. Ibid.

remained precarious. The nature of the relationship of the Jews of the region to government authorities and especially to the medieval kings of France is perhaps best summarized by Theodore Reinach who wrote, in his history of the Jews of France, that the kings of France "treated the Jews like sponges which they would allow to inflate in order to better squeeze them at a given moment so as to benefit the treasury."[20] In addition, there were periodic and dramatic upsurges in violence, especially during the years of the Black Plague in the 1340s, when Jews, who seemed to suffer less from the plague than their Christian neighbors, were repeatedly accused of having poisoned wells. That violence reached a zenith in February 1349 on St. Valentine's Day, when the Jewish quarter of Strasbourg was assaulted by a mob (in spite of efforts by Church officials to prevent the violence) and over two thousand Jews were killed, including many who were taken to their communal cemetery and burned alive. (Today that site, in remembrance of the terrible massacre, is known as rue Brûlée or Burnt Street.)[21]

The cycles of expulsions and readmissions continued, with the Jews of France being viewed as more akin to expropriatable property than subjects. The King Jean le Bon, under great economic pressure related to the early phase of the Hundred Years' War with the English monarchy and in serious need of additional financial resources, recalled the Jews in 1359.[22] But in 1388, all of the Jews then living in Strasbourg (which was still not at that time a part of France and would not become so for some 280 years), who had slowly returned following the horrific violence of less than half a century previously, were expelled.[23]

The final official blow to the French Jewish community came in September 1394 when Charles VI ordered their complete expulsion from the Kingdom of France. Many of the expelled Jews settled as close to France as they could, predominantly in Alsace. Yet despite this definitive de jure expulsion, at considerable risk some Jews remained within very specific circumscribed communities inside France itself as well as on its immediate periphery. Not directly affected by the expulsion order, Jews remained in dozens of small towns and villages on the west bank of the Rhine River

20. Théodore Reinach, *Histoire des Israélites depuis l'époque de leur dispersion jusqu'à nos jours* (Paris: Librairie Hachette et Cie., 1885), 114.
21. Rochette, *Histoire des Juifs d'Alsace*, 31.
22. Rochette, *Histoire des Juifs d'Alsace*, 12–13.
23. Ibid., 40.

that were not then parts of France. These people were mostly very poor, living on the edge and barely making ends meet. Notwithstanding the financial and physical risk, some of the Rhine Valley Jews continued to engage in the long-time and risky Jewish practice of making microloans to their neighbors.

For hundreds of years after 1394, no Jews lived openly with any kind of government sanction in France. Yet, in spite of the official prohibition against the presence of Jews, small groups were tolerated in various eastern areas. In southwestern France, following the expulsion from Spain in 1492 and Portugal in 1497, some periodically received Patent Letters authorizing them to live in specified areas, such as in Bordeaux and its vicinity. These Jews were mostly Marranos who were not officially Jews (and were usually referred to as "New Christians") but continued to practice aspects of their Judaism in secret. They slowly returned openly to their Jewish traditions (without necessarily being officially recognized as Jews) and were generally able to acquire property and carry on their commercial activities with minimal hindrance. Some descendants of those Jews rose to prominence, including notably Michel de Montaigne, the great essayist (whose mother was a Marrano), and Nostradamus, the illustrious prognosticator, whose Jewish father, a physician, converted to Catholicism.

Despite the continuing official prohibition against the presence of Jews within France, Jews were sufficiently numerous in certain areas that, in 1615, the Regent, the Catholic-Italian Marie de Medici, saw fit to order their expulsion.[24] Excluded from the Regent's order were certain Jews living in Metz and in Bordeaux.[25] She appears to have issued her expulsion order as a kind of prophylactic measure to prevent the spread of a blasphemous religion she deemed incompatible with the religious monopoly of Catholicism, since, following the expulsion of 1394, officially no Jews were allowed to reside inside the French borders. The ordinance she issued specified that:

In order not to concede anything which could harm the reputation of the state and the preservation of the blessing that it has pleased God

24. Marie de Medici (1575–1642) was the widow of the assassinated and religiously tolerant Henri IV. In her role as Regent, Marie de Medici was acting on behalf of her son, Louis XIII.
25. Le Chevalier Bail, *L'État des Juifs en France, en Espagne et en Italie depuis le commencement du cinquième siècle de l'ère vulgaire jusqu'à la fin du seizième* (Paris: Alexis Eymery, 1825), 159.

to bring upon it, and, in light of the fact that we have been advised that, in contravention of the edicts and ordinances of our predecessors they [the Jews] have for a number of years surreptitiously expanded within a number of leagues of our kingdom, and being unable to suffer such impiousness without committing a very great fault against His divine goodness, which has suffered from a number of examples of common blasphemy, we have ordered that this be pursued and remedied as promptly as it will be possible for us.[26]

It could be argued that Marie de Medici's attempt to rid France of Jews was not personal but rather that it was a politico-religious act. She expressly allowed her physician, the Portuguese Jew Filoteo Eliua de Montalto (Elijah de Montalto),[27] to remain in France and, at his insistence, to openly practice his Jewish faith.[28] Since in order to practice his faith he needed a *minyan* (ten Jewish men), it would appear that, notwithstanding Marie de Medici's edict, a modest Jewish community, made up primarily of Portuguese conversos, remained discreetly active in Paris during her regency. Even in view of Marie de Medici's ordinance and her preference to keep France relatively free of Jews, the issue of the presence of Jews within the Kingdom of France was on the verge of becoming much more acute.

With the signing of the Treaty of Westphalia in 1648, which brought an end to the internecine religious conflict (Catholic versus Protestant) waged across Europe known as the Thirty Years' War, Alsace and, to some extent, Lorraine, were integrated into France (or came under the hegemonic control of the French monarchy). By the stroke of a pen, the very young king, Louis XIV, was now nominally the ruler of one of the larger concentrations of Jews in western Europe. As a consequence, sooner or later, France would have to face the issue of how to deal with Jews within the French nation. In an initial attempt to do so, Louis XIV issued Patent Letters on September 25, 1657, granting to the Jews of his new province of Alsace the same rights as those then possessed by the Jews of the nearby

---

26. Halphen, *Recueil des Lois Décrets, Ordonnances*, xxxii; cf. Rochette, *Histoire des Juifs d'Alsace*, 13.

27. See Michal Altbauer-Rudnik, *Prescribing Love: Italian Jewish Physicians Writing on Lovesickness in the Sixteenth and Seventeenth Centuries* (Jerusalem: European Forum at the Hebrew University, 2009), 21–29.

28. Richard Henry Popkin, *The Third Force in Seventeenth-Century Thought* (Leiden: Brill, 1991), 229.

German principalities (and, notably, those of the city of Metz).[29] Nearly thirty years after these Patent Letters were issued, Louis XIV would take one of the most intolerant actions of his reign, the revocation of the Edict of Nantes, the statute which granted to Protestants the right to reside within France as members of a tolerated religious minority.

Although the French monarchy seemed willing to accept the newly acquired Jewish populations with some degree of tolerance, with terrifying regularity the Jews of the region were subjected to individual and collective persecution, usually on the flimsiest of excuses. In 1669, the Jewish community of Lorraine (not yet French, but under the protection of the French monarchy) witnessed one of its members become entangled in a particularly egregious miscarriage of justice. The matter involved a dealer in animals named Raphaël Lévy from the town of Boulay. On September 25, 1669, Lévy traveled from his town to Metz (then home to the largest concentration of Jews in France) with his young son. The same day, a little boy from the neighboring town of Glatigny disappeared and was apparently killed by an animal in the forest nearby. However, the family of the boy somehow became aware that a Jew had traveled in the area, and alleged that the Jew, Lévy, had taken their son to Metz and killed him. On the basis of this patently false testimony, Lévy was condemned to be burned alive. After undergoing terrible tortures, during which he stoically refused to confess, he was publicly and brutally executed on January 17, 1670. An obvious and terrifying miscarriage of justice had occurred under cover of the authority of the state. Because of the extensive publicity given to this event, the horror of the matter left an indelible mark on the French Ashkenazi Jewish community for generations. Deeply affected by this and other acts of mistreatment, a strong feeling of hostility and injustice hovered over the relationship between the Ashkenazi Jewish community and its Christian neighbors.[30]

With the arrival of the eighteenth century, there began a slow, but uneven, process of reducing the oppressive legislation against the Jews and of modest integration of the Jewish community into the fabric of France. In 1743, for the first time, a Jew, Moyse Blum de Hoenheim, was able to

29. Moïse Ginsburger, *Cerf Berr et Son Époque: Conference faite à Strasbourg le 17 Janvier 1906* (Paris: Librairie Hachette), 6.
30. See Freddy Raphaël and Robert Weyl, "Les juifs devant leurs juges (1648–1792)," in *Regards Nouveaux sur les Juifs d'Alsace* (Strasbourg: Librairie Istra, 1980), 50–51.

become a major supplier to the French armies. It is recorded that he was an entrepreneur who provided "diverse equipment to the armies of the king [Louis XV] in Germany."[31] In order to carry on his supply business more effectively, he sought permission to open an office in Strasbourg and invoked the assistance of a local aristocrat in his efforts. Those efforts paid off and the city was ordered by Louis XV to permit Blum to establish his business office within the city walls. However, the authorization was limited solely to permitting Blum to conduct commercial activities and, most significantly, he was strictly forbidden from establishing a residence in Strasbourg. The prohibition against any Jew residing overnight within the Strasbourg city limits, a prohibition that dated back hundreds of years, remained, for the time being, inviolable.[32]

The pathway toward tolerance of Jews in the eighteenth century was also punctuated by occasional reversals. In 1750, a royal order required Jews to obtain passports in order to reside in France. This requirement subjected them to the kind of bureaucratic arbitrariness which made the lives of French Jews so precarious. The issuance of passports depended upon the cooperation of inspectors. If they refused to issue the passports, Jews were then subjected to potential arrest for failure to have the required passport, to be followed by ejection from French territory.[33] Periodic restrictions and special legislation against Jews would also take the form of targeted and onerous taxation.[34] Such taxes included impositions assessed against Jews in Alsace on kosher meat, the transportation of goods, the iron trade, access to water, and the right to pasture animals. Special permission, subject to the assessment of high fees, was required whenever a Jew sought to acquire real property (in those areas where such acquisitions were not outright forbidden). Discriminatory restrictions also included the stipulation that property acquired by Jews in repayment of a debt had to be sold within one year and a prohibition against Jews holding a mortgage on the property of Christians.

The impact of centuries of oppressive edicts and an overarching climate of antisemitism caused the situation of the Jewish communities

31. Warschawski, Max, "Strasbourg et les Juifs jusqu'à la Révolution," from *Histoire de Juifs de Strasbourg*. http://judaisme.sdv.fr/histoire/villes/strasbrg/hist/index.htm.
32. Ibid.
33. Rochette, *Histoire des Juifs d'Alsace*, 14.
34. Ginsburger, *Cerf Berr et Son Époque*, 6.

throughout eastern France to be, until the Revolution, characterized by uncertainty and discriminatory treatment. The Jews were effectively, if not juridically, limited to a narrow range of economic pursuits. They generally could neither own land nor manage ordinary retail businesses and they were excluded from the artisan guilds. As a consequence, the Ashkenazi Jews of the region could support themselves only through the performance of menial tasks or a modest number of specific commercial activities, including the sale of livestock and, notably, horses, peddling and dealing in second hand clothing and merchandise and, of course, microlending, which was invariably pejoratively characterized as engaging in usury.[35] The result was that many Alsatian peasants hated their Jewish neighbors without, however, being able to do without them.[36]

Given the difficulty of rural transportation in the Ancien Régime, most peasants had only sporadic direct contact with the town markets where Jews might participate as merchants of certain specific goods, such as animals. As a consequence, except for the gentile Alsatians living in the few villages with a significant Jewish population, where most Jews were extremely impoverished, the only Jews with whom most Alsatians might have any consequential encounter were the microlenders to whom they might turn, reluctantly, in times of dire need for cash, and the Jewish peddlers who might periodically pass through their town. With the variety of wares that he carried on his back for non-Jewish customers in the villages and the countryside, a Jew peddling goods became one of the most likely opportunities for interaction between Jews and gentile peasants. The peddler not only sold a modest number of goods, but he also brought news and acted as an intermediary in the marketing of peasants' crops. Setting out weekly on Sunday, with a sack full of goods carried over his shoulder, the peddler would go from village to village on a regular route for six days of the week, returning home only for the Sabbath.[37] Every aspect of this commercial activity and, for that matter, all commercial activity carried on by Jews, was fraught with risk both economic and physical.

---

35. See Zosa Szajkowski, "The Economic Status of the Jews in Alsace, Metz and Lorraine (1648–1789)," in *Jews and the French Revolutions of 1789, 1830 and 1848* (New York: KTAV, 1970), 152–201.

36. Georges Weill, *L'Alsace française de 1789 à 1870* (Paris: Librarie Félix Alcan, 1916).

37. Paula E. Hyman, *The Emancipation of the Jews of Alsace* (New Haven, CT and London: Yale University Press, 1991), 12.

For the inhabitants of the major cities of Alsace, where Jews were forbidden to live, contact was also infrequent. Until the Revolution, before
entering the major Alsatian cities Jews had to pay a tax similar to the tax
assessed on animals.[38] It is not difficult to imagine the humiliation felt
by these Jews, treated like livestock when they came to the major urban
centers to conduct commercial transactions. This was not dissimilar to
the manner in which slaves were treated in the American colonies, and as
they would continue to be treated for generations in the newly independent United States, where their movement across state lines was taxed "at
a rate not exceeding the average tax rate for all other imports."[39]

Humiliation was augmented in Strasbourg by the blowing of the
Grüsselhorn, a horn that was sounded daily at dusk to remind any
Jews in the city that they could not remain overnight and needed to
leave.[40] For centuries, this horn sounded from the platform at the base
of the cathedral's tower. Although it is not certain, the implementation
of the Grüsselhorn may have evolved from a desire to mimic the sound of
the shofar, the ram's horn blown by Jews notably on the two days of Rosh
Hashanah, the Jewish New Year holiday. It served to proclaim loudly and
overtly blatant discrimination against Jews, who were strictly forbidden
to reside or spend any extended time in Strasbourg.

Another onerous and humiliating special imposition on Jews was the
collective tax on the Jewish residents of the city of Metz, which, as noted,
until the early years of the nineteenth century continued to have the largest Jewish population in France. This tax, referred to as the "*Taxe Brancas*,"
was predicated upon a grant made by Louis XV in the earliest years of his
reign to the noble Brancas family, giving them the right to tax Jews living
within the city. The tax was both an economic burden and a stigma that
created deep resentment. The struggle against this humiliation would be

---

38. For a fuller discussion of the various special taxes imposed on Jews in France,
see David Feuerwerker, "The Abolition of Body Taxes in France" ["Les juifs en
France: l'abolition du péage corporel"] *Annales. Économies, Sociétés, Civilisations*
(1962), vol. 17, no. 5.
39. Richard Beeman, *Plain, Honest Men: The Making of the American Constitution*
(New York: Random House, 2010), 326.
40. The sound emanating from the Grüsselhorn was referred to as the "Juden-
blos" or "Jewish blast." For hundreds of years, this sound could be heard every
day at 8:00 p.m. throughout the city of Strasbourg. See Isidore Singer, & A. Ury,
Jewish Encyclopedia (1906 ed.), s.v. "Strasburg."

a battle all its own.

By the middle of the eighteenth century, the intellectual ferment that was taking hold of French elites helped to bring a new focus on the discrimination and humiliation inflicted upon the Jews, as well as on their generally impoverished condition, all with a special emphasis on the areas where Jews were concentrated, particularly Alsace, Lorraine, and the area known as the Three Bishoprics (the city of Metz and the region around it). As the Revolution approached, non-Jewish political leaders increasingly took note of the situation of France's Jewish population. Changing social and political attitudes also led Jews, especially the wealthier and better educated, to express a desire to bring an end to the centuries-old opprobrium and legal repression that they faced and, most importantly, to contemplate actions that might lead them to achieve that objective.

CHAPTER 12

INTEREST IN THE STATUS
OF THE JEWS GROWS

As French society steadily moved toward its revolutionary upheaval, the Jews of Alsace continued to suffer not only from legal discrimination but also from the resentment and disdain of their non-Jewish neighbors. Obviously, the religious and cultural differences between the Jews and those living in proximity with them generated substantial antagonism. The particularism of the Jews, their different religious practices, their dietary restrictions (which hindered much social interaction), and their strong intra-communal solidarity, as well as their persistent unwillingness to forsake their unique identity and assimilate, generated enormous distrust and dislike. Over the course of centuries of segregation, Alsatian Jews had developed many characteristics that went well beyond their differing religious practices. They spoke an Alsatian Yiddish dialect that sounded very foreign to their neighbors and limited their interaction with those neighbors. They also dressed in their own distinctive manner. Due to their generally extreme poverty, the status of their hygiene and the disorder in their homes left much to be desired (although that situation was likely not markedly different from the condition of their equally poor Christian neighbors).[1]

---

1. See generally, F. Raphaël, "Les Juifs et l'Alsace: Une Rencontre créatrice, une Rencontre douloureuse," in *Regards sur la Culture Judéo-Alsacienne* (Strasbourg: La Nuée Bleue, 2001).

The various factors that separated the Jews from their neighbors highlighted their apparent foreignness, making it relatively easy to see the Jews as being not only religiously different but ethnically differ-ent—essentially a separate nation. At a time when the very notion of a nation-state was still relatively amorphous, the label of "nation" could easily be attached to a group that seemed to live by its own rules and customs within the larger body politic of France. Thus, to most Alsatian Christians, the Jews in their midst were simply strangers who had to be reluctantly tolerated, but could never be absorbed or considered as fellow members of the same political entity. Also, many Jews did not in fact wish to integrate, preferring to live their separate lives awaiting an eventual return to their homeland in Palestine under the aegis of a long-delayed messiah.

Any of these circumstances could by itself have sufficed to alienate the Jews from their neighbors, but it is the role of a relatively modest number of Jewish microlenders, or in the popular parlance of the time, "usurers," that generated the greatest resentment from Christians. In an age when retail banks did not exist and the average Alsatian did not have many choices if he needed to borrow funds, the local microlender was virtually the only resource. In light of the Church's attitude toward lending at interest, frequently (although not by any measure always nor even necessarily mostly), the local microlender was a Jew. As a conse-quence, the Jew became the unremitting object of the anger spawned by the inevitable and unpleasant need to repay loans together with substantial interest.[2]

The anger and distrust that already permeated so many aspects of the relationship between Jews and non-Jews was further heightened by the usually very high interest rate that Jewish lenders charged for their small loans. Most loans were made informally, that is, without reliance upon notarized and registered legal documents, both to facilitate the making of the loans and to save on the very high costs involved in formalizing the loans. However, one of the consequences of that informality was dif-ficulty in enforcing repayment. Since the ability of the lender to recover his loan if the borrower defaulted was very limited, both because the bor-rowers frequently defaulted and because it was exceedingly expensive,

---

2. See Szajkowski, "The Economic Status of the Jews," in *Jews and the French Revolutions of 1789, 1830 and 1848*, pp. 151, et seq.

difficult, and, for Jews especially, risky to attempt to recover defaulted loans through reliance on legal proceedings, high interest rates served as compensation for an elevated risk—but they were deeply resented.

The profound anger and resentment toward the Alsatian Jewish community because of the lending activities of some of its members were dramatically aggravated in the 1770s by one of the region's great scandals.

Beginning in late 1777, the Jews of Alsace who engaged in lending suddenly came face-to-face with an unprecedented crisis. The marketplace of Jewish loans was inundated by counterfeit releases of outstanding loans (so-called *"fausses quittances"*). Since most loans made by Jews were documented only by simple contracts or IOU's, when a loan was repaid, traditionally, the lender would issue a *"quittance,"* a handwritten acknowledgment of repayment or release of debt. Suddenly, thousands of counterfeit *"quittances,"* or releases, began to appear and posed serious obstacles to Jews seeking repayment of loans they had made to Christian neighbors. These counterfeit releases were written and signed in Hebrew script, giving them credibility that would have been inconceivable had they been signed in the commonly used secular script with which Jews were mostly unfamiliar.[3]

This kind of activity was not completely new. Over the course of the eighteenth century there had been many similar, but small-scale, attempts by gentile debtors to escape from debt obligations to Jewish lenders. These efforts had caused extreme hardship to their despised Jewish lenders, but none had been on such a vast scale.[4] It has been suggested that thousands of counterfeit releases were issued at this time, although the actual number is unknown. Regardless of the precise number of these counterfeit releases, their presence in the lending marketplace had a tremendous impact on the entire region and caused significant hardship to a substantial number of Jewish microlenders.

This spree of counterfeiting and the conflicts it spawned as Jews sought to contest the false releases was accompanied by increasing acts of violence against the Alsatian Jews. In 1778, it was alleged that a plan had been concocted to kill Jews while they gathered in their synagogues for Yom Kippur (beginning on the evening of September 30 and continuing until

3. See Szajkowski, "The Case of the Counterfeit Receipts in Alsace, 1777–1789," in *Jews and the French Revolutions of 1789, 1830 and 1848*, 202–19.
4. See Szajkowski, "The Economic Status of the Jews," n355.

shortly after sundown on October 1).[5] Although the pretext of the agitators was a religious one—to rid the region of blasphemous Jews—the
plan was largely materialistic, namely, to liberate themselves from their
economic obligations to Jewish creditors. The notion was to intimidate
Jews and thereby prevent them from seeking recourse in the courts to
nullify the counterfeit releases.

Ultimately, the planned massacres did not take place, while the nul-
lification of the counterfeit releases did. Initially, some gentiles took
action to utilize the counterfeit releases by sending letters to their Jewish
creditors and ordering them to appear before notaries to acknowledge
that they had released their debtors. In some cases, Christians even
audaciously alleged that they had overpaid their Jewish creditors and
that the lenders would have to repay substantial sums. Most Jews refused
to respond to such summonses and then found themselves required to
initiate legal action in order to exonerate themselves.

The question of who actually caused this scandal has never been fully
resolved. It has been suggested that several Jews who had converted from
their religion were the instigators since the releases were written in Hebrew. Jewish apostates have wreaked havoc against Jews at various times
in French history, lending some credence to this theory. However, the
most convincing evidence points to a plot concocted by Alsatians and,
most probably, under the leadership and guidance of Francois-Joseph-
Antoine Hell, the bailiff of the town of Landser (just to the south of the
city of Mulhouse in the Haut-Rhin region).[6]

It is likely that it was, indeed, the very appropriately named Hell who
orchestrated the creation and dissemination of the counterfeit releases.
Various elements point plausibly toward Hell as the perpetrator or, at
least, the chief instigator, of the scandal. Hell was arrested on February

---

5. See *Lettre d'un Alsacien sur les Juifs d'Alsace à M. Reubell*, 15, et seq. (Paris: Imprimerie de Savy le Jeune, 1790). Cf. Veron-Reville, "Les Juifs d'Alsace sous l'Ancien
Régime, le Procès des Fausses Quittances," *Revue d'Alsace*, vol 15 (Colmar, 1864):
273–302.

6. François-Joseph-Antoine Hell (1731–1794) was an avocat who held various
local governmental positions in Alsace. He was actively engaged in a variety of
business ventures, some of which led him to borrow from Jewish lenders. Over
the course of his career, he demonstrated a virulent antisemitism. In 1789, he
was elected to the Estates-General from the town of Hagenau, just to the north
of Strasbourg, and became actively involved in revolutionary politics. He was
executed in the spring of 1794.

18, 1780 and taken to Strasbourg where he was incarcerated in the Citadel of that city. The Royal Intendant for Alsace interrogated him on February 26, 1780. Many counterfeit receipts were found in his house. Furthermore, it became known that he had allegedly bragged about his knowledge of Hebrew, which he had learned along with Latin and Greek. Apparently, he had at one time written a letter in Hebrew to Jewish leaders offering to defend them in a legal proceeding, but had been spurned.[7] Whether he was the guiding hand in this scandal or not, his abiding dislike of his Jewish neighbors and his desire to cause them harm is beyond question.[8]

The royal authority, under the impression that Jews and their lending practices were at fault, initially modestly intervened in this crisis (issuing Patent Letters on November 6, 1778, which proposed a period of time during which individuals who had submitted false receipts could withdraw them without incurring any legal penalty). However, the government quickly came to recognize that the perilous state of the Jews and the serious risk to public order were more urgent issues than any alleged abuse by Jewish lenders, even if its sympathies were clearly with the gentile peasants.[9] As a consequence, criminal proceedings were pursued against certain of the purveyors of the counterfeit releases, two of whom were hanged, several condemned to the galleys, and others banished.

Around the same time as the counterfeit release crisis two anonymous pamphlets with virulently anti-Jewish content appeared in Alsace and were widely disseminated. One was a single-page pamphlet entitled *Malédiction*, which contained the age-old accusation that the Jews had killed Jesus and further alleged that Jews were specifically authorized to deceive Christians.[10] The other was a pamphlet entitled *Observations d'un Alsacien* (Observations of an Alsatian), which was a blatantly anti-Jewish diatribe, and appeared to whitewash the dissemination of counterfeit

---

7. See "Mémoire sur l'état des Juifs en Alsace," in Chr. W. Dohm, *De la Réforme politique des Juifs* (Dessau, 1782), 235–46. Dohm points an accusatory finger directly at Hell, by describing him in detail, although never actually using his name, instead, referring to him only as "*le Sieur....*"

8. Szajkowski, "The Economic Status of the Jews," 208–14.

9. See Mainfroy Maignial, *La Question Juive en France en 1789* (Paris: Arthur Rousseau, 1903), 119.

10. *Malédiction* (Frankfurt, 1778); see Szajkowski, "The Economic Status of the Jews," 203.

releases, alleging that the claim that they were forgeries was actually un-substantiated.[11] The authorship of *Observations d'un Alsacien* has been, with much justification, ascribed to Hell. Beyond attacking Jews for their alleged usurious practices, it is a rehash of old prejudices, accusing Jews of being a deicidal people cursed by God, of corrupting morals, and of impoverishing hardworking Christians. These two documents served to further poison the atmosphere at a time when there was already a growing antagonism between Jews and their Christian neighbors and an increasing sense of uncertain and unwelcome change beginning to hover ominously over the conservative Alsatian region.

The rising resentment against Jews in Alsace was sufficiently worrisome to governmental authorities that the status of the Jews simply had to be addressed. Both the private sector and public authorities began to focus on the problem. In 1779, the "*Société des Philanthropes*" of Strasbourg, an association made up of well-educated private citizens, sponsored an essay contest seeking to address the question of how to improve the condition of the Ashkenazi Jews of Alsace. In spite of the stated objective of the contest, it actually appears to have been more focused on finding ways of eliminat-ing the problems allegedly created, not against, but rather, by Jews. Among the persons who submitted an essay was the liberal cleric Henri Grégoire.[12]

Grégoire's essay was entitled *Sur les moyens de recréer le peuple juif et partout de l'amener au bonheur* (On the methods of recreating the Jewish

---

11. *Observations d'un alsacien sur l'Affaire présente des juifs d'Alsace* (Frankfurt, 1779).

12. Henri Grégoire (1750–1831), usually identified as the Abbé Grégoire, was an ordained priest from the Lorraine region, who, even before the start of the Rev-olution, espoused universalist Enlightenment attitudes toward human rights. He was particularly interested in the plight of Blacks and Jews. He was elected to the Estates-General in 1789, becoming an important participant in the activities of the National Assembly and subsequently served as a member of the National Convention. Although he favored many of the policies that sought to reform the role of the Church in French life, he remained devoted to his religious calling. He continued in politics during the Napoleonic years and the Restoration. An early twentieth-century socialist historian described Grégoire in the following terms: "friend of Negroes and of Jews, the priest who made himself the apostle of toleration and, furthermore, the eloquent defender of the rights of people, the philanthropist who was almost alone in demanding the abolition of the death penalty." Letter of James Guillaume, October 29, 1900, in *La Révolution française: revue d'histoire moderne et contemporaine*, ed. A. Aulard (Paris: Société de l'His-toire de la Révolution, 1900), vol. 39, p. 466.

people and of everywhere leading them to happiness). Regrettably, no copy of this essay has survived, but in light of Grégoire's subsequent writings it can be assumed that the essay was an appeal for improving the status of Jews albeit as a prelude to and with an ultimate goal of persuading them to convert to Catholicism. The fundamental goal of the contest was not lofty but pragmatic—to find a means of stopping Jewish "usurers" from lending money to Alsatian peasants.[13]

In the midst of this terrible onslaught of anti-Jewish activities, in 1781, Alsatian Jews, through the intercession of the communal leader Berr Cerf Berr, appealed to the most prominent Jewish personality of the era, the German-Jewish philosopher Moses Mendelssohn. Mendelssohn, in turn, believing that it would be best to have a Christian write a defense of Jews, asked his friend Christian Wilhelm von Dohm, a high-level bureaucrat of the Prussian state, to write an appeal for Jewish rights.[14] In response, Dohm produced a two-volume work, *Über die Bürgerliche Verbesserung der Juden* (On the Political Reform of the Jews), which Cerf Berr immediately had translated into French and disseminated to the wealthy commercial classes and the intelligentsia.[15] Dohm strongly advocated for equality, arguing that "a Jew is more a man than he is a Jew," even though he suggested that because of their impoverished and unassimilated status it might take several generations before Jews could be fully integrated into society at large.[16] After being translated into French by the great mathematician Johann Bernoulli, as it circulated through the upper echelons of French society Dohm's book became yet one more building block in the construction of a new approach to defining the role of Jews and combating the prevalent popular view of Jews as a malevolent and unassimilable people.

In April 1781 the city of Strasbourg, sensing that some change in the status of the Jews might be in the offing and eager to maintain its status

---

13. Alyssa Goldstein Sepinwall, *The Abbé Grégoire and the French Revolution: The Making of Modern Universalism* (Berkeley: University of California Press, 2005), 29.

14. Robert Badinter, *Libres et Égaux, L'Émancipation des Juifs 1789–1791* (Paris: Fayard, 1989), Chapter 2.

15. Apparently, Cerf Berr's efforts had only limited success since many of the copies of Dohm's book which Cerf Berr attempted to import into France were seized and burned. Ginsburger, *Cerf Berr et son Époque*, 15.

16. "*Le Juif est plus homme encore qu'il n'est Juif...*". Christian Wilhelm von Dohm, *Über die Bürgerliche Verbesserung der Juden*, trans. Jean Bernoulli, 35.

as a Jew-free city, filed a memorandum with the region's royal representative asserting that its anti-Jewish laws were the result of a need to protect Christians from Jewish usurers and should not be suppressed. This same argument was reiterated later that same year in a memorandum filed in support of maintaining the head tax on each Jew entering the city.[17] The elders of Strasbourg fully expected that they would be supported in their struggle against the Jews. Indeed, the military governor of the region, the Maréchal de Contades, and the Cardinal of Strasbourg (Louis-René-Édouard de Rohan, the individual who became a principal actor in the Affair of the Necklace and had Guy Target as his defense attorney) both generally concurred with the anti-Jewish position of the Strasburgers.[18]

However, the times were slowly evolving and the royal government's response was not what Strasbourg authorities had hoped to receive. Instead of acquiescing to the request, the government chose the classic approach of any government seeking to avoid having to reach a decision—it commissioned a study, in this case, a study of the Jewish demands. The report that emerged was prepared by François Nicolas de Spon, the long-time first president of the Sovereign Council of Alsace.[19]

A full report of the Commission headed by Armand Thomas Hue de Miromesnil, then the Minister of Justice, was submitted to the king on August 29, 1783.[20] The result of this maneuvering was the issuance by Louis XVI of a series of orders relating to Alsatian Jews. Initially, in January 1784, the king issued an edict which abolished some of the more obnoxious taxes that targeted Jews. In particular, it brought to an end the degrading tax which was imposed on Jews who entered the Alsatian cities and which seemed to equate Jews with animals. Strasbourg and other cities protested the loss of revenue but were ultimately required to

17. Szajkowski, "The Jewish Problem in Alsace," in *Jews and French Revolutions of 1789, 1830 and 1848*, 299.
18. Louis Georges Érasme de Contades (1704–1795) was a career member of the French military, who, in 1758, became a Maréchal of France. In 1763 he became the commander of all royal forces located in Alsace, a post he would hold until 1788. Through a liaison with a mistress, he was the grandfather of the prominent revolutionary avocat Marie-Jean Hérault de Séchelles, with whom Godard was associated in a number of matters, including in his important case involving the slave Julien Baudelle; as a result of their work the two developed a friendship.
19. Ginsburger, *Cerf Berr et son Époque*, 19.
20. Ibid.

comply with the edict.[21] Then, on July 10, 1784, the king had Patent Letters containing twenty-five articles published. Registration by the Sovereign Council of Alsace occurred shortly thereafter.[22] These Patent Letters represented a very mixed result for the Alsatian Jewish community.

As an initial matter, the Patent Letters sought to limit the number of Jews in Alsace. They called for the expulsion of all Jews without fixed residences and also introduced new, onerous, and humiliating regulations against the Jews already residing there. The letters also imposed severe restrictions on Jews seeking to settle in France, and forbade Jews from owning houses, except for personal use. Although the Patent Letters allowed Jews to own land and factories, they prohibited Jews from employing Christians, which effectively meant that Jews could not own and operate any large-scale businesses.

The Patent Letters of 1784 specified that rabbis were expressly designated to handle adjudication among Jews. Not surprisingly, the religious authorities of the Jewish communities were satisfied with this concept. This was not, however, the case with the secular leadership, since it made the prospect of legal equality for Jews more distant.[23] An already existing schism between Jewish religious leaders and secular authorities was now accentuated.

As a means of making business relations between Jews and Gentiles more difficult, the Patent Letters required that contracts between Jews and Christians had to be witnessed by two government officials—an expensive and detrimental obstacle to normal business relations. A prohibition against any payment from a Christian to a Jew in-kind rather

---

21. *Édit du Roi, portant exemption des Droits de péage corporels sur les Juifs, Du mois de janvier 1784. Enregistré le 17 du même mois* (Colmar, 1784).

22. *Lettres Patentes concernant les juifs d'Alsace* (Versailles, 10 juillet 1784. Reg. Au conseil supérieur d'Alsace le 26 avril 1785); See Abraham Cahen, "L'Émancipation des Juifs devant la Société Royale des Sciences et Arts de Metz en 1787 et M. Roederer," *Revue des Études juives, publication trimestrielle de la Société des Études juives*, vol. 1 (Paris, à la Société des Études juives, 17, rue St. Georges, 1880).

23. Jews had always had a very difficult time using the secular legal system in France. Over the course of centuries, Jews were systematically excluded from the legal professions and were discouraged from recourse to royal law courts. It was only "with the greatest repugnance that they were allowed to seek justice," and they had to do so in person since no avocat would "soil his words" by using them on behalf of a Jew. Jean-François Fournel, *Histoire des Avocats au Parlement et au Barreau de Paris depuis S. Louis jusqu'au 15 octobre 1790*, 109. Reliance upon the local religious courts of the Jewish community was frequently the only viable recourse.

than in funds was set out, presumably as a means of preventing payments that could not be readily calculated and which might serve as an indirect means of imposing high rates of interest on unsophisticated borrowers. Certain prohibitions against the right of Jewish women to benefit from laws establishing that individuals could own property separate from their spouse were promulgated, with a view to nullifying reliance on such separate ownership, especially if it could adversely impact Christians (presumably in the context of insolvency or bankruptcy).

Particularly offensive to the Jews was the newly instituted requirement, intended to limit the number of Jews in Alsace, that no Jew in Alsace could be married without the permission of the king. Finally, the Patent Letters instituted a requirement respecting the manner in which Jews, as distinct from all other Frenchmen, had to take formal oaths. The Letters required Jews taking such oaths to do so only in front of a Torah scroll within a synagogue. This method became known as the *More Judaïco* and was considered as particularly discriminatory since it made it much more difficult for Jews to testify in court and to assume public office. It would also be the longest-lasting of the discriminatory regulations imposed on Jews, surviving until struck down by the highest court during the July Monarchy of Louis-Philippe in the 1840s.

On August 26, 1784, the Patent Letters were acknowledged and registered by the Sovereign Council of Alsace and thereby became the law of the province. There is evidence that the Jews of Alsace retained an avocat, a certain Ignace-Frédéric de Mirbeck from Nancy, to act as their lobbyist in an effort to stop the implementation of the Patent Letters.[24] Mirbeck sent a letter to the Maréchal de Ségur, an Alsatian who was one of Louis XVI's State Secretaries, enclosing a memorandum objecting to various of the provisions of the Patent Letters and requesting the suspension of the implementation.[25] Ségur forwarded the memorandum to Miromesnil,

---

24. Ignace-Frédéric de Mirbeck (1732–1818) was an avocat who served for a decade as a legal advisor to the Polish King Stanislas Leczinski, in his capacity as the ruler of Lorraine. (Leczinski was Louis XV's father-in-law and Louis XVI's great-grandfather.) Mirbeck's service to the Alsatian Jewish community appears to have been a very short-lived matter. He is best remembered for his role as a commissioner appointed by Louis XVI to report on the revolt of Black slaves on the island of Hispaniola. His efforts at putting down the revolt through negotiations failed and the French sent troops to quash the rebellion.

25. *Mémoire de Me. Mirbeck, avocat pour les juifs.* Archives Nationales, K. 1142, cit-

the Minister of Justice. On October 14, 1784. Miromesnil rejected Ségur's appeal, noting, in a classic anti-Jewish diatribe, that Jews "in following what they call their laws could not fulfill precisely their obligations as subjects toward any sovereign."[26]

With the implementation of the Patent Letters, and the provisions setting out a limitation on the immigration of Jews into Alsace, it became necessary to ascertain the size and location of the Alsatian Jewish Community in order to have a baseline from which to enforce the Letters. The means adopted for achieving this objective was a census of the entire community, authorized by the *Conseil souverain d'Alsace* on September 1, 1784. Through the fall and winter of 1784 and 1785 royal census takers traveled throughout Alsace and sought to identify and count all the Jews they could find. The pending prohibition on allowing future Jewish immigration was intended to be a strong incentive for all Jews to respond to the census takers, who were able to identify and list approximately twenty-five thousand Jews living in Alsace. However, general distrust of the royal government likely led many to avoid the census takers, with the consequent undercounting of the actual number of Jews living in the province.

Nonetheless, the census, by providing detailed, albeit incomplete, information on the size and location of the Jewish community, gave new significance to this minority community whose demographic and economic importance could no longer be denied.[27] It also reinforced the need for a clearer legal status for all of these individuals now holding an official identity. The process for achieving this would be given the necessary impetus by the revolutionary fervor that would soon be sweeping over all of France and dramatically transforming French society.

---

ed in Philippe Sagnac, "Les Juifs et la Révolution française (1789–1791)," in *Revue d'Histoire moderne et contemporaine*, vol. 1, no. 1, 1899: 5–23.

26. *Réponse de Miromesnil au Maréchal de Ségur* (Versailles, November 15, 1784, Archives Nationales, K 1142, no. 60).

27. The results of the census were published in 1785 and the document became an especially useful tool for the study of the Jewish population of Alsace, both during the era and in subsequent times. Today, it continues to provide precious assistance to those engaging in genealogical research involving Alsatian ancestors. *Dénombrement Général des Juifs—Qui son tolérés en la Province d'Alsace, en exécution des Lettres Patentes de Sa Majesté, en forme de Règlement du 10 juillet 1784* (Chez Jean-Henri Decker, imprimeur juré du roi & de nosseigneurs du Conseil souverain d'Alsace, 1785).

CHAPTER 13

WRITINGS ABOUT JEWS AND
JEWISH RIGHTS

The Enlightenment generally helped prompt consideration of greater tolerance for Jews. Some Enlightenment *philosophes* demonstrated an interest
in bringing Jews into the ranks of national citizens. The most notable
example was Montesquieu, author of the influential *De l'Esprit des Lois*
[The Spirit of the Laws], a treatise which had a significant influence on
the development of the American system of government, with its emphasis on a separation of government powers. Montesquieu was born and
lived much of his life on his family's property just a few miles south of
Bordeaux. Consequently, most of his encounters with Jews were with the
assimilated Portuguese Jews of his region, with whom it was undoubtedly easier for him to relate than with the more insular Ashkenazim.[1]

Certain *philosophes* were not so open to the concept of granting equality to Jews. Voltaire especially stood out for his dislike of Jews, which
seems to have been born both of his philosophical bent and his personal
encounters with Jews. Generally opposed to organized religion and in
particular to Christianity, Voltaire could not be expected to be favorable
to Judaism, the religion from which Christianity emerged. Furthermore,
Voltaire, as a hedonist, found Judaism's restrictive moral code highly unpalatable. But it is likely that it is the financial losses Voltaire suffered in
transactions involving Jewish financiers in London that most significantly

---

1. Arthur Hertzberg, *The French Enlightenment and the Jews*, 280–86.

colored his view.[2]

Other *philosophes*, such as d'Holbach and Diderot, were either luke-warm or, like Voltaire, hostile in their attitudes toward Jews. Judaism, as the founding component of the Catholic Church, simply could not be viewed very favorably by any of the atheist or deist *philosophes*. To the *philosophes* of eighteenth-century France, seeking to dramatically reori-ent Western thought, Jews appeared retrograde and superstitious, closed to the outside "enlightened" world and more a part of the old order than as potential advocates of the era's new thinking. As such, they were gen-erally considered ideological enemies rather than victims to be assisted.

Major European nations other than France, such as Austria, Holland, and England, initially appeared more open-minded toward Jews. In 1753, England actually adopted a bill in favor of the Jews, the "Jew Bill" of 1753. However, due to the unpopularity of the bill among the population at large, Parliament felt compelled to repeal it the following year—dramatically setting back the cause of Jewish equality in that nation. In Austria, in 1782, the Emperor Joseph II, Marie-Antoinette's older brother, promulgated an Edict of Toleration which granted limited rights to Jews. When enacted, the Edict stood out as an important first, albeit modest, step toward a grant of equality to European Jews.

Throughout the mid-eighteenth century, the champion and very symbol of the opening of Jewish ghettos in central Europe was Moses Mendels-sohn.[3] Of an unprepossessing physical appearance, Mendelssohn's

---

2. Ibid.

3. Moses Mendelssohn (1729–1786) was born in Dessau, a small town located be-tween Berlin and Leipzig, to an impoverished Jewish family. Although steeped in Jewish education from his earliest years, Mendelssohn rapidly absorbed secular learning as well. While serving as tutor for the children of a wealthy Jewish silk merchant in Berlin, Mendelssohn became acquainted with some of Germany's most notable minds. In particular, he struck up a friendship with the philosopher Gotthold Ephraim Lessing. As a result of that friendship, Mendelssohn was able to publish some of his early philosophical writings and became a celebrity in Berlin salon culture. Through his brilliance, Mendelssohn merged his profound under-standing of Jewish texts with a lively involvement in the intellectual secular world around him. Notably, he translated the Bible (the "Old Testament") into German using Hebrew script and thereby made it possible for less-educated Jews to be-gin to transition to the German environment around them. His contributions to Jewish tradition were very significant, as were those he made to Enlightenment philosophy generally. Although he is highly regarded in Jewish tradition, he is a

intellect and his ability to combine his Jewish erudition with an understanding of secular philosophy made him the most influential Jewish thinker of his era. His relationships with the Berlin intelligentsia began the process of changing the perception of Jews in the eyes of enlightened upper-crust society in Germany and, through the interaction between German and French intellectuals, in France as well. His influence on one of the leaders of the earliest phase of the French Revolution would have its particular impact on the achievement of Jewish civil equality.

Among those who, through a familiarity with Mendelssohn's life and writings, were led to focus on the situation of the Jews, Honoré-Gabriel Riqueti, Comte de Mirabeau, stands out.[4] Mirabeau was one of the more eccentric individuals to assume a leadership position in the years leading to the Revolution and in its first phase. He was the son of Victor Riqueti, Marquis de Mirabeau, a distinguished economist of the Physiocratic school. The Physiocrats favored laissez-faire economics, a stark contrast to the regulated, highly centralized French economy, and briefly gained favor at the beginning of Louis XVI's reign when Anne Robert Jacques Turgot oversaw the French economy for a short time.[5] The younger

---

symbol of the risks to tradition posed by assimilation. Mendelssohn's sons, Joseph and Abraham, became very successful bankers. Abraham ultimately converted, together with his children, to Lutheranism. Abraham's son was the immensely talented musical prodigy, Felix Mendelssohn, who became the most popular composer of his era, composing, among other works, a number of Christian-themed oratorios. By the end of the nineteenth century, few of the descendants of Moses Mendelssohn were still practicing Jews.

4. Honoré Gabriel Riqueti, Comte de Mirabeau (1749–1791). Brought up within an aristocratic family, Mirabeau, in spite of his explosive temperament, became a prolific and popular author on a wide variety of topics. When Louis XVI convened the Estates-General, Mirabeau was elected as a member of the Third Estate from two constituencies in Provence. He became a very popular orator for the cause of representative government and an early hero of the Revolution. However, after his death in the spring of 1791, it was discovered that he had been receiving funds from the king and queen to promote the monarchy, which severely tarnished his revolutionary credentials.

5. Anne Robert Jacques Turgot (1727–1781), a leading liberal economic thinker of his time, served for a short period (1774–1776) as one of Louis XVI's ministers with responsibility for the economy. Conscious of France's difficult economic situation, Turgot did not support French assistance to the American colonists. Powerful conservative forces opposed his liberalizing efforts and he was quickly forced out of office. Condorcet, the philosopher and lover of Godard's confidant,

Mirabeau, however, had little interest in economics. Initially, he had no interest in anything beyond the hedonistic pursuits of his tumultuous youth. His marriage to a Provençal aristocrat turned into a public farce as he flagrantly engaged in affairs with other women, squandered familial funds, and violently threatened perceived enemies. He was sent to prison multiple times and was even condemned to death for his reprehensible "abduction and seduction" of the young wife of an elderly aristocrat. As a result of his erratic comportment, Mirabeau's father, in a vain attempt to tame his son, had him imprisoned using a *lettre de cachet*.[6]

The younger Mirabeau spent years in a variety of prisons, including some time in the infamous Chateau d'If in the harbor of Marseille. Subsequently, he was imprisoned in the medieval dungeon of Vincennes, just outside Paris. These lengthy imprisonments did little to alter his behavior, but they allowed him to become well-read. He also became a recognized author, writing on a variety of subjects. Some of his writings had an erotic bent and one of his essays was, not surprisingly, in opposition to *lettres de cachet*. But, with the passage of the years, his interests became more sophisticated.

As the Revolution approached, Mirabeau's attention turned toward the pressing issues of the day, including to an effort to improve the lot of the Jews of France, and especially of the Ashkenazi Jews of the eastern provinces. His interest in the status of the Jews was triggered by a trip he took in July 1786 to Berlin, where he heard about the recently deceased Moses Mendelssohn's distinction as the first Jew in modern times to have achieved an intellectual equality with his non-Jewish peers and of having done so as an observant Jew.

Mirabeau decided to write and publish a book about the Jewish condition beginning with an analysis of Mendelssohn and some of his writings. In 1787, *Sur Moses Mendelssohn sur la Réforme Politique des Juifs* [On Moses Mendelssohn on the Political Reform of the Jews] was published in London and distributed in Paris. The book, which echoed the volume that had been written at the behest of Berr Cerf Berr by the German scholar Christian Wilhelm von Dohm entitled *On the Political Reform of the Jews*, was an odd compilation of disparate subjects. The book began with a lengthy and defensive retort to theological arguments

Amélie Suard, was one of his close friends.
6. See, for example, Edmond Rousse, *Mirabeau* (Paris: Librairie Hachette, 1891).

of Johann Caspar Lavater,[7] who had engaged in a public disputation with Mendelssohn and about whom Mirabeau had published a short pamphlet in German in 1786. After this convoluted and confusing first section, Mirabeau turned his attention to retelling Mendelssohn's life and accomplishments. At one point, Mirabeau cited Mendelssohn's position on religious liberty and noted that Mendelssohn's views had just been put into actual practice by the recently adopted constitution of the American state of Virginia (which Mirabeau, perhaps in a salute to the loose confederation that then existed in the United States, labeled the "Republic of Virginia").[8] Mirabeau conceded that this chapter on Mendelssohn was nothing more than a restatement of Dohm's earlier book, suggesting that he had included it to help publicize that volume.

The next section of the book was the heart of the matter for Mirabeau. Here, Mirabeau sought to indicate that the concerns about Jews were misplaced, that the anti-social behavior of which Jews had been systematically accused was the result of anti-Jewish actions and not of inherent Jewish flaws. The peculiar laws of the Jews, he asserted, were not obstacles to Jewish equality. As proof, he offered the example of Quakers (to whom he referred as "Quackers"), described as having principles inimical to those of the societies in which they live, but who had been accepted as full citizens.[9] He then asserted that no people had suffered persecutions as vile as those to which the Jews had been subjected.[10] He affirmed, echoing Dohm, that, if all the demeaning legislation against the Jews were

---

7. Johann Caspar Lavater (1741–1801) was a Swiss philosopher who achieved a high level of popularity in his time. He is best remembered for his odd pseudo-scientific belief in physiognomy, the study of facial characteristics in order to understand human character. Today, Lavater's theories have been totally discredited. However, in his time, Lavater's theories were known throughout Europe and were widely discussed. Those theories may have had an impact on both Godard and Hérault de Séchelles in prompting them to formulate their argument that, based upon his physical attributes, Julien Baudelle was not really of African ancestry and, therefore, not subject to laws regarding Black slaves. This is rendered more likely since Hérault de Séchelles visited Lavater in the summer of 1789 and, following that visit, wrote that he had never met anyone "who more closely approached perfection." Émile Dard, "Hérault de Séchelles avant la Révolution," 410.
8. Honoré-Gabriel Riqueti, Comte de Mirabeau, *Sur Moses Mendelssohn sur la Réforme Politique des Juifs* (London, 1787).
9. Ibid., 67.
10. Ibid., 73.

to be removed, then Jews would be reformed and would become useful citizens of their nations.

Mirabeau then turned his attention to the legislation adopted in England in 1753 in favor of Jewish emancipation, and its subsequent repeal due to widespread prejudice from the English population and the electoral concerns of British ministers. Mirabeau saw this failed effort as a lost opportunity, since, in his view, if left in place, the legislation would clearly have made the Jews of England more productive for the general good. It seems rather obvious that Mirabeau hoped to encourage his native land to follow the English experiment, and not to allow it to be reversed before its beneficial effects had been felt.

The last portion of the book was devoted to a refutation of Johan David Michaelis' anti-Jewish diatribes, which ascribed to Jews a particularism that was inimical to their integration into Western societies.[11] Michaelis was a prominent non-Jewish scholar of Jewish law, and his opposition to Jewish equality had been part of Dohm's motivation for writing his pro-Jewish book. Mirabeau seemed to believe that the defense of Jewish rights mandated an attack on Michaelis. He concluded his analysis of Michaelis's objections to Jewish equality by suggesting that, if it was true that Jews had certain practices that were an obstacle to a grant of equality, then it was necessary to begin immediately the process of reforming Jews so as to prepare them for equality's inevitable arrival. In this regard, Mirabeau was (unintentionally) anticipating the beginnings of the German-Jewish reform movement that would result in the rise of Reform Judaism, which would eventually come to dominate the American-Jewish community, but which is, to this day, only a marginal part of the French-Jewish community.

Mirabeau was among the earliest French political writers to turn his attention as comprehensively to the plight of the Jews as he addressed more general social change—and he would not be the last. Within just a few months of the publication of his treatise, other writers would provide important contributions to the dialogue about Jewish legal equality. As a consequence of these writings, interest in the place of Jews in enlightened French society was stimulated and would accelerate to a prominent

---

11. Johan David Michaelis (1717–1791), a German Protestant theologian, was a biblical scholar with a profound knowledge of Hebrew, even publishing a Hebrew grammar. For over forty years he served as a professor of Oriental languages at the University of Göttingen.

position on the already crowded French political agenda.

The steady crescendo of attention to Jewish matters in parallel with the political turbulence of the era added intellectual and philosophical interest to the debate surrounding the place of Jews in France. That intellectual curiosity assumed a particular prominence in 1787 and the years immediately following, especially in Metz, at the very moment when Jacques Godard was defending the Germans in the proceedings involving the two Jewish witnesses. In a classic French approach, the issue of the status of the Jews became the topic of a national essay contest—an exercise in theorizing about an issue of immense practical concern—sponsored by the prestigious *Société Royale des Sciences et des Arts de Metz* (Royal Society of Sciences and Arts of Metz).[12] This was the same academy which had given Godard's colleague Lacretelle its award just a couple of years previously and had given a second award that same year to the future revolutionary leader Maximillien Robespierre.

The Royal Society of Sciences and Arts of Metz was established in 1757 under the protection of the Duc de Belle-Isle, governor of the Three Bishoprics region—the northeastern area of France within which Metz is located. In July 1760 the Society was granted Patent Letters by Louis XV, which were registered with the Parlement of Metz on August 28, 1760. The charter enumerated in the Letters specified that the society was being created to promote progress in literature, science, and the arts, as well as to promote the prosperity of agriculture and industry, and to develop cultural relations with other entities having the same objectives. Furthermore, it was charged with the dissemination of the French language. Its motto was the single word *"L'Utile"* (the "Useful"), suggesting that its interest was focused on the realm of the practical rather than on purely theoretical concepts.

In 1785, the city of Metz, as noted, had by far the largest urban concentration of Jews in France, with some four thousand Jews living inside the city. Their living conditions were deplorable. Restricted to a small area, the limited housing available within this district led to drastic overcrowding,

---

12. Many French cities had similar academies. By the mid-eighteenth century no fewer than twenty cities could boast such bodies. Of course, the most prominent of the academies was the Académie Française, founded by Richelieu in 1635, and situated in the heart of Paris. A number of Godard's acquaintances were members of the Académie Française, notably Suard, Marmontel, and Target.

with its accompanying unhygienic conditions.[13] In addition, the Jewish community was required to pay annually the onerous *Taxe Brancas*. This tax, as previously noted, was based upon a right that had been sold to the Brancas family in the early eighteenth century to collect a tax on Metz's Jews. The tax was, obviously, deeply resented by the community and imposed a significant economic burden. Yet, in spite of the miserable conditions under which its members lived, the Jewish community formed an integral part of the fabric of the city. Jews and gentiles interacted with significant frequency and in a reasonably cooperative manner.[14]

On June 23, 1785, Rabbi Lion Asser, the venerated spiritual leader of the Metz Jewish community, died. Because of the prominence of the Jewish community and of the rabbi's reputation as a great scholar, Rabbi Asser's death was noted by the entire city, not just by his Jewish followers.[15] Within the Jewish community, mourning went on for a month (the *shloshim* period), with the gentile community observing the depth of anguish of their Jewish neighbors. Not entirely coincidentally, just one month after the end of the mourning period, on August 25, 1785, the Royal Society of Sciences and Arts announced that the subject matter for the essay contest of 1787 would concern the status of the Jews.

On September 1, 1785, the contest was officially announced in the local newspaper *Les Affiches des Evêchés et Lorraine*: "The Royal Society of the Sciences and the Arts of Metz...announces that for the Contest of 1787, it will award the Prize for the best Essay on the following topic:

---

13. Pierre-André Meyer, "Démographie des Juifs de Metz (1740–1789)," in *Annales de Démographie Historique*/Année 1993 (Paris: Société de Démographie Historique – E.H.E.S.S. 1993), 135–37.

14. Feuerwerker, *L'Émancipation des Juifs en France*, 54. See also Roger Clément *La Condition des Juifs de Metz sous l'Ancien Régime* (Paris: Imprimerie Henri Jouve, 1903).

15. Rabbi Lion Asser (1695–1785) was born Aryeh Leib Gunzberg in Pinsk, then in the Grand Duchy of Lithuania (today Belarus). By the age of thirty he had become the head of the Yeshivah in Minsk, but due to personality clashes he remained in that post but a short time. He then led a congregation in a small village near Minsk, where, in 1755, he authored an important treatise on Jewish law, entitled the *Shaagas Aryeh* [the Roar of a Lion]. He moved to Metz to become that community's chief rabbi in 1765. In Jewish history, in keeping with the tradition of identifying great scholars through their principal works, he is known as the *Shaagas Aryeh* and is considered to have been one of the leading Jewish scholars of his era.

"Are there means of making Jews more useful and happier in France?"[16] A few months later, on February 16, 1786, the *Mercure de France*, the journal that belonged to Charles-Joseph Panckoucke, Suard's brother-in-law, and which was edited by Suard himself, endorsed the merits of the proposed topic in glowing terms, stating that: "no academy has as of yet devoted its prize to so noble an objective."[17]

The enthusiasm shown by the *Mercure de France* was a reflection of the interest the French intelligentsia had in the topic. Note was taken that the very phrasing of the question carried within it certain assumptions regarding the role of the Jews. With the primary emphasis of the topic focused on how to render the Jews useful, it tacitly conveyed that they were considered as being basically parasitical. The matter of their happiness—a concern that rippled throughout Enlightenment thinking, including in the United States, whose Declaration of Independence, with its emphasis on the "pursuit of happiness" as an "unalienable human right," had elevated the human aspiration to a modicum of happiness to a primary position—appeared as the secondary issue.[18] The implication was that Jews were a liability to French society and needed somehow to be transformed into an acceptable presence both for the benefit of France and for their own benefit.

The essay contest generated some interest, prompting seven major submissions and several lesser writings. Nonetheless, in spite of the relatively large number of essays submitted, the committee charged by the Academy to review the essays and award the prize was initially dismayed by the submissions and declined to make an award. Pierre-Louis Roederer, an avocat with the Parlement of Metz, who served as spokesman of the committee, chose instead to provide additional guidance regarding the elements that the committee was hoping to find in the submitted essays and extended the deadline so contestants could provide revised texts and other potential authors could submit new essays.[19]

---

16. *Les Affiches des Evêchés et Lorraine*, no. 35, Thursday, September 1, 1785, p. 279, cols. 1 and 2.

17. *Mercure de France*, February 16, 1786, vol 130, p. 72.

18. Declaration of Independence of the Thirteen United States of America, July 4, 1776, 2nd paragraph.

19. Pierre-Louis Roederer (1754–1835), born in Metz, became an avocat following studies at the University of Strasbourg. In 1771 he was registered with the Parlement of Metz. He was a respected economist and historian and became politically

At the expiration of the additional time period, the Academy found itself still dissatisfied with the submitted essays and unable to decide on a
single winner. Speaking through its committee, the Academy expressed
its disappointment with the texts that had been submitted, indicating
that "all of the authors" had failed to achieve the Academy's objective
because they had all "better demonstrated the need for reform than the
means of achieving it."[20] Nonetheless, on August 25, 1788, the Academy
bestowed its prize on three of the submitted essays. Announcing the
awards, the permanent secretary of the Academy, Le Payen, summarized his assessment of the essays. He began by noting that "all of the
essays that we have received, with one or two exceptions, condemn our
prejudices against the Jews as being the first cause of their vices." But
he gave voice to the basic anti-Jewish prejudice of the times when he
characterized the "dishonesty" of the Jews as the vice "which revolts us
the most."[21] Nonetheless, he conceded that "When we reduce the possibility of their being honest: how would you expect them to be such?" He
then concluded magnanimously and optimistically, albeit patronizingly,
saying "Let us be just toward them so that they are such toward us, this
is the wish of humanity and of reasonable people; everything suggests
that the government has accepted this and will not tarry in realizing it."[22]

    The most significant of the prize-winning essays was authored by the
Catholic priest, Henri Grégoire, already by then a prominent spokesman
for victims of discrimination. Grégoire wrote eloquently on behalf of
Jewish equality in his essay, which he entitled *An Essay on the Physical,
Moral and Political Regeneration of the Jews*.[23] The essay was, as he readily
conceded, based upon a prior essay he had written and submitted in the
earlier contest of the "scientific" academy in Strasbourg, but which was

active at the time of the French Revolution. He remained moderate in his politics
and had to go into hiding during the Terror. He ultimately became a close adviser
to Joseph Bonaparte, Napoleon's older brother and sometime King of Spain. Although the governments of the Bourbon Restoration denied him any posts, he
was elected to the French legislature during the July Monarchy.
20. Feuerwerker, *L'Émancipation des Juifs en France*, 118.
21. "L'Émancipation des Juifs devant la Société Royale des Sciences et Arts de
Metz en 1787 et M. Roederer," *Revue des Études juives*, vol. 1 (Paris, à la Société des
Études juives, 17 rue St. Georges, 1880), 104.
22. Ibid.
23. Henri Grégoire, *Essai sur la Régénération physique, morale et politique des Juifs*
(Metz: Imprimerie de Claude Lamort, 1789).

lost when the Strasbourg academy was dissolved. However, it is clear from Grégoire's essay that the goal of his plea for equality, in spite of its eloquence, was the eventual conversion of the Jews to Catholicism. Grégoire assumed that this process would be a natural consequence of legal equality. He called upon his fellow Christians to extend their mercy to their Jewish brothers and, with that demonstration of lovingkindness, to entice them to relinquish their "abhorrent practices," commercial and religious. Effectively, in summary, he articulated the notion that it was necessary, presumably as an act of Christian charity, to "save the Jews from themselves and save society from the danger that they represented."[24] As an activist in the political turmoil of the years to come, Grégoire would be a powerful spokesman in the forefront of the battle for equality in the new order. However, despite his unflinching adherence to a philosophy of equality based on the notion of natural rights, after an initial active participation in the debate respecting Jewish rights in the summer of 1789 he would remain somewhat of a bystander in the ultimate legislative struggle for Jewish equality.

The second essay that secured a prize was written by a Protestant avocat, Claude-Antoine Thiéry,[25] from the nearby city of Nancy, another urban center with a comparatively significant Jewish population. Thiéry was restrained in his analysis and did not wield the rhetorical flourishes that Grégoire demonstrated. With his strained and convoluted writing style, he noted that when France admitted Jews within its borders it assumed the obligation to make them happy. He deplored the centuries of relentless persecution suffered by the Jews and ascribed their negative attributes to external constraints imposed on them by the societies in which they lived. In summary, he urged that Jews simply be permitted to carry on the activities that were allowed to others and expressed the belief that they would then, as a consequence, naturally flourish.

---

24. Yves Lemoine and Mignard Jean-Pierre, *Le Défi d'Antigone, Promenade parmi des figures du droit naturel* (Paris: Editions Michel de Maule), 136.

25. Claude Thiéry, *Dissertation sur cette question: est-il des moyens de rendre les Juifs plus heureux et plus utiles en France?* (Paris: Knapen Fils et Mme. La Veuve Delaguette, 1788). Claude-Antoine Thiéry (1764–18?) became an avocat in 1782 and was ultimately registered with the Parlement of Paris. He served for a time as a government commissioner for the department of the Meurthe of his native region.

The third prize-winning essay was the work of Zalkind Hourwitz, who identified himself in his essay as "a Polish Jew."[26] Hourwitz was born in a village near Lublin, apparently to an observant Jewish family. Although little is known about his early years, the mere fact that he would have left his Polish-Jewish world for the secular world of Paris suggests that he was something of an adventurer and had a rebellious streak. He appears to have been reasonably learned in Jewish tradition and law and sought in his essay to use his knowledge of Judaism to undermine the religious prejudices that prevailed against Jews and Jewish religious practices. However, he displayed a strong antipathy to rabbinic authority and leveled substantial criticisms at rabbis and rabbinic practices.

Hourwitz did not hesitate to ascribe the anti-social comportment of Jews to their oppression by their Christian neighbors. He was laudatory of his Jewish brethren, depicting them in very favorable terms. Rejecting the notion that Jews were inherently evil, he, instead, referred to them as being "the most peaceful, the most sober and the most industrious of all peoples."[27] In a demonstration of his knowledge of Jewish practices, Hourwitz did not shy away from noting the religious obligations and practices that set Jews apart from their neighbors, but he argued that none of those were obstacles to the Jews being happy and useful. Being a practical sort, Hourwitz went on to propose a ten-point plan intended to make Jews happy and useful and, even more important to Hourwitz, to cause them to become "honest."[28] His plan primarily involved giving Jews full access to all the benefits possessed by non-Jews, including access to secular education, the right to till the soil, and the liberty to pursue all commercial activities. Oddly, one aspect of his plan was distinctly in conflict with Jewish practices: Hourwitz urged that Jews be prohibited from speaking, reading, and writing Hebrew or any language using Hebrew characters (which would include Alsatian Yiddish, whose written form used Hebrew script). In keeping with his dislike of rabbis, he also urged severe curtailment of rabbinic authority "outside of the synagogue."[29] His regimen for Jewish improvement concluded with a ringing condemnation of moneylending, which he proposed be prohibited to Jews. Immodestly,

---

26. Zalkind Hourwitz, *Apologie des Juifs en Réponse à la Question; Est-il des Moyens de rendre les Juifs plus heureux et plus utiles en France?* (Paris: Gattey et Royer, 1789).
27. Ibid., 34.
28. Ibid., 36–41.
29. Ibid., 38.

he boasted that, if his program were adopted, all the bad attributes of Jews would disappear and be converted into positive traits. As he put it, "all of this evil will be changed into as much good."[30] Reinforcing his contrarian outsider attitude,[31] Hourwitz concluded by echoing Grégoire and proposing that granting liberty to Jews was "the best means of converting them to Christianity."[32] This statement may have assisted him in winning a prize from the Metz Academy, and perhaps in ingratiating him to certain French intellectuals—but it could not have won him many friends among his Jewish brethren.

Because of his knowledge of Hebrew—the very language he had proposed that Jews not be allowed to use—in early 1789, with the support of Malesherbes, with whom he carried on a sporadic correspondence on Jewish matters, Hourwitz managed to have himself named to the coveted position of interpreter at the Royal Library.[33] The eccentric, argumentative, and immensely resourceful Hourwitz would become an active patriot in the early days of the Revolution. In October 1789, in spite of his relative poverty, he pledged to give one-quarter of his modest salary to the Nation to assist in the reduction of the national debt. He also joined the National Guard. These acts helped to make him a symbol of Jewish devotion to the cause of the Revolution.[34] In late 1789 and early 1790, he would associate with Jacques Godard in the fight for Jewish equality, becoming an odd and anomalous exemplar of Jewish devotion to the cause of French liberty, bolstered by the prestige of his Metz prize and the importance of his position with the Royal Library.[35]

---

30. Ibid., 41.
31. Frances Molino, whose biography of Hourwitz is incisive and thorough, emphasizes this aspect of Hourwitz's character, noting that "in many ways Hourwitz cherished the role of the outsider; fitting in nowhere liberated him from many constraints." Malino, *A Jew in the French Revolution: The Life of Zalkind Hourwitz* (Oxford: Blackwell Publishers, 1996), 51.
32. Ibid., 72.
33. Ibid., 65.
34. *Le Courier de Versailles à Paris et de Paris à Versailles*, no. 99, par M. Gorsas, October 15, 1789, pp. 209–10; *Journal Politique de Bruxelles*, October 24, 1789, no. 43, p. 259; *Mercure de France*, November 7, 1789, vol. 137, no. 18, pp. 6–11.
35. *DISCOURS prononcé le 28 janvier 1790 par M. Godard, avocat au Parlement, l'un des représentants de la Commune, en présentant à l'Assemblée générale de la Commune, une Députation des Juifs de Paris* (Paris: Imprimerie de Lottin l'aîné et de Lottin de St. Germain, 1790); see, generally, Malino, *A Jew in the French Revolution*.

Although six other essays were submitted, none merited recognition. They were neither intellectually interesting nor constructive. Some contained outrageous or downright absurd proposals. A certain Nicolas Haillecourt, an avocat from Metz who spewed classic anti-Jewish venom in his essay, proposed that all Jews be immediately deported to "the deserts [*sic*] of Guyana."[36] Another, submitted by Dom Chais, a Benedictine monk from the northern city of Charleville, suggested that Jews should be required to become beekeepers and producers of honey and wax. This latter essay was charitably characterized by the Metz judges as "chimerical."[37]

All three prize-winning essays were subsequently published with the permission of the king, and were widely disseminated and cited in public discussions. The essays formed an important part of the political dialogue that was transforming French society and helped to herald the day when Jews would cease to be considered pariahs. Ultimately, it is Grégoire's essay that would come to be cited with the greatest frequency and sometimes even be considered as the true winner of the Metz contest.[38]

Beyond the attention brought to the Jewish issue by the Metz essay contest, the last years of the 1780s saw a great deal of intellectual ferment focusing on the status of the Jews. The government (through the studies conducted by Malesherbes) and some of the leading thinkers in French society turned their attention to this issue. Remaining at the forefront of advocates for Jewish rights in these years before the Revolution stood the firebrand orator Mirabeau, who would, most significantly, become one of the early outspoken opponents of the absolute monarchy and, in the first months of the Revolution, a proponent of the establishment of a national legislature.

---

36. Mainfroy Maignial, *La loi de 1791 et la Condition des juifs en France* (Paris: Arthur Rousseau, 1903), 93.

37. Feuerwerker, *L'Émancipation des Juifs en France*, 100–101.

38. Malino, *A Jew in the French Revolution*, 53. Even the usually very precise Arthur Hertzberg erroneously states without qualification that Grégoire's essay "won first prize" in the essay contest. Hertzberg, *The Jews and the Enlightenment*, 298.

CHAPTER 14

GODARD'S INITIAL ENCOUNTER
WITH JEWS

By the late 1780s, Jacques Godard had increasingly become known as an advocate for the oppressed, the persecuted, and the disadvantaged. He had also begun to take on some of the attributes of what we would today refer to as a professional "lobbyist" through his work with representatives of his native region of Burgundy and of other regions. He assisted, for example, in drafting certain *cahiers de doléances* (the petitions or memorials for redress of grievances that were prepared by the thousands in connection with the summoning of the Estates-General in 1789), one for the Catholic community of his neighborhood, and apparently another, for the community of Mazières-en-Gâtine in the *sénéchaussée* of Niort and Saint-Maixent.[1] This latter participation may well have been a direct result of his role in the Protestant marriage case, since the plaintiff Pierre Brisset had been from this region.[2] Godard's experience as a "lobbyist" combined with his willingness to undertake the defense of the less fortunate made him a desirable advocate for those seeking a place in the

---

1. In pre-revolutionary France, a *sénéchaussée* was an administrative subdivision. The closest Anglo-Saxon concept is that of the bailiwick, an administrative area overseen by a bailiff designated by a higher authority.

2. *Département des Deux-Sèvres, Cahiers de Doléances des Sénéchausées de Niort et Saint-Maixent et des Communautés et Corporations de Niort et Saint-Maixent pour les États-Généraux de 1789, publiés par Léonce Cathelineau* (Niort: Imprimerie Nouvelle G. Clouzot, 1912), 145.

rapidly evolving political situation. The growing restiveness of the Ashkenazi Jewish community and its efforts to join French society as equal
citizens would provide a natural opportunity for an alliance between that
community and Godard.

Godard's participation in the Metz case, which had revolved around
the testimony of members of that region's Jewish community, combined
with his physical proximity to the Paris Jewish community, seem likely
to have caused him to embark on one of the pivotal projects of his brief
career. The impact of his role in the Metz case (in spite of the fact that he
had been adverse to the interests of the Jewish community in that case)
cannot be underestimated since his defense of the Germans coincided
with the essay contest sponsored by the Metz Royal Academy. Godard,
through a kind of inadvertence and coincidence, found himself in the
middle of a matter involving Jews, in which he refrained from displaying
anti-Jewish sentiment, notwithstanding his representation in opposition
to Jewish witnesses. But it was also of obvious importance in reinforcing
the prospective bond between Godard and the Jewish community that,
beginning in 1788, Godard had been residing just a very short distance
from the area of Paris that had the greatest concentration of Jews (both
Ashkenazi and Portuguese). By reason of his residence, he was likely in
daily, even if only casual, contact with Jews. He was probably already
known to some of his Jewish neighbors as an excellent advocate.

Of course, just as Godard was developing his active law practice, dramatic change was altering many aspects of the social fabric of France. The
late 1780s marked the development of a ferment—so well described in
the exchange of letters between Godard and his cousin Cortot—which
would begin the process of reconfiguring every component of French
society. The Enlightenment shined brightly in France, energized in part by
the success, with French assistance, of the American colonists in battling
their British colonial masters and in establishing the first modern democratic society. At the same time, France was heading towards economic and
social paralysis. Combined with natural forces that brought terribly cold
weather and violent storms and their concomitant crop failures, financial
and political problems created the backdrop for revolutionary change.

The late 1780s also witnessed increasing momentum toward greater
religious tolerance, turning back a tide of intolerance unleashed by Louis
XIV in 1685. In that year, Louis XIV had revoked the Edict of Nantes.
The Edict, which had extended a measure of tolerance to Protestants,

had been issued by Henri IV in 1598, shortly after he had converted from Protestantism to Catholicism in order to ascend the French throne. His religious flexibility was best reflected in the statement ascribed to him (but likely apocryphal) that "Paris is well worth a mass." As a by-product of Henry IV's non-dogmatic approach to religion, the Edict had provided France's Protestant minority with a modicum of religious freedom. However, with its revocation, Protestants, who constituted some ten percent of the population of France, had been deprived of any civil status. Many left France to settle elsewhere, including in North America. Those who remained lived on the margins of society—tolerated, but not recognized as equal subjects of the nation. As such, they did not have a legitimate civil existence within the highly regimented order of French society. Unlike the Jews, however, they were not considered to be a separate "Nation," but merely a heretical religious sect. As a "Nation," Jews were alowed to have some of their own laws, to establish their own courts and to benefit from a certain amount of communal autonomy. Protestantism did not create any such structures and did not have such a status. The presence of so large a group of individuals of ill-defined civil status was simply an unsustainable situation in an enlightened society.

In 1785 one of Louis XVI's most senior advisors, the esteemed Chrétien de Lamoignon de Malesherbes, published an essay addressing the issue of Protestant rights entitled *Mémoire sur le Mariage des Protestans* [Memorandum on the Marriage of Protestants].[3] Malesherbes had for many years displayed an interest in bettering the legal status of Protestants. Although he had been a prominent government official during the latter part of Louis XV's reign, he was sent into political exile in the mid-1770s and retired to his estate south of Paris.There he spent considerable time studying the condition of French Protestants. In his seminal essay regarding Protestants, Malesherbes advocated granting them the same right to citizenship as all other residents of France, including the fundamental right to be included in civil registries at birth and at death. Since, officially, no French subject had the right to marry without the blessing of the

---

3. This 132-page essay was the first of two such memoranda that Malesherbes prepared. A second longer memorandum was prepared in 1786. The latter memorandum was published in London in 1787. "Ouvrages de M. de Malesherbes," in *Recueil des Discours, Rapports et Pièces diverses lus dans les séances publiques et particulières de l'Académie française 1840–1849,* part 2 (Paris: Firmin Didot Frères, 1850), 1307.

Catholic Church, he proposed that Protestants should be entitled to be married outside the Church.

On the heels of the publication of his essay, Louis XVI appointed Malesherbes to study the condition of the Protestants and to make recommendations to the government regarding their status. Malesherbes established a commission to analyze the situation and to propose a new approach to Protestants' civil status. Among the members of the commission was Guy Target, who, as the author of the brief in support of the Marquise d'Anglure, was recognized as a leader in the effort to address and resolve this issue. In fact, Target became one of the principal draftsmen of the report that was finally issued in 1787 and which recommended that Protestants become full-fledged citizens of France. The report was quickly followed by the submission of an edict that granted them significant civil rights. On November 17, 1787, Louis XVI issued his Edict at Versailles.[4] Its words, although patronizing to those who did not share the king's Catholic faith, gave hope that all non-Catholics could now aspire to become equal citizens. With the text of his Edict, the king appeared to fully open the door to that possibility. Louis XVI did not hide his hope that Catholicism would soon be the religion of all his subjects, including those Protestants to whom he was extending rights, but he recognized that this might not happen immediately and, therefore, he beneficently sought to offer citizenship to those who did not recognize the same religious "truths" that he professed:

> But while waiting for divine Providence to bless our efforts and carry out this happy revolution, our justice and the best interests of the kingdom do not permit us any longer to exclude from civil rights those of our subjects or foreigners residing in our empire who do not profess the Catholic religion.[5] A sufficiently lengthy experience has demonstrated that these rigorous ordeals have been insufficient to convert them: we must, therefore, not permit our laws to make them suffer unnecessarily merely by reason of the misfortune of their

---

4. *Édit du roi, [Louis XVI] concernant ceux qui ne font pas profession de la religion catholique dit aussi Édit de Tolérance"* [Edict of the king concerning those who do not adhere to the Catholic religion, also called Edict of Toleration] issued on November 7, 1787, and registered by the Parlement of Paris on January 29, 1788.
5. This reference to "foreigners" (*étrangers*) provided particular encouragement to Jews who were, legally, precisely considered as such.

birth, by depriving them of rights which nature does not cease to demand on their behalf. [6]

The issuance of this Edict marked a dramatic turning point in the history of religion in France.

Centuries of brutal struggles between the two principal branches of Christianity had now officially come to an end. Despite the tone of Louis XVI's Edict, this document and the political decision it symbolized represented an important step in the official recognition that Catholicism was not the only form of Christianity practiced in France.[7] Of course, the decision to integrate Protestants into the body politic naturally raised the issue of the status of that other religious group that stood on the margins of French society—the Jews. The text of the Edict itself suggested that all non-Catholics should now be integrated into French civil society. Jews were non-Catholics and were seemingly eligible to benefit from the tolerance accorded by the Edict. However, the term "non-Catholic" in the Edict was, in spite of the absence of any qualifier, presumed to apply only to those who professed a Christian faith other than Catholicism and, notwithstanding the specific reference to the contrary, to those who were already deemed to be citizens of France. Jews, especially Ashkenazi Jews, clearly did not fit into either category.

With but few exceptions (and, most notably, the modest number of Portuguese Jews living in southern and southwestern France), Jews were considered as members of a separate nation and therefore were not deemed to be "subjects" of the king, or citizens. Furthermore, the references in the Edict to Christian practices, specifically baptism, made it readily apparent to most people that Louis XVI's Edict could not be applicable to Jews. Nonetheless, early on, Adrien Duport, a member of the Paris Parlement, proposed that the benefits of the Edict on behalf of non-Catholics be extended to the Jews.[8] The request fell on deaf ears.

---

6. *Édit du roi, [Louis XVI] concernant ceux qui ne font pas profession de la religion catholique*, 2.

7. It has been noted that beyond granting long-sought rights to Protestants, the Edict constituted "the first breach made into the Catholic religion's privileged role as the official religion of the kingdom." Michel Vovelle, *La Chute de la monarchie 1787–1792* (Paris: Editions du Seuil, 1972), 28.

8. Adrien Duport (1759–1798), a member of the Paris Parlement since 1779, was elected to the Estates-General in 1789 as a representative of the nobility from the city of Paris. However, as a member of the National Assembly, he became a

However, Louis XVI is believed to have been prompted by the request to ask Malesherbes to initiate a study of the status of the Jews of France. Although the story is probably apocryphal, the study was initiated after the king is alleged to have said to Malesherbes, "You have made yourself a Protestant, now I will make you a Jew."[9] Malesherbes began the process in early 1788, but by July 1788 was forced to curtail his activities because the general political turmoil proved distracting from all but the most essential aspects of government.[10]

During the course of his brief sojourn into the issue, Malesherbes assembled a commission headed by Target, Pierre-Louis Lacretelle (the elder Lacretelle), and Roederer,[11] and consulted with various Jewish leaders.[12] Following the establishment of the commission, the Portuguese Jews of the southwest hurriedly sent Malesherbes a memorandum of more than one hundred twenty pages in handwritten form divided into three sections. The first two sections set out the history of the Jews in Europe and in France. The last section was entitled "Views and wishes of the leaders of the Jewish Nation on the type of Constitution which the Jews expressly wish to have in France."[13] Although the memorandum advocated for Jewish equality, it also argued forcefully for the preservation of existing rights—rights which the Portuguese Jews had, but the Ashkenazim had never been granted.

---

strong advocate of rights for minorities. In 1791, he would be the individual who would submit for a vote the resolution that finally resulted in legislation granting Jews civil equality.

9. Léon Kahn, *Les Juifs de Paris pendant la Révolution* (Paris: Paul Ollendorff, Éditeur, 1898), 9. Likely equally apocryphal is the frequently cited story that Louis XVI was prompted to initiate the study of the Jewish situation as a consequence of having observed, while traveling in his carriage toward the royal palace, a Jewish funeral procession leaving Versailles to head to a distant Jewish cemetery. Concerned that the Jewish entourage would have to travel such a long distance to bury one of their dead, he was allegedly moved to help the Jews. There is no corroborating testimony or document that gives authenticity to this tale.

10. Feuerwerker, *L'Émancipation des Juifs en France*, 194.

11. Ibid., 162. Lacretelle had defended two Jews in Nancy some years earlier to significant acclaim and, of course, Roederer had served as secretary to the Metz Academy at the time of the essay contest respecting the situation of the Jews.

12. See ibid., 163, et seq.

13. "Les vues et le vœu des Syndics de La Nation Juive sur l'espèce de Constitution que les Juifs désirent particulièrement avoir en France." Feuerwerker, *L'Émancipation des Juifs en France*, 163.

Malesherbes organized meetings with representatives of the Jews. He met with a delegation of Portuguese Jews from Bordeaux, Saint-Esprit, and Bayonne, as well with individuals from the Ashkenazi community.[14] He appears even to have met with Zalkind Hourwitz, the Polish Jew who had been awarded a prize by the Metz Academy, to discuss approaches to the Jewish issue.[15] Because he was confronted not only by two very different types of Jews, but also by dramatically different requests from his several Jewish interlocutors, the meetings must have left Malesherbes perplexed. The Portuguese Jews, officially "New Christians" who already possessed through their Patent Letters most of the rights of French subjects, sought to prevent anything "which might harm [their] principal objective of protecting their corporation."[16] For the Ashkenazi Jews, who were devoid of most civil rights, the objective was dramatically different, and their presentation must have appeared as quite a contrast. Malesherbes' take on the subject and on the internecine disagreement among the Jews is unknown. The Malesherbes commission to study the condition of French Jews never completed its work, and its records, probably destroyed during the Revolution, have never been found.

As activities toward ending inequality based upon religion accelerated, leaders of the Jewish community were not sitting idly by, hoping that they might benefit from the obvious change in the political and legal climate. Both within the comfortable, assimilated, and well-established Portuguese Jewish community in the southwest, and in the much poorer and more marginalized Ashkenazi community of Alsace, Lorraine, and the Three Bishoprics, as well as among the handful of Jews who resided in Paris, Jewish leadership began an effort to capitalize on the dramatic changes sweeping over the country.

In Alsace, the battle for Jewish rights was led principally, as it had been for several decades, by one individual, Berr Cerf Berr, renowned as being the wealthiest Jew in France, with powerful connections within the royal government. Cerf Berr was born around 1726 in Medelsheim, a small town just a couple of miles north of the French-German border

---

14. Ginsburger, *Cerf Berr et son Époque*, 22.

15. Malino, *A Jew in the French Revolution*, 40–41.

16. Gérard Nahon, "Prospective des Portugais du Sud-Ouest de la France à la Veille de la Révolution," in *Politiques et religion dans le judaïsme moderne des communautés à la Révolution*, ed. Daniel Tollet (Paris: Presses de l'Université de Paris-Sorbonne, 1987), 94.

near Sarreguemines and but a few miles from the Grand Duchy of Lux-
embourg.[17] Presumably he adopted the word "*cerf,*" which means stag,
as the first portion of his surname because his Yiddish first name, Hirtz
(usually written as "Hirsch"), also means stag. His father bore the Hebrew
name Dov Berr and presumably from that name he took both his first
name and the second portion of his surname. His Hebrew name, which
he would have used in his religious life and which determined his secular
name, was Naftali Hertz ben Dov Berr.

Cerf Berr appears to have received a thorough Jewish education as
a child and to have remained profoundly observant of Jewish rituals
throughout his life.[18] It is told that at a meeting with Malesherbes, when
Malesherbes was working on his study of the Jewish situation, Cerf Berr
refused to eat, even though his Portuguese brethren seem not to have
had any particular difficulty doing so.[19] Early on, he left his hometown
and ultimately settled in Bischeim, a small town with a substantial Jewish
population located just to the north of Strasbourg. The place of his birth
and his move to Alsace resulted in Cerf Berr being given several different
monikers. He was alternatively referred to as Cerf Berr of Medelsheim,
Hirtz of Medelsheim, and Hirtz of Bischeim. History remembers him
most frequently as Berr Cerf Berr.

Despite the extent of his learning and personal skills, his ability to play
a significant role was ultimately the result of his considerable commercial
success. The Jewish communities of northeastern France had traditionally been involved in animal trading and, especially, the horse trade. Cerf
Berr, whose father already had some involvement in this commercial
activity, became immensely successful in horse commerce and became
an important supplier of horses and other military supplies to the French
royal armies. His services during the Seven Years' War were particularly

17. Ginsburger, *Cerf Berr et son Époque,* 4.
18. Ginsburger, one of Cerf Berr's early biographers, describes a scene where Cerf
Berr, having been granted an audience with the king at Versailles, assumed that
he had sufficient time to recite the prayers of the evening service in a corner of
the antechamber in which he was waiting, before the meeting. Suddenly, while
still engaged in his prayer, Cerf Berr was summoned to meet the king. He did not
budge and insisted on finishing his prayer. When he went to see the king, he presented his excuses for this tardiness by explaining that he had been "presenting
a petition to the king of kings, which had caused [his] delay." Ginsburger, *Cerf
Berr et son Époque,* 18.
19. Ibid., 22.

appreciated by the government. As a reward for his services, despite his membership in the "Jewish Nation," Cerf Berr was made a French citizen by Louis XVI in 1775 at the suggestion of Louis XV's former principal minister and Cerf Berr's friend, the Duc de Choiseul, "for services [rendered to the nation] and which he continues to render to Us, with as much zeal and intelligence as selflessness and honesty."[20] The two had become acquainted during the latter years of the Seven Years' War and their relationship can even be considered a friendship—a very unusual situation between an aristocrat and a commoner, and especially a Jewish commoner. However, Cerf Berr's prominence was such that, as early as 1765, he had become the *"syndic general"* (the official lay leader) of the "Jewish Nation" in Alsace.

Cerf Berr's commercial activities required him to travel frequently to Strasbourg, the center of all commercial activities in Alsace. But he could not live there. For all his wealth and despite his clear importance to the royal government, Cerf Berr, as a Jew, was prohibited from lodging overnight in Strasbourg. When the Grüsselhorn sounded, Cerf Berr, just like all other Jews, had to leave the city and find quarters elsewhere. The local authorities were vehement in the preservation of their prerogative to exclude Jews from a right of residency in their city, and Cerf Berr's importance to the royal government was of no consequence to them.

On August 5, 1767, as a result of having been stopped and robbed by brigands who regularly scoured the countryside of Alsace, Cerf Berr decided to petition the chief magistrate of Strasbourg for the right to rent a bourgeois house for the winter within the walls of the city and, most importantly, for the right to remain overnight in that house along with his family.[21] The authorities simply refused. Cerf Berr then turned to his friend, the Duc de Choiseul, at that time Louis XV's principal minister, to achieve his objective. On December 24, 1767, Choiseul intervened on behalf of Cerf Berr, by means of a letter sent to the city's chief magistrate, requesting that Cerf Berr and his family be allowed to live in Strasbourg. This was followed by a second letter sent on January 22, 1768, to the entire leadership of the city. The letters merely requested a right of temporary residence (*une résidence momentanée*), for which, the Duc suggested,

---

20. Patent Letters issued by Louis XVI in March 1775 and registered with the Parlement of Paris and Nancy and by the Sovereign Council of Alsace (on April 5, 1775). See Szajkowski, *Jews and the French Revolutions of 1789, 1830 and 1848*, p. 305.
21. Ginsburger, *Cerf Berr et son Époque*, 7.

simple humaneness should suffice as a grounds for acceptance.[22] In
February 1768, as a result of the intervention of the duke and Cerf Berr's
persistence, Cerf Berr was given the right to reside in Strasbourg along
with his family and servants, an entourage of approximately sixty people.
For the first time in centuries, a Jew had officially been given the right to
spend the night within the walls of Strasbourg.

But Cerf Berr had bigger plans. He was determined to become a property owner inside the city of Strasbourg and a permanent resident there.
Although property in Strasbourg would provide him with an important
convenience, it is clear that his desire to become a property owner there
was also an assertion of his rights, as a prominent citizen of France, to
benefit from all the rights that citizenship implied. As a consequence, in
1771, he made plans to buy the Hôtel de Ribeaupierre, a large residential
property in the Finkweilerstaden section (today's Quai de Finkwiller,
on the southern bank of the Ill River, which encircles the inner city).[23]
However, despite having received the right to rent a residence and to
reside overnight, Cerf Berr could not persuade the municipal authorities to grant him the right to purchase real estate in the city. Therefore,
he resorted to a legal subterfuge. He arranged to have one of his military
acquaintances, Charles-Joseph de la Touche, the former French Ambassador to the Prussian Court, act as his intermediary.[24] La Touche purchased
the property pursuant to a notarized deed, dated January 16, 1771. On the

---

22. Ibid., 3.

23. The Hôtel de Ribeaupierre is a large structure (today, bearing the address
9 Quai Finkwiller) fronting the River Ill. Originally, it had a wing that reached
south, making this a very large mansion that housed as many as sixty-five people.
It was substantially rebuilt around 1909, but remains an impressive building—
the largest of all of the surrounding houses. Currently, it is a school—the *Université Populaire* (formerly the *École Communale de St. Louis*). When purchased
by Cerf Berr it had a small "oriel" or circular protrusion (bay window) that gave
it an aesthetic and social importance. The Quai Finkwiller was well inside the
fortifications of Strasbourg at the time. It was far from both the Porte des Juifs
(the "Jews' Gate" on the northwest side of the city and rarely used by Jews) and
the Porte Pierre (on the north side of the city through which the largest number
of Jews passed on a regular basis—presumably from Bischeim and Haguenau).
The building is adorned by a plaque that notes it was owned by Cerf Berr and
describes Cerf Berr's role in Alsatian-Jewish history.

24. La Touche served as French Ambassador to Prussia in the early 1750s. *Recueil des Instructions données aux Ambassadeurs et Ministre de France depuis les
Traités de Westphalie jusqu'à la Révolution française*, vol. 16, Prusse. Paris.

same day, he immediately ceded the property to Cerf Berr, but pursuant to a private (that is, a non-notarized and, therefore, unofficial and, most importantly, unregistered) deed deposited on July 9 of the same year with a notary in the nearby city of Colmar.[25] Thus, although the private documentation expressly recognized that Cerf Berr was the actual owner of the property, the official records in Strasbourg indicated that La Touche was the owner. Cerf Berr, his family, and some servants moved into the Hôtel de Ribeaupierre, but nothing was said officially respecting Cerf Berr's title to the property.

When La Touche died in 1784, the city of Strasbourg sought to collect special death duties in respect of the Hôtel de Ribeaupierre since he was the owner of record of the property. Cerf Berr then made it known that he, and not La Touche, was the actual owner of the property. To provide proof, he produced the private deed conveying the property to him. The leaders of the city refused to accept the notion that a Jew (even an important Jew whom the king had made a French citizen with royal protection), could own property in the city—which had been officially closed to Jews for over four centuries. Undoubtedly, there was also significant resentment that Cerf Berr had attempted to circumvent the centuries-long prohibition on Jewish ownership of property by using a subterfuge. The city fathers began legal proceedings to deny Cerf Berr the ownership rights that he was asserting. The matter would never be fully resolved. The legal proceedings were still underway when the Revolution broke out and were permanently suspended without a judgment ever being rendered. In any event, the need for a judgment would be completely mooted by events in Paris.

Frustrated in his personal efforts to achieve the rights he sought, Cerf Berr steadily increased his actions on behalf of his fellow Jews in their efforts to achieve legal parity with their neighbors. He did not hesitate to use his great wealth to promote the cause of the Jews, especially once the Estates-General had been convened. As a consequence, he became an object of villification by Alsatian leaders. The leading Alsatian aristocrat, Strasbourg's Prince de Broglie,[26] characterized Cerf Berr as: "One of these

---

25. Scaramuzza, *Les Juifs d'Alsace doivent-ils être admis au droit de citoyens actifs, Lisez et jugez* (1790), 19–20.

26. Charles-Louis-Victor de Broglie (1756–1794) was a scion of the leading aristocratic family of Alsace. He served in the French force sent to fight in the American War of Independence. In 1789, he was elected to the Estates-General

Jews who has acquired an enormous fortune [and] has for a long time disbursed large sums in order to obtain protectors and assistance in this capital [Paris]."²⁷ Cerf Berr was then maligned by officials of the city of Strasbourg who claimed that he had allegedly provided poor quality wine for the local militia. None of the attacks against him deterred his efforts on behalf of his coreligionists. He would guide and presumably pay for the legal actions that would lead to Jewish equality. Jacques Godard would be the avocat, agent, and lobbyist in this endeavor, making it possible for Cerf Berr to accomplish a task that he himself could not achieve on his own.

---

from Colmar and Sélestat and then served in the National Assembly. He remained a fierce opponent of Jewish rights throughout his political career. His father emigrated from France and Victor chose to defend him. In the process, he began openly to express doubts about the violence engendered by the Revolution and as a result was denounced and brought before the Revolutionary Tribunal. Just a month before the end of the Terror, he was condemned to death and guillotined. His only son married Albertine de Staël, the daughter of Godard's acquaintance Germaine de Staël, herself the daughter of Necker, the Finance Minister, whose dismissal was the spark that set off the Revolution. The younger de Broglie became Prime Minister during the July Monarchy of Louis-Philippe, first in 1830 and again in 1835 and 1836.

27. M. Ginsburger, *Cerf Berr et son Époque*, 24.

CHAPTER 15

THE ROAD TO THE ESTATES-GENERAL

The same American war that had provided an impetus for liberalizing French society had also caused France to spend huge amounts of its scarce capital. The expenses incurred by the French nation in assisting the American rebels, together with decades of squandering and financial mismanagement, brought the government to the edge of bankruptcy. The limited ability of the French monarch to raise additional revenues, combined with a string of difficult winters that, as noted, severely diminished crucial crops and essential food supplies, made the crisis overwhelming. As Godard had discussed in his correspondence with his cousin, one of the few means available to the king to change the country's fundamental taxation structure was through a summoning of the Estates-General, the Assembly made up of representatives of the three principal social orders, whose convening Godard had so feared. The traditional approach to the mode of operation of the Estates-General, with equal voting power being given to each of the three social orders, appeared strikingly anachronistic, at best, to many in 1780s France.

Since, in 1787, the Third Estate consisted of some ninety-seven percent of the population, the prospect of summoning the Estates-General, in which the vast preponderance of the population and especially the rapidly growing and increasingly affluent middle class would have a mere third of the votes, was deemed profoundly offensive, especially to the effectively disenfranchised largest segment of French citizens.[1] Furthermore,

---

1. See Vovelle, *La Chute de la Monarchie 1787–1792*, p. 22, et seq. for an analysis of

the Estates-General was not a functioning entity. It had been summoned very infrequently in past centuries and not at all since 1614. The autocratic Bourbon monarchy had not considered it necessary to consult anyone concerning its governance since the regency following the assassination of Henri IV. Despite prior crises, for over 175 years the Bourbon kings managed to squeeze whatever revenues they needed from the French population without recourse to convening the Estates-General. However, the crisis that now paralyzed the country was far more serious than any of the straits in which the monarchy had found itself in nearly two centuries, and the summoning of the Estates-General was simply unavoidable. In preparation, every aspect of the Estates-General, including the selection process for its members and the manner of its actual operations, would have to be reviewed, refined, and implemented in the midst of a volatile political climate.

Reluctant to relinquish any power, the monarchy considered a variety of approaches to solving its ever-growing fiscal crisis. Attempts to find alternatives short of calling for the Estates-General did not bring about any reasonable solutions. In a final and vain attempt at avoidance, Louis XVI created and convened the Assembly of Notables, an ad hoc group of 147 individuals designated by the king, including seven so-called princes of the blood (senior members of the nobility), seven archbishops, seven bishops, six dukes of the old nobility, six dukes of the new nobility, eight senior military leaders, intendants, certain members of the Parlements and various high-level bureaucrats of the royal administration. Since the vast majority of the members of this Assembly were large-property owners, the Assembly was unremittingly opposed to any meaningful reform and, because of its ad hoc nature, did not have the legitimacy necessary for major structural changes. This last effort to avoid convening the Estates-General seemed doomed from the start.

The Assembly of Notables began its deliberations on February 22, 1787 but was simply unable to address any of the issues that were increasingly destabilizing the French government. It engaged in lengthy, but fruitless debate. By May 25, the very day on which the Constitutional Convention assembled in Philadelphia to create a new governmental structure for the newly independent United States of America, the Assembly of Notables was instructed by Louis XVI to cease its work because of unrelenting

---

the size of the three orders in 1789 and their constituent parts.

opposition from upper echelons of the nobility, including most of the members of the royal family. This last attempt to impose some reform without summoning the Estates-General had failed.

With a king who simply did not have the force of character, charisma, or intellectual agility necessary to impose his will on any of the principal players of his society (whether the high clergy, the most important members of the nobility, or the increasingly important bourgeoisie, with its large cadre of avocats), convening the Estates-General was now a necessity. However, the process was going to be both cumbersome and challenging. Since the Estates-General had last met in 1614, it was impossible to draw upon any recent precedents relating to such an assembly. Thus, not only was the very decision to call the Estates-General a difficult one for the monarchy, but it was also fraught with procedural challenges. Obviously, much had changed since the last time the body had assembled; the Enlightenment concepts of natural rights and the right to representative government had permeated French society. As a consequence, in anticipation of the now inevitable convening of the Estates-General, the power elites began to prepare for their role in the coming gathering.

Certain leaders of the city of Paris were particularly concerned about the influence they would wield if the Estates-General was ultimately convened. On December 18, 1788, 108 prominent Parisians preemptively issued a memorandum to the king, purportedly on the behalf of the residents of Paris addressing the manner in which the city should select its representatives to the Estates-General.[2] The issuance of the memorandum was not an official act, but rather a warning by a large group of self-selected prominent citizens indicating their intention to exert a maximum amount of influence in the process of selecting their representatives. The memorandum was accompanied by a relatively lengthy and analytical Consultation (the kind of legal opinion that usually accompanied pleadings by avocats on behalf of clients before the Parlement and which both Target and Godard had frequently authored). This particular Consultation bears the names of eleven prominent avocats, including Target and Lacretelle.[3] The

2. Charles-Louis Chassin, *Les Elections et les Cahiers de Paris en 1789*, vol. 1 (Paris: Jouast et Sigau, Charles Noblet, Maison Quantin, 1888), 79–101.

3. Target served at this time as a member of the reconvened Assembly of Notables, which had been recalled to provide guidance regarding the procedural

eleventh and last name on the *Consultation* is that of Jacques Godard, who, with his participation in drafting this document, marked the "official" beginning of his political career.

The memorandum and, in particular, the *Consultation*, represent both a lofty assertion of the rights of citizens to representative government and an attempt to find a practical application for this concept. The 108 Parisians, in their very brief memorandum, simply issued a request that the king consider the means and methods for assuring that they would have a role in the selection of their representatives to the Estates-General, and very specifically how they could be assured that past practices (in the convening of the assemblies of 1560, 1576, 1588 and 1614, at which representation of the city of Paris was severely limited) would be avoided.

In the *Consultation*, the avocats applied a legal analysis to the request of the petitioners, but also gave practical advice for the implementation of their request. First, they emphasized that, in order to benefit from a strong dose of legitimacy, the designated representatives would have to satisfy the elementary principle that they had been selected through the free choice of those being represented. They conceded that full democracy, a matter they identified as a "natural right," was practically impossible since Paris was simply too large a city to permit everyone to have a vote.[4] Asserting full participatory democracy as a natural right, they echoed the philosophy of Rousseau, which permeated much of the unrest that was motivating the political class of the time. The avocats, sensitive to the need to find precedent to buttress their argument, looked back with a careful eye at the actions of the kings of France in the most recent convenings of the Estates-General. They noted that, in every case, each of the relevant orders had called for assembling "all of those" within their order for the election of representatives.[5] They then alleged that the written precedent was, in fact, entirely consistent with natural law and, furthermore, that all the municipalities had followed this approach in the past, except for Paris, where the officers of the city had selected the representatives (and only a meager number of representatives, far fewer than proportional representation would have warranted).

---

aspects of the Estates-General. As an example of the absence of strict notions of conflicts of interest at the time, Target assisted in drafting a petition to the very Assembly of which he was a member.

4. Charles-Louis Chassin, *Les Elections et les Cahiers de Paris en 1789*, vol. 1, p. 90.
5. Ibid.

Speculating as to why Paris was excluded from the more equitable selection process, they suggested that it may have been due to the perception that Paris was simply too large a city to permit such participatory democracy. They then proceeded to deconstruct the argument and demonstrate that the claim that Paris's size mandated an undemocratic process was a vastly overstated issue. They noted, with some exaggeration, that Paris had roughly seven hundred thousand inhabitants, then systematically whittled this number down.[6] Half of the people were under the age of twenty-five and did not have the right to vote. Half of the remaining citizens were women (who were, obviously to them, excluded from any political role). Of course, those individuals so poor as to be "denuded of ideas and will power and incapable, in this instance, of participating in a public project" also had to be excluded. Finally, of those remaining, only those who actually paid taxes (of at least six *livres*) could be included. The final number of eligible electors was now down to a paltry fifty thousand. By dividing that number by neighborhoods, with each group to elect an assembly of two hundred, which in turn would each elect two representatives, the whole process would become, in the analysis of the avocats, fully manageable. Thus, the avocats concluded that full proportional representation for the citizens of Paris was entirely possible and rejected the notion that only the officers of the city of Paris, selected by the king, should "elect" the Paris representatives to the Estates-General.[7]

Godard's participation in drafting the *Consultation* on behalf of expanded representation for Paris was an important moment in his career. Although it is not known how much of the *Consultation* he actually wrote, since he was the youngest signatory it is probable that a considerable portion of the drafting was delegated to him. It is clear that Godard's inclusion in the group was a sign that he was well-regarded by his fellow Paris avocats. Furthermore, not only did it indicate that Godard had obtained the esteem of a large number of the political

---

6. Michel Vovelle, in his analysis of the French population in 1789, suggests that the population of Paris was only five hundred fifty thousand. (Vovelle, *La Chute de la monarchie 1787–1792*, p. 49.) That number appears to be on the low side. There is a general consensus that the population of Paris on the eve of the Revolution numbered between six hundred thousand and six hundred fifty thousand. See also T. A. Delaure, *Histoire Civile, Physique et Morale de Paris*, vol. 9 (Paris: Baudoin Frères, Libraires, 1825), 445.

7. Chassin, Les Elections et les Cahiers de Paris en 1789, vol. 1, pp. 91-92.

leaders of Paris, as well as of his peers, it also demonstrated that he had now aligned himself with those whose political principles were about to dominate the incipient societal turmoil.

Yielding to inevitability and despite his obvious trepidations, on January 24, 1789, the king finally issued a formal decree calling for the convening of the Estates-General.[8] In his decree, he specified that the deliberations of the Estates-General would be in keeping with tradition and would therefore involve a vote by Order. The meeting was designated as being an advisory one, intended to provide counsel to the king.[9] Most importantly, however, in the regulations accompanying his decree the king conceded that instead of the past practice of each Order having an identical number of representatives, in 1789, the Third Estate would be entitled to twice as many representatives as the other two Orders, without, however, altering the method of voting with one vote per Order.[10] This very modest concession would be the catalyst for much of the political maneuvering of the months to come.

In the United States, where a new Constitution had just been implemented—less than two weeks after Louis XVI's call for the convening of the Estates-General—on February 4 the Electoral College met to elect the nation's first president. George Washington's unanimous election initiated a period of remarkable stability that would stand in stark contrast to the turmoil that was about to engulf France.[11] A mere two weeks later, on February 19, 1789, Louis XVI sent out a letter to the various authorities, directing them to begin the process for the election of representatives.[12]

---

8. Godard was an enthusiastic supporter of the proposal to convene the Estates-General. He even made reference to his support in the brief he filed on behalf of Pierre Brisset in 1788. In the brief, he praised Louis XVI for his pending decision to do so, rhetorically asking: "and did not the beginning of his [Louis XVI's] reign announce all of the good of which we have already received a part & of which we will not delay in receiving the other, in this memorable Assembly which his royal word solemnly promises to the Nation?" *Mémoire pour Pierre Brisset*, 5.

9. *Règlement général du 24 janvier 1789*, in Armand Brette, *Recueil de Documents Relatifs à la Convocation des États Généraux de 1789*, vol. 1 (Paris: Imprimerie Nationale, 1894), 64–66.

10. Ibid., 612.

11. Washington would be inaugurated as first president of the United States on April 30, just days before the opening of the meeting of the Estates-General which would trigger the French Revolution.

12. *Lettre du Roi Pour la Convocation des États-généraux, à Versailles le 27 Avril 1789*

He wrote:

> We need the support of our loyal subjects to help us overcome all
> of the difficulties in which we find ourselves in relation to the state
> of our finance & to establish, according to our wishes, a constant &
> invariable order in all parts of the Government which are concerned
> with the happiness of our Subjects and the prosperity of our king-
> dom. For these major reasons, we have determined to convene the
> Assembly of the Estates from all provinces obedient to us, both to
> advise & assist us in everything that will be placed before its eyes,
> in order for us to know the wishes & grievances of our People; such
> that, by mutual trust, and by reciprocal love between the Sovereign
> & his Subjects, he will be provided as speedily as possible an effec-
> tive remedy for the problems of the state, and that abuses of all kinds
> will be reformed & prevented by good & solid means that ensure
> public happiness, and that provide to us, in particular, the calm and
> tranquility of which we have been deprived for so long. [13]

Elections for the representatives from the Third Estate to the Estates-
General were scheduled to begin on April 21. All males, whether born in
France or naturalized, aged twenty-five years old and above, who satisfied
at least one of a series of criteria were eligible to vote in their respective
"districts"—the jurisdictions that had been established in order to permit the selection of the electors.[14] The relevant criteria required that
the citizen (i) be the holder of a title to an official position, (ii) be the
recipient of a diploma from a recognized institution, (iii) hold a military
commission or evidence of an employment or (iv) be in possession of a

---

et Règlement Fait Par Le Roi, du 19 Février 1789. Paris: De l'Imprimerie Royale
1789. http://archive.org/details/lettreduroipourl_4.
13. Ibid.
14. Lacroix, Actes de la Commune de Paris Pendant la Révolution, vol. 1, p. v, citing
the minutes of the meeting. Lacroix emphasizes that the Districts were established purely for the purpose of electing the electors who would select the representatives of the city of Paris to the Estates-General, and, once that task had
been accomplished, it was expected that they would cease to exist. However, the
debates that went on during the electoral cycle gave an independent impetus
to the District gatherings, which became District assemblies. After July 14, 1789,
with the sudden disintegration of existing government structures, the District
assemblies, each constituted and functioning as it saw fit, found a new reason for
existence and continued to meet and deliberate.

receipt indicating the payment of taxes of not less than six *livres*. As proof of compliance, each prospective voter was expected to bring a written statement affirming that he satisfied at least one of the criteria. [15]

Once the voting had begun, it would continue for some days—days of political turbulence punctuated by acts of violence. In light of the tight schedule for the selection of the delegates to the Estates-General, a gathering of certain eligible electors took place on April 21 and 22 at the church of the Blancs-Manteaux. The church was a large and austere seventeenth-century edifice that then formed part of an important monastery founded in the twelfth century. (Today it is known as Notre-Dame des Blancs-Manteaux; the monastery that once surrounded it has disappeared.) The church is located on rue des Blancs-Manteaux, just a few dozen yards from the building on the same street where Godard had his office and residence. The gathering was chaired by its duly elected president, who was none other than Guy Target.

The minutes of the meeting were published in a special brochure.[16] Attached to the minutes, as part of the published brochure, was a nineteen-page alphabetical listing of those citizens residing in the Blancs-Manteaux neighborhood who were eligible to vote for representatives to the Estates-General. Godard's name, together with a reference that he was a resident of rue des Blancs-Manteaux, appears on page eighteen.[17] This suggests that Godard was likely in attendance at the extraordinary meeting. It also suggests that he may have had a role in drafting the minutes, which included specific instructions for the representatives being sent to the Estates-General. These instructions emphasized the local assembly's loyalty to the hereditary monarchy, and set out thirteen principles that had been adopted by a vote of the assembly. These principles related to instituting new freedoms, assuring an independent judiciary, affirming respect for persons and property and, in contravention of the expressed wish of Louis XVI, instituting a continuing role for a

---

15. Louis D'Haucour, *L'Hôtel de Ville de Paris à travers les siècles* (Paris: Giard & Brière, 1900), 390.

16. *Procès-verbal de l'Assemblée partielle du Tiers-État de la Ville de Paris tenue en l'Église des Blancs-Manteaux, le Mardi 21 Avril 1789 & le lendemain, sans désemparer,* and *Cahier d'instructions données par l'Assemblée partielle du Tiers-État de la Ville de Paris, tenue en l'Église des Blancs-Manteaux, le Mardi 21 Avril 1789, & le lendemain Mercredi, sans désemparer.* [gallica.bnf.fr]

17. Ibid., 18.

national assembly empowered to make laws, including specifically those relating to the imposition of taxes.[18] The instructions took particular note that the allocated time within which the election of representatives to the Estates-General was to take place was obviously extremely short. This had led to serious complaints among the members of the political class which were expressly stated in the Blancs-Manteaux District minutes and instructions.

Even at this preliminary stage on the road to the Revolution, Godard seems to have been assuming an increasing role in his local assembly, going beyond mere attendance at local meetings. One recorded indication of Godard's growing role arose almost simultaneously with the election of representatives to the Estates-General. The issue of how the three Orders would meet and deliberate at the Estates-General and, in particular, whether they would vote by Order or by head had been hovering over the summoning of the Estates-General since the idea had first been floated. This was the single most pressing issue facing both the government and those who were to participate in the meeting. As the prospective representatives to the Estates-General were being selected, efforts to address the issue were actively underway. The elected representatives of the Second Estate, the nobility, sought to engage in a dialogue with members of the Third Estate, and between April 20 and 23 representatives of the two groups met. Godard was designated as one of his Blancs-Manteaux neighborhood's representatives. The outcome of the gathering of nobles and commoners was inconclusive and Godard's role may have been purely symbolic, but the mere fact that the very young Godard was designated to represent his neighborhood marked an important step in his march along the road to a political role in the coming Revolution.[19]

Just days later, on April 28, the three hundred members of the Paris Assembly of Electors—the limited group of eligible male voters authorized to select the members of the Paris delegation to the Estates-General—met in the great hall of the Palace of the Archbishop of Paris, located just south of Notre Dame Cathedral along the banks of the Seine,[20] to select the

---

18. Ibid. 4–7.

19. Charles-Louis Chassin, *Les élections et les cahiers de Paris en 1789: Les assemblées primaires et les cahiers primitifs*, vol. 2 (Paris: Jouaust et Noblet, Maison Quantin, 1888), 221.

20. The Palace of the Archbishop no longer exists. It was attacked and burned by a mob in 1831. The ruins were demolished a few years later and, today, on the

members of its delegations from the three Orders. The Assembly selected Guy Target to act as its president. Target's prestige both as a former member of the Parlement and as one of the forty members of the Académie Française generated overwhelming support for his election. Jean-Sylvain Bailly, the scientist, who would play a pivotal and ultimately tragic role in the municipal politics of Paris during the years to come, was selected as secretary. Two additional members of the Assembly were selected as supplementary officers: an avocat, Armand-Gaston Camus, as vice-president, and a doctor, Joseph-Ignace Guillotin, as vice-secretary.[21] Dr. Guillotin, of course, came to symbolize the cruelty of the French Revolution because of the instrument of death which he advocated—paradoxically, as a means of making the death penalty less cruel and more egalitarian.

The Assembly of Electors then took care of various administrative matters, including the naming of commissioners who would officially count the votes of the several hundred Electors. Many of Godard's close acquaintances were among the commissioners: Marmontel, Suard, DeSèze, Panckoucke, LaCretelle and, of course, Target (although it was subsequently determined that Target could not be a commissioner and president simultaneously; eventually, he even had to give up his post as president to become a delegate to the Estates-General). The Assembly next turned its attention to reviewing the various grievances that had been submitted by the several districts. Then, finally, began the task of electing representatives. The electoral process was cumbersome and lengthy, extending well past the date of the opening of the Estates-General (with the official naming of all members of the delegation not occurring until May 22). Ultimately, the City of Paris sent a delegation of forty to the Estates-General—ten members of the clergy, ten members of the nobility, and twenty commoners, including LaCretelle. The Paris region outside the city walls also sent sixteen delegates. Target was elected as a representative of the Third Estate from suburban Paris.

Even as France prepared for the momentous event of hosting its first Estates-General in generations, the worsening financial crisis had put

---

site that the Palace once occupied, there is a public park and promenade along the Seine. Just behind that park sits the somber Memorial to the Deportation, commemorating the French victims of the Nazis and Nazi collaborators during World War II.

21. J.-S. Bailly and H.-N.-M. Duveyrier, *Procès-verbal des Séances et Délibérations de l'Assemblée des Electeurs de Paris* (Paris: Baudoin, 1790), 1–85.

the entire country on edge and outbursts of violence were common. This continued as the electoral process advanced. The worst of these violent occurrences took place on April 27 and 28, when employees of the Réveillon firm, a wallpaper manufacturer located in the Faubourg St. Antoine, began to demonstrate against their employer for having reduced their wages due to the economic crisis. Royal forces repressed the demonstration with incredible violence, leaving some two hundred dead and hundreds injured.[22] Soon thereafter, acts of violence began to take place in other French cities. These events fueled popular resentment against the monarchy—a resentment which was growing rapidly.

With the process of selecting representatives to the Estates-General and the drafting of memorials of grievances fully engaged, Jacques Godard remained preoccupied both with his active law practice and with addressing the turmoil that was captivating all of the Paris elites and much of France. Beyond his involvement in preparing the *Consultation* for the members of the Council of the City of Paris, in the months leading up to the convening of the Estates-General Godard had assisted various constituencies in writing *Cahiers de Doléances*. Target, Godard's principal patron, was also actively engaged in the increasing political activities taking place in Paris and in the neighborhood they shared. In addition to presiding over the local elections and securing his own election to the Estates-General, Target assisted the City of Paris in the preparation of its official *Cahier de Doléances*. Ultimately, over sixty thousand of these memorials of grievances were submitted to the king, and, of those, several hundred addressed issues relating to Jews.

Jacques Godard apparently gave some thought to entering the national political arena more directly by seeking election as a representative to the Estates-General. Early on, following the call for the Estates-General, he had indicated to his cousin Cortot that he was considering becoming a candidate, presumably from his home province of Burgundy.[23] But he did not follow through on this intention. He was not a member and there

22. Pierre Kropotkine, *La Grande Révolution (1789–1799)* (Paris: P.-V. Stock, Éditeur, 1909), 69.
23. Letter from Cortot to Godard of February 3, 1789, in which Cortot strongly criticizes Godard and sarcastically urges him to "add to the list that you spread out for me all of the peasants of our Burgundy whose votes you are going to attempt to secure." This is assuredly an allusion to Godard's suggestion that he might seek election from his native province to the Estates-General.

is no indication that he actually ever formally sought a seat. However, several of Godard's friends and acquaintances sought and won seats, in addition to his mentor Target.

The Jewish communities also swung into action in anticipation of the meeting of the Estates-General. With the primary goal being to ascertain whether they could participate in the process of selecting representatives to the assembly, the Jews began to organize. The Portuguese Jewish community of Bordeaux petitioned the Archbishop of Bordeaux, Champion de Cicé, for his assistance.[24] The Archbishop, a strong advocate for the liberalization of the French political environment, issued a ruling in favor of Jewish participation in the election process.[25] As a consequence, the Jews of Bordeaux joined in the gatherings to elect representatives, and one of them, David Gradis, came within just a few votes of being elected. In the city of St. Esprit, which had the largest Jewish community in the southwest, the Jews were treated like all other "non-Catholics" pursuant to the decree of 1787 and participated in the selection of delegates to the Estates-General. Ultimately, no Jews were elected, but Jewish concerns would nonetheless be addressed.

In Alsace, where the Jews continued to be considered a "nation" separate from the French nation, it was beyond imagining that they should be given the right to participate in the process of electing representatives. No Alsatian Jews sought election nor even participated in the process of electing representatives. Still, relatively early on, the leaders of the Alsatian Jewish community sought to have an impact on the deliberations of the Estates-General. Cerf Berr, in particular, made significant efforts to have Jews play a role in the gathering. On April 15 he wrote a letter to Jacques Necker requesting the right of Jews to participate.[26] When he did not receive a response to his letter, he turned to Louis-Pierre de Chastenet, Comte de Puységur, the Minister of War. Puységur, undoubtedly more aware than Necker of the important role that Cerf Berr had played in the

---

24. Jérome-Marie Champion de Cicé (1735–1810) was one of a number of prominent Catholic clerics who became major actors during the early phase of the French Revolution. He was named Minister of Justice by Louis XVI after the start of the Revolution and was one of the principal authors of a declaration of rights that would ultimately serve as the foundation for the Declaration of the Rights of Man and of the Citizen.
25. Feuerwerker, *L'Émancipation des Juifs en France*, 243–44.
26. Ibid., 282.

past in providing supplies to the French armies, was more responsive
and sent Cerf Berr's letter to Necker with a recommendation that Jews
be heard in connection with the convening of the Estates-General.[27] Ultimately, on April 23 the Garde des Sceaux (the Minister of Justice), Charles-
Louis-François de Paule de Barentin,[28] authorized the Jews of each of the
eastern provinces to gather together in their respective regions and for
each regional group to submit a *Cahier de Doléance* to the king, with the
instruction that the three then be combined into a single *Cahier*.[29] It took
some time to organize the gatherings of the Jewish communities and to
have them draw up the *Cahiers*.

The consolidated *Cahier* set out aspirations for "a lessening of [the]
suffering" of the three principal eastern Jewish communities.[30] All three
communities joined in expressing the desire to be recognized as equal
citizens and to be taxed in a manner similar to the taxation borne by their
fellow non-Jewish citizens (as distinguished from being subject to special
and onerous protection taxes); to have the right to carry on all trades and
professions; to own land and to live anywhere in France, but also to have
the right to carry on the practice of their religion, with their own rabbis,
lay leaders, and communal structures.[31]

In spite of the consolidation of the three *Cahiers* into a single document,
each of the three communities set out some specific concerns. The Alsatians asked for the right to have Christian servants for a period of twelve
years (ostensibly in order to learn various agricultural trades from them);
for the untrammeled right to marry (a right that was severely restricted
by the Edict of 1784), and for the prohibition of public officials from using defamatory language against the Jews. The Jews of Metz sought the

---

27. Ibid., 282–83.
28. Charles-Louis-François de Paule de Barentin (1738–1819) was a member of
the nobility of the robe, from a family of avocats. He served for a time as the
advocate general of the Paris Parlement. He succeeded Chrétien-François de
Lamoignon de Bâville as Minister of Justice. Louis XVI dismissed him shortly
after the taking of the Bastille and he was then tried for the crime of *lèse-nation*
at the criminal courts of the Châtelet. However, the charges were dismissed.
In 1790, he left France. He had planned to meet Louis XVI and his family in
Malmédy, when they sought to escape Paris. Shortly after that fiasco, he settled
in England, returning to France only at the time of the Restoration.
29. Henri Grégoire, *Motion en Faveur des Juifs* (Paris: Belin, 1789), 5.
30. Ibid.
31. Grégoire, *Motion en Faveur des Juifs*.

abolition of the Brancas tax and the right to share in the municipal assets of the city (such as the right to benefit from the municipal hospital). Finally, the Jews of Lorraine asked for a variety of rights, including the right to have synagogues, albeit in unmarked buildings. They also asked that their rabbis continue to have the authority to handle communal matters, such as divorces, the appointment of conservators for the young and elderly, and the resolution of disputes between Jews. Additionally, they expressed the wish that the age of majority for religious matters be maintained at fourteen [sic], but that in all other respects it be increased to the general age of twenty-five, that Jews have full access to high schools and universities, and that there be a financial test before a Jew could be authorized to settle in the Jewish community of Nancy (the major city in Lorraine) and in other cities and towns.[32] These requests were quite modest, but also embodied a certain ambivalence. The absence of consensus among the three communities suggests divergent and even conflicting views on the benefits of full equality and a profound skepticism about the prospect of achieving any kind of complete equality.

Once the Cahier had been completed, the six individuals who had drafted it headed to Versailles.[33] When the six Jews finally arrived in Versailles to deliver their *Cahier* and participate as the Estates-General began its deliberations, according to the virulently anti-Jewish (and anti-Grégoire) Abbé Lémann, the Jewish representatives stayed at the home of the Abbé Grégoire, where they waited to be given the opportunity to play a role as the Estates-General pursued its deliberation.[34] The wait would be a long one. The opportunity to engage with the Estates-General (by then the National Assembly) would not come for many weeks.

---

32. Ibid., v–viii.

33. The six are identified as being Gaudchaux Mayer-Cahn and Louis Wolf, from Metz, David Sintzheim (Cerf Berr's brother-in-law) and S. Seligman Wittersheim, from Alsace, and Mayer-Marx and Beer Isaac Beer [sic], from Lorraine. Ibid., v.

34. Lémann, *Les Juifs dans la Révolution française* (Librairie Victor Lecoffre, Paris, 1889), Chapter IV, Part II.

CHAPTER 16

THE ESTATES-GENERAL –
THE REVOLUTION BEGINS

On May 4, 1789, the elected representatives to the Estates-General met for a somber religious ceremony at the church of Saint-Louis in Versailles. The next morning the delegates assembled at 8:00 a.m. and, amidst great splendor, Louis XVI officially opened the proceedings. In this last major ceremony of the Ancien Régime and as a prelude to the dramatic and unprecedented political events that were about to unfold, nearly 1,200 delegates gathered in a great hall near the palace, interestingly named the Hall of Modest Pleasures (*Salles des Menus Plaisirs*). The room measured fifty meters in length, twenty-five in width and ten in height. The sides of the room were lined with columns and it was crowned with a barrel-vaulted ceiling pierced by a large oval glass oculus. At the front of the room was a dais with a highly decorated throne at its center. It was an appropriately impressive venue for the opening plenary session. Three adjacent rooms had been set aside to permit the three Orders to meet separately after the opening ceremonies. The building had originally been built in 1786, but was expanded and extensively renovated for the occasion. Inside the main meeting room, the elected representatives were seated on benches covered with blue velvet.

Due to delays in finalizing the election of the city's representatives, some members of the Paris delegation would miss the opening ceremony and would not join the Estates-General for some days. Once all the Paris delegates had been elected and had arrived in Versailles, they would discover that, among the representatives elected by the Third Estate, the largest group, some four hundred delegates, was composed of avocats. Many colleagues and friends of Jacques Godard were included in that group. Godard's friend and mentor, Guy Target, among the first to be elected to represent the Paris area, would soon play a significant role in the work of the gathering.[1]

At the opening session of the Estates-General, the delegates of each of the Orders were clearly distinguishable by the outfits they wore, which were mandated by royal authorities. The representatives of the First Estate, the Church, were dressed in their traditional ceremonial garb, cardinals in red robes and priests in black robes with white clerical bands. The nobles serving as representatives of the Second Estate were dressed in black outfits with elaborately embroidered gold trim, and wore black hats trimmed with white feathers. The members of the Third Estate were all dressed entirely in black—black shoes, black stockings, black waist-coats, black jackets and black hats.

The deliberations began with an address by the king. His remarks, which lasted about fifteen minutes, generally described the difficulties in which the nation now found itself. He spoke in broad terms, but began, as political leaders in any nation might have, by trying to place some of the blame on his predecessor and on circumstances he deemed to be beyond his control. In an effort to ingratiate himself to the liberal elements of the assembly, he also pointed to the costly, but successful, support for the American Revolution, which he referred to as "an honorable war," as being a principal cause of the looming crisis. But he then conceded that he was simply out of options. He concluded with a note of optimism demonstrating that he was clearly completely oblivious to the avalanche that was about to sweep away the old social and political order and with it many of the old prejudices.[2]

Once he had completed his speech, the king, along with other members of the royal family, left the meeting hall. The *Garde des Sceaux* (the Minister of Justice) then spoke for about an hour, appealing to the

---

1. Of the Paris delegation, seven members were prominent avocats: Target, Tronchet, Treihard, Camus, Martineau, Huteau and Samson (the then-president of the Order of Avocats). François-Étienne Mollot, *Règles sur la Profession d'Avocat* (Paris: Chez Joubert Libraire, 1842), 147.

2. *Ouverture des États-Généraux, Discours du Roi* (A. Strasbourg de l'Imprimerie Ordinaire du Roi, 1789), 3–6.

assembled delegates to remain loyal to the regime and to address only the issues of concern to the king. He provided guidance and a plea for unity, but his plea was laced with a not-so-subtle threat that the representatives had best comply with the king's instructions.[3] These remarks once again disclosed a complete failure of the monarchy to appreciate the depth of the simmering social crisis and an inability to foresee the violence that was about to be unleashed.

Finally, the principal speaker of the opening session, Jacques Necker, the very popular Minister of Finance whose friendship Godard had assiduously sought, spoke at great, even excrutiating, length. The duration of his remarks tested the endurance of even his most fervent supporters. For over four hours he (and when his strength gave out, one of his assistants) addressed in detail the country's dire financial problems and the steps which the king was prepared to take to confront them. However, Necker's remarks studiously avoided confronting fundamental political and social problems and did not propose any dramatic solutions to the financial challenges that were undermining the monarchy.

The tone had been set for a gentlemanly dialogue that would leave the king with the absolute authority to which he believed he was entitled and might result in the implementation of certain modest tax reforms to assist in replenishing the royal treasury. It would not take long, however, for the gathering to take a direction that was dramatically different from the expectations of the ruling clique. The principal focus would not be on the economic straits in which France found itself, but rather on the striking political inequalities that permeated French society.

By the second day of the great gathering, a deadlock respecting the procedures to be followed in deliberations had already developed. The king had commanded that each of the Orders should meet separately for the deliberations. The members of the Third Estate thought otherwise. With twice as many members as each of the other two Orders, the delegates of the Third Estate insisted that all the representatives meet together, with each representative to have one vote on all matters. Conflict was brewing. On May 7 the king prohibited the publication of any summaries of the proceedings of the Estates-General. On May 8, 1789, the electors of the city of Paris (who were not yet fully represented at Versailles) issued a protest against the order, which prohibited publication of the proceedings, as

3. Ibid., 19–21.

being a violation of liberty of the press and as preventing the direct dissemination of information assiduously sought by all of France. Actually, notwithstanding this gag order, information would seep out and become rapidly available in nearby Paris.

Under repeated instructions from Louis XVI, the three Orders were formally directed to meet separately to conduct the process of verification of their members' credentials. However, the representatives of the Third Estate, meeting in the main hall of the *Salle des Menus Plaisirs*, continued to insist, in direct contravention of the king's orders, that this process should occur in a single joint session of all three Orders together. Days passed in a deadlock, with the Third Estate refusing to bow to the wishes of the king and Court. By the time the complete Paris delegation had joined the gathering, the steadily escalating confrontation between the Third Estate and royal authority had already begun to cause a surge in violence on the streets of Paris. The insistence by the Third Estate that all three Orders meet together had initially been met by an outright refusal by most members of both the clergy and the nobility. Efforts were undertaken to break the deadlock. In the delicate negotiations between the Third Estate and the two other Orders, it was Guy Target who led the Third Estate's delegation of negotiators.

By early June, the Third Estate's efforts began to yield some results, with a few members of the clergy, mostly parish priests who came principally from the ranks of the commoners, deciding to join the Third Estate in the main meeting hall. On June 14 the Abbé Grégoire, one of the three winners of the 1787 Metz essay contest and a staunch supporter of Jewish legal equality, left the meeting of the First Estate and joined the Third Estate. The very next day another member of the clergy who had previously chosen to join the Third Estate, Emmanuel-Joseph Sieyès,[4] perhaps

---

4. Emmanuel Joseph Sieyès (the Abbé Sieyès) (1748–1836) was a Roman Catholic priest who became a political polemicist. He rose to prominence in the lead-up to the meeting of the Estates-General, when he published a tract entitled *Qu'est-ce-que le Tiers État?* [What is the Third Estate?]. He asserted correctly that the Third Estate constituted the essence of the nation, but that it was effectively deprived of all real power because of the antiquated structure of the Estates-General. The essay, which was assuredly the most widely read political tract of its time, was a significant component in the battle to alter the balance of power in the Estates-General and to provide political control to the rising bourgeoisie. He remained in the limelight for a generation, notably becoming a member of the Directory in 1799 and playing an active role in the coup d'état of

the most-acclaimed member of the clergy through his popular pamphlet entitled "What is the Third Estate?",[5] proposed that the representatives of the Third Estate, along with the members of the clergy who had joined them, now call themselves the *"Assemblée des representants connus et verifiés de la nation française."*[6]

After a couple days of debate, on June 17 the rump group adopted the name *"Assemblée Nationale"*[7] over the alternative name *"Representants du peuple français"*[8] proposed by the group's most prominent and popular orator, Mirabeau, the individual who, just two years before, had created a stir with his book advocating Jewish rights.

On June 20 the king, at the urging of the queen and of his brothers, sought to reverse the perceived insubordination of the Third Estate and proposed to address the Estates-General. When they arrived at the meeting hall that morning, the members of the Third Estate, accompanied by those members of the clergy and the few nobles who had joined them, were kept out of the area by workmen preparing the space for the gathering. The large group of representatives assumed that they had been intentionally locked out of the space by the king in retaliation for their refusal to comply with his instructions. Angry at being locked out of the hall and deprived of their usual meeting place, the delegates sought an alternative location. They ultimately gathered in an old indoor private tennis court which they found unlocked and unoccupied. There they selected the astronomer Jean-Sylvain Bailly to preside and resumed their deliberations under their new designation as the French National Assembly. Believing that the king was endeavoring to prevent them from meeting and resolved to keep meeting regardless of attempts by the monarchy to suppress their assembly, with only one dissenting vote the members of the newly named Assembly swore and signed an oath (known to history

---

Napoleon Bonaparte. He is considered one of the principal early revolutionary thinkers and political theorists and remained involved in governance through the Napoleonic era.

5. Emmanuel Joseph Sieyès, *Qu'est-ce que le Tiers-État?* (1789).

6. "Assembly of the known and verified representatives of the French nation."

7. The denomination *"Assemblée Nationale"* for the gathering of the Estates-General had actually been proposed many months before by Target in a pamphlet he had published in anticipation of the meeting of the Estates-General in early 1789. Guy Target, *Les États Généraux convoqués par Louis XVI* (1789), 24, 29, and 48.

8. "Representatives of the French people."

as the Oath of the Tennis Court) pledging not to disband until they had promulgated a constitution for France.

After some vacillation, Louis XVI reluctantly and tentatively bowed to the will of those who had gathered in the tennis court. He agreed to meet with all the members of the Estates-General to address the concerns articulated by those members who had declared themselves the National Assembly. At a meeting of all the members of the Estates-General on June 23 the king publicly appeared to accept certain of the National Assembly's demands. However, at the conclusion of his remarks, he instructed the members of the Estates-General to continue meeting separately according to their respective Orders and then demanded that all members disperse and go to their separate meeting areas. After the king had left the room, the members of the Third Estate and their clergy and noble allies, now the self-proclaimed National Assembly, refused to budge, announcing to the Marquis de Dreux-Brézé, the king's Grand Master of Ceremonies, in the memorable words of Mirabeau, that "only the force of bayonets" could persuade them to leave. Unwilling or unable to face the growing confrontation, Louis XVI resignedly acquiesced to the demand that the three Orders meet as a single assembly. With that hesitant concession, the king effectively gave France its first legislative assembly and provided an important impetus to dismantling the absolute monarchy.

By June 23 one hundred fifty members of the clergy had joined the self-proclaimed National Assembly, and just two days later, on June 25, some forty-seven members of the nobility had also joined them. Momentum had by now completely evolved in the direction of the efforts to create a constitutional monarchy with a strong legislature. On June 27, Bailly announced that a preponderance of the nobles had joined the National Assembly and that the events of the day had "rendered the family [the nation] complete; that it had ended forever the divisions which had mutually afflicted" each of the Orders.[9]

However, despite these events and the optimism that enveloped the members of the National Assembly, the king and members of his family were hardly convinced that they would have to relinquish absolute power. Without fanfare, the king summoned various royal regiments—mostly constituted of Swiss and other foreign mercenaries—from different regions of France and ordered them to station themselves near Versailles.

9. *Journal de Versailles*, Saturday, June 27, 1789, Supplement to no. 7, p. 54.

When the activists in the National Assembly and the people of Paris became aware of this movement of troops, they perceived it to be a direct physical threat by the king. This deployment of the troops added considerable stress to an already explosive situation.

Rumors began to spread through Paris that the king was preparing to violently repress the new exuberance. The regiments summoned by the king and gathered near the Royal Court, just outside Paris, appeared increasingly menacing to the activists, who determined to protect themselves against the royal forces. Their fear was somewhat assuaged by the National Assembly's decision to create a National Guard, a militia to be constituted of ordinary citizens eager to help ensure order and prevent a military action by the king's mercenaries. The common people were encouraged to join the National Guard, which was initially peopled by former members of the Royal Guard, and thousands did so. The Marquis de Lafayette, the acclaimed hero of the American War of Independence, was selected to be its leader. As people flocked to join the newly formed militia, many of the Jews of Paris signed on. Of the approximately five hundred Jews who called Paris home, it has been asserted that approximately one hundred joined the National Guard.[10] The willingness of the Parisian Jews to become a part of the local militia in such large numbers and the willingness of their non-Jewish neighbors to accept them as such would become an important asset in the legislative struggle for Jewish equality that would shortly begin.

Even as the prospect of a terrible confrontation with royal troops increased, the National Assembly, on July 9, officially renamed itself as the National Constituent Assembly. This new denomination was intended to serve as a recognition that the Assembly's principal task was no longer an effort to identify some additional tax revenues for France's precarious financial situation, but rather to draft a constitution and to restructure the government into a balanced constitutional monarchy, with a powerful legislative branch.

Events then accelerated at dizzying speed. On July 11, 1789, at the insistence of the queen and other stalwarts of the absolute monarchy, the king dismissed Necker, the Genevan Protestant, who was serving as the king's

---

10. Godard would himself make the assertion in his *Pétition* filed on behalf of the Ashkenazi Jewish community in January 1790.

de facto finance minister and as the government's principal minister.[11] Necker was particularly favored by the Paris bourgeoisie as someone able to bring order to France's finances in a reasonably equitable manner. In Paris, the news of the dismissal was greeted with dismay and anger. The next day, the journalist Camille Desmoulins, one of the young men who had frequented Target's home at the same time as Godard, climbed onto a table at the Café de Foy in the Palais Royal—the personal property of the Duc d'Orléans, the king's distant cousin and ferocious opponent. From that perch, in an eloquent, but inflammatory, speech, Desmoulins announced and denounced the king's dismissal of Necker to the assembled crowd. His speech became the spark that prompted thousands of Parisians to riot. Anger at the perceived arrogance of the Royal Court grew with each passing hour. Roaming mobs of Parisians sought out weapons and looked for targets upon which they could unleash their frustrations.

Ultimately, on the afternoon of July 14, after having raided the arms depot at the Invalides complex on the city's southwestern edge, those who had been rampaging through the streets to assert their opposition to the absolute monarchy focused their anger by launching an assault on the old Bastille. The Bastille was a fourteenth-century fortress, located along the eastern wall of the city adjacent to the popular and vibrant St. Antoine neighborhood. Flanked by eight one-hundred-foot-tall towers with thick walls and defended by heavy cannon on its turrets, the Bastille stood out as a royalist threat to the agitated Parisians. Rather than serving to defend Paris, it had been used as a prison for generations, albeit primarily for aristocratic and affluent prisoners. On July 14 it housed only seven prisoners.[12] And, even though it was without any significant strategic importance, it was an irritating symbol of arbitrary royal power with enormous emotional significance to the local population. Importantly, it also was undermanned and without adequate military supplies.

During the initial assault by the gathering mob, the governor of the Bastille, Bernard-René Jourdan de Launay, authorized his troops to fire on the attackers and nearly one hundred were killed.[13] However, when

---

11. Although Necker was responsible for all the activities of the Ministry of Finance, he had for a second time been denied the title of Minister of Finance because his Protestant faith had been deemed a disqualification by the king and queen.

12. These seven prisoners included two who were mentally unstable individuals confined to the Bastille by their own families.

13. Bernard-René Jourdan de Launay (1740–1789) was born in the Bastille where

faced with the alternative of engaging in a lengthy and likely very bloody battle to hold the fortress by decimating the crowd or relinquishing it without additional bloodshed, de Launay was persuaded to surrender the building to the mob, with the promise that he and the military defenders would not be harmed. De Launay paid for his decision with his life. As he was leaving the Bastille, the crowd turned on him and massacred him. Then they decapitated his body and paraded his head through the streets on a pike. Shortly thereafter, the de facto Mayor of Paris, Jacques de Flesselles, was killed by another mob near the Hôtel de Ville and his head was also placed on a pike and paraded through the streets.[14] Thus, the governor and the mayor became among the first victims of the Paris populace in the French Revolution. The unravelling of royal power was now in full swing and had become unstoppable.

In spite of the terrible violence that swept Paris during the hot July days, just three days after the taking of the Bastille the king and various members of the government came to Paris in an effort to assuage some of the public's anger. Surprisingly, the king was received very warmly both as he made his way from Versailles through the city and as he visited the Paris Hôtel de Ville (the City Hall). He was anomalously acclaimed as the "Restorer of French Liberty" and praised for his alleged support of the reforms that were already beginning. Less surprisingly, when Jacques Necker, after being recalled to the government by Louis XVI, this time with the formal title of Minister of Finance, also came to Paris, he was received as a hero. After the disorder surrounding the storming of the Bastille, a sense of relief and optimism took hold. But this would merely be an interlude in the chaos that the Revolution would spawn.

As early as July 13, 1789, Jacques Godard was swept up by the revolutionary fervor that took hold of Paris.[15] On that day, he attended gatherings in the city where the attendees were inflamed by the emotions of the moment. Having participated in the election of representatives from his district to the Estates-General, he undoubtedly played a role in the political discussions in which those individuals engaged as the turmoil in

---

his father was governor. He, in turn, became governor of the Bastille in 1776 and would end his life where it had begun—within the confines of the Bastille.

14. The position did not carry the title of mayor, but rather of *Prevôt des marchands de Paris* (Provost of the merchants of Paris).

15. *L'Ami des Patriotes ou le Défenseur de la Constitution*, no. 6, November 12 (1791), 180.

Paris accelerated. He would also have been witness to the random and widespread violence that afflicted Paris in the enthusiasm over challenging royal authority. Unlike many fellow Parisians of his age and gender, he did not elect to join the newly established National Guard, the militia of citizens created in Paris in mid-July. (In actuality, the National Guard was not a single unified force, but rather a series of local militias whose creation began with the violence of early July and which was officially authorized in August.) It was generally assumed that the members of the National Guard would protect the population against the forces of reaction and would guard the newly found liberties from those forces.[16] In fact, these militias, with their colorful uniforms and frequent quasi-military exercises, may not have accomplished much—but they were symbolically and psychologically significant. Ceremonies involving and honoring them would become commonplace. Godard would wait many months before he enlisted in the National Guard. At this earliest stage of the Revolution, with the seeds of a new legal order beginning to germinate, he chose, rather, to use his legal and oratorical skills to support the Revolution and its ideals.

The call to convene the Estates-General had already engendered a kind of grass-roots political movement among the more sophisticated classes. The symbolic impact of the capture of the Bastille caused a rapid acceleration of that process. Especially in Paris, there was an effort on the part of political elites to expedite political organizing. De Flesselles, the de facto mayor of the city who was killed on July 14, was immediately replaced by the scientist Jean-Sylvain Bailly. Bailly soon thereafter called for the various neighborhoods of Paris to hold elections and send representatives to the Hôtel de Ville to establish a new governing body. Neighborhood

---

16. See Florence Devenne, " La Garde Nationale, création et évolution (1789-août 1792)," in *Annales historiques de la Révolution française*, vol. 283, no. 1, (1990), pp. 49–66. The Paris National Guard was initially created by resolution of the Paris City Council on July 13, 1789. Most of its members were from the middle classes, since the group was intended both to prevent an aristocratic reaction against the revolutionary fervor and to moderate the excesses of the Paris mobs. At the inception of the National Guard in Paris, the Marquis de Lafayette was named to head the group due to his great popularity as a consequence of his role in the American Revolution. The National Guard would continue in existence (with periodic interruptions) until 1872. In 2016, President François Hollande reinstituted the National Guard as a bulwark against recent violence engendered by Islamist terrorism.

assemblies—the district assemblies that had coalesced around the neighborhood electoral assemblies—began to meet and initiated a process of electing officers and representatives. They also began to take positions on the percolating political and social issues.

Godard's Blancs-Manteaux neighborhood was at the forefront of this process. By July 21 Godard, in spite of his youth—he had just turned twenty-seven—had been elected as one of the presidents of that neighborhood's district and, in that capacity, had signed various declarations.[17] One of these concerned the process of electing new representatives to a municipal assembly to replace the electors who had designated representatives to the Estates-General.[18] The decree called for complete transparency in the electoral process. This would require the publication of the names of all eligible voters. In an apparent effort to control the role of the new representatives and assure they would be fully responsive to the will of the local assembly, the decree called for those representatives to be limited to a term of merely one month. The experiment in democracy was now well underway and Godard had put himself squarely in the middle of the process, where he clearly intended to remain.

---

17. On July 29, 1789, in his capacity as a president of his District, Godard issued a declaration which served as an invitation on behalf of the Assembly of the Blancs-Manteaux District to attend a mass on August 1 at the Église des Blancs-Manteaux. The announced purpose of the mass was to pray for the repose of the souls of the victims of the violence in the battle at the Bastille (*Déclaration du District des Blancs-Manteaux*, Bibliothèque Historique de la Ville de Paris, MS 814, Document 356).

18. *Brochure sur la municipalité et les districts de Paris*, (1789). [gallica.bnf.fr] *District des Blancs-Manteaux, Arrêté du 21 Juillet 1789* (Bibliothèque Historique de la Ville de Paris, Doc. 10065, no. 30bis).

CHAPTER 17

THE SUMMER OF 1789

The summer of 1789 was a heady time for all of France, and especially for Paris. An awareness that something extraordinary was taking place infused every aspect of life in the capital. The tumultuous events of July led to a tremendous amount of agitation, accompanied by periodic mob violence. The wave of newly found freedom that swept across the city unleashed an array of political opinions, with people of all political beliefs publishing tracts of every type to express feelings that had, for so long, been pent up.

Every day, concerns were being addressed in the enthusiasm of a newly found freedom of expression. Presses, which were springing up everywhere, ran overtime printing a vast array of tracts and declarations.[1] Anyone with a political thought seems to have rushed to get that thought in print. Jacques Godard was no exception. No longer constrained to express himself through the legal pleadings that had been his bread and butter for over six years, beginning in 1789 and continuing during the course of the next few years he wrote a variety of short essays on an assortment of political topics, which he had published as pamphlets. According to his assertion to his cousin, Cortot, most of those brochures

---

1. In 1789 alone, 184 new periodicals were launched. That number nearly doubled the next year. See Jeremy Popkin, "Journals: The New Face of News," in *Revolution in Print, the Press in France 1775–1800*, ed. Robert Darnton and Daniel Roche (Berkeley: University of California Press, 1989), 150.

did not bear his name. Regrettably, the brochures can no longer be identified, but it can be assumed that they addressed political issues of the
turbulent era and were likely written in the same logical and careful style
in which Godard prepared all of his writings.[2]

The enthusiasm and ferment then rippling throughout French society
was a major distraction from the serious work facing both members of
the government and the avocats. The ongoing turmoil made it difficult
to organize new governing structures to replace the absolutist regime.
A multitude of issues arose virtually simultaneously as every aspect of
the government began to undergo challenge and change. The newly
self-proclaimed National Assembly, sitting in its temporary home in
Versailles near the Royal Court, was pressured from many sides to debate
societal issues of every sort.

In the city of Paris governing institutions were being assembled and
disassembled. Initially, with the creation of a power vacuum in the municipal government as a result of the events of July 14, the Electors of

---

2. The Bibliothèque Historique de la Ville de Paris holds a collection of eight
anonymous pamphlets which the library ascribes to Jacques Godard. The essays
are entitled: *Lettre Circulaire, Bravoure des Gardes françaises; LeHarangueur, aux
trois Ordres assemblés & réunis; Convoi, service, enterrement; Lettre des députés;
Reproches aux tiers-états de Paris ET aux Electeurs pour l'exclusion des Gens de
Robe à la Députation des États-Généraux; Le véridique,* and *Réponse des femmes
de Paris au Cahier de l'Ordre le plus nombreux du Royaume.* These pamphlets
were contributed to the library by a Jean-François Godard. A handwritten note,
covering the several essays, identifies the contributor as being a builder and
contractor who resided on rue Guisarde on Paris's Left Bank near the church
of Saint-Sulpice. The note lists the various essays by name and indicates that
they are the work of Jacques Godard. Although it is possible that a few may
have been written by Jacques Godard, I am very doubtful regarding Godard's
authorship of any of the pamphlets. Neither the tone nor the style of most of the
pamphlets is consistent with Godard's usual thoughtful and lawyerly approach.
Most are sarcastic and aggressive, even disrespectful in tone. They may very well
have been written by the contributor, Jean-François Godard, himself. Jean-Fran-
cois Godard lived at the time of the Revolution and, based on the very limited
information available about him, appears to have been somewhat of a radical
and rabble-rouser. It is possible that the library may have simply confused the
two Godards. I have not found any apparent familial relationship between
the two Godards, even though there is a possibility, albeit a remote one, that
they were related since Jacques Godard indicated in his correspondence with
Cortot that he had some relatives living in Paris.

Paris—those individuals who had qualified to vote for representatives to the Estates-General—began to act as an interim municipal assembly. The Electors were those who, due to their wealth and status, had been the few citizens given the right to actually vote directly for representatives to the Estates-General. They had remained assembled through the period following the initial meetings and, as the power vacuum developed, purported to be acting as the municipal government of Paris. During the turmoil of the days surrounding the seizure of the Bastille, with organized municipal government paralyzed by disorder and violence, the Electors had found themselves at the forefront of coping with the massive upheaval. Attempting to address a variety of pressing problems, they had acted as though they were a legislative assembly with authority not only to govern the city of Paris, but with rights surpassing even those of the National Assembly.

The Electors represented a rather conservative force amid the turbulence of the Revolution, putting them at odds with the more liberal and dynamic forces of the various district assemblies that had begun to arise throughout Paris. Within a very short time following the fall of the Bastille, however, at the invitation of Bailly, the recently designated mayor of the City, the sixty newly created districts elected a competing one-hundred-twenty-member assembly.[3] By late July this new group took the name of *Assemblée des Représentants de la Commune de Paris* (the Assembly of the Representatives of the Paris Commune or, as we will refer to it, the "Paris Assembly"). On July 30 members of the newly elected Paris Assembly, very unhappy with positions taken by the Electors and believing that only the Paris Assembly was empowered to act on behalf of Parisians, went a few steps from the room where they were meeting in the Hôtel de Ville to the room where the Electors were meeting. They thanked the Electors for their services and dismissed them, an action the Electors chose not to contest.[4] The Paris Assembly was now the sole legislative body for the entire municipality. In that role, it had to confront a plethora of issues, which ran the gamut from mundane matters relating to the everyday operations of a large metropolis to issues relating to political and even philosophical matters, with issues of public order at the forefront of their concerns.[5]

---

3. Godard, *Exposé des Travaux*, 5.
4. Ibid., 7–8.
5. Ibid., generally.

Simultaneously, in these early days of the Revolution, the National Assembly, sitting in Versailles, tried to put some order into its deliberations, which focused on giving France a new political and social structure. Even before the Bastille was taken, drafting a formal constitution had been identified as its primary focus, and resulted in the National Assembly becoming officially known as the National Constituent Assembly.[6] As part of that effort, on July 30, 1789, the National Assembly received a proposal for a "Declaration of the Rights of Man and of the Citizen," which Joseph-Michel-Antoine de Servan, an avocat from the Parlement of Grenoble, proposed should serve as the preamble to the new constitution.[7] Servan, along with many of his fellow Assembly members, was strongly influenced by the French *philosophes*, but also by the American Declaration of Independence, with its lofty assertions regarding the purpose of revolution and the obligations of government, as well as by the United States Constitution, with its framework for representative government, and, very importantly, also by the not-yet-ratified American Bill of Rights.

The draft submitted to the National Assembly by Servan was not intended to be just a preamble with exalted language. Rather, as the representative Jérôme Pétion de Villeneuve,[8] a future mayor of the city of Paris, stated: "This is not a matter of making a declaration of rights solely for France, but for mankind in general."[9] The revolutionaries were intent on creating a new socio-political system that they believed would have world-wide influence. In their enthusiasm for their newly found freedom, these men

---

6. *L'Assemblée Nationale Constituente.*

7. "*Projet de déclaration proposé aux députés des communes aux États-généraux de France par M. Servan, ancien avocat-général au Parlement de Grenoble*" (self-published, 1789).

8. Jérôme Pétion de Villeneuve (1756–1794), born into a family of avocats, also became an avocat. He was elected to the Estates-General from his home district of Chartres, to the southwest of Paris, and briefly served as president of the National Assembly. In November 1791 he became the second Mayor of Paris, succeeding Bailly. Subsequently, he served as the first president of the National Convention in 1792, voting for the death of Louis XVI. However, he ultimately aligned himself with the moderate Girondins faction and, when the Jacobins took control of the National Convention, was placed under arrest. He escaped, but, like Condorcet, chose to commit suicide shortly thereafter to avoid capture by the soldiers of the Convention.

9. *Déclaration de M. Pétion de Villeneuve, Archives Parlementaires*, vol. 8, p. 47.

already saw themselves as proselytizers for the new system of government they were only beginning to develop. Therefore, its authors intended that the Declaration would embody a statement regarding all the fundamental human rights that the new political order would protect. The mere fact that the title to the preamble implied that it applied both to "man" *and* to the "citizen" suggested that the enumerated rights were moral and not just political—that they were rights to which all men were entitled whether or not they were citizens of a particular state. The use of the two terms emphasized that the applicability of the enumerated rights did not depend on legal status, but on human existence itself. However, the debate in the months to come would demonstrate the large gap between high-minded language and practical political realities.

In its first article, the Declaration, echoing the words of Jean-Jacques Rousseau, proclaimed freedom and equality for all men: "Men are born free and remain free and equal in rights; social distinctions can be based only on the public good."[10] A proposed Article 11 was intended as a restraint on the power of any future national legislature, and contained constraints on the various types of laws that could be adopted by a legislative body. One of those categories covered laws infringing on religious freedom. The draft provided that such laws regarding religion would be "deemed to be in conformity with civil liberty [only] when, in prescribing moral acts useful for all, such laws do not infringe on the liberty of men in respect of dogmas and observance so long as such dogmas and observance are necessary to strengthen moral principles."[11] The debate on the actual text of the overall Declaration, including the issue of religious liberty (which would eventually find its place in Article 10), would go on until late August. With the debate on the Declaration playing a central role in the deliberations of the National Assembly during the latter part of August, as part of that debate the Assembly addressed issues specifically relating to freedom of religion.

Shortly following the initial submission of the text intended to incorporate the notion of religious freedom into the Declaration, the issue of the role of Jews in France was brought to the attention of the National Assembly for the first time, in an impassioned plea by the Abbé Henri Grégoire. Grégoire, who had shared the prize for his submission to the

---

10. *Déclaration des Droits de l'Homme et du Citoyen*, Article Premier.
11. *Archives Parlementaires*, vol. 8, p. 306.

Metz essay contest in 1787, on behalf of the Ashkenazi Jews called upon the Assembly to provide this Jewish community, whose condition he deemed to be particularly precarious, with protection and assistance. In the very first discussion of the rights of the Jews of France at the National Assembly, on the evening of August 3 Grégoire addressed the Assembly "on behalf of fifty thousand Jews scattered throughout the kingdom, who 'being men' demand the rights of citizens," and described in detail the "incredible persecutions that have been inflicted on the Jews."[12] He noted that "as a religious leader of a religion that considers all men to be brothers," he was required to demand the intervention of the Assembly in favor of "this proscribed and unfortunate people."[13] Focusing on the issues of primary concern to the Jews of Lorraine, his native region, he submitted, as part of a lengthy address, a multi-faceted resolution. His resolution sought to remove special taxes which afflicted the Jewish community, to give Jews the freedom to exercise their religious practices, to live wherever they chose, and to pursue whatever profession they wished. The resolution also prohibited defamatory remarks about Jews. Missing from Grégoire's resolution, however, was any reference to a grant of full legal equality.[14] Grégoire urged immediate adoption of his proposal. Yet, despite his impassioned plea and notwithstanding his very considerable prestige, the Assembly, faced with so many other pressing issues, rather unceremoniously deferred consideration of the matter without comment. This would occur with frequency, and sometimes with far more acrimony, in the months and years to come.

On August 23, 1789, another debate, a raucous exchange on the subject of religious liberty, took place at the National Assembly. During this boisterous debate, the Protestant deputy, Jean-Paul Rabaut Saint-Étienne, a cleric and representative from the southern city of Nimes, rose to speak in support of the proposed Article 10 of the draft Declaration of the Rights of Man and of the Citizen.[15] In his remarks, Rabaut Saint-Étienne

12. Grégoire, *Motion en faveur des Juifs*, 1.

13. *Moniteur*, August 1–3, 1789, no. 32, p. 135.

14. Grégoire's resolution was published shortly after he submitted it to the National Assembly and appeared in the form of a pamphlet entitled *Motion en faveur des Juifs*.

15. Jean-Paul Rabaut Saint-Étienne (1743–1793) was the son of a Protestant minister who studied for the ministry in Lausanne. In the years leading to the Revolution, he was successful in urging Malesherbes to propose the edict that

made some important and even profound statements about the nature of "tolerance." He began by reminding the Assembly that it had made the pronouncement that "liberty is a common good." "Therefore," he continued, "it belongs to all men; therefore, it belongs to all Frenchmen." He then went on to apply this principle to religious liberty using a syllogism. Declaring that "A cult is a dogma, a dogma relates to an opinion, and an opinion relates to liberty," he then elaborated, "it is thus to attack liberty if there is an attempt to force a man to adopt a dogma that is different from his own." As he continued, he went much further by rejecting the notion of "tolerance." "We must banish forever this notion of tolerance; this barbaric word will not henceforth be pronounced. It is not tolerance that I demand; that word carries with it the notion of compassion, which demeans man; I demand liberty which must be for everyone."[16]

Rabaut Saint-Étienne then applied his analysis to the Jews. He called upon the Assembly to unequivocally grant equal rights to all its religious minorities—specifically to Protestants, his coreligionists, but also to Jews:

I ask, Gentlemen, for French Protestants, for all non-Catholics of the kingdom, what you ask for yourselves: liberty, equality of rights. I ask it for this people [the Jewish people], torn from Asia, always wandering, always banned during eighteen centuries, which would adopt our mores and our customs, if by our laws, they were incorporated into us, and to whose morality we cannot object because that morality is the product of our barbarism and of the humiliation to which we have unjustly condemned them.[17]

During his presentation, Rabaut Saint-Étienne cited the freedom accorded to all religions in the new United States, highlighting the religious liberty that existed in the American state of Pennsylvania. In particular, he noted that the citizens of that state had: "declared that all of those who adore a God, in whatever manner they have chosen to adore Him, must benefit from all of the rights of citizenship."[18] Rabaut Saint-Étienne praised the citizens of Pennsylvania because, as he put it, "they have not

---

granted equality to Protestants. During the Revolution, he held various important legislative posts. However, he aligned himself with the Girondins and, as a consequence, was guillotined in December 1793.

16. *Moniteur*, August 23–26, 1789, no. 46, p. 189.

17. *Archives Parlementaires*, August 23, 1789, vol. 8, p. 479.

18. Ibid.

accepted anyone. A person of any religion has the *right* to benefit from all of the sacred privileges attached to men."[19]

At the conclusion of Rabaut Saint-Étienne's remarks, Jean-Baptiste Gobel, the Bishop of Lydda near Hagenau in Alsace, one of the most liberal members of the clergy in spite of being from Alsace, seconded Rabaut Saint-Étienne's call for religious liberty and his support for the proposed Article 10 to the Declaration.[20] However, he suggested adding a proviso to the text, qualifying the text as follows: "so long as the manifestations of the religious opinion do not trouble the public order." Although there was no further discussion that evening on the rights of Jews, the proposed text establishing a fundamental right to religious liberty was adopted on a voice vote—but, importantly, as amended by Gobel's proviso. Thus, in the preamble of the prospective Constitution of the new France was safely ensconced the principle of religious liberty for all—not just for citizens— but for all: "No one ought to be disturbed on account of his opinions, even religious, provided the manifestation of the religious opinions do not trouble the public order established by law."

Just three days later, on August 26, 1789, the National Assembly adopted the full text of the Declaration of the Rights of Man and of the Citizen. Its adoption specified that it was to be integrated into the French Constitution, as its preamble, once that document had been drafted and ratified. The Declaration addressed the right to religious freedom, but it did so in the somewhat backhanded manner that had been proposed on August 23. Effectively, freedom of religion was addressed by the mere addition of a clarification to the general principle of freedom to express opinions. After extensive and sometimes contentious discussion, the session ended with the adoption of the article.[21] The final language of the Declaration, in its Article 10, included the very text influenced by Rabaut Saint-Étienne,

---

19. Ibid.

20. Jean-Baptiste Gobel (1727–1794) was born in the Alsatian town of Thann. He was an ambitious priest who espoused very liberal policies. He was among the very first priests to accept the Civil Constitution of the Clergy. On March 13, 1791, Gobel became the first elected Archbishop of Paris and served for a brief period in that role, although the Catholic Church did not recognize his election or his service. He became increasingly radicalized in the coming years. In spite of his politics, he eventually ran afoul of the Jacobins and was executed in Paris on April 13, 1794, along with the radical revolutionary Jacques Hébert and a group of his followers.

21. *Archives Parlementaires*, August 23, 1789, vol. 8, p. 480.

Gobel, and the representatives who shared their views. Taken within its historical context, this statement would appear to be a definitive assertion of religious freedom. Notwithstanding the important qualifier respecting limitations on public manifestations, arguably, since the article was applicable, not just to citizens, but also to all "men," the acceptance of this text should have resolved the issue of Jewish equality once and for all. But that was hardly the case. No such simple path to equality was available to the Ashkenazi Jews. The adoption of Article 10 was just one step along a long road yet to be traveled.

The final text of Article 10 of the Declaration clearly reflected the sensitivity of the members of the National Assembly to the role of age-old religious conflict in France. After all, the Wars of Religion of the sixteenth century were not so very distant. The Thirty Years' War—at its heart, a vast European religious conflict between Catholic and Protestant nations that had torn the continent asunder—had occurred less than 150 years before. Yet fresher in the minds of the legislators would have been the Calas Affair, in which Godard's fellow-avocat, Élie de Beaumont, had played a pivotal role, and the torture and execution of the Chevalier de la Barre for having allegedly been disrespectful to Catholic symbols[22]—matters that had profoundly shaken Enlightenment France a relatively short time before the Revolution. Any desire to allow all people in France to freely exercise their religion was tempered by a fear of backlash from the dominant Catholic religious tradition, a tradition to which vast swaths of the French population still adhered fervently. Recognizing that too dramatic a change in public religious practice could trigger a powerful reaction, the legislators put a restraint on public displays of religion. This appeared to be an acceptable and practical compromise. In a nation that had so recently experienced virulent intolerance and was still infused

---

22. The Chevalier de la Barre (François-Jean Lefebvre de la Barre, 1745–1766) was a poignant martyr to the cause of religious tolerance. At the age of nineteen, in 1766, the nobleman was convicted for acting irreverently (specifically, for failing to remove his hat as a crucifix passed in front of him during a religious procession) and for being a promoter of the atheistic philosophy of Voltaire. He was tortured and brutally executed for his alleged crime, with his body then publicly burned. In an allegedly enlightened era, the suffering inflicted upon this young man stood as a particularly tragic miscarriage of justice and flagrant example of Catholic intolerance. His case became one of the *causes célèbres* of the struggle for French religious tolerance.

with deeply embedded religious prejudice, the constraints imposed by
Article 10 must have seemed to be a great step forward with a modest
enough concession to practicality.

Despite the words of the text, which appeared to encompass all minority religious opinions, the dissenting religious opinions (as opposed
to the *philosophes'* non-religious or anti-religious opinions) to which
the Declaration was intending to refer were assuredly just those of
Protestants. France was simply overwhelmingly a Catholic nation and
essentially exclusively a Christian country. Solely the pesky, but relatively inconsequential, Jewish minority held non-Christian religious
opinions. (Muslims were virtually non-existent in France at that time.)
For the moment, in the midst of such unparalleled turmoil, the condition of the Jews of France did not seem especially significant, despite
being a topic of growing interest, and even substantial interest to some.
Indeed, the *Journal de Paris*, in its September 15, 1789 edition, noted that
the issue of France´s relationship with its Jewish population "was of the
most pressing interest."[23] This was echoed in Mirabeau's *Le Courrier de
Provence* a few days later, where, on the subject of altering the status of
the Ashkenazi Jews, it was written that "this political reform will certainly be one of the most important subjects to be addressed subsequently
by the [National] Assembly."[24]

At approximately the time that the Declaration of the Rights of Man
and the Citizen was adopted,[25] an initial petition was submitted to the
National Assembly by eleven prominent members of the Jewish community on behalf of the Jews residing in Paris.[26] The petition was in the form

---

23. *Journal de Paris*, September 15, 1789.
24. *Le Courrier de Provence, pour servir de suite aux lettres du Comte de MIRABEAU
à ses commétans*, September 28, 29 & 30, 1789, no. 47, p. 9.
25. Although the document bears a date of publication of August 26, the day that
the Declaration was adopted, it may have been submitted to the Assembly two
days earlier. The official records of the National Assembly do not record receipt
of the document, nor is there any indication of any kind of official presentation
of the document by a Jewish delegation. It is, therefore, possible that the document was never actually officially received by the Assembly members and merely
represents the early thinking of some of the Jews of Paris regarding their desire
for full citizenship.
26. *Adresse présentée à l'Assemblée Nationale, le 26 août 1789 par les Juifs résidans
à Paris* (Paris: Imp. Prault, 1789). The eleven signatories of the Address were a
mixed group: J.Goldschmit, Abraham Lopès Lagouna, M.Weil, J.Benjamin,

of an "Address." It was a short document, just eight pages of text, but it represented an important initial attempt by Jews to solicit the right to be recognized as equal citizens of the new France. The petitioners noted the history of their persecution. They indicated that they had suffered without complaint—this passive acceptance being the best proof that they were deserving of a better fate. Acknowledging that they had a religion different from that of the majority of Frenchmen, but that they had been faithful to it, they suggested that this fidelity by itself was a guaranty that they would be faithful to their oath to be good citizens. "We are attached to this Religion," they wrote, "but this attachment itself speaks in our favor."[27] After all, they urged, it is better to have people devoted to a religion than to have people without belief. They asked to be made subject to the same laws as all the people of France and thereby suggested their willingness to give up any distinct rights that they had. In concluding their petition, they harkened back to the debate that had just taken place at the National Assembly. Sensitive to the notion that the work of the Revolution was regarded by revolutionary leaders as transcending France itself, they proposed that, by granting citizenship to Jews, the members of the Assembly would have an influence not only on France, but on the entire world. "What blessings are reserved for humane and just men, who, in the entire Universe will have saved the JEWS from proscriptions and will have made them Citizens!"[28]

Although there is no concrete evidence, there is reasoned speculation that Jacques Godard was likely the author of (or at least an important contributor to) this first address to the National Assembly on behalf of a group of Jews.[29] Assuredly, the tone of the petition was reflective of Godard's passion and the language was the flowery and distinguished legal language which Godard adopted in all of his writings. Regrettably,

J. Fernandès, Mardoche Lévi, Jacob Lazard, Trenelle, *père*, Mardoché Elie, Joseph Peyrera Brandon, and Delcampo, *fils*. Their names indicate that they came from both Sephardic and Ashkenazi backgrounds. Therefore, beyond being an initial request to the National Assembly, it is also a rare example of Sephardic (Portuguese)-Ashkenazic cooperation. The Bibliothèque Nationale de France unequivocally ascribes the authorship of this document to Godard, but the actual authorship remains subject to question.

27. Ibid., 5.
28. Ibid., 8.
29. Feuerwerker, *L'Émancipation des Juifs en France*, 336–37.

the absence of any definitive document linking Godard to this initial Address may forever leave its authorship in doubt.

Less than one week later, on August 31, the Ashkenazi Jews of eastern France submitted their own address to the National Assembly. Following the pattern set by the Parisian Jews, the Jews of the Three Bishoprics—the dioceses of Metz, Verdun and Toul and their environs, along with Alsace and Lorraine—styled their presentation: *"Adresse Presentée à l'Assemblée Nationale"* [Address Presented to the National Assembly]. Their document was also relatively brief, just slightly more than fourteen printed pages.[30] The focus of the Address was on the discriminatory taxes assessed against the Jews of the region. In particular, the Jews of Metz objected to the Brancas tax. The Jews of Lorraine and Alsace protested the various offensive taxes and fees to which they were subjected. This Address concluded with an affirmation of loyalty to the French Nation. However, contrary to the unqualified appeal for equality in the document submitted by the Parisian Jews, the eastern Jews asserted an important reservation.

The petitioners proposed that they be allowed to keep their "Synagogues, their Rabbis and their communal Administrators."[31] The request of the petitioners to the National Assembly contained four basic components: 1) that Jews be granted the title and rights of citizens; 2) that Jews be allowed to reside anywhere in France, without exception; 3) that all arbitrary taxes assessed against Jews be abolished; and 4) that Jews be allowed to keep the institutions that they currently have.[32] This petition, more than others submitted to the National Assembly, demonstrated some ambivalence about total Jewish integration and echoed the concerns of the rabbis and leaders of the eastern French Jewish communities. Attached to the Address as a supplement was a two-page more specific request to the National Assembly from representatives of the Jewish community of Metz.[33] The statement enunciated a practical concern which appeared to

---

30. *Adresse Présentée à l'Assemblée Nationale le 31 Août 1789, par les Députés Réunis des Juifs Etablis à Metz, dans les Trois Evêchés, en Alsace & en Lorraine.* The author of this petition is unknown although it may have been Berr Isaac Berr of Nancy, potentially with the assistance of Godard.

31. Ibid., 11.

32. Ibid., 13–14.

33. "Demande Particulière Adressée à l'Assemblée Nationale par les députés des Juifs de Metz," in *Adresses, Mémoires et Pétitions des Juifs 1789-1794,* vol. 5 (Paris: EDHIS, 1968).

contradict the notion of total Jewish equality, but which had a powerful economic motivation. The Jews of Metz wanted the National Assembly to require any Jew electing to leave the Jewish quarter to pay his pro rata share of the outstanding debts of the Metz Jewish community and to assist that community in paying its very heavy debt obligations to non-Jewish creditors.[34] It appears not to have occurred to the petitioners that they should demand the total abolition of the accrued Brancas tax obligations.

Although the two petitions constituted an important volley in the quest for Jewish equality, it was an ambivalent volley. The reluctance of the petitioners from eastern France to squarely renounce their special communal rights, and their attempt to retain certain communal controls over fellow Jews made the plea for full equality less than completely convincing.

---

34. Ibid., 17–18.

CHAPTER 18

GODARD'S FIRST APPEARANCE BEFORE THE NATIONAL ASSEMBLY

As the great debates over rights, privileges, and religious equality were raging in Versailles, Godard, who had regularly been reelected to the assembly of his local district, made his first appearance before the National Assembly. His appearance there, however, was not related to the lofty philosophical issues of the day, nor was it related to the cause of Jewish equality—it concerened a technical and unglamorous legal matter.

On July 31, 1789, Godard went to the Assembly to present a resolution which had been proposed by his Paris District in opposition to two resolutions adopted just days before by the Paris Electors. The conflict between the relatively wealthy and well-established Electors and the more popularly elected district assemblies had been simmering for weeks and had come to a boil.

Amidst the violence of the days around the 14th of July there had occurred acts intended to repress the activists who had seized the Bastille and committed other acts of violence in the context of that event. Unsurprisingly, the royal troops stationed in Paris had sought to constrain the movements of the activists, which led to further violence. The leader of the royal forces in Paris, Pierre-Victor de Besenval, was one of the principal targets of the revolutionaries, who saw him as a tool of the monarchy and a major actor in the effort to repress revolutionary fervor.[1] Shortly after the capture of

---

1. Pierre Victor, Baron de Besenval de Brünstatt (1721–1791), born in Switzerland

the Bastille, Besenval had been arrested on the charge that he had improperly ordered his troops to use force in a vain effort to suppress the violence in Paris. The Electors, in keeping with their conservative bent, had issued an amnesty to Besenval, ordering that he be released from custody. They also ordered that amnesty be given to all the others, mostly soldiers, who had taken actions against the rioters. Many in Paris were angered by the decision to grant such amnesty and sought to reverse it.[2]

The National Assembly, now dominated by an increasingly assertive group of members of the Third Estate, had taken a position contrary to that of the conservative Paris Electors, insisting on pursuing all those who appeared to have committed crimes against the Paris demonstrators, including Besenval himself. Furthermore, they proposed establishing a

---

and a Swiss army officer, had, just as had many of his compatriots with a military bent, joined the French military. He rose through the ranks and by 1789 was placed in charge of all the royal armed forces in the Paris area. In that capacity, he was responsible for maintaining order as Paris became the site of insurrection and violence. He commanded his troops with a firm hand, including in the bloody effort to put down the labor strife at the Reveillon factory, but was frustrated by the royal government's indecisiveness. As a consequence, he pulled his troops back from the center of Paris just as the mobs were growing. His retreat permitted the attack on the munitions barracks at the Invalides and the subsequent assault on the Bastille. Nonetheless, the population of Paris held him responsible for the violence that killed many members of the rampaging crowds, and wanted to try him as a criminal. The king authorized Besenval to leave Paris and seek safety elsewhere. However, as he was attempting to flee, he was discovered in the town of Provins just to Paris's southwest. He was arrested and would have been lynched by his captors had Jacques Necker, the popular former Finance Minister, who was returning from Geneva to reassume his post as principal minister of the king, not intervened on his behalf. After a lengthy legal struggle, Besenval was transferred to Paris, where he was charged with the crime of *lèse-nation* (a vague notion of actual and inchoate acts against the state, which became a rather commonplace accusation in the first years of the Revolution, but which resulted in very few condemnations). See Jean-Christophe Gaven, *Le Crime de lèse-nation. Histoire d'une invention juridique et politique (1789–1791)* (Paris: Presses de Sciences Po, Domaine droit, [2016])). Ultimately, after a trial in which he was represented by Godard's colleague Raymond DeSèze, and which was presided over by Antoine Gaspard Boucher d'Argis (the founder of the Paris legal aid group to which Godard adhered) he was exonerated and liberated. He died on June 2, 1791 of natural causes.

2. As described by Godard in his presentation to the National Assembly. *Archives Parlementaires*, vol. 8, pp. 310–11.

special tribunal to try those accused of violence. A serious conflict had broken out between the Paris Electors and many members of the local districts, who were significantly more radical than the Electors or even than the members of the newly established General Assembly of the Representatives of the Commune of Paris, made up of individuals elected by each of the sixty newly created districts of the City. The members of the local assemblies had been elevated to their offices by voters subject to far less stringent requirements than those imposed for the selection of the Electors, who were drawn mostly from the aristocracy and the moneyed elites. By siding with the National Assembly and acknowledging the National Assembly's supremacy, the nascent district assemblies had determined that they could gain prestige and influence.[3]

As street violence increased in Paris, the National Assembly debated whether to reassert its intention to establish a special tribunal to try those who had fought against the besiegers of the Bastille and harmed others involved in the demonstrations of July 14. Among the members of the National Assembly who spoke out in support of that effort was none other than Godard's mentor, the avocat Target. On July 31 Target addressed the National Assembly and reiterated his position. He stated his belief that "the troubles which are agitating the capital arise from the opinion which [Paris] has derived from the decree of the Electors. [Paris] thought that it was pardoning enemies of France. But this is just an error which

---

3. The circumstances that led to this first appearance by Godard before the National Assembly are further described in *Actes de l'Assemblée des Représentants de la Commune de Paris*, vol. 1, p. 59, as follows: "The [Paris] Assembly, considering that, as a result of the nomination of its representatives at the Hôtel de Ville, the electors had no further pretext for continuing to carry on the functions which necessity alone could have authorized; considering, as a consequence, that it is illegally, without any authorization, without any mission and against the national interests that, prompted by an ill-considered zeal, they [the electors] announced a general pardon; that it is all the stranger that the Assembly of the electors should have adopted such a decree, that the Assembly of the Representatives of the Commune to which Mr. Necker had first read the same speech, stubbornly approved the liberation of Mr. de Besenval; considering that the decree of the Assembly of the Electors effectively destroys the decree of the National Assembly which named a special committee to study the complaints against the traitors [a Research Committee, created by the decree of the Assembly on July 28, 1789, and named two days later]; formally disavows a decree [adopted by the electors] dictated by enthusiasm, which contradicts the wise provisions of the National Assembly and the eternal laws of justice."

must not be disseminated. The City of Paris was simply stating that it was relinquishing the pursuit of justice on its own." Therefore, he went on, "[i]t is simply necessary to provide an explanation which will calm all of Paris." As a means of implementing his proposal, Target then submitted a resolution to the Assembly:

> The National Assembly decrees that, even though the city of Paris honored itself in declaring that the people would no longer be allowed to carry out justice themselves on those who committed lèse-nation, it [the National Assembly] is persisting in its prior decrees; that it intends to pursue punishing the guilty before a tribunal which will be established by the committee with respect to which the Assembly continues to concern itself.[4]

Immediately following the submission of this resolution by Target, several members of the Assembly requested to be heard. However, before a general debate on his resolution could begin, not coincidently, Godard, Target's protégé, entered the National Assembly as the head of a delegation from the Blancs-Manteaux District within which Target himself resided. Godard was then invited to make supporting remarks. Addressing the National Assembly for the first time, in flowery and dramatic language, Godard presented the case for support of the resolution. He set the stage by describing the deep disappointment felt in Paris because of the general pardon given to the opponents of the July 14 demonstrators:

> Gentlemen, an important event brings us to the feet of this august Assembly. It appeared as though the capital had nothing further to wish for, and that calm was to be reinstated forever. It had been fortunate to receive you; it had received its king. Yesterday the Minister [Necker] it had awaited so impatiently had come to crown its joy. This third day, so beautiful, so touching, was one of those where the spirits were most agitated. They still are; and it is to you that we come seeking a cure for this ferment ... If all of Paris had heard Mr. Necker, had been witness to his emotion, had seen his tears flowing, all of Paris would have made a solemn decree of the feelings of this great minister. The Electors, in the name of the City, announced a general amnesty. Their decree produced a most terrible impression.[5]

---

4. *Archives Parlementaires,* vol. 8, p. 310.
5. Ibid.

Then he demanded justice:

Crimes were committed; the laws demand that they be punished; and suddenly a general pardon is announced; it is done on behalf of all citizens, by citizens without authority. The same people who, in a single day, went from slavery to freedom, has been unable to accommodate itself to the sudden change that [the Electors] sought to impose on its mind...It did not recognize, in this order of the Electors, the quality of the law; it did not see an expression of your will, which was, and which is, that the culprits be sought out, judged and punished. This is the spirit of your recent orders, and the respect which those orders inspire in people, joins in its mind, with the hatred it still retains against its enemies, even though they are defeated, and it has caused its complaints to burst out against this order. So we thought that the surest way to calm its agitation was to complain ourselves, to let [the people of Paris] see that they have their advocates and so we have adopted the resolution that we are bringing to you. We are reassured by the purity of our intentions. The need for peace, the necessity to restore public tranquility immediately, the influence you have over all of France, have determined us to proceed with our efforts.[6]

Godard, the man of law, the man devoted to compliance with law and to public order, was making his maiden appearance in the most important political arena of his time by delivering a plea for the pursuit of alleged law breakers. It had to have been a heady moment for the young man from a small provincial town, as he stood before the National Assembly in its grandiose hall in Versailles. His argument, as had been the case in the matters he had pleaded before the beginning of the Revolution, was, very simply, that laws need to be applied and, if applied justly, will achieve justice. The subject evoked great interest at the Assembly.

The president of the Assembly, the Marquis de Lally-Tollendal, responded to Godard's plea.[7] He reminded the Blancs-Manteaux

---

6. Ibid., 310–11.

7. Trophime-Gérard de Lally-Tollendal (1751–1830), the legitimized son of the French descendant of an Irish Jacobite and a French aristocrat, spent part of his youth successfully securing the exoneration of his father, who, after being defeated in French India, had been executed. The younger Lally-Tollendal was elected to the Estates-General as a representative of the nobility of Paris. He quickly became alienated by the anti-monarchist tendencies of the National Assembly

delegation that it was concern for "public welfare and justice" that always guided the Assembly in its deliberations. "This fundamental principle," Lally-Tollendal insisted, "would preside over the deliberations that would take place on the discourse which you [Godard] just made and to the issue which you have just submitted to its wisdom."[8]

In the ensuing debate, Mirabeau clearly concurred with Godard's remarks and spoke strongly in favor of the district's position with respect to the Baron de Besenval and the attempt to grant amnesty.[9] He also reminded his fellow Assembly members that the Assembly existed to make laws, not to enforce them; and then, demonstrating a misunderstanding of the concept of the separation of powers, he declared that the enforcement of the law was vested in the courts (rather than in the executive—the king) and that the Assembly could not usurp that right. He also lauded the Paris districts for their opposition to the pardon that the Electors had issued, thereby supporting Godard's plea on behalf of his own district.

Maximilien Robespierre joined in the discussion, supporting the Assembly's position with the kind of intransigence for which he would become famous a few years later, stating: "I demand the full application of the principles which must subject suspects of crimes against the nation to exemplary judgments. Do you want to calm the people? Speak to them in the language of justice and reason. Let them be certain that their enemies will not escape the vengeance of the laws, and then sentiments of justice will replace those of hate."[10] At the conclusion of the debate, the National Assembly adopted Target's motion, thereby reaffirming the intention to hold Besenval in detention and to prosecute him, as well as to prosecute others who had committed violations against persons. Godard had espoused the winning position in this his first major national political role.

Godard's appearance before the National Assembly garnered him some national recognition. In a letter sent later in the year by an Abbé Defuaus, a priest originally from Godard's hometown of Semur-en-Auxois but then living in a monastery in Lyon, Defuaus made a flattering reference to Godard's appearance before the Assembly. Defuaus suggested that

---

and immigrated to England. He returned during the Restoration, becoming a Peer in the upper legislative chamber and ultimately becoming a member of the Académie Française.

8. *Archives Parlementaires*, vol. 8, 311.

9. Ibid.

10. Ibid., 313.

the importance of Godard's role in national affairs reflected by this appearance indicated he could potentially serve as a representative of provincial interests.[11]

As the revolutionary summer advanced, the National Assembly developed its own dynamic and exhibited an accelerating taste for social and political reform. Drafting the new Constitution was recognized to be a long-term objective, but other more immediate ways of addressing social restructuring were also being contemplated. This process reached its climax on the evening of August 4, when certain members of the nobility, led by the Vicomte de Noailles, a young man who was Lafayette's brother-in-law and who had fought with him at Washington's side in the American Revolution, called for the abolition of the wide range of oppressive feudal rights that still existed throughout France.[12] These rights, vestiges from an era when local nobles controlled the very lives of the peasants who lived within their fiefdoms, ranged from the assessment of taxes on the products of local fields to the right to require peasants to render services without compensation of any kind to the local "lord." In the revolutionary fervor of the moment, these anachronistic rights and obligations appeared particularly repugnant. An assortment of members of the nobility followed de Noailles to the rostrum to personally renounce their vestigial feudal rights. An irresistible enthusiasm swept the Assembly. Within days, many of the privileges that had existed across France for

---

11. Letter dated Lyon, December 21, 1789, to Jacques Godard from "your friend Defuaus." (Unpublished letter from the author's personal collection.) A reference to an Abbé Defuaus can be found on page 2 of *L'Ami de la religion et du roi: journal ecclésiastique, politique et littéraire*, vol. 83 (Paris: Librairie Ecclésiastique d'Ad. LeClere et Cie., 1835).

12. Louis-Marc-Antoine de Noailles (1756–1804) was born in Paris to a prominent noble family. He married a cousin, Anne Jeanne Baptiste Georgette Adrienne Pauline Louise Catherine Dominique de Noailles, whose sister married the Marquis de Lafayette. De Noailles joined Lafayette in America to participate in the fight against the British. He was present at Yorktown with the Comte de Rochambeau when Cornwallis surrendered, effectively ending the military phase of the American Revolution. In spite of his prominent role in the early phase of the French Revolution, as an aristocrat he was compelled to leave France in 1792, immigrating to the United States. His wife, her mother, and grandmother were all guillotined on July 22, 1794, just six days before the end of the Terror. After having returned to France, de Noailles was sent to Haiti to participate in the attempt to supress the revolt of Toussaint l'Ouverture. He died on January 7, 1804, in Havana from wounds he suffered in that effort.

over a millennium had as a matter of official policy ceased to exist.[13]

However, the actual implementation of the termination of ancient feudal rights and privileges would turn out to be an arduous process taking many years, and would give rise to much frustration among the peasant class.[14] That frustration would, in turn, engender uprisings in certain of the provinces. In late 1790 Jacques Godard would be appointed as a royal commissioner to investigate one of the more dramatic peasant uprisings, engaging him in a high-visibility mission and giving him the opportunity to publish one of his most important writings.

As events at Versailles accelerated, Godard's public profile in Paris began to rise. He had been elected a member of the District Assembly of his Paris Blancs-Manteaux neighborhood at the very inception of that body after the capture of the Bastille and had even become one of its earliest presidents, a role he would reprise several times. His activity within that Assembly would continue to increase in the months to come.[15] His name, citing his position as "one of the presidents" of the Blancs-Manteaux District, appears on a number of published Decrees issued by his District Assembly, most, but not all, being ministerial in nature.[16] Of particular interest is a Decree of August 29, 1789.[17] That Decree called for voluntary contributions from private citizens to the national treasury as a stop-gap measure to provide funds to the government pending "the executive power, whose influence is so necessary in a great empire," having reassumed

---

13. As will be noted, the enthusiastic renunciation of privileges and rights to receive special taxes was not universal. Notably, the Brancas family of Metz did not voluntarily renounce its right to collect the tax it annually assessed against the Jewish community of that city.

14. At least one historian has concluded that the resolutions adopted on August 4, 1789, and in the days that followed, were considered by the peasants of France as a "monstrous fraud" because they failed to produce the expected results and prompted tremendous disappointment. P. M. Jones, *The Peasantry in the French Revolution* (Cambridge: Cambridge University Press, 1988), 81.

15. The presidency of the various Paris Districts rotated rapidly and was sometimes held by more than one person simultaneously, giving the many individuals entrusted with that post the ability to claim the prestigious title of "President."

16. Cf. *District des Blancs-Manteaux Arrêté du 21 Juillet 1789* (Bibliothèque Historique de la Ville de Paris, Doc. 10065, no. 30 bis.).

17. *Arrêté du District des Blancs-Manteaux du 29 Août 1789* (de l'Imprimerie de Prault, Imprimeur du Roi, quai des Augustins, 1789).

all aspects of its governing role.[18] It praised the virtue of citizen action in coming to the rescue of the Fatherland, suggesting that such action would not only strengthen the nation, but would also bring citizens closer to each other. Likely drafted by Godard (since the text bears all the marks of Godard's political philosophy and his writing style), the Decree reflects the optimism and enthusiasm that infused the period following the taking of the Bastille.

On September 12, 1789, a ceremony was held to honor and bless the flags of the volunteer National Guard battalion from Godard's district in the church of the Blancs-Manteaux. For the ceremony, Jacques Godard was called upon to deliver some remarks, a singular honor for someone so young.[19] He spoke about his concern respecting the growing divisions that were already emerging within the burgeoning democratic movement in the city of Paris. His remarks, which indirectly seem to be a warning against the power of the local assemblies (including his own local assembly, perhaps with an eye to eventually playing a role in the larger and much more influential Paris municipal assembly), strongly urged unity and coordination among the various and sometimes competing organs of government that were just developing.[20] The remarks foreshadow his future role in Paris municipal—as distinguished from district—politics:

> In the name of Peace, in the name of Liberty, in the name of the public welfare, let each of the sixty Divisions of the Capital restrain its

18. Ibid., 2.

19. *Discours prononcé dans l'église des Blancs-Manteaux le samedi 12 septembre 1789. A l'occasion de la bénédiction des drapeaux du district des Blancs-Manteaux. Par M. Godard, avocat au Parlement, ex-président du District* (Bib. Nat., Lb 40/235, 24 p. in-8e 23, 4 & 10). (*Actes de la Commune de Paris*, 529.)

20. As president of the Blancs-Manteaux District, Godard became an overt supporter of a more centralized municipal government, objecting to the move by some of the districts to act as independent centers of power. On November 3, 1789, Godard, in this capacity, signed a statement in which his district rejected the notion that the districts should retain municipal legislative powers. The statement read, in part: "we cannot at the same time delegate authority to act and retain those same powers ourselves: it is by simple wishes or instructions that we can enlighten our representatives." The minutes of the meeting of the Paris Assembly indicate that one of the members of the Blancs-Manteaux delegation (possibly the president, Godard) read the statement aloud to the Assembly and it, not surprisingly, received unanimous applause. Lacroix, *Actes de la Commune de Paris pendant la Révolution*, vol. 2, p. 534.

concerns and its vigilance to its interior and private administration; that, in this immense city, where the unity, the coordination and the speed of the public operations are of such a great importance, there be a single and unique Assembly charged with these operations.[21]

When his speech was reported in the press, it was noted that "Godard reflected the new feelings of confidence and defiance." Confidence was, in fact, an essential part of Godard's persona. His defiance, however, was muted. Godard's remarks demonstrated a consistent and clear tendency toward moderation, even bordering on conservatism within a revolutionary context. In the course of his remarks, he declared himself satisfied with the accomplishments of the Revolution and did not seem to believe that there was any further need for upheavals. Rather, he evoked caution as he urged consolidation of the dramatic gains that had been achieved, with a warning about the potential for counter-revolution:

> You have no further conquests to make; but you should conserve those that you have made...Remember that a monarch is not accustomed to seeing his will limited so easily; that he watches for a favorable moment when he can break his yoke; that if he is clever, he lulls the people by words.[22]

Godard's remarks suggested a very cautious approach with a view to protecting the newly gained freedoms rather than fighting for additional rights. This was not necessarily the attitude of many of his contemporaries. The press reports noted that Godard had reminded his audience that true liberty lay in submission to law, and that to prevent anarchy they should support their representative assembly. In short, Godard had already placed himself squarely in a centrist position, warning against both a royalist or aristocratic counterrevolution as well as against a radical revolution from the already increasingly radicalizing revolutionary elements.[23]

---

21. Pamphlet published in 1789 setting out the complete text of the address. Collection of the Bibliothèque Historique de la Ville de Paris. See also Godard, *Exposé des Travaux* 160–61.

22. Jacques Godard, *Discours prononcé dans l'église des Blancs-Manteaux le samedi 12 septembre 1789, à l'occasion de la bénédiction des drapeaux du District des Blancs-Manteaux, par M. GODARD, Avocat au Parlement, Ex-Président du District* (Paris: Prault, 1789), cited in Morris Slavin, *The French Revolution in Miniature: Section Droits-de-l'Homme, 1789–1795* (Princeton, NJ: Princeton University Press, 1984), 91.

23. Ibid.

Godard's colleagues in the Blancs-Manteaux District concurred with his moderate patriotic appeal. They determined that the remarks he had delivered at the Blancs-Manteaux church were sufficiently important that they warranted being published and urged Godard to do so. A district decree signed by an individual named Auzolles, one of the District Presidents, and co-signed by Vivier de Launay, a former member of the Paris Parlement and one of the District's Secretaries, announced that in promoting the publication of Godard's remarks the assembly was reflecting the unanimous desire of those who had attended the speech and that it was demonstrating its satisfaction with Godard.[24]

At the time of his speech, Godard was still not a member of the Paris National Guard. However, as his political involvement began to expand, on December 13, 1789, he finally joined. Being a member of the National Guard was undoubtedly politically wise if not a political necessity. It was a statement of good citizenship. The extent of Godard's actual involvement with the National Guard is unclear. With the multitude of activities filling his schedule, it is doubtful he had much extra time to devote to the National Guard.

Godard's prudent approach to the revolutionary activities going on all about him was in stark contrast to some of the attitudes that were developing around Paris and in other parts of France. Contrary to the path chosen by so many of the young revolutionaries populating the political arena, Godard would continue throughout his brief career to counsel order and careful deliberation, eschewing inflammatory and radical rhetoric and displaying a provincial conservatism combined with an abiding respect for legal processes even as he militated for political and social change. His friend Amélie Suard would succinctly highlight his conservatism in her praise of Godard at the time of his death, when she wrote that "his conscience and his reason showed him all of the benefits of the revolution, but prevented him from being swept towards espousing the ideas that could deprive us of all of those benefits."[25]

---

24. *Discours prononcé dans l'église des Blancs-Manteaux le samedi 12 septembre 1789 à l'occasion de la Bénédiction des Drapeaux du District des Blancs-Manteaux, par M. GODARD, Avocat au Parlement, Ex-Président du District* (23-page brochure). Copies of the speech were sold for 12 francs, with proceeds from the sale destined "for the benefit of the poor in the district." *La Chronique de Paris*, September 21, 1789, no. 29, p. 116.

25. Amélie Suard, *Lettres de Madame Suard à son Mari* (A. Dampierre, An X [1802]), 109.

CHAPTER 19

THE JEWISH ISSUE BECOMES
MORE PRESSING

In Alsace, as in many other parts of France, the Revolution brought great turmoil. The convening of the Estates-General and the growing violence in Paris had generated a collective panic. Irrational beliefs of impending attacks by unidentified forces—a "Great Fear"—gripped large segments of the countryside.[1] With rising agitation spreading in Alsace, Jews considered themselves to be in dire danger of attacks from some of their Christian neighbors. The arrival of the Jewish High Holidays in late September triggered well-founded fears in the scattered Jewish communities, as significant elements of the Alsatian population, hostile to Jews for generations, became even more strongly resentful of the Jews than previously. Antagonism began to build in August, around the time of Tisha B'Av, the holiday during which Jews mourn the destruction of the First and Second Temples of Jerusalem, and it accelerated as the Jewish High Holidays approached.[2] This increasing anger was in part motivated by the general turmoil and insecurity that all of French society was then experiencing, but it was also more specifically related to the rising concern among certain segments of the Alsatian population that Jews,

---

1. See Lefebvre, *The Coming of the French Revolution*, 129–32.
2. See *Mercure de France*, August 22, 1789, no. 34; *Le Patriote français*, no. 23; *Le Courrier de Versailles à Paris et de Paris à Versailles*, no. 51, cited in Léon Kahn, *Les Juifs de Paris pendant la Révolution*, 25; see also Grégoire, *Motion en faveur des Juifs*, ix.

a minority they reviled and resented, might be given new rights by the revolutionary forces in Paris. Fearful of the escalating violence and of the prospects of physical harm, the Alsatian Jews turned to the National Assembly for protection.[3]

On the Monday during the ten days between Rosh Hashanah and Yom Kippur, pressed by Jewish leaders, the National Assembly held a debate on the lurking dangers to the Alsatian Jewish community. The plea for protection for that community was made by Stanislas de Clermont-Tonnerre,[4] a young nobleman who was stylish, graceful, and thoughtful. Charles Lacretelle, in his *Memoires*, said of Clermont-Tonnerre's speeches at the National Assembly, "[N]o speeches were more logical than his, nor were any more infused with healthy understanding."[5] Clermont-Tonnerre's several important interventions on behalf of the Jews would bear witness to Lacretelle's judgment. His plea on behalf of the endangered Alsatian Jewish community occurred just after he had stepped down from the presidency of the National Assembly. In this impassioned address, his first speech from the floor of the Assembly since relinquishing the presidency, he called upon his fellow Assembly members to authorize the Assembly President to mandate the local municipalities and public officials in Alsace to put all of the Jews and their belongings "under the protection of the law."[6] Clermont-Tonnerre went on to emphasize that it was his wish that it be "finally recognized that a man, even if he is not a citizen, must not be

---

3. Feuerwerker, *L'Émancipation des Juifs en France*, 303–9.

4. Stanislas de Clermont-Tonnerre (1757–1792), descended from a noble family from the Merthe-et-Moselle region of northeastern France, was elected as a representative of the nobility to the Estates-General. He was a Freemason who aligned himself with members of the liberal nobility, such as the Duc d'Orléans and the Marquis de Lafayette. He was recognized as a skillful and persuasive orator. When, in 1791, his proposals for an English-style bicameral legislature and a monarchical veto were rejected, he left the ranks of the moderates and joined the monarchists. This led to his alienation from the liberal forces and to his ultimate imprisonment. He was released from prison just as the Paris mob began its attack against the monarchy on August 10, 1792. While in proximity to the Tuileries, he was attacked and chased into a building. The mob followed him and he was defenestrated, falling to his death.

5. Charles Lacretelle, *Dix Années d'Epreuves pendant la Révolution*, 48.

6. *Archives Parlementaires*, vol. 9, September 29, 1789, p. 201. See also *Journal de Versailles*, Saturday, October 3, 1789, no. 42, p. 319, reporting on Clermont-Tonnerre's remarks of September 28, 1789.

slaughtered." Henri Grégoire, the "generous defender" of the Jews, albeit for his own theological purposes, "with his customary energy" joined Clermont-Tonnerre in his request.[7] The Assembly then expressly directed its president "to write to the public officials in Alsace, ordering them to put the Jews under the protection of the law and to demand that the king provide the necessary protection."[8] The king acquiesced to the Assembly's decision.

The Comte de Rochambeau, who had been the leader of the French expeditionary force during the American War of Independence, was then serving as the royal military governor of Alsace.[9] In accordance with written instructions from Louis XVI, acting through his Secretary of War Jean-Fréderic de la Tour du Pin, to protect Alsatian Jews, Rochambeau should have immediately used his troops to protect the embattled Jews in accordance with the royally sanctioned decree of the National Assembly.[10] However, initially, instead of doing so, he directed representatives of the Jewish community to turn to the local authorities where, he suggested, they could secure any needed protection. The local authorities, however, were either powerless or unwilling to take any serious measures—something that Rochambeau must have known. Ultimately, in a belated response to unambiguous orders from Versailles, the royal troops under Rochambeau's command did provide some protection and were able to prevent massacres.[11] Despite this protection, however, some Jews deemed it necessary to flee to nearby Switzerland, where they found a

---

7. *Le Courier de Versailles à Paris et de Paris à Versailles*, vol. 4, 1789, p. 17.

8. Ibid.

9. Jean-Baptiste Donatien de Vimeur, Comte de Rochambeau (1725–1807) was a professional member of the French military who served in various campaigns in the War of Austrian Succession and the Seven Years' War. Subsequently, and most notably, he was appointed commander of the French expeditionary force which Louis XVI sent to the American colonies to assist in the war against England. It was to him that General Cornwallis's second in command, Gen. Charles O'Hara, handed his sword in surrender at Yorktown in 1783. However, Rochambeau insisted that O'Hara surrender to George Washington, who in turn directed that the sword be handed over to Gen. Benjamin Lincoln. Rochambeau served in various military roles during the French Revolution. His failures at the northeastern front against Austrian forces led to his arrest by the Revolutionary government. He narrowly escaped execution during the Terror.

10. Grégoire, *Motion en Faveur des Juifs*, x.

11. Feuerwerker, *L'Émancipation des Juifs en France*, 303–4.

temporary degree of safety until sufficient order could be restored in their villages and they could return to their homes in Alsace without fear of violence from their neighbors.

With the multitude of crises threatening public order, the National Assembly could give only limited attention to the problems of the Jewish community. Tackling the issues which undergirded the antagonism between Jews and some of their neighbors would have to await another day. Nonetheless, for the first time the Jews had received a rapid and favorable hearing before the national legislature.

On top of all the disruptions caused by the events of the early summer and the drama of rapid political change, the dearth of bread, then as now the essential food staple of the French population, began to cause growing anger throughout urban centers. In Paris the shortage was especially acute. Difficult wheat harvests and logistical problems arising due to political disruptions were at the heart of the shortage and the concomitant dramatic escalation in the price of bread. Anger at the difficulty in obtaining bread boiled over on October 5.

On that day, a large group of women gathered in front of the Hôtel de Ville, where the Paris Assembly was meeting, to demand that the city government make more bread available at a lower price. The gathering crowd grew increasingly restive, boisterous, and menacing. By the next day, frustrated at the inaction of the Paris Assembly, a number of women from the poorer neighborhoods of the city began a march to Versailles to express their frustration directly to the king. The crowd marching on Versailles grew rapidly, and by the time it arrived at the royal palace it was made up of thousands of women, but also of many men, filled with frustration and anger at the government.

Upon arriving at the palace, some of the male marchers broke into the building, which was surprisingly poorly protected. The safety of the royal family was in jeopardy, and two of the queen's guards were killed by members of the mob. Then, a dramatic intervention by the Marquis de Lafayette, who appeared on one of the palace balconies with the queen and her children, somewhat defused the situation. But the mob refused to leave. They persisted with a demand that the royal government remove itself to Paris. After some vacillation on the part of the king, he acquiesced to the demand of the mob that the royal family leave Versailles and return to Paris, which had been the traditional home of the Bourbon monarchy until the reign of Louis XIV. That evening, a motley procession accompanied the royal family on its trek back to Paris. Hasty preparations were made for them to move into the rather decrepit royal palace of the Tuileries in the city's very heart, a palace that had only infrequently had any royal occupants in well over one hundred years. Once relocated to the Tuileries, the king and his family would effectively become hostages of the Paris populace and of its revolutionary demands.

Just a short time later, on October 19, the National Assembly followed the king and settled into new quarters in Paris. Initially, the Assembly met in the Palace of the Archbishop, a building belonging to the Paris archdiocese which was located on the Ile de la Cité, adjacent to the cathedral of Notre-Dame. But, within a short time, it would permanently relocate to a long, hangar-like former equestrian hall abutting the gardens of the Tuileries palace, just a few yards from Place Vendôme. The hall was reconfigured with six rows of steep stadium seating lining the sides of the hall for the Assembly members. With both the king and the National Assembly now ensconced inside the city, the Revolution would be controlled by events in Paris and subject to the changing moods of the most vociferous activists and the vagaries of the Parisian mobs. The impact of this change of situs on the evolution of the Revolution was to be dramatic.

The struggle for new individual freedoms continued as the political structures of the new order began to take form. In the midst of the growing turmoil, the Ashkenazi Jewish community slowly began to assert itself. On October 14 a small delegation of Jews came to the National Assembly, then still located in Versailles, to raise the issue of their status within revolutionary France.[12] The delegation was headed by Berr Isaac Berr, a wealthy, well-educated Jew from Nancy in Lorraine.[13] Berr both

---

12. *Révolutions de Paris, Dédiées à la Nation et du District des Petits-Augustins, Publiées par L. Prudhomme, à l'époque du 12 juillet 1789, Première Année, Deuxième Trimestre.* Paris 1789, no. 16, p. 42.

13. Berr Isaac Berr de Turique (1744–1828) was a leader of the Jewish community of Lorraine, serving in a number of prominent positions both within the Jewish community and in civic life. He amassed a large fortune through commercial and manufacturing activities, primarily in the tobacco trade and in banking. But he was also a very learned individual. He published a number of books and letters relating to Jewish equality in France. The Jewish community of Nancy elected him as its representative to participate in the political activities in Paris at the beginning of the Revolution. He would be named as a member of the Assembly of Notables convened by Napoleon and then as a member of the Sanhedrin, which Napoleon would organize in 1807.

submitted a lengthy written statement (signed by four members of the Metz Jewish community) and addressed the National Assembly "in the name of the Eternal, author of all justice and of all truth…"[14] In his succinct but moving remarks, he described the delegation's specific request to the Assembly:

> Can we owe to you an existence less painful than that to which we have been condemned! Can the veil of opprobrium which has covered us for so long be torn from our heads so that men will consider us as their brothers; that this divine charity, which is so particularly recommended to you, be extended to us; that an absolute reform to the ignominious institutions to which we are subject be implemented and that this reform, up until now so uselessly wished, which we solicit with tears in our eyes, be your good deed and your work.[15]

The president of the Assembly then assured the members of the Jewish delegation that their eloquent plea could not be disregarded and would be taken into consideration. He directed Berr to so inform his fellow-Jews and urged that they remain "quiet and happy." The president then specified that, even though the Assembly could not just then address their concerns, the Jews could rest assured that their status would be considered "during the present session."[16] With an absence of certainty as to the duration of the legislative session, the assurance was then merely cold comfort—but it would later prove to be a very important pledge.

It is not certain whether Jacques Godard provided any advice to this particular delegation, although it is plausible and even likely. In any event, it is at around this same time that Godard was formally retained to represent and lobby on behalf of the Ashkenazi Jews. It may, in fact, be that he was formally retained because of the failure of the National Assembly to provide a satisfactory assurance to the Jewish delegation. In any case it is clear that he was expressly engaged to provide advice to the Ashkenazi Jews at a point in the late summer or early fall. This may have occurred just prior to the drafting of the August 24 "*Adresse*" that was submitted to the National Assembly, but it is likely that his more formal and broader engagement may not have occurred until September.

---

14. *Archives Parlementaires*, vol. 9, October 16, 1789, p. 444.
15. Ibid.
16. Ibid.

As he noted in a letter to Amélie Suard, dated November 19, 1789, he had been on an extended visit to his native Burgundy for "approximately six weeks," which had "barely ended."[17] He could not have met with his Jewish clients during that six-week absence, but, by the time of his return, he had already been hired. This indicates that he had likely been retained well before Berr Isaac Berr's appearance at the National Assembly.

While the precise date upon which the formal relationship began is unclear, there is further evidence that it must have occurred prior to October 23. On that date, even though he was away from Paris, Godard received a letter from the Marquis de Pastoret, in which Pastoret acknowledged that Godard was then representing the Jewish community.[18] The letter from Pastoret was in response to a request from Godard. Pastoret indicated that, in answer to Godard's request, he was sending him his book on Jewish laws and ethics, which included an extensive analysis of biblical Judaism and a comprehensive analysis of the laws of the Jews. The book in question was Pastoret's nearly 600-page treatise, *Moses, Considered as a Legislator and as a Moralist*,[19] which he had published in 1788—one among the flurry of writings about Jews around that time. Pastoret alluded to Godard having asked for a copy of the book in connection with his representation of the Jewish community, or as Pastoret put it: "for the noble cause that M. Godard is about to defend and which is so worthy of him."[20] Pastoret then briefly summarized his view that the Jews were the people "who has better than any other understood the rights of humanity in its criminal legislation, which has had the best moral laws." He added an expression of great pleasure that it was to Godard that "the opportunity to develop the very important political truths regarding the Jews had been confided." The letter concluded with words that exceeded the usual formulas of regard for a recipient, stating that Pastoret could not

---

17. Unpublished letter from Jacques Godard to Amélie Suard, dated November 19, 1789.

18. Claude-Emmanuel Joseph Pierre, Marquis de Pastoret (1755–1840) played a number of roles in France during the latter part of the seventeenth and the first quarter of the eighteenth centuries. He was trained as an avocat, but achieved fame as an author of legal treatises and as an anthropologist. He was named the first permanent president of the Legislative Assembly which took office in 1791 and in which Godard served briefly as a member.

19. Claude-Emmanuel Joseph Pierre de Pastoret, *Moyse, considéré comme législateur et comme moraliste* (Paris: Buisson, 1788).

20. Feuerwerker, *L'Émancipation des Juifs en France*, 337.

"too sincerely renew the expression of all of his most profound and true esteem."[21] The letter's final salutation further emphasized the author's respect for Godard.

Claude-Emmanuel Joseph Pierre de Pastoret was a particularly interesting individual in an era that abounded with striking and brilliant personalities. A legal scholar, just seven years older than Godard, and originally from Marseille, Pastoret, over the course of a long career, wrote a variety of books on an assortment of topics related to the law and society, including the role of religion in society. He is best remembered for his treatise on criminal law (*Des loix pénales*), published in 1790. One of his other many publications "Remarks in Verse on the Union which must Exist between the Judiciary, Philosophy and Literature," a seventeen-page poem on the philosophy of the law, had as an addendum a letter addressed to a M. Lacretelle.[22] Lacretelle was likely Godard's friend and competitor Pierre Louis de Lacretelle. This would suggest there had been a long association between the two, with the common link being, as it was between so many other avocats of the era, Godard's mentor, Guy Target. Pastoret was generally considered an authority on religious minorities, including Jews (as a consequence of his treatise on Moses and the laws of the Jews). It was, therefore, natural that Godard turned to Pastoret to provide him with information about a group with which he was about to have a very close professional relationship and about which he sought to know more. With the help of Pastoret and several other individuals, Godard would quickly become well-informed about Jews, their customs, their laws, and their history.

Thus, Godard's assumption of an active role as an avocat and lobbyist for the Jewish community occurred precisely in the midst of his rapidly increasing role in Paris politics and at a time of deepening national turmoil. It also occurred when Godard was being pressured not only by his growing political obligations, but also by his actual or self-perceived impecuniousness. Representing a group presumably funded by Cerf Berr and other affluent Jews, and thereby providing some assurance of the payment of his fees, must have given additional impetus to Godard's desire to work with the Jewish group. The financial pressures on Godard

---

21. Ibid.

22. Claude-Emmanuel Joseph Pierre de Pastoret, *Discours en vers sur l'union qui doit regner entre la Magistrature, la philosophie et les lettres* (Paris: Chez Jombert jeune, 1783).

had apparently been increasing at around this time.[23] He had noted in his November 19 letter to Amélie Suard that, although he had had to resign his political positions in order to take his extended trip to Burgundy to address his financial difficulties, he had immediately been reelected president of his District upon his return. Both the turmoil in Paris and his political work were preventing him from pursuing his remunerative professional activities. He strongly suggested as much when he wrote to Suard that he wanted to discuss with her his economic situation because he "saw his condition as being virtually lost." However, he conceded that this was a self-imposed situation. It was, he told Suard, a "sacrifice for the public matter," which he was making "with a full heart." He consoled himself, he wrote, by "endlessly telling himself that by limiting his desires, limited revenue would suffice." And, he added, "I do not feel any kind of regret."[24] His happiness, obviously in addition to the satisfaction he felt from his public service, would come "from the joy of conserving [her] friendship" and spending time with her at the Suard country estate in Fontenay-aux-Roses.[25] He clearly did not recognize, nor could he have known, that his time of sacrifice was only just beginning.

---

23. Godard periodically gave indications of his impoverishment. One such example occurred in his January 1788 letter to his cousin Cortot when, in a postcript, he acknowledged receipt of certain documents from a M. Daubenton, an avocat in Dijon with whom Godard worked on the Hermit of Burgundy matter, but then complained that he had had to pay "48 sous," presumably to retrieve the package from the postal service. Letter from Godard to Cortot, January 1789.

24. Unpublished letter from Jacques Godard to Amélie Suard, dated November 19, 1789 (Archives of the Institut Voltaire in Geneva, Switzerland Cote IMV: MS AS 420).

25. Ibid.

CHAPTER 20

GODARD ENTERS THE PARIS MUNICIPAL STAGE

On December 5, 1789, Jacques Godard presented his candidacy to become a member of the Paris Assembly, the 300 member *Assemblée Générale des Representants de la Commune de Paris* (General Assembly of the Representatives of the Paris Commune), as a representative of the District of the Blancs-Manteaux, where he resided.[1] He was obviously well known in his District since he had been politically active almost from the very beginning of the Revolution and had served several terms as president of his district assembly. His candidacy was successful, and on Monday, December 7, 1789, along with three other newly designated representatives from his District, Godard went to the Hôtel de Ville to be sworn in as an

---

1. *Actes de la Commune* de Paris, vol. 2, pp. 677, et seq. The Paris Assembly had been enlarged from the original 120 members to 300 members on September 18, 1789. This led to the Paris Assembly, from September 19 until its dissolution in October 1790, being referred to as the "Second Assembly." Of the 300 members, 60 were members of the *Conseil de Ville* (a group which advised the Mayor and whose members were frequently antagonistic to the members of the Paris Assembly who did not serve on the *Conseil de Ville*). Although there were 300 members of the Paris Assembly in total, there are frequent references to only 240 members, which is the result of an effort to distinguish the members of the Paris Assembly who served solely in the Paris Assembly from the 60 members who were nominally members of the Paris Assembly, but who also served on the *Conseil de Ville* and for whom that service was the more significant. Godard, in his history of the Paris Assembly, always referred to the Second Assembly as having 300 members.

unpaid member of the Paris Assembly.[2] With this election, he entered upon a new and important phase of his political career. He would not remain a quiet backbencher for very long. Rapidly, he would become an important player in Paris municipal politics, eventually becoming president of the Paris Assembly.

Godard now entered into a period of frenetic political and lobbying activities which would bring him a certain amount of fame.[3] These activities would also engender considerable respect from his colleagues and, inevitably, some disdain from those opposed to his political positions and goals.

The esteem in which he was held by his fellow Paris Assembly representatives was repeatedly demonstrated. He was held in such respect that, on January 30, 1790, in the midst of the great battle Godard was waging on behalf of the Jews, he received the highest number of votes to become the Assembly's Secretary. However, Godard, fully occupied by his lobbying, political, and professional activities, declined the honor.[4] The members of the Assembly would repeat the effort to elect him Secretary on March 29, 1790, and he would yet again decline.[5]

The end of 1789 and the beginning of 1790 marked a period of unparalleled political unrest throughout France and, especially, in Paris. Everyone in Paris had a political opinion and efforts were ongoing to bring people of common opinions together into clubs for discussions and the exercise of influence. Activists, radicals, moderates, and conservatives began to organize themselves into countless and, often, overlapping groups.

---

2. *Actes de la Commune de Paris*, vol 3, 138. None of the members of the Paris Assembly received any compensation. Indeed, when the Assembly's existence came to an end in October 1790, the members were required to confirm that they had not received any payment in rendering services to the Assembly.

3. The extent of Godard's lobbying activities is not entirely clear. However, we can determine that Godard's oratorical skills and his appearances before the National Assembly seem to have attracted some attention in the provinces. Relying upon his rapidly developing reputation, he may have been trying to obtain engagements as an advocate of provincial interests. Toward the end of 1789, he appears to have received at least one offer to represent a religious order in Lyon which was seeking a more favorable treatment for its members from the Ecclesiastical Committee of the Assembly. Letter dated "Lyon, December 21, 1789" to Jacques Godard from "your friend Defuaus." (From the author's personal collection.)

4. Lacroix, *Actes de la Commune de Paris Pendant la Révolution*, vol. 3, p. 645.

5. Lacroix, *Actes de la Commune de Paris Pendant la Révolution*, vol. 4, p. 526.

As 1790 began, the philosopher Condorcet, Godard's erstwhile competitor for Amélie Suard's attentions, made his foray into the political arena by establishing a debating society, which he called the "*Société de 1789*."[6] He sought to bring into his group individuals he believed shared his views about equality and a constitutional monarchy. On January 13, 1790, Condorcet sent Godard (whose name he misspelled as "Godart") an invitation to join the Society. The invitation summarized the Society's purpose as being to "develop, defend, and propagate the principles of a free constitution."[7] Godard and Condorcet shared many political opinions and, most notably, their views on the abolition of slavery. As a consequence, Godard readily accepted the invitation and joined the Society of 1789.[8]

Godard would prove himself to be a joiner, becoming involved in a number of other groups and, in particular, the "*Amis de la Constitution*,"[9] the precursor to the club that would shortly thereafter become known as the Jacobins.[10] He was even listed as a member of the Jacobins toward the end of 1790.[11] At the time, he was in good company. Mirabeau, Grégoire, Léonard Robin and Rochambeau were all listed as members. However, in light of his moderate political views, he was not likely to remain a member of that particular club for long.

Despite his keen interest in individual legal rights, Godard's first major intervention in the debates at the Paris Assembly came during a discussion over an important, but much more mundane, matter. He chose to address the issue of the legal status of the City of Paris. Specifically, he focused on the issue of whether Paris should be included within the system of proposed new political subdivisions to be called "departments" created by the National Assembly. Then, providing it was to be included within that system, the question was whether Paris should be its own "department," or

6. For a short time, the Société issued a newsletter to disseminate its ideals. *Journal de la Société de 1789*, issues nos. 1–15. Paris: EDHIS, 1982.

7. Invitation from M. de Condorcet to Monsieur Godart [sic], January 13, 1790. Bibliothèque Historique de la Ville de Paris (fol. 296, Société de 1789, admission de Godard par Condorcet [Cote 722–1214; catalogue du fonds général, Ms 722 à Ms 1214]).

8. *Règlemens de la Société de 1789 et liste de ses membres* (Paris: Imprimerie de Lejay fils, 1790), 40.

9. "Friends of the Constitution."

10. F. A. Aulard, *La Société des Jacobins, Recueil de Documents pour l'histoire du Club des Jacobins de la Ville de Paris* (Paris: Librarie Jouaust, Librarie Noblet, Maison Quantin, 1889), xxi.

11. Ibid., lii.

just a part of a larger department. The National Assembly had suggested that Paris not be included as a department or within the system of departments both because of its size and because it was the seat of government. On December 13, 1789, less than one week after he had joined the Paris Assembly, Godard delivered a speech before the Assembly (which was then published on orders of the Assembly) in which he declared that he agreed with the Abbé Sieyès that the city of Paris should be included within the new system, but that it should be its own department. The goal was to have Paris fit into the overall legal scheme and to give Paris greater standing, as Godard believed was merited because of its critical role in fomenting the Revolution. Godard, despite his provincial origins, or perhaps because of them, believed strongly in the singular importance of Paris. He knew that it was Paris, more than any other region or locality, which had played the most prominent role in overthrowing the old order and which, as such, was fundamentally responsible for having given France its new liberties. It was his belief that, so long as Paris remained a powerful political force, the changes that had been instituted as a consequence of the Revolution would be protected. However, as an advocate for an even-handed application of the law, he also believed that Paris should fit within the fabric created by the National Assembly for the nation at large.

In his thoughtful remarks, Godard stirred his colleagues in the Paris Assembly by appealing to their loyalty to their city and to the importance of insuring fair and equitable electoral representation.[12] He went into an elaborate defense of Sieyès' theory respecting Paris's integration into the "departmental" system, and his concomitant belief that Paris should be a separate department within that system: "What will be the place of the City of Paris in the new territorial division of the kingdom? What type of organizational structure is destined for her: What structure should she obtain?"[13] His response to his own rhetorical questions was that "[w]e should not ask for anything that will impact adversely on others. We should ask for what is due us, what is necessary, what it is impossible for us not to have, and if so the National Assembly cannot impose on the City of Paris its first act of injustice."[14]

12. *Motion de M. Godard, l'un des Représentans de Commune [sic], faite à l'Assemblée générale de la Commune, le 15 Décembre 1789 (1) sur l'Etendue & l'Organisation du Département de Paris*, 1–16.
13. Ibid., 1.
14. Ibid., 3.

Casting aside his usual prudence, he was unabashedly prepared to disrupt the National Assembly's existing plans for the city. But then he returned to his fundamental faith in careful deliberation and in justice, urging the Assembly to take the time and to exert the effort necessary to achieve a "just" result.[15]

He continued by analyzing the options available to the Parisians in the reorganization of France, concluding that only one was appropriate, namely that Paris should be treated just like the rest of France, which was being divided into departments of approximately thirty-six square leagues each. He suggested that Paris should simply accept this approach and that, by doing so, it would be asking for something that was in conformity with "[j]ustice, regularity, [and] harmony."[16] In spite of his view that Paris was an obviously special place within the French nation, he argued that:

> There is no reason for Paris to be an exception to the general law. Those who support the opposite, claim that there would be inconveniences to Paris if Paris were to be a Department, since the administrative assemblies would meet in different places and would therefore cause the deputies of Paris to have to travel. The other deputies would also have a great deal of influence against those of Paris.[17]

> It is not clear how these Deputies could have such influence. With everyone having the same spirit, the same interest and the same goal in the public administration, how could there be anything other than a common tendency for the general good? Therefore, it is appropriate to disregard this first objection drawn from the chimerical influence of the different districts against Paris.[18]

In his view, there was simply no disadvantage to Paris being part of a department (rather than having a legal status different from the status applicable to all other parts of France), and there were many advantages. By being a department, Paris would have more balanced relationships with neighboring cities. Those neighboring cities would then be more disposed to assist Paris, if such assistance should prove to be necessary. Again emphasizing the practical, he noted that, "as powerful as we [the

---

15. Ibid., 4.
16. Ibid., 5–6.
17. Ibid., 6.
18. Ibid., 7.

Parisians] are, we will be more powerful in an alliance with others and we will cease to be strangers in the midst of the kingdom and put an end to all of the jealousies and rivalries that could someday be so harmful." He also believed that the inevitable dialogue that would exist between Paris and other cities would "provide us with enlightenment, knowledge and resources which we might not have gotten in isolation. Greater commerce with our neighbors will make us better able to maintain the beautiful revolution that we have created and will bring us closer to the simple morality and customs that we praise in them and which we sometimes envy."[19]

Having asserted many positive arguments in support of his position, he now turned to the other side of the matter, the risks and dangers he perceived if his position were not adopted. He went on at excruciating length setting out the prospective parade of horribles that would emerge from a failure to accept his views, including potential violence.[20] Inherent in Godard's concern was the right of Parisians to self-governance. He well understood that if Paris was under the direct rule of the national government, then Parisians would lose their right to govern themselves (and, not incidentally, the Paris Assembly, to which he has just been elected, would cease to have a role to play).[21]

If the importance of Godard's adopted city of Paris in the establishment of liberty was not lost on him, neither was the importance to Parisians, including himself, of benefitting from the city's role and its revolutionary industriousness, as well as its right to control its own destiny. Nonetheless, he seemed to feel compelled to convince his fellow citizens of the vital role that Paris had to play and to do so at great length: "If Paris ceased to exist, soon you would see Liberty disappear from France and Despotism return to its domains."[22] He continued in the same vein, stating " [t]he

---

19. Ibid., 7–8.

20. Ibid., 12–13

21. History would bear out Godard's concern. The tensions between France and Paris erupted in a terrible confrontation at the end of the Franco-Prussian War in 1871. The civil war between the forces of the national government based in Versailles and those of the Paris Commune resulted in thousands of deaths and one of the most destructive internal conflicts in French history. Paris was then placed under the control of a *préfet* named by the national government. It was not until just a few decades ago that Paris was once again given the right to elect its own mayor and to have a measure of self-governance.

22. *Motion de M. Godard, l'un des Représentans de Commune [sic], faite à l'Assemblée générale de la Commune, le 15 Décembre 1789 (1) sur l'Etendue & l'Organisation*

very size of its population gives it insurmountable strength, and so long as it will preserve its liberty, the Provinces are certain to preserve theirs.[23]

Godard went on by setting out his view of the city's political needs: "First, that which is given to all other parts of the kingdom and which cannot be denied for any reason; the option to be a Department. Then, the option of being [in] or being itself a Department, to which we will set the limits and the organization, because without this possibility Paris and then the Provinces will soon suffer the evils which all of France is interested in preventing.[24]

His conclusion was simple and unambiguous: "Paris must be in a Department. Paris must be or have its own Department."[25] Effectively, for Godard, self-governance was essential for the preservation of liberty for the citizens of the capital. Furthermore, the preservation of that liberty would assure the protection of the newly found freedoms for all of France.

Godard's remarks were not only preserved in the minutes of the deliberations of the Paris Assembly, but also in a special publication ordered by the Assembly. The Assembly thought enough of Godard's remarks and their potential to wield an impact on the National Assembly's pending deliberations that their publication took place rapidly. Godard, himself, noted at the bottom of the front page of the published proposal that he "was entitled to some indulgence for a Writing made with such haste in such a short period."[26] The decision to publish Godard's speech may have been made rapidly, but the ultimate decision regarding the matter would not be reached for nearly a month. In any event, this must have been another heady moment for the young avocat, as he savored the respect and confidence of his fellow Paris Assembly members and as his words were injected into a national dialogue.

The debate regarding the status of Paris would continue until January 13, 1790, when the National Assembly created the Department of Paris, which covered not only the city of Paris, but also a number of contiguous municipalities within a twelve-kilometer radius of Notre Dame. In February, the Department was divided into three districts, with one of

du Département de Paris, 14.
23. Ibid.
24. Ibid., 1–16.
25. Ibid.
26. Ibid., 1.

those districts being just the city of Paris. Ultimately, the Department would bear the name of the river that runs through it, "Seine," rather than that of the city of Paris. Godard's proposal had not been adopted, but a reasonable compromise had emerged through the tripartite division of the new Department.

Godard's role in this administrative matter was but a small part of his activities at this time. During these early days of his membership in the Paris Assembly, Godard was active on various fronts. He would simultaneously pursue legal and technical reforms that a new administration needed in order to create an organized democratic process as well as improvements to the status of groups he perceived to be less fortunate.

On January 20 he was named as one of four members of a committee charged with preparing a petition to the National Assembly seeking to establish a school for deaf-mutes. The project had come to the Assembly's attention when, in late December 1789, the Abbé Charles-Michel de l'Épée died.[27] Although not much remembered today, l'Épée was highly regarded in his time. He was instrumental in raising awareness of the plight of hearing-impaired people seeking participation in the world around them and was among the first to systematically assist the hearing-impaired in their struggle for education and social equality.

L'Épée had adopted and promoted a sign language which was particularly geared towards permitting the deaf to participate in civic life and, notably, to defend themselves in court. Actually, there is considerable evidence that l'Épée's sign language was not his invention. Rather, it was a Spanish-Portuguese Jew, Jacob Rodrigues Pereire, who was the creator of the first sign language, which, in large measure, survives as the predominantly accepted sign language today.[28] In acknowledgment of the

---

27. The Abbé Charles-Michel de l'Épée (1712–1789) was an ordained priest and an avocat who devoted his life to assisting the deaf. His work on behalf of the deaf was so extensive that he was, in his time, referred to as the "Father of the Deaf." The sculpture that adorns his tomb in the church of St. Roch in Paris highlights his development of the "*signes méthodiques,*" a sign language for the deaf. A street in Paris's Latin Quarter bears his name. See Ferdinand Berthier, *L'Abbé de l'Épée, sa vie, son apostolat, ses travaux, sa lutte et ses succès* (Project Gutenberg, August 4, 2011 [ebook #36972]).

28. Jacob Rodrigues Pereire (1715–1780) was descended from a Portuguese Marrano family which immigrated to Bordeaux in the mid-eighteenth century and returned to the Judaism it had been forced to forsake at the end of the fifteenth century. Although Pereire's work has assuredly been eclipsed by the renown

significance of his creation, Pereire was granted an audience by Louis XV and received an official pension for his work. However, L'Épée has prevailed in the evaluation of historians as being the more important actor in the development of sign language through his publication of a widely disseminated manual.

L'Épée had established a network of rooming houses in Paris where, in small numbers, young deaf persons could be housed and assisted. The deaf would meet together on Thursday and Sunday of each week to receive special instructions. All of this was conducted through private charities since, even though a couple of official decrees had recognized the Abbé's work, there did not then exist any law that supported schools or provided any other formal assistance for the deaf. With the death of l'Épée his project was in danger of disappearing, and the Paris Assembly sought to preserve l'Épée's good works.

Godard, in his role as a member of the committee charged with persuading the National Assembly to fund l'Épée's project, took up this effort with the energy and enthusiasm that was his whenever he could assist the less fortunate. He prepared a moving speech in homage to l'Épée for delivery to the National Assembly. Although the text of Godard's speech may seem somewhat callous and patronizing to those living in the twenty-first century, it was an important demonstration of concern and compassion in its time. The goal of the remarks was to prompt the National Assembly to create and fund a permanent public establishment for the deaf. In Godard's presentation, he called upon the National Assembly "for the glory and the sensitivity of the French Nation," to establish "an asylum for all of the unfortunates of the empire, which nature has equally disgraced." [29] Of course, there existed hospitals for those who were physically ill and even for the mentally disturbed.

accorded to l'Épée, he is, nonetheless, remembered for his important achievement for the deaf. Today, a street in Bordeaux bears Pereire's name. It is worthy of note that the Pereire family achieved further fame and great wealth when Pereire's grandsons, the bankers and industrialists Émile and Isaac Pereire, made a fortune in the development of various modes of transportation and the installation of infrastructure in the modernization of Paris. They became particuliarly influential during the Second Empire of Napoleon III. A boulevard in Paris's upscale 17th *arrondissement* bears their name.

29. *Adresse des Représentans de la Commune de Paris à l'Assemblée Nationale, sur la formation d'un Etablissement National en faveur des Sourds & Muets* (Imprimerie Lottin, l'ainé, & Lottin de St. Germain, 1790), 6.

However, for those individuals deprived of hearing, but not otherwise afflicted, no such shelter existed. This made the infirmity of deafness subject to distinctly unequal treatment.

Godard and his fellow committee members submitted the text of his proposed address to the Paris Assembly on February 12. The text was unanimously adopted by the Assembly.[30] The Assembly also enacted a resolution directing the members of the committee, led by Godard, to go immediately to the National Assembly to deliver the remarks.[31] Furthermore, Bailly, the Mayor of Paris, in certifying that the Paris Assembly had authorized Godard to speak to the National Assembly, noted that the Paris Assembly had also resolved that Godard's remarks be published for posterity.

As was his wont, Godard had prepared a long and profoundly eloquent speech. His text began with words of praise for l'Épée. He noted that the priest had found the means of "supplementing Nature," of "replacing one of the most necessary senses, through the use of others," namely of permitting those who could neither hear nor speak "to, however, hear with their eyes."[32] Following his panegyric in honor of the late priest, Godard turned to some of his basic themes of justice and of public kindness and beneficence. He urged that, at this time of national regeneration, the French Nation should, "with a unanimous surge of compassion," accomplish that which was both just and decent. He declared that the city of Paris had done all it could to keep l'Épée's institution operational, but that now it was up to the nation as a whole to do so. Noting that the king had already determined to make available the residence and property of the banned Celestine Order (in the Marais section of Paris) for the benefit of the deaf, he urged the National Assembly to follow through on the king's "generous intentions." By taking this step, Godard concluded, the National Assembly would receive the "blessings of the unfortunates for whom [its] justice is a need and with respect to whom [its] humanity is an obligation."[33]

---

30. Lacroix, *Actes de la Commune de Paris pendant la Révolution*, vol. 4 (France, 1789–1794), 80, et seq.

31. Godard, as the head of the delegation from the Paris Assembly, was given an opportunity to address the National Assembly less than a week later, on February 18. *Archives Parlementaires*, vol. 11, pp. 644–45.

32. Ibid.

33. Ibid., 645.

Godard's remarks were delivered to the National Assembly on the evening of February 18, 1790.[34] At the conclusion of his remarks, the then-president of the Assembly, the Bishop of Autun, Charles Maurice de Talleyrand-Périgord, assured the Paris delegation that the Assembly shared their concern for the "unfortunates upon which the Abbé de l'Épée had bestowed so much care."[35] He also assured the delegation that the Assembly would take the matter "under great consideration."[36] In his remarks, Godard did not make any reference to l'Épée's relations to the Jewish community. But he could have. L'Épée had been a staunch supporter of Jewish rights, something that would soon be noted in an official recognition of the Abbé.

On February 23, 1790, Claude Fauchet,[37] a member of the Paris

---

34. Ibid., 644–45. Godard, in his history of the Paris Assembly, generously attributed the remarks to the entire committee; however, the nature of the text itself and the fact that it was Godard who led the delegation to the National Assembly and read the remarks strongly suggest that it was principally his handiwork. Cf. Godard, *Exposé des Travaux*, 124–25, and Ferdinand Berthier, *L'Abbée de l'Épée* (Paris: Michel Lévy Frères, 1852), Chapter 20.

35. Charles Maurice de Talleyrand-Périgord (1754–1838) began his career as a priest, but rapidly entered the political world. He served in the Estates-General and National Assembly. During the second phase of the Revolution, he immigrated to the United States. Napoleon made him his foreign minister. When the Bourbon Restoration replaced the Empire, he remained in government, continuing to serve until the early years of the July Monarchy.

36. *Archives Parlementaires*, vol. 11, p. 645.

37. Claude Fauchet (1744–1793) grew up in the Nièvre region of central France. He became the priest of the church of St. Roch in central Paris and from there was appointed as tutor to the children of the brother of the Duc de Choiseul, at a time when the Duc was one of Louis XV's principal ministers. Fauchet became a preacher to the king and gained a loyal following. However, he began to evolve into a revolutionary, to the point that he was part of a delegation that sought to negotiate the surrender of the royal troops defending the Bastille on July 14, 1789. He was elected to the Paris Assembly and served a number of times as its president. Following the dissolution of the Paris Assembly he formed the *Cercle Social*, which achieved substantial popular success, and eventually became associated with the moderate Girondins. When Charlotte Corday came to Paris from Caen, where Fauchet served as archbishop even as he also served as a member of the National Convention, he brought her to the National Convention to attend a session shortly before she stabbed Jean-Paul Marat to death. Following Corday's assassination of Marat, Fauchet was accused (probably falsely, but conveniently) of complicity in the assassination. He was executed at the end of October 1793.

Assembly and acting as its official representative, delivered a long eulogy of l'Épée at the church of St. Étienne du Mont located just behind the Panthéon (then the still unconsecrated Église Ste. Geneviève) in Paris's Latin Quarter.[38] In tribute to l'Épée, the entire text of Fauchet's eulogy was published as part of the official record of the National Assembly with the minutes of the February 25, 1790, session. A footnote to that text notes that a petition regarding the good works of the late Abbé had been drafted by "Mr. Godard, young jurisconsul gifted with a beautiful soul and a rare talent. He is the same person who drafted the Address of the commune on behalf of the Jews."[39]

Toward the end of the eulogy, among l'Épée's qualities which Fauchet saw fit to laud was l'Épée's relationship to the Jews. Fauchet noted that "a last trait of his charitable tolerance and his universal fraternity, to which the current conditions lend the most touching interest, was his ardent zeal and sweet hopes in favor of the Jews."[40] He then went on to suggest that the late Abbé would have been particularly pleased with the Assembly's promise to provide civil equality to the Jews. "Oh," Fauchet exclaimed, "if he had lived to see them brought closer to us in the name of the laws, and ready to enter the national family, he would have blessed the legislators who are initiating this union and the supreme Providence who arranges all events for the accomplishment of His great designs."[41] The timing was particularly potent since the Paris Assembly would send a delegation to the National Assembly, of which Fauchet would be a member, to petition for Jewish rights that very same week. Was this a mere coincidence or, as Fauchet himself seemed to suggest, was it part of Godard's carefully planned lobbying strategy on behalf of his Jewish clients? Fauchet and Godard were acquainted through their participation in the work of the Paris Assembly [42]

Augustin Bernard, "L'Abbé Claude Fauchet, Membre de la Commune de Paris 1789–90," in *Revue de la Révolution*, published under the Direction of Gustave Bord, vol. 10, 1887 (Paris: Bureau de la Revue de la Révolution, 1887).

38. Claude Fauchet, *Oraison Funèbre de Charles-Michel de l'Épée* (Paris: Chez J. R. Lottin de St. Germain, 1790).

39. *Archives Parlementaires*, vol. 11, p. 709.

40. Fauchet, *Oraison Funèbre de Charles-Michel de l'Épée*, 28.

41. Ibid.

42. Godard had become acquainted with Fauchet substantially earlier. In a letter to Cortot, dated August 17, 1788, Godard indicated that he had recently heard "Fauchet, the famous preacher," preach a rosary regarding, in large part, "*lettres de cachet*, exiled magistrates and the foolishness of ministers." Letter of August

and they would become even more closely associated in the months to come, making it quite likely that the latter is the case.[43] It is also very likely that Godard himself drafted some of Fauchet's remarks, which bore some of Godard's rhetorical flourishes, and that Godard, as a good advocate, incorporated into the eulogy a plea on behalf of his Jewish clients.[44]

Ultimately, it was on July 21, 1791, as the National Assembly was entering its final months of existence, that the Assembly voted to establish the *Institution Nationale des Sourds-Muets* [the National Institution of Deaf-Mutes] in Paris, as a successor to l'Épée's institution, and to fund it with an annual budget of 21,100 *livres*.[45] This new creation would later spawn other similar entities to provide assistance for the deaf. The successor to the Abbé de l'Épée as the director of the institution for the deaf, Roch-Amboise Cucurron Sicard, another cleric, would become an active promoter of education for the deaf in France and elsewhere. Early in the nineteenth century, Sicard was elected a member of the Académie Française and with the resultant prestige was able to develop a comprehensive educational program for the deaf. In that capacity, he encountered Thomas Hopkins Gallaudet, the noted American teacher of the deaf, for whom Gallaudet University in Washington, DC, the leading American institution for teaching the deaf is named, and invited him to visit the *Institution Nationale des Sourds-Muets*.

17, 1788, from Godard to Cortot, Archives départementales de la Côte d'Or, Archives civiles – Série E 642.

43. See Gary Kates, *The Cercle Social, the Girondins and the French Revolution* (Princeton, NJ: Princeton University Press, 1985), 5; See also Jules Charrier, *Claude Fauchet, Évêque Constitutionnel du Calvados*, vol. 1 (Paris, Librarie Ancienne Honoré Champion 1909), 247.

44. It is important to note that Fauchet was not a natural supporter of the Jews. The newspaper *Révolutions de Paris dédiées à la Nation*, in an article published concerning events on September 6, 1789, reported that, around the time of the seizure of the Bastille, at which he had been present, Fauchet had addressed several local District assemblies and had declared that "it is only possible to be free within the Catholic religion, that the perfect Catholic is the only fellow-citizen about which the Fatherland can be certain." The author of the article asked rhetorically whether this formulation was the means of sowing divisions between Catholics, Protestants, and Jews, and strongly criticized Fauchet. *Révolutions de Paris dédiées à la Nation*, vol. 9, p. 16. Godard must have had recourse to his most powerful powers of persuasion to cause Fauchet to be so laudatory of the Abbé de l'Épée's support for Godard's Jewish clients.

45. Lacroix, *Actes de la Commune de Paris pendant la Révolution*, vol. 4, p. 110.

In these early months of his tenure as a member of the Paris Assembly, even as Godard assumed responsibility for important and high-visibility projects, he did not refrain from taking on some of the more routine work. On January 2, 1790, he was appointed one of five members of a special subcommittee charged with reviewing accusations respecting the refusal of an officer of the municipal guard named Guillotte to leave a public space that he was occupying. The matter, originally presented to the Assembly a couple of weeks earlier, raised a series of questions about the right of the districts, the St. Victor District in the southeastern part of Paris in this case, to control publicly owned space and to oversee the selection of members of the local police. Godard, the avocat, must have been added to the subcommittee membership to provide his legal analysis of the issue (which otherwise seems to have been simply a struggle for the control of important municipal assets).[46] Following a substantial amount of wrangling at the St. Victor District level, as well as extensive city-wide lobbying with the various other districts, on January 21, Godard, acting as spokesman for the special subcommittee, went before the Assembly to report the subcommittee's findings in the matter. The press took note of the masterful way Godard had prepared his report. The January 25, 1790, edition of *Le Journal de la Municipalité et des Districts de Paris,* after identifying Godard, went on to note: "There is nothing that we can add to the method and to the clarity of this speech, whose conclusions were adopted by the Assembly."[47] The subcommittee's recommendation, which was adopted by the Paris Assembly, called for the Guillotte dispute to be sent to the city administration for a resolution. The decision from the subcommittee was, not surprisingly, a victory for the municipal administration over the district administration. (Although there is no record of the ultimate decision of the city administration on the matter, it is rather likely that it was favorable to the municipal government.)

As 1790 began, Godard's plate was very full, arguably too full. But he was about to enter into the most dramatic and memorable phase of his professional career.

---

46. Lacroix, *Actes de la Commune de Paris pendant la Révolution,* vol. 3, pp. 343, et seq.

47. Ibid., 503n3, citing *Le Journal de la Municipalité et des Districts de Paris* of January 25, 1790.

CHAPTER 21

THE DEBATE ON JEWISH
EQUALITY BEGINS

Throughout the turbulent summer and fall of 1789, the National Assembly had tackled many issues relating to fundamental human and
political rights. However, it had not completely resolved a question
that had tormented France for centuries: what rights should religious
minorities have? The status of Protestants, which had been the subject of the Malesherbes Commission in 1787 and had resulted in the
Edict of 1787, had, in significant measure, been resolved well before the
outbreak of the Revolution. Protestants were ostensibly now equal citizens with Catholics. Furthermore, the general principles of religious
freedom had been enshrined in the text of the Declaration of the Rights
of Man and of the Citizen adopted during the summer. The Revolution
had cast aside the prejudices of hundreds of years. But, despite its
auspicious beginnings, the fight for complete religious freedom for all
was only beginning. Indeed, from December 21 to 24, 1789, a general
debate respecting the proposition that non-Catholics should have the
right to vote and to have access to government employment—a debate
that should not have been necessary at all in light of the language of
the Declaration of the Rights of Man and of the Citizen—took place at
the National Assembly. The debate was carried on as part of the discussion regarding the restructuring of the government and, in particular,
the reorganization of local governments. As part of that discussion
it became necessary to determine who would be eligible to assume

various municipal offices. It is in that context that the question of the rights and roles of non-Catholics arose before the National Assembly.

Pierre Brunet de Latuque, the representative from Nérac, a small town to the south of Bordeaux, raised the issue at the National Assembly's Monday, December 21 session.[1] He noted that, in many municipalities in his region of the country, large segments of the population were Protestants. (He could have added that some were Jews.) It was therefore, he argued, imperative to decide definitively that those individuals could serve in government. Without that determination, Brunet suggested, many offices might go unfilled. This was, he stated, "a question that is not difficult to resolve."[2] Actually that was hardly the case, since, contrary to Brunet's presumption, he was launching a debate that would drag on for nearly two years.

Brunet concluded his remarks by proposing a simple resolution: "1st. That non-Catholics, who have fulfilled all the conditions prescribed in prior decrees to be electors and eligible citizens, can be elected at all levels of the administration, without exception; 2nd. That non-Catholics are qualified for all civil and military positions, like all other citizens."[3] Stanislas de Clermont-Tonnerre, the young nobleman who had spoken on behalf of the Alsatian Jews when they had sought protection just before Yom Kippur, stood to praise Brunet's proposal, and concluded by saying that he did not want to change the proposal, but merely to suggest a slight wording adjustment. Clermont-Tonnerre's reformulation was subtle, but significant: "The National Assembly decrees that no active citizen, having met all of the conditions of eligibility, can be kept from the registry of eligible citizens, nor excluded from any employment by reason of the faith that he has or the religion that he professes."[4] Of course, contrary to his

---

1. Pierre Brunet de Latuque (1757–1824) was elected to the Estates-General as a member of the Third Estate from a small town near Bordeaux in Lot-et-Garonne. He served as a royal judge during the Ancien Régime and then as a "*juge de paix*" (justice of the peace) in the early years of the Revolution.
2. *Archives Parlementaires*, vol. 10, p. 693.
3. Ibid., 694.
4. Ibid. The term "active citizen" (*citoyen actif*) developed at the time of the Revolution and its invention was ascribed to the Abbé Sieyès. It was intended to apply to all individuals vested with the right to vote. In the early years of the Revolution, that right was limited to males twenty-five years old and up who had been living in their city or region for at least one year, who were registered with the local national guard, who had taken the civic oath, and who paid taxes equal to not

assertion, his proposal constituted a significant modification to Brunet's decree. It was well understood that the term "non-Catholic" was a direct reference to Protestants and was not intended to encompass those who professed a faith other than a Christian one. To those with an interest in the matter, the subtle change engendered by Clermont-Tonnerre's language was readily understood as bringing Jews within the ambit of the proposed decree, and thereby making them fully eligible for all rights ascribed to French citizens.

It did not take long for the opponents of Jewish rights to appreciate what was transpiring and to react accordingly. The virulently anti-Jewish Alsatian representative Jean-François Reubell seized the moment to challenge Clermont-Tonnerre.[5] Reubell audaciously, but not entirely facetiously, proclaimed that he was speaking for the Jews. He exclaimed: "I view the matter like the Jews themselves; they do not believe that they are citizens." Then, he resorted to a devious approach by expressing support for Clermont-Tonnerre's motion, arguing that he considered that Clermont-Tonnerre was excluding the Jews from his motion because of its reference to "active citizens." To Reubell and his Alsatian colleagues, it was self-evident that Jews were not active citizens; they were not citizens at all—they were members of a separate nation. Obviously, that was not Clermont-Tonnerre's position. Clermont-Tonnerre responded to Reubell's assertion with emphasis, asserting that, of course, he meant to include Jews in the definition of active citizens. His response was

---

less than the value of three days' labor. There would be dramatic variations in the requirements for eligibility to vote over the course of the months and years to come. It has been estimated that in 1790, there were approximately four million active citizens in France.

5. Jean-François Reubell (1747–1807) was born in the Alsatian city of Colmar, the son of a royal notary. He was elected to the Estates-General as a representative of the Third Estate from his native city and the nearby town of Sélestat. He served as an active member of the National Assembly and was especially noted for his unwavering anti-Jewish sentiment, reflecting a prevalent attitude in his home province. For a time he was a member of the *Comité de Sureté Générale et de Surveillance de la Convention Nationale* which, for over a year, effectively served as France's executive branch of government. Following the establishment of the Directory, he was elected to serve as a Director and played a prominent role in that capacity, but retired from politics after Napoleon's coup d'état in 1799. In official documents, his last name is sometimes spelled "Rewbell." *The Journal de Paris* frequently spelled his name "Rebbel."

followed by a proposal from Adam-Philippe de Custine, a member of the
nobility and a military hero, that the Assembly should be on record supporting the right of all non-Catholics to freedom of religious exercise.[6]
By making this broad proposal, Custine focused the debate on the heart
of the matter—should Jews be deemed active citizens with all the rights
given to other active citizens?

However, the hour was late (it was 2:00 p.m. and well past the time for
lunch), and, furthermore, the Assembly needed to address the election
of certain of its officers, including a new president since the term of the
sitting president, Fréteau de Saint-Just, had just expired (and the selection of a new president required consultation among the members of the
Assembly). As a consequence, and, perhaps also to avoid a full-fledged
battle on the concerns of the Jews for which some preparations needed to
be made, the Assembly simply adjourned.

Due to yet other pending matters, the National Assembly did not
reopen the debate on Brunet's resolution the next day. It was only on
Wednesday, December 23, that the debate resumed. Clermont-Tonnerre
mounted the podium to express himself yet again on the subject of
granting access to government employment and related rights to Jews,
but, in addition, to executioners and actors (two categories of individuals
who were also deprived of those rights and whose status, deemed to be
particularly lowly, was being debated).[7] This time he was extremely well

---

6. Adam Philippe de Custine (1740–1793) fought in the French armies during
the Seven Years' War. He went on to fight in the American War of Independence as a member of the French expeditionary force. Due to his prominent and
unusual-looking mustache, he was known to his men as "General Mustache."
In 1789 he was elected to the Estates-General from the Metz area. He led the
revolutionary armies to early victories on the Vosges front, but later had to relinquish some of the territory he had won. As a consequence, he was deemed
to have acted against the interests of the Republic and was condemned to death
and executed in August 1793.

7. Both the tone and the duration of the debate about Jews would end up being significantly different from those characterizing the debates about actors
and executioners, who in contradistinction to the Jews would readily achieve
citizenship status. The newspaper *Révolutions de Paris dédiées à la Nation*, sum-
marizing the debates of December 19 through 26, succinctly described that
not-so-subtle difference, writing, "There exist against the Jews, hatreds; against
actors, opinions; against executioners, prejudices." *Révolutions de Paris dédiées à
la Nation*, vol. 24, p. 5.

prepared and delivered a long and thoughtful speech. First, he addressed the issue of civil rights for executioners and actors. His basic premise was very simple. Either a profession is acceptable under the law or it is not. If the profession is acceptable then it cannot possibly be constitutional to deprive those who carry on that profession of rights under the law. He then moved on to the issue of disqualification by reason of religious observance, and very specifically to the issue of the rights of Jews.

It was during the course of these remarks that Clermont-Tonnerre made a statement that would become the most renowned and oft-quoted of the political comments uttered about Jewish equality during the extensive debate respecting Jewish rights. The statement would also reflect the fundamental pivot that would ultimately lead to the acceptance of Jewish equality by the National Assembly and by the French political establishment, albeit not without a protracted struggle. Clermont-Tonnerre reminded the Assembly that it had already affirmed in the Declaration of the Rights of Man and of the Citizen that all individuals had the right to their religious beliefs. He then indicated that the only qualifier that could possibly restrict any form of religious practice was if the religion espoused a concept that undermined public order, for example, a religious endorsement of anti-social practices such as theft or murder. This, he noted, did not apply to Jews. Then, in a broad endorsement of the concept that all individuals (as distinguished from separate national or other groups) are entitled to equal treatment under the law, he declared with respect to Jews that: "It is necessary to refuse everything to the Jews as a Nation and to grant everything to Jews as individuals; it is necessary to disregard their Judges, they must have only ours; we must refuse legal protection to the maintenance of the so-called Laws of their Jewish Corporation; they must, individually, be Citizens..."[8]

Frequently distilled to the phrase: "To the Jews as a Nation, nothing; to the Jews as individuals, everything," Clermont-Tonnerre's statement reflected the need to alter the understanding of the fundamental place of Jews in western Europe. As noted, in France, Jews were generally considered to be an alien Nation within the French nation. They were not viewed as a group of individuals whose only fundamental difference

8. Stanislas Clermont-Tonnerre, *Opinion de M. Le Comte Stanislas de Clermont Tonnerre, Député de Paris, le 23 Décembre 1789* (Chez Baudouin, Paris, 1789); *Moniteur*, December 23, 1789, no. 123, pp. 500, et seq.

from the Catholic majority was their theological outlook and religious practices. Rather, they were considered a homogeneous and separate group living by different laws and ethical standards that simply happened to be scattered within a territory that had French laws, to which these strangers would, allegedly, not adhere. Clermont-Tonnerre was changing the dialogue. He was rejecting the notion that Jews made up a Nation and would have to be admitted into active citizenship as a group, and advocating that they simply be recognized as individual citizens who had different religious beliefs from those held by the majority of Frenchmen.

While this may seem obvious to twenty-first-century minds, it was completely contrary to fundamental notions held by both Jews and gentiles in 1789. In point of fact, Jews, especially those living in Alsace and Lorraine, did rely on many practices and laws that went beyond mere religious observances. To a large extent they conducted their lives with a certain obliviousness to or even outright rejection of the secular environment in which they lived. Fundamentally, they conducted their intra-communal lives and businesses through the institutions of the Jewish community and outside the national framework of France. However, Jewish tradition did not necessarily mandate this. This was rather largely (though not entirely) a result of the fact that Jews generally had no other choice. The secular instruments of society which excluded and mistreated them essentially imposed the situation. But, as Zalkind Hourwitz had emphasized in his essay for the Metz Academy, rabbis also played a powerful role in regulating relationships within their communities and were understandably eager to maintain that role. While some Jews sought civil integration, many of the members of Jewish communities in small towns and villages were deeply attached to their communal structures and reluctant to relinquish them—and not surprisingly, especially the rabbis felt this way. However, it remained a question as to whether this attachment was entirely by choice or was a consequence of the refusal of their surrounding communities to treat them fairly and to do so without imposing Christian practices on them. Once civil equality had actually been granted, the nineteenth century would provide an unambiguous answer to this question.

Clermont-Tonnerre was offering the Ashkenazi Jews a choice and changing the discussion in the process. If Jews wanted to join the French body politic, then they would have to give up their communal autonomy and those aspects of their status and comportment that suggested that they were a separate "Nation." They would have to compromise and become part of the fabric of French society at all levels, with their Jewish identity less part of a way of life and more "religious" in the mold of Christian practices. The choice was not completely evident to all the Jews of Alsace and Lorraine, some of whom cherished the autonomy they had in their status as a "Nation," and many of whom feared that integration would automatically mean assimilation and the alienation of their children from their beloved Jewish traditions.[9]

If the Jews felt some ambivalence, certain members of the National Assembly did not. Deeply concerned that the Assembly was about to adopt the pending resolution, the conservative clergy and the Alsatian delegates to the National Assembly joined together to extend and twist Clermont-Tonnerre's analysis. They sought to distort the ensuing debate by claiming that if Jews were to be considered equal citizens then they could not be protected as a special group and, due to the virulent hatred that had been engendered against them, they would be harmed. The Abbé Maury, the reactionary priest who had been part of Marmontel's salon where Godard had spent time during his early years in Paris, launched a frontal attack on Clermont-Tonnerre and his proposal. He reminded the Assembly that Jews had been proscribed from all nations since time immemorial and had been expelled from many, including seven times from France itself. Then, claiming to speak for the Alsatians, Maury sarcastically sought to reinforce his point by suggesting, falsely, that because of the "12 million mortgages" the Jews allegedly held, they would, if given equality, within a month own half of Alsace and within ten years all of it. He then declared that, "the people have such a hatred for the Jews that this enlargement [of rights] would cause an explosion." Therefore, he urged, for the Jews' own welfare, that the deliberations regarding them should cease.[10] To the deep consternation of the Jews paying attention to this debate, it now became apparent that their precarious position was about to become the very weapon used to deprive them of legal equality.

A short, young, and very meticulously attired member of the Assembly from the northern city of Arras now entered the fray and directly confronted the perverse argument of the Alsatians. Maximilien de

9. *Archives Parlementaires*, vol. 10, pp. 754–56.

10. Ibid., 757. See also Alexandre Seligman, "Les tribulations d'un juif alsacien pendant la terreur." *Le Patriote Français*, December 24, 1789, no. 138, and *Le Courrier de Gorsas*, December 25, 1789, no. 14.

Robespierre, a still little-known avocat whose greatest claim to fame at that time was his outspoken opposition to the death penalty, spoke for the first time in favor of the Jews before the Assembly. He ascended to the podium to voice his outrage, challenging the Alsatians directly: "How can it be that we pose as an objection to the Jews the persecutions of which they have been the victims with different peoples?" He responded to his own rhetorical question, "To the contrary, it is national crimes that we must expiate by giving them the inalienable rights of man, of which no human power can deprive them. We still impute to them vices and prejudices; and the spirit of sectarianism and of self-interest exaggerates those attributes; but to whom can we impute them if not to our own injustice? After having excluded them from all honors, even to the right of public respect, we have left them only objects of lucrative speculation!" Then, he made an eloquent and impassioned plea that they be granted citizenship. "Let us yield them up to happiness, to the nation, to virtue by returning to them the dignity of men and of citizens. Let us realize that it can never be politic, regardless of what anyone may say, to condemn a multitude of men who live in our midst to poverty and oppression."[11] Robespierre had applied on behalf of the Jews his powerful oratorical and rhetorical skills, which would soon project him into the forefront of revolutionary politics.

The next person to address the Assembly was Anne Louis Henri de la Fare, the Archbishop of Nancy, the capital of the Lorraine region—a region with a substantial Jewish population and whose peasantry was infused with a strong anti-Jewish sentiment.[12] He, not surprisingly, associated himself with Maury and reasserted Maury's positions. Echoing the Alsatians, he expressed the fear that a decree that granted the Jews equality could "ignite a great fire."[13] In order to avoid the grant of equality, he proposed the classic political solution; he urged that the matter of Jewish rights be sent to a committee for further review. However, in spite of his dire predictions and his proposal, the debate continued.

As the debate progressed—notwithstanding the support expressed for the Jewish position from various members of the Assembly—the

---

11. *Archives Parlementaires*, vol. 10, p. 757.

12. Anne Louis Henri de La Fare (1752–1829) was elected to the Estates-General in 1789 as a representative of the First Estate. He was called upon by Louis XVI to conduct the mass at the opening of the Estates-General. For decades he served as the Archbishop of Nancy, the capital of Lorraine.

13. *Archives Parlementaires*, vol. 10, p. 758.

delegates favoring Jewish rights seemed fearful that, in a direct vote, the position of the Alsatians might prevail and the cause of Jewish equality would suffer long-term, if not irreparable, harm. As a consequence, one of the strongest of the pro-Jewish advocates, Adrien Duport of Paris, a liberal member of the nobility who would play a pivotal role twenty-one months later, went up to the podium to speak in support of Jewish rights and to attempt to advance that cause with another amendment. "It is not for us to determine if the Jews are being faithful to their laws," he exclaimed. "It will be enough if they fulfill the obligations which we will impose on them; that we will share with them."[14] He then went on to propose a compromise amendment to Clermont-Tonnerre's motion. He suggested that the original resolution be amended to provide that "No Frenchman can have invoked against him, whether in order to be an active citizen or to hold public office, any matter that has not been specified in another decree adopted by the Assembly; subject to all laws and regulations to the contrary." Clermont-Tonnerre readily accepted Duport's amendment to his motion.[15]

However, on a narrowly split procedural vote of 408 to 403, which had to be taken three times due to the closeness of the vote, the compromise resolution was rejected. A vote now had to be taken on the original motion. A modest, but critical amendment was then proposed: that in any further discussion the motion would address only "Christian non-Catholics." This amendment could satisfy the Alsatians and their supporters by avoiding a direct grant of equality to Jews and could also be supported by those who wanted to avoid a negative vote on the Jewish issue which could then be revisited in the near future. A vote was taken and the motion passed, bringing the day's debate to a conclusion.[16]

The closeness of the procedural vote indicated that equality was potentially very near, but still out of reach. This initial defeat of the Jewish position would turn out to have a powerfully motivating effect on the leadership of the Ashkenazi Jewish community. It would stir them to action. They were now resolved to attain for their fellow Jews the equality that the Revolution had promised to all. To that end, they turned to Godard, and, in very short order, he, substantially if not entirely, prepared

---

14. Ibid.
15. Ibid.
16. Ibid.

a document that sought to reverse the obvious setback their cause had just suffered.[17] The document, produced by the very next day, December 24, was entitled *Nouvelle Adresse à l'Assemblée Nationale* [A New Address to the National Assembly].[18] The title harkened back to the Address that had been submitted to the National Assembly on August 26, in the midst of the debate on the article respecting religious liberty for insertion into the Declaration of the Rights of Man and of the Citizen. The very beginning of this new address was infused with a tone of disappointment, even with a kind of desperation: "[t]he hopes that we had been led to conceive & which your Decrees themselves had given us, could they today faint away?"[19] The tract then went on to remind the Assembly that Jews had been exemplary in their conduct since the beginning of the Revolution and had fulfilled all of the obligations of good citizens.

The petitioners took pragmatic stock of the fact that they had opponents among the members of the Assembly and sought to confront the claims of those opponents that Jews had vices that made them unworthy of citizenship. They urged the Assembly to erase the distinctions that separated Jews from their neighbors, asserting that then "we shall be as capable as they are of being virtuous."[20] In a brief analysis, they sought to dispel the notions that Jewish practices made them incapable of being good citizens. They incorporated by reference the observations of the "generous and eloquent pastor from the vicinity of Metz" (the Abbé Grégoire) as the basis for their defense. Then the petitioners called upon the members of the National Assembly to serve as advocates for the fifty thousand Jews of France "in the most beautiful cause that has ever been presented to a tribunal."[21] The plea concluded with an eloquent summary in the form of a supplication: "We beg you, therefore, to consult your customary justice; and the consternation which yesterday took hold of us when we learned of the opposition which was expressed by some members of your assembly with respect to the softening of our fate, which will change by means of the Decree you will adopt, into a soft joy which all

17. David Feuerwerker affirms that he saw a draft of this New Address in Godard's own handwriting in the file of Godard's papers that he reviewed in Geneva in 1944. Feuerwerker, *L'Émancipation des Juifs en France*, 337.

18. *Nouvelle Adresse à l'Assemblée Nationale* (Paris: Imprimerie de Prault, 1789).

19. Ibid., 1.

20. Ibid., 2.

21. Ibid., 3.

Frenchmen will share with us."[22] Unfortunately, the optimism of the petitioners would rapidly be dashed on the shoals of political reality.

On the very same day that the new address was submitted to the National Assembly, the debate at the Assembly respecting the proposal to grant civil equality to actors, public executioners (who, in spite of the very official approval given to their activities, were still being deprived of civil rights) and Jews continued. However, little had changed from the prior day's deliberations. The debate began with a diatribe from François-Joseph-Antoine Hell, the Alsatian who was likely the instigator of the scandal involving forged releases in 1777 and 1778.[23] Hell was seconded by the Prince de Broglie, the senior Alsatian aristocrat, who spoke extensively about all the evils the Jews had allegedly inflicted on Alsatians.[24] Next, the Alsatian representative, Reubell, renewed his efforts to prevent inclusion of the Jews in the resolution respecting full legal equality. He continued with the argument that the hatred of Jews was so profound that there would be an outbreak of violence against them if they were accorded equality. The hatred, he posited, was "essentially incurable." If the Assembly voted to give Jews equality, he could not answer for the terrible consequences that would ensue in his province. He went on to assert that the comportment of the Jews had engendered such strong antipathy that it was simply not prudent to, "at least at this time," grant them equal rights.[25]

Mirabeau entered the fray with a powerful statement on behalf of the Jewish cause. Then, Antoine Barnave,[26] one of the youngest members of

---

22. Ibid., 4.

23. *Archive Parlementaires*, vol. 10, December 24, 1789, pp. 777–79.

24. Ibid., 779–81.

25. Ibid., 781.

26. Antoine Pierre Joseph Marie Barnave (1761–1793) was born to a Protestant family from Grenoble. Barnave became a member of the Grenoble Parlement and was elected in 1789 to the Estates-General. He rapidly assumed a leadership position in the National Assembly, forming a triumvirate with Alexandre de Lameth and Adrien Duport. These three individuals formed the Feuillant Club, which broke away from the Jacobins as the Jacobins became radicalized and came under the sway of Robespierre. He supported a constitutional monarchy and carried on a lengthy correspondence with Marie-Antoinette. Having been appointed as a representative of the government to escort the royal family back from Varennes to Paris, he spent considerable time with them during the long carriage-ride. This proximity to Marie-Antoinette appears to have caused him to become enamored of her. His personal feelings for the queen and the moderate

the National Assembly and an individual already renowned for his oratorical skills, went to the podium to remind the Assembly that the Declaration of the Rights of Man and of the Citizen specified that no one should suffer discrimination because of his beliefs. However, he added as a cautionary note that if the Assembly had serious concerns about the rights to be given to Jews, then it would be best to limit the resolution on equality to Protestants.[27] The representative Bon Albert Briois de Beaumetz attempted to delay the matter by urging that actors be recognized as Frenchmen, and that the motion respecting the status of the Jews be adjourned pending further debate.[28] His remarks were loudly applauded.[29]

The discussion respecting actors continued, but the discussion concerning the status of the Jews did not go further. The version of the decree originally proposed by Brunet de Laturque was adopted with the addition of the proviso: "without intending to prejudge anything with respect to the Jews, whose status the National Assembly reserves the right to decide"—which made it clear that the matter was being intentionally deferred. The issue of the grant of equal rights to the Jews, which had been extracted from the original motion by Beaumetz's amendment, was now officially adjourned and the matter was sent to committee for further consideration.[30] No specific further action was planned for the floor of the Assembly.[31] It was understood that another debate on the matter of the status of the Jews would soon be held, but no date was set.

Although the years have given preeminence to Clermont-Tonnerre's remarks during this phase of the debate, in its coverage of the December 23 National Assembly session, the second installment of which appeared on December 24, it was Robespierre's words that the *Moniteur* cited at

political positions toward the monarchy that they engendered ultimately led to his condemnation by the Revolutionary Tribunal for treason and his execution just a little over a month after the execution of Marie-Antoinette.

27. *Archives Parlementaires*, vol. 10, p. 781.

28. Executioners were also granted full civil rights that same day.

29. *Moniteur*, December 24, 1789, no. 124, p. 504.

30. *Archives Parlementaires*, vol. 10, p. 782. See also *Evènements remarquable et intéressants a l'occasion des décrets de l'auguste Assemblée Nationale, concernant l'éligibilité de MM les comédiens, le bourreau et les juifs*, 1790. [gallica.bnf.fr] (fictional account of the debate viewed by Jean-Jacques Rousseau). "*Et maintenant un mot sur les juifs: je les aime, je ne m'en cache pas…*" p. 11. Most importantly, see the article concerning the debate in *Le Journal de Paris*, December 25, 1789, no. 359.

31. *Archives Parlementaires*, vol. 10, p. 782.

the very beginning of its article and thereby emphasized.[32] Mirabeau's newspaper, the *Courrier de Provence*, echoing Mirabeau's very pro-Jewish position, characterized the decision of December 24 as having been a "victory for the Jews" over those whom Mirabeau sarcastically characterized as the "good Christians, who, having been unfavorable to them [the Jews] during the debates, wanted the matter decided at once in the hope, undoubtedly, that the exclusion [of the Jews from citizenship] would present itself as involving fewer difficulties and consequences."[33] The newspaper went on to elaborate its ecumenical perspective, writing: "It is at a mass that one is a Catholic; it is at a time of preaching that one is a Protestant; it is in a synagogue that one is a Jew. But in the world, before courts, in different social settings, patriots are all of the same religion."[34] Generally, however, the discussion respecting the fate of the Jews was not of significant interest to journalists writing on behalf of various political organizations and the press did not take inordinate notice of the debates. An exception was Jean-Paul Marat,[35] the doctor and editor of the very radical newspaper *L'Ami du Peuple*, who was rapidly evolving into the implacable revolutionary that he would soon become. He expressed himself by first recounting with surprising evenhandedness the arguments both on behalf of the Jews and against them,[36] then giving the Jews a tepid endorsement. He began his brief analysis with a back-handed criticism of the operations of the National Assembly by noting that he did not "have the strength to make any observations on the puerile subjects with which the Assembly [was] currently occupying itself."[37] Nonetheless, he then made the effort to issue a defense of actors and, interestingly in light of his future radical advocacy of mass executions as a means of purging France

---

32. *Moniteur*, December 24, 1789, no. 123, p. 503.

33. *Le Courrier de Provence*, December 23 and 24, 1789, no. 64, p. 151.

34. Ibid., 503.

35. Jean-Paul Marat (1743–1793) became one of the most rabid and blood-thirsty of the radical revolutionaries, using his newspaper as a means of disseminating his ideology. His call for mass executions of alleged opponents of the Revolution led to his assassination by a young woman from Caen, Charlotte Corday, who herself became an anti-revolutionary martyr. Marat's martyrdom served as a symbol of revolutionary fervor during the most radical phase of the Revolution. Over the years he has become one of the most prominent symbols of the excesses of the Revolution.

36. *L'Ami du Peuple ou le Publiciste parisien*, December 24, 1789, no. 76, p. 8.

37. Ibid., December 25, 1789, no. 77, pp. 6–7.

of opponents of the Revolution, to reject giving rights to executioners. Respecting the Jews, however, he wrote that: "even though it does not appear as though one can contemplate seeing them take on diverse jobs in society, this is not a reason to exclude them."[38] This was hardly an effusive endorsement for Jewish equality.

---

38. Kahn, *Les Juifs de Paris pendant la Révolution*, 44–45.

CHAPTER 22

A LOBBYING CAMPAIGN BY THE JEWS OF BORDEAUX

The adjournment of the debate on Jewish civil rights and the absence of concrete forward movement on the Jewish issue now made it clear to the Ashkenazi Jewish leadership that Jewish legal equality simply would not happen without a concerted strategic campaign. The opposition of the Alsatian delegates was just too strong and too adamant. As successful in his business endeavors as Cerf Berr was, he was cognizant that he and his Alsatian colleagues were not capable of elaborating a coherent and effective political strategy, nor were they capable of preparing the sophisticated documents that would be necessary to wage a campaign for Jewish equality.[1] Nor could he or they speak in such a way that would convey the arguments of the Jewish community in an eloquent and polished manner. There was now a dire need to rely on someone capable of providing essential advice and leadership. There was also an obvious need for someone who could articulate both in written form and through oral expression, using the sophisticated language of the elites, the arguments in favor of the Jewish community's objectives.

---

1. Letters written by Cerf Berr indicate that he was not particularly skilled in writing in French. He could write and generally express himself in that language, but he did so with grammatical and stylistic errors. In his short biography of Cerf Berr, Ginsburger emphasizes this point when he notes that Cerf Berr wrote several letters to Godard, in which "he requested advice for his speeches and regarding several laws." Ginsburger, *Cerf Berr et son Époque*, 24.

With his home and office located in the heart of Paris just a short distance from the neighborhood which housed the largest concentration
of Parisian Jews[2] (with Paris's only Ashkenazi synagogue located on rue
Brisemiche, just a few blocks away), as a disciple of the great Target, and
with his by now well-established reputation as a skillful advocate, the
young Jacques Godard was an excellent choice for this task.[3] Godard
was, of course, well known to leaders of the Ashkenazi Jewish community
through his prominent role in the Metz case in which Jewish testimony
had served to condemn several individuals. His statements in favor of
Jewish equality in the Brisset brief may have also been known. Additionally, he had also been previously retained by certain elements of the
Jewish community in connection with their submissions to the National
Assembly in August and October and had played a role behind the scenes
in the most recent debate. As noted, it is possible that Godard's relationship with Jewish leaders had begun as early as August 1789 when he may
have begun to represent the Jewish community of Alsace in its efforts to
have Ashkenazi Jews recognized as equal citizens.[4] However, if that is so,
then that representation had been relatively limited. Now, however, the
issues were joined and everything was at stake—both for the Jews and for
the very concept of liberty and equality for all citizens. Godard must have
been drawn to this representation, which fit very well into his already refined view of the law as an instrument for promoting liberty and equality.

---

2. In his anti-Jewish diatribe, the converted Jew, Joseph Lémann, notes that
"Godard had thus elected to reside in the middle of the Jewish quarter." Lémann,
Les juifs dans la révolution française, 138n213.

3. In the late eighteenth century, Rue Brisemiche was a narrow and congested
street. In some places, its width was barely six meters. Over the course of the last
150 years, the medieval structures which once populated the street have been
largely replaced by larger and more modern buildings. In 1971, the western side
of the street was totally demolished, and the street now opens onto a large plaza with a playful fountain populated by sculptures and mobiles created by Jean
Tinguely and Nikki de Saint-Phalle. Nothing remains of the building in which
the synagogue existed nor of the atmosphere which must have prevailed on the
street at the time of the Revolution.

4. Feuerwerker, *L'Émancipation des Juifs en France*, 337. Rabbi Feuerwerker, the
last scholar known to have seen Godard's file, speculated that Godard's representation of the Jewish community likely began in August 1789, presumably with
the drafting of the short *Adresse des juifs résidans à Paris* that was published on
August 26.

This phase of his representation of the Jewish community would be very time-consuming, but it would also be a high-profile effort and Godard was far from being averse to public recognition. Additionally, it cannot be disregarded that representing the Jewish community presented the prospect of potentially significant legal fees, which, to a financially hard-pressed young man like Godard, had to have had its own attraction.

But Godard was not an inevitable choice. The Metz case had heavily revolved around discrediting Jewish testimony. Dupaty, the lead counsel for the defendants, had argued forcefully that Jews could not be trusted to give truthful testimony and Godard had joined the defense team. He could have been tainted by this role in the eyes of the Jewish community. However, Godard's belief in equal justice and his rejection of the notion that the testimony of Jews was intrinsically unreliable could not but have played a powerful role in persuading the Jews to seek to convince him to become their advisor and spokesman. And it was assuredly necessary to convince him to support the Jewish effort since Godard was already involved in so many other matters at the time. Between his private practice and his public service, Godard's available time for additional work was limited.

In fact, he had just assumed responsibility for another high-profile matter: a dispute in respect to the apartment the police wished to occupy in the St. Victor district of Paris, and he would also soon take on the preservation of the institution for the deaf that had been founded by the Abbé de l'Épée, in addition to fulfilling the ordinary, but time-consuming and unpaid, duties of a member of the Paris Assembly with its frequent meetings and complex agenda of pending matters. The opportunity to act on behalf of the Jewish community was undoubtedly simply too compelling a prospect to refuse. All the burdens on his time notwithstanding, Godard plunged ahead with this representation.

Once Godard had been selected and had agreed to advise the Jewish leaders, it became necessary to develop a comprehensive strategy. Initially, it was hoped that both components of the French Jewish community— the assimilated Portuguese Jews and the far less assimilated Ashkenazim—would coalesce in the pursuit of Jewish equality. Regrettably, that hope would founder rapidly.

Following the adjournment of the Jewish issue by the National Assembly in late December, many of the Sephardic communities in France and, especially, the Portuguese Jewish community of Bordeaux, had immediately concluded that they should mobilize, not to achieve equality, but

rather to protect their existing rights.[5] Far fewer in number and more cohesive, the various components of the Sephardic communities of southwestern France were better able to coalesce in order to engage in political
activities. In particular, the Bordeaux Jewish community had already
developed an organized political effort at the time of the summoning of
the Estates-General (which had nearly resulted in the election of David
Gradis as a delegate) and had created a political infrastructure in the form
of a General Assembly. It was now deemed necessary to bring together
the General Assembly of the Jews of Bordeaux to react to the refusal of
the National Assembly to decide on the status of the Jews.

The General Assembly of the Jews of Bordeaux met on December 30
and designated eight individuals to go as quickly as possible to Paris to
meet with as many members of the National Assembly as they could in
order to protect the interests of the Portuguese Jews.[6] These delegates
were charged with doing everything possible to achieve their objective.
They were authorized to meet with and consider a concerted effort
with the Ashkenzim, but only to the extent that it would not cause the
Sephardic community any harm. The very next day after their appointment three members of the delegation—Lopes-Dubec, de George, and
Salom—were on their way to Paris.[7]

Slowed only by a one-day stop in Poitiers on the Sabbath, the first three
members of the Bordeaux delegation arrived in Paris on the morning of

---

5. Although one of the largest and best organized of the Sephardic Jewish
communities in France, the Bordeaux community consisted of fewer than two
thousand individuals. Szajkowski suggests that in 1752 there were only 1,298
Portuguese Jews in Bordeaux and not more than 3,500 in all of France. See
"Notes on the Demography of the Sephardim in France," in Szajkowski, *Jews
and the French Revolutions of 1789, 1830 and 1848*, 135–50.

6. See *Journal de la Députation des Juifs de Bordeaux auprès de l'Assemblée Nationale 30 décembre 1789 et 17 février 1790* (The Central Archives for the History of the
Jewish People, Jerusalem, Israel, F-Bo-5), a handwritten journal of the Bordeaux
delegation's trip to Paris and their activities while in Paris throughout the month
of January 1790. The eight designated members were: Messrs. Gradis, senior,
Raba, junior, David Dacosta, Rodrigues, Lopes Dubec, B. de George, Salom, and
Furtado, senior. However, Furtado apparently declined his appointment.

7. Lopes-Dubec was already an experienced advocate for the Portuguese Jews.
He had been a member of the two-person delegation which met with Malesherbes in 1788 when the latter began his work on the issue of Jewish rights.

January 4, after a rapid three-day trip.[8] Upon their arrival in Paris, they made their way to the Hôtel de la Chine on rue Neuve des Petits-Champs, near Place Vendôme, and settled in for a long stay.[9] Just a few hours later they headed to the nearby home of Cerf Berr[10] on rue Neuve Saint Augustin for a meeting with the representatives of the Jews of Alsace and Lorraine.[11] The meeting did not go well. At the outset of the meeting, the three members of the Bordeaux delegation informed the Ashkenazi group about the purpose of their mission and of their "good disposition to act in their [the Ashkenzi community's] best interest as in ours."[12] The Ashkenazi representatives were gratified by this expression of fraternal cooperation. They apparently tried assiduously to persuade their Bordelais brethren to join forces with them, giving the Bordeaux delegation an even stronger impression of their desire to become full active citizens, although they did express some concern about being required to perform military service on the Sabbath. (For the far less observant Portuguese Jews such a requirement would not have appeared as a serious impediment.) Cerf Berr and his colleagues delivered to the Bordelais a copy of the August 31 address to the National Assembly as well as a short petition neutrally

---

8. Based upon their description of their activities while in Paris, the stopover in Poitiers on the Sabbath was the only concession that the members of the delegation made to Jewish observance throughout their trip. The text of the unpublished *Journal de la Députation des Juifs de Bordeaux* suggests that for the duration of their more than month-long stay in Paris, the members of the delegation carried on their activities on the Sabbath, without any respite. There is no indication of any religious activity or evidence of any kind of observance of Jewish customs or performance of any ritual by the members of the delegation during the course of their stay. This stands in contrast to the comportment of the Ashkenazi leaders, who appear to have adhered scrupulously to Jewish religious observance throughout their lobbying efforts.

9. This was the same hotel at which John Jay and his wife had stayed (upon the recommendation of William Temple Franklin, Benjamin Franklin's grandson) while Jay was in Paris to negotiate the Treaty of Paris that formalized the independence of the United States. John Jay, *The Correspondence and Public Papers of John Jay: 1781–1782*, vol. 2, p. 308.

10. In their description of meetings with Cerf Berr, the authors of the Journal invariably misspelled Cerf Berr's name as "Cerf Beer."

11. Rue Neuve Saint Augustin was located near today's Avenue de l'Opera, substantially along the same axis as rue Daunou, but it effectively disappeared in the urban renewal carried out by Baron Haussmann in the nineteenth century.

12. *Journal de la Députation des Juifs de Bordeaux*, 1.

entitled *"Réflexions impartiales d'un citoyen sur la question de l'éligibilité des Juifs,"* (Impartial reflections of a citizen regarding the question of Jewish eligibility) which, although published without citing its author, had been prepared by another avocat, Claude-Antoine Thiéry, one of the three individuals who had been awarded a prize by the Metz Academy. Thiéry's text was poorly written, containing long and impenetrable sentences. It was also unconvincing, highlighting anti-Jewish stereotypes with the suggestion that Jews were not ready for immediate integration into the French body politic—"at least for the moment."[13] The statement was a back-handed declaration in support of Jewish equality. To the affluent and well-established Jews of southwest France, this was a profoundly unsavory approach to a problem that did not appear to apply to them.[14] Before parting ways, the Bordelais representatives assured the Ashkenazi group that they very much wanted the Ashkenazi Jews to become citizens and that they would not do anything to prevent them from achieving their goal, "without, however, [the Bordelais Jews' rights] suffering in any manner" since "the rights and the status of the Jews of Bordeaux are titles which no consideration can or may make us abandon."[15]

Although a second meeting was held with the Ashkenazi representatives the very next day, it rapidly became obvious that the Bordeaux community was going to go its own way and, in spite of its expressions of fraternal concern, would not work with the Ashkenazi group. During the second meeting, Cerf Berr and his colleagues made it clear that they intended to prepare a more complete address to the National Assembly setting out all their demands. They promised to provide a copy of the address to the Bordelais and, in exchange, the Bordelais promised to provide

---

13. *"Réflexions impartiales d'un citoyen sur la question de l'éligibilité des Juifs"* (De l'Imprimerie de la Veuve Delaguette), 8.

14. The Thiéry document is so patently badly crafted that its presentation to the Bordelais delegation is perplexing. It is highly unlikely that Cerf Berr and his colleagues truly believed that the document would be considered as a suitable Ashkenazi submission to the National Assembly. Did they provide it to the Bordelais to elicit their assistance by trying to make the Bordelais believe that the Ashkenazim were unprepared and needed the help of the Bordelais? Or, is it possible that they were intentionally misleading their Sephardic brethren into thinking that the approach taken in the Thièry piece was the best they could do, so the Bordelais would be less aggressive towards them? The existing documentation does not provide us with a clear answer.

15. *Journal de la Députation des Juifs de Bordeaux,* 4.

them with a copy of the document they would compose. Even though the meeting between the representatives of the two Jewish groups remained civil, it was obvious that there would be little cooperation between them. Quite simply, the Bordelais delegation had determined that it was not reasonable for them to take the risk of losing their existing rights or even of delaying confirmation of those rights by joining their fate to that of the much less assimilated Ashkenazi Jews. Eventually, the Bordeaux representatives would even go so far as to demean the Ashkenazi demands for civil equality as being "poorly-considered."[16]

Not willing to take any chance that they might not prevail in securing confirmation of their rights, the members of the Bordeaux delegation, in keeping with their instructions from home, engaged in a tireless pursuit of support from members of the National Assembly for their cause, but for their cause alone. Beginning promptly following their second meeting with Cerf Berr and his team, they courted some of the most prominent members of the National Assembly, crisscrossing Paris with the goal of visiting as many of them as they could.

Immediately following their first meeting with Cerf Berr, the Bordelais had sought to meet with Henri Grégoire. Their first attempt failed because when they stopped by his residence Grégoire had not yet returned from that day's National Assembly session. Instead of waiting, the three Bordeaux representatives went back to their hotel and drafted a letter to the leadership of the Jewish community of Bordeaux to keep them apprised of their very first meeting and to demonstrate that they were not squandering any time in fulfilling their mandate. They would send such letters regularly throughout their stay in Paris.

Shortly before their second meeting with Cerf Berr and the Ashkenazi group, the Bordelais delegation was successful in meeting with Grégoire. He greeted them "warmly," embracing them and assuring them that they could "always count on his support."[17] This would be but one of a number of meetings with the great cleric, whose support of the oppressed would remain preeminent, even if his role on behalf of Jews during their legislative efforts would, after the summer of 1789, be relatively modest.

Over the course of the next several weeks, various members of the

---

16. "*Peu réfléchis.*" *Adresse à l'Assemblée Nationale* [of the Jews of Bordeaux] (Paris: Chez Baudouin 1789), 4.
17. Ibid., 5.

Bordelais delegation—a delegation which would grow to six with the arrival of the second group of delegates on January 7—would meet with many different members of the National Assembly, as well as with other notables. To maximize their reach, the members of the Bordelais delegation would frequently split into smaller groups, with one group visiting one or more prominent individuals and others from the delegation meeting with different representatives likely to play a role in the impending debate. When they could not find a person they were seeking, as was frequently the case due to the hectic schedules of the Assembly members and of the other prominent persons they sought to meet, they would simply return repeatedly to the targeted person's lodgings until they were successful. As they pursued their meetings, they also set to work assembling their own submission to the National Assembly in support of their position. After receiving from Bordeaux the basic text which would form the heart of their presentation, they submitted the document for review to the journalist and National Assembly member Dominique-Joseph Garat and engaged the printer François-Jean Baudouin.[18] Following several meetings with Garat and Baudouin they finalized their document, which they simply titled "Address to the National Assembly." Then, they arranged to print their relatively short petition, together with its many exhibits (which included a statement of their credentials).[19]

The Address is a regrettably self-serving document. Instead of promoting Jewish civil equality as a principled proposition, it sought merely to preserve the existing rights of the Jews of Bordeaux and of those who

---

18. Dominique-Joseph Garat (1746–1833) was born in Bayonne. He was a journalist, and served for a time as the literary editor of the *Mercure de France*, the newspaper owned by Amélie Suard's brother and edited by her husband. He became involved in revolutionary politics, and, in the early days of the National Assembly, he reported on its proceedings for the *Journal de Paris*. Associated with the administration of justice in 1792 and 1793, Danton designated him to be a member of the delegation that informed Louis XVI of his death sentence. During the Napoleonic years, he assumed a number of government positions, but was forced to leave government with the arrival of the Restoration. François-Jean Baudouin (1759–1835) served as an alternate member of the Estates-General, and, following its conversion into the National Assembly, he was named the official printer of the Assembly. He continued to serve as the designated printer for the National Convention but was imprisoned during the Terror and narrowly avoided execution.

19. *Adresse à l'Assemblée Nationale* (Paris: Chez Baudouin, 1789).

were identified as being "Portuguese Jews." The eight-page document was unambiguous. In it the Bordelais made it clear that all that they were seeking was confirmation of their existing legal rights. They did not mince any words regarding their Ashkenazi brethren. They expressly stated that they did not wish to be grouped with the Ashkenazi Jews in the battle for equality. They were forthright in asserting that they were not concerned with anything other than to avoid placing their considerable rights in potential jeopardy, a risk which they ascribed entirely to the Ashkenazi efforts. "We dare to believe that our status in France," they wrote, "would not today be submitted to discussion, if certain demands from Jews from Alsace, Lorraine, and the Three Bishoprics had not created a confusion of ideas which appear to envelop us."[20] They even launched a direct attack on their Ashkenazi brethren by indicating that the demands of the Ashkenazi Jews, though unclear, gave the impression that they were seeking "to live in France under a special regime, to have laws that are unique to them and to constitute a class of Citizens separate from all others."[21] This statement not only misrepresented the Ashkenazi position, but it was written with full awareness of its inaccuracy.[22] While it is true that the Ashkenazim were prepared to accept less than full rights as citizens as an interim measure, their ultimate goal, as Godard would so well articulate it, was to be recognized as active citizens vested with all of the rights of such citizens. It is merely that, in recognition of a difficult reality, they were prepared to compromise and accept somewhat less than everything they sought in light of the obvious and vociferous opposition within the Assembly.

The Bordelais, speaking for all the "Portuguese Jews," however, did not believe that they needed to compromise. In fact, they went to great length in their Address to enumerate all their existing rights and civic accomplishments, even expressly contrasting those rights with the dearth of rights granted to the Jews of Alsace and Lorraine. As noted, the Address included an expression of concern that the "poorly-considered demands"

---

20. Ibid., 1–2.

21. Ibid., 2.

22. In the Journal that the Bordelaise delegation kept of its visit to Paris from late December 1789 until late January 1790, it is noted that the Ashkenazi representatives "manifested to us the desire to be recognized as Citizens." It is true that the Journal also notes that the Ashkenazi leaders were prepared to accept a lesser status, but only as a means of improving their situation, not as an ultimate goal. *Journal de la Députation des Juifs de Bordeaux*, 2.

of "a few Jews from Alsace and Lorraine" who had none of the rights that
were already held by the Portuguese-Jewish community could result in
a loss by the Portuguese Jews of their rights.[23] In concluding their petition, the Bordelais Jews presented their excuses to the Assembly for their
"alarm," and assured the Assembly that they were merely seeking to avoid a
"humiliating exclusion" from the right to fulfill their "duties as Citizens."[24]
Attached to the Address were twelve documents intending to demonstrate
the existing rights of the Jews of Bordeaux and to provide testimony of
the esteem in which they were held in their community. When ultimately
submitted to the Assembly, the Address was "signed" (or more accurately,
endorsed) by 215 members of the Bordeaux Jewish community.[25]

Over the course of nearly a month, the Bordelais delegation met with
some of the most prominent members of the National Assembly. They
paid courtesy calls on many of the influential Assembly members, as well as
other political figures. They met with, among others, Clermont-Tonnerre,
Joseph-Alexandre de Ségur, Robespierre, Guillotin, Roederer, the Marquis
de Lafayette and his brother-in-law, the Vicomte de Noailles.[26] They also
met with current and former members of the royal government and most
notably with Jacques Necker, the Minister of Finance, and Charles-Louis-
François de Paule de Barentin, the former Minister of Justice.[27]

Just days after he had been elected president of the National Assembly, on January 20 the delegation went to Target's home in the hope of
encountering him. Target was unavailable. Not to be deterred, they went
back the very next day, but once again without success. They persisted.
Finally, on Sunday, January 24, they succeeded in meeting with Target,

---

23. Ibid., 4.
24. Ibid., 4–5.
25. Ibid., 7–8
26. Joseph-Alexandre Pierre, vicomte de Ségur (1756–1805), was a poet, soldier,
and politician. He was elected to the Estates-General as a member of the Parisian
nobility and remained faithful to the Ancien Régime throughout his brief tenure
in the National Assembly (from which he resigned in 1790). Although he was recognized as being the son of the Marquis de Ségur, a maréchal of France, he was
actually the natural son of the Baron de Besenval, a close friend of the Marquis
(and the individual whose proposed exoneration from the actions of the royalist
military forces around the time of the taking of the Bastille prompted Godard's
first appearance before the National Assembly). See Chapter 18, pp. 231–32n1.
27. *Journal de la Députation des Juifs de Bordeaux*, 41. (The scrivener of the Journal
erroneously spelled Necker's name as "Neker.")

who promised them that their matter "would be addressed within a few days."[28] Although the report does not so indicate, it is likely that Target alluded that the presentation at the National Assembly would take the form of a report from the Constitution Committee, the committee directly charged with analyzing the matter of Jewish rights. This was to be confirmed at a dinner that evening with the Marquis de Perigny,[29] the representative from Saint Domingue, and the Abbé d'Espagnac,[30] who informed the delegates that the Bishop of Autun, Charles-Maurice de Talleyrand-Périgord, the Chairman of the Constitution Committee of the Assembly, would be delivering the formal report.

Fully appreciating the importance of the intelligence they had received from Target, two members of the delegation, along with Perigny and d'Espagnac, hastened to Talleyrand's residence early the next morning, Monday the 25th, to seek a meeting with him. However, the Bishop was not at home. The next day, the delegation continued its visits to various members of the Assembly, some of whom assured the Bordelais that they would urge the "separation of the question which concerned [them] from the one respecting the Jews of Alsace."[31] The Bordelais appeared quite satisfied with this position.

That evening, the Bordelais had a final dinner at Cerf Berr's home. Among Cerf Berr's guests were Roederer, the former secretary of the Metz Academy, and two of the three winners of the Metz Academy contest, the Abbé Grégoire and the avocat Claude-Antoine Thiéry. Also present was Jacques Godard, identified in the Journal of the Bordeaux delegation as "the author of the memorial of the Jews of Alsace." In spite of being given

---

28. Ibid., 33.

29. Louis-Charles-Théodat de Taillevis, Marquis de Perrigny (1766–1827) served as one of the representatives from the island colony of Saint Domingue (today Haiti) to the Estates-General. His properties in Saint Domingue were confiscated during the Revolution, but he succeeded in obtaining compensation from Napoleon in 1808.

30. M. R. Sahuguet, Abbé d'Espagnac (1753–1794) was born in Brive-la-Gaillarde in central France. Although he trained for the clergy, he engaged in financial speculation, which brought him considerable economic success, and sought political appointments, becoming the governor of the Invalides in Paris. He was elected to the Estates-General in 1789 and then became one of the first members of the Jacobin Club. In 1792 and 1793 he became a supplier to the armies but was accused of corruption and ultimately executed in the spring of 1794.

31. Journal de la Députation des Juifs de Bordeaux, 37.

this moniker, the author of the Journal made it a point to emphasize that the Bordelais had not been given a copy of the document that was being prepared by Godard.[32] This led the Bordelais to speculate that Godard had not completed his document and would require two or three more days to do so. They clearly considered it an advantage that they had completed their filing while the Ashkenazim were still bogged down with theirs, and that there was a possibility that the issue would be brought to the National Assembly before Godard's document would be completed.

The dinner was a tense affair, but each side comported itself with decorum and restraint. As the scrivener for the Bordelais put it, "We held ourselves with regard to these gentlemen and they with regard to us with much reserve."[33] Apparently, nothing of substance emerged from the gathering. It would be the last meeting of the two groups before the debate at the National Assembly.

Displaying their customary persistence, two members of the Bordeaux delegation, accompanied by the Marquis de Perigny, went yet again to Talleyrand's home the following morning at 10:00 a.m. This time Talleyrand was available and received his visitors "with great warmth."[34] Over the course of that meeting—a meeting that would turn out to be one of the most important of the many visits conducted by the Bordelais delegation—Talleyrand "disclosed his favorable disposition, but also read to them his report and the draft decree that he [would] propose to the National Assembly."[35] To the great satisfaction of the Bordelais representatives, Talleyrand's report and his draft legislation espoused their positions. Talleyrand also confirmed that the Alsatian Jews were actively soliciting his support and, aware of his conclusions, were urging him not to issue his report. He further divulged that the Ashkenazi Jews had specifically asked him to call for treating all Jews in the same manner, "that the rights and status of active Citizens should be granted to all Jews without distinction."[36]

Talleyrand concluded by indicating that the Alsatian Jews had requested, if their position was not to be espoused, that the debate on the Jewish issue should be delayed. He gave the distinct impression that he was

32. Ibid., 38.
33. Ibid.
34. Ibid., 39.
35. Ibid.
36. Ibid.

disinclined to accept any of the Ashkenazi requests.

Since they fully appreciated that Talleyrand had fundamentally adopted their position, the Bordelais had no reason to further importune the
Bishop. They assuredly did not feel any need to persuade him to alter his
position and support full equality for all Jews. They had made it abundantly clear that this was not a part of their agenda. Having obtained the
precious assurances they had been seeking throughout their stay in Paris,
they did not prolong their meeting with Talleyrand, but left quickly to
continue their visits with other prominent personalities.

Although they would continue their efforts for another day, the members of the delegation from Bordeaux had effectively concluded their
work. All that was left for them to do was to patiently await the expected
outcome of the National Assembly debate and then finalize their report
to their leadership with the inclusion of the salutary result.

The Bordelais representatives demonstrated great discipline, thought-
fulness, and persistence in their lobbying efforts. But these lobbying
efforts cannot in any manner be deemed to have been carried out on
behalf of French Jews. The representatives were exclusively focused on
the "Portuguese" Jews and did not purport to be in support of the Jews
of Alsace, Lorraine, and the Three Bishoprics or even the Jews of Paris.
The sought-for outcome of this campaign was not equality for the Jewish
community; it was merely the preservation of certain rights for a small
select group of affluent and assimilated Jews.

CHAPTER 23

THE ASHKENAZIM PLAN THEIR CAMPAIGN

With the members of the Bordeaux community on their own trajectory, the Ashkenazi Jews had no choice but to develop a separate and distinct strategy to achieve equality. They had actually begun this process after the December 24 vote and well before the meetings with the Bordeaux delegation. A precise strategy was, in fact, discussed, developed, and embraced within mere days of the vote. The Ashkenzim knew that they faced a difficult struggle. Unlike the Portuguese Jews, who were generally well-regarded in their various communities, the Ashkenazim were loathed by many of their neighbors and knew it. Also, they could not anchor their claims on preexisting rights since they had virtually none. Furthermore, with an appreciation that the Thiéry document was wholly inadequate, the very first task was the preparation of a new and more comprehensive petition to the National Assembly for which they needed to rely on a skilled, experienced, and respected writer. Godard would very well fulfill that role.

The work on the document and the lobbying efforts began in earnest during the first days of 1790 while it was still unclear when the Jewish issue would be taken up by the National Assembly, but at a time when it was hoped that it would be done relatively quickly. It was also evident that the Bordelais delegation was working assiduously to have their rights confirmed as quickly as possible and that the Ashkenazim needed to put forth a maximum of effort if they hoped to achieve their own goal.

The Ashkenazi Jewish leaders and their avocat, Godard, decided that their petition to the National Assembly would be a full-throated document addressing all the legal and moral reasons for the Jews' entitlement to the rights of active citizens, as well as confronting all the previously articulated objections to Jewish equality. Simultaneously, they wanted to dispel a variety of myths about Jews and to depict Jews as being fully suited to becoming citizens. In preparing this petition, Godard realized that he needed to acquire a great deal more knowledge about Jews and Jewish practices. Consequently, he held many meetings with Cerf Berr's group of representatives of the Ashkenazi Jewish communities. As an avocat seeking to represent a client about which he did not know enough, the process of becoming more familiar with Jews, Judaism, and Jewish practices was vital to his ability to counter the various arguments that were being brought forth in opposition to Jewish equality. It was also entirely consistent with Godard's approach both as an avocat and as a political actor. He was always extremely thorough in his preparations regardless of the task and assuredly intended to follow this practice now.

Preparing to battle on behalf of his Jewish clients was a laborious process. Godard, as was his wont, sought to know everything that he could about his clients—a process he had begun in the fall, as demonstrated by his exchange with Pastoret. The letters found in Godard's client files indicate that he quickly plunged into his task.[1]

A working group was created for the launch of a political operation to achieve the goal of Jewish equality. The group was headed by Berr Isaac Berr, the wealthy and erudite manufacturer from Nancy, who had addressed the National Assembly back in October. Berr, who was the

---

1. Godard's client file survived into the twentieth century. However, regrettably, the file can no longer be located. The last scholar to have seen the papers was Rabbi David Feuerwerker in 1944, at a time when they were owned by Henri de Tolédo, who then resided in Geneva. Through contact with Mr. de Tolédo's descendants, I ascertained that it is possible that Mr. de Tolédo bequeathed his archives to the Jewish community of Geneva. However, my multiple efforts to try to locate the documents have not been fruitful. Leaders of the Geneva Jewish community, although eager to be of assistance, did not seem to know anything about the documents or their whereabouts. They very kindly gave me full access to the community's library and archives, which I scoured at length, but without success. Despite my failure to locate the Godard file, I remain hopeful that it may yet be found. It would be truly unfortunate if this precious evidence of Godard's handiwork had been destroyed through inattention or inadvertence.

official representative of Nancy's Jewish community, was a practicing Jew who had received a comprehensive Jewish education, making him an invaluable resource. The team also included Theodore Cerf Berr, the eldest son of Berr Cerf Berr, the wealthy Alsatian. Although it is less certain, other members of the working group likely included two Parisian Jews, Jacob Lazard and Trenelle, *père* (the elder),[2] Mayer Marx from Lorraine, and possibly David Sintzheim, a rabbi who also happened to be Cerf Berr's brother-in-law.[3] Sintzheim would go on to play an important role in the French-Jewish community when he was elected to serve as the first Chief Rabbi of France, a role which would be created under the auspices of Napoleon. Zalkind Hourwitz, the proudly self-described "Polish Jew" who had shared the Metz Academy prize and was now an official interpreter in the Royal Library in Paris, was likely also a part of the group.

The group members met regularly to discuss issues and strategy. They supplied their counsel with the information, both religious and secular, that he requested and responded to his questions, working with him in a closely coordinated manner. The exchanges among the legal team

2. Trenelle, *père,* is likely Marc Akiba Trenel (also known as Jacob Trenel[le]) (1748–1826), a resident of Metz. Apparently, because he used the name Jacob, which was also the name given to his son (Jacob Trenel, 1775–1840), he is referred to as "*père*" to distinguish him from his son. His descendants have played a prominent role in French society. Trenel's great-granddaughter Marianne married Simon Debré, who became the chief rabbi of the Paris suburb of Neuilly. Their son was the noted pediatrician Robert Debré, whose name adorns a Paris hospital. Dr. Debré's son was Michel Debré, one of the authors of the Constitution of France's Fifth Republic, who served as finance minister, defense minister, foreign minister and prime minister of France during the presidencies of Charles de Gaulle and Georges Pompidou. Michel Debré's son, Jean-Louis Debré, a judge by training, has served as minister of the interior, president of the National Assembly and as president of France's Constitutional Council.

3. David Sintzheim (1745–1812) was a German-born rabbi, who, in 1765, married Berr Cerf Berr's sister. He became the *Rosh Yeshivah* (headmaster) of the rabbinical academy in Bishcheim in 1785. Following the end of the Revolution, he became the chief rabbi of the growing Jewish community of Strasbourg. During the Napoleonic Empire, Sintzheim was a delegate to the Assembly of Notables assembled by Napoleon and was named as the head of the Sandhedrin that Napoleon organized subsequently. Following Napoleon's creation of the Consistoire and the establishment of a formal Jewish clerical hierarchy, he became the first Chief Rabbi of France in 1807. He is buried in a prominent tomb in Paris's Père Lachaise cemetery.

covered biblical texts, talmudic texts, Jewish prayers and praying methods, as well as information about Jewish social and legal practices. The team also paid close attention to recent secular writings which advocated for Jewish equality.[4]

On December 30, 1789, as Godard was just beginning his work, Berr Isaac Berr sent Godard a letter highlighting certain documentation that the team had been able to collect for his review and demonstrating a dramatic sense of self-deprecation:

> Mr. Berr Isaac Berr has the honor of saluting Mr. Godard and of sending him enclosed herewith a number of copies, which he has succeeded in procuring, of *"Reflexions d'un Citoyen sur l'Eligibilité des Juifs"* ("Reflections of a Citizen on the Eligibility of Jews"). The passage from the prophesy of Jeremiah which Mr. Berr cited this morning will be found at Chap. 29, vs. 4, 5, 6, and 7.
>
> Here, Sir, is approximately the contents of the four verses in Hebrew which I have translated as well as it is possible for a translator to do, who is absolutely ignorant of both of the languages in which he wishes to work. Mr. Godard will undoubtedly have the Latin translation in order to judge the faithfulness of the cited passage.
>
> Tomorrow Mr. Berr will have the honor of sending to Mr. Godard the work of M. Mirabeau on the reform of the Jews by Mendelssohn.
>
> This Wednesday, in the evening, 30th December.[5]

Presumably in keeping with this promise, the next day Godard must have received a copy of Mirabeau's extensive 1787 review of the matter of Jewish reform: *On Moses Mendelssohn, The Political Reform of the Jews: And in Particular the Revolution Attempted on Their behalf in 1753 in Great Britain,* which he had had published in London and which had been one of the significant documents that helped to bring the Jewish struggle into the French public arena prior to the beginning of the Revolution. Since

---

4. Fortunately, both David Feuerwerker and Joseph Lémann, each of whom personally reviewed Godard's file, have quoted extensively from that file and, since the quotes they each cite are consistent, there is a strong presumption that they accurately reflect the content of Godard's correspondence. Feuerwerker, *L'Émancipation des Juifs en France,* 332–38, and Lémann, *Les Juifs dans la Révolution française,* Chapter 7.

5. Cited in Feuerwerker, *L'Émancipation des Juifs en France,* 333.

Godard had undoubtedly met Mirabeau previously during his appearances before the National Assembly or at sessions of the political clubs he frequented, he must have taken great comfort in knowing that his clients' goal was fully consistent with an important literary work by the Assembly's most brilliant orator and most renowned member.

With the arrival of the new year and following the disappointing initial meetings with the representatives of the Jews of Bordeaux, the Jewish delegates and Godard began their work in earnest. How could they best persuade the recalcitrant National Assembly that Jewish equality had to be addressed and granted? Of course, serious arguments in favor of Jewish equality would have to be presented, but it was clear that political pressure would also need to be generated in order to create the necessary momentum and to overcome the opposition of the Alsatians and the conservatives. Unlike the Portuguese Jews whose focus was entirely on the National Assembly, Godard, in his capacity as a member of the Paris Assembly, clearly saw Paris as the primary source of revolutionary fervor and as the vehicle for providing the impetus through which to overcome the opposition of Alsatian and other conservative members of the National Assembly. Not being subject to contemporary standards, he does not seem to have felt that there was any conflict of interest in lobbying the very Assembly in which he sat on behalf of his clients. Therefore, he devised a two-pronged approach. The serious and well-articulated petition would be drafted for submission to the National Assembly, and would be made available for general distribution. But, simultaneously, the Paris Assembly and all the district assemblies would be enlisted in the battle. Paris would become the engine that would overcome the inevitable opposition of the conservative members of the National Assembly and would serve to persuade the National Assembly that it was the will of the people of Paris, the true revolutionary leaders of the new France, that the Jews should become equal citizens.

So, with the advice of Godard, the members of the group mustered all their best arguments in favor of Jewish equality and against the objections repeatedly expressed by their opponents. They would present those arguments in the two fora simultaneously: they would prepare their comprehensive brief for submission at the national level when the National Assembly would resume its deliberations on the question of Jewish rights, then, travelling just a short distance along rue St. Honoré to Place de Grève where Paris's City Hall, the Hôtel de Ville, is located, they would address the Paris Assembly and rally the Parisians to exert crucial pressure on the National Assembly. The Paris component of the strategy would also have two prongs: a direct appeal would be made to the Paris Assembly to be followed by an appeal to each of the sixty district assemblies, which would provide the impetus for a confirmation of support for Jewish rights at the Paris Assembly. With this powerful base of support, the Paris Assembly could then formally articulate the pro-Jewish sentiments of all Parisians to the National Assembly. The hope was to coordinate all aspects of these efforts and to carry them out at virtually the same time. The strategy was a realistic one, but it would be difficult to coordinate and was likely exhausting even to contemplate.

Once the overall strategy had been determined, the Jewish clients and their counsel turned to an analysis of the arguments to be presented. How could they overcome the opposition of the anti-Jewish National Assembly members, who had already repeatedly cited the "danger" that the Jews would encounter from their incensed non-Jewish neighbors if they were granted equal rights? How could they overcome the perception that they were a separate nation that could not integrate into the general population of France due to their particular and peculiar habits?

Godard intended to address all these issues and more. Not yet certain as to when the issue of Jewish rights would be brought to the National Assembly, but aware that the deadline was looming, he had to learn about Jewish history, customs, and religious practices, and quickly. To rapidly enhance his knowledge, he requested yet more documents and information he had determined he needed in order to draft the petition on behalf of the Jews.

Cerf Berr's eldest son, Theodore Cerf Berr, served as an intermediary between the Jewish working group and their avocat. In a short period of time, avocat and clients had many exchanges, in writing and in person. Those exchanges included the delivery of documents as well as explanations of Jewish theological principles, customs, and practices. As January progressed and the as-yet-unspecified date for the two-pronged presentation was inevitably drawing closer these exchanges accelerated.

On January 12 Theodore wrote to Godard: "Mr. Theodore Cerfbeer has the honor to wish Mr. Godard a good day; he also has the honor to send him enclosed the items which he has requested. This 12th of January 90."[6]

---

6. Feuerwerker, *L'Émancipation des Juifs en France,* 334.

The letter does not specify which items were enclosed with the letter, but it must be assumed that the items were additional texts relating to Jewish practices and beliefs.

Two days later, the younger Cerf Berr wrote again:

> Mr. Theodore Cerfberr has the honor of greeting Mr. Godard. As it was agreed upon with you last Monday that you would trouble yourself to come to his home Saturday with your Brief to discuss it together. He begs you, therefore, to let him know if you would like to come tomorrow evening at 6 o'clock; whereupon he will in consequence alert the Gentlemen, the Jews of Paris.
>
> This 14th of January 90.[7]
>
> I beg you to favor me with a response.

The letter noted that the Jewish clients and their avocat were engaged in regular meetings, but it also indicated that, unlike their assimilated Sephardic brethren, the Ashkenazi Jews were very mindful not to violate the Sabbath. The Saturday meeting was scheduled to take place long enough after sundown in order to permit them to have celebrated *havdalah*—the brief ceremony that marks the end of the Sabbath and the beginning of the secular week—before beginning their work, which, for observant Jews, would be prohibited on the Sabbath.

Additional letters sent to Godard by his clients indicate that yet more meetings were held; however, the absence of dates on some letters and the incomplete nature of the Godard file make it difficult to trace with precision the intense work that must have been ongoing. In one such letter, Theodore Cerf Berr wrote to Jacques Godard:

> Theodore Cerfberr has the honor of wishing a good evening to Mr. Godard and prays him to let him know if he can come to his home tomorrow between noon and two o'clock accompanied by his colleagues.
>
> This Saturday. [Undated][8]

As Godard's preparations progressed, he delved ever more intensively into religious issues, especially as they related to the role of Jews as

---

7. Ibid.
8. Lémann, *Les Juifs dans la révolution française*, 91.

moneylenders. He was well aware that Jews were constantly castigated for their alleged obsession with moneylending and he determined to confront that issue head-on and thoroughly. It became readily apparent that he needed to know a great deal more about the Jewish position on charging interest to non-Jews. To that end, Godard turned to Berr Isaac Berr for additional assistance. Berr had already given Godard some biblical texts regarding the rights and obligations of Jews with respect to moneylending. Now, however, he began to provide Godard with a much more in-depth analysis, introducing the young avocat to the Jewish approach to the interpretation of biblical text through the use of post-biblical commentary.

In a letter dated January 18 Berr resorted to the Talmud in an effort to provide Godard with additional arguments for his brief. He wrote to Godard:

> Mr. Berr Isaac Berr has the honor of wishing Mr. Godard a very good evening and is sending him two passages from the Talmud translated into French. Who will now dare to assert: The Bible or the Talmud authorize Jews to engage in usury?
>
> Who would still doubt that those who have forced the Jews to live only from usury, have forced them to violate at the same time their own laws and those of the Prince?
>
> This Monday, January 18.[9]

Enclosed with the letter were some talmudic excerpts, in the original Hebrew and Aramaic, as well as in French translation. The first excerpt was from the talmudic tractate Bava Metzi'a (folio 70b), which served as the starting point for Berr Isaac Berr's explanation regarding Jewish rules concerning the lending of money:[10]

> Verse 8 Chapter 28 of Proverbs: He who accumulates a fortune by interest and usury, G-d will share it with the poor.

---

9. Feuerwerker, *L'Émancipation des Juifs en France*, 336.
10. Bava Metzi'a means "middle gate" in Aramaic. The name reflects this tractate's position as being the middle talmudic tractate of three which appear under the overarching name of "Neziqin" or "damages." Bava Metzi'a concerns itself principally with business matters, including the issue of whether and when interest may be charged in connection with the lending of money.

Commentary of Rabbi Nachman: King Solomon did not need to defend interest between one Jew to another Jew because the law of Moses expressly prohibited it, but he was concerned that the biblical text would not be respected (you will lend with interest to the stranger). This is why he uses his allegory as an interpretation of the above passage:

You will lend to the stranger at ordinary interest rates to live and to sustain yourself, but you will not lend to him at usurious rates in order to accumulate a fortune, because he who accumulates a fortune, etc.[11]

A second excerpt from the Talmud was also described:

Talmud tractate Makkot, fol. 24a Ver5, Chp. 15 of Psalms. [King] David identifying the virtues which a wise man should have, includes not lending money at interest.[12]

Rabbi Samloy [Simlai][13] concludes that since lending money for interest to one's brother is expressly prohibited by the Law, David recommends not to lend money at interest to a stranger and deems this to be one of the principles of virtue and wisdom.[14]

This second talmudic reference analyzed the 15th Psalm's poetic summary of eleven fundamental principles of Judaism (rendering more succinct the 613 commandments deemed to be set out in the Torah). In the Psalm, the author, presumed to be King David, asks rhetorically: "Who will dwell in Your tabernacle? Who will dwell in Your holy mountain?"[15] He responds by identifying meritorious individuals who either carry out or refrain from carrying out certain actions. The tenth of these is "the individual

---

11. Feuerwerker, *L'Émancipation des Juifs en France*, 334–35.
12. Tractate Makkot, whose title translates to "plagues," is the fifth talmudic tractate in the order Neziqim. It primarily focuses on issues of court procedures and legal punishments.
13. Rabbi Simlai was an Amoraic rabbi (part of the second wave of great rabbinic scholars interpreting the oral or Mishnaic laws) who lived in the third century in the land of Israel. The origin of the notion that there are 613 specific positive and negative commandments (*mitzvot*) in the text of the Torah is generally ascribed to him and is found in Tractate Makkot (Plagues) in the Talmud.
14. Feuerwerker, *L'Émancipation des Juifs en France*, 335.
15. Psalms 15:1.

who does not lend money for interest."[16] Isaac Berr was emphasizing the disfavor which basic Jewish law, both biblical and talmudic, ascribes to those who engage in the process of lending for interest to anyone—Jew or gentile.

Even though the extant exchanges of correspondence between Godard and his clients are modest in number and incomplete, it is nonetheless clear that the meetings of the working group must have been frequent so as to provide Godard with the necessary backup for the completion of his work before the next National Assembly debate, which was anticipated for the end of January.[17] This was especially the case because Godard was not one to prepare cursory documents. His pleadings on behalf of his prior clients had always been both thorough and voluminous. He did not intend to act differently for his Jewish clients. It was his intention to draft and submit an extensive petition that would assemble all the arguments in favor of his clients, setting out a case which would seek to diminish, if not destroy, all the arguments against them.

---

16. Psalms 15:5.

17. As noted above, in light of the author's inability to find the original Godard dossier, the letters and documents cited are exclusively from the transcriptions of these items provided by Joseph Lémann and David Feuerwerker in their respective writings.

CHAPTER 24

THE PÉTITION TO THE NATIONAL
ASSEMBLY – ANALYZING THE ISSUES

Throughout much of January it was uncertain when the Jewish matter would be brought before the National Assembly. The Portuguese Jews, eager to advance their cause as expeditiously as possible, finished their document relatively quickly. Only the delays caused by their printer Baudouin prevented an earlier issuance and distribution of their Address. Godard's much more ambitious document was taking substantially longer to produce. But Godard had one advantage. On January 16 Target had been elected president of the Assembly and, since it was the president who had the ability to set the Assembly's agenda, the schedule for the next discussion of the Jewish issue was now placed squarely in his hands. In light of Godard's close relationship with Target, it appears likely that Godard was able to prevail upon his mentor to hold the debate in abeyance until he had finished his document. Nonetheless, despite his relationship with the Assembly President, he was clearly not able to delay the debate for more than a few days.

After weeks of intense work, on January 27, 1790, acting on behalf of the Ashkenazi French Jewish community and in the name of his clients, Godard finished, had printed, and filed his comprehensive petition (dated January 28) with the National Assembly. This was the lengthiest pleading he had prepared on behalf of any cause to date. It reflected an enormous amount of effort and a thoughtful and elaborate analysis of all the principal issues related to the matter of Jewish civil equality. The

305

document was signed by Mayer Marx, Berr Isaac Berr, David Sintzheim, Theodore Cerf Berr, Jacob Lazare, and Trenelle, *père*. Cerf Berr placed his signature on the *Pétition* in his official capacity as the administrative leader (*syndic*) of the Alsatian Jewish community. All the signatories were clearly Ashkenazi. (The Bordelais Jews had submitted their petition with 215 signatories/endorsers, all of them Portuguese Jews from Bordeaux.) Two of the signatories of Godard's petition, Lazare Jacob and Trenelle, *père*, had signed the August 26, 1789, submission to the Assembly and, of course, Berr Isaac Berr had previously appeared before the National Assembly in October.

Godard's document was entitled: "A Pétition by the Jews Living in France to the National Assembly with respect to the Adjournment of December 24, 1789."[1] This title suggested that the *Pétition* was focused on a technical procedural issue, but the text prepared by Godard was, to the contrary, quite broad in scope. The 107-page printed document sought both to address the fundamental reasons underlying the desires of the Jewish community for legal equality and to evoke and respond to the various objections that had been articulated in recent debates by those opposed to making Jews equal citizens, each of which was systematically refuted. It was an appeal to logic, to principle, and to justice, but it was not a radical document. Rather, it was a typical legal pleading in the style of briefs and opinions submitted to the Parlement, intended to persuade its audience by means of reasoned argumentation. In order to maximize the impact of his pleading on his targeted readers, Godard and his clients arranged to have the *Pétition* published and widely disseminated.

The *Pétition* was delivered under cover of a letter from the seven petitioners to Target, the president of the National Assembly.[2] Humble in tone and purporting merely to request that the Ashkenazi Jews be treated in a manner similar to the manner in which the Portuguese Jews of the Bordeaux region were being treated and to have their status addressed at the same time as the status of the favored Portuguese Jews, the petitioners' letter was crafted so as to appeal to the most elementary egalitarian instincts of the majority of National Assembly members. "Our principal demands are the same as theirs," Godard had his clients write

1. *Une Pétition des Juifs établis en France Adressée à l'Assemblée National sur l'ajournement du 24 décembre 1789* (Paris: L'Imprimerie de Prault, 1790.)
2. *Lettre des Juifs établis en France, à Monsieur le Président de l'Assemblée Nationale* (Paris: L'Imprimerie de Prault, 1790).

to the members of the Assembly, referring to the Portuguese Jews.[3] But, highlighting the important difference between the Ashkenazi Jews and the Portuguese Jews, Godard had the Ashkenazi petitioners declare that "what they [our Bordeaux brothers][4] seek to preserve, we seek to obtain."[5] And, in an obvious effort to give the Portuguese Jews a stake in their effort, he added that there were rights that the Portuguese Jewish community did not have but that they should have and that the Paris delegation would also be requesting.[6] The call was not for revolutionary action, but rather for elementary fairness. The petitioners were respectful, dignified, restrained, and brief in their letter. The *Pétition* was quite different both in tone and content.

Godard's *Pétition* stands out as one of the most thorough pieces of advocacy for Jewish civil aspirations in an era that abounded with documents addressing civil rights generally and even Jewish rights more specifically. It sought to undermine the long-standing prejudices that plagued Jews in the western European diaspora, with reliance upon the philosophical underpinnings of the new French society that was emerging from the revolutionary ferment. It debunked the notions that Jews were fundamentally different from their neighbors, that they wished to remain separate, and that they could not live within the legal and social framework that was being created in revolutionary France. More than two centuries after it was written and disseminated, the *Pétition* remains a stirring statement of Jewish aspiration for full integration into Western society. However, it has also been considered as a major rhetorical step toward assimilation and the dilution of Jewish life within that society.

As a good advocate, Godard began the *Pétition* by flattering his target audience, the members of the National Assembly, even though it is clear he had a much wider audience in mind. He diplomatically suggested that the Assembly's decision of December 24, 1789, to defer a vote on the fate of the Jews, demonstrated the prudence and wisdom of the Assembly since, he asserted, if it had been taken on the spot, the vote would have been adverse to the Jews and would, consequently, have been a detrimental action. Not without stretching credulity, he lauded the unwillingness of the Assembly to take the very decision that the Jews were now seeking

---

3. Ibid., ii.
4. "[N]os frères de Bordeaux." Ibid.
5. Ibid., iii.
6. Ibid., ii

as the reflection of a deliberative and thoughtful approach.[7]

Then, relying upon his customary lawyerly approach, Godard indicated that it was important to consider all sides of the issue. Using this approach he made it possible to present the arguments that were being propounded by anti-Jewish forces in a manner that he believed made them appear as weak as possible. This dialectical methodology allowed him to maximize the opportunity to undermine those arguments (*Pétition*, p. 4).

He went on to note that the desire of the Jews was already well known to the National Assembly. This was his way of proposing that the objectives of the Jews were self-evident (in spite of the confusion sown by the document submitted by the Bordeaux delegation) and did not really require much elaboration (as he began his long and detailed presentation). Nonetheless, Godard proposed that, if it was deemed necessary (a proposition that he clearly deemed obvious), he was prepared to set the objectives out in detail. Importantly, following the lead of Clermont-Tonnerre, he sought to lay to rest the very notion that Jews were seeking to keep their status as a separate "nation" and simultaneously obtain full legal equality (p. 5).

As if to make certain that the objectives of his Jewish clients were unambiguous, when he published his *Pétition*, Godard, in noting that Jews wanted to be full citizens, had the word "CITIZENS" printed entirely in capital letters (p. 6). He then stated that he would not engage in a philosophical polemic, but rather that he was pursuing a practical goal. He indicated that the legislators—"who are guided by the immutable source of reason and justice"—did not need to have every aim specified, since they knew what had to be accomplished. He went on to posit that even if Jews did not themselves wish to seek all the rights to which they were entitled, the National Assembly could not fail to raise the Jews out of their servile state and to the status of full Frenchmen in light of the elevated goals the Assembly had set for itself (p. 6).

In his customary fashion, Godard set out a road map of how he intended to present his *Pétition*. He promised his audience that he would be thorough and would not fail to address every relevant argument. The benefits his *Pétition* was seeking, he insisted, would be derived from an act, not of grace, but of justice (p. 8).

---

7. *Une Pétition des Juifs établis en France Adressée à l'Assemblée Nationale sur l'ajournement du 24 décembre 1789*, p. 4.

Godard then asserted that, as a practical matter, the Jews could have left this task to others (and he made an allusion to the Abbé Grégoire). However, with a matter of such importance (their societal life or death, as he put it), it was their duty to defend themselves (p. 8). Indeed, he continued, if the Jews had failed to take up their own defense, they would have been accused of an inability to do so or of indifference (p. 9).

Continuing in his lawyerly fashion and to facilitate an understanding of his *Pétition*, Godard then presented an outline of the arguments he was submitting. He informed his readers that he was proposing to make four major points. He would, he announced:

1. Establish the basic principles for Jewish citizenship generally;
2. Prove that this would be in the best interest of France;
3. Review and refute all the objections to Jewish citizenship; and
4. Demonstrate why Jews must become full citizens immediately and not at some indefinite future time (p. 9).

Once he had set out his road map, Godard plunged into his substantive text, beginning by describing the basic principles which, in his view, demanded that Jews should be elevated to the rank of full active citizens. He began with an argument that harkened back to the writings of Jean-Jacques Rousseau. Godard's premise was that all people in a nation should have the same rights and obligations (p. 11). Based upon that premise, he asserted that logic then demanded that Jews, because they lived in France and were subjects of France, had an obligation to serve (and, he affirmed, had served) their nation (p. 11). As a consequence, Godard continued, it would be unjust for the Nation not to give back to the Jews of the Nation in the same proportion as it had received from those Jews (p. 12).

Of course, this gave rise to the fundamental legal question of whether Jews who lived in France were actually "domiciled" there. In other words, were the Jews a foreign group which was merely passing through—just as visiting Turks might be passing through the kingdom and did not intend to remain there permanently? Godard responded by asserting that it was certainly not possible to call Jews "FOREIGNERS" (p. 12). (Once again, in the printed version, Godard resorted to capital letters for emphasis.) But, in order to answer his question fully, and echoing contemporary arguments that are often heard in the context of immigration issues, Godard first reminded his readers that Jews did not have another country to which they could go, that many had been living in France with their families for generations, and that most now residing in France had actually been born in France. He also noted that Jews had even sometimes been assigned places to live by the French government itself. But, most importantly, he reminded his readers that Jews paid taxes (a matter of particular significance at a time when the French government was confronting its most critical fiscal crisis) (p. 12).

To complement his logic, Godard emphasized that in every country there could only be two categories of people: (i) foreigners and (ii) citizens. With that simple analysis, Godard concluded that it was logical that Jews were and should be recognized as citizens of France (p. 13).

He then took on one of the more obvious issues lurking just beneath the surface of the debate on Jewish equality, namely, that Judaism was considered heretical by the dominant Catholic religion and its followers, who still constituted the vast majority of the French. He acknowledged that this had been the case, but, he went on, France was long past a time when the dominant religion could impose its tenets on others. In fact, he reminded his readers, Protestants had already been given full rights. Once again, concluding a simple syllogism with a question, he asked, if intolerance of Protestants no longer existed, how could intolerance of Jews be permitted? (pp. 12–13)

Godard also noted that civil rights were entirely independent of religious principles. So long as religious principles did not offend a "pure and severe" morality, he proposed that the adherents of the religion that espoused those principles had to have all of the rights of citizens (p. 14). He then asked the rhetorical question: what would be the consequence of letting only adherents of the dominant religion (and related religions) have rights? The response, Godard asserted, was that it would establish the principle that force prevails over weakness, that the majority dominates over the minority. He added that, if this were the case, then, where Catholics are in the minority, they could be subject to all the restrictions applicable to Jews (p. 15).

In his continuing effort to depict Jews as "normal" individuals similar in character to their neighbors, Godard then emphasized that Jews were attached to their religion just like others are attached to theirs. Only God, he asserted, could call men to account for their opinions of Him (p. 16). No religion can dominate by itself; each religion must be persuasive on its own and not everyone is persuaded by the same evidence (p. 17).

He proceeded to advance the argument that echoed the remarks that the liberal Protestant cleric Rabaut Saint-Étienne had made on August 23 before the National Assembly. Mere tolerance, he declared, was no longer appropriate or adequate (p. 17). To tolerate, he stated, was to suffer something that could be prohibited. But, Godard affirmed, the dominant religion simply did not have the right to prohibit another religion (p. 19). The fundamental point, he argued, was that all religions have equal rights (p. 18). Then, once again emulating the approach taken by Rabaut Saint-Étienne, Godard cast his gaze across the Atlantic toward the newly independent United States, asserting that the world would owe many useful lessons to the United States, which, in his view, had rejected tolerance as compromising individual liberty (p. 17).

Gingerly beginning to focus on the political aspects of Jewish rights, Godard asked whether, in order to fulfill one's public obligations, it was necessary to be of a particular religion or if religious affiliation really made any difference? Then, returning to the issue of citizenship, he noted that two uncontestable principles assured that Jews should have all the rights of citizens. First, their position as subjects of the kingdom assured them this right (as Godard claimed that he had already proven) (p. 19). Second, the particular religion of the Jews could not take away their rights (and Godard once again noted that he already proven this). Thus, he considered it a necessary consequence of these authentic principles that Jews be declared to be CITIZENS (yet again, in capital letters in the published text), and that it was impossible that they should not be so declared (p. 20).

Godard then suggested that, with respect to the question of Jewish rights, France should act in its own self-interest. He indicated that Jews could readily see and were naturally attracted to the spread of liberty all around them in enlightened societies. If they could not benefit from it in France, then they might choose to go elsewhere where they might enjoy happiness and tranquility. (This was an allusion to Austria, where the Emperor Joseph II, Marie-Antoinette's brother, had granted Jews certain rights (p. 20). Godard wryly noted that Jews had left other nations in the past, so why would they not leave France? (p. 22)

But, he reminded his audience, France had now declared that all men were equal in rights. This suggested that, if Jews did not receive those same rights, then it would mean that, in France, Jews would not be considered to be men. Godard highlighted the proximity of Austria, which, he suggested, could welcome certain of the individuals that France might treat as slaves in its midst and that the French would regret this loss.[8]

Godard asserted, not entirely correctly, that most Jews engaged in commerce. He complemented that observation with a question: Was France prepared to make a gift to its neighbors of the activities and wealth of its Jewish residents? (p. 23). He noted that every time France had expelled its Jews, it had had to recall them. He also cast his eyes across the Pyrenées and pointed out the dire consequences that had befallen Spain when it expelled its Jews in 1492. But, he noted, some might say that Jews are accustomed to oppression and therefore would not leave (p. 24). He warned against this assumption, indicating that if Jews continued to live in the midst of the French without being made citizens, they would consume without producing; this is how they would avenge themselves (p. 25). If Jews were made equals, however, he posited, commerce would flourish in their hands. They would take up new arts—maybe even agriculture—as their ancestors had in Palestine (p. 26). Able to engage in all pursuits, they would end their isolation for the benefit of the French nation.

Identifying a French demographic obsession that has continued to this day, he observed that, by accepting Jews as citizens, a very substantial increase in the size of the population would occur (p. 27). He argued that, were France a small and poor country, a bigger population could be more of a problem than a benefit. However, in light of its wealth, an increase in population could only be a great benefit. This, Godard emphasized, would happen if Jews were made citizens (p. 28). Additionally, he suggested that the laws and habits of the Jews encouraged population growth. The more Jews there are, he posited, the more hands there will be in the service of the nation. And, with a grant of Jewish equality, France would attract even more Jews, thereby further increasing the productive population of the nation.

Yet again projecting concerns which have remained relevant to this day, he wrote that it would be a good thing for France to become a safe haven for persecuted humanity (p. 30). He seems to have been contemplating a France that would come into being only a century later, when it would indeed become a haven for persecuted immigrants, including

8. Ibid. This argument was also a not-so-subtle allusion to the loss of many Huguenots, who, following the revocation of the Edict of Nantes in 1685, moved to various other nations and notably to Brandenburg, where the elector welcomed them and they became an important element in the industrial development of that principality.

many Jewish immigrants seeking to escape the persecutions in eastern European nations.

Godard then compared the advantages and disadvantages of granting Jews equality. Justice, France's self-interest, and France's glory, all, in his view, militated in favor of giving Jews equal rights (p. 30). Only very specific considerations could detract from the force of these beneficial consequences, and such considerations would have to be powerful and based on character, morals, customs, and laws.

Drawing on the experience of the National Assembly with the issue of Protestant civil equality, of which he was well aware because of the role Target had played in these efforts, as well as through his own study of the matter in handling the Brisset case, Godard analogized that the objections being raised to Jewish equality were effectively the same as those that had been made against Protestants (p. 33).

Godard then made the astute observation that all innovations encounter some opposition. He asserted that prejudice begins to fall away when demanded by the public and as the necessity for its removal is recognized (p. 33). Considering that granting rights to Jews would be an innovation, Godard then reviewed the various objections to the admission of Jews to citizenship.

He suggested that a quick review of the cruel and bizarre destiny of the Jews would reduce the disfavor from which they suffered and would indicate whether it was truly appropriate to reproach them for their conduct. Coming to a theme that would be repeated many times, Godard reminded his readers that Jews had systematically been persecuted in so many different ways (p. 34). And, with all of this persecution, he admonished, it was inappropriate to complain about their lowly state. Echoing the words of the Abbé Grégoire, Robespierre, and others, he urged that the Jews not be accused of inappropriate behavior since such an accusation would simply ricochet against Christians (p. 35).

Continuing with this analysis, Godard wrote that the vices of a few Jews were the product of the actions of the peoples who provided the Jews with asylum and then mistreated them. He conceded that some Jews might have shown their belief in the superiority of their religion—and as a result may have incited jealousy and hatred since people do not long accept a spirit of pride (p. 36). Suggesting a kind of spiral of intolerance, he conceded that it was as a means of avenging themselves or coping that Jews had become obsequious and slowly had became vile in the eyes of some of their neighbors. Godard reemphasized that the vices of the Jews were to be understood as the fault of the people who gave them shelter, namely France itself. These vices were, he urged, the effect and not the cause of injustice (p. 38).

Godard then went into greater detail respecting the reproaches to which Jews were subjected, first enumerating those reproaches and then systematically refuting them.

The first reproach—the prevailing argument repeated endlessly by the Alsatians and others—concerned the Jewish propensity toward moneylending and the charging of "usurious" interest. Godard dispensed with this argument by noting that, in reality, only a few Jews were actually "usurers" and that this was only because Jews had generally been excluded from most other gainful occupations. This served as a kind of preface to a historical analysis of the legal framework that forced Jews into "usurious" practices.

The second reproach, Godard asserted, related to the alleged baseness and ignorance of the Jews. Here again, Godard turned this accusation into an indictment of society at large. It was not surprising that the Jews were uneducated, he observed, since it had to be asked: given the restrictions under which they lived, what benefit would Jews get from education? (Presumably, here he was referring to secular education, since virtually all Jewish men had to learn to read and write in order to comply with certain religious imperatives, including, notably, the need to study religious texts.) Furthermore, he noted that, actually, it was surprising that the situation was not worse. To make his point, he observed that, despite their situation, there were Jews (and here he was assuredly writing about his own clients) who had made public sacrifices, who had studied philosophy and literature (pp. 43–44). He then turned his sights to places where Jews appeared to be accepted and reminded his readers that when Jews had had a state, they had studied science and public administration and had distinguished individuals in their community (p. 45). Reflecting information gleaned from Mirabeau's recent publication about Moses Mendelssohn, he also highlighted the fact that, in Berlin and Vienna, where Jews had relative freedom, there were Jews who were scholars. He specifically cited Mendelssohn, [Marcus Elieser] Bloch and [Markus] Herz, three of the most distinguished German Jewish academic elites (p. 46). He continued to cast his gaze beyond Paris and Alsace, first to Bordeaux, where there was less persecution and no one accused Jews of poor behavior, and then to Poland where he alleged that Jews successfully engaged in agriculture (p. 47) and where, with some exaggeration, he asserted—seeming to reflect the influence of Zalkind Hourwitz—that commerce was almost entirely given over to the Jews (p. 48).

Godard then restated the various anti-social accusations leveled at Jews: that their religion authorizes deceit and bad faith; that usury against non-Jews is an essential part of the Jewish religion; that Jews are commanded to hate strangers; that they have so many holidays; that their religion promotes indolence; that they are opposed to military service; that their dietary laws set them apart, and that they cannot be loyal to the nations they inhabit (pp. 49–50).

He systematically addressed each of these accusations (p. 51). He noted that there was no Jewish principle that authorized deceit and bad faith and that it was certainly not from badly interpreted commentaries or apostates that judgments should be made respecting Jewish concepts. Indeed, he asked with undisguised sarcasm (and perhaps recalling his own pleadings in the case involving the priest Bée de Belicour), what would the Catholic faith look like if a similar approach were applied to that religion? (p. 52)

Regarding usury, Godard demonstrated his recently acquired under-standing of Jewish juridical concepts by emphasizing that a few verses in Deuteronomy addressing the issue of lending had simply been misinter-preted. For example, he noted that there was no distinction in Hebrew between the words "interest" and "usury," citing verses from Chapter 23 of the Book of Deuteronomy: "You shall not charge interest to your brother...But you may lend with interest to a stranger."[9] This, he stated, meant that Jews are merely allowed to charge a legitimate interest, but that between Jews, in order to promote good relations within a commu-nity, no interest is to be charged.[10]

---

9. Godard erroneously cited the two verses as Deuteronomy 23: 19–20. The correct verses are 20 and 21.

10. *Une Pétition des Juifs établis en France Adressée à l'Assemblée Nationale sur l'ajournement du 24 décembre 1789*, p. 53. Rabbinic interpretation of the prohibi-tion on Jews charging interest to one another suggests that it was presumed that if a Jew asked his fellow-Jew for a loan, it was because he was in dire difficulty and a Jew should not take advantage of a brother's difficulty. However, if a stranger asked a Jew for a loan, it was presumably for a business reason and it was deemed ethical to charge a fair amount of interest in a business context.

Godard then challenged the notion that Judaism reviles the stranger. To the contrary, he asserted, Judaism insists that no one should hate anyone else, but rather that Jews should always expand the circle of good deeds (p. 55). Godard emphasized that the Bible only speaks of hatred of the inhabitants of Canaan, whose immoral conduct was repulsive to the Jews. Everywhere else, he stated, God has expressly commanded that Jews care for the stranger. As proof of his assertion, he highlighted the biblical requirement that farmers leave a portion of their crops for gleaners,[11] and the text of the prophet Jeremiah's appeal (Jeremiah 29:7) to the Jews to: "Work for the peace of the city where I have sent you." (This was one of the verses specifically cited by Berr Isaac Berr in his letter to Godard of December 30, 1789.) In fact, Godard noted that the Jewish obligation to care for the stranger is so clearly enunciated that it cannot be misinterpreted. (As a proof text, he relied on the verse first articulated in the Book of Leviticus,[12] reiterated in a Gemara (an explanatory text) in the Talmud attributed to Hillel: "Love your neighbor like yourself."[13]) He rhetorically inquired, how could a religion that demands so much kindness to strangers seek to do them harm through usury? (p. 57).

Godard then addressed the issue of the allegedly cumbersome Jewish calendar, which was frequently invoked to assert that Jews could not be good citizens because of their numerous holidays. (Of course, this observation has a peculiar echo in modern France, where workers have more paid holidays than their counterparts in virtually any other part of the world.) He affirmed that the Jewish calendar has only thirteen holidays, not fifty-six, as has been sometimes claimed, (p. 59) while conceding that Jews have fifty-two Sabbaths and that those Sabbaths do not occur on the same days as the Christian Sabbaths. This merely means, he indicated, that Jews will suffer from being unable to work on the Christian Sabbath (a notion that Godard did not see fit to challenge) in addition to resting during the Jewish Sabbath. However, he noted that this did not suggest that Jews were lazy. The Jewish calendar, he concluded, was an inconvenience, but did not in any manner impose a detriment on others (pp. 59–60).

With respect to constraints imposed on Jews by their calendar of holy days, there remained the very sensitive topic of military service, and

---

11. Leviticus, 19: 9–10.

12. "You will love your neighbor as yourself: I am the Lord." Lev. 19:18.

13. Babylonian Talmud, Tractate Shabbat, 31A.

Godard now turned to that matter. At a time of perceived increasing en-
dangerment from forces outside the nation and turmoil within, there was
a powerful and pervasive belief that all male citizens had to bear responsibility for protecting the homeland. Godard tackled the issue head on. First,
he observed, even if Jews were forbidden from performing military service, this would not be grounds for denying them citizenship (p. 61). There
were, he reminded his readers, other groups that did not perform military
service (e.g., Quakers and Anabaptists), and these groups were nonetheless deemed to be good citizens (p. 62). However, he went on, there was no
prohibition on Jews being soldiers. Even the prohibition on Jews carrying
arms on the Sabbath was, he asserted rather broadly, no longer binding on
Jews (p. 63). As proof of his position, Godard asked rhetorically where in
the Bible is it suggested that Moses, who trained the Jews for war, prohibited them from fighting on any day of the week? (p. 64).

Godard conceded that it was possible that, after their return from their
exile in Persia, the Jews may have foolishly thought that they did not
need to fight on the Sabbath and that God would defend them. However,
during subsequent wars they discovered that they might have to defend
themselves on the Sabbath. As a consequence, the only restriction the
Jews now believed to be imposed on them was to avoid conducting an
aggressive war on the Sabbath. In fact, he continued, the Talmud (citing
tractate Eruvin, folios 19 and 45)[14] expressly states that a Jew can perform
work on the Sabbath in order to save a life (a concept which is known in
Judaism as *"pekuach nefesh"* or "the saving of a soul" and which exempts
a Jew from certain strictures of *halakhah* [Jewish law]) and, he went on,
history has borne this out (p. 65). Godard then personalized the point
by citing the specific example of the bravery of a Portuguese Jew in the
service of Holland (p. 66).[15]

---

14. The reference to folio 19 of tractate Eruvin (which literally means "mixtures,"
but addresses issues relating to permissible activities on the Sabbath) appears to
be a slight error since the reference to the right to perform certain work on the
Sabbath actually appears in the very next folio (20a). Godard's second reference
should have more specifically been to Eruvin 45a. The latter reference is to the
statement in the Gemara that "All who go out to save lives may return to their
original location on the Sabbath." This has been interpreted to mean that if, on
the Sabbath, a Jew engages in work otherwise prohibited, but such work is being
carried out in order to save a life, he is not considered to have violated the prohibition; rather he is deemed to have observed the Sabbath.

15. Events in the twentieth century would provide support to Godard's argu-

Continuing his argument regarding Jewish military service, Godard unqualifiedly asserted that there was simply no obstacle to Jews serving in the military and that, furthermore, there was always the option for Jews to serve in the National Guard, where participation required service only on certain days, which could be adjusted to avoid Jewish holidays and the Sabbath. But, he emphasized, in case of genuine necessity, Jews would be available at any time, consistent, even though he did not expressly say so, with the concept of *pekuach nefesh* (p. 68).[16] He added that, even if military service were to be impossible, it would not be an impediment to citizenship since there are other tasks that Jews could perform in the service of the nation. This led Godard to yet another issue regarding the allegation that Jews were unsuited for military service—their lack of propensity to be good fighters. Godard, in proposing a response, reminded his readers that, in the past (meaning during biblical times and during the Greek and Roman eras), Jews had been great warriors. He did observe that Jews tended to marry young, which could be seen as precluding their participation in the military, but he remarked that no one had said that only bachelors should be in the military and, in addition, that those who chose to be in the military could defer marriage (p. 70).

Godard noted, using his lawyerly approach of anticipating objections, that there was another issue that allegedly made Jews unsuitable for military service: their unique dietary laws. He took that issue on directly. His fundamental premise was that dietary differences should hardly be a criterion for separating peoples and, more specifically, for denying people the right to be citizens. Furthermore, he reminded his readers that, despite Jewish dietary restrictions, Jews and non-Jews ate many of the same foodstuffs and (with a passing allusion to the continuing importance of meals to the French) sharing meals was not the sole means of bringing people together. Finally, he suggested that, where necessary, Jews could simply abstain from eating foods that were offensive to them (p. 71).

Of course, underlying many of the objections to Jewish citizenship was the dogged issue of disloyalty or dual loyalty. Godard sought to remove the notion that Jews were not loyal to the nations where they lived. Yet again turning to the Talmud, he cited it for the proposition that Jews will

---

ment. In the State of Israel, Jews, including observant Jews, stand in defense of the State every day of the year, including during the Sabbath and on holidays.
16. See the discussion of *"pekuach nefesh"* above.

seek to return to Palestine only when the Messiah is about to arrive (p. 72). The Jewish religion did not, he affirmed, prohibit loyalty to the nation in which Jews resided and, in any event, their personal interest would make loyalty to the nation in which they resided their duty (p. 72).

Having demonstrated that nothing in their religion, their morals, or their rituals and customs posed obstacles to Jews becoming citizens, Godard offered that Jews needed to explain their religion, morals, and rituals (as his clients had just done for him) in order to overcome prejudice, but conceded that they had not done so very well in the past. He then proceeded to present a brief disquisition on Judaism itself, but a disquisition focused mostly on the issues relating to Jewish integration into contemporary society.

Judaism, he posited not entirely accurately, has three basic tenets: one God, the immortality of the soul, and a belief in future punishments and rewards (pp. 73–74). Similarly, he stated over-simplistically that Judaism has three basic rituals: circumcision, the observance of the Sabbath, and the observance of holidays (p. 74).

Next, once again not entirely correctly, he asserted that many of the old and complex laws found in the Bible and other Jewish writings were no longer applicable. He specifically cited the ancient Jewish custom of Levirate marriage (*halitza*), where the younger brother of a deceased Levite was required to marry his widowed sister-in-law (but could be relieved of the obligation by performing a ceremony involving the throwing of footwear). He also highlighted that, for Jews, divorce was permissible (as opposed to the religious prohibition imposed by the Catholic Church), but that it was rare (p. 74). Most importantly, attempting to sweep away once and for all the canard of dual loyalty, he emphasized that Jews believe that all citizens of a large empire should be subject to a single law, by which he meant the law of the land (p. 75).[17]

Turning his attention to Judaism's morals and customs, he indicated that there were six principal moral rules and customs applicable to Jews (pp. 75–76). First, Godard emphasized charity, which he proffered as being one of the most important Jewish virtues. In that context, he noted that Jews tithed voluntarily. Then he went on to list other virtues,

---

17. Godard did not cite, but could have cited, the famous Jewish rabbinic dictum: "*Dina d'malchuta dina*" ("the law of the land is the law,") which is derived from a number of talmudic pronouncements.

including some that would appear rather ordinary. He stated that Jews respect their parents, that they do not die without either receiving the blessing of their fathers or giving a blessing to their children, that they honor their teachers, and that they profoundly venerate their elderly (p. 76). Then he rather unexpectedly cited that Jews prohibit wholesale commerce in grains and that they object to those who hoard this product of primary necessity. In light of the then current concerns about food scarcities in France, this seems more of an attempt to address a contemporary issue than a matter specifically affecting Jews and their predilections.

Godard proposed that the principles of Jewish morality were as touching as they were pure (p. 76). Anticipating criticism from those who found Jewish behavior objectionable, he stated that, if the actions of Jews had not always appeared in conformity with these principles, it was because of the hatred to which they had been subjected and the injustices proffered against them, rather than due to the moral underpinnings of Jewish tradition.

Yet again addressing an oft-levelled charge that Jews were standoffish, he affirmed that there was no aspect of the Jewish religion which was anti-social (p. 77). He reiterated that Jews were just like all other members of society—ready to be citizens (without capitalization this time). He affirmed that their religion was constituted of a collection of dogmas and ceremonies that did not adversely impact the welfare of the state.

He then turned to a frontal attack on the objections cited repeatedly by opponents of the Jews and, especially, by the Alsatians: that by giving Jews civil rights, the prejudice of the people around them would be brought to the fore—that equality for Jews would be destructive to the Jews and that they themselves should oppose equality for that reason (p. 78). It was, to the contrary, Godard asserted, in the interest of the Jews for them to be given what they were demanding (p. 78). In fact, he retorted, a refusal would give credibility to popular hatred. Rejection of the Jews' desire to be recognized as humans would further strengthen the popular prejudices and, as a result, hatred of the Jews would become "inextinguishable" (p. 79).

With these observations, Godard concluded the first portion of his document, the analytical portion. He now pivoted and converted his presentation into a direct appeal to the members of the National Assembly, urging them to act as moral leaders, calling upon the "Representatives of the Nation" to make their wish known and suggesting that, if they did so, the people who respected them would obey them and would see every Jew as a fellow citizen and brother (p. 79).

CHAPTER 25

THE PÉTITION TO THE NATIONAL ASSEMBLY – ADDRESSING THE MEMBERS OF THE NATIONAL ASSEMBLY DIRECTLY

Godard began his direct appeal to the members of the National Assembly by once again addressing the tactics of the Alsatian opponents, noting that in remarks before the National Assembly the Abbé Maury had said that the Jews held more than twelve million mortgages and that, if granted equality, they would in one month own Alsace, such that it would become a "Jewish colony" (p. 80). Godard flatly rejected that proposition, questioning its accuracy and its logic. He asked rhetorically: would Jews really try to seize everything and thereby antagonize all their neighbors? Furthermore, he indicated, if the claims held by the Jews were, in fact, legitimate, then, arguably, they would have a perfect right to seize the lands on which they held mortgages (p. 81).

Godard pursued the question of whether Jews really posed a danger by asking whether they were actually sufficiently numerous to constitute any sort of threat. There were, according to him, fifty thousand Jews in France. But, he noted, even if there were one hundred thousand Jews, out of a total population of twenty-five million people this would not be very significant (p. 83).

At this point, Godard indicated that he had now exhausted all the purely "human" objections to Jews being equal citizens of France. As a consequence, he turned to the religious arguments that the conservative clergy and their allies, especially those in the National Asembly, had been

321

asserting (p. 83). The first was the classic allegation by Catholics that God had condemned the Jews and that, therefore, Catholics should not stand in the way of a divine plan. His response to that argument was simple. Ceasing all human injustice against the Jews would not alter a divine plan, if this was, in fact, the true divine plan (which would, in any event, be independent of human action) (p. 84). Furthermore, he questioned whether it was really up to men to interpret divine judgments, asking: Is it really for men to take charge of vengeance? Godard answered his own theoretical theological question with a resounding "No." Rather, he declared, "it is up to God to execute his plans. And it is up to man to fulfill his mission on earth—to render all men happy!" (p. 85).

Continuing with his theological analysis, Godard noted that some people would say that the destiny of the Jews cannot be changed—that their destiny is simply an unhappy one. He recalled that one of the "proofs" for that proposition advanced in recent years was the rejection by the population of England of the so-called "Jew Bill" of 1753, which, after its adoption by Parliament, was revoked due to the massive objections of the local population. However, Godard retorted that the revocation could not be surprising when the strength of English prejudice against the Jews (which, he asserted, was even greater than that in France) was fully understood (p. 86).

Diplomatically and patriotically, Godard proceeded to draw a contrast between France and England, thereby appealing to the National Assembly's patriotic impulse. In France, he asserted, prejudice was tempered by the gentleness of French morality. The Enlightenment, which had, according to Godard, destroyed prejudices, was, he suggested, stronger in France than it was in England in 1753 (p. 88). As a consequence, a law adopted in France would not need to be revoked. As an example, Godard turned to Austria, where the edict in favor of the Jews promulgated by Joseph II had not been revoked. In fact, Godard affirmed, people in Austria were quite satisfied with the legislation (p. 89).

Punctuating his arguments, Godard now reasserted that no objection could resist the justice which the Jews were seeking. All objections, he proclaimed, had been refuted, vanquished, and defeated. There was generally, in France, a firm recognition of the need for a law favorable to the request of his Jewish clients (p. 90). The logical conclusion was that the members of the National Assembly had no alternative but to respect the will of the French people.

As Godard perceived it, the remaining issue was only a question of timing: now versus later. He returned to the assertion, made mainly by the Alsatian members of the National Assembly, that there were people who had expressed the need for more time before giving Jews equal rights, that giving Jews rights immediately would create a danger (p. 90). Godard categorically rejected this argument. Instead, he posited that, if it was just a matter of making Jews citizens, then it would be unjust to delay. It would be unjust not to automatically remedy an injustice. Turning to his legal training and echoing the arguments he had made in the Metz case on behalf of the German defendants, he dramatically stated that it was important to remember the axiom (an axiom that the radical revolutionaries would soon cast aside), that it is better to spare 100 guilty persons than to see a single innocent individual perish. The same principle must, he continued, apply to citizenship—but in this case, he suggested, there was not just one person at stake, but rather all the Jews (p. 92).

Once again he turned to a rhetorical question: Should a single Jew be deprived of citizenship just because some Jews may arguably be debased or may not currently be worthy of citizenship? His answer conformed to his faith in the legal system—a legal system that, if appropriate, could punish any Jews who might actually commit crimes. In summary, he observed that, just because there may be some Jews who are not yet worthy of civil rights, there must not be a proscription of all Jews. Justice, he extolled, consistent with his fundamental faith in the law and its beneficial effects, rejects all delays (p. 93).

Godard then listed all the problems that would be generated if members of the National Assembly imposed further delays. Such delays would make people believe that Jews are different from other men. They would strengthen and perpetuate prejudice. They might engender special laws, such as limiting the number of Jews in particular places or forcing them to move to designated locations (p. 94). In Godard's analysis, such delays would purely and simply promote injustice.

Next, Godard rejected an incremental approach to the granting of equal rights to Jews. He noted that almost all authors on the subject had adopted the erroneous notion of softening laws against the Jews by steps. In a tribute to one of the early leaders in the fight for Jewish equality and to political pragmatism, Godard then flattered the National Assembly leader Mirabeau, whom, he affirmed, had avoided this error (p. 94n1). Furthermore, the incremental approach could result in Jews being required to assume special burdens, or in being required to obtain special instructions, or even in having restrictions placed on their religious practices. Such special requirements would, Godard stated, accentuate the division between Jews and Christians (p. 95).

In this context, Godard now turned to the generations-old claim that Jews were a separate nation. He categorically rejected that claim. It was permissible, he wrote, for Jews to have their own religious laws, but with respect to all civil matters, it was necessary for all distinctions to be avoided in order to refrain from encouraging old hatreds. At this point, he espoused the assimilationist agenda: let the Jews be completely integrated with the French, he urged. This, he declared, is the principle that is appropriate, and which can create peace and concord (pp. 95–96).

Godard next put the grant of Jewish equality within the revolutionary context, appealing to the National Assembly in its role as the leading force in the struggle to bring legal reform to France. Things that might not have been done otherwise, he argued, should be done now at a time of universal regeneration, as society was heading in a new direction (p. 96). He posed another rhetorical question: Could society really fear an old prejudice at a time when all prejudices were being destroyed? Everything was changing, therefore, the destiny of the Jews also had to change. The people would not be any more startled by this change than by the other changes that were then ongoing (pp. 96–97).

This was the time to act, he declared to the members of the National Assembly. Link an improvement in the status of the Jews to the flow of the Revolution, he urged. There would not be any real resistance to this and there would be no substantial obstacles. Therefore, he felt compelled to urge that the legislators, who had just shown such respect for human rights generally, should not now suddenly hold back—an attitude which would be simultaneously combative (against Jewish rights) and unjust (pp. 97–98).

Godard's plea on behalf of the Jews turned into an appeal for fundamental human rights—so often in the past the underlying goal of his legal efforts. It was true, he acknowledged, that Jews were no longer being persecuted as in the past. They were no longer being forced to choose between baptism and death, nor were their children being taken from them and raised as Catholics. Their belongings were no longer being seized; they were no longer being burned (presumably a specific reference to the massacre in Strasbourg in 1349); they were no longer being legally massacred; they were no longer being subjected to humiliating ceremonies (pp. 98–99). But, after having reminded his audience of all the evils that France had imposed on the Jews in the past, he bemoaned that they were still treated "as slaves" (a status that he had vociferously condemned in his pleadings on behalf of Julien Baudelle) and were segregated in certain locations. They still bore arbitrary taxes (notably the Brancas tax on the Jews of Metz and the discriminatory taxes imposed when they entered Alsatian cities). Although he did note that a few Jews had been exempted (including, of course, one of his principal clients, Berr Cerf Berr), he reminded his readers that many restrictions remained in place (pp. 101–2).

Once again, he urged the National Assembly to stop delaying and to act. He reiterated his view that what remained to be done was simply to complete a task already largely accomplished by the Enlightenment itself, and that it would be inappropriate for the National Assembly to suddenly become deaf to so many voices which urged it to speak and act. This would be chimerical and the very thought of it simply inappropriate, he declared (p. 104).

In his final appeal, Godard made a powerful plea to the members of the National Assembly and to the French population at-large, with a kind of indignation worthy of the prophets of the Bible:

> You are human—you will end the suffering of the Jews; you are just, you will give them the title and rights they seek. Hasten the time of justice; they are justifiably impatient…Hasten because you have promised to resolve their destiny "this session" and the Jews could become victims of any delay you might cause to the determination of their fate. And you, the people, [will] see without worry or concern the elevation of a people you have [previously] persecuted; you have gained rights which are so dear to you; do not impede the Jews in their efforts to, in their turn, conquer the rights to which they are entitled…Make Jews happy and you will benefit. Let all wrongs, yours to the Jews and those of the Jews to you, be buried in the past. Let the same spirit guide Jews and Christians toward a common goal, and the act of justice from the National Assembly will be an act of reconciliation. They will have their separate religion, but common public laws (pp. 104–6).

As he brought his *Pétition* to a climactic close, Godard stated on behalf of his Jewish clients that they would become CITZENS AND FRENCH-MEN (with Godard once again supplying the emphasis) and, for everything related to the welfare of the nation, they would be united with their fellow citizens. Jews and Christians, he asserted "would compete in their patriotic fervor and in their virtues" (pp. 106–7).

The eloquent *Pétition* was a significant political and moral declaration that combined Enlightenment philosophy with the practical issues related to the rights of individuals who had lived on the margins of western European society for more than a thousand years. In just over one hundred pages, prepared in a mere four weeks, it sought to address all the common prejudices that had been leveled at Jews over the centuries, as well as those that were particularly being bandied about in the Revolutionary era. It informed its readers in direct and practical terms that Jews were fundamentally no different from other residents of France, but that it was the prejudicial treatment they had received over centuries that had forced them to behave differently. Judaism, it forcefully posited, was entirely compatible with the requirements of citizenship in an enlightened society, and it pledged that Jews were fully prepared to take the steps necessary to assimilate into French society. Within the pamphlet, Godard endeavored to address all the issues relating to Jewish integration into French society, analyzing them both philosophically and practically and mapping out a future for the full assimilation of the Ashkenazi Jews. Most significantly, the *Pétition* constituted an important offer by his Jewish clients: Allow us to become equal citizens and we will relinquish all our special rights. Accept us and we will become like you—to the extent that our particularism prevents us from becoming full-fledged Frenchmen, we are prepared to renounce that particularism, at least, in the public square. Jews were prepared, according to Godard, to become Frenchmen, distinguished from their fellow Frenchmen only by religious practices, but asserting that in all other respects they were the same as Frenchmen of other religions, with the same feelings of devotion and loyalty to the newly emerging France.

Godard's proposal on behalf of his Jewish clients represented a compromise that would become a model for Jewish integration into Western societies. While retaining the essence of their traditions, Jews would begin a process of blending into the nation in which they lived. They would retain their religious practices and unique traditions, but they would learn the ways of the majority population around them so as to minimize differences and the inevitable conflicts that arise from sharp cultural differences within a largely homogeneous society. The *Pétition* would ultimately achieve its stated objective, but would be a bargain with very mixed results.

The *Pétition* was a stark contrast to the short self-serving document submitted to the National Assembly by the Bordelais. It was a document of broad scope intended to appeal to the best instincts of the revolutionaries. Godard was not just trying to persuade a group of legislators to adopt a piece of legislation. He was trying, as he had in so many of his prior pleadings, to convince his fellow Frenchmen to perform an act of justice, to induce them to right a wrong and to elevate both the victims of that wrong and French society generally. It was an eloquent statement in the cause of religious and human rights.

The *Pétition* was well received and bestowed upon its author merited credit and public recognition. Shortly following its publication, the *Pétition* received a glowing review by an author identified only as "G" in the *Moniteur* of February 15, 1790. (It is worth remembering that the *Moniteur* was owned by Charles Panckoucke, the brother of Amélie Suard, Godard's long-time friend and admirer.) The reviewer described the *Pétition* as having been written "with philosophy, eloquence and sensibility." He further commented that the *Pétition* "was worthy, from all standpoints, of the talent Godard had previously evidenced in all of the circumstances for which he had used his pen to further the interests of humanity."[1]

Sometime later, the *Mercure de France* (also owned by Charles Panckoucke and edited by Jean-Baptiste-Antoine Suard) published an extensive and favorable review of the *Pétition* in its "*Nouvelles Litteraires*" section. The reviewer, identified only as "C..." (possibly Charles Panckoucke, himself), suggested that Godard, as the avocat for the Jews, could be considered to be merely repeating arguments previously articulated in favor of the Jews, but that "he devotes himself also to demonstrating that political conveniences and [French] self-interest are aligned with the notions of justice calling for the designation of the Jews living in France as citizens." The author noted that Godard was making a persuasive argument for justice. In identifying Godard as the author of the *Pétition*, the reviewer praised him as "a young avocat as distinguished by his talent as by his patriotism," thereby reminding the readers that Godard was,

---

1. *Moniteur*, February 15, 1790.

despite his youth, already quite well known.[2] At the time of Godard's death, *L'Ami des Patriotes, ou le Défenseur de la Constitution* would praise the *Pétition* with a very few powerful words, referring to it as a work "full of energy and humanity."[3]

Godard, clearly proud of his work, appears to have sent his *Pétition*, just as he had previously disseminated his other published writings, to friends and acquaintances. On February 3, 1790, Jacques Necker wrote to Godard to thank him for a copy of the *Pétition* and of his speech (the speech that he would shortly deliver to the Paris Assembly) "in favor of the Jews."[4] Later in the year, on July 2, in a letter written to Godard, his friend, the priest Defuaus, acknowledged receipt of a copy of the *Pétition*. Defuaus was clearly impressed by the document and wrote to Godard that he believed that "the Jews will owe you a great deal, since it appears difficult to deny the strong arguments contained in the *Pétition*."[5]

Defuaus also relied on the strength of the *Pétition* to urge his friend to remain active as an avocat in the public arena, suggesting that either Godard was giving consideration to ending his role as a private avocat and taking a position with the government, or that he was contemplating that he would be summoned to government service on the basis of his work.

Beyond being a compelling piece of advocacy, the *Pétition* would serve as a kind of certificate of good standing for the Ashkenazi Jews of France, attesting to the goodness of their character and to their ability to integrate themselves into the newly emerging society. It was designed to appeal to the developing consciousness of a France that was purporting to live by the Enlightenment principles that were the prime movers of the Revolution. It was not a call to arms, but rather a plea for a grant of civil equality to Jews in the name of elementary justice and patriotic duty. It was a respectful request to French leaders to take another critical step in the civic regeneration of France itself.

In the years to come, it is for this document and the important advance

---

2. *Mercure de France*, March 27, 1790, vol. 138, no. 13, pp. 115–19.

3. *L'Ami des Patriotes ou le Défenseur de la Constitution*, November 12, 1791, no. 6, p. 181.

4. Unpublished letter from Jacques Necker to Jacques Godard, dated February 3, 1790, Lot no. 319, sold at Alde, Maison de Vente auction on April 20, 2009.

5. Letter dated July 2, 1790, from Defuaus to Jacques Godard. (Unpublished letter from the author's personal collection.)

that it represented in his efforts on behalf of the Ashkenazi Jews that God-ard would be remembered. Yet, in spite of the strength of the *Pétition*—its powerful arguments and its appeal to the essence of the Revolutionary ideal—it did not, indeed it could not, by itself achieve its objective. The political reality in the National Assembly, with a considerable and vo-cal minority of reactionary members (primarily from Alsace and from among the conservative clergy), would continue to serve as a breakwater to the wave of support engendered by the *Pétition* and by the elaborate lobbying campaign pursued by Godard and his clients. Nonetheless, the *Pétition* served as a vital step and a critical volley in the battle for Jewish legal equality in France—a battle which would continue for nearly twen-ty more months of active political maneuvering in a context of increasing social and political disorder.

Godard had served his clients well. His efforts on their behalf would continue through this early phase of the Revolution, as would his work on behalf of other clients and causes.

CHAPTER 26

THE DEBATE AT THE NATIONAL ASSEMBLY

On January 28, 1790, the day after each member of the National Assembly had received a copy of Godard's *Pétition* and the day on which a debate on the issue of Jewish rights had finally been scheduled, the president of the Assembly was Guy Target, who had been serving in that role since January 16. The relationship between Target and Godard had to have been a significant factor in the initial phase of the lobbying campaign that now went into high gear and especially, as noted, in the coordination of dates for the Jewish presentation. However, due to illness,[1] Target was not present on this important day, and when the Assembly convened at 9:00 a.m., a prior president, Jean-Nicolas Démeunier was sitting in the presiding officer's chair.[2]

---

1. *Archives Parlementaires*, vol. 11, p. 354.

2. Jean-Nicolas Démeunier (1751–1814) served as a representative from the city of Paris to the Estates-General. On two occasions he served as president of the National Assembly and was a member of the Constitution Committee. He was an author of various essays primarily focused on political matters. In 1790 he published a compilation of essays about the United States and included in his book copies of all the principal documents related to the governance of the United States, including its founding documents and the constitutions of the various states. In 1792 he immigrated to the United States where he remained for a number of years. He was invited to write an essay about the United States for Charles Panckoucke's *Encyclopédie Méthodique*, an attempt to update Diderot and d'Alembert's original *Encyclopédie*, and secured the assistance of Thomas

After a lengthy discussion regarding some administrative matters, the Assembly took up the Jewish issue. As the delegation from Bordeaux had been informed, it was Charles-Maurice de Talleyrand-Périgord, the Bishop of Autun—the renegade aristocratic priest who would later serve as Napoleon's wily foreign minister—who slowly ascended to the podium in his capacity as Chairman of the Constitution Committee to read the Committee's report.[3] He began, as expected, by speaking, not about the status of the Jews of France generally, but solely about the petition of the Jews of Bordeaux requesting confirmation of their existing legal rights and the affirmation that they were already active citizens. Noting the presence in Paris of the Bordeaux delegation, he reminded the Assembly that the petition in support of their request was signed by 215 individuals. The leaders of the Bordeaux Jewish community had, just like their Ashkenazi brethren, also hand-delivered copies of their pleading to each member of the Assembly at their homes the prior evening.

As he proceeded with his remarks, Talleyrand asserted that the adjournment of the debate respecting the Jews which had occurred on December 24, 1789, should not affect the dialogue about the Jews of Bordeaux. He cumulated the Jews of Bordeaux with the other Sephardic Jews of the region together with those from Bayonne and Avignon, reiterating that the adjournment had been based upon the notion that the Ashkenazi Jews were different, and had their own laws, courts and community leaders—attributes of separate nationhood. He also reminded the Assembly that the Ashkenazi Jews could not own real property and did not pay the same taxes as their neighbors. Talleyrand emphasized that none of these attributes were applicable to the Portuguese Jews, who had benefited from Patent Letters issued as long ago as the reign of Henri II in the sixteenth century and reissued just a very few years previously by Louis XVI.[4] Although it is not certain whether any representatives of the Ashkenazi Jews were present as Talleyrand made his remarks, if they were their hearts must have begun to sink. Talleyrand's presentation began with an exhaustive articulation of the position of the Portuguese Jews and an undermining of theirs.

Accepting the tactical position of the Portuguese Jews, Talleyrand

---

Jefferson in the preparation of his entry.

3. *Moniteur,* January 31, 1790, no. 31, p. 126.

4. *Archives Parlementaires,* vol. 11, pp. 363–64.

enumerated the differences between the two groups of Jews. He reasserted in detail that, in contrast to the Alsatian Jews, the Jews of Bordeaux and their coreligionists of the region did not have particular laws, tribunals, or officers; that they had an undefined (and, therefore, unlimited) right to acquire property; that they actually possessed all types of property; that they were subject to all manner of taxation on the same basis as other Frenchmen; that they had the rights of the bourgeoisie generally; that they took part on all occasions in public assemblies as citizens and as businessmen; that they had participated recently in the elections for delegates to the Estates-General (indeed, almost electing one of their own as a delegate); and that they served at that very moment in the national militias, where they held ranks and played important roles on all days of the week without distinction (a detail intended to undermine the notion that the prohibition of work on the Sabbath and the multitude of Jewish holidays made it impossible for Jews to fulfill their civic duties as citizens).[5]

Talleyrand was drawing a sharp and unavoidable distinction between the assimilated Portuguese Jews and their unassimilated Ashkenazi brethren—the very distinction the Bordelais Jews wanted drawn as a means of preserving their rights. He was reminding the National Assembly that the Portuguese Jews shared in all the basic rights of bourgeois French citizens. By especially emphasizing that these Jews held public offices, served in the National Guard, paid taxes, and were in all respects analogous to other Frenchmen, Talleyrand was reiterating to the Assembly that the issue of equality had effectively already been decided with respect to the Portuguese Jews. He sealed his point by repeating that these Jews had for two hundred forty years been recognized as citizens of France pursuant to Patent Letters issued by several kings, and reissued as recently as in 1776 and 1780. (He conveniently omitted to mention that some of those Patent Letters had been addressed to "New Christians" rather than to Jews.) In essence, the request of the Portuguese Jewish citizens was merely an effort to confirm an existing reality; it did not involve a juridical modification of any kind.

Talleyrand affirmed that the Committee fully concurred with this analysis. Therefore, he concluded his remarks to his fellow National Assembly members by saying: "your Constitution Committee believes, without prejudicing anything with respect to the question of the Jews

---

5. *Moniteur*, Sunday, January 31, 1790, no. 31, p. 251.

more generally, it would be just and appropriate for you to decree at this time for the Jews to whom ancient laws have granted the status of citizen, as well as for those who have had such protection since time immemorial, to continue to benefit from it, to preserve it and, as a consequence, to be active citizens."[6] Talleyrand's conclusion was accepted by the acting president of the Assembly as a resolution being submitted for adoption. Although he clearly did not so intend, due to the breadth of Talleyrand's remarks the resolution was interpreted by some Assembly members as covering all the Jews of the kingdom, including the Ashkenazi Jews of Alsace, Lorraine, and the Three Bishoprics.

As a consequence, Talleyrand's presentation unleashed a strong reaction. The Alsatian Reubell immediately demanded the right to speak and was given permission to ascend to the podium. Unwilling to yield an inch when it came to granting rights to Jews, Reubell spoke in strong opposition to Talleyrand's presentation. He was promptly interrupted. The aristocrat Louis-Marc-Antoine de Noailles, the Marquis de Lafayette's brother-in-law and one of the leaders of the debate to abolish feudal rights less than six months earlier, jumped to the defense of the Jews. Noailles made an impassioned plea—not just on behalf of the Portuguese Jews, but on behalf of all Jews.[7] The *Moniteur* described his intervention as a "crying out."[8] He argued with vehemence that the Jews, not just the Jews of Bordeaux, but Jews throughout France, had been patriotic and supportive of the national interest since the beginning of the Revolution.

Reubell was not to be deterred and quickly resumed his remarks with a reiteration of his dire warnings of the consequences of giving the Jews equal rights. He restated his prior assertion that the Jews were a separate nation and dramatically affirmed that they were trying to seize all the property of the Alsatians. He concluded with the technical and facile observation, which he knew to be a false premise, that, if the Jews were already active citizens, then no new legislation was really necessary.[9]

With Reubell's diatribe concluded, several representatives sought to be heard in response on behalf of the Jews of Bordeaux. Raymond DeSèze, the avocat who had been part of Marmontel's pre-Revolutionary social circle which had also included Godard, and who had collaborated on a number

6. *Archives Parlementaires*, vol. 11, 364.
7. Ibid.
8. Ibid.
9. Ibid.

of legal matters with Godard, ascended to the podium. DeSèze represented the Guyenne region, which encompassed the city of Bordeaux, where
he had been born and raised and with which he retained deep ties. He had
also previously had occasion to delve into the situation of the Jews in his
professional capacity. In 1785, he had played an important role in the defense of a Jewish individual named Worms, accused of the "crime" of usury
by a young soldier seeking to avoid repayment of his debts. DeSèze's pleading, in the successful support of his Jewish client, had sought to normalize
Jews and had elicited much praise.[10] Of course, the Bordeaux delegation
had met with DeSèze during January and had undoubtedly anticipated his
role in the Assembly debate. Invoking his extensive and cordial contacts
with Bordeaux's Portuguese Jewish population and his wide knowledge of
Jewish matters, he expressed his solidarity with the Jewish community's
efforts. DeSèze noted that he had had the support of the Jewish community in Bordeaux throughout his political career, and described that support
as an indication of the community's involvement in political life. In other
words, he used his personal experience to support the notion that Jews
were already exercising the prerogatives of active citizens. He went so far
as to indicate, accurately, that if no Jews had been elected to the Assembly,
it was simply a matter of randomness; that a Jew could readily have been
sent to the Assembly as a representative.[11] He also ascribed any failure to
have Jews hold municipal offices in his region simply to the failure of some
French citizens to overcome their ancient prejudices.[12]

The reactionary cleric, the Abbé Maury, then tried to limit the damage
that he perceived the Assembly was about to cause. First, he argued that

---

10. According to the account of the case in a contemporary publication, in his
brief, DeSèze, erroneously referred to as "Me. De Seize," had "sown [semés] many
curious episodes about the Jews, their customs and privileges in France." He
had done so, according to the author of the analysis of the case, in order to raise
interest about the Jewish religion throughout France, "but in such a manner so
as not to shock." The commentator bestowed high praise on DeSèze for his work
on the case, noting that DeSèze's pleadings had made a "great sensation not only
because the substance of the matter is already important, but also through the
talent that he has demonstrated." *Mémoires Secrets pour servir à l'histoire de la
République des Lettres en France depuis MDCCLXII*, vol. 28, pp. 93–94.

11. David Gradis, a leader of the Bordeaux Jewish community, had by only a mere
handful of votes failed to be elected as a delegate to the Estates-General from his
home region of Bordeaux.

12. *Archives Parlementaires*, vol. 11, pp. 364–65.

if the Jews of Bordeaux had received "privileges" this was an indication that they were not citizens, since those who are granted "privileges" do not have "rights." Then, as a fallback argument, he proposed, yet again, to explicitly separate the question of the rights of the Portuguese Jews from the issue of the rights of the Jews of Alsace and Lorraine. He suggested that the Assembly should be unambiguous in limiting the scope of its resolution to an affirmation of the existing rights of the Portuguese Jews, since going beyond such a step would, he declared, irremediably change the status of the Alsatian Jews.[13]

When Maury had concluded his remarks, in an attempt to break the logjam and move on to other business, Isaac Le Chapelier, one of the individuals with whom the Bordelais had met multiple times during their lobbying campaign, urged that the status of the "Jews of Bordeaux" be completely separated from the status of the Alsatian Jews. He then tried to call the question.[14]

It was at that moment that the Vicomte Alexandre de Beauharnais,[15] a young aristocrat, married to a woman raised on Martinique named Marie Josephe Rose Tascher de la Pagerie—the woman who would, a few years later, after Beauharnais's execution, marry Napoleon Bonaparte and become the Empress Josephine—rose to propose a more precise and much more limiting motion. He moved that "The Jews of Bordeaux shall continue

---

13. Ibid., 365. See also *Journal de Paris*, January 29, 1790, no. 29, p. 115.
14. Isaac René Guy Le Chapelier (1754–1794) was descended from a long line of avocats and was himself registered with the Parlement of Rennes. He was elected to the Estates-General from the Third Estate and went on to become an active participant in the work of the National Assembly, including as a member of the Constitution Committee of that body. He is best remembered for the Le Chapelier Laws, which sought to limit the role of guilds and labor associations and which resulted in bans on trade unions in France until 1884. At the height of the Terror, Le Chapelier immigrated to England, but returned to France in a vain attempt to prevent the confiscation of his property. He was arrested and sentenced to death by the Revolutionary Tribunal. His execution took place on April 22, 1794, the same day that Malesherbes and his family were guillotined.
15. Alexandre François Marie, Viscount of Beauharnais (1760–1794) would go on to serve as a general in the revolutionary armies. He would ultimately be judged by the Revolutionary Tribunal for his failures at the battle of Mainz and would be executed on the guillotine just five days before the execution of Robespierre. With his death, his young widow was free to remarry, and, several years later, following numerous intimate relationships with an assortment of government officials, she married the young military hero, Napoleon Bonaparte.

to benefit from the rights from which they have benefitted to the present through the Patent Letters."[16] The Assembly now had to determine whether it would adopt the broad motion of the Constitution Committee, as presented by Talleyrand, or the much more restrained and constraining Beauharnais proposal.[17]

DeSèze stood up yet again and made a slightly different proposal. He urged that the Assembly decree that "the Jews of Bordeaux continue to exercise their rights as active citizens." This motion went beyond the mere precarious legal status given by the Patent Letters to a full acknowledgment of the equal civil status of the Portuguese Jews of Bordeaux. Thus, the Assembly was now faced with three proposals. It appeared as though Beauharnais' proposal would be given priority. However, more amendments were submitted. Bon Albert Briois de Beaumetz suggested that the rights of the Jews of Bordeaux be extended to those of Bayonne. Then, the Abbé Grégoire, the great proponent of the era for rights for the downtrodden, proposed that the rights of the Jews of Bordeaux simply be extended to all of the Portuguese, Spanish, and Avignonnais Jews, namely, to all of the Sephardic Jews in France, regardless of their place of origin or residence. He further urged that a decision on the fate of the Alsatian Jews (by which he meant the Ashkenazi Jews) be deferred for a time—but, he emphasized, only for a time. He also declared that he would in due course systematically and comprehensively tackle and, presumably, demolish the Abbé Maury's "illogical" arguments against full Jewish equality.[18]

Another young nobleman then stood up to be heard. Louis-Michel le Peletier de Saint-Fargeau, who was just beginning his evolution toward anti-monarchical politics, proposed a single resolution that was a synthesis of the original resolution and the various amendments.[19] However, a

---

16. *Archives Parlementaires*, vol. 11, p. 365.

17. Ibid.

18. Ibid.

19. Louis-Michel le Peletier de Saint-Fargeau (1760–1793) was an avocat who was elected to the Estates-General as a member of the Second Estate. In late 1790 he would advocate for the abolition of the branding of criminals and for the substitution of beheading for hanging. However, he is best remembered for his vote for the death of Louis XVI and for having been stabbed to death by a royalist sympathizer the evening before the execution of the king. Le Peletier de Saint-Fargeau's assassination resulted in a tremendous outpouring of public grief and seems to have elicited more of a reaction from the public than did the king's execution.

motion was made to call all the amendments to a vote separate from the original resolution. Alexandre de Lameth,[20] an aristocratic veteran of the American War of Independence, objected, noting that the amendments were not consistent with each other. It was then determined that each of the amendments would be voted upon in turn. Despite several attempts to prevent a vote on the amendments, the Assembly, nonetheless, proceeded to do so.[21]

The first amendment provided that the words "Jews who are Portuguese, Spanish, and Avignonnais" should be added to the original resolution, so as to assure that the resolution would unequivocally apply to all Portuguese Jews and expressly exclude the Ashkenazim. The amendment was approved.[22] It was then proposed that the amendment be supplemented to provide that the Jews who had done so in the past would be required to continue to pay municipal charges. A member of the Assembly noted that it was necessary that, as a preliminary matter, a decision be made as to whether the Jews were to be considered as active citizens. Crafted into an amendment, this issue now became the critical and preeminent matter before the Assembly.

However, efforts to vote on this amendment were frustrated by an increasing rowdiness in the Assembly. According to the journalist Brissot de Warville, a great tumult, which lasted for some two hours, spread through the ranks, primarily caused by the Alsatians and other conservative opponents of citizenship for Jews and therefore opposed to an affirmation of citizenship for Portuguese Jews as well.[23] The level of shouting and noisemaking made the process of voice voting extremely difficult.

---

20. Alexandre-Théodore-Victor, Comte de Lameth (1760–1829) was one of three brothers (the other being Charles and Théodore) who played significant roles during the French Revolution. During the American Revolution he served as a colonel in the army led by Rochambeau. In 1789, he was elected to the Estates-General as a member of the Second Estate, but rapidly joined the Third Estate as it formed the National Assembly. He helped found the Club des Jacobins, over which he presided for a time, but was forced out by the rise of Robespierre. In 1792, he joined the army defending the eastern border of France. Ultimately, however, together with Lafayette, he defected to the Austrians and spent years in foreign prisons. He subsequently returned to France and continued to engage in political activity until his death during the Restoration.

21. *Archives Parlementaires*, vol. 11, p. 365.

22. Ibid.

23. *Le Patriote Français*, Saturday, January 30, 1790, no. 175, p. 2.

Several attempts to vote on the pending amendment were made, but to no avail. The din was simply too great. After a long delay, the Assembly was finally able to proceed. The vote was taken by means of members of the Assembly standing to express their support or opposition to the motion. However, once the vote had actually taken place, due to the chaos on the floor of the Assembly the presiding officer was unable to ascertain whether the amendment had been adopted or rejected. Several attempts were made to count the votes, without success. Opponents of the resolution and its amendments began to gather to the right side of the podium and shouted their demand that the matter be delayed until another session. This disruptive and frustrating process continued for at least one hour.[24]

Then, François Alexandre Frédéric de La Rochefoucauld-Liancourt,[25] a prominent and outspoken member of the nobility (best remembered as the individual who, on July 14, awakened Louis XVI to inform him of the taking of the Bastille and who in response to the king's observation that the event constituted a revolt said, "No, Sire, it is a revolution") ascended to the podium. He demanded that order be established so as to permit a proper vote to take place for the sake of the duty and honor of the Assembly. He invoked the rule that once a vote had begun on a matter, it had to be continued to its full conclusion. Objections were voiced and it was then observed that the hour was late and that a large number of priests had already left.[26]

Unable to prevent the continuing "disorder and tumult," the Assembly's

---

24. *Archives Parlementaires*, vol. 11, p. 365.
25. François-Alexandre-Frédéric, Duc de La Rochefoucauld-Liancourt (1747–1827), was descended from a prominent aristocratic family, and was elected to the Estates-General as a member of the Second Estate. Shortly after the capture of the Bastille he served briefly as the president of the National Assembly. Although liberal in his outlook, including his strong advocacy for the elimination of slavery, La Rochefoucauld-Liancourt remained a staunch royalist. When the monarchy was overthrown in 1792, he fled to England and then to the United States. In 1796, he exchanged letters with George Washington, soliciting, unsuccessfully, the assistance of the U.S. president in seeking the liberation of the Marquis de Lafayette, who was then being held as a prisoner of war by the Austrians. Upon his return to France in 1799 and until his death during the Restoration, he advocated for various innovative measures to improve the quality of life of his fellow citizens, including mandatory innoculation against smallpox, the establishment of banks for individuals, and improvements in education.
26. Ibid.

presiding officer, Démeunier, expressed his frustration by declaring that
the chaos would not deter a vote and that he would require the members
of the Assembly to stay in session "all night, if necessary."[27] As a consequence, after some additional confusion, the question was again called,
including the amendment recognizing the so-called Portuguese, Spanish,
and Avignonnais Jews as full citizens of France. The amended resolution
was finally adopted by a vote of 374 for and 224 against. The definitive text
of the adopted resolution as read into the official record of the session
effectively accepted Grégoire's more expansive view of the rights of the
Sephardim. The resolution provided: "The National Assembly recog-
nizes that all of the Jews of France known as Portuguese, Spanish, and
Avignonnais Jews will continue to benefit from the rights to which they
have benefited to the present and which have been consecrated by Patent
Letters; and, as a consequence, they will benefit from the rights of active
citizens when they fulfill the obligations of active citizens prescribed by
the decrees of the Assembly."[28]

    With the resolution adopted, the members of the Assembly were eager
to go to their homes or to other gathering places. The lengthy and tumultuous session was finally brought to an end at 8:00 p.m., having lasted
over ten hours.[29] Only the Portuguese Jews had received a hearing. The
fate of the Ashkenazi Jews had been discussed only tangentially. Neither
Talleyrand nor any other member of the Assembly had made any reference to Godard's *Pétition* and virtually none of its arguments had been
given consideration. The sole unambiguous result that had emerged from
the National Assembly's deliberation was that the status of those Portuguese Jews who had previously benefitted from Patent Letters had been
decided. They were now confirmed in their position as being full active
citizens of France, regardless of their place of residence. This constituted
an important and decisive victory for the Portuguese Jews, but it also
served to emphasize the deep and regrettable divisions between the two
principal components of the Jews in France. It would, however, provide

---

27. *Journal de Paris*, January 30, 1790, no. 30, p. 117.
28. Ibid.
29. Adrien Duquesnoy, the representative of the city of Bar-le-Duc in Lorraine,
provides a particularly vivid description of the tumultuous nature of the January 18, 1790 session of the National Assembly in his published memoirs. *Journal
d'Adrien Duquesnoy, député du Tiers état de Bar-le-Duc, sur l'Assemblée constituante,
3 mai 1789–3 avril 1790* (Paris: Alphonse Picard et Fils, 1894), 324–30.

one additional arrow to the quiver of arguments that the Ashkenazi Jews could put forward. In Paris, where both Portuguese and Ashkenazi Jews lived in very close proximity, sometimes in the very same buildings, there would now exist the anomaly of having individuals of the same religion in the same area with dramatically different rights. This would ultimately prove to be an untenable position for the enlightened revolutionaries.

In spite of the long and emotional debate, the king and his ministers had chosen to stay out of the matter. The very Catholic royal family had not previously and did not in this debate directly intervene in any aspect of the discussion respecting the Jews. They studiously refrained from making any official comment. However, a clue to their attitude can be found in a private letter written by the king's sister, the twenty-five-year-old Madame Elisabeth, on the evening of the decision regarding the status of the Portuguese Jews by the National Assembly.[30] Writing to her friend Marie-Angélique de Bombelles, in a rather convoluted and confusing style, the Princess—who likely had never had a direct encounter with a Jew in her life—aware of the limited scope of the adopted resolution, but seemingly terrified at the prospect of a grant of full equality to the Christ-killers that she believed Jews to be, complained bitterly about the Assembly's decision:

> Yesterday, the Assembly put a finishing touch on all of its nonsense and irreligious actions by giving Jews the opportunity to be admitted to all occupations. The discussion was very long, but reasonable people have, as usual, had the worst of it. Thus far, it is still only the Jews who already had privileges that are admitted [to citizenship], but soon you will see that it is the entire [Jewish] nation that will have the same benefits. It was reserved for our century to receive as a friend the only nation that God has marked with a sign of disapproval, to forget the death that it caused Our Lord to suffer and the blessings

---

30. Elisabeth de Bourbon, Princess of France (1764–1794), who, in spite of having remained unmarried throughout her brief life was known as "Madame Elisabeth," was Louis XVI's youngest sibling. When her two brothers left France at the beginning of the Revolution, she chose to stay with the royal family and remained steadfast in her determination not to abandon her brother and sister-in-law even though it was obviously increasingly dangerous to stay with them. After the executions of both the king and queen, in the spring of 1794 she was tried by the Revolutionary Tribunal and was also sent to the guillotine. She went to her death calmly and with dignity, seemingly fortified by her strong Catholic faith.

that this same Lord bestowed on France, by permitting these enemies to triumph and, with joy, exposing our breast [to humiliation].
I cannot tell you how much I am angered by this decree. It would be
far better to submit to and wait submissively for the punishment that
Heaven holds for us, because It [Heaven] will not allow this error to
remain unavenged, and It suffers evil for some time, however then
It will punish it with no less force when the ingratitude of men has
made it rise to the greatest heights [sic].[31]

The old religious prejudices that had permeated French society for centuries, frequently propagated by the Catholic Church, were obviously still
very much alive. The conservative forces, led by the royal family, were
certainly not ready for the dramatic changes in the status of the Jews that
were wending their way through the national legislature.

Many Paris newspapers noted the Assembly's actions of January 28 in
their editions of the following days. The *Moniteur* of February 1 provided
a specific and elaborate description of the debate that had taken place on
the floor of the Assembly. This was in rather stark contrast to the succinct,
even dry, summaries debates usually received.[32] The fate of the Jews of
France was increasingly a matter of import to the French elites, and they
were eagerly following the National Assembly's consideration of the matter. The *Journal de Paris* devoted a number of columns to a vivid description
of the Assembly's January 28 debate on the Jewish issue and lauded the
outcome with extravagant words: "The cause of the Spanish, Portuguese
and Avignonese Jews is therefore won. May Heaven be blessed and may
human reason rejoice! It is a triumph for it [human reason]."[33] Even in
Godard's home province of Bourgogne, the action taken by the National

---

31. Letter of Madame Elisabeth to Mme. de Bombelles (January 29, 1790). F.
Feuillet de Conches, *Louis XVI, Marie-Antoinette et Madame Elisabeth, Lettres et
documents inédits*, vol. 1 (Paris: Henri Plon, 1864), 301–2.

32. *Moniteur*, no. 32, p. 122.

33. The *Journal de Paris* added a biblical touch to its praise for the Assembly's
decision by noting that it was regrettable that the Jews of Alsace and Lorraine
had not been included in that decision and that, as a consequence, those Jews
could with justification say to the Assembly, "like Esau to his father, 'Have you
only one blessing to give?'" The *Journal* then expressed the hope that "there is
no injustice that will not be repaired" by the Assembly and that "light which is
everywhere prepares for reason a universal triumph." *Journal de Paris*, January 30,
1790, no. 30, p. 117.

Assembly attracted press attention. The *Journal Patriotique de Bourgogne*, published by Jean-Baptiste Capel, Dijon's most prominent bookseller (from whom Godard's father had purchased the *Encyclopédie*), not only noted the grant of equal rights to the Portuguese Jews, but also denigrated the Abbé Maury's efforts to prevent the Assembly's decision. In an effort to make the Assembly's decision more relevant to his readers, the liberal Capel drew an analogy between the Assembly's acknowledgment of the Portuguese Jews' "rights" (as distinguished from "privileges") and the appropriateness of this exchange of "ancient privileges" for "rights" in this revolutionary period.[34]

---

34. Capel erroneously wrote that the National Assembly made its important decision on January 21. *Journal Patriotique de Bourgogne par une Société de Gens de Lettres*, no. 5, p. 44.

CHAPTER 27

"A WELL-PREPARED COINCIDENCE"

The second prong of Jacques Godard's lobbying strategy was put into effect on the very same day the National Assembly adopted its resolution in favor of the Portuguese Jews. Paris had always been at the heart of Godard's lobbying campaign. Although he knew, and it was clear to the Jewish group, that any law granting all French Jews full equality had to emerge from the National Assembly, it was equally clear that the road to persuading the National Assembly, with its recalcitrant Alsatian and other conservative members who would endeavor by every means to block Jewish equality, was through Parisian pressure. If Paris could be won over, then assuredly the National Assembly would follow. Therefore, a presentation to the Paris Assembly was a critical and dramatic step in the lobbying effort Godard was orchestrating.

On the evening of January 28, as the debate on Jewish rights was raging at the National Assembly, less than a half mile away at the Paris Hôtel de Ville another debate about the status of the Jews was about to begin. A delegation made up of a group of Ashkenazi Jews, likely including Berr Cerf Berr, Berr Isaac Berr, Berr Cerf Berr's son Théodore, Mardoché Pollak, Jacob Trenel, a certain J. Goldschmidt (identified solely as a "rentier," i.e., an individual who lived from rental income),[1] Jacob Lazard, a jeweler,

---

1. This was likely Jacob Goldschmidt, a banker who became a secular leader of the Paris Jewish community. Haïm Harboun, *Les Voyageurs juifs du XVIIIe siècle:*

and the eccentric Polish Jew and co-winner of the Metz essay contest, Zal-kind Hourwitz (who was dressed in his National Guard uniform), slowly made its way into the *grande salle* of the Hôtel de Ville, as the members of the delegation prepared to submit their plea for Jewish equality.[2] Godard would, at the appropriate moment, rise from his seat among the stadi-um-style bleachers along the sides of the chamber and stride to the front of the hall to join the Jewish delegation as its leader and as its spokesman.[3]

In a carefully planned and tactically impressive maneuver, the two most important legislative bodies of France, the National Assembly and the Assembly of the Representatives of the Commune of Paris, engaged in deliberations related to Jewish civil rights on the very same day. The noted commentator, Sigismond Lacroix, in an understated tribute to Godard's lobbying strategy, referred to this as a "well-prepared coinci-dence."[4] However, as a consequence of Godard's tactical adaptability,

---

1773–1794, vol. 2 (Editions Massoreth, 1997), 207.

2. There is some speculation that David Sintzheim, the rabbi who was Cerf Berr's brother-in-law, was also part of the delegation. However, it is not very likely that this was the case since the presence of a rabbi, in his austere and unfamiliar at-tire, would have served to highlight the particularism of the Jews, contravening the approach taken by Godard of attempting to limit perceptions that Jews were substantively different from their fellow Frenchmen.

3. Sigismond Lacroix indicates that the Paris Assembly moved from the *salle des Gouverneurs* of the Hôtel de Ville into the *grande salle* on November 30, 1789, because it was a larger hall to which the public could be invited to observe the Assembly's deliberations. He describes the room as a semi-octogon with a sta-dium seating arrangement and a small stage at the front of the hall, where the of-ficers of the Assembly sat at a long table. In one of his descriptions, he alludes to an etching of the room made by Pierre-Gabriel Berthault and Jean-Louis Prieur depicting a ceremony during which a young English captain named Nesham was given an award for having saved a Frenchman from a mob that sought to kill him while the Frenchman was endeavoring to deliver food to Paris. Lacroix expresses doubts about the accuracy of the etching, which depicts the room as a rectangle. However, the etching is the only image of a meeting of the Par-is Assembly known to exist. (The room was destroyed during the fire which devasted the Hôtel de Ville during the Paris Commune uprising in 1871.) The ceremony in question actually occurred on January 15, 1790 and Godard made extensive reference to it in his *Exposé* about the work of the Paris Assembly. See Lacroix, *Actes de la Commune de Paris pendant la Révolution*, vol. 3, pp. 70 and 463, and Godard, *Exposé des Travaux*, 129–33.

4. Lacroix, *Actes de la Commune de Paris pendant la Révolution*, vol. 3, 625. Feuer-werker, describing the simultaneity of the debates at the National Assembly and

the process which unfolded before the Paris Assembly was quite unlike what had taken place earlier in the day at the National Assembly. At the Paris Assembly, the matter was one of first impressions and the prime movers were Ashkenazi Jews, not the Portuguese Jews. Importantly, the presentation on behalf of the Jews was orchestrated and would be led by their official representative, who would also be the principal actor in the debate. The very subject of the debate was also to be dramatically different. The matter before the National Assembly had focused almost exclusively on the status of the relatively assimilated Portuguese Jews. At the Paris Assembly, notwithstanding the reticence of the Portuguese Jews about intertwining their own battle for rights with the Ashkenazi Jewish struggle, the fate of all the Jews, ostensibly of Paris, but, in reality, of all of France, was to be considered.

The debate at the Paris Hôtel de Ville began with the dramatic entrance of the delegation of members of the Jewish community into the elaborately decorated great hall. As the members of the Jewish delegation filed in, their presence was acknowledged by the Abbé Mulot,[5] who was presiding the Assembly. Godard strode from his seat and joined the members of the small group as they approached the slightly elevated stage at the front of the hall.

The combined group—the eight visitors and Godard—then stood in

the Paris Assembly, notes that "the harmonization of the efforts is patent." Feuerwerker, *L'Émancipation des Juifs en France*, 342. Godard would himself modestly refer to the coordination as "this extraordinary confluence of circumstances." *Exposé des Travaux*, 134.

5. François-Valentin Mulot (1749–1804) was an ordained priest who was strongly influenced by the philosophy of Rousseau. Highly educated, he earned a doctorate in theology. He was a member of the Paris Assembly and then was elected to the Legislative Assembly in September 1791. He took the civic oath of the clergy, thereby alienating himself from the Catholic hierarchy. Ultimately, he left the priesthood and married. The Jewish apostate, the Abbé Joseph Lémann, in his virulently anti-Jewish tract about the supposedly nefarious impact of the grant of equality to Jews, seeking to demean Mulot's warm embrace of Jewish equality played on the meaning of Mulot's name. (Mulot is the French word for field mouse.) Lémann sarcastically noted that Mulot (the mouse), "gnawed" on the obstacles or dams constructed by the beavers (meaning the conservative Catholics) against the grant of Jewish equality. Lémann, *Les Juifs dans la Révolution française*, 93. Over the course of the years of the Revolution, Mulot served in various legislative bodies, including the Paris Assembly, the Legislative Assembly, and the Convention. He also served as a Paris elector.

front of the table at which sat the Assembly's officers. The eight Jews were a somber group of older men, with the exception of Zalkind Hourwitz, who clearly stood out in his distinctive blue, white, and red uniform of the Paris National Guard.[6] As they huddled near the elevated officers' table, Godard and the Jewish delegation were officially welcomed by Mulot. In what was obviously a well-choreographed act, Mulot invited Godard to address the Assembly on behalf of the Jewish delegation. All the other members of the delegation moved to the side as Godard, in the flowery syntax common to the era in general and especially common among avocats, began his remarks by emphasizing his role as a frequent defender of the downtrodden: "I have left for just a moment the place that I occupy in your midst to assume the one that suits me when I speak on behalf of supplicants and I serve as the interpreter for the unfortunate."[7] Then, he went on to identify the clients on whose behalf he was petitioning, being careful not to overstate the nature of his representation:

> Charged by most of the Jews of the kingdom to defend their cause within the National Assembly, I am, at the same time, charged by those in Paris, gentlemen, to offer you the homage of their respect, the assurance of their dedication, and even the testimony of their gratitude.[8]

Continuing, he alluded to the purpose and nature of his mission in greater detail:

> ...the generous people of this city have, to a certain extent, preempted for the Jews the benefits of the law by seizing this memorable revolution as an occasion to mingle with them, to make them their comrades in arms, to cover them with the appearance of citizenship, under which several of them appear here in front of you; finally, to treat them as brothers even before treating them as actual citizens.[9]

Godard then acknowledged the difficult role that he was asking the Assembly to play, not just in enacting new legislation, but in setting a tone

---

6. Malino, *A Jew in the French Revolution,* 92.

7. *Discours prononcé, le 28 Janvier 1790, par M. GODARD, Avocat au Parlement, l'un des Représentans de la Commune, en présentant à l'Assemblée générale de la Commune, une Députation des JUIFS de Paris* (Paris: L'Imprimerie de Lottin l'aîné & Lottin de St. Germain, 1790), 1. Cf. *Moniteur,* February 2, 1790, no. 32, p. 265.

8. Ibid., 1–2.

9. Ibid., 2.

and paving the way for a major attitudinal change. He continued, in the tradition of all lobbyists, by not forgetting to flatter his audience:

> This is not by itself to make law, but rather this is to prepare for a law by means of public opinion; this is to exercise the highest of powers; this is to render easier the work of the legislator and to transform, so to speak, in advance its intentions into decrees; such that all aspects of glory, Gentlemen, seem to be reserved to you. Sometimes you second a law already made by promptly consecrating it through public opinion, and by placing next to principle memorable examples that give to that law an irrevocable empire. Sometimes, it is a law that is yet to be made that you prepare by means of actions, by means of events, by means of an ensemble of conduct that the legislators seem to ask of you, and which they need in order to effectuate all of the good that it is in their desire to accomplish for you. There are no prejudices that can withstand the incalculable power of opinion that prepares the law, or of the law which is assisted and consecrated by public opinion.[10]

Godard now revealed his true purpose in addressing the Paris Assembly, namely, to use the Assembly as a tool of persuasion to cause the National Assembly to adopt a law granting to all Jews the status of active citizens of the new France. He explained his objective eloquently and in detail, not forgetting to indirectly give himself some credit:

> The Jews, who are seeking from the National Assembly and who are expecting from its wisdom a law which will be favorable to them, place a great deal of confidence in the honorable voters who surround them in this capital and from whom they have already received such beneficial impact. They will dare to say, Gentlemen, that they are worthy of it by dint of the patriotic zeal which since the very beginning of the Revolution has moved their souls.

> I must say it to their credit, gentlemen; although, in all the steps that it has taken in order to endeavor to win their rights, they did nothing for themselves, and they needed to be guided by others, it is they, nevertheless, who, first, had the idea to offer their homage, because this idea is only a feeling, and feeling does not need a guide.

He continued to unveil his strategy, emphasizing his request on behalf of

---

10. Ibid., 2–3.

his Jewish clients that the Paris Assembly become the instrument through which they could achieve their civil equality throughout the nation:

> They also thought, Gentlemen, that the goodness of this capital toward them would, perhaps, give them the right to beg you to raise your voice in their favor, and to issue a wish that could hasten the decision on their fate, but they fear to ask you for this new testimonial of their goodness and they abandon themselves, they confide themselves for this purpose to your wisdom.

> They ask of you only to permit them to express pride at all the former testimonials that they have received. They beg you to give them the justice they deserve, by saying loudly that you do not have anything with which to reproach them; that public order has never been troubled by them, that even in the excess of their misfortune, they have not murmured against any man nor against the law; that a pure and civic zealousness animates them today for the common defense and the general welfare, and, by this solemn attestation which will merely be an homage rendered to the truth, you will have the satisfaction, so sweet for true friends of the public interest, to serve not only the cause of the Jews of Paris in particular, but the cause of all of the Jews of the kingdom generally and thereby prepare the well-being of fifty thousand individuals.

In this time of ostentatious displays of national pride, Godard buttressed his appeal on behalf of the Jews by giving testimony to the Jewish community's ardent nationalism and its contribution to the protection of the gains of the young Revolution:

> You will not hesitate, gentlemen, to give them this moral certificate that I have the honor of requesting on their behalf, when you become aware that, of the five hundred who reside in Paris more than one hundred serve in the National Guard and sacrifice all of their time, all of their zeal, all of their energy in the defense of the Constitution.[11]

Then, in a manner that appears to have anticipated the modern American presidency's frequent approach to speechmaking in which an individual is highlighted as a means of exemplifying worthy conduct, Godard used Zalkind Hourwitz—the "famous Hourwitz"—as his dramatic prop:

---

11. Ibid., 3–6.

When you will know that, in the midst of the representatives that I have the honor of presenting to you, is to be found the famous Hourwitz, Author of an excellent work, crowned by the Academy of Metz, Interpreter of Oriental Languages at the King's Library, having for his entire fortune, only 900 *livres* of salary and having determined these 900 *livres* to be too much for himself; since he has just made an irrevocable Patriotic gift of a quarter of this amount, and when he was informed that a Patriotic Contribution was only imposed upon one year's revenue, he responded that he was abandoning, forever, the quarter of his salary because the 900 *livres* was an amount in excess of the amount which was due to him for the kind of work he was performing at the King's Library.[12]

Having used this small interlude to highlight the quality of his clients and their patriotic fervor, Godard continued with his presentation:

These, Gentlemen, are the men for whom I solicit your justice. And if, as I hope, you will not refuse it to them; if you show yourselves to be, simultaneously, humane and just; if, finally, this day could end with the fulfillment of our desires; you will not have had a more memorable nor a more complete day since the beginning of the Revolution.[13]

Godard brought his remarks to a conclusion by urging the Paris Assembly to take immediate action in order to set an example for the entire French nation, and prompting the members of the Assembly to give to their short-term existence as an assembly a kind of immortality by taking an action that would be remembered through the generations:

It will, therefore, be from these precincts that will emerge, to spread thereafter throughout the entire kingdom, the irrevocable prohibition on all the prejudices which dishonor the French nation. You are only provisional administrators of this capital; but you will have accomplished that which will not be temporary; which will be, instead, unperishable; & for which all of the generations and all of the centuries will owe you recognition.[14]

Godard's appeal to his legislative colleagues had contained all the

---

12. Ibid., 7–8.
13. Ibid., 8.
14. Ibid., 9–10.

rhetorical components of persuasion and flattery that a lobbyist must invariably use in order to succeed. It was a skillful and impressive presentation.

Upon completion of Godard's remarks, the presiding officer of the Assembly, the Abbé Mulot, who was a practicing, albeit very liberal, Catholic priest and who was then serving as the principal clergyman at the Left Bank church of Saint-Victor, responded warmly:

> You come, gentlemen, to request the Assembly of the Commune to issue a wish which will support before the legislators of the nation a request that you have made in the name of nature.

> I am proud, Gentlemen, that I can be the spokesman for this Assembly and that you are not afraid to appear before it while I am exercising the powers of its presidency.

> Yes, Gentlemen, you bring honor to my heart; and that which must flatter me the most is that I can respond to your confidence without wounding the severity of my principles.[15]

Consistent with the perspective of the Catholic Church generally and even of the enlightened members of the clergy of which he was among the most prominent, Mulot, in spite of his willingness to support the Jewish quest for equality, felt compelled to reassert the truth that he perceived in the Church's religious beliefs and the concomitant error that underlay Jewish theology. But he did so in a relatively generous manner:

> The distance of your religious opinions from the religious truths that we all profess as Christians do not prevent us, as men, from coming closer to you; and if, mutually, we believe ourselves in error, if mutually we believe it to be our obligation to complain, we can nonetheless love one another.[16]

Taking Godard's lead, he then sought to make the grant of equality to Jews a far broader matter:

> Your request is not so personal that it will not spread any benefit to

---

15. *Discours prononcé, le 28 Janvier 1790, par M. GODARD, Avocat au Parlement, l'un des Représentans de la Commune, en présentant à l'Assemblée générale de la Commune, une Députation des JUIFS de Paris,* 10–11.
16. Ibid., 11.

all of society; and if it tends to have us confirm the rights which you
acquired by being born as subjects of the law, it also tends to banish all of the vices of which our nation has been accused, to make
the virtues which you cultivate in secret blossom and to open for
the State new sources of enrichment. I cannot announce what will
precisely be the wish of the Assembly with respect to the substance
of this request; but, I can at least assure you simultaneously that its
pronouncements will be in conformity with the laws of reason and
of humanity and that I will be the first to applaud that which will be
determined to be favorable for your nation.

Mulot concluded his remarks by a show of hospitality, inviting the delegation of Jews to remain for the balance of the evening's meeting.[17]

Godard then returned once again to the officers' table at the front of the
great hall to express his thanks to the Assembly and to its president. At the
conclusion of this exchange, the Assembly adjourned the discussion until
the day after next (Saturday, January 30, 1790), with a formal invitation
for the delegation to attend. This adjournment was undoubtedly another
well-planned tactic to provide the Paris Assembly with an opportunity to
wait and see what decision would emerge from the ongoing discussion
at the National Assembly. For the Jewish members of the delegation, the
scheduling of a meeting on the Jewish Sabbath meant that they would
not be able to attend in person. This arrangement was also likely planned
well in advance in order to give the Paris Assembly's deliberations a greater sense of objectivity. And the Jews, of course, knew that their very able
agent, Godard, would be there in their stead to promote their interests. In
any event, even if the scheduling of the next deliberations on a Saturday
was not planned in advance, Godard understood that it would not be
wise to raise the issue of the inability of his clients to be present at a Saturday session since that would highlight an aspect of their particularism at
the very moment when he was endeavoring to minimize the differences
between his Jewish clients and the population at-large.

As a final gesture to the Jewish petitioners, yet again an action likely
planned in advance, the Paris Assembly decided to publish Godard's and
Mulot's remarks, since "each merited general admiration."[18] The speech

---

17. Ibid., 12.
18. *Journal de la Municipalité et des Districts de Paris*, January 29, 1790, quoted in

soon appeared as a brochure bearing the title "REMARKS made on the
28th of January, by Mr. GODARD, avocat with the Parlement, one of
the representatives of the Commune, in presenting to the Assembly of the
Commune a delegation of Jews of Paris," with, just below, a statement that
the publication had been carried out "On the orders of the Assembly."[19]

This presentation to the Paris Assembly was merely the first step, indeed, only a preliminary first step, of Godard's strategy with respect to
the Paris prong of his lobbying on behalf of the Jews. No one understood
better than Godard the tension between the central governing bodies of
the city of Paris and the local assemblies. In his short political career, he
had already served at both levels. He knew well that the district bodies
cherished their rights and privileges and were loath to cede them to the
city Assembly or to the mayor. Thus, Godard was fully cognizant that
the municipal component of his lobbying strategy had to have two
phases. He had just begun the first part, with his appeal to the communal
Assembly, and he would not delay in launching the second part—an
appeal to the local district assemblies.

Lémann, at page 94. The *Journal* was not unqualified in its praise of Mulot's remarks. In its article concerning the Paris Assembly's meeting, reflecting the res-
idue of anti-Jewish sentiment that existed in Paris, it referred to Mulot's remarks
as being "an embarrassing response for a clergyman," but then noted that Mulot
had "known how to reconcile the austerity of his ministry with the intentions of
the Assembly of which he was the spokesman as its president."
19. *DISCOURS prononcé le 28 janvier 1790 par M. Godard, avocat au Parlement,
l'un des représentants de la Commune, en présentant à l'Assemblée générale de la
Commune, une Députation des Juifs de Paris*, 1.

CHAPTER 28

THE CARMELITES TAKE THE LEAD

Even before the full debate on Jewish rights was held by the Paris Assembly, the assembly of the Carmelite District,[1] where the preponderance of the Jews of Paris lived and worked, convened to discuss the matter of Jewish equality. It can safely be presumed that Jacques Godard had planned this gathering, and it is clear that he and some of his clients were present for the district assembly's discussion. Being able to demonstrate to all of Paris and, ultimately to all of France, that the Paris neighborhood with the greatest concentration of Jews was favorable to their quest for equal status would be a brilliant and convincing stroke. The occurrence of this deliberation directly on the heels of the presentation to the Paris Assembly was likely yet another "well-prepared coincidence."

On Friday, January 29, 1790, the members of the local assembly of the Carmelite District deliberated on the issue.[2] Godard used a format for this meeting similar to the one that he had orchestrated for the Paris Assembly the previous day. He brought with him a delegation of Jews.[3]

---

1. The Carmelite District was located immediately to the west of the Blancs-Manteaux District and just a short distance from Godard's residence on rue des Blancs-Manteaux.

2. Lacroix, *Actes de la Commune de Paris Pendant la Révolution,* vol. 3, p. 646, citing the minutes of the meeting (Arch. Nat., D IV 3, no. 24).

3. It is not certain precisely which individuals were members of the Jewish delegation, but it is clear that such a delegation appeared before the Carmelite District

A short presentation was made and deliberations took place after the Jewish delegation had left. The minutes of the meeting described the proceedings as having been conducted as follows:

> The president informed the assembly about the appearance of a delegation that had attended the General Assembly of the Representatives of the Commune representing the Jewish nation residing in Paris, to request the support of the Commune before the National Assembly, for the purpose of being admitted to the honor of sharing, with other French citizens, without distinction, the rights of active citizens which prejudice and laws had until now refused them.

> Following a reading of the address delivered to the National Assembly on the prior August 26, in the name of the Jewish nation—this address is published with a date of August 24, 1789—the president requested that the Assembly debate the question of whether this District would vote in favor of their admission to the rights of active citizens, whereupon the Jews who were then present left.[4]

Godard had clearly done his homework. The District Assembly engaged in a "lengthy and sufficient" debate.[5] At the conclusion of the debate, the Assembly adopted a comprehensive and laudatory resolution (likely crafted by Godard) in strong support of the Jewish effort:

> Considering that, since the beginning of the Revolution, the Jews residing within the *arrondissement* of the District have always comported themselves with the greatest zeal, the purest and most generous patriotism;

> Considering that the petition submitted by them to the National Assembly incorporates their complete submission to the laws and courts of the kingdom, and their renunciation of the privilege of having their own particular chiefs and other privileges of which they have always appeared to have jealously guarded;

Assembly in light of the press reports and because the minutes of the meeting indicate that, at a particular point in the District Assembly's deliberations, "the Jews present at the assembly left." Ibid. See also "Second Établissement des Israélites à Paris," in *Archives Israélites de France, Année 1841*, vol. 2, p. 502.

4. Lacroix, *Actes de la Commune de Paris Pendant la Révolution*, vol. 3, p. 646, citing the minutes of the meeting (Arch. Nat., D IV 3, no. 24).

5. Ibid.

Considering also that the terrible prejudice, which has until the present time kept them in the depth of degradation, was not conducive to inspiring within them the sentiments of good and loyal citizens; that the means of giving to all of the Jews the energy that is appropriate to free men, is to make them participate in this honorable capacity;

Considering, finally, that the Carmelite District, the one in which are located the most Jews, was, just as it still is, in the best position to know about their public conduct and to render justice to their zeal and to the patriotism which they have always demonstrated; thinking also that thanks are due to them;

Has unanimously decided to bring to the Assembly of the Representatives of the Commune the wish formulated by the District that the Jews, to whose good conduct and complete devotion to the public interest they attest, should benefit henceforth from the rights of active citizens, as soon as they have fulfilled the other conditions which are imposed by the decrees of the National Assembly.[6]

With the resolution in favor of Jewish citizenship adopted, the District Assembly then determined to send a large delegation of representatives of the District to the Paris Assembly. It further resolved, on its own initiative (but undoubtedly with some encouragement from Godard), to notify both the National Assembly and the other Paris Districts of its decision:

To that effect the Assembly has designated six representatives to present its resolution to the Assembly of the Representatives of the Commune; has furthermore decided that this resolution will be sent to the president of the National Assembly and to the fifty-nine other Districts.[7]

In fact, the District followed through on its determination to be in direct contact with the National Assembly. On February 18, 1790, presumably at the behest of Godard and probably with the assistance of his pen, the Carmelite District, represented by its president, issued a letter to the National Assembly, confirming its support:[8]

---

6. Sigismond Lacroix, "Les Juifs à Paris en 1790." *Revue Bleu*, series 4, vol. 9 (Paris: Bureau des Revues, 1898): 418–19.
7. Ibid., 419.
8. Archives nationales, D IV, 49–1425. Sigismond Lacroix cites a different date of February 18 and the signature of Robin, president (Lacroix, *Actes de la Commune*

Mr. President:

The General Assembly of my District honored me by authorizing me to convey its wishes on the subject of the Jews of Paris. . .

It is the first which has issued one [a resolution] in their favor, and our District is the one which contains perhaps the largest number in its midst; we have voted for their legal existence; the National Assembly, on the basis of a petition from the municipality, which joined with us, believed that it was necessary to adjourn this great question with respect to those in Paris who do not benefit from Patent Letters from our kings; wise and political reasons undoubtedly caused the National Assembly to not have as of yet taken care of their fate.

But at this time when all men seek the title of active citizen, we are daily requested by families whose children bear arms in our battalion, to cause them to receive from the National Assembly a decree which will be favorable to them and will erase their original stain.

Deign, Mr. President, to take into consideration the tender concern of the Carmelite District for its brothers, the Jews of Paris, and present to the August Assembly which you preside, and at the head of which your merit and your civic devotion have undoubtedly placed you, the demand, the respect, and the devotion of the Jews of our District and of the citizens who support their just claims.

I am, with respect,

Leverdier, President of the Carmelites[9]

The National Assembly did not officially respond to the letter from the Carmelite District, but the letter was deposited into the Assembly's file relating to the Jews. The Constitution Committee must have undoubtedly taken note of it as it prepared its report on the issue of Ashkenazi citizenship to the entire National Assembly.

---

de Paris pendant la Révolution, vol. 3, p. 201; also cited in Kahn, *Les Juifs de Paris pendant la Révolution*, 90–91.

9. Nicolas-Vincent Leverdier (1754–1820), born in Rouen, was an avocat who served as a judge in the early years of the Revolution. He lived in the Marais area of Paris on rue de Montmorency in the Carmelite District. In 1794 he was arrested and imprisoned, in part due to the positions he had taken at the beginning of the Revolution, but he managed to avoid execution.

The Carmelite District Assembly's delegation to the Paris Assembly, which immediately prepared to head to the Hôtel de Ville, was made up of Bon-Claude Cahier de Gerville,[10] Leverdier, and four other members of the District Assembly identified as le Nain, d'Ailly, Chiboult, and Cholé. Cahier de Gerville was designated to head the delegation and to serve as its spokesman. Just as Godard and his clients had intended, the district with the largest Jewish population in Paris would lead the way in advocating for Jewish equality.

---

10. Bon-Claude Cahier de Gerville (1751–1796) was selected in 1789 as a Paris elector and as a representative of the Sepulcher (future Carmelite) District of central Paris. In October 1789 he was designated as an assistant prosecutor. Subsequently, he was sent to Nancy to assist in resisting the revolt of the soldiers in Châteauvieux (August 1790). More importantly, in November 1791 Louis XVI named him Minister of the Interior at the request of the Legislative Assembly as a consequence of his role in putting down the soldiers' revolt in Nancy. However, he resigned the post on March 10, 1792, and left Paris, thereby retiring from politics and probably saving his life. He died four years later without having returned to the political arena.

CHAPTER 29

A RETURN TO THE PARIS ASSEMBLY

In accordance with its prior decision, the Paris Assembly met to debate the Jewish matter on Saturday, January 30. Since it was the Jewish Sabbath, in spite of the invitation from the Assembly to the entire Jewish delegation to be in attendance, Godard's clients were not present. The Assembly was again presided over by the Abbé Mulot, who immediately called upon the delegation from the Carmelite District to read the lengthy resolution that had been adopted the prior day by the District Assembly. The text of the resolution was read in its entirety to the Assembly by Cahier de Gerville.

At the conclusion of the reading, Cahier de Gerville added his own remarks. He bestowed unabashed additional praise on his district's Jewish community, praising their civic virtues:

> No citizens have shown themselves more ardent in the conquest of liberty than the Jews; none have been in a greater hurry to take on national responsibilities; none have been better friends of order and justice; none have been more disposed towards acts of kindness toward the poor and voluntary contributions required for the needs of the District.[1]

---

1. Lacroix, *Actes de la Commune de Paris pendant la Révolution*, vol. 3, p. 647. Cf. Lacroix, *Les Juifs à Paris en 1790*, p. 419.

Then he took the argument in favor of the Jews one step further, suggesting that the decision to make Jews full citizens, had, in reality, already been superseded by events:

> Dare I admit it? The Jews are already Frenchmen amongst us. Yes, Gentlemen, the Carmelite District has not wanted to draw a distinction between them and other citizens: we admit them to our councils; they share in the honors and difficulties of military service, and not the slightest murmuring is heard against their possession of these rights of the city, from which, nonetheless, the seal of the law is still missing.[2]

He concluded by reminding the representatives that, in securing for the Jews the status that they were seeking, they would merely be giving to the Jews of Paris the very rights that other Jews, the Jews of Spanish and Portuguese origin and those from Avignon, already possessed. This was, of course, an appeal against discrimination leveled at one class of Jews as opposed to another and it was also a plea for a kind of equal protection for all Jews residing within France—an argument that Godard had expressed previously.

With the principal arguments in favor of Jewish equality now fully and favorably articulated before the Paris Assembly, the discussion that followed Cahier de Gerville's presentation was in large part very supportive of the Jewish position. The only condition that the Assembly members wished to impose on the grant of Jewish equality was that the Jews be required, just as all other citizens of Revolutionary France were required, to take the oath "of loyalty to the Nation, to the law and to the king" ("*de fidelité à la nation, à la loi et au roi*").[3]

However, even though the written record does not include them, the remarks of the Abbé Bertolio,[4] delivered toward the end of the debate, suggest that certain members of the Assembly had evoked the old

---

2. Ibid.

3. In French, this phrase has a kind of poetic quality to it, with the last two components actually rhyming. It was the customary expression of loyalty to the new regime until the overthrow of the monarchy in August 1792.

4. Antoine-René-Constance Bertolio (1741–1812) was an ordained Catholic priest who served for a time as an avocat at the Paris Parlement. Beyond his service as president of the Paris Assembly in 1790, he went on to serve as France's Ambassador to Rome during the Directory and as a judge in Guadeloupe during the Consulate.

prejudices, notably by identifying the Jews as being reviled by the heavens themselves. Bertolio refuted those arguments and then, demonstrating that his intervention in the debate had not been without some significant pre-planning with Godard, proposed that, in order to develop a full consensus throughout the city, all the Districts should be canvassed.[5]

Following Bertolio's suggestion, Jean-Claude-Antoine Debourge,[6] a representative from the District of the Enfants-Rouge (Godard's home district) and a close colleague of his fellow representative, spoke to the Assembly. His eloquent address, which echoed Godard's own earlier remarks, was deemed worthy of publication and was, in fact, published soon after its delivery. The haste with which it was published is obvious from the various factual and grammatical errors that the published version contains, including even an erroneous reference to the date upon which Godard's *Pétition* on behalf of the Jews was officially submitted to the National Assembly, identifying that date as January 27 rather than the 28th.

Debourge's remarks were another important volley in the Jewish struggle and appear to have been made in close coordination with the efforts of Godard, if they were not actually prepared by Godard himself (which is quite likely since they are lawyerly in tone and Debourge did not have any legal training). Debourge reiterated many of Godard's arguments. He began with Godard's fundamental argument debunking the notion that Jews were foreigners and not entitled to French citizenship. To be a citizen, he asserted, it is "merely sufficient to reside in a State, to pay taxes to it and to

5. Lacroix, *Actes de la Commune de Paris pendant la Révolution*, 648.
6. Jean-Claude-Antoine Debourge, who served in the Paris Assembly as a representative of the Enfants-Rouge District, is an obscure character about whom not much is known. Apparently, he served as the administrator of a hospital in Paris at one point, but, otherwise, there is little information respecting his background or career. In addition to writing on behalf of Jews, it is known that in early 1791 and for a number of months thereafter he was one of three commissioners sent down to Provence as an emissary of the royal government to investigate certain riots that had taken place. Together with the other two commissioners he submitted a report on their investigation to the king in February, 1792. *Catalogue général des livres imprimés de la Bibliothèque*, vol. 17, Bibliothèque Nationale (France). Département des imprimés, Léopold Delisle. See also C. Lourde, *Histoire de la révolution à Marseille et en Provence: depuis 1789 jusqu'au Consulat*, vol. 1 (Marseille: Senes Imprimeur, 1838), 335; also Georges Guibal, *Mirabeau et la Provence: Deuxième Partie. Du 5 mai 1789 au 4 avril 1791* (Paris: Ernest Thorin, Editeur, 1891), 480.

fulfill the requirements imposed by law."[7] He went on to reassert the notion that religion is a private matter between a person and God and is not related to any legal duties. He then reminded his audience that the issue of Jewish rights had in actuality already been decided by the provisions of Article 10 of the Declaration of the Rights of Man and of the Citizen.

Attempting to weaken the common prejudice that Jews were merely usurers, Debourge noted that administrative restrictions and even actions of the tribunals had imposed this activity on Jews, but also that many non-Jews were in the same business and were not prevented from being citizens. As a consequence, he reasoned that the "cause of the Jews is, therefore, no longer problematic in the eyes of reason or equity."[8] He emphasized that most members of the National Assembly did not disagree with his analysis and that when the Assembly had delayed a decision on Jewish rights in December it had not taken a stand against them, but rather had merely sought to provide some time for the prejudices against the Jews to dissipate.

Echoing Godard's plea of two days earlier, Debourge urged that the time to act in favor of the Jews had now come. As a tactical matter he asked that the Paris Assembly send a representative to plead for the cause of the Jews before the National Assembly and recommended that this representative be a member of the Catholic clergy. Specifically, he identified the Abbé Sieyès as his choice, intending to use Sieyès' enormous prestige to promote the cause of Jewish equality. Sieyès had become one of the most renown clerics among the liberal elites when, in anticipation of the convening of the Estates-General, he had published his immensely popular political tract entitled *What is the Third Estate?*[9] The pamphlet, arguing in favor of a preponderant allocation of legislative authority to the Third Estate, had marked an important milestone in the political conversion of France. His overt assistance to the Jewish cause was seen by some as certain to bring with it a wide swath of support.

Debourge concluded his remarks by making the following specific proposal, which included his recommendation for the intercession of the Abbé Sieyès:

---

7. Jean-Claude-Antoine Debourge, *Discours Prononcé le 30 Janvier dans l'Assemblée générale des Représentans de la Commune par M. DEBOURGE, l'un des Représentans de la Commune à l'occasion de la Demande faite le 27, par les Juifs de Paris,* 4
8. Ibid., 6.
9. Emmanuel Joseph Sieyès, *Qu'est-ce que le Tiers-État?* (1789).

First. To give to the Jews of Paris testimony of satisfaction with their conduct before and since the Revolution;

Second. To have the mayor summon the representatives of Paris at the National Assembly and to direct them to invite, in the name of the representatives of the Commune, the Abbé Sieyès to take up the cause of the Jews, and to act in concert with his fellow representatives to take advantage of the first moment when it will be possible to set a specific time to address the issue.[10]

The long session ended with the adoption by the Assembly of a comprehensive resolution that reflected Debourge's proposal:

Considering that all people residing in an empire and who are subjects of that empire must participate with the same status and the same rights; that differences in religious opinions should not create any such differences within civil status and it is at the time when a people gives itself a Constitution that it must hasten to shake off the yoke of prejudice and reestablish the ignored rights to equality;

Considering, furthermore, that the Jews living in Paris have always comported themselves with integrity and zealousness, and that, in this Revolution, especially, they have provided the most meritorious proof of their patriotism;

Has resolved:

1. That there should be provided to the Jews of Paris public and authentic testimony of the good conduct that they have always evidenced, of the patriotism of which they have given proof, of the virtues that, we know from the testimony of the Carmelite District within which the largest of their number live, they have practiced in secret;

2. That the desire for their admission to civil status and to all of the rights of active citizens would be formally declared; but that it would be brought to the National Assembly only once it has received the approval of the districts, which will be invited to meet in extraordinary sessions for this purpose, as much because it is in the districts that all power resides for this purpose as because the wish of all of

10. Lacroix, *Actes de la Commune de Paris pendant la Révolution*, vol. 3, p. 649. Cf. Lacroix, *Les Juifs à Paris en 1790*, p. 419.

the districts or a majority of the districts would constitute a more authentic and more solemn expression for the Jews than the expression of just the Assembly of the Representatives of the Commune.[11]

The adoption of the resolution was followed by general applause from the Assembly.[12] In accordance with the terms of the resolution, a copy of the resolution was sent to all the Paris districts. When the resolution was submitted to the districts, it was signed both by the Mayor and all the officers of the Paris Assembly: "BAILLY, Mayor, MULOT, Président; GUILLOT DE BLANCHEVILLE, CELLIER, BERTOLIS, CHAN-LAIRE, CHARPENTIER, Secretaries." The number of signatories was intended to emphasize the resolution's importance.[13]

The Abbé Mulot, president of the Assembly and representative of the District of the Mathurins—the only district which would ultimately oppose the Jewish initiative—then returned to the podium and enthusiastically endorsed the decision, stating that he "applauded it with all my heart, and if my name is not to be found among those priests who have defended you [the Jews], I consider myself happy to be able to be the last on the list."

The final word of the day was left to Jacques Godard. He stood in front of the officers' table and, on behalf of his clients, responded to the decision of the Assembly (which he had so well and so successfully engineered) and to the remarks of the Abbé Mulot:

Gentlemen, I had invoked your justice for the Jews of Paris; I must now thank you in their name, because you have rendered it.

However, it is not by an oratorical speech that I will try to paint their

---

11. Lacroix, *Actes de la Commune de Paris pendant la Révolution*, vol. 3, p. 639.
12. The importance of the decision to seek the approval of the districts of Paris was highlighted later that summer. In a report entitled "Address presented by the General Assembly of the Representatives of the Paris Commune with respect to rights of entry, fraud, contraband, so conceived" submitted to the National Assembly on August 19, 1790, the Paris Assembly stated that whenever the Paris Assembly had to decide a matter "on an important proposition on which opinions are divided, then our powers are limited: we have always made it our duty to so recognize it; we would cite here only those decrees on the department of Paris, on the civil status of the Jews and on the federation of Brittany and Anjou, that we sent to the sixty Districts before presenting them to the National Assembly." *Archives Parlementaires*, vol. 28, p. 167.
13. Ibid.

gratitude. I will insist upon repeating the moving words [words that had been expressed by the Mayor Bailly during a prior debate relating to the coal carriers of Paris] that were heard here with pleasure, that resounded thereafter with enthusiasm in every mouth and which are the most beautiful thanks that can be addressed to you: "Let us bless the Revolution which makes us all brothers."[14]

The two days that had been devoted to considering the status of the Jews were undeniably a great triumph for Godard and his clients. They had received rousing support for their position. Nonetheless, serious work remained to be carried out and Godard and the Jewish delegation were prepared to proceed with the next step of their lobbying efforts.

In this era, the dissemination of information was hardly instantaneous. Therefore, it was not until its February 2 edition that the *Moniteur* reported the presentation made by Godard on behalf of the Jews before the Paris Assembly. The coverage was significant. The editor, Charles Panckoucke (the brother of Godard's friend Amélie Suard) reprinted Godard's remarks in their entirety. In an interesting twist, the same edition of the *Moniteur*, even as it followed closely the debate on Jewish rights at both the National Assembly and the Paris Assembly, also contained an article (directly above the description of the deliberations of the Paris Assembly) describing remarks made in October by Quakers in the United States to President George Washington (repeatedly referred to in the article as "General Washington") expressing their loyalty to him and to the people of the United States. As the article noted, the Quaker action was taken in an effort to refute accusations of disloyalty being asserted against them. The *Moniteur* also contained the text of a response from President Washington, according to which Washington wrote:

The freedom to honor God in accordance with the lights of our conscience is less an indulgence of civil government than an inalienable right of man; so long as he fulfills his obligations as a citizen, society has nothing more to ask of him. It is only before the tribunal of God that men have to give account of their religious opinions. I have some knowledge of your principles and your conduct and I am doing nothing other than to give Quakers the justice which no one can deny them they are entitled, when I say that excepting only their

---

14. Lacroix, *Actes de la Commune de Paris pendant la Révolution*, vol. 3, p. 649.

refusal to defend the common cause of their fellow citizens during the war, there are no sects which can glorify themselves of a greater number of useful and exemplary individuals.[15]

The *Moniteur* then went on to say that: "Such an honorable testimonial about the Quakers by the most impartial judge and the legislator the most enlightened that America has produced should impose an eternal silence on their detractors and exonerates them fully from all of the calumnies spread about them."[16]

The *Moniteur's* article was both timely and helpful. That Quakers, a group long ostracized in the nations of Europe, should receive the assurance of equality from the highly respected General Washington could not but be noticed, especially as another long-ostracized religious community was seeking its place in French society.[17]

---

15. *Moniteur*, February 2, 1790, no. 33, p. 132.

16. In the original French, the article uses a formulation for exoneration based upon the French word for "wash" (*et les lave bien de toutes les calomnies répandues contre eux*).

17. Other newspapers also took note of Godard's presentation on Jewish rights before the Paris Assembly. *La Chronique de Paris*, in its February 6, 1790 edition, was particularly lavish in its praise, referring to Godard's remarks as being "full of nobility and of sensibility." *La Chronique de Paris*, February 6, 1790, no. 37, p. 146.

CHAPTER 30

LOBBYING THE PARIS DISTRICTS

With the knowledge that the Paris Assembly had been fully responsive to his pleas and that the Assembly had specifically requested that it be strengthened in its endorsement of his goal by the support of each of the districts, Godard now began a whirlwind lobbying campaign to persuade each of those neighborhood assemblies of the city of Paris, all sixty of them, to support the equality being sought by his Jewish clients. It would appear as though he and representatives of his clients went before all sixty assemblies within less than a month.[1] The effort had to have been exhausting and must have required significant preparatory work. Each meeting had to be scheduled and choreographed. The presentations suggest a kind of political onslaught with packaged speeches and prepared proposals for each of the assemblies. The effort conjures up images of more modern attempts to influence legislators.

Godard—the spokesman, the orchestrator, and the conductor—attended the many presentations. According to one eyewitness who reported his recollections over fifty years later, the delegation also consisted of four prominent members of the Paris Jewish community: Mardochée Pollak, Jacob Trenel, Jacob Lazard, and J. Goldschmidt, all of whom had been members of the delegation that had appeared before the Paris Assembly.[2]

---

1. Feuerwerker, *L'Émancipation des Juifs en France*, 350–54.
2. "Second Établissement des Israélites à Paris," p. 502.

It is interesting to note that the most prominent of Godard's clients, the Alsatian Jewish leaders, did not participate in the effort. Presumably, they would have appeared as foreign (with their undoubtedly pronounced Alsatian accents and provincial appearances) to the Parisian districts. Godard, the consummate politician and tactician, recognized that for this grassroots undertaking it would be best if the participants in the lobbying effort were all Parisians.

Over the the next several weeks, all the district assemblies met to consider the matter, and the delegation led by Godard appears to have attended all the gatherings. Although incomplete, the existing record provides a thorough picture of the extensive lobbying effort that Godard and his clients carried out in the early days of February. Godard himself summarized his successful effort in an address to the Paris Assembly on February 24.[3] Based upon the extant record and the results of the efforts, it is clear that Godard had made comprehensive and detailed preparations for the lobbying blitz. Not only did he meet with representatives of each district, but he seems to have varied his arguments to the districts, presumably to show awareness of each districts' unique features and concerns and, perhaps, to provide the impression of a measure of spontaneity and diversity of opinion.

The meetings with the district assemblies took place in rapid-fire succession, beginning immediately after the January 28 session of the Paris Assembly with the meeting at the Carmelite District Assembly. This was quickly followed, on February 4, by a meeting with the Saint Joseph District Assembly, at which the assembly members determined to support the request of the Jews. Then, on the same day, a favorable decision was issued by the assembly of the Notre-Dame de Nazareth District on the northeastern fringe of the city. That decision was based upon observations of the "good comportment that they [the Jews] have always displayed, the virtues that we knew they practiced in secret, the proofs that they have given, as citizens, as good brothers, of their entire devotion to the public interest."[4] The next day, it was the Left Bank Petit-Pères and Saint Marcel Districts whose assemblies reached their decisions. At

3. *Adresse de l'Assemblée des Représentants de la Commune de Paris à l'Assemblée Nationale sur l'admission des JUIFS à l'Etat Civil*, (Paris: Imprimerie de Lottin l'aîné & Lottin de St. Germain, 1790).
4. Lacroix, *Actes de la Commune de Paris pendant la Révolution*, vol. 4, p. 194; cf. Feuerwerker, *L'Émancipation des Juifs en France*, 351.

the Petits-Pères assembly, it was noted that "while some of the specific dogmas of the Jews seemed to be in contradiction with the laws of the French empire, the deepest recesses of conscience cannot be opposed to the Jews,"[5] so long as "on the exterior they cannot be distinguished from other citizens." By February 11, 1790, the assembly of another Left Bank district, the District of Saint-Étienne du Mont, let it be known that it also favored the resolution of January 30.[6]

On February 20 Godard was able to report to the Paris Assembly that, of the sixty districts, thus far "more than forty-five" had accepted the Resolution, and that none had objected. He informed the Assembly that:

> Several Districts have anticipated the transmittal of your decree; they have already treated the Jews as citizens, and they have issued a vow similar to yours. Other districts have awaited your resolution, they have assembled in accordance with the invitation made to them, and also pronounced their wish for the admission of the Jews to civil status. Not a single one has arisen against this group, too long unhappy, of our future fellow-citizens; more than forty-five have already adhered to their demand, ask you to support it at the National Assembly, express their congratulations at their welcome by the representatives of the nation, and in most of the decrees we note these words: unanimously, with perfect unanimity, with the most perfect unanimity, expressions which establish a very precise and well-defined wish.[7]

Certain of the ultimate success of his tour of the districts, Godard urged his fellow representatives of the Paris Assembly to act promptly:

> We can therefore act immediately, since we have the great majority of the districts in our favor, and I dare to guarantee that before two days have passed, the fifteen others will have expressed a wish similar to that of the first.[8]

His guarantee would prove to be somewhat of an overstatement. But, confident of his impending success, Godard then presented a draft set of remarks in support of the Jewish cause which he proposed be finalized and submitted to the National Assembly. A committee, composed

5. Lacroix, *Actes de la Commune de Paris pendant la Révolution*, vol. 4, p. 193.
6. Ibid., 199.
7. Ibid., 159.
8. Ibid.

of the Abbé Bertolio, the Abbé Fauchet (the fiery cleric who had been among the leaders of the demonstrators in the attack on the Bastille),[9] and Honoré-Nicolas-Marie Duveyrier, was established to study Godard's proposal.[10] Godard played a significant role in the ad hoc committee's deliberations and in influencing its actions, reflecting yet again that concepts of conflicts of interests were not as finely honed as they are in the contemporary political world.

Just days later, on February 24, Godard returned to the Assembly together with the committee members. He reminded the members of the Assembly that the vast majority of the sixty district assemblies had voted in favor of the Jewish position (and by then forty-nine had done so). He went on to declare that the balance of the district assemblies simply had not yet had time to meet and discuss the subject, but would assuredly concur with the other districts.[11]

Godard's statement was not entirely accurate. On February 20, the very day that Godard had made his first report to the Paris Assembly on the outcome of the canvassing of the districts, one of the districts, the District of the Mathurins, represented at the Paris Assembly by the staunch supporter of the Jewish cause, the Abbé Mulot, had strongly rejected the resolution in favor of the Jews after allegedly holding four sessions to discuss the matter.[12] Arguing that Jews, due to their particularism and, especially, their unique laws and legal system, were not ready for admission into the French body politic, the District urged that a national referendum on the Jewish issue be held before a decision was taken.[13] The actual reason for the district's decision, however, may have been significantly less motivated by democratic ideals than by mercenary ones. Many of the residents of the district were involved in the cloth and clothing trade.

9. Fauchet would later become the constitutional bishop of the Calvados Department and, ultimately, a member of both the Legislative Assembly and the National Convention before his life ended under the blade of the guillotine in October 1793.
10. Honoré-Nicolas-Marie Duveyrier served as an avocat with the Parlement of Paris. He was admitted to the Parlement in 1779 and resided on rue St. Jacques in the Mathurins district. His selection to be a member of the delegation was particularly interesting since his district was the only one that opposed the quest for Jewish rights. *Almanach Royal*, 1790, p. 361.
11. LaCroix, *Actes de la Commune de Paris pendant la Révolution*, vol. 4, p. 194n4.
12. Mainfroy Maignial, *La loi de 1791 et la condition des juifs en France*, 184.
13. *Extrait du Procès-Verbal du District des Mathurins, du vingt Février mil sept cent quatre-vingt-dix* (Paris: EDHIS, 1968).

Jews had begun to enter that trade and it appears likely that members of the district assembly were hoping to limit Jewish competition by depriving them of full civil rights.

Godard then proceeded to read the final version of the remarks he had prepared in conjunction with his three fellow committee members for submission on behalf of the Paris Assembly to the National Assembly.[14] The remarks were a stirring restatement of his earlier presentation to the Paris Assembly, but now buttressed by the support of a preponderance of the district representatives of the city of Paris:

> The destiny of most of the Jews of the kingdom is still undecided; or rather it is only too certain that they are still laden with their irons; and that their chains seem every day to weigh upon them more, proportionately as the benefits of liberty multiply around them. Perhaps you expected a strongly pronounced opinion to strengthen your generous intentions and to accelerate the moment of your justice. We are pleased to be the first to bring you this opinion; it is not ours alone; it is the opinion of many districts of this Capital; and it is Paris as a whole which speaks to you at this moment through us.
>
> A considerable number of Jews live in this city. Some are scattered throughout the different districts of Paris. Others, and in a greater quantity, in order to render their gatherings amongst themselves easier, and to compensate themselves for their isolation while they were amongst other men, placed themselves in specific neighborhoods, where it was impossible for them to escape from public surveillance. All of them, and everywhere, have been irreproachable in their conduct. No complaint has been asserted against them. They have never disturbed public order; and, if they have been the most unhappy, perhaps also, which is quite extraordinary, they have been the most peaceful of all Citizens.
>
> At the moment of the Revolution, their courage, their zeal, and their patriotism gave them rights to public gratitude. We have seen them in our midst, decorated with the national insignia, helping us to

14. David Feuerwerker, who, as noted, may have been the last scholar to review the complete Godard file in Geneva, reports that he found the text of the speech in Godard's handwriting, signed by the three committee members, in that file. Feuerwerker, *L'Émancipation des Juifs en France*, 356.

conquer liberty; and every day they help us to preserve our common heritage.[15]

He continued with the rhetorical flourishes typical of his legal pleadings as he argued on behalf of his Jewish clients:

Ah! Gentlemen, if they have contributed to the conquest of liberty, can they be condemned not to enjoy their own work? If they are real Citizens, under what pretext would the title be refused to them? We dare to say that they would deserve it as a reward, if it were not due to them as an act of justice.[16]

Next, Godard used the grant of equality that had been confirmed to the Portuguese Jews less than one month before as an additional argument in favor of the Ashkenazi Jews:

Their Religion is no longer incompatible with this title and with the rights which emanate from it, since the Portuguese, Spanish, and Avignonese Jews, who have received from you the status of active Citizens, have the same religion, the same principles, the same usages as the other Jews of the kingdom, designated under the title of Polish and German.[17]

He went on to make an equal protection argument. Granting rights to some Jews and then discriminating against other Jews living in proximity was, he observed, obviously incompatible with the new social order:

You will not suffer, then, that a mere difference in an accessory denomination should have a different influence on two classes of men, who bear the same name, which the same principles unite, and who must now blend with each other. If old injustices or extraordinary prejudices have separated them for a long time, you will not allow that in the same city, where there will be Portuguese Jews and German Jews, some are everything, and others nothing; and that, for example, in Paris, where Portuguese Jews are domiciled next to the Germans, the former are blessed by the favors of the nation, and the latter burdened with contempt.

---

15. Lacroix, *Actes de la Commune de Paris pendant la Révolution*, vol. 4, p. 195.
16. Ibid.
17. Ibid., 196.

Neither reason nor liberty can any longer tolerate such a monstrous-
ly unequal treatment.

Patent Letters had been obtained by the Portuguese Jews; and
though founded on nature and justice, they were, however, but
a preference expressed by arbitrary authority. Could it be the title
alone that would have made you decide? And would you have granted only one privilege?[18]

As was his wont, Godard ended his proposed remarks with a powerful
plea on behalf of his clients, urging that they be granted the rights that
they sought as a matter of elementary decency:

In the name of humanity and of the fatherland, in the name of the
social qualities of the Jews, of their patriotic virtues, of their powerful
love of liberty, we beg you to give them the title and the rights of which
it would be unjust to deprive them any longer. We consider them to
be our brothers; we are impatient to call them our fellow citizens. Ah!
Already we treat them as such; our interest causes us to want to be
integrated with them; our interest gives us the right to demand your
justice for them and for us. Accelerate their happiness and ours![19]

Following his reading of the proposed remarks, and notwithstanding the
opposition from the Mathurins District (which Godard had conveniently
failed to mention), at the conclusion of the debate, on the basis of the
approval given by the vast preponderance of the districts, the Paris Assembly voted that same day to ask the National Assembly to "accelerate
its justice" in favor of the Jews. A resolution, crafted almost certainly by
Godard as an amalgamation of the various supportive arguments made
by some of the districts, was submitted to the Assembly for adoption.

The resolution, read to the Assembly by the Abbé Mulot, summarized the collective and almost unanimous view of the districts of Paris
regarding the grant of equal rights to Paris's Jewish residents. It lauded
the virtues of the Jews and echoed the position initially expressed by
the Carmelite District by suggesting that the National Assembly would
merely be recognizing a fundamental reality if it went ahead and officially
recognized the Jews as full citizens:

---

18. Ibid.
19. Ibid.

Considering that at this time, which has fixed the destiny of the Empire, the Jews of this capital have hastened to join the good citizens;
that the patriotic zeal which they have demonstrated has, by anticipation, incorporated them into the French nation, because, like all
other citizens, they have supported and support even now the expenses of the service of the National Guard, having thus served with
ardor the cause of liberty, the good conduct which they have always
demonstrated, the virtues which we have known that they have practiced in secret, the proofs that they have given as citizens, like good
brothers, of their entire devotion to the public cause, testify powerfully in their favor;

Considering, finally that, for many years, many Jews living in Paris
have acquired in this large city a good will based upon their zeal to
fulfill their duties as citizens, their faithfulness in their commercial
engagement, their exemplary conduct and their service in the current Revolution; that this people once viewed as citizens, will be
what every good Frenchman should be, a good citizen, a good father,
a good spouse, a good son, and in a word, an honest man....[20]

As the debate on the Jewish issue drew to a close, the Assembly voted its
support for Godard's resolution.

Immediately following the vote, a delegation of Jews entered the Paris
Assembly's chamber and expressed thanks for the Assembly's support.[21]
This seemingly spontaneous, but obviously well-planned, appearance by
the Jewish group was yet one more part of Godard's continuing campaign
on behalf of his clients. After the Jews had expressed their gratitude for
the action of the Assembly, it was, once again, Mulot who responded. He
opined that the National Assembly would now heed the request of the
Paris Assembly and grant the Jews the equality they were seeking.[22]

With the Paris Assembly's affirmative vote, the initial phase of Godard's
Paris strategy had reached a successful conclusion. Strengthened by the
weight of a favorable determination by most of the district assemblies and
the express opposition of only one, the Paris Assembly was motivated to
flex its muscle and eloquently petition the National Assembly in favor of

20. Kahn, *Les Juifs de Paris pendant la Révolution*, 93.
21. Lacroix, *Actes de la Commune de Paris, pendant le Révolution*, vol. 4, 196.
22. Ibid., 197.

the Ashkenazi Jews. Since the Parisian delegates to the National Assembly already played a dominant role, Godard and his Jewish clients seemed justified in their assumption that a favorable outcome would be achieved quickly at the national level.

CHAPTER 31

A PARIS DELEGATION HEADS TO THE NATIONAL ASSEMBLY

Following its vote in support of Jewish civil equality, the Paris Assembly, in an effort to join action to its important resolution, designated a large delegation to head promptly to the National Assembly to present the resolution it had just adopted. The delegation was made up of Godard, the Abbés Fauchet and Bertolio, and another avocat, the secretary of the Assembly of Paris Electors, Honoré-Nicolas-Marie Duveyrier. Additional members of the delegation were the representatives Faureau de la Tour, Ravault, and the Abbé Mulot.[1] The delegation designated the Abbé Mulot as its spokesman. That designation was particularly meaningful both because Mulot was a priest and because he was a representative of the Mathurins District, the only Paris district that had voted against supporting the efforts of the Jews.

The delegation did not waste any time. On the very next day, February 25, 1790, they appeared before the National Assembly.[2] The priests made a point of wearing their distinctive clerical garb, overtly identifying themselves as Church leaders in a show of ecumenical support and in an important effort to bring the prestige of the newly enlightened clergy to the Jewish cause.

On the day when the delegation appeared, the officer presiding over

---

1. Ibid., 92.
2. *Archives Parlementaires*, vol. 11, pp. 698, et seq.

the National Assembly was none other than the renegade Bishop of Autun, Charles-Maurice de Talleyrand-Perigord. Talleyrand had been a strong supporter of the confirmation of the rights of the Portuguese Jews, but was much more lukewarm in his support of the grant of rights to the Ashkenazim. Following Talleyrand's welcome to the delegation, Mulot addressed the Assembly, as spokesman for the Paris delegation and in the name of the entire city, with eloquent words that had been drafted by Godard and approved by the Paris Assembly.[3]

Talleyrand accepted the text of the petition of the city of Paris, and responded to Mulot's remarks with his own brief, but rather moving words:[4]

> The National Assembly has made it its sacred duty to give to all men their rights; it has decreed the conditions necessary to be an active citizen. It is in this spirit, it is in bringing itself closer to these conditions that it will examine, in its justice, the reasons that you are exposing in such a touching manner in favor of the Jews.[5]

In his response, Talleyrand was blending together his two careers as priest and as political operative, ascribing a kind of religious sacredness to the political work he was performing at the National Assembly, endorsing the reordering of civil society with a quasi-religious imprimatur. Thus, for Talleyrand, his role as a bishop of the Church of Rome was not inconsistent with his political duties. But then again, he tended generally to carry out his sacerdotal duties without rigid adherence to Church doctrine and practice. He was a renowned philanderer, with a number of illegitimate children to his credit, and he was an amazingly adept schemer. Over the course of his lengthy career Talleyrand would demonstrate an astounding blend of political flexibility and boundless ambition. He was sufficiently resourceful that he was one of the very few revolutionaries who ended up able to serve whatever political regime cropped up, whether revolutionary, Napoleonic, or royalist (Bourbon or Orléans), with seemingly equal devotion, but assuredly with equal disdain and self-interest.

To demonstrate the good will that Talleyrand sought to portray (not without some component of hypocrisy, since a substantial segment of the Assembly could hardly be qualified as friendly to the Jewish cause),

---

3. Ibid., 698.
4. Lémann, *La Prépondérance Juive*, 97.
5. Lacroix, *Actes de la Commune de Paris pendant la Révolution*, 423.

he then invited the Paris delegation to stay in the Assembly chamber throughout the day's deliberations, declaring that "The National Assembly invites you to attend its session."[6] The invitation was considered a sign of respect, and was expressed as though the Assembly was united in its support for the Jewish cause. Of course, that was hardly the case.

Reporting the events of that day, the *Journal de Paris* took stock of the composition of the delegation and of its presentation to the National Assembly and reserved special recognition for Godard.[7] The *Journal de Paris* pointedly observed:

> Among the other Deputies we noted a young Avocat, Mr. Godard, Author of the Address of the Jews to the National Assembly, a Work worthy of so noble a cause due to its logic and its style, a Work where there is so manifestly demonstrated enlightened reasoning and a pure soul and which announces to the Nation one more man to guard over its interests.[8]

The next day, February 26, at the National Assembly's regular session, an attempt was made to continue consideration of the Jewish concerns. The Duc de la Rochefoucauld-Liancourt urged that Jewish equality be enacted. He specifically requested that a date be set for a final debate on the matter, with a subsequent vote. However, he was stymied in his efforts by another member of the National Assembly, who retorted to the Duke's request, saying: "I note that the matter respecting the Jews is undoubtedly very important, however, we have other important matters pending..."[9] The member went on to cite the need to continue the debate on the pending judicial reforms, on the size of the new French army, and regarding the adoption of new financial regulations, which, as the member noted, were more pressing than resolving the Jewish issue because, as he emphasized, those latter subjects "interest the entire kingdom."[10] Oddly, the *Archives Parlementaires* indicates that the member in question was none other than Godard's mentor, Target. It is surprising that Target would have expressly opposed Godard's most important public effort, and there is reason to

---

6. Ibid.
7. *Journal de Paris*, February 27, 1790, no. 58, pp. 230–13.
8. Ibid. Cf. *Tableau des Operations de l'Assemblée Nationale d'après le Journal de Paris*, vol. 2 (A. Lausanne, chez Hignou & Compe. Imprimeurs, 1789), 319.
9. *Archives Parlementaires*, vol. 11, p. 710.
10. *Moniteur*, February 27, 1790, no. 58, p. 233.

believe that the *Archives Parlementaires*, which were assembled from notes and newspaper reports nearly one hundred years after the actual National Assembly sessions had taken place, may have been mistaken. The *Moniteur* of February 27, which reported on the National Assembly session of February 26 and noted the exchange, specifically identified La Rochefoucauld-Liancourt, but did not identify the member who opposed La Rochefoucauld-Liancourt's request. Since Target was one of the best-known members of the National Assembly and readily identifiable, it seems peculiar that, if Target was indeed the individual who opposed La Rochefoucauld-Liancourt, he was not expressly named.

The absence of extant correspondence between the mentor and the mentee leaves open to speculation the question why Target would have opposed this important component of Godard's effort on behalf of his Jewish clients—if he actually did so. Target had, after all, been in the forefront of the recent battle for Protestant equality, beginning with his pleading on behalf of the Marquise d'Anglure. He had also been a close collaborator of Malesherbes as Malesherbes prepared the edict that granted civil equality to Protestants, thereby demonstrating a certain commitment to religious tolerance. Beyond the factor of his close personal relationship with Godard, Target should have been a natural supporter of Jewish equality. However, if Target did, in fact, oppose Godard's efforts on behalf of the Jews, it suggests that there may have been a falling out between the two, perhaps over Godard's insistent approach for an immediate grant of Jewish equality or perhaps over other matters. Is it possible that Target, in spite of his reputation for loyalty to his friends, resented his protégé's growing prominence? Or, alternatively, is it possible that Target was, in fact, assisting Godard by delaying a consideration by the National Assembly that might very well have had a negative outcome and might have set back the cause of Jewish equality?

Whether it was Target who led the effort or not, the member who opposed La Rochefoucauld-Liancourt was successful: the majority of the Assembly concurred with his position against going forward on the Jewish issue. And so, in spite of the cordial reception afforded to the Paris delegation and the elegant exchange of words, no decision was forthcoming from the Assembly, not even the setting of a date upon which a decision would be taken. Later, the National Assembly's evening session of March 23 would be set as the time for the resumption of the debate on the Jewish matter.

Although still engaged with his Jewish clients, by early March Godard's attention was focused on a very different matter: the issue of censorship. This new focus arose as a consequence of the production of a three-act play entitled *Le Baron de Wolza ou les Religieuses danoises* [Baron Wolza or the Danish Nuns] by a little-remembered playwright named Bartin d'Antilly.[11] Following the play's first performance, some groups determined that it was offensive to public morality. The precise nature of the offensive qualities is now unknown since the text of the play has been lost. However, its general topic, about moral comportment within monastic orders, alluded to a serious problem afflicting the French Catholic Church at a time when the Church had not yet lost all of its political sway in France, but was already under attack from many quarters, with its property having been nationalized just months before. In its time, the play was clearly a sensation and a cause for alarm. The Mayor of Paris, Jean-Sylvain Bailly, banned the play on his own initiative after receiving complaints following its opening performance. The members of the Paris Assembly, always sensitive to protecting their prerogatives, especially when the mayor was infringing on those prerogatives, then took up the matter. A heated debate on the question of banning the play took place at the Assembly.[12] In an effort to resolve the issue of whether to allow the play to be performed, on March 13 the Assembly designated three of its members, Étienne Vigée,[13] the Abbé Mulot, and Jacques Godard, as special commissioners charged with reviewing the matter. Vigée was himself a reasonably well-known author. However, today, he is best remembered not because of his writings but as the brother of the extraordinarily talented portrait painter, Élisabeth Vigée-Lebrun, whose paintings of the nobility of her era, including of Marie-Antoinette and her children and other prominent citizens of the time, are among the best illustrations of

---

11. Louis Auguste Bartin d'Antilly (1760–1804) was the author/composer of a number of comic operas and plays that were of consequence in their time. The most prominent of these were *L'École de l'Adolescent*, produced in 1789, and *La Vieillesse d'Annette et de Lubin*, produced in 1790.

12. Victor Hallays-Dabot, *Histoire de la Censure théâtrale en France* (Paris: E. Dentu, Editeur 1862), 151.

13. Louis-Jean-Baptiste-Étienne Vigée (1758–1820) was a playwright of some renown, who wrote dozens of plays and a substantial number of poems, although his accomplishments are now forgotten. His name arouses interest solely because of his sibling, the painter Élisabeth Vigée-Lebrun, whose reputation has grown dramatically in recent years.

the personalities and styles of those years.[14]

Vigée, Mulot, and Godard reported their findings to the Assembly on March 18, recommending that the play be banned. However, Bertin d'Antilly refused to be discouraged. He quickly made some changes to his play and added incidental music, seeking to recharacterize it as a comic opera (a format which was less likely to be subjected to censorship than a play). He then resubmitted the altered piece to the Assembly. On April 16 the Assembly requested that the commissioners review the play in its altered form. This time, however, Godard was no longer one of the commissioners and Vigée and Mulot were joined by Georges d'Epinay for the second review. The newly constituted group reported its findings to the Assembly on May 3 and approved the work in its new form as a comic opera, embellished with music by the prolific but now largely forgotten composer Louis-Emmanuel Jadin.[15] The comic opera opened on December 13 at the Theater of Mlle. Montansier in the Palais Royal complex under a slightly different name, *Le Duc de Waldeza ou la Communauté de Copenhague* ["The Duke de Waldeza or the Community of Copenhagen"]. The play's and the comic opera's fame seem to have rapidly subsided, as both disappeared from the repertoire of the French theater and from the annals of history.[16]

Godard's removal from the group charged with reviewing Bertin d'Antilly's play was not the result of any disapproval of his role. It was rather the result of his growing prominence. He had just been elected president of the Paris Assembly and, according to the rules of the Assembly, he could not simultaneously serve as president and as a member of a committee. It is also possible that too many matters were filling his plate. Godard was still involved in his work with the Jewish community, and would have

---

14. Élisabeth Vigée-Lebrun painted a portrait of her brother in 1773. The portrait of the fifteen-year-old Étienne is in the collection of the St. Louis Art Museum.

15. Louis-Emmanuel Jadin (1768–1853) wrote forty operas and numerous orchestral and instrumental works over the course of a long life. During the Revolution he became a musician in the National Guard. His operas are no longer part of the repertoire of any major opera company and his other music is infrequently played. The few available recordings of Jadin's orchestral works, and notably of his *Fantaisie Concertante* in G-minor for harp, piano, and orchestra, suggest that, in spite of his current obscurity, he was a talented and creative composer in the early romantic vein.

16. Maurice Tourneux, *Bibliographie de l'histoire de Paris pendant la Révolution française*, vol. 3 (Paris: Imprimerie Nouvelle [Association Ouvrière] 1900), 696.

further opportunity to be of assistance to his Jewish clients and, on their behalf, to use the extensive knowledge about Jews and their practices that he had rapidly accumulated in the course of his lobbying efforts.

One such opportunity had already presented itself in March of 1790. In its political section, the *Mercure Historique et Politique de Bruxelles* reproduced an article written by an author identified only as "a distinguished Author from Germany" under the rubric "Germany." The article extensively criticized Jews and their practices and traditions, and asserted that those practices were incompatible with life under the new enlightened order.[17] Godard did not wait long before writing a response to those assertions. His letter, which appeared in the March 22, 1790, edition of the *Moniteur*, and which represents a remarkable and quite erudite presentation of Jewish religious concepts by a non-Jew, went into surprising detail with respect to certain Jewish prayers, engaging in a kind of analysis usually reserved for rabbis or Jewish scholars.[18] Even though Godard was undoubtedly closely coached by his clients in the preparation of his letter, his articulation demonstrated a profound understanding of components of Jewish life and practice.

Godard began by systematically refuting the classic anti-Jewish arguments asserted by the German author. Then, he specifically rejected the argument that Portuguese Jews were more suitable for integration because they relied only on the Old Testament and the "Jerusalemma" (meaning the Jerusalem Talmud, as distinguished from the much more widely-consulted Babylonian Talmud), in contrast with Ashkenazi Jews who place great reliance on "the Mishnah and the Talmud" (presumably referring to the Babylonian Talmud). Godard noted that all Jews rely on the "Mishnah and Talmud" (not correcting the error contained in this statement, namely that the Mishnah, along with the Gemara, which interprets and elaborates upon the laws set out in the Mishnah, is itself part of the Talmud).

He then refuted the allegation that the Talmud is fundamentally incompatible with the "social instruction" of Christians and that therefore Jews could not live in harmony with Christians. As proof of the fallacious nature of this allegation, Godard simply pointed to the Jews of Paris, who, he noted (as had been observed during the January and February

17. *Mercure Historique et Politique de Bruxelles*, March 6, 1790, no. 10, pp. 10–15.
18. *Moniteur*, "*Mélanges*," March 22, 1790, p. 663.

debates), were already fulfilling all of the civic obligations of French citizens. Then Godard tackled the writer's accusation that Jews used the term *"goyim"* to denigrate Christians by characterizing them as pagans. Godard accurately reminded his readers that the Hebrew word *"goyim"* simply means "nations." He further emphasized that Jews do not denigrate other nations, but rather call upon God to bestow his blessings "on the entire universe."

Godard especially took issue with the author's claims regarding one of the most important prayers in the daily and holiday services of the Jews, the *"Aleinu"* prayer.[19] With an exegetical analysis worthy of a rabbi, Godard refuted the accusations leveled against the Jews on the basis of this prayer. He was also aware, and indicated, that a portion of the prayer that had been deemed offensive in prior centuries had for a generation been expressly expunged from all the prayer books used by Ashkenazi Jews.[20] In a volley against the "distinguished German Author," Godard wrote that he, Godard, probably should not have bothered to respond in such detail since the observations that he had refuted "came from a nation where the rights of man are so unknown and the prejudices against Jews are so deeply rooted that one can read at the entrance to a public promenade this gross insult against humanity: Jews and pigs are prohibited from entering here."[21] Godard's letter was also remarkable in its concluding paragraph, in which he seized the opportunity to reiterate to the *Moniteur's* large readership his clarion call for Jewish equality. Godard noted, with insightful pragmatism, that:

---

19. *"Aleinu"* is a Hebrew word which means "it is our [duty to praise"]. The *Aleinu* prayer is recited toward the end of most Jewish prayer services. It is an aspirational prayer that looks to a time when all humankind will acknowledge the existence of a single deity.

20. The deleted sentence can be translated as "For they prostrate themselves to vanity and emptiness and pray to a god that cannot save" and was considered by some as an allusion to, and a condemnation of, Christians praying to Jesus. Godard did not note that many Ashkenazi Jews carried on the peculiar practice of spitting during the recitation of the *Aleinu* prayer as a reminder of the deleted sentence. The Hebrew word for "emptiness," as it appears in the Aleinu prayer, is *"riq,"* and the Hebrew word for "saliva" or "spitting" is *"liroq."* The latter word has a similar consonance to the former and thus, to some Jews, the act of spitting conjured up the recollection of the deleted phrase and served as a substitute for its recitation.

21. *Moniteur,* "Mélanges," March 22, 1790, p. 663.

…we are at the veritable moment when the admission of the Jews to civil status can be achieved; maybe later it will no longer be the appropriate time; in the middle of all of the changes which are enveloping the people, the change relative to the Jews will make only a modest impression, whereas in a more distant time this same people might not accustom itself to this change as readily…[22]

While devoted to the cause of his clients, Godard clearly understood the difficulty of attempting to overcome centuries of deeply ingrained prejudice. He saw, as he had declared in the *Pétition*, that the moment was propitious and had to be seized. Granting Jews full equality at a time when so many other segments of society were being given new rights presented a unique opportunity. In some ways it was, to put it in the modern vernacular, a "teachable moment."

For all of Godard's enthusiasm for the changes going on about him, his vision of the potential for a reversal of the attitudes that were prompting those changes demonstrates an understanding of the difficulty in securing the acceptance of people who are different from the majority and of the reluctance of people to shed old prejudices. With that parting shot, he was demonstrating his contempt for the anti-Jewish sentiment that still permeated much of Europe, as distinguished from revolutionary France. This was a fitting close to his letter, which would be one of the last public pronouncements on the Jewish issue to which he would affix his name, even though he would continue to play a role behind the scenes in the months to come.

Even as Jacques Godard's career continued its ascent in the turbulent Parisian political world, his father also continued his more modest political rise on his home turf in Burgundy. On March 26, 1790, the *Moniteur* noted that Godard's father had been named the public prosecutor (*procureur au cours royal*) in the city of Dijon. (The appointment had actually occurred on February 3, but, reflecting the slow pace at which news travelled in that era, the Parisian press did not take note of it for a number of weeks.)[23] This position was a considerable honor, but it was to lead the elder Godard into significant difficulty several years later. On October 16, 1793, he would be arrested by the revolutionary authorities

---

22. Ibid., 664.
23. Justin Ledeuil, *1789–1795 La Révolution à Dijon* (Paris: Librairie Historique et Archéologique J.-B. Dumoulin, 1872), 16.

on a variety of charges, including that he had "made very inappropriate remarks" regarding the Revolution, and he would be incarcerated in the chateau of Dijon, which served as a revolutionary prison. The decree of accusation which landed the elder Godard in prison would draw a link between father and son. It stated that Godard had initially been "a friend" of the Revolution, but that "since and perhaps shortly before the death of his son, a member of the Legislature, he appears to have changed his opinion."[24] The elder Godard was fortunate to escape the fate of so many who were incarcerated in this period. He would be released from prison 375 days later on the 5th of Brumaire of Year III (October 26, 1794), some three months after the fall of Robespierre and the end of the Terror.[25] In another ironic twist of history, the order which decreed the sixty-five-year old Godard's "immediate liberation" from prison was signed by eight members of the Committee on Public Safety of the National Convention, with the first signature being that of Reubell, the Alsatian who led and symbolized the opposition to the efforts for Jewish equality that were led by the younger Jacques Godard.[26]

Despite the apparent support for the Jewish cause within the National Assembly and the continuing efforts of the Jewish community—presumably still with the advice of Godard—as the months passed, the debate on Jewish equality was repeatedly adjourned and left in abeyance. The debate was initially placed on the agenda for the March 23 session. But, as a Catholic newspaper urging a further slowdown of the steady progress of the Jewish lobbying effort noted, "Their [the Jews'] agents should suspend their efforts during the week that we are about to enter [Holy Week]..." Invoking a pattern of Catholic anti-Jewish sentiment, which was traditionally especially acute around the time of the confluence of the Catholic holidays of Good Friday and Easter and the Jewish festival of Passover, the newspaper suggested that the lobbyists "must be aware that it [Holy Week] is full of memories that are very unfavorable to them

---

24. Extract from the Register of the Committee of Surveillance of the Mons Section of the Commune of Semur in the Department of the Côte d'Or, 16 Nivose, Year II (Archives de la Côte d'Or).

25. Vaulabelle, *Histoire générale de Semur-en-Auxois*, 84.

26. Decree of the *Comité de Sureté Générale et de Surveillance de la Convention Nationale*, 5 Brumaire an III (an unpublished document from the Archives de la Côte d'Or).

[the Jews]."²⁷ To opponents of Jewish rights and the liberalizing influence of the Revolution, this observation was likely as valid as any other to prevent progress toward Jewish equality.

As Godard and his clients pursued their efforts, support for the Jewish cause emerged from a variety of sources. It emanated from clerics, from random individuals, and even from Alsatians. While it is unclear whether this support was prompted by Godard and his clients or was spontaneous, it is clear that Godard had helped to provide the impetus and momentum for the continuing efforts on behalf of the Jewish cause. In large part, the support took the form of pamphlets—the preferred mode of expression in the heady days of this first phase of the Revolution—which articulated arguments in favor of the Jews and which confronted those who were in opposition to Jewish equality.

One such tract was written by a Philippe Vieillard, a former French envoy to China with an extensive familiarity with Asia, who became a Paris elector and ultimately an administrator of the city. Entitled *Dissertation sur la demande des Juifs de Paris tendante à être admis au rang de citoyens actifs*, the fourteen-page essay was published in February 1790, not long after Godard's lobbying efforts on behalf of his Jewish clients had begun, and was in direct support of that effort.²⁸ Vieillard, who read his essay to his Saint-Roch District Assembly on February 13, 1790²⁹ (during Godard's whirlwind lobbying campaign to the Paris districts), devoted a large portion of his text to comparing Jews to Armenians, suggesting that it was the relentless persecution of the Jews that had turned them into an isolated people, just like the perennial persecution of the Armenians had made them a pariah people in south central Asia. By diminishing the uniqueness of the Jews, he sought to persuade his fellow-citizens that Jews could readily be integrated into the French nation. Concluding his text with the declaration that all people residing in France, including Jews, should become brothers, Vieillard expressed the hope that France would be the Jewish Promised Land with Paris its Jerusalem, and powerfully urged that Jews be granted civil equality.³⁰

27. *Journal de la Cour et de la Ville*, March 28, 1790, no. 87.
28. "Dissertation on the request of the Jews of Paris seeking to be admitted to the ranks of active citizens."
29. Sigismond Lacroix, *Actes de la Commune de Paris*, vol. 4 (Paris: Librairie Léopold Cerf, Charles Noblet, Maison Quentin, 1896), 199.
30. Philippe Vieillard, *Dissertation sur la demande des Juifs de Paris tendante à être*

In a twenty-four-page pamphlet issued shortly after the decision to delay the debate on the rights to be granted to the Ashkenazi Jews, an unidentified "Alsatian" confronted Reubell directly and contradicted his presumption that all Alsatians were ill-disposed toward the Jews. This Alsatian not only supported equality for the Jews of his province, but even indicated that with the arrival of the Revolution negative feelings toward the Jews in Alsace had begun to dissipate. Specifically, the author of the pamphlet emphasized that since the adoption of the Declaration of the Rights of Man and of the Citizen, "the unfavorable opinion which still subsisted against the Jews in certain communities in Alsace, is weakening by the day."[31] Strongly taking issue with all of Reubell's threats and alleged fears, the author made a broad-based appeal for Jewish equality. He declared that "[t]he cause of the Jews is reasonable, it is just, it is constitutional, it is favored, even in Alsace, by public opinion[;] nothing, therefore, militates for an indefinite adjournment [of the matter]."[32] Although there is no proof, the hand of Godard appears to be not very distant from this pamphlet, in inspiration, if not through actual use of a pen.

Yet another pamphlet in strong support of the Ashkenazim came from a cleric, who chose to hide his identity behind the label "M. l'Abbé L***."[33] The anonymous priest focused his argument on the remarks of the Abbé Maury during the December debate.[34] The pamphlet made a powerful argument against using the particularisms of the Jewish religion to oppose the full integration of the Jews into the French nation. Taking express issue with Maury's assertions that Jews could not be good citizens because of their religious practices, the author of this pamphlet reminded Maury that he too, due to his religion, had certain constraints. In an especially intriguing footnote, the author suggested that, notwithstanding the Catholic prohibition on eating meat on Friday, Maury, for

---

admis au rang de citoyens actifs [sic] (Bib. Nat. Lb 40/106), 2–15.

31. Lettre d'un Alsacien sur les Juifs d'Alsace à M. Reubell, deputé de cette Province à l'Assemblée nationale.

32. Ibid., 21.

33. Observations sur l'État civil des Juifs adressées à l'Assemblée nationale par M. l'Abbé L***, (Paris: Chez Belin, 1790).

34. Arthur Hertzberg suggests that the anonymous priest was actually Antoine-Adrien Lamourette (1742–1794), a liberal priest who joined the Girondins and was guillotined in January 1794. Since Lamourette was a close ally of Mirabeau and an advocate of religious tolerance, Hertzberg's conjecture is likely correct.

the sake of the nation, would undoubtedly be willing to violate this proscription, implying that even the most religious person had to be willing
to contravene sacred religious principles for the sake of patriotism and
that, therefore, the various Jewish prohibitions cited by Maury would not
constitute obstacles to Jews being good citizens.[35] Overall, the pamphlet
was an elegant refutation of Maury's narrow-minded attempt to restrict
Jewish rights. Once again, there is no specific indication that Godard had
a hand in the preparation of this pamphlet. However, there does seem
to be a skilled invisible hand at work in the issuance of a frontal attack
on the leading clerical opponent of the Jewish effort by another cleric,
just as there is a similar sense of careful planning in having an Alsatian
attack Reubell, the leading secular Alsatian opponent to Jewish rights.
All in all, the issuance of these tracts gives the impression of yet another
well-prepared coincidence in a coordinated effort to persuade the national legislature of the need to take the appropriate decision for the benefit
of the Ashkenazi Jews.[36]

The most significant of the Alsatian pamphlets supportive of the Jewish position was a report issued by the Society of the Friends of the Constitution of the City of Strasbourg in February 1790, just days after the
issuance of Godard's *Pétition*.[37] This report, written by an unidentified
author and submitted to the members of the Society for their approval,
sought to combat the notion that Alsatians were generally opposed to
granting civil equality to Jews. It argued at length that the prejudice
against Jews was overstated and propounded multiple arguments to suggest that Christian Alsatians, as well as Alsatian Jews, would benefit from
a grant of equality to all Jews. Taking particular issue with the strong

---

35. *Observations sur l'État civil des Juifs*, 14n1.

36. Other pamphlets echoed those of the anonymous "Alsatian" and the "Abbé
L***." In particular, a pamphlet entitled *Reflexions Impartiales d'un Citoyen, Sur la
question de l'égilibilité des Juifs, proposée et discutée dans les séances de l'Assemblée
nationale, des 23 & 24 Décembre & ajournée par la même Assemblée* [Impartial Reflections of a Citizen on the question of the eligibility of the Jews, proposed and
discussed during the sessions of the National Assembly on 23 and 24 December,
and adjourned by the same Assembly] (Imprimerie de la Veuve Delaguette [un-
dated]) also took vigorous issue with the arguments Reubell and the Abbé Maury
articulated at the National Assembly.

37. *Rapport lu à l'assemblée de la Société des Amis de la Constitution, le 27 fevrier mil
sept cent quatre-vingt dix sur la Quéstion de l'État Civil des Juifs d'Alsace*. [gallica.
bnf.fr]

anti-Jewish sentiments that the leaders of Strasbourg had demonstrated for generations and were continuing to articulate during the debate, the report's author urged the immediate cessation of the blowing of the Grüsselhorn, the horn which sounded daily to warn Jews that they needed to leave the city by nightfall. He also called upon the people of Strasbourg to atone for their past prejudice.

Attached to the Society's report was a resolution adopted by the Strasbourg Society fully endorsing the favorable report and directing that the resolution be transmitted to the Paris Society of Friends of the Constitution with the request that the Strasbourg Society's position be conveyed to the National Assembly. Interestingly, various portions of the report strongly echoed some of Godard's arguments, and, at one point, the report's author even cited Godard's document. The author, taking note of the allegation that the enhancement of the status of the Jews would result in a negative impact on other Alsatians, then indicated that the fallacious nature of this argument had already been made clear by "the author of the *Pétition* of the Jews addressed to the National Assembly on the last January 28."[38] This specific reference to Godard's *Pétition* demonstrated both the strength of Godard's arguments and the wide dissemination of his document. Importantly, it suggested that, through his tract and his strategy, Godard may have helped to sway opinions in favor of his clients well beyond the Paris area, engendering support for the Jewish position even in the section of France most hostile to that position.

One unexpected expression of assistance was voiced in a pamphlet written by a British (although Belgian-born) aristocrat, the Baroness Cornélie Wouters de Vasse.[39] De Vasse was a widely published author at a time when female authors were not numerous. She primarily wrote fiction and also translated books from English into French. In a dramatic

---

38. Ibid., 16.

39. Cornélie Wouters de Vasse (1737–1802) was a Belgian-born author, who lived much of her life in England and France, but identified herself as an "Englishwoman." She was a prolific author of works of fiction, some of which were deemed scandalous in their time. Her non-fiction advocacy writings were limited and she does not appear to have engaged in polemical writing. There is no indication that she demonstrated any interest in the status of the Jews other than on the one occasion cited here. See Carrie F. Klaus, "*Une école des moeurs & de la morale*": How the Wouters Sisters made English Theater French." *Palimpsestes* 20 (2007) https://doi.org/10.4000/palimpsestes.95

shift from the topics that usually preoccupied her, in March 1790 de Vasse published an undated Memorial addressed to the National Assembly, in support of Godard's efforts, which she entitled "To demonstrate to the French, the reasons which must determine them to admit the Jews without any distinction to the rights of citizenship."[40] She urged tolerance for the Jews ("Believe me, Frenchmen; consolidate your happiness by being tolerant; it is the triumph of reason."), and did so with a variation on one of the arguments Godard had set out in his *Pétition*. She urged France to swiftly grant equality to the Jews not just on the basis of Enlightenment principles, but also because that action would bestow on France the honor of being the first nation to act in a manner consistent with justice, acting even sooner than England. This, the Baroness argued, would prevent productive Jewish families, who might now, due to the revolutionary fervor of the times, be inclined to gravitate toward France, from being attracted to other nations which might grant Jews equality before France did so. She blended high motives, practicality, and an obvious admiration for revolutionary France.[41]

There are strong indications that de Vassse's pamphlet may have been part of Godard's concerted lobbying campaign. Apparently, Godard and de Vasse knew one another, probably from attendance at Paris salons prior to the onset of the Revolution. There is written evidence of that relationship. In early 1786, de Vasse was awarded two gold medals by the Swedish King Gustavus III.[42] She had dedicated her multi-volumed *Traduction du Plutarque anglois* to the Swedish king, and in response he awarded her two medals "as a token of the pleasure that His Majesty had in reading" the translation.[43] Sweden's ambassador to France, Baron Erik Magnus de Staël de Holstein, sent her a letter on January 11, 1786, announcing that she was the recipient of the medals. Some months after

40. Cornélie Wouters de Vasse, *Mémoire à l'Assemblée Nationale, pour démontrer aux François, les raisons qui doivent les déterminer à admettre les Juifs indistinctement aux droits de Citoyens* (Paris: Chez Baudouin, 1790), 6. The Friday, March 12, 1790 edition of *La Chronique de Paris* noted that "the Jews have found another defender in Mme. the Baronesse de Vasse," suggesting that she had just published her pamphlet. *La Chronique de Paris*, March 12, 1790, no. 71.
41. Ibid., 2.
42. *L'Année littéraire XXXIII* (1786), vol. 1 (Geneva: Slatkine Reprints, 1966), 278.
43. Cornélie Wouters, *Mortimer Thomas, Traduction du Plutarque anglois*, vol. 8 (Paris: Couturier Belin 1785–1786).

receiving the award, de Vasse apparently decided to express appreciation for the medals to the Ambassador's wife, who was none other than
Germaine de Staël, the daughter of Jacques and Suzanne Necker, with
whom Godard had sought to develop a relationship in the years before
the Revolution. On September 25, 1786, Godard penned a draft letter to
de Staël, clearly intended for de Vasse's signature, expressing appreciation
for the honor bestowed upon her by Sweden. Whether Godard ghost-
wrote this letter as a legal service to de Vasse or as an act of friendship,
it points to the existence of a relationship between the two and serves to
provide a potential explanation for de Vasse's surprising intervention in
the debate on Jewish equality.[44] It is logical that Godard would have called
upon his friend, a very popular author of bestselling books, to assist him
in his campaign on behalf of his Jewish clients. The likelihood that de
Vasse's essay was the product of Godard's request is further reinforced
by the actual text of de Vasse's pamphlet, which has a lawyerly tone far

---

44. There exists a draft of a thank-you letter in Godard's handwriting expressing
appreciation for certain gifts. This draft letter is addressed to a woman identified
as an "*ambassadrice*," almost certainly Germaine de Staël, thus giving credence to
the notion that the draft is of a letter being ghost-written by Godard for de Vasse's
signature. The date on the draft is September 25, 1786. Indeed, Germaine Necker
had married the Baron Erik Magnus de Staël von Holstein, then Ambassador of
Sweden to the French Court, on January 14, 1786—a marriage that brought her
important status, but not much happiness. In the draft letter, Godard notes that
he believes that the unspecified gifts (which must have been the two gold medals
from the king) that the intended recipient of the draft letter has given "is a tribute
which Sweden is giving me" (although the reason for the gifts is not specified). He
goes on to say that "[i]t is your favor that Sweden gives me," presumably through
the unspecified gifts. There are several additional references to Sweden in the
draft, including to a certain M. von Rosenstein (Nils von Rosenstein [1752–1824],
the most renowned Swedish philosopher and orator of his time, as well as a tutor
at the Court of Gustavus III and the son of the reputed founder of pediatric medicine), with whom Germaine de Staël would carry on a lengthy correspondence
throughout her life. Apparently, von Rosenstein may have been the instigator of
the award to de Vasse. It is not clear whether a final version of the letter was ever
written or if the letter was ever sent to Germaine de Staël. (The various extant
compilations of her correspondence do not refer to such a letter from de Vasse.)
The draft letter, written in very flowery, and, as was Godard's wont, somewhat
sycophantic language, is part of a package of documents that had belonged to
Godard which was acquired by the author. Unpublished draft, dated September
25, 1786, of a letter from Godard to an unidentified "*ambassadrice*." (From the author's personal collection.)

more reflective of Godard's writing style than that of a writer of fiction or a translator of ancient Greek philosophy. Furthermore, the arguments set forth in the pamphlet succinctly echo certain of those made in the *Pétition*. All of this lends credence to the notion that de Vasse's seemingly spontaneous contribution to the campaign for Jewish equality may have been yet another component of Godard's carefully crafted service to his clients. It is difficult to know whether her pamphlet had any influence, but it does serve to demonstrate that Godard was able to muster support for the Jewish cause, even in unlikely quarters.

These elements of support constituted an important buttress in the struggle for Jewish equality. Yet, in spite of the assistance of other contributors to the cause and the carefully crafted lobbying campaign, the struggle would continue for many months to come, to the continuing frustration of the Ashkenazi leadership and their allies.

CHAPTER 32

CONTINUING OBSTACLES ON THE PATH TO EQUALITY

Dilatory tactics by opponents of the Jews had their effect. The status of the Ashkenazi Jews had been placed on the agenda of the National Assembly for debate on March 23. But, that day's evening session, when the issue had been scheduled to be debated, came and went without an additional debate. However, one of the representatives, Jean-Georges-Charles Voidel,[1] objected, asserting that "a major discussion" needed to be held at a morning session, when, presumably, a greater number of the members would be in attendance and would be more attentive.[2] The presiding officer, Fréteau de Saint-Just (Sophie de Condorcet's uncle), reminded Voidel and the members of the Assembly that it had been previously decided that morning sessions were to be reserved for discussions regarding the Constitution and matters relating to finances.[3] He went on to remind the members that a discussion regarding criminal statutes was pending and that this was by far the

---

1. Jean-Georges-Charles Voidel (1758–1812) was an avocat from the Moselle region of northeastern France. He is best remembered as the author of the resolution adopted by the National Assembly calling for the clergy to swear allegiance to the nation. Although he would become a Jacobin, he served as the unsuccessful defense counsel for the Duc d'Orléans when the Duke was tried before the National Convention. Voidel was arrested in 1793, along with Alexandre de Beauharnais, but he was freed in 1794 after the fall of Robespierre.

2. *Archives Parlementaires*, vol. 12, p. 309.

3. Ibid.

more important matter to be addressed. Antoine-César de Choiseul-Pralin, a cousin of the Duc de Choiseul (Louis XV's principal minister and the individual who befriended the Alsatian Jewish leader, Berr Cerf Berr), then rose to support Fréteau's position.[4] A vote was taken and the matter was adjourned, ostensibly until the evening session.[5] However, in reality, the matter was adjourned for much longer, since the Assembly did not take it up at its evening session nor, indeed, the next day. It was not until mid-April that the Assembly would again debate the issue of Jewish rights. The status of the Jews had to take second place to other more pressing matters.[6] When the next round of debate involving the status of the Jews began, it was in a peculiar context. On April 12 the National Assembly was engaged in a debate respecting compensation for clergy in light of the nationalization of Church property which had been decreed back in October of 1789. During the discussion, unexpectedly, an eccentric member of the clergy, Antoine Christophe Gerle, more commonly known as Dom Gerle, began to speak, purportedly on the topic being discussed, in spite of not having been properly recognized by the president.[7] As he was speaking, he rapidly veered off topic to propose to the surprise of all and to the consternation of many that the Catholic religion be declared "to be and to remain the sole Religion of the Nation, the only one authorized to be practiced in public."[8]

---

4. Antoine-César de Choiseul-Praslin (1756–1808) served as a general in the French armies both before and during the Revolution. His grandfather served briefly as one of Louis XV's foreign ministers, and the grandfather's eulogy was delivered in 1785 by Condorcet. Choiseul-Praslin was elected as an alternate to the Estates-General. When in August 1789 the representative for whom he was the alternate died, he became a full member of the National Assembly. Arrested in 1793, he narrowly avoided execution. He later served in the Senate during the Napoleonic Empire.

5. *Archives Parlementaires*, vol. 12, p. 309.

6. Not without a dose of sarcasm, the *Journal de Paris* took note of the continuing delays respecting the anticipated debate on the Jewish issue. In its April 12, 1790 edition, the *Journal* wrote: "It appears that it is the destiny of the matter of the Jews of Alsace and Lorraine to be forever set aside from being discussed by some unexpected circumstance." *Journal de Paris*, April 12, 1790, no. 102, p. 409.

7. Antoine Christophe Gerle (1736–1801), a cleric from Riom in central France, was elected from his home district to the Estates-General as a member of the clergy. He joined the more radical elements of the National Assembly, but remained peculiarly enamored of religion and mysticism. Imprisoned during the Terror, he was liberated after the fall of Robespierre. His obsession with mysticism led him to leave the priesthood, after which he married his mistress.

8. *Journal de Paris*, April 12, 1790.

Considering the nature of the discussions about religion at the Assembly during the prior months, including, importantly, about the Jews, this proposal was anomalous at best. The reaction of many Assembly members was one of shock. But from the conservative groups in the Assembly came cries of support and a demand that the proposal be adopted immediately. Others in the Assembly called for a rejection of the proposal primarily on the grounds that it was out of order. Quickly Charles de Lameth, the brother of Alexandre de Lameth, the deputy who had participated in the debate on the Jewish matter in late January, objected strenuously to the proposal, noting that it was a financial matter that was being discussed—not a theological one.[9] Sensing the risk that the Assembly ran if the issue was further discussed, he tried to end the discussion by speaking to the Catholic members of the Assembly on their terms. He argued that all the Assembly's work had been guided by the Gospels and that the very notions of equality and fraternity, written into the Declaration of the Rights of Man and of the Citizen, were at the base of the Catholic faith and thus that it was unnecessary to make any statements about a state religion. The notion that the subject of affirming a state religion should even have been brought to the floor of the Assembly took many of the members by surprise. Mirabeau attempted to speak, presumably against Gerle's proposal, but was shouted down. Chaos spread through the hall. The president adjourned the session to bring an end to the confusion.[10]

The next day, April 13, at the opening of the session, the president of the Assembly, the Marquis de Bonnay,[11] announced that he had received a letter

9. Charles-Malo-François de Lameth (1757–1832) served, along with his two brothers, in the American Revolution as an assistant to Rochambeau. He was wounded during the siege of Yorktown that effectively ended the war. In 1789, he was elected to the Estates-General as a member of the nobility from the Artois region. He was a strong supporter of certain executive power being vested in the National Assembly, including the power to declare war. In 1791, he served a term as president of the National Assembly. However, ultimately, he emigrated, spending a number of years in Germany before returning to France after Napoleon Bonaparte had come to power.

10. *Archives Parlementaires*, vol. 12, pp. 702–3; see also *Mercure Historique et Politique de Bruxelles*, April 12, 1790, no. 17, pp. 381–83.

11. Charles-François, Marquis de Bonnay (1750–1725) was from a noble family from the Nivernais area of central France. He was elected to the Estates-General as an alternate and became a full-fledged member in July 1789. He served twice briefly as president of the National Assembly, but resigned from the Assembly

from officials of the city of Strasbourg regarding the request of the Alsatian Jews for full civil rights.[12] The letter, not surprisingly, expressed strong opposition to the admission of Jews to the rank of active citizens.[13] It focused on Jewish particularism, suggesting that full integration was impossible and regurgitating many of the standard prejudices against the Jews. The letter was signed by the mayor of Strasbourg and fifteen local citizens. However, the president noted that, in light of other pressing matters, a discussion on the letter from Strasbourg would be deferred until the evening session. At that point, the debate of the previous day on Gerle's proposal resumed.

The first speaker was Philippe Samary, the presiding priest of the cathedral of his native city of Carcassonne in the foothills of the Pyrenées, who began his remarks with a disquisition on the Catholic religion.[14] But from the floor of the Assembly there were calls for the discussion to refocus on the issue at hand, namely the payment of compensation to the clergy. This was followed by vigorous and contentious exchanges. Certain members of the Assembly asserted their Catholic faith, but then expressed their view that faith was a private, not a public, matter. Mirabeau demanded to be recognized. He ascended to the podium and, with his usual forcefulness and sarcasm, unsurprisingly declared his opposition to any notion of a state religion. Among other things, he reminded the Assembly that they were seated just steps from where a prior French king, Charles IX, had, in August 1572, launched a massacre of Protestants as a means of asserting Catholicism's primacy.

and emigrated from France with the Comte de Provence, Louis XVI's brother and the future Louis XVIII. He remained by the Comte de Provence's side throughout the years of the Napoleonic Empire. During the Restoration he served as a diplomat and member of the Parliament, as well as a close adviser to the Comte once he had ascended the throne as Louis XVIII.

12. *Archives Parlementaires*, vol. 12, p. 711.

13. Ibid., 711–14. See also *Procès-verbal des Séances du Conseil Général de la Commune de Strasbourg* (Strasbourg: Ph. J. Dannbach, 1791), 18.

14. Philippe Samary (1731–1803) served as a parish priest in various churches in his native city of Carcassonne. Shortly before the outbreak of the Revolution, he was named the officiating priest of the cathedral of that city. He became renowned throughout France for his orations, which were widely circulated both during his lifetime and following his death. In 1789 he was elected to the Estates-General as a member of the clergy from Carcassonne. Samary was an advocate of Catholic tradition, remaining strongly attached to conservative values. After his tenure as a member of the National Assembly, he left France and settled in Rome, returning to France only after Napoleon signed a Concordat with the Vatican in 1802.

The acrimonious debate continued.[15] One of the speakers who rose to support the notion of endorsing Roman Catholicism as a state religion was Godard's old acquaintance and colleague, Duval d'Eprémesnil, with whom, as Godard had informed his cousin Cortot, he had had some significant disagreements. In the course of his remarks, d'Eprémesnil suddenly began to suggest that the tepid support for Catholicism should be contrasted to the Assembly's support for the Jews. He was not even allowed to finish his thought as loud "murmurings" forced him to abandon the podium.[16]

After some parliamentary maneuvering, Gerle's motion was replaced by another, after which the replacement motion was subjected to numerous amendments, none of which obtained sufficient support to be adopted. Finally La Rochefoucault-Liancourt proposed a resolution that called for the Assembly to end the debate and return to the official agenda. The motion was adopted but the discussion did not end, with chaos ensuing and shouts echoing throughout the Assembly. Among the cries heard were seemingly mock professions of adherence to the Catholic faith by Mirabeau and some of his colleagues, as they "raised their hands to the sky, saying 'We swear in the name of God and of the religion which we profess' before being drowned out by the din on the floor of the Assembly."[17]

The Assembly president struggled to restore order. Once he had done so, the discussion was rescheduled for the evening of April 15. Reubell, however, asked for a further postponement by asserting, as had Voidel the prior month, that a "constitutional" question should be considered during a morning session and not "hidden" from public view during an evening session.[18]

At the evening session of April 15, when the Marquis de Bonnay, still serving as president of the Assembly, was compelled to leave the podium to hand-deliver certain decrees to the king for his signature, the Baron de Menou assumed the role as temporary presiding officer.[19] Menou was an

15. *Archives Parlementaires*, vol. 12, pp. 714–19.
16. Ibid., 717.
17. Ibid., 718–19.
18. Kahn, *Les Juifs de Paris pendant la Révolution*, 95, citing the *Journal de Paris*, April 17, 1790, no. 107. The *Archives Parlementaires* do not include this statement by Reubell.
19. Jacques-François de Menou (1750–1810) was a noble elected to the Estates-General from the Tourraine region. He became a general during the Revolution and

odd character. He would serve in the revolutionary army that violently suppressed the royalist uprising in Vendée in 1793, and then would join Napoleon Bonaparte in the conquest of Egypt. There he would meet a woman whom he would marry and for whom he would convert to Islam, even changing his first name to Abdallah. In spite of his religious evolution, he continued in the service of French diplomacy until his death in 1808, while serving as the French governor of Venice. In his role as the acting president of the Assembly, Menou began by noting that the day's agenda called for a discussion on the status of the Jews. Ever the vigilant opponent of any rights for Jews, the Abbé Maury immediately asked for an adjournment of the question. He cited the need for the Jews to take cognizance of a memorandum that he had just delivered to the Assembly as the reason for this adjournment.[20] With sarcastic generosity, Maury suggested that it would not be fair if the Jews did not have adequate time to respond to his arguments. Reubell piled on further assertions. He proposed that it was necessary to await the review of the report from "the province of Alsace" which had been delivered on April 13 in order to have the latest observations respecting the position of the authorities there.[21] Reubell used yet other arguments, including his cynical "concern" for the safety of the Jews, whose usurious credits would, he asserted, expose them to great risks, as well as his fear for the welfare of the territory which would, in his words "drown in Jews."[22]

The Duc de La Rochefoucauld-Liancourt immediately saw through the Alsatians' tactics and once again demanded that the debate be

---

fought on behalf of the Revolution during the Vendée royalist uprising. He went to Egypt in 1798, where he became the commander of French troops. It is there that his life took an unlikely turn. While in Egypt he was compelled to surrender French forces to the British and, as part of the terms of surrender, relinquished possession of the Rosetta Stone, which had been found by French soldiers early during Napoleon Bonaparte's expedition to Egypt.

20. In *La Chronique de Paris* of May 4, 1790 (no. 124, p. 495), Zalkind Hourwitz attacked Maury for his memorandum. He calumniated Maury for being "intolerant and impious." He asserted that it was only possible to understand the Abbé's conduct "by supposing that you ignore the principles of your religion." "Learn them then," Hourwitz concluded, "they can be reduced to the following: love your neighbor as yourself, love your fatherland more than your benefits, & consider as your brother Zalkind Hourvitz [*sic*], Jew."

21. *Archives Parlementaires*, vol. 13, p. 69.

22. Kahn, *Les Juifs de Paris pendant la Révolution*, 95.

rescheduled to a specific date. He expressed the view that by delaying further, the Assembly was putting the Jewish community at risk since representatives of the Jews believed they would not be safe until the Assembly had granted them full citizenship. Then, he demanded that the matter be returned to the Constitution Committee and that this committee report to the full Assembly at the earliest possible date. The Assembly approved La Rochefoucauld-Liancourt's motion and the matter was again sent back to the Constitution Committee.[23]

In its edition of April 14–15 Mirabeau's *Le Courrier de Provence*[24] reported on the tumultuous deliberations of the immediate past and suggested that, for most of the members of the Assembly, the discussion regarding Jewish rights now boiled down to just a few questions of doctrine (*catéchisme*): "Gentlemen, are our laws your laws? Are our tribunals your tribunals? Are you legally our fellow citizens? Can you mentally and orally take the civil oath? If yes, well then, you are good Frenchmen, you will be active citizens. If not, stay as passive citizens, while awaiting the reestablishment of Jerusalem where you will be active or passive, as you see fit."[25] This was simply a reformulation of Clermont-Tonnerre's analysis of the late fall. Were Jews prepared to acknowledge that their unique Jewish practices were religious practices and did not create a separate legal system? Did Jews consider themselves to be a separate nation or were they part of the French body politic who simply espoused a different form of religious practice from the majority of French citizens, but who otherwise shared French values and loyalty to the French nation? An unequivocal answer affirming Jewish willingness to assimilate into the French body politic could open the path to equality. The newspaper was failing to recall that, on behalf of his Jewish clients, Godard had already provided powerful responses to the questions it was posing.

Almost as if to give credibility to Reubell's and his Alsatian colleagues' warnings, the very next day, April 16, the Assembly received a plea from the Alsatian-Jewish communities. With the Passover holiday pending and with virulently anti-Jewish sentiments reinforced by the Good Friday liturgy, including the view that "perfidious" Jews were responsible for the death of Jesus, there was great fear among the Alsatian Jews.

---

23. Ibid., 69–70.
24. *Le Courrier de Provence*, April 14–15, 1790, no. 131.
25. Cited in Kahn, *Les Juifs de Paris pendant la Révolution*, 95.

Pierre-Louis Roederer, the avocat from Metz, who had been one of the
reviewers of the submissions made in the Metz essay contest and was
now a member of the Assembly, submitted the text of a decree for the
approbation of the Assembly:

> The Assembly once again places the Jews of Alsace and others under
> the safeguard of the Law; prohibits all persons from endangering
> them and orders the Municipalities and the National Guard to use
> all their power to protect their persons and their property.[26]

At least one representative, Voidel (who had sought to prevent the discussion on the Jewish issue in March), asserted that the adoption of such a
decree was unnecessary since the Assembly had already adopted a similar
decree in September.[27] However, following a plea by Roederer that the request was well-founded, the Assembly adopted his proposed resolution.[28]
The king then issued a decree to this effect on April 18.[29]

Yet again on April 30 the National Assembly addressed the issue of the
means whereby foreigners (a category applicable to Jews according to
those who saw the Jewish community as a separate nation) could become
active French citizens. Target, in his role as a member of the Constitution
Committee, submitted a proposed decree seeking to grant active citizenship to foreigners residing in France:

> All those who, although born outside the kingdom of foreign parents,
> are established in France, will be deemed French, and admitted, by
> taking the civil oath, to exercise the rights of active citizens after five
> years of continuous residence in the kingdom, if they have, moreover,
> either acquired real property, or married a Frenchwoman, or formed
> an establishment of commerce, or received in some city letters of cit-
> izenship, notwithstanding all contrary regulations, to which deroga-
> tion is made, without, however, relying upon the present decree, to
> cause any election to be reheld. [30]

26. *Archives Parlementaires*, vol. 13, p. 76. Cf. *Mercure Historique et Politique de Bruxelles*, April 16, 1790, p. 403.
27. *Archives Parlementaires*, vol. 13, p. 76.
28. Ibid., 77.
29. *Proclamation du Roi sur un Décret de l'Assemblée Nationale concernant les Juifs*, April 18, 1790.
30. *Archives Parlementaires*, vol. 15, p. 340.

Target's proposal was adopted.[31]

Nothing in the decree addressed the status of the Jews, nor did anything allude to them. Nevertheless, the next day, as the minutes of the prior session were being read, Reubell, ever attempting to prevent the Jews of Alsace from achieving full citizenship, went to the podium to "clarify" the matter. Just to avoid, in his words, "any ambiguity," he proposed that a qualifier be added to the prior day's resolution to specify that the resolution had been adopted "without intending to determine anything with respect to the civil status of the Jews, which remains adjourned." The Assembly adopted Reubell's amendment without discussion,[32] and on May 2 the king issued Patent Letters echoing the text adopted by the National Assembly, with its express exclusion of Jews from the benefits of the Letters.[33] Yet again, the Jewish issue had been put on the back burner.

Just days later, at its morning session on May 10, 1790, the National Assembly received a letter, dated May 4, signed by three members of the Paris Jewish community. The letter was an emotional appeal to the Assembly to grant equal rights to the Jews of Paris in conjunction with the adoption of legislation respecting the reorganization of the Paris municipal government (a matter about which Godard had published a lengthy dissertation some months earlier). The authors of the letter appeared ready to cast aside Ashkenazi solidarity and to acknowledge that the strong opposition from the Alsatian representatives was an almost insurmountable obstacle to a grant of equality to all the Jews of France. Therefore, they were suggesting that the Assembly could, at least as a next step, grant such equality to the Jews of Paris.[34] Citing the overwhelming support that the Jews had received from the various districts in the city, as well as the "zealous" support that the Paris Jewish community had manifested for "this happy Revolution," the signatories of the letter urged immediate action.[35] They concluded their plea with a pledge of their loyalty, using the then prevalent formula, "to the nation, to the law and to the king," and a commitment to defend "to our last drop of blood,

31. Ibid.
32. Ibid., 349. Cf. *La Chronique de Paris*, May 2, 1790, no. 122, p. 487.
33. Henry Lucien-Brun, *La Condition des Juifs en France depuis 1789* (Lyon: Librairie A. Cote, 1900), 76.
34. *Archives Parlementaires*, vol. 15, p. 452.
35. The letter was signed by Trenelle, *père*, M. Weil and Lazare Jacob, "Deputies." Lacroix, *Actes de la Commune de Paris Pendant la Révolution*, vol. 7, p. 554.

the constitution and the decrees of the National Assembly, accepted and confirmed by the king."[36]

As had become all too customary, the letter was referred to the Constitution Committee for consideration. The record does not indicate who, if anyone other than the signatories, had drafted the letter. However, even though the letter's plea on behalf of the Jews of Paris rather than for all the Ashkenazi Jews seems contrary to the interests of Godard's principal clients as a group, it is possible that Godard had significant input into the letter. It is possible that Godard, ever pragmatic, had advised his clients to try to use a grant of equal rights to only the Parisian Jews as a stepping stone to full Jewish equality; to plead for the more readily doable as a means of achieving the ultimate, but as yet unattainable, goal. In any event, the letter made ample use of Godard's lobbying technique by referring prominently to the massive support that the Jewish community had garnered in the Paris districts during the previous winter.

On May 21, 1790, the Paris Assembly took note of yet another lengthy letter sent to the Constitution Committee of the National Assembly. This time, the letter, which bore the signature of Debourge, had been sent in the name of the Paris Assembly, even though it appears that the Paris Assembly had not formally approved the letter or its transmittal nor had even been fully aware of its existence. The letter, thoughtful and lawyerly, continued a barrage of appeals arguing forcefully for immediate equality for the Ashkenazi Jews.[37] It was really more of a legal brief than a letter. A substantial part of the format adopted by the author was the presentation of objections articulated against Jewish equality and responses intended to refute those arguments. The conclusion (at the end of forty-four printed pages) was that the Constitution Committee should propose to the National Assembly a resolution that called upon the Assembly to recognize that any man who fulfilled all of the requirements respecting government assemblies could be a voter regardless of his profession or religion. (In order to give greater emphasis to the conclusion, the entire proposed resolution was printed in capital letters.) In light of the close relationship between Debourge and Godard and the legal style and tone of the document, it is very probable that Debourge's letter was in large part

---

36. Ibid., 554–55.

37. See Jean Claude Antoine De Bourge, *Lettre au comité de constitution sur l'affaire des juifs: 19 Mai 1790* (Paris: Imprimerie du Patriote Français, 1790); *Actes de la Commune de Paris pendant la Révolution*, vol. 5 (France, 1789–1794), 498–593.

(if not entirely) Godard's handiwork.[38] Its preparation and dissemination were also entirely consistent with Godard's grand lobbying plan to cause the National Assembly to achieve his clients' goal.

The fact that the letter had been sent directly to the National Assembly, bypassing the Paris Assembly, may have been an expression of Godard's frustration with the Paris Assembly's failure to act more decisively or persuasively on the Jewish issue. This was a strategy that carried with it some risk of offense to the Paris Assembly. (However, Godard, who by then was no longer a member of the Paris Assembly, may not have been overly worried about causing such an offense.) Indeed, following confirmation by the Paris Assembly that Debourge's letter had already been sent, a resolution was adopted by the Assembly naming a committee consisting of Jacques-Pierre Brissot de Warville, Condorcet, and Léonard Robin[39] to review the matter and to prepare an analysis of Debourge's letter.[40]

Within a week, on May 29, Brissot de Warville, on behalf of his small committee, submitted a report on the Debourge letter in an oral presentation to the Paris Assembly.[41] His laudatory report began by noting that the Assembly was already very familiar with the issues regarding the Jews

38. Since the little that is known about Debourge suggests that it is not likely that he would have known how to draft a persuasive letter of a type tantamount to a legal brief, it is all the more probable that he would have relied on his friend and colleague Godard to draft the letter.

39. Léonard Robin (1745–1802), the son of a printer from the southwestern city of Angoulême, studied law at a university in Poitiers, where he became an avocat registered with the Parlement of that city. He subsequently moved to Paris and was registered with the Paris Parlement. In 1789, he became active in Paris politics, joining the National Guard and being elected to the Paris Assembly. As will be noted later, in late 1790 and early 1791 he served as a special commissioner with Jacques Godard. He was incarcerated during the Terror, but survived and became a judge serving through the early years of Napoleon's Consulat. At his death, the Abbé Mulot delivered and published a lengthy eulogy praising Robin, inexplicably failing to make any reference to the close association that Robin (and he) had with Godard. François-Valentin Mulot, *À la Mémoire de Léonard Robin, Tribun et Membre de l'Académie de Législation, discours prononcé à la séance publique du 1er Germinal An XI par le Cit. Mulot, ex-Législateur.*

40. *Actes de la Commune de Paris*, vol. 5, p. 498.

41. Ibid., 593–96. See *Rapport sur la Lettre de M. de Bourges au Comité de Constitution, Concernant l'Affaire des Juifs, fait par M. Brissot de Warville, à l'Assemblée générale des Représentans de la Commune de Paris, le 29 Mai 1790.* Imprimé par l'ordre de l'Assemblée.

by reason of the "enthusiasm" with which two members of the Assembly had devoted themselves to this "important cause."[42] Brissot was, of course, referring to Godard and Debourge. Brissot went on to describe Debourge's letter and noted that it "pulverized" the arguments which had been put forth to delay the National Assembly's deliberations on the Jewish matter. At the conclusion of his report he proposed that the Paris Assembly adopt another resolution of support for Jewish equality, the text of which he read out to the Assembly:

> The General Assembly of the Representatives of the Paris Commune based upon the report of its commissioners nominated to examine the printed letter sent to the Constitution Committee regarding the matter of the Jews written by Mr. Debourge, a Representative of the Assembly of the Representatives of the Paris Commune, having reflected that on the eve of the creation of the new Paris Municipality it is important not to leave any doubt as to the rights of the Jews as active citizens, believes that it is appropriate to recommend to the most serious attention of the members of the Constitution Committee of the National Assembly this writing where the rights of all of the Jews of the kingdom are proven by the most recent evidence.[43]

A number of members of the Assembly rose in support of the resolution, including, notably, the Abbé Mulot, the staunch supporter of Jewish rights.[44] Following a brief discussion, the resolution was readily adopted. It was ordered that it be printed and distributed to the district assemblies of all sixty districts of the city. Although the record is not clear on the point, it is highly likely that the resolution was also forwarded to the National Assembly's Constitution Committee.

42. Ibid., 593.
43. Ibid., 596.
44. *Journal de la Municipalité et des Districts*, June 1, 1790.

CHAPTER 33

PRESIDENT GODARD

Addressing the issue of Jewish rights formed a significant part of the work of the Paris Assembly during the early months of 1790, and especially for Godard as the primary spokesman for the Paris Jewish community and for the Ashkenazi community more generally. However, between February and March 1790 the public's attention was also focused on a far different battle being waged in Paris. A new power struggle was rapidly taking center stage on the political scene. The French national government, whose very foundation had been shattered by the events of the summer of 1789, was being restructured. The notion of a federal government, influenced by the experiment in the nascent United States of America, was being proposed. The Paris Assembly enthusiastically endorsed the federal concept and sent a proposal to the various districts of the capital, with a request for expressions of support. However, the Paris Assembly could not but take note that the districts were accelerating a process that had begun as early as July 1789 to act on their own, circumventing and even disregarding the Paris Assembly. As Godard would later note, the districts not only decided to name their own representatives to the planned *Fête de la Fédération* (Festival of the Federation), which was to be a massive outdoor celebration scheduled to take place on the first anniversary of the capture of the Bastille, but had already named special representatives to address issues relating to the confiscation of Church property, as well as to consider other issues affecting the general operations of the

409

city.[1] These smaller representative assemblies were seen by the more conservative elements in the Paris Assembly as posing a direct threat to their authority. In Godard's dramatic and dire words, these (the district) assemblies "destroyed the equilibrium of the City, the center of power disappeared and the rival authorities which had grown up next to each other plunged the Capital into the most disastrous anarchy."[2]

The power struggle broke out into the open in March. A plan for the reorganization of the Paris municipal government had been developed by certain of the districts and was presented by Bailly, the mayor, to the National Assembly on March 23. However, a majority of the districts opposed the plan and supported an alternative that called for an end to the Paris Assembly, advocating that the districts make decisions by themselves on behalf of the Paris Commune. This plan was adopted by forty of the sixty districts and was presented to the National Assembly on April 10. In spite of his earlier support for the initial plan, Bailly accepted this second proposal, causing a confrontation between the Paris Assembly and the district assemblies, which would ultimately have a significant impact on Godard's role.

As the spring progressed, acrimony increased between the more militant district assemblies and the Paris Assembly. One manifestation of the conflict occurred when an accusation of the crime of *lèse-nation* was leveled against Georges-Jacques Danton.[3] Danton, an avocat and a

1. Godard, *Exposé des Travaux*, 158–59.
2. Ibid.
3. Georges-Jacques Danton (1759–1794), born into a modest family from Arcis-sur-Aube, a small town in the Champagne region, studied to become an avocat in Rheims. He would become one of the most popular and powerful politicians in Paris during the Revolution. He served in various government posts and, most importantly, as a member of the Committee of Public Safety that became the de facto governing body of France in 1793–94. Ultimately, he became a competitor of Robespierre in the battle to control the direction of the Revolution and when he lost that competition he was arrested and sentenced to death by the Revolutionary Tribunal. On his way to the guillotine, in April 1794, he dramatically and accurately predicted that Robespierre would follow him. The sense of drama that characterized his political career did not fail him as he mounted the scaffold. His last words, addressed to the executioner, were a request that his head be shown to the people because, as he put it, "it is well worth the trouble." Among those who accompanied Danton to his death and were executed with him was the avocat-turned-journalist Camille Desmoulins, who had been one of Target's cadre of young followers, and Hérault de Séchelles,

fiery orator in the mold of Mirabeau, was a larger-than-life personality. He dominated his particularly radical District of the Cordeliers on Paris's Left Bank, using his oratorical skills to promote his aggressive agenda. In the years to come, he would become one of the most prominent of the Paris revolutionaries, extremely popular with the lower classes. Notwithstanding suspicions (which were ultimately substantiated) that he was receiving bribes from the king and various royalists, he came to play an important role in the national government, serving for a time as Minister of Justice. He would also briefly be named president of the Committee of Public Safety, thereby effectively becoming the de facto head of the French government. During the Terror, the effervescent and bon vivant Danton, just months following the death of his wife while giving birth, married a young woman of sixteen, barely half his own age. He would clash with the ascetic Robespierre, whose lifestyle and austere approach to life stood in stark and irreconcilable conflict with Danton's. The clash would ultimately result in Danton's arrest and his execution on the guillotine in April 1794, several months before Robespierre's own execution.

When the act of indictment for the novel crime of *lèse-nation* was handed down against Danton, his Cordeliers District petitioned the National Assembly to adopt legislation that would establish a special new tribunal distinct from the criminal court of the Châtelet to try such crimes. An attempt was made to secure the support of the Paris Assembly for the special legislation being proposed on Danton's behalf, and the Abbé Fauchet addressed the Assembly to this end. However, during a debate on the exception requested by Danton's district, Godard, in spite of his general political alignment with Fauchet, spoke up, along with several other members, in opposition. Godard argued that members of the Paris legislature were compelled to oppose the special treatment being requested on behalf of Danton by reason of the "duties of fraternity, honor and liberty." He questioned whether the fraternal bonds of fellow-members of the Paris Assembly "could remove from Mr. Danton his status as a 'Citizen' and from the Law its dominion." He then asserted, echoing the theme that had been a recurrent one throughout his career, that honor consisted "of respecting the Law and using all of our power to engender respect for the Ministers." Finally, he summarized his view by saying that

---

who worked closely with Godard on the Julien Baudelle matter.

liberty's "veritable character was a scrupulous adherence to the Law."[4] Danton was to be given no advantage. To Godard, the consummate avocat, the law was applicable equally to all.[5]

Following Godard's remarks, the Paris Assembly determined not to intervene on behalf of Danton.[6] Undoubtedly, Danton—who would later wield enormous power as a member of the Committee on Public Safety, which would govern France for over a year—must have been particularly displeased with Godard's intervention. Fortunately, he never had an opportunity to carry out any act of vengeance against Godard. But it can be fairly surmised that, had such an opportunity presented itself, he would have seized upon it.[7]

The conflict between the Paris Assembly and the districts escalated dramatically in April. On April 9, 1790, Godard was charged by the Assembly with the responsibility of drafting an address to the districts explaining the risks posed by their contentious relations with the Assembly.[8] At the April 10, 1790, session Godard stood up to decry the situation, which he described as being one of "anarchy."[9] Displaying his growing conservatism and his opposition to the increasingly radicalized Parisian populace, Godard took note of the disorder being sown by the competing poles of power that were emerging. He, obviously, was seeking to defend the authority and power of the Paris Assembly of which he was a member, but he was likely also manifesting his innate dislike of disorder. He proposed a dramatic and grand gesture in an effort to bring the conflict to an end: that all the members of the Assembly resign, thereby bringing into focus

---

4. *Mercure Historique et Politique de Bruxelles*, Saturday 27 March 1790, no. 13, pp. 343–44.

5. Ibid. However, the then-radical (it would later veer to the center) *Révolutions de Paris* did not much appreciate Godard's opposition to Danton's situation, referring to Godard and others (such as Mulot and Vigée) who stood with him as "*grands faiseurs de phrases aristocratiques*" (great makers of aristocratic phrases). *Révolutions de Paris dédiées à la Nation*, vol. 37, p. 16.

6. *Mercure Historique et Politique de Bruxelles*, Saturday 27 March 1790, no. 13, pp. 344–45.

7. Cf. Louise Elizabeth Tourzel (Duchesse de), *Memoirs of the Duchess de Tourzel: Governess to the Children of France*, vol. 1 (London: Remington & Co. 1886), 96.

8. Lacroix, *Actes de la Commune de Paris pendant la Révolution*, vol. 4, p. 650.

9. *Adresse de l'Assemblée Générale des deux-cents quarante Représentans de la Commune, à ses Commettans*, April 10, 1790 (Paris: Imprimerie de Lottin, l'aîné, & Lottin de St. Germain,1790), 5.

the real struggle. He disseminated an address to all the districts.[10] The *Journal de la Municipalité et des Districts* took note:

> Mr. Godard, Deputy from the Blancs-Manteaux District, explained the state of anarchy in which the Capital finds itself; all of the rival authorities which arose one next to the other and crossed each other in all directions; the necessity to side with someone who, while satisfying those with ambition, can bring back all of the powers to a common center....[11]

Then, reporting in significant detail on the tumultuous session of the Paris Assembly, the *Journal de la Municipalité et des Districts* showered praise on the young Godard. The *Journal* reminded its readers that Godard had already participated in many matters relating to honor and liberty and wrote that his motion "was worthy of his heart, it was worthy of Parisians, conquerors of liberty, worthy of the Assembly before which he read it."[12] The newspaper then went on to describe its perspective on the extraordinary legislative session, which it referred to as being "memorable in the annals of the Revolution," and focused very specifically on Godard's role at the session:

> The presentation of his [Godard's] sentiments and of his principles on liberty, principles which it is not possible to assume to have been born just for the present circumstances, since he professed them before joining the Commune, served as a first basis for the proposition that he wanted to make. The present state of the Representatives of the Commune, despoiled of the authority which was entrusted to them, placed between defiance, suspicion, and envy, insulted in all of the press, held in contempt in a thousand delegations, barely known by a rival assembly, although [that assembly] is itself legal, and the chief of the Municipality presides also and more often over it; finally, reduced to refraining from attempting anything other than the good, with being able to have it recognized as such; the depiction of anarchy and of the confusion of power, the fruit of a lack of restraint and destructive of liberty, these are the second basis that Mr. Godard expounded and

10. Lacroix, *Actes de la Commune de Paris pendant la Révolution*, 654–57.
11. *Journal de la Municipalité et des Districts*, April 13, 1790, as cited in Lacroix, *Actes de la Commune de Paris pendant la Révolution*, vol. 4, pp. 654–55.
12. Ibid.

upon which he supports his proposition: that it would be indispen-
sable to make an appeal to the Districts on the evils which abound
and which are about to sink the vessel of liberty; to hand in a collective resignation while assuring the Districts that the representatives
would depart only when their successors had been designated to replace them and would be received in the communal hall; to draft the
address for the next day and to have it delivered as rapidly as possible
to the Districts; to convene together with the mayor the [various mu-
nicipal] sections so that they might elect their successors.[13]

Godard's motion was strongly supported by many of his fellow representatives, some of whom went to the podium to express that support. One
of the representatives, Lepelletier, proposed to add to Godard's resolution the requirement that a delegation be sent to the National Assembly
to describe the intolerable situation in which the Paris Assembly found
itself and the need to remedy the problem. Certain members of the Assembly were less convinced by Godard's arguments and some opposition
to Godard's motion was heard.

However, after a long discussion, the Abbé Mulot addressed the Paris
Assembly, bringing to bear his considerable standing and prestige. Mulot
proposed that Godard's motion, as modified by Lepelletier's amendment,
be adopted. With the Abbé's public support, it was then unanimously
decided that each of the districts would be notified of the Assembly's
position that the general resignation of all the representatives would take
place by means of the dissemination of Godard's remarks, but that no representative would leave his position until his successor had been selected
pursuant to a summons for new elections from the mayor.[14]

Godard had just achieved an important legislative success and the press
provided him with extensive coverage. Panckoucke's *Moniteur* was lavish
in its praise of Godard's address, suggesting that "few writings emanating
from the Commune bore a character of reason and a spirit of principles
better enunciated than this work of M. Godard, the reading of which
merits the most enthusiastic applause."[15] All the members of the Paris
Assembly then tendered their resignations.

---

13. Ibid.
14. *Actes de la Commune de Paris pendant la Révolution*, vol. 4. Commune de Paris
(France, 1789–1794), 655.
15. *Moniteur*, April 25, 1790, no. 115, p. 468.

With this success, Godard's prestige within the Paris Assembly rose to new heights, and on April 13 he was elected the Assembly's president. The minutes of that day's proceedings indicate that "a plurality of the votes were cast in favor of Mr. Godard, who took the oath of office from the hands of his predecessor and thanked the Assembly."[16] Sigismond Lacroix, the foremost nineteenth-century chronicler of legislative activity during the Revolution, in his commentary on this election, notes that Godard, rather than obtaining the plurality mentioned in the minutes, had obtained the vast majority of the votes, but that it took some persuasion on the part of his colleagues to secure his consent to assume the office. In Lacroix's words, members of the Assembly had "to do violence to [Godard's] modesty in order to have him accept the office."[17]

It was then decided that the Paris Assembly would send a delegation to the National Assembly to express its position regarding the role of the Paris Assembly. Although a delegation was constituted, the Paris mayor, Bailly, refused to lead it, and, as a consequence, on April 20 it was Godard who, as president of the Paris Assembly, led the delegation to the National Assembly and had the opportunity to make another presentation to the national legislature.[18]

After taking note of Godard's and his delegation's presentation, the then president of the National Assembly, the Marquis de Bonnay, sent a brief response to the Paris Assembly. Courteously, but without making any commitments, he wrote simply:

The National Assembly has received various plans for the organization of the Paris Municipality; it will weigh them all in its wisdom, and will give particular attention to the one which was presented in the name of the Assembly of the Representatives of the Commune of Paris.[19]

Godard was charged with drafting a letter on behalf of the Paris Assembly to the president of the National Assembly thanking the National Assembly for its support of the Paris Assembly's position on the governance of the city and for facilitating the implementation of the reorganization.

16. Lacroix, *Actes de la Commune de Paris pendant la Révolution* , vol. 4, p. 710.
17. Ibid., n. 2.
18. Lacroix, *Actes de la Commune de Paris pendant la Révolution*, series 2, vol. 1, October 9–December 31, 1790, p. xii.
19. Lacroix, *Actes de la Commune de Paris pendant la Révolution*, vol. 5, p. 110.

One of the secretaries of the Paris Assembly read Godard's letter to the National Assembly on April 30, 1790:

Mr. President:

We should be grateful to the National Assembly for each of its decrees, which are homages to freedom, and the means of securing public happiness; but when we participate with the whole nation in the benefits of its wisdom, we confine ourselves to mingling our applause with that of the provinces, and we should fear distracting it by particular testimonials of gratitude. It has just issued, Mr. President, a decree which concerns only the capital, which concerns it alone; it has penetrated our hearts with the most lively sensitivity; we cannot observe, without the most touching joy and without largely abandoning ourselves to expressions of the most profound sentiments, the measures which the National Assembly has taken to enable us to enjoy promptly the organization to which we aspire and which has become a pressing need for the capital. The Assembly of the representatives of the Commune instructs me to express to you the extent of its gratitude, and to ask you, Mr. President, to express its respects to the august Assembly of which you are the representative.

I am with respect, etc.

Signed: M. Godard President of the Paris Commune[20]

In spite of the Paris Assembly's energetic exercise of its authority, its ability to accomplish very much was being hampered by the short period of time before it would be replaced by a new assembly in the early fall.

Taking cognizance of the limited amount of time left to the Paris Assembly, but also fully aware of the historic role it had played during a most tumultuous time in the history of France and of the city of Paris, the members of the Paris Assembly, as early as March 9, 1790, adopted a resolution calling for the preparation of a comprehensive summary of its accomplishments. A committee of twelve members was established and Étienne Vigée was given the task of preparing the report. However, other obligations forced Vigée to relinquish this responsibility. In his stead, Jacques Godard, by now one of the most vocal members of the Assembly and soon to be named its president, was designated as the draftsman

20. *Archives Parlementaires*, vol. 15, p. 338.

of the report.[21] This task suited Godard admirably. He was, indeed, an excellent writer and he was thorough, arguably even compulsively so, in the performance of his assigned tasks. Godard would work actively on the history of the Paris Assembly for many months, as the Assembly's existence ebbed. Of necessity, this task severely limited his ability to engage actively in many other matters, including remunerative matters. However, Godard was not deterred. He seems to have appreciated that a historian not only writes history, but can also shape it. He clearly saw an opportunity to influence the judgment of future generations regarding the work of the Paris Assembly, which was, in part, his own work.

It was difficult to imagine that, even with his prodigious energy, Godard would have the time and the physical wherewithal needed to address this monumental task. Godard, however, soon found himself with more time to devote to the drafting of the history of the Paris Assembly than he had anticipated.

In the struggle between the Paris Assembly and Jean-Sylvain Bailly, the mayor, the acrimony grew so great that it turned into an outright test of wills. In spite of the general consensus against the mayor, the members of the Assembly apparently did not do a very effective job persuading their constituencies of their position. Many of the districts sided with the mayor. As a consequence, a number of the districts turned on their representatives and voted them out of office. On April 23 Godard's Blancs-Manteaux District elected new representatives to the Assembly and, to his great dismay, voted to replace him. A delegation of the National Guard battalion of that district, however, in marked contrast to the district assembly, expressed its regrets to the Paris Assembly on the resignation of its representatives. Godard replied graciously and thanked the members of the National Guard delegation for their "heroic role" in the past.[22] Understandably, Godard was deeply distressed with his district's decision and resisted its effort to replace him.

When the new representatives of the Blancs-Manteaux District arrived at the Assembly, Godard, in his role as president of the Assembly, received them coolly. While lauding their personal qualities and even the fact that they had merited the confidence of their fellow citizens, he chastised the district for having taken the decision it had. As one commentator noted

21. Lacroix, *Actes de la Commune de Paris pendant la Révolution*, vol. 4, p. 348.
22. Slavin, *The Revolution in Miniature*, 98.

with understatement, Godard's situation was a "delicate" one.[23] However, both practically and philosophically, as a believer in the established rules there was little that Godard could do to retain his seat.

Just five days after Godard's district had voted to elect new representatives, the Paris Assembly elected the Abbé Mulot to replace Godard as president. Godard then had the difficult and clearly unpleasant task of announcing the election of his successor. Interestingly, Mulot had been president of the Assembly when Godard had played his most important role there, when he had stood up to advocate on behalf of his Jewish clients. Godard took this opportunity to deliver his valedictory address to the Assembly. In a bittersweet speech, characterized as "a speech remarkable by its noble and sensible tone which reflects his character," Godard seized the occasion to emphasize his gratitude for the trust that had been placed in him.[24] He displayed suitable modesty, but also sincere regret, in his remarks:

> Gentlemen:
>
> When you deemed it appropriate to elevate me to lead you, your intention was to reward the zeal which I demonstrated to you and to encourage the efforts of my youth. But so shining an encourage-ment, a reward so disproportionate with my service and especially with the talents necessary to preside over you had always been so far from my thoughts, such that at the first instant when I heard myself proclaimed by your votes the head of this Assembly the sentiment of surprise almost prevailed in my heart over the sentiment of gratitude.
>
> I was unable to explain to myself, Gentlemen, the motivations of your choice other than to attribute it to one of these movements of gener-osity which you have demonstrated, at all times, that it was so easy for you to make. You thought that there was a kind of convenience that the one of your colleagues whom you have selected for the brave step that you have taken should be the first to consummate a sacrifice and should walk at the head of your funeral procession.

He then recognized and bowed to the unavoidable, acknowledging that he was leaving the Paris Assembly and his role within it:

> It is now to another that this glory is reserved, since your existence

---

23. Lacroix, *Actes de la Commune de Paris pendant la Révolution*, vol. 5, 119.
24. *Journal Municipal et des Districts*, May 1, 1790.

has been prolonged beyond your hopes. Calumny has retreated from before you by the honorable challenge that you have brought to it; and while generally it [calumny] survives good men whose reputations it has endeavored to alter, we can say of this Assembly before it dissolves that we have truly survived it.

I will see the Assembly's triumph from afar, Gentlemen, and I will applaud with emotion; since my successors have been designated. Even if they were present in your midst, and I believe that I see them within these precincts, such that today I must descend from this important place which eludes me to resume the role of a simple citizen; that my thanks to the Assembly, my farewell and this speech which I have the privilege of addressing to you is to be a kind of civic testament.

But, if I now cease to be your colleague, Gentlemen, I will not cease in my thoughts to be in your midst. It will be impossible for me to forget your indefatigable devotion to the public welfare and your touching kindness towards me. The names of each of you, as citizens, will always be with me in my thoughts and, as colleagues who are dear to me, you will live forever in my heart. I do not commend myself to your memories, because one is always involuntarily attached and even with a kind of joy, to the men whom one has created and who are in some respects our handiwork.

He seemed to apologize for his errors, ascribing them to his young age, but in this manner at least giving a hint that he expected to be back in the political arena:

I place in your hands, Sir [Abbé Mulot], the responsibility that had been entrusted to me. I tried as best I could to preserve it in the same manner as I received it. If on some occasions I demonstrated a severity that was not proportionate to my age, it was mandated by the role with which I was honored and it will be believed without much effort that I never sought to offend any of my colleagues.

The Assembly proved to me by awarding me its votes that it permitted itself to be, for once, indulgent; it proves today, in choosing you as my successor, that it is compensating for its act of indulgence toward me by the multiple acts of justice that it is happily rendering to you.[25]

---

25. Lacroix, *Actes de la Commune de Paris pendant la Révolution*, vol. 5, (France,

At the conclusion of Godard's remarks, Mulot assumed the president's seat at the table at the front of the Paris Assembly's meeting hall and, after thanking the Assembly for having bestowed upon him its confidence by electing him president for the third time, showered his praise on his predecessor. He expressed his regret at having to bid farewell to Godard:

> In spite of the pleasure which I must naturally feel as a consequence of this new honor which you are bestowing on me, I feel, nonetheless, some pain: it is to see the end of the term of the presidency of my predecessor become the end of his presence amongst us. At the flower of his age, he has demonstrated by his firm and generous conduct, all of the maturity of old age; and if his District is withdrawing him from our Assembly, we will always keep within our hearts the memory both of his person and of the heroic act which he inspired in us.[26]

If Godard had good reason to be hurt and saddened by his sudden removal from his august position at the Paris Assembly, he must nonetheless have basked in Mulot's words. Since his own words had made clear, by a careful blend of flattery and self-congratulation, that he was not leaving the political arena forever, the praise must have sounded like a blessing for his continuing ambitions. He had bid his colleagues farewell, but he had also demonstrated, with just the appropriate expression of modesty leavened by a restrained display of ambition, that he did not intend to be forgotten.

Mere days after Godard stepped down from the presidency and had left the Assembly, the Assembly was called upon to address a question of religious tolerance that echoed certain aspects of Godard's pleading on behalf of his Jewish clients. It had been ascertained that the mother superior who oversaw one of Paris's hospitals, the La Salpêtrière Hospital on the Left Bank, was requiring that patients sign statements affirming their Catholic religious faith before they would be given medical assistance.[27] On May 12, 1790, the Abbé Fauchet proposed a motion to ban

---

1789–1794), 178–79.

26. Ibid., 179. Presumably, the heroic act to which Mulot was making reference was the mass resignation of the members.

27. The Hôpital de la Salpêtrière was founded in the 1660s during the reign of Louis XIV. By the late eighteenth century it was Paris's largest hospital complex, as it remains today. Already during the eighteenth century, La Salpêtrière had begun to develop a more humane approach to the treatment of mental illness and, by the mid-nineteenth century, its psychiatric department was considered

such behavior, which was quickly approved by the Paris Assembly. The
Assembly then went on to protest the hospital's policy to the National
Assembly, but it went well beyond, directing the Paris Department of
Hospitals to enforce the existing legislation, which, as Godard would put
it in his history of the Paris Assembly, assured "that religious liberty be
precisely observed at the Salpetrière as well as in other Hospitals."[28] He
must have been pleased that his former colleagues had acted in support of
the religious freedom he had been so strongly advocating.

In spite of Godard's obvious political setback and his departure from
center stage, he would continue to play a role in the work of the Paris
Assembly,[29] as well as of his local district assembly, serving in various
advisory capacities over the coming months.[30] And, in addition, he still
held within his hands a very important tool for his future. He had not
relinquished his role as the scrivener who would be documenting all the
work of the Paris Assembly. By use of his pen, Godard would be in a position to preserve and enhance the Assembly's reputation, as well as that
of some of his colleagues, and his own, for posterity. His assiduous work
on the history of the Paris Assembly was an effort he would refer to as
"an enormous task with which the Commune has charged me and which
overwhelms me with fatigue."[31]

As he pursued his monumental task of documenting the work of the
Paris Assembly, Godard remained vigilant in defending the Assembly in

one of Europe's most advanced.

28. Godard, *Exposé des Travaux*, 168.

29. Despite no longer being a member of the Paris Assembly, Godard was appointed by members of the Assembly to serve on certain ad hoc commissions. See, e.g.,
Sigismond Lacroix, *Actes de la Commune de Paris pendant la Révolution*, vol. 6, p.
224. One such commission related to a request for a prohibition on the wearing
of all cockades other than the tricolor national cockade. When the king issued a
proclamation to that effect, Godard was part of a delegation sent to thank the king.
Lacroix, *Actes de la Commune de Paris Pendant la Révolution*, vol. 5, p. 603.

30. As an example, on June 1, 1791, Godard's local Enfants Rouge assembly would
name him a commissioner to report on the "advantages and disadvantages of the
Revolution in Poland" and to propose means and methods of providing support
to the Polish people. Lacroix, *Actes de la Commune de Paris pendant la Révolution*,
series 2 (October 9–August 10 1790), vol. 1, p. 243.

31. Unpublished letter from Jacques Godard to Amélie Suard, dated July 27 (year
illegible, but almost certainly 1790), Archives de l'Institut Voltaire, Geneva,
Switzerland (Cote IMV: MS AS 421).

which he had played a major role. On July 13 there appeared in the columns of the *Moniteur* a letter from a priest named Debois, from the parish of St. André des Arts on Paris's Left Bank. Debois attacked the Paris Assembly for allegedly failing to designate an appropriate priest to participate in the ceremonies commemorating the first anniversary of the fall of the Bastille.[32] The Assembly had appointed the chaplain of the Paris National Guard to perform this role. According to Debois, the Chaplain of the National Guard, whom he claimed not to know, was not worthy of the honor. He went further, writing that the members of the Paris Assembly had even created the position of chaplain simply in order to be able to name one of their own to that position. An obviously displeased Godard rushed to respond. With his extensive knowledge of the actions of the Paris Assembly, he was in an excellent position to undermine the priest's arguments. He castigated Debois for being "unjust" in his criticism. As was his wont, Godard homed in on the misstatement of the facts and, in his eyes, the priest's consequent hypocrisy. He attacked the priest with indignation, telling his readers that not only did the priest know the chaplain, but that he had, in fact, voted for his appointment. Then, moving in for the kill and, as a final blow to Debois, he wrote with ample sarcasm that, if the priest had been reelected to his position instead of being turned out by his district, he would have been in a better position to express his views.[33] It was apparent that when defending causes in which he believed, Godard was not reluctant to use every argument available.

However, less than three weeks later, on August 13, 1790, it was Godard's turn to be attacked in the pages of the *Moniteur*. He had proposed that the members of the Paris Assembly write to the provincial municipal assemblies to urge that they "favor by all means possible the collection of taxes." He had written that the failure to pay taxes would cause the new edifice (of revolutionary France) "constructed with such glory, but also with such pain, to crumble from all of its parts."[34] Therefore, he wanted the Paris Assembly to urge all citizens to do their civic duty, explaining the importance of doing so as being a patriotic obligation. However, the author of the article reporting Godard's proposal, a certain Jacques Peuchet,[35] unceremoniously rejected

---

32. *Moniteur*, July 25, 1790, no. 194, p. 795.

33. Ibid., July 25, 1790, no. 206, p. 847.

34. Ibid., no. 225, p. 930.

35. Jacques Peuchet (1758–1830) was an avocat who evolved into a journalist, becoming one of the editors of the *Moniteur*. He also served as an elector for

Godard's approach. He suggested that the obligation to pay legislated taxes should not be the subject of "prayers" from municipal assemblies. Rather, Peuchet argued that it was up to the executive (the king) simply to enforce the law.[36] For once, Godard, the staunch and unflinching advocate of the strict application of the law, was being upbraided for failing to insist on its forceful enforcement. Godard did not react to this public reprimand, but it can safely be assumed that he did not appreciate it.

In late July Godard submitted his first version of the summary of the accomplishments of the Paris Assembly to its members. The text, entitled "Exposé of the Work of the General Assembly of the Representatives of the Paris Municipality," ran over two hundred pages.[37] It was not only lengthy, but extremely detailed, with extensive explanations of the various decisions taken by the Assembly. In spite of its length and complexity, Godard read the text aloud in its entirety to the Paris Assembly over the course of several sessions beginning on July 24, continuing on July 30, and concluding on August 6.[38] Once the reading had ended, at Godard's request a committee was appointed to study the text and make any appropriate corrections. On August 19 Godard received the official thanks of the Paris Assembly for his history.[39] It was also decided that Godard should continue his work until the scheduled expiration of the term of the Paris Assembly in October. When the committee completed its work and reported to the Assembly on October 4, the report was glowing. Ultimately, Godard's 223-page history was published on October 20. The final work was impressive and thorough; however, it could hardly be qualified as an objective document.

While acknowledging that the Assembly had made some errors, Godard's history was overwhelmingly laudatory. Its primary emphasis was on the Assembly's role as an instrument of stability at a time of strife. Interestingly, Godard did not focus on his own significant work with the Assembly,

---

the selection of representatives to the Estates-General. In his role as a journalist, he penned many articles before becoming a director of the Ministry of Police. After the Revolution, he became the chief archivist of the Ministry of Police. He authored books regarding crime statistics and the role of the police.

36. *Moniteur*, August 13, 1790, no. 225, p. 931.

37. Godard, *Exposé des Travaux*, 1790.

38. Lacroix, *Actes de la Commune de Paris pendant la Révolution*, vol. 6, pp. 572, 624–25, 667.

39. Ibid., 754.

making only occasional and modest observations about his personal efforts. Notably, at the very end of this text—using the artifice of posing the rhetorical question: which institution had pioneered important revolutionary reforms?—he summarized the fourteen great accomplishments of the Assembly, praising two of the matters to which he had devoted much effort and with respect to which he played a leading part, asking: "Who supported and elevated an institution for the Deaf and Mute? Who was the first to raise a voice in favor of the Jews?"[40] Otherwise, he demonstrated an uncharacteristic modesty about his role in the Assembly's work. This self-restraint provided more credibility to the history than it might otherwise have had. Godard's text remains the most comprehensive overview of the Paris Assembly and its accomplishments, and provides important, even invaluable, insights into the social and political environment in Paris during the turbulence of the first year of the Revolution.

As a member of the review committee that evaluated Godard's history, Médéric Louis Élie Moreau de St.-Méry rose before the Assembly at its October 4 session to praise the document.[41] Moreau was not a natural ally of Godard; he was an opponent of equality for Blacks and strongly supported the continuation and spread of slavery throughout France. Yet, he did not hide his high regard for Godard's work and submitted a resolution that called upon each member of the Assembly to pay nine *livres* for the purpose of having the document printed and distributed. He added to his resolution the proposition that, to the extent the members' contributions exceeded the cost of printing and distribution, the excess funds would go to benefit freed prisoners. His motion was unanimously adopted.

When, several weeks later, Godard's document was finally published and disseminated, it was widely praised.[42] The *Moniteur* commented that

---

40. Ibid., vol. 7, p. 222.

41. Médéric Louis Élie Moreau de Saint-Méry (1750–1819) was one of the more peculiar actors in the French Revolution. He was a slaveholder who argued against equal rights for Blacks in an apparent effort to protect his own property. He was elected to the Paris Assembly in the spring of 1789 and then to the National Assembly in September of the same year, serving in both for short periods of time. He is best remembered as an opponent of freedom for Blacks living in France— the freedom that Godard had sought for Julien Baudelle. Ultimately, he had to leave France to save his life and, after spending time in various places in Europe, he spent his last years as the owner of a bookstore at the corner of Fourth and Walnut Streets in Philadelphia, which became a gathering place for French exiles.

42. The poet and playwright Augustin-Louis de Ximénès (1728–1817) wrote a

this work would be a precious document in setting out the history of the French Revolution, complimenting the author by noting that Godard had confirmed "in a convincing manner that the Assembly, in selecting him, had chosen a vehicle worthy of itself..."[43] Similarly, the *Journal de Paris* praised the *Exposé*, citing "the uncommon talent" that Godard, "the young lawyer, already known for his excellent pleadings" had demonstrated in the selection of the matters to be discussed and the manner in which they were presented.[44] On October 20 the National Assembly itself issued a tribute acknowledging the quality of the *Exposé*.[45]

Indeed, the document was a monumental work. Beyond its sheer length, especially considering the short period of time which Godard had been given to prepare it, it was a comprehensive and informative document, prepared without the full cooperation of those who could have assisted Godard as he pursued his research. In fact, in September, as he was endeavoring to complete the report, Godard had come to the Assembly to report the lack of cooperation that he had received from the office of the Mayor of Paris (the Paris Assembly's antagonist, Bailly) as he sought to obtain copies of various documents. The competing *Conseil de la Ville de Paris*, controlled by Bailly, according to Godard, would not provide any information since it "was not supposed to have any contact with the Paris Assembly," as it had declared in an ordinance it adopted on September 7.[46] Of course, Godard's prior run-in with the mayor during the struggle earlier that spring between the Paris Assembly and Bailly must not have militated in his favor.

In his description of the work of the Assembly in which he had served as a member for approximately five months and briefly as its president, Godard sought to be comprehensive, but clearly he did not attempt to be objective. His need to defend the actions of his colleagues (and, as a consequence, at least indirectly his own actions) dominated the text and

---

letter to Godard on October 12, 1790, expressing his praise for Godard's history of the Paris Assembly and extolling its style as being "precise and exciting." Ximénès suggested that, as a consequence of his history, Godard would "benefit from the respect of even those who are not your friends." Unpublished letter from the Bibliothèque Historique de la Ville de Paris, MS 814, Document 335.

43. *Moniteur*, October 29, 1790, no. 302, p. 1252.

44. *Journal de Paris*, October 16, 1790, no. 289, p. 2178.

45. Lacroix, *Actes de la Commune de Paris pendant la Révolution*, vol. 7, p. 385n1.

46. Ibid., 133.

turned it into a kind of paean. Also permeating his text is a moderate tone, perhaps displaying his evident concern with the rule of law, order, and decorum and probably his increasing discomfort with the radicalization of the Revolution. He focused heavily on the efforts of the Assembly to preserve order in Paris even as the Revolution was steadily destroying both existing institutions and the fabric of Ancien Régime society.

Godard's history remains to this day an important tool for documenting the first phase of the French Revolution. In spite of its subjectivity, it provides significant insights into the thinking of those who initiated the fundamental changes that created a new political order, with special insights into the men who were the leaders of the city of Paris during that dynamic time.

As the Paris Assembly's existence came to an end, Godard's principal work of publicly lobbying for his Jewish clients was also substantially at an end. But he still had much to accomplish. Godard's attention, along with the attention of other actors in the Revolution, began to turn to more urgent matters. The Revolution was gaining momentum. Economic pressures and rising demands from the people of Paris were coming to the fore, and the issue of Jewish rights, although far from being resolved, began to recede.

CHAPTER 34

LIFE AFTER THE PARIS ASSEMBLY

The summer of 1790 saw the National Assembly revisit the issue of Jewish rights on two occasions. The Constitution Committee also gave additional consideration to Jewish rights, but only relating to the Portuguese Jewish community.

On June 15 the Prince de Broglie, the representative from Strasbourg, submitted yet another petition from his Jewish constituents. De Broglie was merely acting as a conduit for constituents and not as an advocate for their interests. In light of his general obstructionism on the Jewish matter, not surprisingly he did not make any remarks in support of the petition that he was submitting. The petition was promptly sent to the Constitution Committee to join other similar efforts on a one-way trip to oblivion.[1]

However, on July 20, 1790, an important step forward in the battle for Jewish equality took place when the *Comité des Domaines* issued a report: "On the protection tax assessed against the Jews."[2] The report was presented to the Assembly by Jacques François Laurent de Visme, the representative from Laon, a town north of Paris.[3] The report recommend-

---

1. *Archives Parlementaires*, vol. 16, p. 229.
2. *"Sur le droit de protection levé sur les Juifs."*
3. *Rapport fait le 20 juillet sur le droit de protection levé sur les Juifs. Par M. de Visme, Député de Vermandois. Et Décret rendu sur ce Rapport;* Cf. *Archives Parlementaires*, vol. 17, pp. 215–18. Jacques François Laurent de Visme (1749–1830) pursued a

ed the elimination of the onerous and humiliating *Taxe Brancas* imposed
for generations on the Jews of the city of Metz for the benefit of the holder
of the title "Duc de Brancas." The theory of the tax was that it served (as
had been asserted with respect to the tax assessed on Jews entering the city
of Strasbourg) to pay for the protection of Jews entering the city. However,
the *Comité des Domaines*'s recommendation for abolition of the tax was
based upon the syllogism that Jews were residents of France, that as such
they were entitled to protection by the government as a matter of right and
that, therefore, they did not need to pay a supplemental tax for such protection. The words of the report were both unambiguous and eloquent:

> According to the general thesis, anyone who has come to live in a
> country, with the approval of the sovereign; whoever is, above all,
> born of parents domiciled in that country, is by right a member of the
> social body. As such, he cannot be deprived of the right to continue
> his residence there, so long as he has not become unworthy through
> some offenses, and, consequently, he must be protected by the gov-
> ernment. This right of all citizens is incontestable, not only because
> it is in the interest of all that public tranquility should not ever be
> troubled by particular quarrels, but also because the protection of
> the public authority is an obligation of the government, which is paid
> for by means of the collection of taxes.[4]

The report then took an important new step forward in the cause of Jewish equality, asserting the equal status of the Jews of Metz, stating that:
"The condition of the Jews of Metz cannot be different in this regard from
that of other inhabitants of this kingdom."[5]

According to the report, the only issue remaining to be considered was
whether the Brancas family was entitled to compensation for the elimination of the tax. The report then noted that the right to collect the tax was
given gratuitously by Louis XV to the Brancas family and suggested that,
as such, there was a strong argument for not paying any compensation

---

number of different careers, including trading in jewelry, before becoming an
avocat. He was elected to the Estates-General in 1789, but retired to his estates
as the Revolution veered toward radicalism. He returned to public life only after
Napoleon's coup d'état in 1799. He spent his last years writing history, including
a history of the city of Laon.

4. *Archives Parlementaires*, vol. 17, p. 217.

5. Ibid.

for its elimination. The report recommended the complete abolition of the tax, but, despite the arguments to the contrary, concluded with the suggestion that compensation should be paid.

Vismes had barely finished reading the report when, with his usual fervor, Reubell ran to the podium to express his disagreement with the report. He alleged that the Jews had always been willing to pay the tax because they were aware that they were not citizens and simply benefitted from the privilege of living in Metz. Objections to this assertion were immediately voiced by members of the Assembly. Reubell, refusing to be stymied, then tried to force the issue by suggesting that abolishing the Brancas tax would be tantamount to granting full citizenship to the Jews, something that the Assembly had not yet determined. He continued in that vein for some minutes.[6] When he had concluded, Robespierre rose to speak in support of the report, but objected to the notion that any compensation should be paid in connection with abolition of the Brancas tax:

> I do not believe that a society can prohibit any men from living on its land so long as they do not disturb the social order. I conclude that the title to Mr. de Brancas's claim is illegitimate and I concur with the first part of the decree of the committee. As regards the second, which promises an indemnity to the Brancas family, I reject it, because an indemnity can be granted to a possessor only when the title of the initial holder is just, which is not to be found in the proposed hypothesis.[7]

Others then rose in support of the report, including Pierre-Samuel du Pont de Nemours, whose son, Éleuthère-Irenée, would a few years later immigrate to the United States and found a gunpowder manufacturing company that would become the Dupont Company. At the conclusion of the discussion, the Assembly adopted a resolution implementing the substance of the report, namely abolishing the tax altogether. However, Reubell was not finished. The next day he attempted to reopen the discussion, but for once, his efforts were unsuccessful.[8] On August 7 the king, vacationing in his residence in St. Cloud just outside of Paris, issued Patent Letters that "eliminated and abolished" the Brancas tax and all special taxes on Jews without any indemnification whatsoever to those entitled to

---

6. Ibid., 218.
7. Ibid., 218–19.
8. See *Mercure Historique et Politique de Bruxelles*, July 31, 1790, no. 31, p. 343.

collect them.⁹ The Brancas tax, together with the slew of other obnoxious taxes on Jews—the vile remnants of blatant discrimination—were now just a historical footnote. Another important barrier to Jewish equality had been eliminated.

In spite of sporadic attention to the issue of Jewish rights, the deteriorating economic situation in France brought to the fore far more pressing matters, and, of course, the Alsatian representatives, ever vigilant to obstruct any effort to advance the cause of full Jewish civil equality, remained an apparently insurmountable obstacle to any progress. The National Assembly chose to wrestle with a growing assortment of complex reforms and crises and put the matter of Jewish equality to the side.

Nonetheless, during the summer of 1790, there was yet one more attempt to persuade the National Assembly to act on behalf of the Ashkenazi Jews. This effort emerged from the Parisian district with the largest Jewish population, the Carmelite District. On their own initiative (but probably at the urging of Godard and Debourge), on July 2 the members of the district assembly adopted a decree which lauded the district's Jewish citizens, and designated a delegation of four of its members, Nicolas Leverdier, Léonard Robin (then the district president), Jean-Louis Ravault, and Bon Claude Cahier de Gerville, to appear before the National Assembly's Constitution Committee to plead for Jewish equality.¹⁰ Apparently concluding that this would not be sufficient, the decision to send the delegation was followed just three weeks later by a letter addressed directly to the president of the National Assembly, signed by the new president of the District, Leverdier. Leverdier began by reminding the National Assembly that the Carmelite District, which had "perhaps" the largest concentration of Jews in Paris, had been the very first governmental entity to call for Jewish equality. Then, echoing an argument that had been articulated in Godard's *Pétition*, the letter (with at least a modest dose of sarcasm) commended the National Assembly for its cautious approach in addressing the issue. The letter then went on to indicate that "daily" the district assembly was being solicited with demands by Jews, whose "sons bear arms in our battalion," that they be granted a favorable decree from the National Assembly that "would erase their original sin." In his concluding paragraph,

9. *Lettres Patentes du Roi du 7 août 1790* (Laon: Imprimerie d'Augustin-Pierre Courtois, Imprimeur du Département de l'Aisne, 1790).
10. Lacroix, *Actes de la Commune de Paris pendant la Révolution*, vol. 7, pp. 557–58.

Leverdier asked the National Assembly's president to "take into consideration the tender solicitude of the Carmelite District for its brothers, the Jews of Paris, and present to the august assembly which you preside... the request, the respect, and the devotion of the Jews of our District and of the citizens who support their just demands."[11] For all of its eloquence and convincing arguments, this letter suffered the same fate as that which had befallen so many of the other pleas since January. The requested action was not granted.

Although the National Assembly would not again consider the issue of nationwide Jewish equality in a plenary session during 1790, the Portuguese Jews were able to persuade the Constitution Committee to give further consideration to their status. On October 28 the Committee issued a *"Décision"* in response to a petition submitted earlier in the year by David Sylveira, the official representative of the "Portuguese" Jews. Sylveira had requested confirmation that the January 28 decree which affirmed that the "Portuguese and Spanish" Jews were active citizens extended to all Jews who benefited from the Patent Letters issued to those Jews regardless of where they resided. He noted that if the "Portuguese and Spanish" Jews were active citizens through those Patent Letters then there was assuredly no need for any additional action on the part of the National Assembly to confirm that all Jews benefitting from such Patent Letters were full citizens of France, whether they were to be found in Bordeaux and Bayonne or in Paris, Marseille, or Lyon.[12] This was another attempt by the Portuguese Jews to consolidate their legal position by distancing themselves from the continuing battle involving the Ashkenazi Jews. The Constitution Committee sided squarely with the Portuguese Jews. Under the signature of several of its members, including notably Talleyrand and Target, the Committee clarified that "there is no doubt that those Jews who hold specific Patent Letters, can, just like the Portuguese, Spanish, and Avignonais Jews invoke [the benefits of] the January 28 decree..."[13] With this clarification, for the Portuguese Jews the battle for civil equality was over.

---

11. Ibid., 558–59.

12. *Adresse Présentée à l'Assemblée Nationale par le Député des Juifs Espagnols et Portugais établis au Bourg Saint-Esprit-les-Bayonne* (D'Houry & Debure, 1790).

13. *Décision du Comité de Constitution Requise par David Sylveira, Syndic Agent des Juifs François Patentées*, October 28, 1790, in *Adresses, Mémoires et Pétitions des Juifs 1789–1794* (Paris: EDHIS, 1968).

The Jews of Paris, however, seized upon the decision of the Constitution Committee to submit another petition for consideration, invoking
the notion that the blatant discrimination sowed by having one group
of Jews given rights while another was deprived of the same rights was
contrary to the principles of the Revolution. The petitioners noted the
anomaly that Jews who had been residing in Paris for generations would
not have the same rights as either foreigners who could obtain citizenship
within five years of becoming residents of France or other Jews who could
invoke their Patent Letters. They also reminded the National Assembly of
the consensus in favor of the Jews that had been demonstrated by the
various Paris districts through the efforts of Jacques Godard as another
reason to grant the ever-elusive equality to the Jews of Paris. Interestingly,
this petition bore the signatures of Mardoché Élie, one of the signatories
of the August 26, 1789, petition, and David Sylveira.[14] In this instance, the
interests of the Portuguese Jews and those of their Ashkenazi brethren
living in Paris brought about a brief moment of relative Jewish unity, as
the Portuguese Jewish representative joined with the Parisian Mardoché
Élie (albeit also a Portuguese Jew) in seeking National Assembly recognition of equal rights for all of the Parisian Jews. However, the petition did
not result in any immediate action.

Godard was no longer an elected representative of his district. Nonetheless, beyond the apparent assistance that he had provided in drafting some
of the latest decrees and letters on behalf of his Jewish clients, Godard
remained active in the political sphere. Early in 1790, Claude Fauchet, the
Abbé who would deliver the eulogy for the Abbé de l'Épée and would
praise Godard in the process, had created a new political group, the *"Cercle
Social"* (whose name evolved to become the more descriptive *"l'Assemblée
fédérative des amis de la verité"* (The Federated Assembly of Friends of
Truth). Jacques Godard became part of the small initial group of members
during the latter part of 1790.[15] The *Cercle Social*, which met in the *"Cirque
National"*—the large hippodrome-shaped amphitheater located partially
underground within the precincts of the Duc d'Orléans's Palais Royal—
was intended to bring together professionals, philosophers, and priests to
discuss the pressing issues of the day. Fauchet gave it the altruistic motto:

14. *Adresse présentée à l'Assemblée Nationale par les Juifs domiciliés à Paris* (Imprimerie de Momoro, 1790).
15. Kates, *The Cercle Social*, 5–6.

"To banish hate from the world, and to allow only love to rule."[16] In creating his *Cercle Social*, Fauchet, who has been referred to as "the most popular priest of revolutionary Paris," brought together a small group of like-minded individuals with a moderate orientation and gave the group a distinctly philosophical and intellectual bent.[17] Among the dozen or so who formed the core of the club were Condorcet, Brissot, de Bonneville,[18] Roland,[19] and Garran-Coulon,[20] in addition to Jacques Godard. Fauchet served as the anchor for the group, which resembled a debating society, giving it its philosophical orientation and its dynamism. He had a flair for oratory, and, within a short time, thousands of people of diverse backgrounds and positions flocked to his lectures. Godard's mentor, Target, also joined the club, and Godard's erstwhile romantic competitor, Condorcet, had a great

---

16. Étienne Caubet, *Histoire Populaire de la Révolution Française, de 1789 à 1839*, vol. 2 (Paris: Pagnerre Editeur, 1839), 199.

17. Kates, *The Cercle Social*, 48.

18. Nicolas de Bonneville (1760–1828), originally from Normandy, moved to Paris where he was at various times the keeper of a bookshop, a journalist, and a writer. Around the time of the storming of the Bastille, he began publishing a newspaper, and advocated for the attack on the fortress. He was closely associated with Fauchet in founding the *Cercle Social*. In the late 1790s he became close friends with Thomas Paine, the English-American pamphleteer, who ultimately moved into de Bonneville's residence. In 1802, Paine left for the United States with de Bonneville's wife and three sons and they all settled together in New Rochelle, New York. De Bonneville came to the United States in 1814, but stayed only four years before returning to France.

19. Jean-Marie Roland (1734–1793) was an economist from Lyon who became a leader of the Girondins. He would serve briefly as France's Interior Minister. In 1781 he married Jeanne-Marie Phlippon, who became active in Girondins politics in support of her husband. Her execution, which took place in conjunction with the beheading of a number of Girondins leaders, was a source of drama that made her a legendary figure. Just moments before being beheaded, Mme. Roland allegedly uttered one of the memorable statements of the era: "Oh Liberty, what crimes are committed in your name." Roland, himself, upon hearing of her execution chose to commit suicide rather than face revolutionary justice.

20. Jean Philippe Garran de Coulon (1748–1816), was originally from Saint-Maixent, the locality where Pierre Brisset, whom Godard had defended in 1788, lived. He became an avocat in Paris and engaged in radical politics in the early days of the Revolution. Allegedly, it was he who turned the then Mayor of Paris, de Flesselles, over to the mob, which then murdered him. However, his politics moderated and he survived the Revolution to serve in subsequent governments. He became a strong abolitionist, advocating for the elimination of slavery in France's colonies.

deal of influence on the group, leading it to espouse advocacy for the rights of women. Although the group maintained some secrecy regarding the identity of its members, it is possible to ascertain that Godard remained active for so long as it continued its brief existence.

One of the matters that brought Godard and Fauchet together was their shared dislike of Paris's domineering and arrogant mayor, Jean-Sylvain Bailly. Godard had crossed swords with Bailly during his service as president of the Paris Assembly when, in late April, the mayor had failed to support the Paris Assembly in its power struggle with the districts. Godard undoubtedly attributed his own ouster from the Assembly following that confrontation to Bailly's perceived duplicitous behavior. That behavior, compounded by the mayor's general high-handedness, must have left Godard with a desire to confront and weaken Bailly. Godard's opportunity came just days after his history of the Paris Assembly had been formally adopted and had received extensive praise. With Fauchet serving as president, in the Paris Assembly's last days of existence the Assembly debated the role the mayor had played in having had several citizens of Paris incarcerated on his personal order without other legal process. Following the debate, the Assembly adopted a resolution which called for sending a report to the National Assembly citing the mayor's abuse of power. It was also determined that the mayor should, like other municipal officers, be required to swear an oath affirming his probity. This requirement was clearly intended as a slight to the mayor.

Bailly was deeply offended at the very thought that he should have to take an oath. As a consequence, battle lines were drawn. With the struggle out in the open, Fauchet used the newspaper of his *Cercle Social, La Bouche de Fer* [The Iron Mouth], to stir up popular discontent over Bailly's conduct. Furthermore, Fauchet sought to take a petition to the National Assembly complaining about Bailly's comportment in the hope that the mayor would be condemned by the Assembly. However, in spite of Fauchet's efforts, the National Assembly refused to allow him to read his complaint or even to enter the Assembly chamber to submit his petition.[21]

Bailly was not a person to take a perceived offense lightly. He therefore penned a letter to the National Assembly in defense of his conduct and of his refusal to take the prescribed oath. The long letter, dated October 13, 1790 (but written on October 10), was a full-throated defense by the

21. Lacroix, *Actes de la Commune de Paris pendant la Révolution*, vol. 7, pp. 408–9.

Mayor of his conduct. He attempted to justify his actions in incarcerating individuals he deemed a danger to society, arguing that he held the ultimate police power of the city of Paris and the responsibility for its safety. He also rejected the notion that an "honest man" should have to take an oath to affirm his honesty.[22]

Fauchet determined that it was critical to answer Bailly's letter even though the Paris Assembly no longer even existed. He tasked the individual he deemed to be most qualified to do so: Jacques Godard. Godard was a natural choice to write this response. He had just received accolades for his history of the Paris Assembly. Furthermore, he and Fauchet were now close allies in the *Cercle Social* and had the same very negative view of Bailly. Godard accepted the task and undertook it with his usual skill. He gave his response to Bailly the rather long-winded title: "A Refutation of the Principles Discussed by the Mayor of Paris in his Letter to the President of the National Assembly by a Society of Citizens Legally United for the Public Welfare at the *Cirque National* and in Coalition with the General Confederation of the Friends of Truth."[23]

The letter was written in Godard's customary lawyerly style, filled with the flowery language he always used in articulating his detailed legal arguments. It began with a powerful accusation against Bailly, stating that the Mayor had "arrogated to himself the right to pronounce sentences of imprisonment" and that "ideas of civil liberty are totally foreign" to him.[24] To Godard a failure to abide by recognized legal procedures had always been unacceptable, and he did not hide his contempt for Bailly's attempt to bypass legal processes. He also denigrated Bailly's refusal to take an oath, which Bailly defended with a self-serving assertion of his own honesty. Logically and somewhat sarcastically, Godard noted that by that analysis no one would ever take an oath. Instead, he asserted, the requirement motivated people to consider carefully whether they could honorably take an oath and, therefore, engendered honesty.[25]

---

22. Ibid., 410–13.
23. "Réfutation des principes exposés par M. le Maire de Paris dans sa lettre à M. le président de l'Assemblée nationale, par une Société de citoyens légalement réunis, en vue du bien public, au Cirque national, et coalisés à la Confédération générale des Amis de la vérité." Lacroix, *Actes de la Commune de Paris pendant la Révolution*, vol. 7, 413–15.
24. Ibid., 413.
25. Ibid., 414.

Moving past his obvious dislike of Bailly, Godard turned to his more principled objections to Bailly's conduct. He reminded his readers that public authorities only had the power given to them by law. As he succinctly put it, "All public power which is not expressly given by law, is illegal."[26] He then suggested that if Bailly's approach to the exercise of municipal power was accepted, then all mayors would have unlimited power over their constituents. This, he posited, was contrary to principles of liberty. In order to protect liberty, he argued, power had to be divided among different components of government. Most significantly, echoing Montesquieu's philosophy of the separation of governmental powers, he insisted that all parts of government needed to be limited in their authority and supervised in order to prevent abuses of power. Godard concluded his "Refutation" of Bailly's positions with the clarion call that everyone's very liberty depended upon vigilance.[27] Bailly did not respond to Godard's attack.

Ultimately, the war with Bailly fell by the wayside, the victim of distractions and new tasks. In the spring of 1791, Fauchet was named Archbishop of Caen in the Calvados region of northwestern France, and left Paris. Godard's close relationship with and regard for Fauchet was such that Godard was one of the few intimates who gathered with Fauchet after he delivered his farewell sermon at the church of Saint-Roch and then, along with a large contingent of Parisians (including the Marquis de Lafayette), travelled the considerable distance to Caen to attend the ceremony that marked Fauchet's installation as Archbishop.[28] However, Fauchet's departure left the *Cercle Social* without his charismatic leadership. Shortly following Fauchet's assumption of his new duties, the group stopped meeting and effectively dissolved. But Godard would not be left without responsibilities. In fact, in the late fall of 1790 he would be given a new responsibility that would take him away from Paris and far from his struggle with the municipal authorities.

Although when the "Refutation" was published, Godard's name was not attached to it, it is quite clear that he was the author. The absence of his name on the document is consistent with the general reluctance of the *Cercle Social* to identify any of its members. The style, however,

---

26. Ibid., 415.
27. Ibid.
28. Lacroix, *Actes de la Commune de Paris pendant la Révolution*, vol. 7, 451. See also J. Charrier, *Claude Fauchet, Évêque Constitutionel du Calvados*, vol.1 (Paris: Librairie Ancienne Honoré Champion, 1909), 246–47.

is certainly Godard's and the document serves as an addendum to his previously published history of the Paris Assembly.

At around the same time, on October 8, 1790, Godard and a number of other former members of the now dissolved Paris Assembly formed yet another group, which they called the *"Société fraternelle des anciens Représentants de la Commune de Paris"* (the Fraternal Society of Former Representatives of the Paris Commune). Although, as its name implies, the group purported to continue the relationships among members of the former Paris Assembly, it appears as though it was both prompted by Fauchet and was actually intended to provide him with a group of supporters. It also had as one of its principal purposes to highlight and defend the work done by the Paris Assembly, as is demonstrated by its very first decision, namely, to send each member of the newly established *Conseil général de la Commune* (which replaced the Paris Assembly) a copy of Godard's history of the Paris Assembly.[29] Ultimately, the group of former members of the Paris Assembly merged into the *Cercle Social* and accompanied it as it faded into oblivion. Nonetheless, for a short time it must have provided Godard with a natural group of allies with whom he could reminisce about his past actions as he positioned himself for his next role in the turbulent politics of the times.[30]

During its relatively brief existence, the *Cercle Social* managed to provoke the ire of other political groups, some of which developed into ultimately far more powerful formations. In particular, the Jacobins did not take kindly to the creation of a competing club and lashed out at the group. However, a number of Jacobins, including, notably, Camille Desmoulins, stood up to defend the *Cercle Social*.[31] The scars resulting from the competition between the *Cercle Social* and the Jacobins would have its impact on future power struggles. Ultimately, some of the most prominent members of the *Cercle Social* would become the leaders of the Girondins, the more moderate political formation that would be swept

29. Lacroix, *Actes de la Commune de Paris pendant la Révolution*, vol. 7, p. 446.

30. One of the few tangible actions taken by the group was the establishment of a subscription for the purchase of a bust of Jean-Jacques Rousseau. In spite of repeated protestations of his impoverishment, Godard was among the twenty or so individuals who contributed to this effort. However, there is no indication that the bust was ever actually purchased by the group. Lacroix, *Actes de la Commune de Paris pendant la Révolution*, vol. 7, p. 452.

31. Ibid., 392, et seq.

away by the Jacobins in late 1793. Although he was far from being the only politician to have taken membership in a number of such groups, including competing groups, Godard's membership in both of the prominent clubs of the times suggests a continuation of his energetic networking and a certain hedging of his bets with respect to the future political scene and his role within it. Based upon his writings and pleadings, he clearly must have felt more at home in the embrace of the relative moderation of the *Cercle Social* than among the increasingly radical Jacobins. It is very likely that over time Godard would have sided with the Girondins in their struggle with the Jacobins, with the result that he might very well have shared their fate when the confrontation turned deadly.

In the last months of 1790, the French legal system was undergoing profound reforms. On September 30 the Parlements, which had been at the apex of the French legal system and were the judicial bodies where Jacques Godard, his father, grandfathers, and many of their ancestors had built their careers, were unceremoniously abolished. With the National Assembly as the ultimate legislature, the Parlements had already lost their primary function of registering and rendering enforceable legislative pronouncements. Now that a new judicial structure was being developed, the Parlements could no longer serve as courts of appeals. As a consequence, the vestigial Parlements were simply eliminated. The Parlements of France, which had played such an important role for hundreds of years and which had been virtually the only stalwart insitutions standing as a bulwark against the absolute monarchy, had simply become superfluous. Although the Parlements had, in large part, become insignificant once the National Assembly had evolved into France's national legislature, nonetheless, their final elimination marked a signficant step in the creation of the new French governing structure. Jacques Godard must have felt at least a twinge of emotion as the institution which had been his introduction into the world of law and revolution disappeared from the scene.

Just a little over two months after the abolition of the Parlements, as the new judicial system was being implemented, Godard became the object of a conspicuous and dramatic display of both his ambitions and the esteem in which he and his legal skills were held. On the 9th of December, 1790, the *tribunal criminel provisoire* (provisional criminal court) of Paris unanimously designated Godard "to assume the role of public prosecutor."[32]

---

32. See *Journal de la Municipalité et des Sections*, December 11–15, 1790, and *La*

This may have been a spontaneous decision at the gathering that was convened for the election since Godard was actually too young for the position (which had a minimum age requirement of thirty). Perhaps, due to the important positions that he had already held, it was assumed that Godard was actually older than he was, or at least that his considerable experience in the public sector would compensate for the age requirement. Godard was compelled to inform the tribunal of his actual age:

> As soon as he learned of the selection with which he was being honored, he indicated that he was only twenty-eight years old and that he therefore did not satisfy the requirement that one had to be thirty in order to be designated a prosecutor. The tribunal had assumed that the decree regarding the establishment of a provisional tribunal required that the individual had to have appropriate credentials, but without specifying any age. [33]

In fact, initially, Godard's age did not appear to pose an insurmountable problem and the very next day he came before the tribunal, was sworn in, and delivered extemporaneous remarks. These remarks disclosed significant elements of his character. They also reaffirmed his abiding faith in the rule of law and the importance of judicial order. Godard began with a concerted show of modesty:

> I was far from expecting the honor of sitting in this temple as one of the new ministers of the law and to have to prepare, through my opinion, the irrevocable decisions of the first judges freely and legally elected by the city. My age, in some respects, unconstitutional in the judicial order; the awesome importance of the functions that you have unfurled, the multitude of wise and experienced men who reside within the capital and who sought your attention, all seemed to distance me from your votes; and it is with surprise blended with terror that I was informed that they were directed toward me.[34]

He went on to speak of his devotion to the law and of his respect for those individuals more experienced and seasoned than himself:

> I have come, with fearful obedience, to bring you my respect, to

---

Chronique de Paris, December 17, 1790.
33. Ibid.
34. Ibid.

promise my devotion and to swear [before you] to assist you with all of my power to fulfill the holy ministry which has been confided in you. My zeal will be the supplement to my age and your good counsels will also supplement it because it is my hope, gentlemen, that you will serve as my guides, that you will watch carefully over your handiwork, that you will draw some glory from the fact that the man you have created will not be completely unworthy of you. I still have the consolation to think that my faults, if some elude me, will immediately find their cure in your wisdom and will never cause any detriment to society.

He continued with a blend of optimism and a kind of tragic prescience about the duration of his career:

Finally, I can see, just a short distance from the present moment, the end of the career in which I am today taking the first steps, and all of these considerations, explaining to me the motivations for your choice, rekindles, if you will, my courage and seems to double my strength. [35]

Seasoning his remarks with his customary flair for hyperbole, he then expressed his perspective on the role of the law in society and his view of the awesome responsibility imposed on one serving as a prosecutor:

Nonetheless, it is impossible to consider coldly the frightful functions that I am to fulfill. If an accused is guilty, it is I, who the very first, must prove to you that he really is guilty; it will be up to me to indicate to you the penalty which must be imposed upon him; it is by my mouth that will have to pass, in a certain manner, the judgment which will thereafter be pronounced by yours. Oh, may you be required to issue only a small number of these terrible judgments which cause humanity to tremble, but which social order renders necessary. May most of the accused who groan daily in prisons, have only modest errors of which to reproach themselves or only false accusations. It is then that I will embrace their defense; it is then that I will be, in a certain manner, their first counsel, and it would be very pleasant for me to see myself brought back to my usual and cherished role [as a defender of the innocent].[36]

---

35. Ibid.
36. Ibid.

Finally, reflecting thoughts that he had articulated in some of his earlier pleadings and, notably, in the case involving the Jewish complainants in Metz, Godard concluded his remarks by describing his philosophy of judicial and even prosecutorial neutrality with respect to the actual application of law in society:

> But under all circumstances, gentlemen, it will be solely the law that I will invoke; it is always its holy name that I will arrange to have echo through these vaults; my efforts against the guilty or for the innocent will never be either against the one or against the other, nor for the one against the other, but always for the law. You will never forget, gentlemen, that you have been its first ministers after having assured by your principles and by your writings the success of the revolution; and I will also never forget that it is to your goodwill and to your esteem that I owe the honorable but perilous prerogative to also be one of its instruments.[37]

Godard's remarks were particularly well received. However, when it became more widely known that he was under the age of thirty, in spite of the initial impression that this qualification for the position might be merely a kind of alternative to other prerequisites (which Godard fully satisfied) rather than a firm minimum age requirement, it quickly became apparent that the age threshold was fundamental and Godard's failure to meet it was disqualifying. As a consequence, shortly after he had been sworn into office, the National Assembly's Constitution Committee affirmed unequivocally that the prosecutor had to be at least thirty years old.[38] Godard clearly did not meet this minimum criterion. Without hesitation, Godard immediately and voluntarily stepped down from the position.

The press took note of how Godard had been named to the position and had then been forced to relinquish it. *La Chronique de Paris* of December 17 included an article about the episode:

> The court has unanimously named to fulfill the position of public prosecutor, Mr. GODARD, an attorney, former president of the Representatives of the Municipality.

---

37. *La Chronique de Paris,* December 17, 1790, p. 1402.

38. *Révolutions de France et de Brabant,* vol. 5, no. 53, p. 177; See also *Journal de Paris,* no. 346, p. 1406.

At the hearing of the following day, the 10th, Mr. GODARD was sworn in and delivered a speech that was loudly applauded. But having restated its concerns about his failure to qualify because of his age, the court determined that it was appropriate to rely upon the decision of the Constitution Committee, which has declared that, in the spirit of the decree, it is necessary to be at least thirty years of age in order to assume the position of public prosecutor.[39]

Upon Godard's resignation, Charles-Francois de La Saudade, another member of the Paris Assembly and an avocat who had previously been registered with the Paris Parlement, was immediately selected to replace him.[40] Although this episode ended as something of a fiasco for Godard's professional development, his comportment during the event earned him substantial respect from his peers and suggested that, in spite of this setback, he had a bright future. Within a matter of days, the debacle of the prosecutorial appointment would be forgotten as Godard received another important appointment, this time from the hands of the king.

---

39. Ibid.
40. Ibid.

CHAPTER 35

THE ROYAL COMMISSIONER

The reforms of the Revolution had raised expectations of dramatic change. In Paris, change was relatively apparent, albeit chaotic. However, in the provinces, change was much less evident. The peasant class continued to suffer under the yoke of obligations to the regional nobles and from the more subtle oppression of the Church. Promised land reform was especially slow to materialize.[1] As a consequence, there was a growing restiveness among peasants and particularly an unwillingness to continue making rental payments to property owners who had lost much of their standing when the nobility had relinquished its feudal rights. In the late fall of 1790, riots broke out in le Quercy in the south central Périgord region and throughout the Lot Department just to its south. Increasingly concerned about the growing insurrection, on December 13, 1790, the National Assembly, on an emergency basis, agreed to hear a report respecting the troubles in the Lot Department from one of its members, a certain Vieillard (de Coutances).[2] The Assembly then adopted a decree requesting its president to meet immediately ("*à l'instant*") with the king in order to have him investigate the causes of the disorders, appropriately prosecute those who were breaking the laws, and send commissioners to investigate the matter.[3]

---

1. See P. M. Jones, *The Peasantry in the French Revolution.*
2. Pierre-Jacques Vieillard (1756–1815), from the bailiwick of Coutances, was an avocat who served as a member of the Estates-General and then of the National Assembly.
3. *Archives parlementaires*, vol. 21, p. 458.

The next day, December 14, the king named the two commissioners who were to head to the Lot region and report on the budding insurrection. Jacques Godard was the first individual selected for the task. His designation as a royal commissioner very likely was an appointment he had actively sought. This appointment is entirely consistent with an allusion to the possibility that Godard might be seeking employment with the government in a letter to Godard, dated July 2, 1790, from his friend Defuaus.[4] In that letter, Defuaus, trying to steer Godard away from government service, wrote that "it would be a shame that with such talent in your profession [*pour votre État*], you would abandon it to throw yourself into the Administration." However, the turmoil of the times had made it more difficult for Godard to find legal work and he was no longer occupied by his political activities. Rendering services to the government was assuredly a means of generating steady income, but it could also serve to raise Godard's public profile and underpin his continuing and unassuaged political ambitions.

The second individual named by the king was Léonard Robin, a former colleague of Godard's from the Paris Assembly. Appointment of the commissioners drew some press attention. The *Mercure de France*, the newspaper edited by Suard, noted their appointment in its January 22, 1791, edition, showering special praise upon Godard, of whom the *Mercure* noted, "[he] is personally known to us by his talents and his very estimable qualities."[5] The article went on to suggest that the new commissioners were embarking upon a thankless mission, apparently with insufficient resources to accomplish their tasks. But in spite of whatever financial or logistical handicaps they may have faced, the commissioners neither hesitated nor tarried. By December 26 the two men were on their way to Cahors, the seat of the local government of the Lot Department, accompanied by Robin's son and by Pierre-Denis Durouzeau,[6] who acted

---

4. Letter dated July 2, 1790, from Defuaus to Jacques Godard. (Unpublished letter from the author's personal collection.)
5. *Mercure de France*, no. 4, January 22, 1791, p. 310.
6. Pierre-Denis Durouzeau (1766–1837) was one of Godard's colleagues at the Parlement of Paris. Just like Godard, Durouzeau came from a family of *Parlementaires*. Durouzeau's father had become a member of the Paris Parlement in 1755. The younger Durouzeau went on to have a distinguished legal career, assuming various positions with local courts in Paris. He also become a member of the *Académie des Sciences, Belles-Lettres et Arts de Rouen* during the Restoration. (See

as secretaries to the commissioners.[7] Their express mission was both to investigate the situation and to pacify the region.[8]

The mission would result in the issuance of a very long report (some one hundred thirty-nine pages in the printed version and over sixty lengthy columns in the record of the debates of the National Assembly), written entirely by Jacques Godard and one of his three most important written products.[9] Nearly four months after his appointment, Godard would submit the comprehensive description of the mission, together with an analysis of some of the major issues of concern to provincial France arising from the revolutionary changes being imported from Paris. According to the *Moniteur's* March 16, 1791 edition, Godard had promised to submit his report by March 15.[10] Ultimately, he did not file the report until early April, but its length and detailed nature explain the delay. In one of his few recorded direct encounters with Louis XVI,[11] Godard met with the king and the *"Garde des Sceaux"* on April 6, 1791 to personally hand over his report,

---

Aristide Douarche, *Les Tribunaux civil de Paris pendant la Révolution (1791–1800)*, vol. 2 (Paris: Librairie Léopold Cerf, Charles Noblet, Maison Quantin), 888.

7. *Archives Parlementaires*, vol. 25, p. 288.

8. Both Godard and Robin were members of the Electoral Assembly of Paris, charged with electing various officials to the multitude of posts which needed to be filled within the developing governmental structure. On December 24 they sent a letter to the president of the Assembly notifying him that they had been named commissioners to the Lot department by the king and that they would not be able participate in the Electoral Assembly's deliberations while fulfilling their obligations as royal commissioners. They assured the president of the Assembly that they would again participate in the Electoral Assembly's deliberations "once the purpose of our mission is completed," in order "to join our zeal to that of our colleagues." Étienne Charavay, *Assemblée Electorale de Paris 18 novembre 1790–15 juin 1791*, p. 286.

9. According to a footnote in the *Archives Parlementaires*, Robin was sent by the king on another mission to the Gard Department and, therefore, he was not available to draft the report. However, the substance of the report had apparently been agreed upon by the two commissioners before Robin left on the new mission. *Archives Parlementaires*, vol. 25, p. 309n1.

10. *Moniteur*, March 16, 1791, no. 76, p. 307.

11. As noted above, Godard had previously met the king when, on May 30, 1790, he was a member of a delegation of the Paris Assembly that thanked the king for having issued a proclamation forbidding all cockades other than the national blue, white, and red cockade. Lacroix, *Actes de la Commune de Paris pendant la Révolution*, vol. 5, p. 605.

which was submitted to the National Assembly the following month.[12] The report is hardly an objective analysis, since Godard immodestly depicts himself and his fellow commissioner as peacemakers and saviors of the revolutionary ideals in the Lot region, doubtless in his eagerness to elevate and laud the benefits that all of France was receiving from the changes wrought by the Revolution.

Godard's report is suffused with an optimism and faith in the new governing principles that had just transformed the nation. This optimism reflects the kind of naïve idealism that permeated a large portion of France's new governing elites in the early days of the Revolution. Godard sprinkled the report with aphorisms and elegant principles, reflective of his general legal philosophy and of his profound and rigid faith in legal processes. At one point he noted that if the people did not respect "the Constitution" (merely a work in progress at that time), it would be "substituting the tyrannical despotism of force for the saintly authority of the law."[13] Later in his report, he wrote that "one should only seek to vindicate one's rights before tribunals and it is criminal to seek to impose justice oneself."[14] When certain individuals asked for the liberation of prisoners, Godard and Robin told them that "indulgence is for errors, but crime must carry a penalty."[15] Reflecting his respect for the army, Godard informed his listeners in the city of Montauban that "discipline is the nerve and safeguard of the army."[16] He could also wax eloquent with his optimism for universal well-being: "the spirit of man being the same in all nations, it is equally everywhere susceptible of receiving the light which it has been offered."[17] The report also provides an important contemporary perspective on the impact the new government

---

12. By April 1791 the *Chancellerie*, which fulfilled the functions of a Ministry of Justice, had been abolished, but the new Ministry of Justice had not yet been established. This would occur only later during April 1791. Therefore, at that time, the senior official in the administration of justice was the Keeper of the Seals (*le Garde des Sceaux*). That position was then held by Marguerite-Louis-François Duport du Tertre, whose signature would ultimately appear on the decree that granted Godard's Jewish clients their equality.

13. *Archives Parlementaires*, vol. 25, 278.

14. Ibid., 282.

15. Ibid., 286.

16. Ibid.

17. Ibid., 288.

in Paris was having on the heartland of France.[18] Upon issuance of the report, the press provided complimentary coverage of Godard's and Robin's work. The *Journal de Paris* noted that "we know how happily this mission has been accomplished and the choice of the individuals to whom it was entrusted presaged this outcome."[19]

The Godard report began with a description of the logistics of the mission. According to the report, by December 26 Léonard Robin and Jacques Godard, along with their secretaries, were on their way to Cahors, the administrative center of the Lot region. Considering the difficulties of traveling within France in the late eighteenth century, they made the four-hundred-mile trip to Cahors in a rather rapid four days. The morning following their arrival, the two commissioners met with the local council that had notified the National Assembly of the insurrection. They quickly determined that the ongoing civil strife was severe. The local peasantry had attacked the national militia throughout the area and had prevailed over them. Allegedly, among the reasons for the violence was the failure of some of the peasants to pay their *rentes* to the local landlord (invariably a nobleman) and the consequent attempts by the landlords to collect those payments. It is important to remember that most peasants in the Lot region did not own their lands, but were sharecroppers. They were obligated to pay rent to a local nobleman pursuant to a single regional ground lease. If anyone defaulted, in theory, the noble landlord had to pursue all the tenants and all the tenants were liable to the landlord. This resulted in major difficulties for both the landlord and the tenants. The tenants were always at risk if any one of them failed to make his payments on time, and the landlord had the difficult legal problem of pursuing all the tenants for the default of just one.[20] One of the overriding questions that faced the commissioners was a determination of whether there was merit to the claim that the insurrection was due to a desire on the part of the peasants not to pay their *rentes*. Godard and Robin, according to the report prepared in March 1791, determined that, before they could take any action, they

---

18. A law (*"Le Code Rural de 1791"*) reforming France's agricultural practices, including certain reforms proposed by Godard in his report, was enacted on September 28, 1791, in one of the National Assembly's last acts before it was replaced by the Legislative Assembly. See J.-B. Pérot, *Le Code Rural de 1791, commenté & expliqué* (Reims: Matot-Braine, 1865).

19. *Journal de Paris*, April 25, 1791, no. 115, p. 462.

20. See generally P. M. Jones, *The Peasantry in the French Revolution*.

needed to "find in the events, in the character of the inhabitants, in the principles which must govern a people which has achieved its freedom, the true means of repressing excesses and to restore order."[21]

By January 2 the two commissioners had requested that a small force of ninety soldiers be assembled to permit "pacification" of the area. They sent a request to the Minister of War emphasizing the need to assemble this force and requesting that it be sent promptly. Godard did, however, note that he and Robin would, "to the extent possible" act "only by the empire of persuasion and have recourse only in extreme need to the military apparatus."[22] They also sent a letter to the Mayor of Cahors asking him to distribute throughout the region a declaration "whose purpose is to announce to all of the Citizens of the Department of the Lot our important mission and our views."[23] In their proclamation, Robin and Godard called upon all the residents of the region to remain calm. Then they began a series of meetings with locals in order to better understand the nature of the discontent. Having completed their preliminary research, the two commissioners began a journey that reads rather like a guided tour of the region.

They first headed north some forty miles to the town of Gourdon, which was at the heart of the most serious disturbances. Godard sought to demonstrate his belief in the fundamental decency of the people as he and Robin headed into the heart of the rebellion. Having emerged from the visit without encountering any physical danger, he later asserted that "there was nothing to fear from a people in whom one demonstrated confidence."[24] He even noted that their travels through the region around Cahors had the feeling of a triumphal march. The people were, according to Godard, eager to greet the Parisian representatives and to find out the true status of rules and regulations emanating from the National Assembly. With a kind of poetic ecstasy, he described the "signs of joy that burst out the moment that we entered within their walls."[25]

Godard then went into excruciating detail about the various aspects of the mission. He depicted every encounter with officials, with those

21. *Archives Parlementaires*, vol. 25, p. 275.
22. Ibid., 276.
23. Letter to the Mayor of Cahors from Robin, Godard, Commissaires Civils, "*envoyée par le Roi dans le Department du Lot*," January 3, 1791.
24. Ibid., 277.
25. Ibid., 278.

who were accused of rebellion, and with ordinary citizens. He vividly described events that had prompted people to challenge order and had aggravated the situation, and those that demonstrated support for the National Assembly. Confrontations and amicable discussions were given equal space. The report recounted numerous conversations virtually verbatim and Godard transcribed at considerable length each of the many speeches he and Robin delivered at various stops on their trip.

In a second section of the report, Godard described the causes of the insurrection in the Lot region.[26] He denied that a desire to undermine the new order was at the heart of the troubles. He also dismissed the notion that the people of the region did not wish to fulfill their obligations to make payments of *rentes*. Rather, he posited that there were many diverse causes for the rebellion. Among those causes were misunderstandings respecting the presence of troops in the region, and the destruction of symbolic and talismanic wooden posts, called "*mais*," that the locals had erected.[27] Most significantly, rumors—false rumors according to Godard—of counter-revolutionary activities set off a series of events that caused major disorders, with each rebellious act serving as grounds for additional such acts. Godard went out of his way to deny that there was any fundamental opposition to the Revolution. He ascribed the rebellious occurrences to actions that were either simply ill-advised or misinterpreted by the local population and which had set off chain reactions of violence.

In the last section of his report, entitled "Definitive means of strengthening tranquility in the Department of the Lot," Godard discussed methods for pacifying the region.[28] He began by suggesting, with considerable self-satisfaction, that he and Robin had been persuasive in calming spirits throughout the area. Addressing the king in his report,

---

26. "*Moyens définitifs de raffermir la tranquilité dans le département du Lot.*" Ibid., 301–5.

27. In his report to the king, Godard defined "*mais*" as being "tall and very straight trees planted in the public square or in the most spacious space of a village." They were decorated with "ribbons and were topped by a crown of laurel or a bouquet of flowers" and bore "the civic inscription: 'Long live the nation, the law, and the king.'" In some cases, they were a symbol of sedition and were sometimes believed by the locals to represent a release of villages from their obligation to pay *rentes. Archives Parlementaires*, vol. 25, p. 280.

28. Ibid., 305–9.

he wrote, "The people, Sire, docile upon hearing the voices of your commissioners, appeared convinced that the fires and pillaging were crimes
worthy of the severity of the law; they demonstrated the most sincere
repentance..."[29] Godard tried to demonstrate an even-handedness as
he ascribed the root of the problems to both peasants who had acted
unreasonably and in haste and to "former" nobles who had taken inappropriate actions against the locals.

As a concrete measure and in keeping with wise legal practice, he
proposed a change of venue for any legal proceedings initiated against
the troublemakers. The courts which had previously acted, he suggested,
were not perceived as independent—a factor that was necessary for a
court to act appropriately. On the technical point of the payment of *rentes*,
Godard proposed simplifying the process so the landlord could collect
the *rentes* from the municipality, which would in turn collect the pro rata
share from each tenant. He also proposed that the National Assembly
adopt legislation that would provide clarity in matters involving titles to
land which generated *rentes*, as well as resolve the claims of creditors and
debtors of *rentes*. To that end, he suggested that the legislation should
specify that the electors of each of the communities in the Department
should designate four commissioners to definitively ascertain the ownership of properties, the actual *rentes* due, and from whom and to whom
they should be paid. In this way, Godard thought, the payment of *rentes*,
which had long been in abeyance, could resume and strife could then
be significantly lessened. With respect to the indemnities that needed
to be paid to those who had suffered property damage as a result of the
insurrection, Godard believed that the prosecutions already in process
should be pursued and concluded. Once liability for damages had been
determined, he proposed that each of the various districts should "be in
a condition to decide that which its humanity and its justice will suggest
to it."[30]

Notwithstanding Godard's persistent faith in the people and in their
adherence to the laws promulgated by the National Assembly, he cautiously made a last practical suggestion to the king: "But, until all of
the measures that we have proposed to Your Majesty are implemented,
it is essential, in spite of the confidence to be given to the people, and

---

29. Ibid., 305.
30. Ibid., 308.

the intimate conviction that we have of its desire for order and peace, to maintain in the department a force sufficient to guarantee this same people from the instigators who might continue to obsess them."[31]

Once the field trip had been completed, the two commissioners participated in a series of conferences with local officials from all the major municipalities within the region, addressing many significant policy issues which Godard's report would emphasize, including the importance of having a fair judiciary to resolve disputes.

The mission was deemed to have been a great success. Godard and Robin were given credit for having pacified the Lot region. The *Journal de Paris* went so far as to posit that this pacification had occurred solely as a consequence of the "power of reason and persuasion" used by the commissioners. In the *Journal de Paris's* laudatory view, when they arrived everything was in disorder, but when they left "everything was peaceful."[32]

While Godard was occupied with his mission to central France and far from the political jostling in Paris, the National Assembly yet again addressed the issue of Jewish rights, albeit briefly and merely on a technical point. At its January 18, 1791 evening session, with the Abbé Grégoire presiding, Louis-Simon Martineau (who had worked with Godard while both were avocats with the Paris Parlement) went to the rostrum. He reproached the Assembly for the narrowness of its resolution of January 28, 1790, when it had confirmed the right to active citizenship to all "Portuguese, Spanish and Avignonais" Jews who possessed patent letters. He expressed his dismay that Jews "of other nationalities" who held patent letters did not qualify. As a consequence, he offered a resolution: "The National Assembly, based upon what has been disclosed by several Jews, who have been given French nationality pursuant to patent letters, and are disturbed in the exercise of their rights as active citizens, on the pretext that they are neither Portuguese, nor Spanish, nor Avignonais, declares that the decree of January 28, 1790, applies without distinction to all Jews of whatsoever nation and under whatever denomination there is, so long as they have obtained naturalization patent letters, and that all those who have otherwise satisfied the requirements established by the

---

31. Ibid.
32. *Journal de Paris*, April 25, 1791, no. 115, p. 462.

law must benefit from the rights of active citizens."[33]

An inevitable debate ensued. One (unidentified) member of the National Assembly noted that the resolution was in full conformity with the original report of the Constitution Committee. Another (Toustain de Viray[34]) disingenuously suggested that, since this was merely a matter of enforcing an existing law, the Jews needed simply to petition the king for its enforcement. But the Alsatians could not be deterred from their customary obstructionism and, when yet another member (Charles Alquier[35]) alluded to the resolution as acquiescing to the request of the Alsatian Jews for broad rights and urged that the matter be referred to the Constitution Committee, de Broglie, leader of the aristocratic Alsatians, intervened energetically. He objected to Martineau's resolution and expressed his surprise at its submission, declaring that the resolution would extend rights to the Jews of Alsace, a matter that the Assembly had "wisely chosen to adjourn for several months."[36] He then once again expressed concern that such a resolution would "raise the alarm in the provinces of Lorraine and Alsace, which assuredly do not need, at this time, the germ of heat and fermentation," a germ he ascribed to "four or five Jews"[37] (presumably Cerf Berr and his group of activists). Despite objections to de Broglie's statements, the matter was sent to the Constitution Committee for further consideration and no decision was taken either on Martineau's resolution or on the fundamental question of full citizenship. A pattern of short presentations about the Jewish matter followed by inaction was now in full evidence at the National Assembly.

May 1791 bore particular witness to this pattern, as a series of public discussions relating to matters of religion took place, but without any significant action. On May 7 Talleyrand, in his capacity as the Chairman of the Constitution Committee, reported to the National Assembly

33. *Archives Parlementaires*, vol. 22, p. 318.
34. Joseph-Maurice, Comte de Toustain-Viray (1728–1809), born in Nancy, was a career member of the military when he was elected as a member of the nobility to the Estates-General. He consistently voted with the conservative forces and emigrated from France in 1791. He returned to France in 1801, abstaining from any further political activities.
35. Charles Jean-Marie Alquier (1752–1826), from the Vendée region of western France, served both in the National Assembly and, subsequently, as a member of the National Convention.
36. *Archives Parlementaires*, vol. 22, p. 318.
37. Ibid.

regarding the use of public buildings for religious activities based upon a decree that the Paris Department had adopted on April 11. He delivered a strong plea on behalf of full religious freedom, citing the text of the Declaration of the Rights of Man and of the Citizen, as well as lofty Enlightenment principles that demanded, in his view, acceptance of all religious rites. Echoing comments heard more than a year before during the debate on rights for the Jews and expressed by Godard in the *Pétition*, he decried those who advocated "tolerance," rejecting that notion as being patronizing and unworthy of the new French social order. He nobly declared that "it is, therefore, necessary that the form of worship which they [any Frenchmen] may wish to adopt, whether it differs or not from ours, must be as free as any other form of worship, for, without this, religious liberty is but a vain name."[38] In spite of its seeming breadth, his plea was limited to an appeal for rights for Protestants and for priests who chose not to take the civil oath. (It is important to remember that Talleyrand was officially the Bishop of Autun, albeit far more of a politician than a spiritual leader.) In spite of his wide-ranging plea for the right of all to their own religious practices, not once did he mention Jews.[39]

Ultimately, after much debate, including an impassioned address by the Abbé Sieyès, the Assembly adopted a resolution which, in its first article, reasserted the right to religious liberty stated in the Declaration of the Rights of Man and of the Citizen and provided that the failure of any priest to take the civil oath could not be invoked to prevent that individual from leading a prayer service in a public church. The resolution also provided in a second article that any seditious activity (namely activity against the civil oath of the clergy by members of the clergy) could result in the closure of a religious edifice and prosecution of the person having advocated such a notion. The debate leading to the adoption of the resolution involved some of the most inspiring oratory in favor of freedom of religion of the era. But, except for a couple of passing references to synagogues, the Jews were entirely left out of both the dialogue and the resolution.[40]

Perhaps inspired by the speeches of May 7, on May 16, 1791, certain Jews from the city of Paris submitted yet another petition to the National Assembly seeking to be designated as active citizens. The minutes of the

---

38. Ibid., vol. 25, p. 645.
39. Ibid., 643.
40. Ibid., 643–53.

National Assembly for that date note in a succinct summary that "the Jews stated that they have always comported themselves as good citizens, that they have stood guard, that they have made patriotic contributions in accordance with their means; that they wish to be declared active citizens."[41] However, the tone of this latest petition was far more eloquent than the minutes would suggest and bore the striking imprimatur of Godard's approach. It contained a powerful appeal, asserting that "the civil enslavement of the Jews continues and yet, if they [the Jews] have received the right to build their synagogues, is it possible that they will not receive the title and rights of citizens? Can they be citizens in their synagogue only and outside, strangers and slaves? …Their religion is now elevated to the level of others by the universal system, not of tolerance, but of the justice which must prevail amongst a free and enlightened people. Where can now be found a reason to separate their civil status from the status of other citizens?"[42] The tone of the petition, reminiscent of the January 1790 *Pétition*, makes it reasonable to suspect that Godard was, in fact, the author of this latest submission.[43] Expeditiously, though, this petition, just like the preceding ones, was sent to the Constitution Committee for further and uncertain consideration.[44]

Yet another discussion regarding the Jewish community occurred at the morning session on May 20. The representative Théodore Vernier de Montorient, a member of the National Assembly's Finance Committee, addressed the Assembly in the name of the Committee.[45] He reported on

---

41. *Archives Parlementaires*, vol. 26, p. 98.

42. Lataulade, *Les Juifs sous l'ancien régime: leur émancipation* (Bordeaux: Imprimerie Y. Cadoret, 1906), 248.

43. In his anti-Jewish diatribe, *Les Juifs sous l'ancien régime: leur émancipation*, Lataulade affirms that this petition was, indeed, the work of Godard. Lataulade, *Les Juifs sous l'ancien régime: leur émancipation*, 248.

44. *Archives Parlementaires*, vol. 26, p. 98; cf. *Journal Général de France*, May 17, 1791, no. 135, p. 545. It is relevant to note that the National Assembly had a substantial agenda of other matters that day. In particular, it considered the matter of who would be eligible for election to the Legislative Assembly which was to replace the National Assembly on October 1. After a long and contentious debate, it is at this session that, on the motion of Robespierre, the National Assembly voted that no member of the National Assembly would be allowed to serve in the Legislative Assembly, thereby opening the door for the candidacies of an entire cadre of potential new legislators.

45. Théodore Vernier de Montorient (1731–1818), the son of an avocat, became an

the debts which had been incurred by the Jewish community of Metz. Then he submitted a proposal respecting the resolution of disputes in connection with payment of those debts for adoption by the Assembly:

> The National Assembly, having heard the report of its Finance Committee, decrees provisionally that all disputes which could result from the list established by the Jews of Metz for the purpose of recovering the sum of 439,727 l[ivres]; 12 s[ous], 6 d[eniers] from all of those whom they believe to be responsible on the stated list or from those who could appear on other lists to be drawn up, will be brought to the directory of Metz, Department of Moselle, to be decided on the basis of the opinion of the municipality, except that as a last resort the matter will be decided by the Department, if applicable; all new lists are to be certified solely by the directorate of the District of Metz. [46]

Without any discussion, the resolution was adopted.

Then, at the opening of the evening session that same day, immediately following the reading of the minutes, the secretary of the Assembly read a new petition from the Jews of Paris requesting, yet again, a grant of civil rights. This petition was signed by the Portuguese Jew, Mardoché Élie, one of the Jews who had signed the petition submitted to the National Assembly on August 26, 1789. The petition emphasized the fundamental unfairness of preventing Jews who had resided in Paris for generations ("for more than one hundred years") from receiving the benefits of citizenship that were now readily available to any stranger who had lived in France for five years. It cited the anomaly of Jews of different backgrounds living in the same buildings in Paris, but not having the same rights. The petition exuded a kind of despair, asserting that the petitioners could not "remain in this state of cruel perplexity." It warned that a failure to act might be deemed in the future as a tacit assertion that Jews should always be excluded from the French body politic. Interestingly (and as an indication that Godard had a hand in the preparation of the petition), the petition made a point of citing the support that had been generated by the various districts of the city of Paris for the grant of active citizenship

---

avocat registered with the Parlement of Franche-Comté. He was elected to the Estates-General from his native region and then remained active throughout the Revolution, specializing in matters relating to taxes. In spite of his revolutionary activities, he was elevated to a peerage by Louis XVIII during the Restoration.
46. *Archives Parlementaires*, vol. 26, p. 247.

to the Jewish residents of Paris and the presentation that had been made to the National Assembly by the delegation of representatives of the Paris Assembly (which had included Godard) on February 25, 1790.[47]

The short petition was an eloquent plea for reconsideration of the matter of Jewish citizenship. And, although it focused strictly on the Jews residing in Paris and not on all Ashkenazi Jews, the document echoed in abbreviated form many of the arguments articulated by Godard in his *Pétition*.[48] Once the petition had been read into the record, the National Assembly moved on to other business. The Assembly would not again consider matters relating to the Jews until September.

Toward the end of May, Godard's Jewish clients sought once again to raise the Jewish issue before the new municipal government of Paris in a further effort to prompt the National Assembly to act on the matter. On May 26 a new petition, once again prepared by Godard, was submitted to the Paris government.[49] In response to the petition, the new Paris governing council adopted a resolution that lauded the persistence of the Jewish community and called for the preparation and submission of a letter that would "put before the eyes [of the National Assembly] both the petition of the Jews and the wish of the municipality to press it to extend formally to the Jews of the Capital the beneficent consequences that it has already consecrated with respect to religious opinions."[50] The resolution was signed by the long-time Mayor of Paris and Godard antagonist, Jean-Sylvain Bailly. A letter was then submitted to the National Assembly, but that body did not take any immediate action. Too many other matters were already taking up its attention, most importantly the completion of the new French Constitution. Furthermore, events occurring outside of the National Assembly would yet again divert all attention from the pleas of the Jewish community.

In May 1791, Godard had an opportunity to render one more service

---

47. Oddly, the petition erroneously referenced February 24, 1790, as the date of the presentation to the National Assembly, when the actual date was the next day, February 25. (See *Archives Parlementaires*, vol. 11, pp. 698, et seq.)

48. Ibid., 253–54.

49. Sigismond Lacroix, "Ce qu'on Pensait des Juifs à Paris en 1790," in *La Révolution française: revue d'histoire moderne et contemporaine*, ed. A. Aulard, vol. 35 (Paris: 1898), 117; cf. *Moniteur*, June 11, 1791, no. 162, p. 670.

50. "Municipalité de Paris, par le maire et les officiers municipaux," *Extraits du registre des délibérations du Corps Municipal*, May 26, 1791, no. 162.

to his Jewish clients. He went to the municipal authorities of the city of Paris to solicit consent for the Jews to purchase or rent a building in which to install a new synagogue.[51] The chapel that the Jews of the center city had been using was clearly too small to accommodate all those who wished to worship there. Permission from the authorities was needed in order to convert another space into a Jewish place of prayer, and Godard managed to obtain the requisite permits without very much difficulty. A new synagogue was promptly installed in a room in an apartment on rue du Renard (not far from the existing synagogue on rue Brisemiche and very near the Louvre).[52] This was Godard's last known public service to the Jewish community. It is possible he had become discouraged by the lack of progress at the National Assembly, or he may have simply been diverted by other matters as well as by his own growing political ambitions. It is likely, however, that he continued discreetly to lobby members of the National Assembly behind the scenes and played an important role in the dramatic evolution of the Jewish struggle which would soon occur.

As the summer of 1791 waned, the deadline for the fulfillment of the commitment made back in 1789, promising that the matter of Jewish equality would be addressed during the first session of the National Assembly loomed. No concrete steps were publicly being taken to fulfill that promise and time was rapidly running out. The National Assembly was very focused on finalizing its work on the new Constitution and on organizing forthcoming elections for the new Legislative Assembly. It would not be deterred from this work. And yet, although no one was aware of it, in spite of the many demands facing the National Assembly a very tangible result on the Jewish matter was but a few months away.

---

51. *Moniteur*, June 11, 1791, no. 162, p. 628; cf. Lacroix, *Actes de la Commune de Paris pendant la Révolution*, vol. 4, p. 409.
52. Hillairet, *Dictionnaire historique des Rues de Paris*, vol. L/Z, p. 330.

CHAPTER 36

THE ROAD TO THE LEGISLATIVE ASSEMBLY

During May, the process of electing representatives to a new Legislative Assembly, which was anticipated to occur as soon as the National Assembly completed the adoption of a Constitution for the nation, actually began. On May 28 the Assembly adopted a decree which set out the criteria for the designation of active citizens authorized to vote in their local electoral assemblies for "electors" who would then in turn elect the new representatives. The very next day, the king signed the decree.[1]

Initial gatherings of the local electoral assemblies of the Paris region were scheduled to begin on June 16. All active citizens were summoned to meet in their districts where each 100 eligible voters would be entitled to one electoral representative. The districts took varying amounts of time to designate their electors. The Enfants-Rouges District which encompassed Godard's residence had 1,784 eligible voters. However, only 236 to 245 of them (depending on the day of the deliberations) actually participated in the lengthy process of selection. (Low active citizen turnout plagued all the Paris districts due to the work responsibilities of the active citizens and the cumbersome and time-consuming electoral process.) When the Enfants-Rouges District concluded its selection process on

---

1. Étienne Charavay, *Assemblée Electorale de Paris, 26 août 1791–12 août 1792, Procès-verbaux de l'Election* (Paris: Librairie Léopold Cerf, Charles Noblet, Maison Quentin, 1894), iii–xvi.

July 2, Godard had been designated as one of the electors who would go on to participate in the Paris Electoral Assembly. Among the members of the Electoral Assembly were the author Beaumarchais (most famous for writing *The Barber of Seville*), the philosophers Pastoret (who had provided Godard with some of his early information about Jewish customs) and Condorcet, the avocats Cahier de Gerville, Danton, and Léonard Robin, several prominent scientists, and a number of journalists, including Camille Desmoulins from Target's circle of friends, and Target himself.[2]

Although in June and July the process of selecting electors was in full swing, increasing turmoil throughout France caused considerable delays. The rebellion in the Lot region was merely one of the growing domestic and international crises that were increasingly plaguing France in the late spring and early summer of 1791. Among these, perhaps the most significant was the rapidly increasing antagonism between the National Assembly and the monarchy, which would become particularly acute in late June.

Louis XVI had always been resistant to challenges to the absolute monarchy posed by the Revolution. But, even more importantly, as a deeply committed Catholic he was especially troubled by the secularization of society and attacks on the Catholic Church. He increasingly realized that he would never be able to stop the momentum of the Revolution so long as he remained effectively a prisoner of the Paris populace in the Tuileries Palace. Frustrated by the situation and prodded by members of his family, and especially the queen, he plotted to find a means of escaping his royal prison. Late on the evening of June 20 Louis XVI and his family, with the help of monarchical supporters, surreptitiously left Paris in an effort to reach the royalist fortress near the border with the Austrian Netherlands at Montmédy, where many of the emigrants who had previously left France congregated. He hoped that, from there, he could return to Paris at the head of an army of loyal troops to wrest power from the revolutionary forces and reinstate the absolute monarchy. He was so confident of his ability to escape successfully that he foolishly left behind a lengthy declaration explaining his opposition to the Revolution and his intention to retake control of the government when he returned.

Louis XVI's effort to evade his Parisian captors nearly succeeded. However, the king—whose escape was slowed by his need to travel in

---

2. Ibid.

comfort, in a large and cumbersome carriage, and with too large an entourage—was recognized when the convoy stopped for refreshments a few dozen miles from the border at Ste. Ménéhould. Two of the men who had recognized the king rushed ahead on horseback to warn authorities at the next major town that the royal family was fleeing. When the king and his family arrived at Varennes, only a short distance from the border, they were prevented from leaving long enough for a warrant for the king's arrest to arrive from authorities in Paris. After having been formally identified by a judge, the king was placed under arrest and the royal family was escorted back to Paris by a revolutionary militia. As they reentered Paris surrounded by troops, the populace was demonstrably hostile. Whatever good will the king had retained in the months following the storming of the Bastille evaporated. Once they were again ensconced in their Tuileries Palace residence, the members of the royal family were now truly prisoners of the Revolution and would never again escape.[3]

The king's flight put the entire notion of a constitutional monarchy in jeopardy and caused major political turmoil. The ill-planned adventure and the declaration the king had unwisely left behind would ultimately dramatically alter the trajectory of the Revolution, undermining the moderates and giving impetus to the radicals. As an immediate reaction, the king was temporarily suspended from his constitutional position. However, the National Assembly refrained from removing him from the throne, believing that a constitutional monarchy was still a realistic possibility. For the time being, plans for a constitutional monarchy went ahead. However, in a little more than a year the monarchy would be dismantled, and just months later the king would be tried on charges of treason against the nation and executed.

In the midst of the political crisis caused by the king's flight and capture, another event shook France. Within several weeks of the attempted royal escape, in connection with a commemoration of the second anniversary of the attack on the Bastille, a large crowd gathered at the Champ de Mars, the large open field on the southeastern end of Paris where the Eiffel Tower would be erected a century later. When the crowd became unruly, representatives of the National Assembly and the Parisian authorities, specifically prompted by Godard's nemesis, the Mayor Bailly, sought to restore order. Troops fired on the crowd and dozens of participants were

---

3. See M. A. Thiers, *The History of the French Revolution*, vol. 1, 177–88.

killed.[4] The Paris populace was profoundly angered, and a growing sense of violent discontent began simmering barely below the surface.

Frustration and anger were growing, but despite the turbulence of the times certain components of daily life continued uninterrupted. The political activities of the ruling class went on unabated as France pursued its legal transformation. In particular, preparations for the elections to the Legislative Assembly stipulated by the new Constitution continued as did the need for ordinary citizens to carry on whatever remunerative activities they could. For Godard, that meant simultaneously pursuing his political activities and endeavoring to carry on a legal practice. Although the disorder spreading throughout French society, along with the increasingly severe revolutionary regulations, made record-keeping less accurate, including of the activities at the various Paris courts, it is still possible to identify certain of the legal matters that Godard took on in this period, even though he did so in a new capacity.

In September 1790, as part of the general movement to eliminate "corporatism," the *Ordre des Avocats*—a vestige of the professional guild system that had existed for hundreds of years in France and other European countries—was abolished.[5] The legal profession, as a formally recognized and organized profession, officially no longer existed. As a consequence, Godard, like all his fellow-avocats, could now only serve as a counselor, as a "*defenseur officieux*" (an unofficial defender), and not as an *avocat* since, officially, that status no longer existed. Undoubtedly, in spite of Godard's statement to his cousin of half a decade earlier that the status of "avocat" was of the least importance, the loss of his status must have been a double blow. He was clearly conscious of his position in society, and being a man of the law (*un homme de loi*) was a vital part of

---

4. Some two-and-a-half years later, Jean-Sylvain Bailly, who was accused of having ordered the troops to fire upon the crowd, was held liable for the deaths of those killed and was sent to the guillotine. His execution was marked by particular cruelty with the assembled crowd pelting him with rocks and insulting him while he was compelled to wait for hours as, at the demand of the mob, the guillotine was dismantled and moved from its original location on the Champ de Mars to be reassembled in a less "sacred" location, where the execution could proceed. In spite of the humiliation and physical harm inflicted on him, Bailly retained his composure throughout the ordeal and went to his death with dignity.

5. David Bell, *Lawyers and Citizens*, 190; cf. Camus, *Lettres sur la Profession d'Avocat* (Brussels: Librairie de Jurisprudence de H. Tarlier, 1833), 65. Cf. Hervé Leuwers, *L'Invention du Barreau Français*, 1660–1830, p. 255.

his identity. However, with the law adopted by the National Assembly on January 29, 1791, giving every citizen the right to act as counsel in legal disputes, a component of that status had simply been eliminated. Furthermore, Godard's very economic survival was in jeopardy. In theory, the *defenseurs officieux* were not allowed to receive compensation for their services. Furthermore, Godard and other former *avocats* were now faced with unregulated competition from all the would-be avocats in French society. In spite of the new legislation, although many of his former avocat colleagues abandoned the profession, Godard, and some of those former colleagues, continued their law practices as best they could under the new legislation.[6] As it would rapidly become apparent, the complexity of the French legal apparatus remained sufficiently daunting that, in spite of the official abolition of the profession, the former avocats continued to dominate the legal system, especially with respect to complex civil cases. Less than a decade later, the profession of avocat was reauthorized and resumed its role in French society.[7]

As part of his effort to earn a living while relying on his legal skills, toward the end of the tumultuous spring of 1791 Godard served as the unofficial counsel of an individual named Moni in a legal battle with a member of the nobility named Villemain. The litigation revolved around the consequences arising from the extinguishment by the National Assembly of yet another symbol of status: noble privileges. Godard's client, Moni, had sought to become a nobleman, a status that could, under certain circumstances, actually be acquired in pre-Revolutionary France. One method of doing so was through a payment to a person having the status of "*secrétaire du Roi*" (secretary to the king), who had a limited capacity to sell noble status. In 1782, for the sum of 18,000 *livres*, Moni, a notary, had purchased from Villemain a life estate or the usufruct (*usufruit*) in a portion of certain of Villemain's rights, which carried with them economic benefits in the form of various payments. After the passage of twenty years, these rights would provide the beneficiary with the same attributes of nobility as those held by the grantor.

In August of 1789 all privileges of this sort had been abolished by the National Assembly. Villemain received a payment of 120,000 *livres* in

6. Leuwers, *L'Invention du Barreau Français, 1660–1830*.
7. Nicolas Derasse, "Les Défenseurs officieux: une défense sans barreaux," in *Annales Historiques de la Révolution française*, October–December, 2007, vol. 350, pp. 49–67.

compensation for the abolition of his rights as *secrétaire du Roi*, but Moni found himself without the cash flow he thought he had purchased and also found himself deprived of any hope of attaining the now abolished noble status. He did not contest the loss of his expectation of that status, but he demanded compensation for the loss of his economic benefits. Godard argued on behalf of Moni that the outcome of the change in status of the parties was clearly inequitable. Villemain had received the benefits of the compensation for the abolition of his title and Moni had received nothing. Moni's claim, as Godard articulated it, was that, without the assistance of the courts, "the annuitant [Moni] would have lost everything and the owner [Villemain] would have won everything." To Godard, "such a system [was] the height of iniquity and of absurdity."[8]

Relying on principles of Roman law as well as on French treatises, Godard argued that, if the source of the annuity ceased, then it should continue on the basis of the replacement of that source. He took as his example a house and noted that if that house, from which the annuitant had rights to receive a cash flow, was destroyed, the annuitant had a claim on the cash flow generated by whatever its replacement might be. Similarly, he argued that "the usufruct of an office [the role of secretary to the king, in this instance] which is abolished, is transported to the compensation."[9] Villemain's counsel claimed that all that had been transferred was a fractional interest in the "title" and nothing further. Godard vehemently rejected this argument, stating that, if that was the case, then Moni "should never have received any emoluments." However, the agreement between the parties assured Moni that he would receive various specific payments arising from some of the privileges attached to Villemain's position. Godard then put forward his strongest argument. He noted that Villemain had reserved for himself only a modest portion of the emoluments of his office, but that the National Assembly had awarded him an amount that reflected the value of the total amount of the emoluments, including those that had been transferred to Moni. As a consequence, Godard insisted, Moni was entitled to his share of the payment from the National Assembly. Otherwise, Villemain would receive an unjust enrichment (a violation of the equitable principle that "no one can enrich himself to the detriment of another").[10]

8. *Journal des Tribunaux, et Journal du Tribunal de Cassation; réunis; par une Société d'Hommes de Loi*, Friday, June 3, 1791, no. 37, p. 100.
9. Ibid., 103.
10. Ibid., 106.

Villemain defended himself on the grounds that a *force majeure* had deprived the parties of their bargain and that, furthermore, if Moni had died before the passage of twenty years, he would not have benefitted from the critical portion of the bargain, i.e., becoming a noble. On May 28, 1791, the Court rendered its decision. It ordered Villemain to set aside a portion of the National Assembly's award of 120,000 *livres* for the benefit of Moni so as to generate as much revenue as the original payment of 18,000 *livres* would have generated for so long as Moni remained alive, whereupon the sum would revert to Villemain or his heirs. Alternatively, Villemain was given the option to reimburse Moni the sum of 18,000 *livres* with interest thereon from the date upon which Moni had made demand on Villemain for payment. Villemain was also ordered to pay all the costs of the proceedings. The result was a complete victory for Godard and set an important precedent respecting obligations arising in connection with the abolition of privileges.

At around the same time, Godard undertook the defense, again as a *défenseur officieux*, of the owners of the prestigious and widely read *Journal de Paris* in an appellate procedure that also related to the extinguishment of privileges, albeit of a somewhat different kind. The *Journal de Paris* case arose in the context of an agreement between the owners of the *Journal de Paris* and a Mme. Fauconnier, who had the official and exclusive right to the publication of the obituaries of personalities at the Royal Court in *Le Journal des deuils de Cour et du Nécrologie des homes célèbres*. In 1782 she assigned this right to the *Journal de Paris* in consideration of an annual payment of 4,000 *livres*, to be transfered upon her death to two other individuals, a M. Palissot and a Mme. Devaux. The contractual provision respecting the transfer of Mme. Fauconnier's right expressly provided that the obligation to make the annual payment would cease in the event that, contrary to the wishes of the parties, the exclusive right to publish the detailed announcements of deaths at the Court and of other prominent individuals was to come to an end. Since in August of 1789 many privileges, including the exclusive rights to publish certain information, had been abolished by the National Assembly, the *Journal de Paris* refused to continue to pay the annual amount. Palissot and Devaux brought an action at the court at the Châtelet against the *Journal de Paris* for non-payment of the sums allegedly due. The judges at the Châtelet, on May 18, 1790, ordered the implementation of the agreement and the *Journal de Paris* to pay 1,000 *livres* for the prior quarter.

The owners of the *Journal de Paris* engaged Godard to represent them in an appeal to the Tribunal of the second *arrondissement*. Godard argued that the underlying basis of the transfer had been the "reunion of a privilege for a privilege" and since "privileges no longer exist, there is no basis, no cause, no motive, everything which bound the parties is dissolved... The condition under which the agreements were made have swooned away, the agreement can no longer be implemented."[11] He also resorted to a careful textual analysis of the agreement and noted that it expressly recited that it was not the sale to the *Journal de Paris* that had been arranged, but the transfer of the "privilege," a word that the agreement repeated multiple times. Godard then went into excruciating detail deconstructing the plaintiffs' arguments. He had a worthy opponent in Jean-François Fournel. Fournel, as the digest reporting on the case noted, did not yield an inch. He resorted to an equitable argument—namely that regardless of the actual words of the agreement, the *Journal de Paris* had benefitted immensely from the arrangement with Mme. Fauconnier by a dramatically increased readership, and that it would simply be dishonest to deprive her successors of the modest payments that constituted consideration for those important benefits—to undermine Godard's textual ones. Nonetheless, on July 22 the Tribunal adopted Godard's logic and decided that the obligation to pay could not survive the extinguishment of "the undertaking which was the object of the contract," namely the transfer of an exclusive right. Thus, the court declared that the defendants no longer had an obligation to make the annual payment. Godard had completely prevailed.[12]

During the busy summer of 1791, Godard would be involved in yet one more major legal matter. This time he assumed the role of a lobbyist rather than an avocat (or a *defenseur officieux*, as it would have had to have been at the time). The matter involved conflicting claims, similar to the multitude of such claims that clogged the law courts and the legislature due to the abolition of the various rights and privileges that had thrived during the Ancien Régime, but which had been eliminated

---

11. *Journal des Tribunaux, et Journal du Tribunal de Cassation; réunis; par une Société d'Hommes de Loi*, Friday August 12, 1791, no. 57, pp. 422–23.

12. Ibid., 426–27; cf. Casenave, *Les Tribunaux civils de Paris pendant la Révolution [1791–1800]*, documents inédits recueillis avant l'incendie du Palais de justice de 1871, vol. 1 (Paris: L. Cerf/Noblet, 1905–1907, pp. 94–95); *La Gazette des Nouveaux Tribunaux*, vol. 3, p. 132. See also *Moniteur*, Saturday August 27, 1791, no. 239, p. 490.

by the Revolution. The claims being defended by Godard were based upon the establishment of a series of eight *"fondations,"* (foundations), arguably the equivalent of Anglo-Saxon trusts, which had been created in the 1730s by a nobleman and legal scholar from Godard's native region of Burgundy, Melchior Cochet de Saint-Valier.[13] Ostensibly the trusts were intended to assist less fortunate members of the nobility of the Provence region. Seven of the trusts were expressly intended to provide revenue to persons in difficult straits who were required to be, in the words of the texts establishing the trusts, "true nobles." The eighth was more generic and was intended to provide funds for the benefit of churches and the giving of religious instructions, but without any requirement that nobles specifically benefit. Each of the trust instruments provided that, if the purpose of the specific trust was frustrated and became impossible to fulfill, the corpus of each of the trusts should revert to Cochet's descendants.

When titles of nobility were abolished in 1790, members of the Cochet family invoked the reversionary clauses of the trusts and asserted that they were now entitled to the corpuses. On the other hand, public authorities in Paris, where the trusts were managed, realized that the abolition of titles of nobility provided them with an opportunity to declare that the substantial amounts of funds held in each of the trusts were now public property. Thus, the city of Paris seized the corpuses of the Cochet trusts and placed them in an escrow fund, at least temporarily, pending the issuance by the National Assembly of a law clarifying their status.

In July 1790 the National Assembly attempted to address generically the issue of trusts whose purposes could no longer be fulfilled, but the text of the 1790 decree focused specifically on trusts that had religious objectives. This focus was not surprising. Many trusts had been established to benefit the Church and its activities and, in light of the prior fall's decision to nationalize Church property, it was logical that the resources intended to benefit the nationalized properties should themselves be nationalized. The Assembly had determined that if such a trust's purpose

---

13. French law did not then and does not now provide for the concept of trusts as they have developed in Anglo-Saxon jurisdictions. However, the *"foundations"* that were in question in this matter are very much analogous to Anglo-Saxon trusts and, therefore, for the sake of ease of explanation of this case, I have taken the liberty of referring to them as such.

was now impossible to fulfill, the trust would come under the control of the government, "notwithstanding all clauses, even reversionary clauses, incorporated in the trust instrument."[14]

In spite of the July 1790 decree, Cochet family members sought to claim the corpuses of the seven trusts intended to benefit nobles, but not the one intended to benefit the Church. In light of the broad language against the enforcement of reversionary clauses in the 1790 decree, their chances of success seemed remote. However, on May 5, 1791, the Assembly adopted another decree which, while it confirmed that current trust distributions could continue, acknowledged that additional legislation would be necessary to fully clarify the enforceability of express provisions of a trust instrument. It provided and decreed that no other disposition could proceed pending a definitive law to be issued by the Assembly. Specifically, the new decree indicated that the prior decree was merely a provisional law and that the Assembly would have to issue additional legislation.[15] The Cochet family now had a new impetus to try to recover the seven trust corpuses. The National Assembly had effectively recognized that the 1790 decree that addressed trusts exclusively for the benefit of religious causes did not fully resolve the issue of who could be entitled to the corpuses of the seven trusts established by Cochet to benefit members of the nobility. So long as no new legislation was adopted, the Cochet family could ask the courts to determine their rights based upon the existing decree, which left the issue open to a favorable interpretation for the family.

The Cochet family then hired Godard to act as their advocate to lobby members of the National Assembly. Godard's objective was to prevent the National Assembly from adopting a law that would definitively deprive the Cochet family of their right to invoke the reversionary clause, or, alternatively, to have the National Assembly adopt a law that reaffirmed the enforceability of reversionary clauses such as the ones incorporated in the seven frustrated trusts. Godard apparently drafted an initial set of brief observations immediately following the issuance of the May decree. However, he and his clients determined that a more concerted and dramatic effort needed to be pursued, reminiscent of Godard's effort on behalf of his Jewish clients, albeit on a smaller scale.

14. *Archives Parlementaires*, vol. 16, p. 615.
15. *Archives Parlementaires*, vol. 25, p. 612.

Godard then drafted and published a fourteen-page petition he entitled "New Observations addressed to the National Assembly by the Family of Mr. Cochet de Saint-Valier."[16]

The petition began with a precise and systematic description of the Cochet trusts, including an emphasis on the fact that seven of the eight trusts were intended to benefit nobles. Then, demonstrating his full awareness of the political climate of the times and his ability to use that climate to his clients' benefit, Godard made a spirited attack on the notion of special privileges for a noble class. He drew a distinction between the "enlightened beneficence" that motivated the creation of the last trust benefiting religious and educational objectives and the "extraordinarily purile homage to vanity" that he deemed to have motivated the creation of the other trusts, established for the benefit of "nobles." Godard ridiculed the grantor's insistence that the beneficiaries of seven of the trusts had to demonstrate with certitude their status as members of the nobility. With a cadence worthy of Shakespeare's Marc Antony at Caesar's funeral, Godard repeated again and again that the beneficiaries had to be "truly noble," "nobles without qualification," and "nobles whose nobility is established with certitude," effectively turning the word "noble" into an object of ridicule.[17]

Godard then turned his attention to the specific language of the instruments that had established the trusts and noted that in each case, it was expressly stated that the terms of the trust could not be altered in any manner. Here, he was trying to avoid an equivalent of the Anglo-Saxon cy-près (from the old French: the next closest) doctrine which can permit trusts whose purposes have been frustrated to be reinterpreted by courts to achieve an alternative and closely related objective. He also quoted the very unambiguous reversionary clause of the trusts, which expressly provided that the trusts could not "due to any eventuality be converted to a different purpose," and that in the event of an impossibility to achieve the stated purpose of the trusts, "they were to be extinguished" and that the corpuses "were to be returned to his family."[18] The evident conclusion, Godard asserted, was that once the status of "noble" had been abolished,

---

16. *Nouvelles Observations adressées à l'Assemblée Nationale par les Parens de M. Cochet de Saint-Valier*, J. Godard, Rédacteur (Paris: Imprimerie des Amis de l'Ordre, 1791).

17. Ibid., 3–4.

18. Ibid., 12.

it was no longer possible to comply with the terms of the trusts and the principal amounts held by the trusts had to be returned to Cochet's family.

In response to the proposal that the National Assembly should further legislate on the matter and extend the prohibition on reversions of trust assets beyond the world of religious trusts, Godard invoked the notion of the separation of legislative and judicial powers. Reminding the members of the Assembly that they had both extinguished titles of nobility and adopted legislation regarding *"fondations,"* he urged them to refrain from adopting more legislation and to leave it up to the courts to interpret the import of the actions of the national legislature. He rejected the notion that the issue of determining the validity of the Cochet trusts' reversionary provisions should be decided by a clarifying decree from the National Assembly. Acting in this manner, would, he asserted, deprive the Cochet family of the opportunity to be heard by an impartial judge. It would, he insisted, be an intrusion by the legislature on the prerogatives of the courts. Rather, he argued, the courts should make the just decision, namely the return of the trust assets to the Cochet family based upon the existing legislation and principles of elementary justice. Would it not be the height of injustice, Godard insisted, to declare to be national assets those assets which the Grantor had properly and in keeping with the then applicable law declared to belong to his family? He concluded by asserting his profound belief in justice through the application of law, stating, "The first duty of a great people is to be just: and justice consists principally in respecting all of the agreements made under the authority of the laws..."[19]

The issue of the validity of reversionary clauses in private trusts was presented to the National Assembly just days before it was about to go out of existence. On September 26, 1791, the representative Armand-Gaston Camus, speaking in the name of the Assembly's Committee on Sales and Pensions, proposed new legislation to clarify the issues that had been raised by Godard.[20] The proposal was intended to place the assets of trusts in the hands of the government for the purpose of administering and disposing of them, declaring them to be national assets. But this was not at all what Godard had sought. As the debate on Camus' proposal began, the first speaker, echoing Godard's arguments, immediately noted that by

19. Ibid. 13.

20. Armand-Gaston Camus (1740–1804) was an avocat who headed the Archives Committee in the National Assembly and became the founder of the French National Archives.

passing this legislation the National Assembly would effectively deprive
the Cochet family of the Cochet trust corpuses. Thus, those individuals
would be deprived of assets without the opportunity to be heard before
the courts. Camus retorted that he was not interested in any specific matter, but that his proposal was intended to benefit the entire nation. Then,
obviously well aware that the members of the National Assembly had
been given the petition regarding the Cochet trusts, he addressed the issue
of those trusts directly. He postulated that when the National Assembly
had abolished titles of nobility, it had not caused nobles to disappear; it
had merely declared that the nobility no longer existed as a class—not as
individuals. This suggested that the purposes of the trusts were not being
frustrated. As a result, he argued, the legislation would not deprive the
Cochet claimants of anything, since they were not entitled to anything.
Another representative, Jean-Nicolas Démeunier, then urged that the proposed law be amended to "provide citizens the right to assert their claims
before the courts."[21] There was a surge of support from the floor for such
an amendment and Camus, as a result, agreed to modify his proposal to
provide that the Assembly reserved to the legislature the right to adopt
rules that would be developed as a consequence of specific trust clauses.
Camus's proposal as so amended passed, effectively deferring consideration of the very specific matter of interest to Godard and his clients.[22] It
was left to a later time to develop specific regulations to fully address this
matter. With only four days left in the life of the Assembly, it was almost
certain that this would not be soon and that the matter would not be
decided by the National Assembly, but would have to be considered by
the new Legislative Assembly. Much time would assuredly elapse before
a more precise law would be developed that would address the validity
of reversionary clauses in trust arrangements, leaving open the possibility
that such clauses could be enforced. Godard had won a partial victory for
his clients. Their claims remained viable, at least for the moment.

While the legislative outcome (or the deferred outcome) left the door
open for a successful result to Godard's efforts, the courts do not appear to
have ever rendered a decision in favor of the Cochet family. Nonetheless,
Godard had every reason to be optimistic about what he had achieved.

21. Démeunier (1751–1814) was, of course, the individual who presided over the
tumultuous session of the National Assembly at which it was voted to confirm
the civil rights of the Sephardim.
22. *Archives Parlementaires*, vol. 31, pp. 343–45.

Within a couple of years, however, the National Convention would put a very unfavorable end to the matter. On May 10, 1795, the Convention adopted a decree that specifically targeted the Cochet trusts, decreeing that the trusts were being definitively terminated, provided only that the then current recipients of pensions and other assistance could continue to receive those pensions and that assistance. At such time as the existing beneficiaries were no longer receiving benefits, the trust corpuses were, according to the Convention's legislation, to be liquidated for the benefit of the nation.[23]

In the short term, Godard's logical presentation and persuasive writing had won the day. But logic and elegant arguments would soon yield to radical ideology, and the ultimate objective that he had sought in this, the last of his important legal writings, eluded him. Notwithstanding that failure, we are left with yet one more thoughtful, well-reasoned, and principled legal document crafted by a brilliant young avocat, whose career seemed so very promising and filled with untapped potential.

---

23. *Collection Générale des Décrets rendus par la Convention Nationale avec la mention de leur date. Floréal An III* (Paris: Chez Baudouin, 1795), 127.

CHAPTER 37

ELECTIONS FOR THE LEGISLATIVE ASSEMBLY

With the summer of 1791 drawing to a close, just a couple of weeks after filing the Cochet pleading, on August 22 Godard was designated as the advisor for the Chevalier Charles de la Rivière. De la Rivière was a fifty-three-year-old native of Quincy in Champagne, who lived near Godard in the Marais at 56 rue Ste. Anne. Godard's role was to assist de la Rivière in connection with an interrogation at the radical Club des Cordeliers. The club, dominated by Jean-Paul Marat and Danton, had organized the demonstration at the Champ de Mars in July to commemorate the anniversary of the taking of the Bastille. The heavy loss of life that occurred at that time had incensed the club members, who sought to conduct an extra-judicial investigation into the event.[1] Godard seems merely to have acted in this matter as a protector of de la Rivière's rights—as a *defenseur officieux*—during the inquiry into the violence of the Champ de Mars events. It is not clear that the interrogation of de la Rivière was further pursued after the initial questioning. In any event, even if it had been, Godard would not have had very much time to assist de la Rivière due to other pressing circumstances.

In the midst of the revolutionary turmoil of late summer 1791, on August 26 the Paris Assembly of Electors met in the great hall of the Palace of the

---

1. Albert Mathiez, *Le Club des Cordeliers pendant La Crise de Varennes et Le Massacre du Champ de Mars, Documents en Grande Partie Inédits* (Librairie Ancienne: H. Champion, Ed. 1910).

Archbishop of Paris, located on the Ile de la Cité in the area between Notre Dame and the Seine, to begin its deliberations. The deliberations were
intended to lead to the election of representatives to the new Legislative
Assembly that was to be created pursuant to a Constitution that had been
debated since 1789 but had not yet been finally adopted.[2] On September 3,
after a lengthy deliberative process during which Godard's mentor Target
had played a major role, a new Constitution was approved by the National
Assembly and sent to the king for his signature. The king, who had amply
demonstrated his unwillingness to serve as a constitutional monarch when
he had fled Paris earlier in the summer, came to the National Assembly
chamber on September 14, and amidst much acclamation reluctantly af-
fixed his signature to the Constitution and with equal reluctance pledged
his support for it. For the first time in its history, France now had a formal,
written Constitution. Although the Constitution's complexity seemed to
doom the document from its very inception, the process of implementing
its legislative component proceeded in earnest. The steps for the election
of representatives to the new Legislative Assembly moved rapidly toward
an electoral conclusion.

Long before the king had ratified the new Constitution, the political
establishment had turned its full attention to the election of a new assembly, which was to be called the National Legislative Assembly or,
more commonly, the Legislative Assembly.[3] In a remarkably unselfish
(but arguably foolish) act, the members of the National Assembly had,
at Robespierre's urging, incorporated into the Constitution a provision
that specified that no individual who had been a member of the National
Assembly could stand for election to the Legislative Assembly.[4] This provision created an opening for many ambitious individuals who had been
watching the ongoing political changes from the sidelines, but were eager

2. Étienne Chavaray, *Assemblée Electorale de Paris, 26 août 1791–12 août 1792,
Procès-verbaux de l'Election*, xi.
3. *L'Assemblée Legislative*.
4. The decision to exclude all the members of the National Assembly from eligibility for the new Legislative Assembly deprived the new Assembly of the only
group of experienced legislators then available. Some of the subsequent failures
of the Legislative Assembly can assuredly be ascribed to the complete absence of
any legislative experience of its members. Combined with all the dysfunction in
the governing structure and the blatant hostility of the executive (the king), this
dearth of experience would, within less than one year, ultimately prove fatal to the
Legislative Assembly and the monarchy.

to participate more directly.

Even as he pursued his legal and lobbying practice, Godard was edging closer to a new phase of his life. He had flirted with running for a seat in the Estates-General in the spring of 1789 but had not done so. Now, he saw his opportunity. He determined to become a member of the new Legislative Assembly. As an active citizen and as a member of the Paris Assembly of Electors he was fully eligible to be elected.[5] He was also well known through his comparatively long service as a member of the Blancs-Manteaux District Assembly, where he had served as a president. More importantly, he was well known as a former member and former president of the Paris Assembly. His role as the defender of the Jews and as the chronicler of the Paris Assembly were particularly well recognized and would also serve him well.[6] Finally, his adherence to certain political groups would prove to be decisive in this pursuit.

As the Paris electors began their meetings in August, it rapidly became obvious that there were fundamental and evolving divergences in the political positions of the over eight hundred electors. These growing differences caused serious divisions within the Assembly of Electors as they planned the process for selecting representatives to the Legislative Assembly. Initially some of the more radical electors began to meet regularly in a separate room at the Palace of the Archbishop, where the full Assembly was holding its meeting. This group became known as the *Club de l'Evêché*.[7] Rapidly, the meetings of the Assembly of Electors came to be dominated by a cadre of vocal and increasingly radicalized individuals, which alienated many of the more moderate and conservative electors. As a result, some of those latter electors began to separately engage in their own strategizing for the elections to the Legislative Assembly. They first met in a hall of the Palace of Justice, which rapidly became too small to accommodate them. Eventually, they would move to the *Sainte-Chapelle*, the beautiful gothic chapel built by Louis IX in the thirteenth century to house a purported fragment of the true cross and which was also located within the precincts of the Palace of Justice. Following

---

5. Being an elector was not a prerequisite to being elected to the Legislative Assembly, but it was assuredly an advantage since it meant that the individual could attend all the deliberations of the Assembly of Electors and engage in politicking during those sessions.

6. Chavaray, *Assemblée Electorale de Paris*, xxxii.

7. Club of the Bishop's Palace.

their move, the members of the group, which included some 375 electors (or roughly two-fifths of the electors), began calling themselves the *Club de la Sainte-Chapelle* to distinguish themselves from the radicals meeting at the Palace of the Archbishop.[8]

Godard joined the *Club de la Sainte-Chapelle*. This was undoubtedly due to his generally moderate to conservative political orientation, but it was also a wise tactical move.[9] With this club constituting a large voting bloc, any Paris elector wishing to be elected to the Legislative Assembly had a far better chance of election as a member of the group and with its support.[10] Godard was an enthusiastic member of the club. Jean-Joseph Hurel, also an elector and, like Godard, from the Enfants-Rouge District, in recanting his membership in the club in 1793, at a time when moderation was viewed as a dangerous attribute, would ascribe his brief membership to Godard's influence. He would write that he had been resistant to joining until "[a] Citizen (M. Godard) particularly honored by the Confidence of the Section insisted."[11] Godard was both a strong advocate for the club and ultimately an important beneficiary of the club's support.

Throughout France, the electoral process proved to be slow and cumbersome. Every regional Assembly of Electors went through a series of elections, one for each of the 745 representatives to be elected to the Legislative Assembly. The Paris Assembly of Electors followed the general pattern, holding numerous meetings in order to select the twenty-four representatives and eight alternates to which the Paris Department was entitled. They began the process of deliberating on August 26. The very next day, in keeping with long-standing tradition, all the electors participated in a mass at Notre Dame conducted by the archbishop, Gobel, who had been elected to his ecclesiastical post less than six months before. Then,

---

8. Ibid., *Compte rendu des séances de l'assemblée électorale de 1791 par Nau-Deville*, 20, et seq.

9. It was a wise tactical move, but it would have had a nefarious impact on Godard had he lived longer. In 1792, following the overthrow of the monarchy, as the National Convention—the new legislative body—was being constituted, individuals who had been members of the *Club de la Sainte-Chapelle* were prohibited from running for seats in the Convention because they were deemed to be far too conservative, even anti-revolutionary.

10. Melvin Edelstein, *The French Revolution and the Birth of Electoral Democracy* (London & New York: Routledge Taylor & Francis Group, 2014), 249.

11. Jean-Joseph Hurel, *Aux Citoyens de la Section du Marais ci-devant Enfans-Rouges* (Paris: Mayer & Compagnie, rue St. Martin, 1793).

the Assembly engaged in organizational activities, beginning with the verification of the electors' credentials and the review of claims from some who had not been selected. The next order of business was the selection of an official printer for the Assembly, a somewhat delicate matter since nine printers were among the Assembly's members. Having concluded the various organizational tasks and set aside certain preliminary political skirmishes, the Assembly of Electors finally began the actual process of electing representatives to the Legislative Assembly on September 1.

In the initial rounds of elections, a number of individuals with whom Godard had been associated were elected. Garran de Coulon, one of the founders of the *Cercle Social* and a close collaborator of Fauchet, was the very first elected. The third person selected to serve was Pastoret, who would be elected president of the Electoral Assembly a few days later. But during these early days of voting, Godard's name did not come up. He was, however, selected as an alternate vote-counter on September 11, a small step toward the center of the local political stage.

In spite of Godard's active participation in the electoral activities from the very beginning of the process in August, it was not until mid-September that he began to emerge as a serious candidate. On September 12, in the first round of voting in which he received any votes, he received a mere two. The next day, in a round of voting which resulted in the election of Brissot, Godard's vote total increased to six. On September 15 he received fifteen votes, and the next day, when Hérault de Séchelles, the long-time avocat-général who had supported Godard's position in the Julien Baudelle case, was elected, Godard received sixteen votes. September 17 saw Godard's vote total increase dramatically to thirty-nine. Then, in the balloting held on September 19, which resulted in François-Valentin Mulot, who had been so laudatory of Godard and his Jewish clients back in January of 1790, being elected as the fifteenth deputy, Godard saw his vote total surge to 287, bringing him very close to election.

Finally, the next day, on Tuesday, September 20, at the twenty-fifth session of the Electoral Assembly, although some twenty individuals (including Godard's colleague Léonard Robin, and the fiery revolutionary Georges-Jacques Danton who had received forty votes the previous day) were among those receiving votes, the contest had been reduced essentially to a race between Godard and the renowned philosopher and former lover of Amélie Suard, Nicolas de Condorcet. Condorcet, a long-time republican and now a member of the more radical *Club de l'Evêché*, had, at this late date, emerged for the first time as a serious contender. However, Godard's affiliation with the *Club de la Sainte-Chapelle* was assuredly helpful, probably even decisive, and on this day he emerged victorious.[12] The number of electors present (608) set the minimum number of votes required for election at 305. In two rounds of voting, Godard defeated Condorcet by 343 votes to 119 (with Danton receiving fifteen votes), thereby becoming the sixteenth elected representative from the Paris Department. The minutes of the Assembly noted that:

> The result of the vote was announced by one of the general vote counters, who declared that M. Godard, man of laws and elector, had obtained 343 votes, thirty-eight more that the absolute plurality set at 305. The president, in accordance with this result, declared, in the name of the Assembly, that M. Jacques Godard, man of laws, unofficial defender, elector from the Enfants-Rouges District, twenty-nine years of age, residing at rue des Blancs-Manteaux, no. 56, had become a deputy from the Department of Paris to the legislative corps.[13]

Godard, who was present at the Assembly session, then requested to be heard. He ascended to the podium to make a statement that could be characterized as a declaration of victory (although it also sounded as though he was trying to convince his audience that he merited his election). His remarks appropriately also served as a kind of summary of his entire legal and public career, as well as of his political philosophy. These remarks would be his last public address.

He began by asserting his devotion to the ideals of the Revolution:

> Gentlemen, I have loved and defended liberty before the Revolution; I have not ceased to defend it since this memorable era. This uniform conduct on my part throughout my existence is a certain guaranty for you of my future conduct in the legislative body.[14]

---

12. The more radical political elements among the Paris electors, including Jacques-Pierre Brissot (who, as a member of the Paris Assembly had favorably reviewed the letter from Debourge regarding the status of the Jews), were clearly not very happy with Godard's defeat of the far better-known Condorcet and squarely ascribed the victory to "intrigues" by the conservatives associated with the *Club de la Sainte-Chapelle*. J.-P. Brissot, *Correspondance et Papiers*, ed. Claude Perroud (Paris: Librairie Alphonse Picard & Fils, 1911), vol. 2, p. 209.
13. Ibid.
14. Étienne Charavay, *L'Assemblée Électorale de Paris, 26 août 1791–10 août 1792*,

He went on to assure the electors that he was not an opportunist and that he would not alter his behavior as a result of his election to the Assembly:

> By linking in this manner in your thoughts the present and the future, you will not have to fear, Gentlemen, that I will resemble those men who, formerly at the feet of the ministers of the various powers of the time, became friends of the Revolution in the same spirit of servitude which dominated them previously, and are incapable of ever having an independent attitude and of being proud of liberty. Unwavering in my principles, I will defend with constant ardor the interests of the people and I will attach myself with equal attention to thwart the crowd, still far too numerous, of schemers and the ambitious who abuse the sacred name of the people to serve their own passions and to become, in turn, the oppressors.[15]

Consistent with his remarks of September 1789 at the blessing of the flags at the church of the Blancs-Manteaux, Godard affirmed his desire to consolidate the gains of the Revolution and to put an end to the violence and disorder that was increasingly tormenting France and harming its economic welfare. He concluded his remarks by reaffirming his faith in the legal processes to which he had devoted his entire, albeit brief, career:

> I will arm myself with all of the courage which I have within myself against these other men who would seek to have succeed a revolution other than the one that has been accomplished and who would seek to keep us forever in the midst of these convulsions which may be preferable to them, but which would ultimately ruin the body politic. It is time that commerce began its activity and its splendor once again, that the nervous arm be returned to agriculture, that the artisan live from his labor, that order be reborn in all portions of the Empire. It is to bring back this order, sole safeguard of liberty; it is to strengthen the power of law without which also liberty would be an impotent word that I will dedicate my most vigilant and most energetic efforts. I place in your hands, Gentlemen, these genuine promises and it is by them and by them alone that I want to be worthy today of the favor of your votes.[16]

Procès-verbaux de l'élection, 254.

15. Ibid., 254–55.

16. Ibid., 255.

The president of the Electoral Assembly, Pastoret, responded to Godard, extolling his virtues and emphasizing several of his principal accomplishments: his defense of wrongly condemned individuals, his service as an emissary to the troubled Lot region and, importantly, his role as the spokesman for the Jewish community:

> Sir, in the exercise of an honorable profession, you have distinguished yourself by your labors and made yourself cherished by your virtues. Depending, to some extent, on magistrates, you combatted with even more courage the errors of the judiciary. He [sic] spoke especially against this barbarous code, which often made the sword of justice the axe of executioners. More recently, you pleaded energetically for reason and humanity for these astonishing people [the Jews] whose laws have survived their political existence, and whose fate has always been to be led astray by their needs and deceived by their hopes; more recently still, in a part of the Empire, troubles were excited by these armed robbers, who, as their fellows always do, dishonored the holy name of the people…, [but] you appeared, and in response to your voice, murder and fire ceased their ravages [an allusion to Godard's trip to the Department of the Lot].[17]

The president ended his remarks with high praise, "These are your titles, as an orator, as a philosopher, as a citizen. May all those who will be elected have the same right to our votes!"[18]

Following Godard's election, the Electoral Assembly continued the process of electing representatives to the Legislative Assembly. Less than a week later, on September 26, Condorcet was also elected. The elections now came to an end. Each successful candidate was issued a document certifying his election. Godard's certificate bears the date of September 27, 1791, a date that would be of particular significance in his efforts on behalf of his Jewish clients.[19]

Within days following Godard's election to the new Legislative Assembly, the National Assembly, with a now firm expiration date of September 30, began to conclude the many matters that it had left pending over the

17. Ibid.
18. Ibid.
19. Certificate for a member of the "Députation à la Première Législature," dated September 27, 1791, signed by the Garde des Archives Nationales. (From the author's personal collection.)

course of the preceding months and years. Since none of the members of the existing Assembly would be returning to the new Legislative Assembly, there was some urgency to concluding the unfinished business. It is in this context that the issue of Jewish civil rights would suddenly and dramatically reemerge.

The newly ratified Constitution, even beyond the lofty provisions of its preamble (the Declaration of the Rights of Man and of the Citizen) which proclaimed that no one was to be disturbed because of his religious beliefs, appeared to have already addressed the issue of Jewish equality, and its adoption could have been deemed to resolve the matter. Very specifically, in its Title II, Article 2, the Constitution provided:

> The following are French citizens:
> Those born in France of a French father;
> Those who, born in France of a foreign father, have established their residence in the kingdom;
> Those who, born in a foreign country of a French father, have established themselves in France and have taken the civic oath;
> Finally, those who, born in a foreign country and descended in any degree whatsoever from a French man or a French woman expatriated because of religion, come to reside in France and take the civil oath. [20]

By these standards explicitly set out in the new Constitution, Jews—the preponderance of whom had been living within France for many years, if not for multiple generations—fulfilled all the prerequisites of citizenship. Therefore, with the ratification of a constitutional framework for citizenship in place which would set the stage for resolving the question of Jewish citizenship, it could now reasonably be expected that the matter would either be resolved expeditiously or could even be deemed resolved by the very provisions of the Constitution.

Yet, once again, the hopes for a quick and non-controversial resolution were dashed. The mere adoption of the new Constitution had not elicited any immediate reaction regarding the issue of Jewish citizenship. Because of the repeated exceptions cited by the National Assembly with respect to Jewish rights and the continuing delays in formally addressing their status, the legal position of the Jews remained uncertain. The frequently

---

20. Constitution of 1791, Title II, sec. 2.

reaffirmed resolution expressly deferring through adjournment a decision regarding the status of the Ashkenazi Jews remained ostensibly as the single legal obstacle to a recognition of an unqualified right to French citizenship for all Jews residing in France.

But, doubtless lurking in the minds of certain members of the National Assembly was the promise made almost two years earlier during the exuberant summer of 1789 that the status of the Jews would be resolved during the National Assembly's existence. The Assembly was just days away from being dissolved and nothing suggested that the promise would be kept.

CHAPTER 38

A PROMISE KEPT –
ACHIEVING LEGAL EQUALITY

During its morning session on September 27, the day following the debate on the Cochet matter and a mere three days before the National Assembly was set to dissolve, Adrien Duport, one of the representatives from Paris and a stalwart supporter of the rights of the Jews, suddenly brought the issue of Jewish equality to the floor. The Assembly had been discussing the consequences to be imposed on individuals who continued to use their former titles of nobility—titles that had been abolished just months before by the National Assembly, as Godard had so skillfully highlighted in his pleading in the Cochet case. Following an extensive debate, the Assembly adopted a decree that made it a punishable offense to use such titles in legal transactions. Duport addressed the Assembly several times during the debate. When the vote was over, he simply returned to the podium and began yet again to address the Assembly, indicating that he wanted to present "a short observation." He continued by clarifying his statement and telling the Assembly that this observation "appears to me to be of the utmost importance and requires all of its [the Assembly's] attention."[1] Duport then plunged into the heart of the matter:

> You have resolved, Gentlemen, by the Constitution, what qualities are necessary to become a French citizen, then to be deemed an active French citizen: this is sufficient, I think, to settle all the inci-

---

1. *Archives Parlementaires*, vol. 31, p. 372.

dental questions which may have been raised in the Assembly relative to certain professions, to certain persons. But there is a decree
of adjournment which seems to impose a kind of infringement to
these general rights; I am speaking of the Jews; to decide the question which concerns them, it will be sufficient to eliminate the decree
of adjournment which you have rendered, and which seems to put
the matter respecting them in suspense. Thus, if you had not issued
a decree of adjournment on the question of the Jews, there would be
nothing to be done at all; since having declared by your Constitution
how all the peoples of the earth can become French citizens and how
all French citizens can become active citizens, there would be no difficulty regarding this subject.[2]

He went on to describe his simple request of the Assembly:

I therefore ask that the decree of adjournment [regarding the status of
the Ashkenazi Jews] be revoked and that it be declared that, in relation
to the Jews, they may become active citizens, like all the peoples of the
world, by fulfilling the conditions prescribed by the Constitution. I
believe that freedom of religion no longer allows that any distinction
be made between the political rights of citizens on the basis of their
beliefs, and I also believe that the Jews cannot alone be excepted from
the enjoyment of these rights, while pagans, Turks, Muslims, even the
Chinese, in a word, men of all sects, are so admitted.[3]

His remarks were followed by applause and with shouts calling for an
immediate vote, even though Duport had not formally submitted the text
of a resolution. The Assembly's reaction suggested that it was very recep-
tive to Duport's position, but there were also expressions of opposition.
Various members reacted vociferously to these objections, shouting out
their impatience with those apparently seeking to stop Duport and prevent a vote on his proposal. Undoubtedly, some politicking and possibly
a substantial amount of lobbying behind the scenes had set the stage for
Duport's presentation and for the boisterous expressions of support.

But, despite the general enthusiasm for Duport's proposal, opposition
was audible and irrepressible. Leading the opposition was Reubell, the
unrelenting Alsatian representative, who remained adamantly opposed to

2. Ibid.
3. Ibid.

Jewish equality. In response to Reubell's efforts to speak against Duport's "motion," Michel Louis Étienne Regnaud de Saint-Jean d'Angély[4] forcefully demanded that the matter be brought to a vote without giving those opposed to it an opportunity to express themselves because, as he succinctly put it, "to combat against it [Duport's proposal] is to combat the Constitution itself."[5] Reubell was determined to get to the podium in an effort to stop the vote, but was unsuccessful. At the insistence of the vast majority of its members, who repeatedly shouted out their demand for an immediate vote, the Assembly cut off all debate and immediately proceeded to a vote without any further discussion. Duport's proposal was then promptly adopted.

However, once the vote had been taken, Reubell charged to the fore again. He insisted once more on being heard. In an effort to reverse the action just taken by the Assembly, he asserted from the podium that the vote was not valid. It was necessary, Reubell insisted, for the actual text of the resolution to be read since the issue was so controversial a matter that a vote on a concept rather than on a specific text was unacceptable. Aggressively, he declared:

> I demand that the decree be drafted and read immediately so that we will be able to know what is being decreed and so that we do not incorporate into the minutes a decree that was not adopted. At least, it will be known that I wanted to be heard to prove that the Assembly was caused to adopt a decree that only ignorance could have led it to adopt.[6]

Even if Duport had merely made a general proposal, he and those organizing his presentation were prepared with a very specific text, which Duport

---

4. Michel Louis Étienne Regnaud de Saint-Jean d'Angély (1760–1819), originally from the town of Saint-Jean d'Angély, located just to the north of Bordeaux, became an avocat and a journalist. He was an admirer of Jacques Necker and a friend of his daughter, Germaine de Staël. Barely surviving the Terror, he became an active supporter of Napoleon. When the Bourbons came back to power he fled to the United States, returning to France in 1819 and dying on the very day he returned to Paris. It is likely that Regnaud knew Godard well, being a contemporary and moving in the same social circle. We can reasonably speculate that his intervention in this crucial debate on behalf of the Jews was the result of some coordination with Godard.

5. *Archives Parlementaires*, vol. 31, p. 372.

6. *Archives Parlementaires*, vol. 31, p. 372.

proceeded to hand to the Assembly's president, Jacques Guillaume Thouret.[7] Thouret then read Duport's resolution to the entire body:

> The National Assembly, considering that the conditions necessary to become a French citizen, and to become an active citizen, are set by the Constitution, and every man who, having satisfied all of those conditions, taking the civil oath and agreeing to fulfill all of the obligations which the Constitution imposes, has the right to all of the benefits which it assures: revokes all adjournments, reserves and exceptions inserted in prior decrees.[8]

Within just moments, by a voice vote, the Assembly adopted Duport's now formalized motion.

Duport and his Paris colleagues had skillfully used the advantage of incumbency and the lame-duck status of the Assembly to finish the work begun in the fall of 1789 and advanced in January 1790 when Godard had filed his *Pétition* on behalf of the Jews. Not surprisingly, the royalist press uncharitably qualified his carefully arranged approach as being predicated upon "the indulgence by the majority for the sects that are the enemies of our religion."[9]

With this vote, the matter of Jewish equality appeared to be fully resolved. In spite of its opposition to the Assembly's decision, even the royalist newspaper *L'Ami du Roi* believed that the matter was closed when it reported with expected sarcasm and with a charge that had echoed through the ages that the adoption of the resolution demonstrated that the Assembly had chosen to terminate its work by doing "a great good deed to those who blaspheme the divine author."[10]

However, Reubell and the Alsatians were not finished with their attempts to obstruct the grant of civil equality to Jews. Far from it. They

---

7. Jacques Guillaume Thouret (1746–1794) was an avocat registered with the Parlement in Rouen in Normandy. He was elected to the Estates-General as a member of the Third Estate and served as a member of the Constitution Committee. He was elected president of the National Assembly on four different occasions, more than any other individual. Associated with the moderate Girondins, he was condemned to death by the Revolutionary Tribunal and was guillotined along with Malsherbes and his family in April 1794.

8. *Archives Parlementaires*, vol. 31, p. 372.

9. *L'Ami du Roi, des Français, de l'Ordre et Sur-tout de la Vérité*, Wednesday, September 28, 1791, no. 272, p. 1083.

10. Ibid.

had a further procedural card to play.

The next day, when the secretary of the Assembly began reading the minutes of the September 27 morning session, one of the representatives from Strasbourg, Prince Charles Louis Victor de Broglie, interrupted the reading as the text reached the discussion of Duport's resolution. He suggested that, for the benefit of the welfare of Alsace, it was important to clarify the actual words of the adopted resolution:

> Gentlemen, it is necessary that the Assembly take precautions in order that the decree, adopted yesterday relative to the Jews who will take the civil oath, not have bad effects in Alsace; because, in light of the intrigues whose influence can already be felt, there could be some very bad effects. It is therefore necessary that it not be possible to badly interpret it and that it be said that the taking of the civil oath by the Jews will be regarded as a formal renunciation of the civil and political laws to which individual Jews believe that they are particularly subject.[11]

De Broglie's words, which were deemed to be a kind of amendment to Duport's text, seemed relatively benign and received a general expression of approval.

Louis-Pierre-Joseph Prugnon, an avocat from Nancy in Lorraine, then ascended to the podium.[12] He put forward a modification to de Broglie's proposal. He suggested that, in lieu of inserting: "will be regarded as a renunciation of their civil laws, etc.," the words: "will be regarded as a renunciation of their privileges" be added because, as Prugnon asserted, "the civil laws of the Jews are identified with their religious laws; and it is not part of our intention to demand that they abjure their religion."[13] Although it should now have become apparent that this text was yet another attempt to highlight Jewish particularism, for most members of the Assembly the matter was innocuous enough. The fundamental principle of Jewish equality was embodied in the resolution and its adoption could bring to an end the debate that had been ongoing for months. Further arguments against Prugnon's addition did not appear particularly necessary.

---

11. Ibid., 441.

12. Louis-Pierre-Joseph Prugnon (1745–1828) was an avocat registered with the Parlement of Nancy. He played a significant role in the judicial reforms of the National Assembly.

13. *Archives Parlementaires*, vol. 31, p. 441.

LOBBYING FOR EQUALITY

Duport's original resolution with Prugnon's additional caveat and more specific focus, including a specific reference to Jews, was now reread to the Assembly:

> The National Assembly, considering that the conditions necessary to become a French citizen and to become an active citizen, are set by the Constitution, and every man who, having satisfied all of those conditions, takes the civil oath and agrees to fulfill all of the obligations which the Constitution imposes, has the right to all of the benefits which it assures:
>
> Revokes all adjournments, reserves and exceptions inserted in prior decrees relative to individual Jews who take the civil oath, which will be regarded as a renunciation of all privileges and exceptions previously introduced in their favor.[14]

Without any additional discussion, the modified text was put to a formal vote and was immediately approved.

With the adoption of this text, the last legislative act necessary to permit the Jews of France to ascend to the ranks of active citizens appeared to have been taken. But Reubell was not yet willing to give up and raced back to the podium. He asserted:

> The manner in which the decree was adopted yesterday, without discussion, without examination, the difficulties that could be the consequence, will determine, I hope, the Assembly to permit me today to express certain reflections on its language.[15]

There was an attempt to prevent Reubell from continuing his remarks. Some members shouted out that the decree had already been adopted. But Reubell was not to be denied and stubbornly continued: "We propose today a new version," he began. Then he proceeded to describe all the problems that the Jews had allegedly caused to their Christian neighbors through their "usurious" practices. He argued that it was necessary to provide some relief to non-Jews from the risks posed by the outstanding loans owed to the Jews. At the conclusion of his diatribe, he put forward a concrete proposal:

14. Ibid.
15. Ibid.

The National Assembly decrees:

1. That within the month, the Jews of the former Province of Alsace shall give to the Directories of the Districts of the Debtors, a detailed statement of their claims, both in regards to principal and interest, with respect to non-Jewish individuals, named in the old regulations of the former class of the people of the same province.

2. That the Directories of the Districts shall immediately take all the information necessary to ascertain the means known to the debtors to pay these debts; that they will provide this information, with their advice as to the mode of liquidating these debts, to the Directories of the Departments of the Upper and Lower Rhine;

3. That the Directories of the Departments of the Upper and Lower Rhine will provide, without delay, their opinion on this mode of liquidation, that they will communicate this opinion to the Jews, and that they will send it, together with the observations of the latter, to the legislative body, to have legislated that which needs to be.[16]

The members of the Assembly discussed the proposal briefly and then, eager to put the whole matter behind them and move on to the many other issues still pending in these last days of the session, proceeded with a vote. The resolution was adopted and, finally, with its adoption, the National Assembly concluded its ultimate consideration of the legal treatment of Jews. The hasty treatment of both Duport's and then Reubell's motions certainly made the outcome less than perfect. On the one hand, once and for all, Jews were now deemed to be qualified to be active citizens with all the rights and responsibilities attendant to such a status. On the other hand, the Alsatians had managed to attach a special treatment to the loans held by Jews, as Jews, thus leaving a slight doubt as to the absolute equality given to Jews by Duport's resolution. In the final analysis, the Reubell resolution had almost no impact. It was generally forgotten and seems to never have actually been implemented. Its adoption could appear to have been merely a means of placating the Alsatians. Only the Duport resolution, which gave unqualified legal equality to all Jews in France, was thereafter deemed to govern the status of French Jews.

With the National Assembly about to end its existence and the Legislative Assembly soon to come into being, the press took little note of the motion

---

16. Ibid., 442.

on behalf of Jewish rights. The *Moniteur* devoted just two short paragraphs to the discussion that led to the adoption of Duport's motion and did not bother to mention the subsequent debate.[17] In fact, this ultimate outcome was rather anti-climactic. The protracted struggle over Jewish equality had apparently drained most of the public interest in the matter, and the strong emotions that had characterized the early phases of the effort had been defused. Other issues had become far more pressing and the implementation of the new Constitution and the convening of the new Legislative Assembly were certainly much more important to the public.

There is no tangible evidence that Godard was directly involved in this dispositive action on the matter of Jewish equality. However, it is important to note that the principal proponent of this final act in the process toward legal equality for the Ashkenazi Jewish community was a member of the Paris delegation at the National Assembly. It can be assumed that Godard's lobbying efforts within the Paris political structure had a significant effect that reinforced the resolve of Parisian political leaders to put an end to the struggle and to give Jewish residents the rights they had been seeking for years. It is also likely that Godard was included in the coordination of the legislative activities led by the Paris representatives during the final days of the National Assembly that resulted in the resolution affirming Jewish equality. All the efforts that Godard and his clients had expended in pursuing their goal may not have been the sole impetus toward this legislative accomplishment, but they were assuredly of great importance. They altered the political atmosphere and context within which the decision to consider Jewish equality was debated such that, when the last step was taken, it seemed both almost effortless and of only modest consequence.

Effectively, the legislative struggle for Jewish legal equality had come to an end. The objective for which Ashkenazi Jews had striven for a generation and for which Godard had been retained by the community had, at long last, been achieved. Only the signature of the king was now necessary for the decree to become law. The king would sign the decree on November 13, 1791. The lengthy delay in achieving this final act has been ascribed to the large amount of legislation which piled up on the king's desk as a result of the hectic activity of the National Assembly in its last days and the king's rather lethargic approach to the fulfillment of his formal

---

17. *Moniteur*, September 29, 1791, no. 272, p. 1132.

duties.[18] Most importantly, contrary to all the predictions of the Alsatians and their allies, the decree did not engender any violence. With all the changes being instituted by the Revolution, the grant of civil equality to the Ashkenazi Jews passed without any great fanfare or outcry among other French citizens—even in the province where they lived in the greatest concentration and where anti-Jewish sentiment was the strongest.

Of course, not all Jews were pleased with the grant of equality by the Legislative Assembly, nor were they all prepared to take up the new rights that they had just been given. Among very religious Jews who lived in small communities in Alsace and Lorraine, the new legislation brought with it fear of a loss of communal cohesiveness. Similarly, among leaders of the community, both religious and secular, there was a natural concern that their authority would be diminished by the new legal regime for Jews. Furthermore, the grant of legal equality was one thing, but the actual exercise of the rights emanating from the status of active citizen would be quite another. Berr Isaac Berr articulated this challenge in a letter to his fellow Jews in Lorraine shortly after the adoption of Duport's motion.[19] Berr expressed his gratitude to God, to Louis XVI, and to the French nation for having made Jews equal citizens. But he also reminded his fellow Jews that they now had to prove themselves worthy of the rights bestowed upon them. He did not seek to alter compliance with Jewish religious principles nor did he propose any compromise with the religious practices of his community, but he strongly recommended that all Jews take the civil oath of loyalty to the country, the law, and the king so as to integrate into the nation that had just extended to them basic legal rights.[20] He reminded his coreligionists that, if they were giving up some of their communal rights, it was more than a fair exchange. By renouncing their "privileges," the Jews would be gaining the rights of active citizens, of being "French Jews."[21] Berr was not naïve and he did not minimize the problems that would face the Jews as they began to benefit

18. See Feuerwerker, *L'Émancipation des Juifs en France*, 407, et seq., regarding the administrative process which resulted in a delay of forty-eight days before the decree was signed by Louis XVI.
19. Berr Isaac Berr, *Lettre d'un Citoyen Membre de la Ci-devant Communauté des Juifs de Lorraine à ses Confrères, à l'occasion du Droit de Citoyen actif, rendu aux Juifs par le Décret du 28 [sic] septembre 1791* (Nancy: Chez H. Haener, 1791).
20. Ibid., 4.
21. Ibid., 11.

from their new rights. He highlighted those challenges: the need to learn to speak French, to shed their isolated lifestyles and to actively participate in French civic life. Berr concluded his letter with an exhortation to his fellow-Jews not to waste any time in preparing to benefit from the newly given rights.[22] His words would be echoed by the actions of the preponderance of the Ashkenazi Jews who would within but a few months take the civil oath, usually collectively as entire communities.[23]

Once the National Assembly had voted on Reubell's supplement to the Duport motion and thereby completed its work on the issue of Jewish civil rights, the very next matter that was brought to its attention was another issue that had been of particular interest to Jacques Godard. A representative named Edmond Louis Alexis Dubois de Crancé[24] stood and made an important request of the Assembly: "I ask," he said, "that, in accordance with ancient laws, it be decreed that all men of color are free the moment that they touch French soil."[25] Suddenly, the issue that had been at the core of the case that Godard had unsuccessfully handled in 1787 on behalf of Julien Baudelle was before the Assembly. A brief debate ensued. Some members affirmed that the matter was already resolved by existing law and that no further action was necessary. Most members were inclined to agree with Dubois de Crancé and unwilling to engage in a protracted dialogue. At the conclusion of a brief debate, the Assembly adopted a simple text:

> Article 1: Every individual is free as soon as he enters France.
> Article 2: Every person, of whatever color, has in France all the rights of an active citizen, if he complies with the requirements specified by the Constitution in order to benefit from them.[26]

The resolution enacted into law the very principle that Godard had asserted in his defense of Julien Baudelle as he sought to win Baudelle's

---

22. Ibid., 22.

23. For the process of civil oathtaking in Alsace and Lorraine, see Feuerwerker, *L'Émancipation des Juifs en France*, 429–55.

24. Edmond Louis Alexis Dubois de Crancé (1747–1814) was a military man who became active in revolutionary politics. He is best remembered for having urged the implementation of universal military service for all Frenchmen. While he served in the Assembly of the Paris Electors he became the president of the *Club de l'Evêché*.

25. *Archives Parlementaires*, vol. 31, p. 441.

26. Ibid.

freedom, namely, that no one could be a slave within the boundaries of France itself. All the rules and regulations that had served as obstacles to Baudelle's quest for freedom were now effectively removed. The new decree was nothing less than a formal reversal of the disappointing adverse decision that had been handed down in the Julien Baudelle matter. It was a small but a very important step toward the abolition of slavery in France (which it accomplished) and in its colonial empire (which would not be unqualifiedly accomplished for another half century).

In what appears to be a truly felicitous coincidence, two causes that had been at the heart of Jacques Godard's legal and political careers were addressed and ostensibly resolved at essentially the same time: the grant of equality to his Jewish clients and the achievement of freedom for all persons of color when they arrived on French soil. It must have been a moment of deep satisfaction for the young man. He had every reason to believe that these two victories were merely the prelude to what would become a very successful political career.

CHAPTER 39

"A MIND FULL OF CLARITY AND JUSTICE"

With many considerable accomplishments behind him, Godard, a man of not yet thirty, was now about to embark upon a new phase of his career. He was joining the first freely elected French national legislature when much serious work in the effort toward creating a new French society remained to be done.

On October 1, 1791, Godard and the other elected members of the new Legislative Assembly convened for a short ceremonial session in the *Manège*, the hangar-like building contiguous to the Tuileries Gardens, where the National Assembly had been meeting. On the second day of the Assembly's existence, the members addressed issues regarding its operations. Confirming the status of the elected representatives was the first matter on the agenda: that very day, Godard's election was certified along with the election of twenty-three other representatives from the Paris region.[1] Godard was the youngest member of this first popularly elected French legislature.

On the Assembly's third day of existence, the members elected their first permanent president. Their choice was none other than Claude-Emmanuel-Joseph-Pierre Pastoret, who had provided Godard with materials about Jewish belief and custom in October 1789 as Godard began his representation of the Jewish community. Then, on October

---

1. *Archives Parlementaires*, vol. 34, p. 64.

4, all the newly elected members of the Legislative Assembly took their oath of office. The minutes of that day's meeting indicate that Godard joined his fellow Paris representatives in taking that oath.[2]

Throughout the first month of the opening session, the Assembly spent much of its time organizing itself. Importantly, it set up its committees and elected members to sit on those committees. Toward the end of October, on the 26th, Godard was unsurprisingly elected to serve as one of forty-eight members of the Civil and Criminal Legislation Committee.[3] His selection for this committee was a logical one in light of his well-known legal skills. Of course, he was hardly the only individual with that qualification since the Legislative Assembly, just like its predecessor assembly, had a sizeable number of members who had been avocats. In fact, former avocats constituted the new Assembly's single largest professional group.

During these early weeks, Godard did not have occasion to make any speeches before the body. His past political activities suggest that he was not reticent about standing before large legislative bodies and expressing himself. During this early organizational phase of the Assembly's existence, perhaps he was biding his time, awaiting the right opportunity for his maiden speech.

That opportunity would not come. Near the end of October he fell seriously ill. Word of his "dangerous illness" spread to both the Legislative Assembly and the Assembly of the Paris Electors, of which he was still a member. Many of his colleagues were very concerned for his welfare.[4] After just a few days, at seven o'clock on the morning of November 4, 1791, Jacques Godard, aged only 29, died. His death, the first of a member of the new Legislative Assembly, was ascribed to a "putrid fever." The illness, referred to by contemporary writers as a *"fièvre maligne,"* was most likely typhoid fever. It is possible that Godard's susceptibility to the disease would have been the result of exhaustion brought on by his relentlessly hard work. His impecuniousness as well could have left him undernourished and a candidate for illness, and would have compounded the nefarious consequences that would be brought on by any illness at a time of poor hygiene and limited medical care.

---

2. Ibid., 78.
3. Ibid., 429.
4. Chavaray, *Assemblée Electorale de Paris,* 534.

On that same day, Godard's passing was announced from the Assembly's podium. Léonard Robin, Godard's colleague in the mission to the Lot region in late 1790, was invited to officially inform his fellow Assembly members that their youngest colleague had just died. He spoke briefly and personally about Godard:

> Gentlemen, I am obliged to inform you of some news that is very painful for me and woeful for the nation. Mr. Godard was my colleague on an important mission which we were assigned; he was appointed as an attorney and as a representative of the Paris Commune. Everywhere I had occasion to recognize and admire his virtues, his intelligence and his talents. His fellow citizens had just given him justice; he was, Gentlemen, our colleague; but he had barely appeared in our midst; death has come and taken him away from the nation.[5]

Then, Robin requested that the Assembly "name a delegation of twelve of its members to participate in his funeral procession." The deputy Delacroix rose and followed Robin at the podium. He suggested that a delegation of twelve was insufficient under the circumstances and proposed that the delegation should consist of twenty-four deputies, which the Assembly voted to authorize. Shortly before the Assembly adjourned for the day, the president designated the twenty-four members of the delegation.[6]

It was also decided that both Robin's and Delacroix's remarks should be inserted verbatim into the minutes of Assembly's proceedings and that they should be published.[7] Other than the procedural references to Godard's election to the Legislative Assembly and to the committee on which he was to serve, the remarks about his death and the announcement on November 7 of his replacement by J-L Lacretelle (one of the alternate representatives to the Legislative Assembly and an individual who had been a member of the coterie of young avocats around Target) are the only places where Godard's name appears in the minutes of the Legislative Assembly as part of the activities of the Assembly. Death had deprived him of any role in the Assembly's work. He had not cast any votes nor participated in any meaningful debates. He had not even had the time to make his first remarks from the podium.

---

5. *Archives Parlementaires*, vol. 34, p. 626.

6. Ibid., 639.

7. Chavaray, *Assemblée Electorale de Paris*, 254–55.

News of Godard's death was also delivered to the Assembly of the Paris Electors, of which Godard had been a member for some years and in which he had been especially active since the beginning of the process to select the members of the Legislative Assembly in May. The Electoral Assembly, riven with factions and fraught with tensions, was at this time in the final throes of its work and even of its very existence, since the Legislative Assembly was now fully constituted. After announcing Godard's death, Jacques Delavigne, the president of the Electoral Assembly and a member of the *Club de la Sainte-Chapelle*, relayed the wish of Godard's family that a delegation of electors accompany his funeral procession. The elector Claude-Antoine Nau-Deville immediately informed the Assembly that the Legislative Assembly had already determined to send a large delegation to participate in Godard's funeral procession and suggested that it would be appropriate for the electors to emulate this gesture.[8] Of course, as a member of one of the two major clubs that had split the Electoral Assembly, Godard had not been uniformly admired at the Assembly and, as a consequence, a strikingly discordant note entered the discussion. One of the members of the Assembly, not specifically identified (but probably Jean Rousseau),[9] reminded the group that, in accordance with its prior decrees, "the Assembly [of Paris Electors] was not allowed to take any external action, as a group, such as sending a delegation [to a funeral]."[10]

As a consequence of the elector's observation, there was an attempt to hold an immediate vote on the question of whether to send the proposed delegation to Godard's funeral. An odd debate ensued, during which the precedent set with the funeral of a certain Brizard was cited. In that case, in 1790, the Electoral Assembly had sent a delegation to the funeral.[11] However, another member of the Assembly stood to oppose the sending of an official delegation, noting, as an example, that the National Assembly had determined never to send an official delegation to the funeral of one of its members so as to avoid impinging on the Assembly's operations. He further presumed that if the Legislative Assembly had just decided to the

---

8. Claude-Antoine Nau-Deuville (?–1805) was an elector from the Louvre District. Little is known about him other than that he served in the National Guard and authored at least one brochure regarding an art exposition at the Louvre.

9. Chavaray, *Assemblée Electorale de Paris*, 534.

10. Ibid., 385.

11. Ibid., xlvi–xlvii. (See reference on p. 40 to Jacques Godard: "*GODARD (Jacques), homme de lois, défenseur officieux, 29 ans, rue des Blancs-Manteaux, 56.*")

contrary, it was because the new Assembly was simply not aware of the precedent. The creation of an impediment to the Assembly's operations, he declared, would not be appropriate for a public institution.

In a peculiar and somewhat disturbing development regarding the young avocat who had himself been attached to proper procedure and respect for the law, a debate on procedure then took place. Honoring the deceased Godard had fallen prey to the political discord among Parisian factions. The question before the Assembly was whether the discussion should continue or if it was now time to vote on the matter without further discussion. A vote determined that all further debate was futile, and that no delegation would be sent. This then led to a discussion of whether members should be individually invited to attend the Godard funeral and whether the invitation made by Godard's family should be published. This time the result of the vote was in the affirmative. The discussion about Assembly member participation at Godard's funeral was protracted; the minutes of the meeting indicate that it was adjourned at 2:30 in the morning.[12]

Godard's funeral service took place at the *Église des Blancs-Manteaux,* just a short distance down rue des Blancs-Manteaux from his residence. The elector Nau-Deville, who had urged that a large delegation of the electors attend the funeral, reported that he personally was in attendance.[13] He described an odd encounter he had while sitting in a café near the church, awaiting the arrival of the funeral procession. He engaged in a conversation with another patron of the café, who presumed that Nau-Deville was in the neighborhood to attend Godard's funeral. Nau-Deville confirmed that he was indeed about to attend the service because "he very much missed this young man."[14] According to Nau-Deville, there then ensued an exchange which revealed the ambivalent views of Godard on the streets of his neighborhood. The other patron told Nau-Deville that Godard had been very helpful to him in a matter of significance, involving some 20,000 francs. He went on to describe Godard as having been "so kind, so honest." But then, notwithstanding his obvious respect and gratitude, he chose to deplore Godard's political association with the *Club de la Sainte-Chapelle* (a club to which Nau-Deville himself adhered). To underpin his negative

---

12. Chavaray, *Assemblée Electorale de Paris,* 385–86.
13. Ibid., 553.
14. Ibid.

opinion of the club and, by implication of Godard, he indicated that a local doctor, a member of the rapidly growing Jacobin Club, had told him that all of the members of the *Club de la Sainte-Chapelle* were "bad citizens."[15] Clearly distressed by this analysis, Nau-Deville tried to disabuse his interlocutor of an opinion that he believed to be unjust. However, he did not indicate whether he was successful in his effort. The report of this unfortunate encounter stands as one of the very few testimonials of events relating to Godard's funeral.

The absence of unanimity regarding Godard is reinforced by a comment regarding his funeral made many months later, on February 3, 1792, from the podium of the Legislative Assembly. This occurred when another member of the Paris delegation to the Assembly, Joseph-Antoine-Joachim Cerutti, had died. A resolution had just been adopted by the Assembly calling, as had been the case for Godard, for twenty-four members to attend Cerutti's funeral as an official delegation. A representative named Audrein stood up and reminded the Assembly that a similar resolution had been adopted when Jacques Godard had died. He went on to observe, however, that only three members of the Assembly had actually attended Godard's funeral and chastised the Assembly by noting that this "had caused much pain to the persons who expected a much more numerous delegation and which were very much affected by this indifference."[16] These rather sad observations about Godard's funeral serve to highlight the growing political fractures that were already afflicting France and which would soon erupt into fratricidal violence—the very fractures that Godard had deplored and had frequently sought to prevent.

The Paris press, however, took ample note of Godard's death, repeatedly identifying him as the youngest member of the Legislative Assembly. In these early days of the Revolution, the death of a politician was not yet quite so common an occurrence as it would soon become. Various newspapers published eloquent tributes to Godard. *La Chronique de Paris* of November 5, 1791 included a long obituary which noted that Godard had presided over the District des Blancs-Manteaux and then, conflating the parallel roles he played at the time of the debate over the status of the Jews, went on to state that he was the person who "took up the defense of the Jews in his role as a representative of the Commune." The obituary

---

15. Ibid.
16. *Archives Parlementaires*, vol. 38, pp. 111–12.

went on further to note that "he was of an advantageous appearance; he had intellect, he was well-educated and articulate."[17] In the *Courrier des 83 départements*,[18] the editor, Gorsas (who had assisted the Bordelais in the preparation of their petition to the National Assembly), announced Godard's death rather succinctly: "Mr. Godard, deputy from Paris, has just died: he was a young man with many talents and who gave rise to much hope. His death will make us forget and will erase pages from his life. He is being replaced by Mr. Lacretelle."[19] An especially laudatory article appeared on the front page of the November 5 edition of the *Annales Patriotiques et Litteraires de la France*. The author of the obituary described Godard as "a representative from Paris, recommended by his known talents, by his tested patriotism, by his amiable qualities, and even by his youth, of which he had the principal attributes, strength and beauty."[20] Not surprisingly, the royalist *L'Ami du Roi* took a more negative approach, and seized upon the event ominously to suggest that Godard's death might represent a kind of divine intervention and portend the impending death of all of the members of the new legislature. "And here are our legislators, who are falling victim to death," the newspaper reported.[21] It continued by inaccurately indicating that "Mr. Godard, a deputy from Paris will be buried tomorrow; the Assembly is invited to his funeral procession, it will send a delegation of twelve [*sic*] members."[22]

None of the tributes to Godard, however, matched the emotional words of his long-time friend Amélie Suard, in a letter to her husband, published on November 8 in the *Journal de Paris* (and which she would later publish in a compilation of such letters).[23] The letter was preceded by a short, but

---

17. *La Chronique de Paris*, November 5, 1791. *"Il était d'une figure avantageuse; il avait de l'esprit, de l'instruction et de la facilité de parler."*

18. *Courrier des 83 départements*, November 6, 1791, p. 89.

19. Chavaray, *Assemblée Electorale de Paris*, xlvi, n3.

20. *Annales Patriotiques et Litteraires de la France*, November 5, 1791, no. 764.

21. Although hardly a fulfillment of the royalist prophecy, barely two weeks later another young member of the Legislative Assembly, A. M. Thallier, a representative from the Puy de Dôme region, succumbed to illness and died at the age of 33. *The Journal de Paris*, in reporting Thallier's death, noted that the Assembly had lost, "a precious individual worthy, like Mr. Godard, of the regret of the friends of liberty and public order." *Journal de Paris*, Friday, November 18, 1791, no. 322, p. 1307.

22. *L'Ami du Roi, des Français, de l'Ordre et Sur-tout de la Vérité*, Saturday, November 5, no. 310, p. 1234.

23. Amélie Suard, *Lettres de Mme. Suard à son Mari* (A. Dampierre, An X (1802),

moving tribute from the *Journal de Paris*, whose owners Godard had successfully represented in a legal proceeding just a few months previously (a fact that was not disclosed to the readers of the newspaper, but to which it merely alluded). As a preface to Amélie Suard's letter, the *Journal de Paris* wrote that "The Fatherland, by the death of this young man, has suffered a loss which only those who have known him well can fully appreciate."[24] Indeed, her letter compellingly made the *Journal de Paris's* point. Clearly deeply saddened by the passing of her young friend, Amélie wrote at length and emotionally, in a manner that suggests that she was writing not only to her husband and contemporary readers but for posterity. Her letter provides us with significant insights into Godard's brief life.

After having praised his good looks and refined manners, Amélie touched upon his legal career, noting that he had a reasonable approach to handling legal matters and had also been systematic and organized. "His mind was full of clarity and justice, and of a very pure manner. He had a natural method, which permitted him to put everything in its place."[25] She then praised his eloquence and his devotion to justice, offering to her husband and her readers her belief that Godard did not plead for any cause that was not consistent with his conscience. "His talent," she wrote, "was only in the service of truth."[26] This was also the case, she emphasized, in his political endeavors. "With what ardor did he embrace the hopes of our political regeneration?" she asked rhetorically. Answering her own question, she noted that Godard applied all his faculties to this goal, adding that he was "always guided by his love of liberty." [27]

Following her praise of Godard's history of the Paris Assembly and his report on the disturbances in the Lot region, both of which she urged her husband to read, Amélie turned her thoughts to the cause of Godard's death and the lost opportunity that his untimely demise represented for France and, specifically, for the newly constituted Legislative Assembly to which Godard had just been elected:

Unfortunate young man! The ardor of serving the Fatherland, the

106–12.
24. *Journal de Paris*, November 8, 1791, no. 312, p. 1268. Cf. *Journal de Paris*, November 18, 1791, no. 322, p. 1307.
25. Suard, *Lettres de Mme. Suard à son Mari*, 107–8.
26. Ibid., 109.
27. Ibid.

hope of seeing our liberty astride respect for the Law, inspired you completely; the glory, even the glory was forgotten; the public good, the happiness of all your fellow-citizens absorbed all of your wishes.[28] Alas! It is this so noble devotion which hastened you into the tomb. You did not apply any moderation to a sentiment, whose excess itself was a virtue. You exhausted nature by work, when nature, already weakened, demanded rest from you; and when you saw it detracted from your projects, your hopes, your affections, you trembled for a moment in the clutch of friendship from having exhausted all of the resources; but soon your soul, as courageous as it was sweet, submitted to destiny, and leaves in tears your devastated friends.[29]

Suard ascribed Godard's notable successes to his sincerity. "Almost always he persuaded, because he himself was persuaded."[30] She also recalled that his personal attributes, his physical appearance, and his charm, combined with his youthfulness and his talents, all served to blend emotion with reason and made Godard a brilliant advocate.

It is interesting to note that, for all the praise that she heaped upon his memory, Amélie Suard did not cite Godard's efforts on behalf of the Jews of France, nor even mention his lengthy treatise in support of Jewish equality. She praised Godard's two other major writings, the history of the Paris Assembly and the report on the disturbances in the Lot region. But, there was not a single word in her letter about the writing and the effort for which Godard is best remembered today.

Amélie Suard's reticence notwithstanding, history would lavish its blessings of immortality on Godard, principally, although not exclusively, because of his work for the Jewish community. The entry on Jacques Godard in the official dictionary of the members of the various French legislatures has a summary of his political accomplishments. It does not fail to highlight his role on behalf of the Jews:

In this capacity, and as one of the presidents of the Blancs-Manteaux District, he spoke on July 31, 1789, to disavow the electors. On the 28th of January, 1790, he presented a delegation of Jews to the general assembly of the Commune of Paris, and demanded that they

28. Here Amélie Suard evolves from using the more formal "*vous*" to the more familiar and, at the time, rarely used, "*tu*" in addressing Godard in her letter.
29. Suard, *Lettres de Mme. Suard à son Mari*, 111–12.
30. Ibid., 110.

be granted a certificate of patriotism; in October of the same year, he published the "History of the work of the general assembly of the representatives of the Commune of Paris," which the *Moniteur* praised. Elected on September 20, 1791, Deputy of the Department of Paris to the Legislative Assembly, 16th out of 24, with 343 votes out of 608 voters, he died less than two months later. [31]

Not surprisingly, as would be expected with the death of any politician, the comments on Godard's death were not unanimously laudatory. The newspaper, *L'Ami des Patriotes ou le Défenseur de la Constitution*, carried a flattering obituary. However, in a footnote, the author of the obituary, the avocat, J.B.L.J. Billecocq, alluded to criticism about Godard voiced at the time of his death. He wrote, "With indignation, I have heard it said that in a respectable assembly [presumably the Assembly of Paris Electors] there were men who had carried their animosity and lack of shame to the point of applauding at the news of the death of Mr. Godard. They are unknown to me; for, if I knew their names, I would denounce them for public contempt and public indignation."[32]

Just nine days after Godard's death, on November 13, 1791, Louis XVI signed the law that had been adopted by the National Assembly with respect to the Jews. With this signature, the resolution became the law of the land. Little note was paid to this rather ministerial act that consecrated years of efforts, frustrations, and delays. Godard was already fading into obscurity. However, with the simple act of signing the decree, Louis XVI crowned Godard's principal lobbying effort with success and finally made it possible for Jews to join their fellow citizens as full participants in the benefits bestowed upon the French population by the Revolution. Jews could now flock to the nearest municipal office and take the oath that had been prescribed as a requirement for all who would become active citizens of France. In many communities, groups would join to take the oath as a collectivity. In Nancy, on July 2, 1791, led by their rabbi, every male member of Jewish community went to the city hall to be collectively administered the oath.[33] Once the oath was taken, each

---

31. Adolphe Robert, Edgar Bouloton and Gaston Cougny, *Biographie extraite du dictionnaire des parlementaires français de 1789 à 1889* (Paris: Bourloton Ed., 1891).
32. *L'ami des Patriotes ou le Défenseur de la Constitution*, November 12, 1791, vol. 4, no. 6, p. 178.
33. Jacques Godechot, "Les Juifs de Nancy de 1789 à 1795." *Revue des Études juives*

Jewish male would, henceforth, at least theoretically, benefit from all the rights, and assume all the responsibilities, of a citizen of the French nation. Within but a few months, thousands of Jews had done exactly that and had by that simple act become full and equal active citizens of the nation in which they resided—the first major modern nation where this had become possible.[34] Taking the oath, however, was not always easy. In certain jurisdictions, notably in smaller villages in Alsace, local officials placed obstacles in the path of Jews seeking to fulfill the requirements for citizenship.[35] Nonetheless, in contradiction to the many dire predictions pronounced at the National Assembly by the enemies of Jewish equality, the transition to full Jewish civil equality took place without any measurable violence and with relative ease.

It was only a month later, on December 15, 1791, that the United States joined France in enshrining the principle of religious liberty (which had been a primary motivator in the establishment of many of the British American colonies) as a fundamental pillar of American democracy with the ratification of the Bill of Rights. Although the new Constitution of the United States had in 1788 assured American citizens that "no religious Test shall ever be required as a Qualification to any Office or public Trust under the United States,"[36] it was not until the adoption of the first article of the Bill of Rights—the First Amendment—that American citizens were assured that the Federal Government would not make any law "respecting an establishment of religion, or prohibiting the free exercise thereof."[37] George Washington had already made it clear, in

(Paris: Librairie A. Durlacher, 1928): 11.

34. See Feuerwerker, *L'Émancipation des Juifs en France*, described on p. 492n23, above.

35. Gary Kates describes the obstacles placed in the path of the Jews of Bischheim, a town near Strasbourg with a rather large Jewish population, where, beginning in March 1792, town officials kept refusing Jews the opportunity to take the required oath of citizenship until the regional government, acting at the behest of the central government, ordered the officials to stop their obstructionism. By the end of April 1792, as a result of the intervention of the regional government, all the citizens of Bischheim who wished to do so were able to take the oath of citizenship. Gary Kates, "Jews into Frenchmen: Nationality and Representation in Revolutionary France," in *The French Revolution and the Birth of Modernity*, ed. Ferenc Fehér (Berkeley: University of California Press, 1990), 103–4.

36. *The Constitution of the United States*, Article VI, third paragraph.

37. Amendment I to the Constitution of the United States.

a letter to the Jewish Congregation in Newport, Rhode Island (at that time a Sephardic congregation) sent on August 17, 1790, following his visit there, that, in the United States, the government (by which he meant the Federal Government) would "give to bigotry no sanction, to persecution no assistance."[38] However, that lofty notion would not be enshrined in the American Constitution for more than a year. And, the full benefits of legal equality for all American Jews still had to wait. It would not be until ratification of the Fourteenth Amendment in 1868, with its extension of the protections of the Constitution to the states, that American Jews would be assured the full legal benefits of equality throughout all of the United States—benefits that Jacques Godard had helped to obtain for his Jewish compatriots in September 1791.

Notwithstanding the important legal victory of September 27, 1791, as ratified by Louis XVI in November, it would take generations for full equality to be achieved. Many of the reservations that had been articulated by opponents of Jewish equality about the ability of the Jews to become fully integrated citizens of the new French state, as distinguished from merely de jure citizens, would turn out to have some validity. Jews would demonstrate an understandable reluctance to discard certain of the attributes they had developed over the course of centuries and which highlighted their differences from their non-Jewish neighbors, preventing their full integration into secular society. Even de jure recognition would go through dramatic reversals and challenges as France encountered repeated crises and alternated regimes over the course of the ensuing more than two and a quarter centuries. Nonetheless, Jacques Godard had helped the Jews of France break through a critical barrier and take a dramatic step toward overcoming the prejudice of centuries. For this important and pivotal accomplishment alone he assuredly deserves to be remembered.

---

38. Letter of President George Washington to the Hebrew Congregation of Newport, RI, August 18, 1790, *The Papers of George Washington Digital Edition*, ed. Theodore J. Crackel (Charlottesville: Univ. of Virginia Press, Rotunda, 2007).

EPILOGUE

Jacques Godard died while the French Revolution was in its first phase. Ideas molded by the Enlightenment, the American experiment with democratic government, and Anglo-Saxon principles of self-governance, ideas so avidly embraced by Godard, dominated this phase of the Revolution. However, the early euphoria with such liberal and moderate concepts was rapidly challenged by the hard realities of coping with the rising expectations of the French populace and of the increasingly radical politics of the revolutionaries—all while trying to address ever-pressing financial and geopolitical problems in a context of unremitting turmoil.

By the late spring of 1792, the Paris mob—hungry, angry, and impatient with the seemingly slow progress in creating the advantages promised by the early revolutionary activities—invaded the Tuileries Palace and, for a short period, held the king hostage as an initial indication of an impending destitution. Then, as domestic chaos grew and the threat of foreign invasion by conservative monarchical forces from Austria and Prussia became acute, the Paris mob truly flexed its muscle. On August 10 the mob again stormed the Tuileries, but this time unrestrained violence resulted in the deaths of hundreds of Swiss guards and forced the royal family to flee through the palace gardens to the Legislative Assembly for protection. Within less than two months, the monarchy was overthrown, a Republic declared, and the Legislative Assembly had ceased to exist. In its place, a new body, a more radical National Convention, elected by

nearly universal male suffrage, was established to create yet a new political order. Escalating violence became the dominant backdrop to the
Revolution, as it now entered its second and much more turbulent phase.
In September, massacres of aristocrats, priests, and others held in Paris's
prisons ushered in an era of horrific bloodshed and violence. Following
the execution in January 1793 of Louis XVI, who had been convicted of
treason against the nation, and the growing military conflict on France's
northeastern borders, a dictatorship of the more radical revolutionaries
steadily took control of France. The dictatorship instituted a regime of
Terror, intended to remove those perceived to be enemies of the Revolution. In an ever-increasing frenzy of righteous violence, many of the
idealistic young revolutionaries who had been Jacques Godard's friends
and colleagues turned on each other in a legally sanctioned bloodbath.

Concerns about civil rights, whether for Jews, Blacks, or others, were
now replaced by fears of foreign invasion and the purging of those believed
to be opponents of the increasingly radical Revolution. The result was a
regime where summary execution was the favored punishment, and the
anxiety this engendered put moderates on the defensive and annihilated
many of those who had helped shape the first phase of the Revolution.
Stanislas Clermont-Tonnerre, whose rousing speech on behalf of Jewish
equality had made such an impact in the fall of 1789, was imprisoned, then
released, only to be defenestrated and killed by the mob that attacked the
Tuileries in August 1792. In 1793, Condorcet, Godard's competitor in politics and, perhaps, in love, committed suicide in prison rather than face
certain decapitation. The more moderate Girondins, including Godard's
ally, the Abbé Fauchet, went in rapid succession to their deaths in a purge
prompted by the Jacobins. In the spring of 1794, Camille Desmoulins, the
young journalist who had been one of the youthful admirers of Guy Target, was accused of betraying the Revolution he had sparked and was sent
to the guillotine with his political mentor and erstwhile Godard antagonist, Georges-Jacques Danton. Hérault de Séchelles, the avocat-général
who worked closely with Godard on the Julien Baudelle case, accompanied Danton and Desmoulins to the scaffold. Desmoulins' young wife
followed her husband to the guillotine just days later. Moderates who
were not executed fled into hiding or exile. Of course, Godard had been
just such a moderate. Likely, he too would have been swept away in the
paroxysm of revolutionary violence. His illness and early death perhaps
spared him a violent end in the Terror, but also likely deprived him of the

glory that participation in the revolutionary events and even martyrdom might have provided.

Robespierre, who had been among the first members of the National Assembly to enthusiastically endorse the quest for Jewish equality, after having spent some months as the de facto dictator of France ultimately also met the same fate as had many moderates and other opponents he had sent to the guillotine previously. By the spring of 1794, Robespierre had become the virtually absolute ruler of France. But when in the summer of the same year many of the remaining revolutionaries became fearful that they too would be sent to their deaths by Robespierre and his clique, it was Robespierre and his followers who were overthrown. The death of the "incorruptible" Robespierre marked the end of the second phase of the Revolution and the beginning of a slow return to a semblance of stability and the consolidation of fundamental revolutionary gains.

Berr Cerf Berr, the Jew who was the spear-carrier and financier for the Ashkenazi community in the battle for Jewish equality, would only very briefly benefit from the legal rights he had fought so diligently to obtain. In 1793 he appears to have been imprisoned for a short time in Strasbourg for ill-defined offenses—undoubtedly his wealth alone made him suspect of promoting anti-revolutionary activities. His imprisonment allegedly caused a serious deterioration in his health, and he died on December 7, 1793, shortly following his release. He was buried in the oldest Jewish cemetery in Alsace on the outskirts of the town of Rosenwiller, just a few miles from Strasbourg, the city which was the principal object of his efforts for Jewish equality. He was denied a dignified funeral and burial. Due to the then prevailing anti-religious climate (a climate that was not particularly anti-Jewish, but rather ecumenically anti-religious), he had to be buried quickly and at night. His grave marker, which had at one point disappeared, now proudly denotes, in Hebrew, his accomplishments as an important champion of Jewish rights.

The violence of the second phase of the Revolution impinged heavily upon the rights that had been gained at the outset of the Revolution, including those obtained for Jews through Godard's lobbying efforts. Along with many other rights, Jewish rights took a violent step backwards as the virulently anti-religious radicals took control of France. Synagogues were closed and Jewish property was seized, not as part of specifically anti-Jewish actions, but rather as part of a further curtailment of the power of the Church and of all organized religion generally. To the radical revolutionaries, notwithstanding the stirring words of the Declaration of the Rights of Man and of the Citizen, religion was considered a reactionary force and, logically enough, Judaism was viewed in a similar vein. The constraints instituted against Jews, in spite of their legal equality, marked the beginning of a rollercoaster ride for the French Jewish community that would continue to the present day.

At the very end of the eighteenth century and the beginning of the nineteenth, Napoleon Bonaparte emerged as the dominant actor on the French stage. He appeared to be convinced that the Jews were an unassimilated and potentially unassimilable foreign group living within a France that he was trying to unite with an unparalleled uniformity and order. They were both an irritant and a challenge. To that challenge, he brought his usual organizational talents. Initially, he instituted some beneficial organizational changes to France's Jews, convening first an assembly of "Jewish notables" and then, in 1807, a "Sanhedrin" of Jewish leaders, both religious and secular.[1] He then established a Consistory (the *Consistoire*) as a central organization for the Jewish community. However, he also imposed special limitations on Jewish commercial activities, which reinstituted some of the old constraints and thereby nullified a substantial portion of the important advances the Jews had made during the Revolution. Ironically, it was the Bourbon Restoration, following the defeat and abdication of Napoleon, under Louis XVI's two younger brothers who would rule until 1830 (Louis XVIII from 1815 until 1824 and then Charles X until the July Revolution of 1830), which would eliminate Napoleonic restrictions and reinstate some of the gains achieved during the early years of the Revolution of 1789.

With the arrival of a more liberal and bourgeois monarchy under Louis-Philippe, a descendant of the Orléans line of the royal family who would rule from 1830 until his overthrow in 1848—Jews began to thrive. They began to fully benefit from the legal rights they had acquired in 1791, and the few remaining legal barriers to their full equality, including the particularly odious *more judaïco* (the special form of oath that Jews

---

1. During the years of Jewish self-rule in the land of Israel two thousand years ago, the most important court was a seventy-person tribunal made up of rabbinical scholars, which was called the "Sanhedrin." The Talmud relies extensively on discussions and decisions of the the members of the Sanhedrin in elucidating Jewish jurisprudence.

were required to take in order to be considered credible witnesses), were suppressed. Large numbers of Jews who had been born in the villages of Alsace and Lorraine began to make their way to Paris and other major French cities. They became increasingly educated and assimilated (sometimes at the cost of conversion to Catholicism), moving into the mainstream of French life. Some of them achieved remarkable success in business as the French economy began to thrive with increasing industrialization. During the short-lived Second Republic (1848–1852), France saw its first Jewish cabinet ministers when Adolphe Crémieux became Minister of Justice and the banker Achille Fould served as Minister of Finance. Fould would ultimately serve in that capacity under four different prime ministers.

By the Second Empire of Napoleon III (1852–1870), a significant segment of the Jewish community had achieved marked success at many levels of French society. These Jews joined the ranks of government, with several becoming government ministers. They played a role in the development of railroads and major banks, as well as in the growth of commercial activities of all types. The arts, including music and especially opera, saw an important Jewish presence, with Jews achieving great success in certain of those fields of endeavor.[2]

But this success and the increasingly higher profile of the prosperous elements of the French-Jewish community brought with it significant undercurrents of anti-Jewish sentiment. After France's dramatic defeat in the Franco-Prussian War of 1870, a growing nationalism associated with a search for scapegoats for France's abject military failure engendered a toxic political antisemitism, which jeopardized so many of the gains that had been achieved by French Jews. This culminated in 1894 with the Dreyfus Affair, in which Alfred Dreyfus, a French army captain, who had been born in Alsace to an affluent Jewish family, was accused of spying for the Germans. With Dreyfus quickly, and wrongly, convicted of espionage, overt antisemitism emerged with an unparalleled virulence. Although Dreyfus was ultimately exonerated with the support of the more liberal

---

2. As a symbol of that success, one need only note that of the seven statues that adorn the front façade of the Opera Garnier of Paris, two are of Jews: Giacomo Meyerbeer and Jacques-Fromental Halévy (one of whose daughters married Georges Bizet, the composer of perhaps the most popular opera of all time, "Carmen," and whose mother was likely from a Jewish family, although he was not a practicing Jew).

elements of French society, his prosecution and the persecution of the Jewish community, together with the enormous political turmoil that the Affair fomented, served as a serious setback to the cause of Jewish equality.

The struggle on behalf of Dreyfus had its beneficial side. Once Dreyfus had been exonerated, the monarchical and nationalist forces in France stood discredited and a new era of relative calm emerged for the Jewish community. The power and influence of the Catholic Church began to wane, with that diminution in status being formalized by the legal separation of Church and State in 1905. These developments led many in the French-Jewish community to believe that they would now irrevocably have the true equality for which they had striven for so many years. In fact, France would come to be viewed as a haven for Jews, especially in comparison to Russia and central Europe, where Jews suffered from terrible poverty and ever-present violence. Jehiel Levyne, the father of Emmanuel Levinas, one of France's most renowned twentieth-century Jewish scholars, was reported to have commented with respect to France and its struggles during the Dreyfus Affair that, "any nation that would tear itself apart over the fate of a little Jewish captain, is a nation to which we [Jews] should go immediately."[3]

The new era also gave rise to the Yiddish phrase "Gliklekh vi Got in Frankraikh" ("As happy as God in France"), an aphorism which for generations highlighted the equality granted to Jews by the French Revolution and the vast opportunities which seemed to exist for Jews in a France whose borders remained open to immigrants, even as those of other prospective havens, and most prominently the United States, were steadily closed. The promise of equality and of equal opportunity drew thousands of persecuted eastern European Jews to France.

As if to prove their gratitude to France, young Jews died by the thousands in the trenches of World War I defending French territory and values. When the war was over, the Jewish community justifiably expected that this enormous sacrifice would solidify and sanctify the French-Jewish relationship. However, within little more than a decade, economic struggles once again gave rise to growing French nationalism

3. He could have added to his commentary that a nation whose leaders had spent as much time as the French revolutionaries had in giving consideration to the grant of equality to the very modest group of Jews living in France during the first phase of the Revolution had already demonstrated its potential desirability as a haven for Jews.

with its antisemitic accompaniment. Even though Jews rose to the pinnacles of power, with Léon Blum becoming the first Jewish Prime Minister in 1936, the toxic stew of anger, frustration, and rising fascism put the Jews of France yet again in a precarious position. Eastern European Jews who, as the doors to the United States slammed shut, had flocked to France following World War I—becoming a large presence in France, generally, and in Paris in particular—initially were welcomed as a means of repopulating a society depleted by the bloodletting of the war. But their presence rapidly became a very visible irritant. Following the defeat of France by Nazi Germany in 1940, the French Jewish community, and especially immigrant eastern European Jews, were victimized in a cauldron of persecution and extermination, with French collaborators joining the Nazi occupiers in an attempt to destroy the entire community. Before World War II had come to an end, over seventy-five thousand Jews living in France had been deported to death camps in eastern Europe, where most were murdered.

The post-World War II era saw the Jewish community in France begin efforts to revivify itself. It was, however, the arrival in the early 1960s of thousands of North African Jews from the former French colonies of Algeria, Tunisia, and Morocco—Sephardim who had been naturalized as French citizens in the mid-nineteenth century—which provided a new and powerful dynamism to the French Jewish community. By the 1970s, the French Jewish population had grown to nearly seven hundred fifty thousand. For some decades, prosperity and growing assimilation brought a sense of stability to the community. However, the arrival of large numbers of North African and Sub-Saharan Muslims, many with their own negative attitude toward Jews, frequently in the guise of anti-Zionism, has most recently generated a new antisemitism that is once again posing a threat to the full integration of Jews into French society. There is no threat to Jewish legal equality; those gains are not in jeopardy. But there is a perceived threat to the safety and security of Jews. As a result, a new exodus of Jews has begun. Only this time, it is an exodus out of France and toward Israel and, to a lesser extent, the United States.

The continuing rollercoaster-like quality of the status of Jews in France leaves us with the question of whether the efforts of Jacques Godard, in his representation of the small, marginalized, and unassimilated Jewish community in 1789, have resulted in a successful outcome. Did the lobbying work of a young Christian lawyer over 225 years ago achieve the objective of genuine equality for the Jews of France for which he was retained and toward which he devoted so much thought and energy?

The answer to that question may lie in the wisdom of a twentieth-century Chinese leader. The story is told—it is perhaps apocryphal, but it has sufficient basis in fact to be credible—that during one of their meetings in the 1970s, when there was a break in the conversation, the American Secretary of State Henry Kissinger, seeking to make small talk and enliven their suddenly silent meeting, turned to Chinese Premier Chou En-lai and asked him, "Mr. Premier, what do you think of the French Revolution?" The intellectual Chinese politician hesitated a moment and then responded, "It is too early to tell."

Was Jacques Godard successful in his efforts on behalf of his Jewish clients? Perhaps, it is simply too early to tell.

ACKNOWLEDGMENTS

I was prompted to write this book as a result of two rather unrelated events. Many years ago, when I was a teenager living in Chicago, my uncle, Jean Geissmann, very generously invited my brother and me to spend part of a summer in Paris with our grandparents, Robert and Jeanne Geissmann, whom we had not seen for many years following our immigration to the United States. During the course of that summer, our grandfather, then retired from his position as *Secretaire-Général* of the *Consistoire Central de Paris* (the principal administrative arm of the Paris Jewish Community established by Napoleon in 1807), took us to the *Archives Nationales*, where he was conducting some research into French Jewish history. During that visit, I was fascinated by the availability of important historic documents, especially those about France's Jewish community. Our grandfather's research was being carried out to assist his friend, Rabbi David Feuerwerker, a practicing rabbi and a brilliant scholar. At one point during that summer, we were invited to hear an erudite lecture about the history of the Jews of France given by Rabbi Feuerwerker to a group of American students. Both the visit to the Archives and the lecture by Rabbi Feuerwerker left their mark on me.

Some years later, during one of my many visits to Paris, but long after our grandfather had passed away, I had occasion to stroll down rue des Rosiers in the Marais neighborhood and to walk into a large Jewish-themed book store named "Bibliophane." While scanning the shelves, I found Rabbi

515

Feuerwerker's book, *L'Emancipation des Juifs de France*—the book for which our grandfather had been doing research during that summer years before. I bought the massive book (containing over seven hundred pages) and put it on a bookshelf, but I did not read it for many years. When I did get around to reading the large tome, I had become a practicing attorney and I remember taking special note of the various references to the young lawyer who had worked with the Ashkenazi Jewish community of France at the time of the French Revolution.

Years later, one of my distant cousins, Philip Hamburger (like me, a descendant of Alsatian Jews who so benefitted from Jacques Godard's efforts), then a professor of law at my alma mater, The University of Chicago, and today a professor at Columbia University Law School, kindly gave me a set of books published by EDHIS containing copies of all of the principal documents relating to the grant of equality to France's Jews, including, notably, the *Pétition* drafted by Godard in early 1790. In giving me these volumes, Philip noted that they were likely to be of greater importance to me than they were to him. Indeed, they turned out to be of very great importance to me and I am most grateful that Philip thought of giving them to me since they gave new, albeit slow, impetus to my interest in Godard.

Initially, my inquiries into Godard's life story suggested that I might write an essay about his efforts. However, as I began to delve into Godard's work, I became convinced that this virtually forgotten young man deserved more and that his role in connection with the grant of legal equality to Jews in France was worthy of a more extensive analysis. As a consequence, I resolved to write a longer biography of Godard. This book is the result of that resolve.

In the preparation of this book, I have benefitted from the assistance and encouragement of many individuals and institutions, for which I am very grateful.

The staffs of the Archives Nationales de France, the Bibliothèque Maza-rine, the Bibliothèque Historique de la Ville de Paris, the Bibliothèque de l'Hôtel de Ville de Paris, the Bibliothèque Nationale de France (at both the Tolbiac and Richelieu sites), the Archives de Paris, the Archives de la Côte d'Or, the Bibliothèque Municipale de Semur-en-Auxois, the Archives Historiques du Diocèse de Paris, the New York City Public Library and The Central Archives for the History of the Jewish People Jerusalem (CAHJP) have been of great assistance. The president of the

Jewish community of Geneva, Philippe Grumbach, and the staff of the community's library and archives, as well as members of the family of Henri de Toledo, did their best to assist me in my, unfortunately, unsuccessful efforts to locate the Godard files in Geneva. The Jewish community of Zurich and the archivists at the ETHZ in Zurich also kindly aided me in my search for the Godard files. My thanks to Janice Rosen of the Alex Dworkin Canadian Jewish Archives, where the archives of Rabbi David Feuerwerker, the last person to have studied the Godard files, are now kept, whom I was induced to contact as a result of a conversation with the rabbi's son, Hillel, a childhood acquaintance and today an architect in southern France.

I have been the recipient of generous doses of advice and counsel from many individuals in the United States and in France, who kindly reviewed the manuscript. Prof. David Bell of Princeton University, certainly the foremost American expert on French lawyers at the time of the French Revolution, provided me with important suggestions, as did Prof. Frances Malino, long-time professor at Wellesley College and author of a remarkable book on the "Polish Jew" Zalkind Hourwitz, to whom I was introduced by my good friends Raphaël and Mireille Hadas-Lebel. I had occasion to speak with Prof. Hervé Leuwers, a French specialist on French revolutionaries about the manuscript. Prof. Miranda Spieler of the American University of Paris provided invaluable insights into the Julien Baudelle matter and Prof. Carrie F. Klaus of DePauw University assisted me in gaining a better understanding of the Belgian-British writer, Cornélie Wouters de Vasse. The Chief Rabbi of France, Haïm Korsia, did me the honor of reading the manuscript and providing me with his comments and insights. My good friend, Prof. Gershon Greenberg of American University in Washington, was particularly generous with his praise, which became an important source of encouragement for my writing. Similarly, Prof. Jeremy Rabkin of George Mason University's Antonin Scalia Law School provided sound advice and encouraging words, as did François Legros, President of Rochambeau, The French International School. I am grateful to have had the opportunity to speak with a descendant of family members of Raymond DeSèze, Me. Ghislaine Sèze, and with descendants of Guy Target. Yves Ozanam, the kindly archivist of the Paris Ordre des Avocats at the Paris Palais de Justice, devoted considerable time to assisting me in locating information respecting Godard's legal career in Paris. I was introduced to Mr. Ozanam by my very good friend and colleague Me. Louis-Bernard Buchman of Paris.

My cousin Daniel Hayem assisted me in obtaining copies of the extant letters between Godard and Amélie Suard at the Institut Voltaire in Geneva. His son, Laurent, served as my eyes in evaluating certain documents concerning Godard located in Paris at a time when I could not do so myself and has generously given of his time to assist me in locating the missing Godard file. Philippe Bézamat of *Passé-Présent* made it possible for me to acquire documents related to the Godard family that brought me a sense of proximity to Jacques Godard that only tangible items sometimes can. My friend Howard Rosen became my emissary to procure a critical document at the Central Archives for the History of the Jewish People in Jerusalem, where he was kindly assisted by Inka Arroyo-Antezana. I am grateful to Mme. Chantal Céceille for having agreed to let me purchase the only known portrait of Jacques Godard, which was in her personal collection.

As I confronted the product of my extensive research and felt confused, almost paralyzed, as to the best way to proceed with the mountain of materials about Jacques Godard I had gathered, some straightforward advice from Prof. Steven Katz of Boston University, one of our era's greatest Holocaust scholars, put me on the right path. "Just start writing," Prof. Katz told me. He was right and I am grateful for his seemingly obvious, but insightful and very helpful, advice.

My colleagues at Arent Fox, LLP, the Washington, DC law firm with which I have been affiliated for forty years, provided me with assistance, even though they may not be aware that they did so. On many occasions, I would stay in my office in the evenings to use my office computer (invariably a better computer than my home computer) and to make copies of critical documents that I had gathered over the Internet. By using the firm's facilities, my work advanced much more rapidly and with much greater ease. My thanks to my law partners and colleagues and, especially to Michael Gordon, who spent considerable time proofreading the manuscript and providing his valuable insights.

Special thanks go to Sonja Rethy, my editor at HUC Press, whose guidance, advice and diligent efforts have been invaluable in making this book a reality.

Over the years, members of my immediate family have had to cope with my incessant isolation in our family library as I worked on this manuscript. I always received encouragement and was given all of the time that I needed to pursue this project. However, particular thanks must be given to my wife, Lisa, who not only gave me the time and space to pursue my work and was a good-natured captive audience as she had to listen to repeated oral readings of the manuscript. She also proofread the manuscript several times and accompanied me on trips to archives in France, serving as my most-valued assistant as I gathered critical information. She, in spite of her serious health challenges, but with the extraordinary courage with which she confronted them, has created and maintained the precious world in which I have been able to engage in research and writing. Without her, my life would not have been as blessed as it has been and this manuscript would assuredly never have seen the light of day.

A final word of acknowledgment and gratitude goes to my late grandparents, Robert and Jeanne Geissmann, to whom this volume is dedicated. They instilled in me the profound appreciation that I have for my French heritage. In the somewhat gloomy post-World War II years, in the midst of family turmoil and illness, it is they who, in spite of their own meager resources, provided my family with a home and with precious stability. Notwithstanding the suffering they endured during the German Occupation of France and the betrayal that had been visited upon them by some of their compatriots, they remained deeply devoted to France and its culture while adhering to the Jewish traditions of their ancestors. That devotion became a gift that they bestowed on me and which has played such an important role throughout my life, including in connection with the writing of this book.

For all the express and tacit assistance I received during the many years that I worked on this biography, I am very appreciative. However, I take full and sole responsibility for any errors that may have crept into my work in spite of my determined efforts to be as precise and careful as possible.

This book has been a labor of love and remembrance: of the French and Jewish traditions that are mine, of those who made those traditions a part of my life, and of all of those who over the course of years have so kindly extended encouragement and a helping hand to me as I prepared for this project and then pursued it.

BIBLIOGRAPHY

ARCHIVES AND LIBRARIES

Archives de la Côte d'Or, Archives Civiles - Serie E, Nos. 642 & 643
Archives de l'Institut Voltaire (Geneva, Switzerland); Archives Suard;
    Cote IMV: MS AS 420
Archives Nationales de France
Author's Personal Collection
Bibliothèque Historique de la Ville de Paris
Bibliothèque de l'Hôtel de Ville de Paris
Bibliothèque Mazarine
Bibliothèque Nationale de France (Richelieu and Tolbiac)
Central Archives for the History of the Jewish People
État civil de la Côte-d'Or
Georgetown University Library
HathiTrust Digital Library
Stanford University Archives

PRINTED PRIMARY SOURCES

PERIODICALS

Les Affiches des Evêchés et Lorraine
L'Ami des Patriotes, ou le Défenseur de la Constitution

L'Ami du Peuple ou le Publiciste parisien
L'Ami du Roi, des Français, de l'Ordre et Sur-tout de la Vérité
Annales patriotiques et litteraires de la France
Archives Israélites de France, Revue Mensuelle, Année 1841, vol. 2.
   Paris: Au Bureau des Archives Israélites de France, 1841
La Chronique de Paris
Le Courrier de Provence
Le Courrier de Versailles
La Gazette Nationale ou Le Moniteur Universel
Journal de la Cour et de la Ville
Journal de la Municipalité et des Districts de Paris
Journal de Paris
Journal Patriotique de Bourgogne par une Société de Gens de Lettres
Journal politique, ou Gazette des Gazettes
*Journal des Tribunaux et Journal du Tribunal de Cassation; réunis; par une
   Société d'Hommes de Loi*
Journal de Versailles
Le Patriote Français!
Mercure de France
Révolutions de France et de Brabant
Révolutions de Paris dédiées à la Nation
Revue d'Histoire moderne et contemporaine
Revue du Lyonnais

BOOKS, PAMPHLETS, DOCUMENTS

*Adresse de l'Assemblée des Représentants de la Commune de Paris à l'Assem-
   blée Nationale sur l'admission des Juifs à l'Etat Civil.* Paris, Imprimerie
   de Lottin l'ainé & Lottin de St. Germain,1790.
*Adresse Présentée à l'Assemblée Nationale le 31 Août 1789, par les Députés
   Réunis des Juifs Etablis à Metz, dans les Trois Evêchés, en Alsace & en
   Lorraine.*
*Adresse des Représentans de la Commune de Paris à l'Assemblée Nationale,
   sur la formation d'un Etablissement National en faveur des Sourds &
   Muets.* Imprimerie de Lottin, l'ainé & Lottin de St. Germain 1790.
Almanach Royal, 1790. Imprimerie de la Veuve d'Houry & Debure.
Berr, Berr Isaac. *Lettre d'un Citoyen Membre de la Ci-devant Communauté
   des Juifs de Lorraine à ses Confrères, à l'occasion du Droit de Citoyen*

actif, rendu aux Juifs par le Décret du 28 [sic] septembre 1791. Nancy: Chez H. Haener, 1791.

Billecocq, Jean Baptiste Louis Joseph. Letter of November 5 1791. *Mercure Universel*, vol. 9, no. 230, pp. 86–88 and *L'Ami des Patriotes, ou le Défenseur de la Constitution*, vol. 4, no. 6, pp. 177–83.

Brissot, J.-P. *Correspondance et Papiers*, edited by Claude Perroud. Paris: Librairie Alphonse Picard & Fils, 1911.

Brochure sur la municipalité et les districts de Paris (1789), District des Blancs-Manteaux, Arrêté du 21 Juillet 1789, du matin. [gallica.bnf.fr]

Buffon, Henri Nadault de. *Correspondance inédite de Buffon*, vol. 2. Paris: Hachette, 1860.

Cahiers de Doléances des Bailliages des Généralités de Metz et Nancy pour les États-Généraux de 1789, series 1, Département de Meurthe-et-Moselle, vol. 2, *Cahiers du Bailliage de Dieuze*, published by Charles Étienne. Nancy: Imprimerie Berger-Levrault, 1912.

Cahiers de doléances des Sénéchaussées de Niort et de Saint-Maixent et des communautés et corporations de Niort et Saint-Maixent pour les États-Généraux de 1789, edited by Léonce Cathelineau. Niort: Imprimerie Nouvelle G. Clouzot, 1912.

Collection Générale des Décrets rendus par la Convention Nationale avec la mention de leur date. Floréal An III. Paris: Chez Baudouin, 1795.

The Collection of John Boyd Thacher of the Library of Congress, vol. 3, Catalogue of Autographs Relating to the French Revolution. United States Government Printing Office, 1931.

Clermont-Tonnerre, Stanislas de. *Opinion de M. Le Comte Stanislas de Clermont Tonnerre, Député de Paris, le 23 Décembre 1789.* Paris: Chez Baudouin, 1789.

Condorcet (J.A.N Caritat), Marquis de. *Lettres et manuscrits de J.A.N. Caritat, Marquis de Condorcet*, compiled February 1932. New Acquisition 23639, Bibliothèque Nationale de France.

Correspondance de Cortot et de Godard (1788–1789). Archives de la Côte d'Or, Serie E, Nos. 642 & 643.

Debourge, Jean-Claude-Antoine. *Discours Prononcé le 30 Janvier dans l'Assemblée générale des Représentans de la Commune par M. DEBOURGE, l'un des Représentans de la Commune à l'occasion de la Demande faite le 27, par les Juifs de Paris.*

———. *Lettre au comité de constitution sur l'affaire des juifs: 19 Mai 1790.* Paris: Imprimerie du Patriote Français, 1790.

Décision du Comité de Constitution Requise par David Sylveira, Syndic Agent des Juifs François Patentées, October 28, 1790. *Adresses, Mémoires et Pétitions des Juifs 1789–1794. Paris: EDHIS, 1968.*

Déclaration des Droits de l'Homme et du Citoyen.

Déclaration du District des Blancs-Manteaux. MS 814, Document 356, Bibliothèque Historique de la Ville de Paris.

Declaration of Independence of the Thirteen United States of America

"Demande Particulière Adressée à l'Assemblée Nationale par les députés des Juifs de Metz." *Adresses, Mémoires et Pétitions des Juifs 1789–1794,* vol. 5. Paris: EDHIS, 1968.

Dénombrement Général des Juifs—Qui sont tolérés en la Province d'Alsace, en exécution des Lettres Patentes de Sa Majesté, en forme de Règlement du 10 juillet 1784. Chez Jean-Henri Decker, imprimeur juré du roi & de nosseigneurs du Conseil souverain d'Alsace, 1785.

Dupaty, Charles-Marguerite Mercier. *Justification de sept hommes condamnés par le Parlement de Metz en 1769 sur les seules dépositions de juifs plaignants,* 1787.

Édit du Roi, concernant ceux qui ne font pas profession de la religion Catholique, November 28, 1787.

Élie de Beaumont, Jean-Baptiste Jacques. *Mémoire à Consulter pour la Dame Anne-Rose Caribel, veuve Calas, & pour les Enfans.* Imprimerie de Le Breton, 1762.

Fauchet, Claude. *Oraison Funèbre de Charles-Michel de l'Épée.* Paris: Chez J. R. Lottin de St. Germain, 1790.

Franklin, Benjamin. *The Papers of Benjamin Franklin,* vol. 37, March 16 through August 15, 1782, edited by Ellen R. Cohn. New Haven, CT and London: Yale University Press, 2003.

Godard, Jacques. Letters to Amélie Suard, dated November 18, 1789. Archives of the Institut Voltaire, Geneva, Switzerland (Cote IMV: MS AS 420), and dated July 27 (presumably 1790). Archives of the Institut Voltaire, Geneva, Switzerland. Cote IMV: MS AS 421.

———. *Consultation à un Mémoire intitulé Justification de Sept Hommes Condamnés par le Parlement de Metz, en 1769,* in Dupaty, Charles-Marguerite Mercier, *Justification de sept hommes condamnés par le Parlement de Metz en 1769 sur les seules dépositions de juifs plaignants,* 1787.

———. *Consultation à un Mémoire pour Antoine Lefevre, dit Barré, et al.* Imprimerie de C. Simon, 1788.

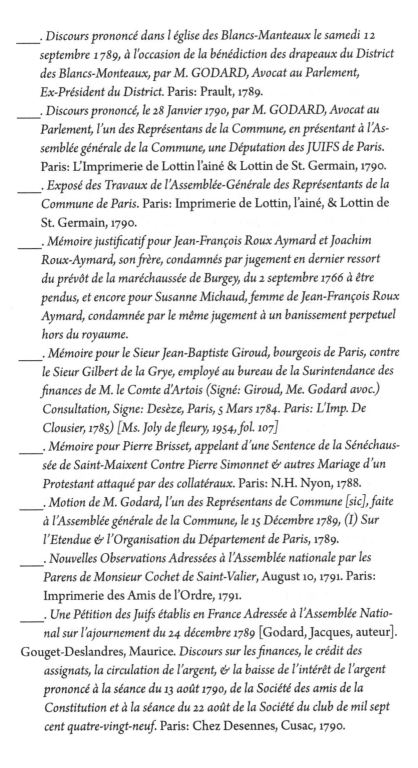

____. *Discours prononcé dans l église des Blancs-Manteaux le samedi 12 septembre 1789, à l'occasion de la bénédiction des drapeaux du District des Blancs-Monteaux, par M. GODARD, Avocat au Parlement, Ex-Président du District.* Paris: Prault, 1789.

____. *Discours prononcé, le 28 Janvier 1790, par M. GODARD, Avocat au Parlement, l'un des Représentans de la Commune, en présentant à l'Assemblée générale de la Commune, une Députation des JUIFS de Paris.* Paris: L'Imprimerie de Lottin l'ainé & Lottin de St. Germain, 1790.

____. *Exposé des Travaux de l'Assemblée-Générale des Représentants de la Commune de Paris.* Paris: Imprimerie de Lottin, l'ainé, & Lottin de St. Germain, 1790.

____. *Mémoire justificatif pour Jean-François Roux Aymard et Joachim Roux-Aymard, son frère, condamnés par jugement en dernier ressort du prévôt de la maréchaussée de Burgey, du 2 septembre 1766 à être pendus, et encore pour Susanne Michaud, femme de Jean-François Roux Aymard, condamnée par le même jugement à un banissement perpetuel hors du royaume.*

____. *Mémoire pour le Sieur Jean-Baptiste Giroud, bourgeois de Paris, contre le Sieur Gilbert de la Grye, employé au bureau de la Surintendance des finances de M. le Comte d'Artois (Signé: Giroud, Me. Godard avoc.) Consultation, Signe: Desèze, Paris, 5 Mars 1784. Paris: L'Imp. De Clousier, 1785) [Ms. Joly de fleury, 1954, fol. 107]*

____. *Mémoire pour Pierre Brisset, appelant d'une Sentence de la Sénéchaussée de Saint-Maixent Contre Pierre Simonnet & autres Mariage d'un Protestant attaqué par des collatéraux.* Paris: N.H. Nyon, 1788.

____. *Motion de M. Godard, l'un des Représentans de Commune [sic], faite à l'Assemblée générale de la Commune, le 15 Décembre 1789, (I) Sur l'Etendue & l'Organisation du Département de Paris, 1789.*

____. *Nouvelles Observations Adressées à l'Assemblée nationale par les Parens de Monsieur Cochet de Saint-Valier, August 10, 1791.* Paris: Imprimerie des Amis de l'Ordre, 1791.

____. *Une Pétition des Juifs établis en France Adressée à l'Assemblée National sur l'ajournement du 24 décembre 1789* [Godard, Jacques, auteur].

Gouget-Deslandres, Maurice. *Discours sur les finances, le crédit des assignats, la circulation de l'argent, & la baisse de l'intérêt de l'argent prononcé à la séance du 13 août 1790, de la Société des amis de la Constitution et à la séance du 22 août de la Société du club de mil sept cent quatre-vingt-neuf.* Paris: Chez Desennes, Cusac, 1790.

Grégoire, Henri. *Essai sur la Regénération physique, morale et politique des Juifs.* Metz: L'Imprimerie de Claude Lamort, 1789.

____. *Motion en Faveur des Juifs.* Paris: Belin, 1789.

Hell, François Joseph Antoine, *Observations d'un alsacien sur l'Affaire présente des juifs d'Alsace.* Frankfurt, 1779.

Hérault de Séchelles, Marie-Jean. *Voyage à Montbard,* edited by Aulard, F.-A. Paris: Librairie de Bibliophiles, 1890.

Jay, John. *The Correspondence and Public Papers of John Jay: 1781–1782,* vol. 2, edited by Henry P. Johnston. New York: G. P. Putnam's Sons, 1891.

Journal de la Députation des Juifs de Bordeaux auprès de l'Assemblée Nationale, 30 décembre 1789 et 17 février 1790. The Central Archives for the History of the Jewish People, Jerusalem, Israel, F-B0-5.

Journal de la Société de 1789, issues nos. 1–15. Paris: EDHIS, 1982.

L…, Abbé [Lamourette, Antoine Adrien]. *Observations sur l'État civil des Juifs adressées à l'Assemblée nationale par M. l'Abbé L***.* Paris: Chez Belin, 1790.

Lacretelle, Charles. *Dix Années d'Épreuves pendant la Révolution.* Paris: Chez A. Allouard, Librairie, 1842.

Lacretelle, Pierre-Louis. *Discours sur le Préjugé des Peines Infamantes.* Paris: Chez Cuchet, 1784.

____. *Oeuvres de P-L LaCretelle, Aîné,* vol. 1. Paris: Bossange Frères, 1823.

Lettre d'un Alsacien sur les Juifs d'Alsace à M. Reubell, député de cette Province à l'Assemblée nationale. Paris: Imprimerie de Savy, le Jeune, 1790.

Lettres Patentes concernant les juifs d'Alsace. Versailles, 10 juillet 1784. Reg. Au conseil supérieur d'Alsace le 26 avril 1785.

Lettre du Roi pour la Convocation des États-généraux, à Versailles le 27 Avril 1789 et Règlement Fait par Le Roi, du 19 Février 1789. Paris: De l'Imprimerie Royale 1789. http://archive.org/details/lettreduroipourl_4.

Malédiction. Frankfurt, 1778.

Malesherbes, Chrétien-Guillaume Lamoignon de. *Mémoire sur le Mariage des Protestans,* 1785.

Marmontel, Jean-François. *Essai sur les Révolutions de la Musique en France,* lu et approuvé, ce 16 avril 1777, de Sauvigny, permis d'Imprimerie, ce 19 avril 1777, Le Noir.

____. *Mémoires de Marmontel, Secrétaire Perpétuelle de l'Académie*

Française. Paris: Librairie de Firmin Didot Frères, Imprimeurs de
l'Institut, 1846.

*Mémoire à Consulter et Consultation pour Dame Sara Mendez d'Acosta,
épouse du Sieur Samuel Peixotto, 1777.*

*Mémoire pour Julien Baudelle, Américain, Intimé; Contre le sieur Ruste de
Rezeville, Négociant à la Martinique, & Demoiselle Reine Baudelle, son
épouse, Appellans; En présence de M. le Procureur Général, Plaignant &
Accusateur; contre la Dame Ruste & le sieur Ozenne.* Paris: Chez N. H.
Nyon, Imprimeur du Parlement, rue Mignon Saint André-des-Arcs,
1787.

Mémoire de Me. Mirbeck, avocat pour les juifs. Archives Nationales, K.
1142, cited in Philippe Sagnac, "Les Juifs et la Révolution française,
1789–1791." *Revue d'Histoire moderne et contemporaine*, vol. 1, no. 1,
1899.

*Mémoires Secrets pour servir à l'histoire de la République des Lettres en
France depuis MDCCLXII jusqu'à nos jours ou Journal d'un Observa-
teur*, vols. 27 & 35, edited by Louis Petit de Bachaumont. London:
John Adamson, 1789.

Menassier de l'Este, François. *De l'honneur des deux sexes, et principes
généraux sur les différentes espèces de rapts, de séduction, de subornation
et de violence.* Paris: N.H. Nyon, imprimeur du Parlement, 1784.

Mirabeau, André-Boniface-Louis Riqueti, Vicomte de. *Facéties du
Vicomte de Mirabeau, "Cinquième Bulletin de couches de Me. Target,
Père et mère de la Constitution…,"* March 20, 1790. Côte Rôtie:
Imprimerie Boivin, 1790.

Mirabeau, Honoré-Gabriel Riqueti, Comte de. *Sur Moses Mendelssohn
sur la Réforme politique des Juifs.* London, 1787.

Mulot, François-Valentin. *À la Mémoire de Léonard Robin, Tribun et
Membre de l'Académie de Législation, discours prononcé à la séance
publique du 1er Germinal An XI par le Cit. Mulot, ex-Legislateur.*
[gallica.bnf.fr]

Muraire, M. *Éloge de G.J.B. Target.* Paris: Imprimerie de Xhrouet, 1807.

Necker, Jacques. *De l'Importance des opinions religieuses.* London, 1788.

Observations d'un alsacien sur l'Affaire présente des juifs d'Alsace.
Frankfurt, 1779.

*Ouverture des États-Généraux, Discours du Roi, Discours de M. le Garde
des Sceaux; Rapport de M. le Directeur General des Finances, Fait par
Ordre du Roi.* A Strasbourg de l'Imprimerie Ordinaire du Roi, 1789.

Pastoret, Claude-Emmanuel Joseph Pierre de. *Discours en vers sur l'union qui doit regner entre la Magistrature, la philosophie et les lettres*. Paris: Chez Jombert jeune, 1783.

_____. *Moyse, considéré comme législateur et comme moraliste*. Paris: Buisson, 1788.

Procès-verbal de l'Assemblée partielle du Tiers-État de la Ville de Paris tenue en l'Église des Blancs-Manteaux, le Mardi 21 Avril 1789 & le lendemain, sans désemparer, and *Cahier d'instructions données par l'Assemblée partielle du Tiers-État de la Ville de Paris, tenue en l'Eglise des Blancs-Manteaux, le Mardi 21 Avril 1789, & le lendemain Mercredi, sans désemparer*. [gallica.bnf.fr]

Procès-verbal de la confédération des gardes nationales des quatre départements formans ci-devant la province de Bourgogne et pays adjacens faite sous les murs de Dijon, le 18 mai 1790. Dijon: l'Imprimerie de P. Causse, 1790.

Procès-Verbal des Séances du Conseil Général de la Commune de Strasbourg. Strasbourg: Ph. J. Dannbach, 1791.

Proclamation du Roi sur un Décret de l'Assemblée Nationale concernant les Juifs, April 18, 1790.

Rapport lu à l'assemblée de la Société des Amis de la Constitution, le 27 fevrier mil sept cent quatre-vingt dix sur la Quéstion de l'Etat Civil des Juifs d'Alsace. Extrait du procès-verbal de la société des Amis de la Constitution à Strasbourg, du 27 février 1790. [gallica.bnf.fr]

Rapport sur la Lettre de M. de Bourges au Comité de Constitution, Concernant l'Affaire des Juifs, fait par M. Brissot de Warville, à l'Assemblée générale des Représentans de la Commune de Paris, le 29 Mai 1790. Imprimé par l'ordre de l'Assemblée.

Reflexions Impartiales d'un Citoyen, sur la question de l'egilibilité des Juifs, proposée et discutée dans les séances de l'Assemblée nationale, des 23 & 24 Décembre & ajournée par la même Assemblée. Imprimerie de la Veuve Delaguette [undated].

Règlemens de la Société de 1789 et liste de ses membres. Paris: L'Imprimerie de Lejay fils, 1790.

Réponse de Miromesnil au Maréchal de Ségur. Versailles, November 15, 1784, Archives Nationales, K 1142, no. 60.

Scaramuzza. *Les Juifs d'Alsace doivent-ils être admis au droit de citoyens actifs, Lisez et jugez* (1790).

Sechehaye, Jules. *Allocution de M. le Bâtonnier et Éloge de P.-L. Lacretelle*.

Metz: Typographie Rousseau-Pallez, Editeur, 1867.

Sieyès, Emmanuel Joseph. *Qu'est-ce que le Tiers-Etat?* (1789). [gallica.bnf. fr]

Soulavie, Jean-Louis Giraud. *L'Histoire naturelle de la France méridionale.* Paris: Chez Quillau, Mérigot, Belin, 1782.

de Staël, Anne Louise Germaine. *Considerations on the Principal Events of the French Revolution* (new translation of the 1818 English edition, edited by Aurelian Craiutu). Indianapolis, IN: Liberty Fund, Inc., 2008.

Suard, Amélie Panckouke. *Essais de Mémoires sur M. Suard.* Paris: Imp. P. Didot, 1820.

_____. *Lettres de Mme. Suard à son Mari sur son Voyage de Ferney, Suivies de quelques autres inserées dans le Journal de Paris.* A. Dampierre, An X, 1802.

Suard, J.B.A. *Mélanges de Littérature; Publiés par J.B.A. Suard.* Paris: Dentu, Impr.-Libraire, 1806.

Tableau des opérations de l'Assemblée Nationale: d'après le Journal de Paris, vol. 1. Lausanne: Chez Hignou et Compagnie, 1789.

Target, Guy. *Consultation sur l'Affaire de la dame Marquise d'Anglure contre les Sieurs Petit, au Conseil des Dépêches, dans laquelle l'on traite du mariage et de l'état des Protestants.* Paris: Imp. Nyon, 1788.

_____. *Les États Généraux convoqués par Louis XVI,* 1789.

_____. *Observations de Target sur le procès de Louis XVI.* Paris, 1792.

Thiéry, Claude-Antoine. *Dissertation sur cette question: est-il des moyens de rendre les Juifs plus heureux et plus utiles en France?* Paris: Knapen, Fils & Madame la Veuve Delaguette et Fils, 1788.

Vasse, Baronne de. *Mémoire à l'Assemblée Nationale, pour démontrer aux Français les raisons qui doivent les déterminer à admettre les Juifs indistinctement aux droits de Citoyens.* Paris: Chez Baudouin, Imprimeur de l'Assemblée Nationale, 1790.

Vieillard, Philippe. *Dissertation sur la demande des Juifs de Paris tendante à être admis au rang de citoyens actifs* [Bib. Nat. Lb 40/106], 1791.

SECONDARY SOURCES

"À la fidelité et à la vertu des suisses, Christian-Frederic-Dagobert, premier comte de Waldner de Freundenstein, 1711–1783, bourgeois suisse au service du roi de France." *En passant par Soultz, Haut Rhin,* 2018: http://www. amisdesoultz.fr/index.php/site-er/

christian-frederic-dagobert-premier-comte-de-waldner-de-freunstein.

Alexandre, Seligman. "Les tribulations d'un juif alsacien pendant la terreur." *Le Patriote Français*, no. 138, December 24, 1789.

Altbauer-Rudnik, Michal. *Prescribing Love: Italian Jewish Physicians Writing on Lovesickness in the Sixteenth and Seventeenths Centuries.* Jerusalem: European Forum at the Hebrew University, 2009.

L'Ami de la religion et du roi: journal ecclésiastique, politique et littéraire, vol. 83. Paris: Librairie Ecclésiastique d'Ad. LeClere et Cie., 1835.

Amiable, Louis. *Une loge maçonnique d'avant 1789: la loge des Neuf Sœurs. Augmenté d'un commentaire et de notes critiques de Charles Porset, 1989.* Paris: Felix Alcan, 1897.

Annales du Barreau français ou choix des plaidoyers et mémoires les plus remarquables, vol. 5. Paris: B. Warée, 1824, 457, et seq.

Arbaumont, Jules d'. *Armorial de la Chambre des Comptes de Dijon, d'après le manuscrit inédit du Père Gautier.* Dijon: Lamarche, Librairie-Editeur, 1881.

Archives parlementaires de 1787 à 1860, recueil complet des débats, edited by M.J. Mavidal & M.E. Laurent. Paris: Société d'Imprimerie et Librairie Administrative et des Chemins de Fers, Paul Dupont, 1886.

Aulard, F.-A. *La Société des Jacobins, Recueil de Documents pour l'Histoire du Club des Jacobins de la Ville de Paris, vol. 1.* Paris: Librairie Jouaust, Librairie Noblet, Maison Quantin, 1889.

Badinter, Robert. *Libres et Égaux, L'Émancipation des Juifs 1789–1791.* Paris: Fayard, 1989.

Bail, Le Chevalier. *L'État des Juifs en France, en Espagne et en Italie depuis le commencement du cinquième siècle de l'ère vulgaire jusqu'à la fin du seizième.* Paris: Alexis Eymery, 1825.

Beaune, Henri and Jules d'Arbaumont. *La Noblesse aux États de Bourgogne de 1350 à 1789.* Dijon: La Marche Libraire-Editeur, 1864.

Beeman, Richard. *Plain, Honest Men: The Making of the American Constitution.* New York: Random House, 2010.

Bell, David A., *Lawyers and Citizens: The Making of a Political Elite in Old Regime France.* New York: Oxford University Press, 1994.

Bernard, Augustin. "L'Abbé Claude Fauchet, Membre de la Commune de Paris 1789–90." *Revue de la Révolution*, published under the Direction of Gustave Bord, vol. 10, 1887. Paris: Bureau de la Revue de la Révolution, 1887.

Berthier, Ferdinand. *L'Abbé de l'Épée, sa vie, son apostolat, ses travaux, sa lutte et ses succés*. Paris: Michel Lévy Frères, 1852.

Boucher d'Argis. "Histoire abrégée de l'Ordre des Avocats," in Dupin, aîné, M., *Profession d'Avocat*, third edition. Brussels: Louis Haumann & Cie.Libraires, 1834.

Boulloche, M.P. *Un Avocat du XVIIIe siècle* Paris: Alcan-Lévy Imprimeur de l'Ordre des Avocats, 1893.

Brette, Armand. *Recueil de Documents Relatifs à la Convocation des États Généraux de 1789*. Paris: Imprimerie Nationale, 1894.

Brodie, Fawn M. *Thomas Jefferson: An Intimate History*. New York: W. W. Norton & Co., 1974.

Cahen, Abraham. "L'Emancipation des Juifs devant la Société Royale des Sciences et Arts de Metz en 1787 et M. Roederer." *Revue des Études juives, publication trimestrielle de la Société des Études juives*, vol. 1.Paris: à la Société des Études juives, 17, rue St. Georges, 1880.

Camus, Armand-Gaston. *Lettres sur la Profession d'Avocat*. Brussels: Librairie de Jurisprudence de H. Tarlier, 1833.

Capefigue, Baptiste. *Histoire de Philippe-Auguste*, vol. 1, 1180–1191. Paris: Dufey, Libraire, 1829.

Carré, Henri. "La Tactique et les Idées de l'Opposition Parlementaire d'après la Correspondance Inédite de Cortot et de Godard (1788–1789)," in Aulard, vol. 29, *La Révolution française: Revue d'histoire moderne et contemporaine*. Paris: La Société de l'Histoire de la Révolution, 1895.

Catalogue général des livres imprimés de la Bibliothèque, vol. 17, Bibliothèque Nationale (France). Département des imprimés, Léopold Delisle, 1903.

Caubet, Étienne. *Histoire Populaire de la Révolution Française, de 1789 à 1839*, vol. 2. Paris: Pagnerre Editeur, 1839.

Charet, Pierre. "L'affaire Julien Baudelle, une affaire d'état Pierre Ferdinand Ozenne et le marquis de La Fayette," *Généalogie et Histoire de la Caraïbe*. http://www.ghcaraibe.org/articles/2017-art25.pdf

Charrier, Jules. *Claude Fauchet, Évêque Constitutionel du Calvados*, vol. 1. Paris: Librairie Ancienne Honoré Champion, 1909.

Chassin, Charles-Louis. *Les Élections et les Cahiers de Paris en 1789*, vol. 1: *La Convocation de Paris aux Derniers États Généraux*. Paris: Jouast et Sigaux, Charles Noblet, Maison Quantin, 1888.

_____. *Les Élections et les Cahiers de Paris en 1789, vol. 2: Les Assemblées*

primaires et les Cahiers primitifs. Paris: Jouaust et Sigaux, Charles Noblet, Maison Quantin, 1888.

Chavaray, Étienne. *L'Assemblée Electorale de Paris, 26 août 1791 –10 août 1792, Procès-verbaux de l'élection.* Paris: Léopold Cerf, Charles Noblet, Maison Quantin, 1894.

Clément, Roger. *La Condition des Juifs de Metz sous l'Ancien Régime.* Paris: Imprimerie Henri Jouve, 1903.

Dard, Émile. "Hérault de Séchelles avant la Révolution." *La Revue de Paris*, vol. 4. Paris: Bureaux de la Revue de Paris, 1906.

Darnton, Robert and Daniel Roche, eds. *Revolution in Print: The Press in France 1775–1800.* Berkeley: University of California Press, 1989.

DeJean, Joan. *How Paris Became Paris: The Invention of the Modern City.* New York: Bloomsbury, 2014.

Delaure, T. A. *Histoire Civile, Physique et Morale de Paris*, vol. 9. Paris: Baudoin Frères, Libraires, 1825.

Derasse, Nicolas. "Les Défenseurs officieux: une défense sans barreaux." *Annales historiques de la Révolution française*, vol. 350 (October-December, 2007): 49–67.

D'Haucour, Louis. *L'Hôtel de Ville de Paris à travers les siècles.* Paris: Giard & Brière, 1900.

D'Hozier, Charles. *Armorial Général de France, Receuil Officiel dressé en vertu de l'Édit de 1696*, Généralité de Bourgogne, vol. 1. Dijon: Imprimerie Darantière, 1875.

Dohm, Christian W. *De la Réforme politique des Juifs*, translated from the German by Jean Bernoulli. Dessau, 1782.

Douarche, Aristide. *Les Tribunaux civil de Paris pendant la Révolution (1791–1800)*, vol. 2. Paris: Librairie Léopold Cerf, Librairie Noblet, Maison Quantin.

Doumic, René. "Lettres d'un Philosophe et d'une Femme sensible— Condorcet et Madame Suard, d'après une Correspondence inédite." *Revue des Deux Mondes*, vols. 5, 6 & 8, 1911–1912.

Duchaine, Gustave and Picard, Edmond, *Manuel Pratique de la Profession d'Avocat.* Paris: A Durand et Pedone Lauriel, 1869.

Dusquesnoy, Adrien. *Journal d'Adrien Duquesnoy, député du Tiers état de Bar-le-Duc, sur l'Assemblée constituante, 3 mai 1789–3 avril 1790.* Paris: Alphonse Picard et Fils, 1894.

Edelstein, Melvin. *The French Revolution and the Birth of Electoral Democracy.* London & New York: Routledge Taylor & Francis

Group, 2014.

Encrevé, André. "La Réception des Ouvrages de J. Necker sur la Religion d'après sa correspondance privée." *Cahiers Staëliens, organe de la Société des études staëliens*, n.s., no. 55–2004.

État et société en France aux XVIIe et XVIIIe siècles: Mélanges offerts à Yves Durand, edited by Jean-Pierre Bardet. Paris: Presses de l'Université de Paris-Sorbonne, 2000.

Faucher, Jean-André and Achille Ricker. *Histoire de la Franc-maçonnerie en France (avec Lettre liminaire de Me Richard Dupuy)*. Paris: Nouvelles Editions Latines, 1967.

Feuerwerker, David. "The Abolition of Body Taxes in France" ["Les juifs en France: l'abolition du péage corporel"] *Annales. Économies, Sociétés, Civilisations*, vol. 17, no. 5, 1962.

____. *L'Émancipation des Juifs en France*. Paris: Editions Albin Michel, 1976.

Feuillet de Conches, Felix-Sébastien. *Louis XVI, Marie-Antoinette et Madame Elisabeth, Lettres et documents inédits*, vol. 1. Paris: Henri Plon, 1864.

Fitzsimmons, Michael P. *The Parisian Order of Barristers and the French Revolution*. Cambridge, MA: Harvard, 1987.

Fournel, Jean-François. *Histoire du Barreau de Paris dans les cours de la Révolution*. Paris: Maradan, 1816.

Gaudry, Joachim, *Histoire du Barreau de Paris*. vol. 2, Paris: Auguste Durand Éditeur, 1864.

Gaven, Jean-Christophe. *Le Crime de lèse-nation. Histoire d'une invention juridique et politique (1789–1791)*. Paris: Presses de Sciences Po, Domaine droit, 2016.

Ginsberger, Moïse. *Cerf Berr et Son Époque*, Conférence faite à Strasbourg le 17 janvier 1906. Paris: Hachette, 1908. gallica.bnf.fr/ ark/12148/bpt6k5427849p/f2

Godechot, Jacques. "Les Juifs de Nancy de 1789 à 1795." *Revue des Études juives* (Paris: Librairie A. Durlacher, 1928).

Graetz, Heinrich. *Popular History of the Jews*. New York: Hebrew Publishing Company, 1919.

Guérard, Benjamin. "Semur-en-Auxois," in *Histoire des Villes de France*, edited by Aristide Guilbert. Paris: Furne et Cie. – Perrotin – H. Fournier, 1848.

Guibal, Georges. *Mirabeau et la Provence: Deuxième Partie. du 5 mai 1789 au 4 avril 1791.* Paris: Ernest Thorin, Editeur, 1891.

Guillaume, James. Letter dated October 23, 1900 in *La Révolution française: revue d'histoire moderne et contemporaine,* edited by A. Aulard. Paris: Société de l'Histoire de la Révolution, 1900, vol. 39.

Guillois, Antoine. *Le salon de Madame Helvétius: Cabanis et les idéologues.* Paris: Calmann-Lévy, Editeur, 1894.

_____. *La Marquise de Condorcet, sa famille, son salon, ses amis 1764–1822.* Paris: Paul Ollendorff, ed., 1897.

Hallays-Dabot, Victor. *Histoire de la Censure théâtrale en France.* Paris: E. Dentu, Editeur 1862.

Halphen, Achille-Edmond. *Recueil des Lois Décrets, Ordonnances, Avis du Conseil d'Etat, Arrêtés et Règlements Concernant les Israélites depuis la Révolution de 1789.* Paris: Aux Bureau des Archives Israélites, 1851.

Harboun, Häim. *Les Voyageurs juifs du XVIII siècle: 1773–1794,* vol. 2. Editions Massoreth, 1997.

Hayes, Kevin, J. *The Road to Monticello: The Life and Mind of Thomas Jefferson.* New York: Oxford University Press, 2008.

Hell, François Joseph Antoine. *Observations d'un alsacien sur l'affaire présente des juifs d'Alsace,* 1779 (published anonymously).

Hertzberg, Arthur. *The French Enlightenment and the Jews: The Origins of Modern Anti-Semitism.* New York: Schocken, 1968.

Hillairet, Jacques. *Dictionnaire Historique des Rues de Paris.* Paris: Editions de Minuit, 1961, vols.1 and 2.

Hurel, Jean-Joseph. *Aux Citoyens de la Section du Marais ci-devant Enfans-Rouges.* Paris: Mayer & Compagnie, rue St. Martin, 1793.

Hyman, Paula E. *The Emancipation of the Jews of Alsace.* New Haven, CT and London: Yale University Press, 1991.

Kahn, Léon. *Les Juifs de Paris pendant la Révolution.* Paris: Paul Ollendorff, Éditeur, 1898.

Kates, Gary. *The Cercle Social, the Girondins and the French Revolution.* Princeton, NJ: Princeton University Press, 1985.

_____. "Jews into Frenchmen: Nationality and Representation in Revolutionary France," in *The French Revolution and the Birth of Modernity,* edited by Ferenc Fehér. Berkeley: University of California Press, 1990.

Klaus, Carrie F. "Une école des moeurs & de la morale": How the Wouters Sisters made English Theater French." *Palimpsestes* 20 (2007) https://doi.org/10.4000/palimpsestes.95.

Kropotkine, Pierre. *La Grande Révolution* (1789–1799). Paris: P.-V. Stock Éditeur, 1909.

Lacroix, Sigismond. *Actes de la Commune de Paris pendant la Révolution*, Série 1. Paris: L. Cerf, Charles Noblet, Société Française d'Éditions d'Art 1894–1900.

____. *Actes de la Commune de Paris pendant la Révolution*, publiés et annotés. Série 2. Paris: L. Cerf, Charles Noblet, Ancienne Quentin, 1900–1905.

____. "Ce qu'on Pensait des Juifs à Paris en 1790." *Revue Politique et Littéraire Revue Bleue*, no. 14. Directeur: M. Henry Ferrari, 2 avril 1898 (lecture given at the annual meeting of the Société de l'Histoire de la Révolution Française, March 27, 1898).

____. "Les Juifs à Paris en 1790." *Revue Bleu*, series 4, vol. 9. Paris: Bureau des Revues, 1898.

Lamourette, Abbé A.-A. *Observations sur l'état civil des juifs adressées à l'Assemblée Nationale.* Paris: Chez Belin, 1790.

Lataulade, Joseph de. *Les Juifs sous l'ancien régime: leur émancipation.* Bordeaux: Imprimerie Y. Cadoret, 1906.

Ledeuil, Justin. *1789–1795. La Révolution à Dijon.* Paris: Librairie Historique et Archéologique J.-B. Dumoulin, 1872.

Lefebvre, Georges. *The Coming of the French Revolution, 1789*, translated by R.R. Palmer. New York: Vintage Books, 1947.

Lémann, (Abbé) Joseph. *La Prépondérance Juive, première partie, ses origines (1789–1791), d'après des documents nouveaux.* Paris: Librairie Victor Legouffre, 1889.

____. *L'Entrée des Israélites dans la société française.* Paris: Librarie Victor Lecoffre, 1886.

Lemoine, Yves and Jean-Pierre Mignard. *Le Défi d'Antigone, Promenade parmi des figures du droit naturel.* Paris: Éditions Michel de Maule.

Le Moyne des Esscarts, Nicolas-Toussaint, ed., *Causes célèbres curieuses et intéressantes de toutes les cours souveraines du royaume avec les jugemens qui les ont decidées*, vol. 167. Paris, 1788.

Leuwers, Hervé. *L'Invention du Barreau Français, 1660–1830. La Construction Nationale d'un Groupe Professionnel.* Paris: Éditions de l'École des hautes études en sciences sociales, 2006.

Lévy, Michel Louis. *Recherches sur la démographie des juifs d'Alsace du viii siècle*, INED, France. https://www.erudit.org/fr/livres/ actes-des-colloques-de-lassociation-internationale-des-demog-

raphes-de-langue-francaise/demographie-destin-sous-popula-
tions-actes-colloque-liege-1981/000706c0.pdf

Lourde, C. *Histoire de la révolution à Marseille et en Provence: depuis 1789 jusqu'au Consulat*, vol. 1. Marseille: Senès Imprimeur, 1838.

Lucien-Brun, Henry. *La Condition des Juifs en France depuis 1789.* Lyon: Librairie A. Cote, 1900. Bibliothèque de l'Alliance israélite universelle.

J. Madival and E. Laurent, et al., eds. *Archives parlementaires de 1789 à 1860: recueil complet des débats législatifs & politiques des Chambres françaises.* Paris: Librairie administrative de P. Dupont, 1862.

Maignial, Mainfroy. *La loi de 1791 et la condition des juifs en France.* Paris: Arthur Rousseau, 1903.

Malino, Frances. *A Jew in the French Revolution: The Life of Zalkind Hourwitz.* Oxford: Blackwell, 1996.

Mancini Nivernois, Louis-Jules-Barbon. "Essai sur la Vie de J.J. Bar-thélémy," in *Voyage du Jeune Anacharsis en Grèce dans le milieu du quatrième siècle avant l'ére vulgaire*, vol. 1. London: Chez Charles Dilly, 1796.

Marignan, A. *Études sur la Civilisation française*, vol. 1, *La Société Mérovingienne.* Paris: Librairie Émile Bouillon, 1899.

Martin, Xavier. "À Propos d'un livre, Target, Bentham et le Code Civil." *Revue d'Histoire des Facultés de Droit.* SHFD/Librairie générale de droit et de jurisprudence, 2001.

Mathiez, Albert. *Le Club des Cordeliers pendant la Crise de Varennes et Le Massacre du Champ de Mars.* Paris: Librairie Ancienne H. Champion, Éditeur, 1910.

Mazon, Albin. *Histoire de Soulavie (Naturaliste, Diplomate, Historien)*, vol. 1. Paris: Librairie Fischbacher, 1893.

McRoberts, Meg. "The French Philosophes and the Jews: An Historiographical Inquiry." *Proceedings of the Second Meeting of the Western Society for French History*, Nov. 21–23, 1974, edited by Brison D. Gooch. College Station: Texas A & M University, 1974, 208–15.

Meyer, Pierre-André, "Démographie des Juifs de Metz (1740-1789)," in *Annales de Démographie Historique*/Année 1993. Paris: *Société de Démographie Historique* – E.H.E.S.S. 1993), 127–60.

Michelet, Jules. *Les Femmes de la Révolution.* Paris: Adolphe Delahays, Libraire-Editeur, 1855.

____. *History of the French Revolution*, translated by Charles Cocks.

Chicago, IL: The University of Chicago Press, 1967.

Mollot, François-Étienne. *Règles sur la Profession d'Avocat*. Paris: Chez Joubert Libraire, 1842.

Nahon, Gérard. "Prospective des Portugais du Sud-Ouest de la France à la Veille de la Révolution," in *Politiques et religion dans le judaïsme moderne: des communautés à la Révolution*, edited by Daniel Tollet. Paris: Presses de l'Université de Paris-Sorbonne, 1987.

Pérot, J.-B. *Le Code Rural de 1791, commenté & expliqué*. Reims: Matot-Braine, 1865.

Peyrusse, Louis-Eugene. *Éloge de Lamoignon de Malesherbes*. Toulouse: Imprimerie de Jean-Matthieu Douladoure, 1840.

Popkin, Richard Henry. *The Third Force in Seventeenth-Century Thought*. Leiden: Brill, 1991.

Raphaël, F. "Les Juifs et l'Alsace: Une Rencontre créatrice, une Rencontre douloureuse," in his *Regards sur la Culture Judéo-Alsacienne*. Strasbourg: La Nuée Bleue, 2001.

Raphaël, F., and R. Weyl. *Regards nouveaux sur les juifs d'Alsace*. Librairie Istra, 1980.

Recueil des Instructions données aux Ambassadeurs et Ministre de France depuis les Traités de Westphalie jusqu'à la Révolution française, vol. 16, Prusse. Paris: Félix Alcan, Éditeur, 1901.

Recueil de pièces concernant l'Association de Bienfaisance Judiciaire, Fondée en 1787. Paris: Clousier, 1789.

Reinach, Théodore. *Histoire des Israélites depuis l'époque de leur dispersion jusqu'à nos jours*. Paris: Librairie Hachette et Cie., 1885.

Rittiez, F. *Histoire du Palais de Justice de Paris et du Parlement, 860–1789*. Paris: Schlesinger Frères, 1863.

Robb, Graham. *Parisian: An Adventure History of Paris*. London & Paris: W.W. Norton & Company, 2010.

Robert, Adolphe, Edgard Bourloton, and Gaston Cougny. *Dictionnaire des Parlementaires français*. Paris: Bourloton Ed., 1891.

Robin-Aizertin, Régine. "Les structures sociales à Semur-en-Auxois en 1789." *Actes du Quatre-vingt onzième Congrès National des Sociétés Savantes*, Rennes 1966, Section d'Histoire Moderne et Contemporaine, vol.2 , *Ancien Régime et Révolution*. Paris: Bibliothèque Nationale, 1969.

Rochette, Jacqueline. *Histoire des Juifs d'Alsace des Origines à la Révolution*. Paris: Librairie Lipshutz, 1938.

Rousse, Edmond. *Mirabeau*. Paris: Librairie Hachette, 1891.

Sagnac, Philippe. "Les Juifs et la Révolution française, 1789–1791." *Revue d'Histoire moderne et contemporaine*, vol. 1, no. 1, 1899.

Semach, Y. D. *L'Abbé Grégoire et l'Émancipation des Juifs*. Paris: Librarie Larose, 1931.

Sepinwall, Alyssa Goldstein. *The Abbé Grégoire and the French Revolution: The Making of Modern Universalism*. Berkeley: University of California Press, 2005.

Slavin, Morris. *The French Revolution in Miniature, Section Droits-de-l'Homme, 1789–1795*. Princeton, NJ: Princeton University Press, 2014.

Szajkowski, Zosa. *Jews and the French Revolutions of 1789, 1830 and 1848*. New York: KTAV, 1970.

Target, Paul-Louis. *Un Avocat du XVIIIème siècle*. Paris: Alcan-Levy, Imprimeur de l'Ordre des Avocats, 1893.

Thiéblin, Henri. *Éloge de Gerbier*. Paris: Typographie de E. Plon, 1875.

Tourzel (Duchesse de), Louise Elisabeth. *Memoirs of the Duchess de Tourzel: Governess to the Children of France*, vol. 1. London: Remington & Co. 1886.

Vaulabelle, Alfred de. *Histoire générale de Semur-en-Auxois*. Semur-en-Auxois: L. Horry Imprimeur-Editeur, 1905.

Vovelle, Michel. *La Chute de la monarchie 1787–1792*. Paris: Editions du Seuil, 1972.

Waldner de Freudenstein, Henriette-Louise de. *Mémoires de la Baronne d'Oberkirch*, vols. 1 and 2, edited by Comte de Montbrison. Paris: Charpentier, Libraire-Editeur, 1853.

Warschawski, Max. *Histoire des Juifs d'Alsace*. http://judaisme.sdv.fr/histoire/historiq/histo/index.htm

____. "Strasbourg et les Juifs jusqu'à la Révolution," from *Histoire de Juifs de Strasbourg*. http://judaisme.sdv.fr/histoire/villes/strasbrg/hist/index.htm

Weill, Georges. *L'Alsace française de 1789 à 1870*. Paris: Librairie Félix Alcan, 1916.

INDEX

185, 228, 289, 293, 334

Tisha B'Av, 243

Tocqueville, Alexis de, 32n65

Treaty of Westphalia, 146

Trenel(le), Jacob, 226–7n26, 297,
297n2, 306, 345, 369, 405n35

tricolor national cockade, 421n29

Tronchet, François-Denis, 40, 40n17

Tuileries (Palace and Gardens), 31n65,
244n4, 247, 460–61, 495, 507–8

Turgot, Anne Robert Jacques,
167, 167n5

U

Usury. *See* microlending

V

Vasse, Cornélie Wouters de, 392–95

Victoires, Place des, 12, 12n2, 34, 68n3

Vieillard, Philippe 389

Vigée, Louis-Jean-Baptiste-Étienne,
383, 383n13, 384, 412n5, 416

Vigée-Lebrun, Élisabeth, 383–84,
383n13, 384n14

Voidel, Jean-Georges-Charles, 397,
397n1, 401, 404

Voltaire, 19, 24, 36n3, 165–66, 225n22

W

Wagner, Richard, 37n5

Waldner de Freundenstein,
Christian-Frederic-Dagobert de,
57–58

Waldner de Freundstein,
François-Louis Baron de, 57–59

War of Austrian Succession, 245n9

Washington, George, 7, 196, 196n11,
237, 245n9, 339n25, 367–68, 505–6

Waterloo, Battle of, 43

Women's March on Versailles, 246–47

X

Ximénès, Augustin-Louis de, 424n42